*Major Problems in American
Environmental History*

MAJOR PROBLEMS IN AMERICAN HISTORY SERIES

GENERAL EDITOR
THOMAS G. PATERSON

Major Problems in American Environmental History

DOCUMENTS AND ESSAYS

SECOND EDITION

EDITED BY

CAROLYN MERCHANT

UNIVERSITY OF CALIFORNIA-BERKELEY

HOUGHTON MIFFLIN COMPANY
Boston   New York

Publisher: Charles Hartford
Senior Consulting Editor: Jean L. Woy
Senior Development Editor: Frances Gay
Editorial Assistant: Rachel Zanders
Senior Art and Design Coordinator: Jill Haber
Senior Composition Buyer: Sarah Ambrose
Manufacturing Coordinator: Renée Ostrowski
Senior Marketing Manager: Sandra McGuire
Marketing Associate: Ilana Gordon

Cover image: Collection of Governor & Mrs. John Y. Brown (Phyllis George)/Jane Wooster Scott/SuperStock.

Printed in the U.S.A.

Library of Congress Catalog Card Number: 2003109877

ISBN: 0-618-30805-9

6789-MP-09

Contents

CHAPTER 3

The New England Forest in the Seventeenth Century

Page 65

CHAPTER 4

Tobacco and Rice in the Colonial South

Page 95

CHAPTER 5

Farms and Cities in the Early Republic

Page 129

CHAPTER 6

Nature and the Market in the Nineteenth Century

Page 166

C H A P T E R   9
Great Plains Grasslands Exploited
Page 274

C H A P T E R   1 0
Resource Conservation in the Twentieth Century
Page 312

CHAPTER 13
The Emergence of Ecology in the Twentieth Century
Page 427

CHAPTER 14
Water, Energy, and Population in the Twentieth Century
Page 467

CHAPTER 15
Globalization: The United States in the Wider World
Page 502

APPENDIX
Page A-1

Preface

Caribou or oil? Preservation of pristine wilderness or energy source for an ever-growing population? Democratic commitment to the environment or Republican exploitation of natural resources? Late in the year 2000, as outgoing President Bill Clinton approved the preservation of millions of acres of land in Alaska's Tongass National Forest, President-elect George W. Bush was in the process of appointing cabinet secretaries committed to the drilling of oil in the Arctic National Wildlife Refuge. The nation was in the throes of a new energy crisis—symptomatic of its dependence on foreign oil and its place in a globally interlinked world economy. The major political parties were at odds on environmental policy.

Yet, as environmental historian William Cronon notes, there was a time when the two parties were both committed to conservation, a time "When the G.O.P Was Green." Theodore Roosevelt in the early twentieth century created the nation's first wildlife refuges and national monuments. Dwight D. Eisenhower in the 1950s set aside the lands that protected the caribou herds in the Arctic National Wildlife Refuge. And Richard Nixon in the early 1970s, with broad support from both parties, signed into law the National Environmental Policy Act (NEPA), the Clean Air and Clean Water Acts, and established the Environmental Protection Agency (EPA). Cronon's points remind us of past policies and show how environmental history can help us to understand competing political approaches to solving environmental problems.

Why do people study environmental history? Today, interest in the earth—its past, present, and future—commands worldwide attention. The 2002 Earth Summit in Johannesburg, South Africa, brought together government leaders and environmental organizations from around the globe to address sustainable development, one of the topics explored in Chapter 15. As concern mounts over the quality of environments and human life in the future, the study of past environments—how they were used and how they changed—provides guidance for the formation of governmental policy. Leaders can learn from environmental history. For example, the rise of salmon fisheries in the Pacific Northwest and the role played in their depletion by the construction of dams for energy and flood control affects future policies on whether to build dams (or to decommission existing dams), a topic that is explored in Chapters 8 and 14. Environmental conditions also influence policy decisions. Urbanization of the American West, where droughts are all too frequent, prompts governmental funding of reclamation projects and soil conservation, as well as the interstate highway system linking east with west—themes explored in Chapters 9, 10, and 14 of this volume. Environmental history, moreover, instills an appreciation of the complexity of human interactions with nature and in this way contributes to a fuller understanding of history. Thus knowledge of rice cultivation by African slaves in the Southeast and of corn cultivation by Pueblo Indians in the Southwest casts new light on the conflicts that arose among the races and cultures of those regions, as Chapters 2 and 4 examine. Further, environmental history illuminates the different effects that forests, farms, and cities have on local environments, as Chapters 3, 5, and 12 reveal.

And there are still other reasons to study environmental history. Historical writings about nature offer aesthetic or spiritual perceptions of humans' place in the natural world that continue to inspire respect and reverence for nature and to foster the conservation and preservation of nature. Poets who wrote about the natural world, such as Puritan Anne Bradstreet and slave Phyllis Wheatley; the Hudson River school of painters; New England transcendentalists, among them Ralph Waldo Emerson and Henry David Thoreau; and nature writers John Muir and Mary Austin initiated an appreciation of wilderness that influenced the creation of the national parks, a subject treated in Chapters 6 and 11. Gender and race also play critical roles in environmental activism. Women and men, blacks and whites, often perceive the environment differently and contribute different approaches to environmental movements as revealed in Chapters 13 and 15. Such histories and case studies offer valuable perspectives to a world whose very survival depends on shifting from exploitative to environmentally sustainable development, and from inequality to environmental justice.

The second edition of *Major Problems in American Environmental History* retains the broad goals of the first edition set out in the above paragraphs, the basic structure of the book, and many of its most popular and successful documents and essays, making for a smooth transition from the first to second editions in the classroom. The second edition, however, includes new topics and new scholarship in this rapidly expanding field.

New material is included on water, energy, urbanization, the automobile, environmental health, suburbanization, population growth, environmental justice, and globalization. New essays on water, for example, include the work of Theodore Steinberg on dams in the Northeast, Richard White on salmon in the Northwest, and water in the American West by Charles Wilkinson. An increased emphasis has been placed on the twentieth century, and all chapters have been brought forward in time. Included here are essays by Martin Melosi, Robert Gottlieb, and Adam Rome on urban and suburban pollution and reform, energy sources and their impacts on the twentieth-century environment by David Nye, and the role of the automobile and the interstate highway system in promoting national park tourism by James Flink.

The roles of minorities and their interactions with each other and the environment are emphasized in essays by Andrew Isenberg on Indians and bison on the Great Plains, Judith Carney on "black rice" in South Carolina, William Katz on "black Indians," Elizabeth Blum on slave women's views of wilderness, Philip Burnham on Indians and the National Parks, and Eileen McGurty on the origins of the environmental justice movement. Greater attention is likewise paid to international connections and globalization that reveal the historical and current roles played by the United States in the wider world. Historical influences on the North American environment, in addition to those of Europeans and Africans on the East Coast, include those of the French in Canada, the Spanish in Mexico and New Mexico, and the Russians in Alaska. Current international issues are reflected in the Kyoto Protocol, the Johannesburg Earth Summit, and an essay by Fritjof Capra on the meaning of globalization, included in this volume. The chapters also incorporate new directions taken in the field over the past decade, such as Jared Diamond on "guns, germs, and steel," Mark Stoll on the New England Puritans, William Cronon on the meaning and value of wilderness, Edmund Russell III on environmental regulation, and Linda Lear on Rachel Carson's ecological vision.

The second edition of *Major Problems in American Environmental History* is the result of more than three decades of the growth of the field of environmental history. This volume, like its companions in the Major Problems in American History series, draws on both documents and essays. It is intended as a primary text in a one- or two-term environmental history or environmental studies course, but it also may be assigned to provide an environmental dimension to introductory classes in United States history. Chapter introductions discuss the place, period, and particular focus of each case history. The documents for each chapter provide a variety of perspectives written or spoken by those who lived in and helped to create the history of a specific environment. These primary sources stimulate students to form their own opinions on environmental history and, through discussion with others, to develop confidence in their own interpretations. The essays offer a range of views, demonstrating that scholars often draw conflicting conclusions from the same primary sources. This format encourages students to evaluate each interpretation, as well as to gain an understanding of the ways in which different underlying assumptions and positions influence the writing of history. It is hoped that the second edition, like the first, engages and challenges students to think critically about the American past and the role the environment has played and will play in the global future. This edition includes the glossary from the first edition, plus a timeline and a set of maps for reference to geographical regions, natural resources, and environmental conditions encountered in various places and periods of history.

In approaching environmental history, it may be helpful to ask students to construct their own personal environmental histories. Some students are descended from people long native to the Americas, but most are the descendants of more recent newcomers, either free or enslaved. These past generations have used and shaped their environments, often with very different goals and values from generations living today. In inquiring about the environments in which they, their parents, and their grandparents grew up, students might ask what natural resources sustained their families' livelihoods and how their families participated in environmental change. To what extent were their environments "natural" as distinct from human-made; to what degree were they native as distinct from exotic (that is, transformed by nonnative species)? Students might also explore the roles that race, ethnicity, class, and gender have played in the way their ancestors have interacted with their environments. And they might ponder how their forebears' personal values with regard to the world around them differed from their own values. Finally, readers might reflect on what kind of environment they want for the future. Then, after reading and discussing the documents and essays in this book, students might consider how these investigations, and the new insights gained from them, might have altered their original interpretations of their families' past. Instructors and students also might decide to collaborate on a supplementary chapter of documents and essays highlighting their own particular region or unique experiences.

In compiling this updated volume, as well as the first, I am grateful for contributions, suggestions, and evaluations from my students and teaching assistants over the past several years, in particular Michael Allen, Elisa Cooper, Dylan Esson, Yaakov Garb, Debora Hammond, Michael Heiman, David Igler, Barbara Leibhardt, Jeffrey Mann, Jessica Owley, Tina Stevens, Sarah Thomas, Sarah Trainor, Laura Watt, Thomas Wellock, Jennifer Wells, Rob Weinberg, Robert Weyeneth, Tamara Whited, and Ken Worthy. Shana Cohen assisted in the evaluation and selection of dozens of articles for the second edition. Earth Duarte-Trattner helped in updating the additional readings. Sara Friedman and Lisa Zhuo scanned the documents and essays and helped to prepare the manuscript.

Colleagues who shared their ideas and syllabi helped broaden the scope of both editions of the book, as did reviewers who provided formal written comments on the table of contents. For the second edition: Dianne Glave, Loyola Marymount University; Sandra Lin Marburg, University of California Berkeley Extension Online; James E. Sherow, Kansas State University; Mark Stoll, Texas Tech University; Nancy Unger, Santa Clara University; and for the first edition: William Cronon, University of Wisconsin, Madison; Matthew Dennis, University of Oregon; Wesley A. Dick, Albion College; Gordon B. Dodds, Portland State University; Arthur F. McEvoy, University of Wisconsin; Martin V. Melosi, University of Houston; Donald J. Pisani, University of Oklahoma; William F. Steirer, Clemson University; Richard White, Stanford University; and Donald Worster, University of Kansas. Thomas Paterson, general editor of the Major Problems in American History series, was extraordinarily helpful in framing the scope of both editions. The second edition was prepared at Houghton Mifflin under the editorship of Jean Woy, whose astute comments and sense of what readers wanted to hear vastly improved the book, and with the assistance of Frances Gay who provided expertise on overall composition and Rachel Zanders who prepared the volume for print. Finally, I am deeply indebted to Charles Sellers, who over the years has profoundly influenced my interpretation of American history and helped me to conceptualize my course in environmental history.

I welcome readers' feedback on and suggestions for improving this anthology. I also would be interested in receiving copies of supplementary chapters that instructors or students create or other projects that grow out of the study of this volume.

C. M.

CHAPTER
1

What Is Environmental History?

❦

Environmental history offers an earth's-eye view of the past. It addresses the many ways in which human beings have interacted with the natural environment over time. As one of the newest perspectives within the discipline of history, it is a field that is still in the process of self-definition. It therefore offers the exciting challenge of engaging in a dialogue with the documents of the past and with historians of the present to create individual interpretations of history.

For environmental historians, the term environment refers to the natural and human-created surroundings that affect a living organism or group of organisms' ability to maintain itself and develop over time. Ecology deals with the relationships between these organisms and their surroundings. In the case of humans, it also includes social and cultural patterns. Ecological history is therefore somewhat broader than environmental history, but the two terms are often used interchangeably.

Environmental history's pictures of the past come from a colorful palette of sources. From the natural history side of the picture come data on climatic fluctuations, geological changes, plant and animal ecology, and microbial life. From human history, it draws on tools for extracting resources; account books of traders; journals of explorers; court records of births and deaths; laws; diaries of farmers; interviews with slaves; Indian myths and legends; paintings, poetry, and essays about nature; scientific investigations; and the musings of philosophers.

Environmental historians ask a number of questions of these sources. How and why did people living in a particular place at a particular time use and transform their environment? How did people of different cultural backgrounds and of both genders perceive, manage, exploit, and conserve their environments? What differing economic forms, or modes of production (such as gathering, hunting, fishing, farming, ranching, mining, and forestry), evolved in particular habitats? What problems of pollution and depletion arose under industrialization and urbanization? What political and legal conflicts, struggles, and compromises emerged over resource use and conservation? How did people's attitudes toward nature and their mental constructions of nature change over time? And how do changing concepts of ecology influence the interpretations of environmental historians? In attempting to answer these kinds of questions, environmental historians

1

have developed a number of different conceptual approaches, four of which are considered in this chapter. (See Maps 1, 2, and 3 in the Appendix.)

❦ E S S A Y S

The four essays in this chapter offer contrasting frameworks for interpreting environmental history. In the first essay, Donald Worster, Hall Distinguished Professor of American History at the University of Kansas, discusses three of the environmental historian's most important sources: ecology, modes of production, and ideas, using these three levels of interpretation as the framework for doing environmental history. The second essay is by Jared Diamond of the Geography Department at the University of California, Los Angeles. Diamond argues that Europeans were able to take over the New World because the Eurasian environment had many more species of domesticatable animals than did the Americas, leading to settled agriculture and complex political organizations supported by metal technologies. Europeans thus had an ecological advantage in colonizing the globe. The third essay is by William Cronon, Villas Professor of History at the University of Wisconsin, Madison. Cronon suggests that environmental historians may tell stories about environmental degradation as parables to raise people's consciousness about healing and restoring nature to an earlier ideal. But that romanticized ideal never really exists. Nature is never static or stable, and the awesome human power to change nature means that transformed biotic actors may in turn have immense consequences for humanity. The fourth essay, by Carolyn Merchant, professor of environmental history at the University of California at Berkeley, looks at the importance of gender, race, and class in interpreting environmental history and argues that we also need to consider the category of reproduction when doing environmental history. Together the essays introduce important concepts about nature and society that provide a toolkit for doing and interpreting environmental history.

Doing Environmental History

DONALD WORSTER

In the old days, the discipline of history had an altogether easier task. Everyone knew that the only important subject was politics and the only important terrain was the nation-state. One was supposed to investigate the connivings of presidents and prime ministers, the passing of laws, the struggles between courts and legislatures, and the negotiations of diplomats. That old, self-assured history was actually not so old after all—a mere century or two at most. It emerged with the power and influence of the nation-state, reaching a peak of acceptance in the nineteenth and early twentieth centuries. Often its practitioners were men of intensely nationalistic feelings, who were patriotically moved to trace the rise of their individual countries, the formation of political leadership in them, and their rivalries with other states for wealth and power. They knew what mattered, or thought they did.

From Donald Worster, "Doing Environmental History," in Donald Worster, ed., *The Ends of the Earth: Perspectives on Modern Environmental History.* New York: Cambridge University Press, 1988, pp. 289–299, 301–303, 305–306. Reprinted with the permission of Cambridge University Press.

But some time back that history as "past politics" began to lose ground, as the world evolved toward a more global point of view and, some would say, toward a more democratic one. Historians lost some of their confidence that the past had been so thoroughly controlled or summed up by a few great men acting in positions of national power. Scholars began uncovering long submerged layers, the lives and thoughts of ordinary people, and tried to reconceive history "from the bottom up." Down, down we must go, they maintained, down to the hidden layers of class, gender, race, and caste. There we will find what truly has shaped the surface layers of politics. Now enter still another group of reformers, the environmental historians, who insist that we have got to go still deeper yet, down to the earth itself as an agent and presence in history. Here we will discover even more fundamental forces at work over time. And to appreciate those forces we must now and then get out of parliamentary chambers, out of birthing rooms and factories, get out of doors altogether, and ramble into fields, woods, and the open air. It is time we bought a good set of walking shoes, and we cannot avoid getting some mud on them.

So far this extending of the scope of history to include a deeper and broader range of subjects has not challenged the primacy of the nation-state as the proper territory of the historian. Social, economic, and cultural history are all still commonly pursued within national boundaries. Thus, to an extent that is quite extraordinary among the disciplines of learning, history (at least for the modern period) has tended to remain the insular study of the United States, Brazil, France, and the rest. Such a way of organizing the past has the undeniable virtue of preserving some semblance of order in the face of a threatening chaos—some way of synthesizing all the layers and forces. But at the same time it may set up obstacles to new inquiries that do not neatly fit within national borders, environmental history among them. Many of the issues in this new field defy a narrow nationality: the wanderings of Tuareg nomads in the African Sahel, for instance, or the pursuit of the great whales through all the world's oceans. . . .

Environmental history is, in sum, part of a revisionist effort to make the discipline far more inclusive in its narratives than it has traditionally been. Above all, it rejects the conventional assumption that human experience has been exempt from natural constraints, that people are a separate and "supernatural" species, that the ecological consequences of their past deeds can be ignored. The old history could hardly deny that we have been living for a long while on this planet, but it assumed by its general disregard of that fact that we have not been and are not truly part of the planet. Environmental historians, on the other hand, realize that we can no longer afford to be so naive.

The idea of environmental history first appeared in the 1970s, as conferences on the global predicament were taking place and popular environmentalist movements were gathering momentum in several countries. It was launched, in other words, in a time of worldwide cultural reassessment and reform. History was hardly alone in being touched by that rising mood of public concern; scholarship in law, philosophy, economics, sociology, and other areas was similarly responsive. Long after popular interest in environmental issues crested and ebbed, as the issues themselves came to appear more and more complicated, without easy resolution, the scholarly interest continued to expand and take on greater and greater sophistication. Environmental history was, therefore, born out of a moral purpose, with strong political commitments behind it, but also became, as it matured, a scholarly enterprise that had neither any simple, nor any single, moral or political agenda to promote. Its principal goal became one of deepening our understanding of how humans have been affected by their natural environment through time and, conversely, how they have affected that environment and with what results. . . .

Much of the material for environmental history has . . . been around for generations, if not for centuries, and is only being reorganized in the light of recent experience. It includes data on tides and winds, on ocean currents, on the position of continents in relation to each other, on the geological and hydrological forces creating our land and water base. It includes the history of climate and weather, as these have made for good or bad harvests, sent prices up or down, ended or promoted epidemics, led to population increase or decline. All these have been powerful influences over the course of history, and continue to be so, as when massive earthquakes destroy cities or starvation follows in the wake of drought or rivers determine the flow of settlement. The fact that such influences continue in the late twentieth century is evidence of how far we are yet from controlling the environment to our complete satisfaction. . . .

Put in the vernacular then, environmental history is about the role and place of nature in human life. By common understanding we mean by "nature" the nonhuman world, the world we have not in any primary sense created. . . . The built environment is wholly expressive of culture; its study is already well advanced in the history of architecture, technology, and the city. But with such phenomena as the forest and the water cycle, we encounter autonomous energies that do not derive from us. Those forces impinge on human life, stimulating some reaction, some defense, some ambition. Thus, when we step beyond the self-reflecting world of humankind to encounter the nonhuman sphere, environmental history finds its main theme of study.

There are three levels on which the new history proceeds, three clusters of issues it addresses, though not necessarily all in the same project, three sets of questions it seeks to answer, each drawing on a range of outside disciplines and employing special methods of analysis. The first deals with understanding nature itself, as organized and functioning in past times; we include both organic and inorganic aspects of nature, and not least the human organism as it has been a link in nature's food chains, now functioning as womb, now belly, now eater, now eaten, now a host for microorganisms, now a kind of parasite. The second level in this history brings in the socioeconomic realm as it interacts with the environment. Here we are concerned with tools and work, with the social relations that grow out of that work, with the various modes people have devised of producing goods from natural resources. A community organized to catch fish at sea may have very different institutions, gender roles, or seasonal rhythms than one raising sheep in high mountain pastures. Power to make decisions, environmental or other, is seldom distributed through a society with perfect equality, so locating the configurations of power is part of this level of analysis. Then, forming a third level for the historian is that more intangible and uniquely human type of encounter—the purely mental or intellectual, in which perceptions, ethics, laws, myths, and other structures of meaning become part of an individual's or group's dialogue with nature. People are constantly engaged in constructing maps of the world around them, in defining what a resource is, in determining which sorts of behavior may be environmentally degrading and ought to be prohibited, and generally in choosing the ends of their lives. Though for the purposes of clarification, we may try to distinguish between these three levels of environmental study, in fact they constitute a single dynamic inquiry in which nature, social and economic organization, thought and desire are treated as one whole. And this whole changes as nature changes, as people change, forming a dialectic that runs through all of the past down to the present.

This in general is the program of the new environmental history. It brings together a wide array of subjects, familiar and unfamiliar, rather than setting up some new, esoteric specialty. From that synthesis, we hope, new questions and answers will come.

Natural Environments of the Past

The environmental historian must learn to speak some new languages as well as ask some new questions. Undoubtedly, the most outlandish language that must be learned is the natural scientist's. So full of numbers, laws, terms, and experiments, it is as foreign to the historian as Chinese was to Marco Polo. Yet, with even a smattering of vocabulary, what treasures are here to be understood and taken back home! Concepts from geology, pushing our notions of history back into the Pleistocene, the Silurian, the Precambrian. Graphs from climatology, on which temperatures and precipitation oscillate up and down through the centuries, with no regard for the security of kings or empires. The chemistry of the soil with its cycles of carbon and nitrogen, its pH balances wavering with the presences of salts and acids, setting the terms of agriculture. Any one of these might add a powerful tool to the study of the rise of civilizations. Together, the natural sciences are indispensable aids for the environmental historian, who must begin by reconstructing past landscapes, learning what they were and how they functioned before human societies entered and rearranged them.

But above all it is ecology, which examines the interactions among organisms and between them and their physical environments, that offers the environmental historian the greatest help. This is so in part because, ever since Charles Darwin, ecology has been concerned with past as well as present interactions; it has been integral to the study of evolution. Equally significant, ecology is at heart concerned with the origins, dispersal, and organization of all plant life. Plants form by far the major portion of the earth's biomass. All through history people have depended critically on them for food, medicine, building materials, hunting habitat, and a buffer against the rest of nature. Far more often than not, plants have been humans' allies in the struggle to survive and thrive. Therefore, where people and vegetation come together more issues in environmental history cluster than anywhere else. Take away plant ecology and environmental history loses its foundation, its coherence, its first step.

So impressed are they with this fact that some scholars speak of doing, not environmental, but "ecological history" or "historical ecology." They mean to insist on a tighter alliance with the science. Some years back the scientist and conservationist Aldo Leopold projected such an alliance when he spoke of "an ecological interpretation of history." His own illustration of how that might work had to do with the competition among native Indians, French and English traders, and American settlers for the land of Kentucky, pivotal in the westward movement. The canebrakes growing along Kentucky bottomlands were a formidable barrier to any agricultural settlement, but as luck would have it for the Americans, when the cane was burned and grazed and chopped out, bluegrass sprouted in its place. And bluegrass was all that any farmer, looking for a homestead and a pasture for his livestock, could want. American farmers entered Kentucky by the thousands, and the struggle was soon over. "What if," Leopold wondered, "the plant succession inherent in this dark and bloody ground had, under the impact of forces, given us some worthless sedge, shrub, or weed?" Would Kentucky have become American property as and when it did? . . .

When organisms of many species come together, they form communities, usually highly diverse in makeup, or as they are more commonly called now, ecosystems. An ecosystem is the largest generalization made in the science, encompassing both the organic and inorganic elements of nature bound together in a single place, all in active, reciprocating relationship. Some ecosystems are fairly small and readily demarcated, like a pond in New England, while others are sprawling and ill-defined, as large as the Amazonian rain forest or the Serengeti plain or even the whole earth. All are commonly described, in language derived heavily from physical mechanics and cybernetics, as self-equilibrating like a machine that runs on and on automatically, checking itself when it gets too hot, speeding up when it slows and begins to sputter. Outside disturbances may affect that equilibrium, throwing the machine temporarily off its regular rhythm, but always (or almost always) it returns to some steady state condition. The numbers of species constituting an ecosystem fluctuate around some determinable point; the flow of energy through the machine stays constant. The ecologist is interested in how such systems go on functioning in the midst of continual perturbations, and how and why they break down.

But right there occurs a difficult issue on which the science of ecology has reached no clear consensus. How stable are those natural systems and how susceptible to upset? Is it accurate to describe them as balanced and stable until humans arrive? And if so, then at what point does a change in their equilibrium become excessive, damaging or destroying them? Damage to the individual organism is easy enough to define: It is an impairment of health or, ultimately, it is death. Likewise, damage to a population is not very hard to determine, simply, when its numbers decline. But damage to whole ecosystems is a more controversial matter. No one would dispute that the death of all its trees, birds, and insects would mean the death of a rain-forest ecosystem, or that the draining of a pond would spell the end of that system. But most changes are less catastrophic, and the degree of damage has no easy method of measurement. . . .

There is a further unresolved problem in translating ecology into history. Few scientists have perceived people or human societies as being integral parts of their ecosystems. They leave them out as distractions, imponderables. But people are what the historian mainly studies; consequently, his or her job is to join together what scientists have put asunder.

Human beings participate in ecosystems either as biological organisms akin to other organisms or as culture bearers, though the distinction between the two roles is seldom clear-cut. Suffice it here to say that, as organisms, people have never been able to live in splendid, invulnerable isolation. They breed, of course, like other species, and their offspring must survive or perish by the quality of food, air, and water and by the number of microorganisms that are constantly invading their bodies. In these ways and more, humans have inextricably been part of the earth's ecological order. Therefore, any reconstruction of past environments must include not only forests and deserts, boas and rattlesnakes, but also the human animal and its success or failure in reproducing itself.

Human Modes of Production

Nothing distinguishes people from other creatures more sharply than the fact that it is people who create culture. Precisely what culture really is, however, is anybody's guess. There are literally scores of definitions. For preliminary purposes it can be said that the definitions tend to divide between those including both mental and material activities and those emphasizing mental activities exclusively, and that these distinctions between the mental and material correspond to the second and third levels of analysis in our environmental history. In this section we are concerned with the material culture of a society, its implications for social organization, and its interplay with the natural environment.

   In any particular place nature offers the humans dwelling there a flexible but limited set of possibilities for getting a living. The Eskimos of the northern polar regions, to take an extreme case of limits, cannot expect to become farmers. Instead, they have ingeniously derived a sustenance, not by marshaling seed, plows, and draft animals of other, warmer latitudes, but through hunting. Their food choices have focused on stalking caribou over the tundra and pursuing bowhead whales among floating cakes of ice, on gathering blueberries in season and gaffing fish. Narrow though those possibilities are, they are the gift of technology as much as nature. Technology is the application of skills and knowledge to exploiting the environment. Among the Eskimos technology has traditionally amounted to fish hooks, harpoons, sled runners, and the like. Though constrained by nature, that technology has nonetheless opened up for them a nutritional field otherwise out of reach, as when a sealskin boat allowed them to venture farther out to sea in pursuit of prey. . . .

   As historians address these elemental issues of tools and sustenance, they soon become aware that there have been other disciplines at work here too, and for a long time. Among them is the discipline of anthropologists, and environmental historians have been reading their work with great interest. They have begun to search for clues from anthropologists to critical pieces of the ecological puzzle: What is the best way to understand the relation of human material cultures to nature? Is technology to be viewed as an integral part of the natural world, akin to the fur coat of the polar bear, the sharp teeth of the tiger, the fleet agility of the gazelle, all adaptive mechanisms functioning within ecosystems? Or should cultures be viewed as setting people apart from and outside of nature? Everything in the ecosystem, we are told by natural scientists, has a role and therefore an influence on the workings of the whole; conversely, everything is shaped by its presence in the ecosystem. Are cultures and the societies that create them also to be seen in that double position, both acting on and being acted on? Or are they better described as forming their own kind of "cultural systems" that mesh with ecosystems only in rare, isolated cases? Or, to make the puzzle more complicated still, do humans create with their technology a series of new, artificial ecosystems—a rice paddy in Indonesia or a carefully managed German forest—that require constant human supervision? There is, of course, no single or consistent set of answers to be given to such questions; but anthropologists, who

are among the most wide-ranging and theory-conscious observers of human behavior, can offer some provocative insights. . . .

The modes of production are an endless parade of strategies, as complex in their
taxonomies as the myriad species of insects thriving in the canopy of a rain forest or
the brightly colored fish in a coral reef. In broad terms, we may speak of such modes
as hunting and gathering, agriculture, and modern industrial capitalism. . . . [T]he
environmental historian wants to know what role nature had in shaping the productive
methods and, conversely, what impact those methods had on nature.

This is the age-old dialogue between ecology and economy. Though deriving
from the same etymological roots, the two words have come to denote two separate
spheres, and for good reason: Not all economic modes are ecologically sustainable. Some last for centuries, even millennia, while others appear only briefly and
then fade away, failures in adaptation. And ultimately, over the long stretch of time,
no modes have ever been perfectly adapted to their environment, or there would be
little history.

Perception, Ideology, and Value

Humans are animals with ideas as well as tools, and one of the largest, most conse-
quential of those ideas bears the name "nature." More accurately, "nature" is not
one idea but many ideas, meanings, thoughts, feelings, all piled on top of one another, often in the most unsystematic fashion. Every individual and every culture
has created such agglomerations. We may think we know what we are saying when
we use the word, but frequently we mean several things at once and listeners may
have to work at getting our meaning. We may suppose too that nature refers to
something radically separate from ourselves, that it is "out there" someplace, sitting
solidly, concretely, unambiguously. In a sense, that is so. Nature is an order and a
process that we did not create, and in our absence it will continue to exist; only the
most strident solipsist would argue to the contrary. All the same, nature is a creation
of our minds too, and no matter how hard we may try to see what it is objectively,
in and by and for itself, we are to a considerable extent trapped in the prison of our
own consciousness and web of meanings.

Environmental historians have done some of their best work on this level of cultural analysis, studying the perceptions and values people have held about the nonhuman world. They have, that is, put people thinking about nature under scrutiny. So
impressed have they been by the enduring, pervasive power of ideas that sometimes
they have blamed present environmental abuse on attitudes that go far back into the
recesses of time: as far back as the book of Genesis and the ancient Hebraic ethos of
asserting dominion over the earth; or the Greco-Roman determination to master the
environment through reason; or the still more archaic drive among patriarchal males
to lord it over nature (the "feminine" principle) as well as women. The actual effects
of such ideas, in the past or in the present, are extremely difficult to trace empirically,
but that has not deterred scholars from making some very large claims here. Nor
should it altogether. Perhaps we have too wildly exaggerated a notion of our mental
prowess and its impact on the rest of nature. Perhaps we spend too much time talking
about our ideas, neglecting to examine our behavior. But however overblown some
of these claims may be, it is certainly true that our ideas have been interesting to

contemplate, and nothing among them has been more interesting than our reflections on other animals, plants, soils, and the entire biosphere that gave birth to us. So, for good reason, environmental history must include in its program the study of aspects of esthetics and ethics, myth and folklore, literature and landscape gardening, science and religion—must go wherever the human mind has grappled with the meaning of nature.

For the historian, the main object must be to discover how a whole culture, rather than exceptional individuals in it, perceived and valued nature. Even the most materially primitive society may have had quite sophisticated, complex views. Complexity, of course, may come from unresolved ambiguities and contradictions as well as from profundity. People in industrial countries especially seem to abound in these contradictions: They may chew up the land wholesale and at a frightful speed through real estate development, mining, and deforestation but then turn around and pass laws to protect a handful of fish swimming in a desert spring. Some of this is simply confusion, some of it may be quite reasonable. Given the protean qualities of nature, the fact that the environment presents real dangers as well as benefits to people, this contradictoriness is inescapable. It has everywhere been true of the human reaction. Yet not a few scholars have fallen into the trap of speaking of "the Buddhist view of nature" or "the Christian view" or "the American Indian view," as though people in those cultures were all simple-minded, uncomplicated, unanimous, and totally lacking in ambivalence. Every culture, we should assume, has within it a range of perceptions and values, and no culture has ever really wanted to live in total harmony with its surroundings.

But ideas should not be left floating in some empyrean realm, free from the dust and sweat of the material world. They should be studied in their relations with those modes of subsistence discussed in the preceding section. Without reducing all thought and value to some material base, as though the human imagination was a mere rationalization of the belly's needs, the historian must understand that mental culture does not spring up all on its own. One way to put this relationship is to say that ideas are socially constructed and, therefore, reflect the organization of those societies, their techno-environments and hierarchies of power. Ideas differ from person to person within societies according to gender, class, race, and region. Men and women, set apart almost everywhere into more or less distinctive spheres, have arrived at different ways of regarding nature, sometimes radically so. So too have slaves and their masters, factory owners and workers, agrarian and industrial peoples. They may live together or in close proximity but still see and value the natural world differently. The historian must be alert to these differences and resist easy generalizations about the "mind" of a people or of an age. . . .

As it tries to redefine the search into the human past, environmental history has, as indicated above, been drawing on a number of other disciplines, ranging from the natural sciences to anthropology to theology. It has resisted any attempt to put strict disciplinary fences around its work, which would force it to devise all its own methods of analysis, or to require all these overlapping disciplines to stay within their own discrete spheres. Each may have its tradition, to be sure, its unique way of approaching questions. But if this is an age of global interdependence, it is surely also the moment for some cross-disciplinary cooperation. Scholars need it, environmental history needs it, and so does the earth.

Predicting Environmental History

JARED DIAMOND

This [essay] sets itself the modest task of explaining the broad pattern of history on all the continents for the last 13,000 years. Why did history take such different courses for peoples of different continents?

Eurasians, especially peoples of Europe and eastern Asia, have spread around the globe. They and their overseas descendants now dominate the modern world in wealth and power. Other peoples, including most Africans, survived and have thrown off European domination but remain far behind in wealth and power. Still other peoples, including the original inhabitants of Australia, the Americas and southern Africa, are no longer masters of their own lands but have been decimated, subjugated and even exterminated by European colonialists. Why did history turn out that way, instead of the opposite way? Why were American Indians, Africans and Aboriginal Australians not the ones who conquered or exterminated Europeans and Asians?

This question can easily be pushed back one step further. By the year 1500 [C.E.], the approximate year when Europe's overseas expansion was just beginning, peoples of the different continents already differed greatly in technology and political organization. Much of Eurasia and North Africa was occupied by Iron Age states and empires, some of them on the verge of industrialization. Two Native American peoples, the Incas and Aztecs, ruled over Stone Age or nearly Bronze Age empires. Parts of sub-Saharan Africa were divided among small indigenous Iron Age states or chiefdoms. All peoples of Australia, New Guinea and the Pacific Islands, and many peoples of the Americas and sub-Saharan Africa, lived as Stone Age farmers or hunter–gatherers.

Obviously, those differences as of 1500 [C.E.] were the immediate cause of the modern world's inequalities. Iron Age empires conquered or exterminated Stone Age tribes. But how did the world get to be the way that it was in the year 1500 [C.E.]?

This question, too, can be pushed back a further step, with the help of written histories and archaeological discoveries. Until the end of the last Ice Age around 11,000 B.C.[E.], all humans on all continents were still living as Stone Age hunter–gatherers. Different rates of development on different continents, from 11,000 B.C.[E.] to 1500 [C.E.], were what produced the inequalities of 1500 [C.E.]. While Aboriginal Australians and Native American peoples remained Stone Age hunter–gatherers, most Eurasian peoples and many peoples of the Americas and sub-Saharan Africa gradually developed agriculture, herding, metallurgy and complex political organization. Parts of Eurasia, and one area of the Americas, developed indigenous writing as well. But each of these new developments appeared earlier in Eurasia than elsewhere. For instance, mass production of copper tools was only beginning to spread in the South American Andes in the centuries before 1500 [C.E.], but was already spreading in parts of Eurasia 5,000 years before that. The stone technology of Native Tasmanians in 1500 [C.E.] was simpler than that of Upper Palaeolithic Europe tens of thousands of years earlier.

From Jared Diamond, "The Evolution of Guns and Germs," in A. C. Fabian, ed., *Evolution: Society, Science, and the Universe* (Cambridge: Cambridge University Press, 1998), pp. 46–47, 49–55, 61–62. Reprinted with the permission of Cambridge University Press.

Hence we can finally rephrase our question about the origin of the modern world's inequalities as follows. Why did human development proceed at such different rates on different continents for the last 13,000 years? Those differing rates constitute the broadest pattern of history. . . .

. . . I shall show that the answer to the question about history's broadest pattern has nothing to do with differences among peoples themselves, but instead lies in differences among the biological and geographical environments in which different peoples found themselves.

Europe and the New World: Proximate Factors

. . . Most of us are familiar with the stories of how a few hundred Spaniards under Hernan Cortes overthrew the Aztec Empire, and how another few hundred Spaniards under Francisco Pizarro overthrew the Inca Empire. The populations of each of those empires numbered millions, possibly tens of millions. At the Inca city of Cajamarca in modern Peru, when Pizarro captured the Inca Emperor Atahualpa in 1532, Pizarro's Spaniards consisted of only 62 soldiers on horseback plus 106 foot soldiers, while Atahualpa was leading an Inca army of about 40,000 soldiers.

Most of us are also familiar with the frequently gruesome details of how other Europeans conquered other parts of the New World. The result is that Europeans came to settle and dominate most of the New World, while the Native American population declined drastically from its level as of 1492 [C.E.]. Why did it happen that way? Why did it not happen that Montezuma or Atahualpa led the Aztecs or Incas to conquer Europe?

The *proximate* reasons are obvious. Invading Europeans had steel swords and guns, while Native Americans had only stone and wooden weapons. Just as elsewhere in the world, horses gave the invading Spaniards another big advantage in their conquests of the Incas and Aztecs. Horses had been playing a decisive role in military history ever since they were domesticated at around 4000 B.C.[E.] in the Ukraine. Horses revolutionized warfare in the eastern Mediterranean after 2000 B.C.[E.], later let the Huns and Mongols terrorize Europe and provided the military basis for the kingdoms emerging in West Africa around 1000 [C.E.]. From prehistoric times until the First World War, the speed of attack and retreat that a horse permitted, the shock of its charge and the raised fighting platform that it provided left foot soldiers nearly helpless in the open. Steel swords, guns and horses were the military advantages that repeatedly enabled troops of a few dozen mounted Spaniards to defeat South American Indian armies numbering in the thousands.

Nevertheless, guns, steel swords and horses were not the sole proximate factors in the European conquest of the New World. The Indians killed in battle by guns and swords were far outnumbered by those killed at home by infectious diseases such as smallpox and measles. Those diseases were endemic in Europe, and Europeans had had time to develop both genetic and immune resistance to them, but Indians initially had no such resistance. Diseases that were introduced with the Europeans spread from one Indian tribe to another, far in advance of the Europeans themselves, and killed an estimated 95% of the New World's Indian population. . . .

Finally, there is still another set of proximate factors to be considered. How is it that Pizarro and Cortes reached the New World at all, before Aztec and Inca conquistadores could reach Europe? That depended in the first instance on ships reliably capable of crossing oceans. Europeans had such ships, while the Aztecs and Incas did not. Those ships were backed by the political organization that enabled Spain and other European countries to finance, build, staff and equip the ships. Equally crucial was the role of writing in permitting the quick spread of accurate detailed information, including maps, sailing directions and accounts by earlier voyagers to motivate later explorers. Writing may also be relevant to what seems to us today the incredible naïveté that permitted Atahualpa to walk into Pizarro's trap and permitted Montezuma to mistake Cortes for a returning god. Since the Incas had no writing and the Aztecs had only a short tradition of writing, they did not inherit knowledge of thousands of years of written history. That may have left them less able to anticipate a wide range of human behavior and dirty tricks, and made Pizarro and Cortes better able to do so.

Europe and the New World: Ultimate Factors

So far, we have identified a series of proximate factors behind European colonization of the New World: ships, political organization and writing that brought Europeans to the New World; European germs that killed most Indians before they could reach the battle field; and guns, steel swords and horses that gave Europeans a big advantage on the battle field. Now, let us try to push the chain of causation back further. Why did these proximate advantages go to the Old World rather than to the New World? Theoretically, American Indians might have been the ones to develop steel swords and guns first, to develop ocean-going ships and empires and writing first, to be mounted on domestic animals more terrifying than horses and to bear germs worse than smallpox.

The part of that question that is easiest to answer concerns the reasons why Eurasia evolved the nastiest germs. It is striking that American Indians evolved no devastating epidemic diseases to give to Europeans, in return for the many devastating epidemic diseases that they received from the Old World.

There are two straightforward reasons for this gross imbalance. First, most of our familiar epidemic diseases can sustain themselves only in large dense human populations concentrated into villages and cities, which arose much earlier in the Old World than in the New World. Second, most human epidemic diseases evolved from similar epidemic diseases of the domestic animals with which we came into close contact. For example, measles arose from a disease of our cattle, influenza from a disease of pigs, smallpox from a disease of cows and falciparum malaria from a disease of birds such as chickens. The Americas had a very few native domesticated animal species from which humans could acquire diseases: just the llama/alpaca (varieties of the same ancestral species) and guinea pig in the Andes, the Muscovy duck in tropical South America, the turkey in Mexico and the dog throughout the Americas. In contrast, think of all the domesticated animal species native to Eurasia: the horse, cow, sheep, goat, pig and dog throughout Eurasia; many local domesticates, such as water buffalo and reindeer; many domesticated small mammals, such as cats and rabbits; and many domesticated birds, including chickens, geese and mallard ducks.

Let us now push the chain of reasoning back one step further. Why were there far more species of domesticated animals in Eurasia than in the Americas? Since the Americas harbour over a thousand native wild mammal species and several thousand wild bird species, you might initially suppose that the Americas offered plenty of starting material for domestication.

In fact, only a tiny fraction of wild mammal and bird species has been successfully domesticated, because domestication requires that a wild animal fulfil many prerequisites: a diet that humans can supply, a sufficiently rapid growth rate, willingness to breed in captivity, tractable disposition, a social structure involving submissive behaviour towards dominant members of the same species (a behaviour transferrable to dominant humans) and lack of a tendency to panic when fenced. Thousands of years ago, humans domesticated every possible large wild mammal species worth domesticating, with the result that there have been no significant additions in modern times, despite the efforts of modern science.

Eurasia ended up with the most domesticated animal species in part because it is the world's largest land mass and offered the most wild species to begin with. That pre-existing difference was magnified 13,000 years ago at the end of the last Ice Age, when more than 80% of the large mammal species of North and South America became extinct, probably exterminated by the first arriving Indians. Those extinctions included several species that might have furnished useful domesticated animals had they survived, such as North American horses and camels. As a result, American Indians inherited far fewer species of big wild mammals than did Eurasians, leaving them only with the llama/alpaca as a domesticate. Differences between the Old and New Worlds in domesticated plants are qualitatively similar to these differences in domesticated mammals, though the difference is not so extreme.

A further reason for the higher local diversity of domesticated plants and animals in Eurasia than in the Americas is that Eurasia's main axis is east/west, whereas the main axis of the Americas is north/south. . . . Eurasia's east/west axis meant that species domesticated in one part of Eurasia could easily spread thousands of miles at the same latitude, encountering the same daylength and climate to which they were already adapted. As a result, chickens and citrus fruit domesticated in Southeast Asia quickly spread westwards to Europe, horses domesticated in the Ukraine quickly spread eastwards to China and the sheep, goats, cattle, wheat and barley of the Middle East quickly spread both west and east.

In contrast, the north/south axis of the Americas meant that species domesticated in one area could not spread far without encountering daylengths and climates to which they were not adapted. As a result, the turkey never spread from Mexico to the Andes; llamas/alpacas never spread from the Andes to Mexico, so that the Indian civilizations of Central and North America remained entirely without pack animals; and it took thousands of years for the corn that evolved in Mexico's climate to become modified into a corn adapted to the shorter growing season and seasonally changing daylength of North America. That seems to be the main reason why North America's Mississippi Valley, which you might think should have been fertile enough to support a populous and politically advanced Indian society, did not give rise to one until around 1000 [C.E.], when a variety of corn adapted to temperate latitudes was finally developed.

Eurasia's domesticated plants and animals were important for several other reasons besides letting Europeans develop nasty germs. Domesticated plants and animals yield far more calories per acre than do wild habitats, in which most species are inedible to humans. As a result, populations of farmers and herders are typically ten to 100 times greater than those of hunter–gatherers. That fact alone explains why farmers and herders almost everywhere in the world have been able to push hunter–gatherers out of land suitable for farming and herding. Domestic animals revolutionized land transport. They also revolutionized agriculture, by letting one farmer plough and manure much more land than the farmer could till or manure by his/her own efforts. In addition, hunter–gatherer societies tend to be egalitarian and have no political organization beyond the level of the band or tribe, whereas the food surpluses and storage made possible by agriculture permitted the development of stratified societies with political elites. The food surpluses produced by farmers also accelerated the development of technology, by supporting craftspeople who did not raise their own food and could instead devote themselves to developing metallurgy, writing, swords and guns. . . .

Thus, we began by identifying a series of proximate explanations—guns, germs and so on—for the conquest of the Americas by Europeans. Those proximate factors seem to me ultimately traceable in large part to the Old World's greater number of domesticated plants, much greater number of domesticated animals and east/west axis. The chain of causation is most direct in explaining the Old World's advantages of horses and nasty germs. But domesticated plants and animals also led more indirectly to Eurasia's advantage in guns, swords, ocean-going ships, political organization and writing, all of which were products of the large, dense, sedentary, stratified societies made possible by agriculture. . . .

Conclusion and Outlook

As for the overall meaning of this whirlwind tour through human history, it is that our history has been moulded by our environment. The broadest pattern of human history—namely, the differences between human societies on different continents—seems to me to be attributable to differences in continental environments. In particular, the availability of wild plant and animal species suitable for domestication, and the ease with which those species could spread without encountering unsuitable climates, have contributed decisively to the varying rates of rise of agriculture and herding, which in turn have contributed decisively to human population numbers, population densities and food surpluses, which in turn contributed decisively to the development of writing, technology and political organization.

Using Environmental History

WILLIAM CRONON

When I first started teaching a lecture course on American environmental history at Yale over half a decade ago, I came to the end of the semester feeling that despite all the rough spots and gaps, it had gone as well as I could have expected. My ordinary practice on such occasions is to distribute teaching evaluations during the penultimate week of classes so I can read students' comments and report back to them on what they collectively see as the strengths and weaknesses of the course. When I did this for the new environmental history class, I was taken aback to discover that despite my students' enthusiasm for the course, the vast majority seemed profoundly depressed by what they had learned in it. I was unprepared for this reaction. What my students had apparently concluded from their encounter with my subject was that the American environment had gone from good to bad in an unrelentingly depressing story that left little or no hope for the future. Because my own feelings about the matter were not nearly so bleak, I had not intended to lead students to this dreary conclusion, and the more I thought about it, the more it seemed to me that I had no right to end the course on such a note. Whether or not my students' sense of despair was justified, I did not think it was a particularly useful emotion, either personally or politically. To conclude that the environmental past teaches the hopelessness of the environmental future struck me as a profoundly disempowering lesson—albeit a potentially self-fulfilling one—and I felt that my responsibility both as a teacher and as someone who cares about the future must be to resist such a conclusion.

I therefore wrote a final lecture that ended the class on a deliberately upbeat note with a very personal set of reflections about lessons I had extracted from my study of environmental history—the morals I drew from its stories—and the reasons why I continue to remain hopeful despite all the apparent reasons for feeling otherwise. Leaving aside my own worries about the appropriateness of temporarily turning my lectern into the secular equivalent of a pulpit, I'm persuaded that it was the right thing to do, for my students seemed genuinely grateful for this unusual bout of sermonizing on my part. I still end my environmental history course with a similar lecture. And yet I also think there's something odd about an academic subject that seems to require such an antidote against despair. Certainly I've never felt the need for a comparable closing lecture in my classes on the history of the American West, where I suspect that a residue of frontier optimism and high spiritedness somehow combine with moral outrage and regional pride to produce more ambiguous lessons. Because I've also encountered this sense of despair not just among students but among readers as well, I think it's worth asking why environmental history seems regularly to provoke such a response. A more general way of framing the question is to ask how our study of the environmental past affects our sense of the environmental present and future. Perhaps the simplest way to put this is just to ask: what are the uses of environmental history?

Do practitioners of environmental history have special reason to worry about their field's usefulness? Yes. Like the several other "new" histories born or reenergized in the wake of the 1960s—women's history, African-American history, Chicano history, gay and lesbian history, and the new social history generally—environmental history has always had an undeniable relation to the political movement that helped spawn it. The majority (but not quite all) of those who become environmental historians tend also to regard themselves as environmentalists. And so it is no accident that many of the most important works in the field approach their subjects with explicitly present-day concerns. Any number of environmental histories have clearly been framed to make contemporary political interventions. Roderick Nash's *Wilderness and the American Mind* has played a significant role in helping frame debates about wilderness protection in the three decades since its publication. Samuel Hays's *Conservation and the Gospel of Efficiency* and *Beauty, Health, and Permanence,* though less obviously partisan in their politics than Nash's book, speak just as powerfully to major trends in conservation and environmental politics in the twentieth century. Among the most consistently interventionist of environmental historians has been Donald Worster, whose unflinching moral vision has never failed to produce works of history that are also passionately committed to change. *Nature's Economy* critiqued the twentieth-century evolution of ecological science by seeking to rehabilitate an older natural-history tradition that had fallen into disrepute with many modern ecologists, while *Dust Bowl* and *Rivers of Empire* located the origins of environmental degradation in capitalist world-views and modes of production that are as alive in the present as they have been in the past. Carolyn Merchant joined Worster in bringing an environmentalist perspective to the history of science, but combined it with a more feminist approach to argue in *The Death of Nature* that western science has harmed nature and women in parallel ways; her *Radical Ecology,* though less historical, is still more activist in its efforts to intervene in contemporary political struggles. Even scholars whose work has been less explicitly political have consciously sought to make it relevant to contemporary environmental concerns. Joel Tarr's many studies of pollution and waste streams have always aimed to address the concerns of contemporary policymakers, while Steven Pyne's epic histories of fire have consistently tried to persuade present-day resource managers of the complexity of their task. Pyne has even gone so far as to author a textbook on fire management practices. And so on and on. The list of such interventions is long, and applies in varying degrees to the majority of historians who work in this field. So I think we can take it as a given that many if not most environmental historians aspire to contribute to contemporary environmental politics: they want their histories to be useful not just in helping us understand the past, but in helping us change the future. . . .

One reason I emphasize the importance of our historical practice is that there are impulses within environmentalism that are quite strongly *a*historical or even *anti*historical, placing environmental history in some considerable but little noticed tension with the larger political movement that helped spawn it. This tension is fascinating in its own right, and it significantly complicates the already difficult task that environmental historians face in trying to make themselves "useful" to their fellow environmentalists. One of the longstanding impulses that environmentalism shares with its great ancestor, romanticism, has been to see human societies, especially those affected by capitalist urban-industrialism and the cultural forces of modernity, in opposition to nature. Ironically, environmentalism often commits itself to a fundamentally dualistic vision even as it appeals for holism. According to the standard terms of this dualism, nature is assumed to be stable, balanced, homeostatic, self-healing, purifying, and benign, while modern humanity, in contrast, is assumed to be environmentally unstable, unbalanced, disequilibrating, self-wounding, corrupting, and malign.

Implicit in this opposition is the belief that ideal nature is essentially without history as we know it, save on the very long time-scales that affect plate tectonics, biological evolution, and climatic change. Another way of putting this is to say that natural time is cyclical time, while the time of modern humanity is linear. Time's cycle is the proof of nature's self-healing homeostasis and equilibrium, while time's arrow is the proof of humanity's self-corrupting instability and disequilibrium. Humanity's arrow is the fall, while nature's cycle is salvation. These metaphorical dualisms are among the most powerful in our culture, with roots that stretch back literally to Biblical times, and by stating them in this way I do not intend to critique one or the other half of their implied dialectic. As with most dualisms, both poles of the opposition reveal important truths even as they work to disguise their mutual interdependence. I simply want to note that the environmentalist affection for natural equilibrium and cyclical time as the Archimidean foundation from which to judge the human drama as it unfolds in linear time necessarily implies a not-so-disguised flight from history. The natural or primitive utopia which serves as counterpoint for so many environmentalist critiques of modern society posits a rupture between past and future so radical as to imply what Francis Fukuyama would call an "end of history."

However one may feel about this utopian environmentalist vision—and it has many attractive features—it collides at numerous points with the intellectual agenda that environmental historians have set for themselves. Our task, after all, far from trying to escape from history into nature, is to pull nature itself into the stream of human history. Whatever affection we may feel for the attractions of cyclical time and natural equilibrium, our chief stock in trade is linear time and disequilibrium: we study change. Perhaps one might argue that this is a temporary phenomenon. Maybe, for instance, we tell linear narratives of environmental degradation as moral fables whose purpose is to transform people's consciousness and behavior in ways that will ultimately mean an end to linear time, heralding the coming millennium when cyclical time will reign once again over a stable equilibrium that applies as much to humanity as to nature. But I'm frankly dubious that many of us really believe this: most historians have pretty powerful negative reactions to pronouncements like Fukuyama's about "the end of history"—and not just because we have a professional vested interest in linear time! . . .

Let me move toward a close by offering what seem to me to be some of the core lessons that make environmental history useful not just in its specific claims but in its habits of thought. I'll state these as a general set of very broad, very simple morals for the stories we've been telling. They are among the deepest articles of faith for at least this environmental historian, articles of faith which I suspect many of my colleagues share.

1. All human history has a natural context.

This is so obvious to most environmental historians that it is almost a truism of our subfield, and yet it is also the claim that seems to come as the greatest surprise to our colleagues. History since the 1930s has had a powerful bias toward cultural determinism, spawned in part as a reaction against the extreme environmental determinism that characterized some fields of history and geography in the pre-World War II era when racialist theories held sway. The chief defenders of materialist history in the intervening period were Marxists who had their own reasons for deemphasizing the natural context of human history. Their critics in turn used the attack on Marxism as a reason to reject all determinisms as inherently destructive to human freedom. One important contribution of environmental history, then, has been to reintroduce materialist styles of analysis to the study of past human-environment interactions while trying to finesse a full-blown determinism. Our strategy has been to argue for a dialogue between humanity and nature in which cultural and environmental systems powerfully interact, shaping and influencing each other, without either side wholly determining the outcome. One can restate this prescriptively as follows: *in studying*

environmental change, it is best to assume that most human activities have envi-
ronmental consequences, and that change in natural systems (whether induced by
humans or by nature itself) almost inevitably affects human beings. As a corollary,
most environmental historians would add that human beings are not the only actors
who make history. Other creatures do too, as do large natural processes, and any
history that ignores their effects is likely to be woefully incomplete.

2. Neither nature nor culture is static.

This is the historicist argument I've already mentioned. Any vision of a past human
place in nature that posits an ideal relationship of permanent stability or balance must
defend itself against almost overwhelming evidence to the contrary. Descriptions of
historical eras in which human populations were supposedly in eternal equilibrium
with equally stable natural systems are almost surely golden-age myths. A comparable rejection of stasis has occurred within the modern science of ecology, where
the notion of a permanent climax community as postulated by Frederic Clements
and his followers now seems thoroughly discredited. In its stead, we have a newly
dynamic, even stochastic or chaotic ecology in which history plays a crucial role in
shaping the pattern and process of ecosystems whether or not people are involved.

Recognizing the dynamism of natural and cultural systems does not, of course,
mean that all change is good or that there are no benchmarks for comparing one
kind of change with another. Most past societies, for instance, have not altered the
natural world at anything like the rate or scale that has typified the modern era. To
argue otherwise would be to engage in a different form of myth-making, in which
the values and behaviors of different cultures toward nature are assumed to be
everywhere and always the same—"economic man" being undoubtedly the most
familiar subspecies of the genre. The insights of environmental history tend to be
powerfully anti-essentialist, lying in the middle ground between the golden-age
myth of permanent equilibrium and the economistic myth of a reductively universal
human nature. Our work suggests that nature and culture change all the time, but
that the *rate* and *scale* of such change can vary enormously. . . . Restated prescriptively, this suggests that *the relationship between nature and culture should always*
be viewed as a problem in comparative dynamics, not statics. Naive assumptions
about the stability of natural systems can produce behavior that is as environmentally destructive as it is culturally inappropriate. As a corollary, essentialist arguments about past cultures and environments are almost always historically suspect.

3. All environmental knowledge is culturally constructed
and historically contingent—including our own.

On the surface, this will probably seem the most radical challenge that environmental history has to offer environmentalists who regard nature as a source of absolute
authority for their vision of how people ought to behave in the world. Here again we
encounter the problem of sacred versus historical time. If one is inclined to regard
nature as an eternal realm of absolute facts, stable processes, and permanent values,
it is not at all reassuring to discover that such beliefs have clear historical roots and
that people in other times and other places and other cultures have held very different
views. Much of what they took to be permanent and absolute has since changed, and

the same will likely happen to many of our own most cherished beliefs as well. The historicist impulse seems to undermine sacred knowledge and replace it with a relativist world in which nature is apparently no more than what we think it is, with literally everything up for grabs. If static nature is our moral compass, then historicism threatens to set us adrift on an unfamiliar sea with no way of taking our bearings. . . .

Let me sum up this third lesson more prescriptively: *recognizing the historical contingency of all knowledge helps us guard against the dangers of absolute, decontextualized "laws" or "truths" which can all too easily obscure the diversity and subtlety of environments and cultures alike.* An historical, social-constructionist perspective takes seemingly transparent, absolute environmental "facts" and places them in cultural contexts which render them at once more problematic, more interesting, and more instructive. Paradoxically, by making reality more contingent the historicist approach to knowledge lends greater realism to our understanding of nature and culture alike.

My final lesson may seem oddly put, but seems to me the core of what sets environmental history apart from most other fields that seek to understand and influence the way we relate to the natural world. It describes a peculiar quality that characterizes most historical writing and sets it apart from the social and natural sciences. It is simply this:

4. Historical wisdom usually comes in the form of parables, not policy recommendations or certainties.

The significance of this point is hardly intuitive for anyone who is not a historian. Whenever I lecture to the general public or to scholars in the social or natural sciences, I'm invariably asked afterwards for my predictions about the future course of environmental change. Just as invariably, I explain that historians usually make reluctant prophets, despite the teleological similarities between the stories we tell about the past and the prophecies that others may wish us to make about what will happen in the future. The power of our history derives from the fact that, when speaking about the past, we can at least pretend that we know the end of the story. Doing so enables us to make our arguments and narratives point toward the present and hence seem to explain it, if only for the brief period in which that supposed "ending" continues to hold good. This sense of narrative closure is never available to us for the future, the very contingency of which is what prophecy seeks to contain and resist. Because historians cannot help but respect the awesome, terrifying complexity of past cause and effect, and because we recognize the dangers of teleology even as we embrace it as a necessary consequence of the narrative form, most of us—unlike many of our colleagues in the sciences—are reluctant to predict the future course of events.

This is not to say that we are silent about the future, or that we regard our histories as irrelevant to present concerns. Instead we adopt a much older, albeit less seductively scientific, rhetorical strategy. Rather than make *predictions* about what *will* happen, we offer *parables* about how to interpret what *may* happen. Strange as it may sound, I believe this may be the most important contribution we environmental historians can make in a world where expert knowledge has for the most part forgotten the peculiar form of wisdom that the parable represents. . . .

Ground for Hope

Is telling parables about nature and the human past a useful thing to do? Yes. I believe so in my bones, which is what I told my students when they expressed despair about the seemingly hopeless lessons they thought they had learned from our course in environmental history. Let me close by returning for a moment to my secular pulpit to repeat some of the articles of faith I shared with those students.

The answers we environmental historians give to the question "What's the story?" have the great virtue that they remind people of the immense human power to alter and find meaning in the natural world—and the even more immense power of nature to respond. At the same time, they remind us that whatever we do in nature, we can never know in advance all the consequences of our actions. This need not necessarily point toward despair or cynicism, but rather toward a healthy respect for the complexity and unpredictability of history, which is much akin to the complexity and unpredictability of nature itself. The proper lesson of such complexity, I believe, should be to teach us humility. It should make us more critical of our own certainty and self-righteousness, and deepen our respect for the subtlety and mystery of the lives we lead on this planet, entangled as we are in the warp and woof of linear and cyclical, secular and sacred time. . . .

. . . All of us change the world around us, and yet different people choose to confront their problems and make their changes in strikingly different ways. The diversity of their experiences, past and present, can serve almost as a laboratory for exploring the multitude of choices we ourselves face. Stories about the past lives of such people teach us how difficult it is to act in ways that benefit humanity and nature both—and yet how crucial it is to try. By telling parables that trace the often obscure connections between human history and ecological change, environmental history suggests where we ought to go looking if we wish to reflect on the ethical implications of our own lives.

And that, on reflection, seems quite a useful thing to do.

Interpreting Environmental History

CAROLYN MERCHANT

In *The Hidden Wound,* published in 1989, environmentalist Wendell Berry writes that "the psychic wound of racism has resulted inevitably in wounds in the land, the country itself." When he began writing the book in 1968 during the civil rights movement, he tells us, "I was trying to establish the outlines of an understanding of myself, in regard to what was fated to be the continuing crisis of my life, the crisis of racial awareness." Berry's book is an effort to come to terms with the environmental history of race as reflected in his family's history as slaveholders, in his own childhood on a Kentucky farm in the segregated South, and in his adult life as a conservationist and environmentalist.

Adapted from Carolyn Merchant, "Shades of Darkness: Race and Environmental History," *Environmental History,* 8, no. 3 (July 2003): 380–394 and Merchant, "Gender and Environmental History," *Journal of American History,* 76, no. 4 (March 1990): 1117–1121.

Over the past several decades, environmental historians, like other historians, have become increasingly conscious of the place of race, gender, and class in the interpretation of history. Environmental history has widened its scope to include questions of the meanings and relationships between the environment and the roles played by people of color, by women and men, and by rich and poor. Environmental historians have questioned prejudices such as using environmental conditions and apparent human adaptations to justify slavery in the hot, humid South. They have looked at how women have used and changed the environment in arid, treeless locales, such as the Great Plains. And they have studied environmental conditions and human health in urban neighborhoods and industries in which poor people live and work in a capitalist society that exploits wage labor for the sake of wealth, power, and privilege.

In interpreting environmental history, therefore, one needs to ask probing questions such as: What is race and how is it historically and socially constructed at different times and places? What is gender and how do gender roles change over time in different environments and under different social circumstances? How do different types of societies in different environments, from Native American tribal groupings, to rural farming communities, to industrial capitalist economies foster various egalitarian, hierarchical, or class structures that define people and their access to a good life? What is the character of a just society in which environmental goods and services are distributed in humane ways and in which all people have access to a high quality of life? Historical documents and essays help to answer such questions and to reveal hidden assumptions underlying the writer's own race, gender, and class background. What follows are some examples of the ways in which race, class, and gender enter into the interpretation of environmental history.

In recent years, environmental historians have reflected on the place of racial awareness in the field and have begun the process of writing an environmental history of race. They have explored the negative connections between wilderness and race, cities and race, toxic wastes and race, and their reversal in environmental justice and have analyzed the ideology and practice of environmental racism. These include the following perspectives:

• Native Americans were removed from the lands they had managed for centuries, not only during settlement, as is well known, but during the creation of the national parks and national forests. Indians resisted these moves in an effort to maintain autonomy and access to resources.

• American Indians and African Americans perceived wilderness in ways that differed markedly from those of white Americans.

• Slavery and soil degradation are interlinked systems of exploitation and deep-seated connections exist between the enslavement of human bodies and the enslavement of the land. Blacks resisted that enslavement in complex ways that maintained African culture and created unique African American ways of living on the land.

• A "coincidental order of injustice"—in environmentalist Jeffrey Romm's terminology—reigned in post-Civil War America as emancipated blacks in the South were expected to pay for land with wages at the same time that free lands taken from Indians were being promoted to whites via the Homestead Act and other land acts.

• African Americans bore the brunt of early forms of environmental pollution and disease as whites fled urban areas to the new streetcar suburbs. Black neighborhoods became toxic dumps and black bodies became toxic sites. Out of such experiences

arose African American environmental activism in the Progressive Era and the environmental justice movement of the late twentieth century.
•   Over time the meanings attached to skin colors have been redefined in ways that reinforce environmental and institutional racism.

Viewed from the perspective of race, the rich resources of the American environment were developed at the expense of Indians and blacks. From the ideological standpoint of European settlers, the wilderness and its native peoples needed to be tamed, improved, and civilized. Native American lands were appropriated by Europeans as free lands, while Africans were enslaved to provide the free labor that enabled many European Americans to claim political freedom. Warfare, disease, and dependency on trade goods all undercut Indian power to resist European expansion. As Indian populations declined, African American populations increased, first from the slave trade and then, after its official demise in 1808, through smuggling and natural increase as tobacco dominance gave way to the cotton boom. On economic grounds, the slave system both caused the destruction of black bodies and contributed to the rapid degradation of Southern soils, as tobacco, rice, sugar, and cotton became cash crops in an expanding world market.

Despite their racial degradation, however, Native and African Americans maintained their cultural identities, making significant contributions to agriculture and hence to environmental history. Indians contributed maize (corn), beans, squash, and pumpkins to America as well as Europe. African foods were stowed on slave ships and then grown in provision gardens. As a result, African, Native American, and European foods became mixed together, mutually influencing each other. Slave traders, as well as slaves, introduced crops, having obtained them in other parts of the world. Yams were brought by slaves from Africa. Eggplant came from Africa to South America, whence it was brought by Portuguese slave trading ships to the United States. Peanuts came from South America and were introduced into Virginia by African cooks who arrived aboard slave ships. But food is also a cultural construct and is therefore not only good to eat, but is important to people in maintaining historical and cultural identities. Rituals and traditions, such as songs and dances, were important in association with the foods grown by Indians and brought by black people from Africa. And from an environmental standpoint, both Native American and African American gardens exhibited ecological effects that enhanced food production. Crops grown together kept down insect pests and weeds, hence gardens packed with crops might result in relatively higher yields per acre than fields of monocultures grown alone. A racial perspective is therefore an important element in understanding environmental history.

A class perspective is likewise important for interpreting environmental history. People at all levels of society use natural resources and contribute to environmental pollution. Working class people often interact most directly with the land in extracting resources for the market. Fishers, loggers, trappers, farmworkers, ironworkers, coal miners, and industrial workers supply much of the labor for the food and fuel on which society depends. They are in turn the most vulnerable to environmental disasters such as droughts, fires, fishery collapses, mine accidents, fluctuations in the labor supply, and market prices. Middle- and upper-class citizens are often the most conspicuous consumers of environmental goods and energy sources. From automobiles and gasoline to television sets and computers, those with the most wealth and status often extract the most from nature and return the most waste.

On the other hand, many of those who are closest to the land practice conservation and have developed an intimate environmental awareness, while many middle- and upper-class individuals become environmental leaders and activists who help to spear conservation movements and to develop environmentally friendly technologies. Knowing who is writing environmental history is also important. Lower-class workers are usually too busy making a living to write their stories or leave literary legacies, while educated elites contribute much of the material that can be replicated in printable sources. In reading environmental history, therefore, it is important to ask who is writing, what they are advocating, and from what class or environmental perspective they are making their argument.

A gender perspective can also add to environmental history in important ways. Women and men have historically had different roles in production relative to the environment. In subsistence modes of production such as those of native peoples, women's impact on nature is immediate and direct. In gathering-hunting-fishing economies, women collect and process plants, small animals, bird eggs, and shellfish and fabricate tools, baskets, mats, slings, and clothing, while men hunt larger animals, fish, construct weirs and hut frames, and burn forests and brush. Because water and fuelwood availability affect cooking and food preservation, decisions over environmental degradation that dictate when to move camp and village sites may lie in the hands of women. In horticultural communities, women are often the primary producers of crops and fabricators of hoes, planters, and digging sticks, but when such economies are transformed by markets, the cash economies and environmental impacts that ensue are often controlled by men. Women's access to resources to fulfill basic needs may come into direct conflict with male roles in the market economy, as in Seneca women's loss of control over horticulture to male agriculture and men's access to cash through greater mobility in nineteenth-century America or in India's chipco (tree-hugging) movement of the past decade, wherein women literally hugged trees to protest declining access to fuelwood for cooking as male-dominated lumbering expanded.

In the agrarian economy of colonial and frontier America, women's outdoor production, like men's, had immediate impact on the environment. While men's work in cutting forests, planting and fertilizing fields, and hunting or fishing affected the larger homestead environment, women's dairying activities, free-ranging barnyard fowl, and vegetable, flower, and herbal gardens all affected the quality of the nearby soils and waters and the level of insect pests, altering the effects of the microenvironment on human health. In the nineteenth century, however, as agriculture became more specialized and oriented toward market production, men took over dairying, poultry-raising, and truck farming, resulting in a decline in women's outdoor production. Although the traditional contributions of women to the farm economy continued in many rural areas and some women assisted in farm as well as home management, the general trend toward capitalist agribusiness increasingly turned chickens, cows, and vegetables into efficient components of factories within fields managed for profits by male farmers.

In the industrial era, as middle-class women turned more of their energies to deliberate child rearing and domesticity, they defined a new but still distinctly female relation to the natural world. In their socially constructed roles as moral mothers, they often taught children about nature and science at home and in the elementary schools. By the Progressive era, women's focus on maintaining a home for husbands and children led many women . . . to spearhead a nationwide conservation movement to save forest and waters and to create national and local parks. Although the gains of the movement have been attributed by historians to men such as President Theodore Roosevelt, forester Gifford Pinchot and preservationist John Muir, the efforts of thousands of women were directly responsible for many of the country's most significant conservation achievements. Women writers on nature such as Isabella Bird, Mary Austin, and Rachel Carson have been among the most influential commentators on the American response to nature.

At the level of cognition as well, a sensitivity to gender enriches environmental history. Native Americans, for example, construed the natural world as animated and created by spirits and gods. Origin stories included tales of mother earth and father sky, grandmother woodchucks and coyote tricksters, corn mothers and tree spirits. Such deities mediated between nature and humans, inspiring rituals and behaviors that helped to regulate environmental use and exploitation. An animate earth and an I/thou relationship between humans and the natural world does not prevent the exploitation of resources for human use, but it entails an ethic of restraint and propitiation by setting up rituals to be followed before mining ores, damming brooks, or planting and harvesting crops. The human relationship to the land is intimately connected to daily survival. Environmental history can thus be made more complete by including a gender analysis of the effects of women and men on ecology and their roles in production.

When mercantile capitalism, industrialization, and urbanization began to distance increasing numbers of male elites from the land in seventeenth-century England and in nineteenth-century America, the mechanistic framework created by the "fathers" of modern science legitimated the use of nature for human profit making. The conception that nature was dead, made up of inert atoms moved by external forces, that God was an engineer and mathematician, and that human perception was the result of particles of light bouncing off objects and conveyed to the brain as discrete sensations meant that nature responded to human interventions, not as active participant, but as passive instrument. Thus the way in which world views, myths, and perceptions are constructed by gender at the cognitive level can be made an integral part of environmental history.

Additionally, ideas drawn from feminist theory suggest the usefulness of another level of analysis—reproduction—that has both biological and social aspects. First, all species reproduce themselves generationally and their population levels have impacts on the local ecology. But for humans, the numbers that can be sustained are related to the mode of production: More people can occupy a given ecosystem under a horticultural than a gathering-hunting-fishing mode, and still more under an industrial mode. Humans reproduce themselves biologically in accordance with the social and ethical norms of the culture into which they are born. Native peoples adopted an array of benign and malign population control techniques such as long lactation, abstention, coitus interruptus, the use of native plants to induce abortion, infanticide, and senilicide. Carrying capacity, nutritional factors, and tribally accepted customs dictated the numbers of infants that survived to adulthood in order to reproduce the tribal whole. Colonial Americans, by contrast, encouraged high numbers of births owing to the scarcity of labor in the new lands. With the onset of industrialization in the nineteenth century, a demographic transition resulted in fewer births per female. Intergenerational reproduction, therefore, mediated through production, has impact on the local ecology.

Second, people (as well as other living things) must reproduce their own energy on a daily basis through food and must conserve that energy through clothing (skins, furs, or other methods of bodily temperature control) and shelter. Gathering or planting food crops, fabricating clothing, and constructing houses are directed toward the reproduction of daily life.

In addition to these biological aspects of reproduction, human communities reproduce themselves socially in two additional ways. People pass on skills and behavioral norms to the next generation of producers, and that allows a culture to reproduce itself over time. They also structure systems of governance and laws that maintain the social order of the tribe, town, or nation. Many such laws and policies deal with the allocation and regulation of natural resources, land, and property rights. They are passed by legislative bodies and administered through government agencies and a system of justice. Law in this interpretation is a means of maintaining and modifying a particular social order. These four aspects of reproduction (two biological and two social) interact with ecology as mediated by a particular mode of production.

While in most societies governance may have been vested in the hands of men (hence patriarchy), the balance of power between the sexes differed. In gatherer-hunter and horticultural communities, extraction and production of food may have been either equally shared by or dominated by women, so that male (or female) power in tribal reproduction (chiefs and shamans) was balanced by female power in production. In subsistence-oriented communities in colonial and frontier America, men and women shared power in production, although men played dominant roles in legal-political reproduction of the social whole. Under industrial capitalism in the nineteenth century, women's loss of power in outdoor farm production was compensated by a gain of power in the reproduction of daily life (domesticity) and in the socialization of children and husbands (the moral mother) in the sphere of reproduction. A gender perspective on environmental history therefore both offers a more balanced and complete picture of past human interactions with nature and advances its theoretical frameworks.

Race, gender, and class are lenses through which to view history and interpret human interactions with the environment. How these three categories are constructed socially and culturally, how and why they change over time, and why they are important add to the complexity of history. They help us to envision the possibility of a socially just world that could be a better place in which to live.

ψ *F U R T H E R   R E A D I N G*

Kendall E. Bailes, ed., *Environmental History: Critical Issues in Comparative Perspective* (1985)

William Beinart and Peter Coates, *Environment and History: The Taming of Nature in the USA and South Africa* (1995)

William Cronon, "Kennecott Journey: The Paths out of Town," in William Cronon, George Miles, and Jay Gitlin, eds. *Under an Open Sky: Rethinking America's Western Past* (1992)
———, "A Place for Stories: Nature, History, and Narrative," *Journal of American History* 78, no. 4 (March 1992), 1347–1376

————, "The Uses of Environmental History," *Environmental History Review* 17 (Fall 1993), 1–22

Alfred W. Crosby, *The Columbian Exchange: Biological and Cultural Consequences of 1492* (1972), reprint (2003)

————, *Ecological Imperialism: The Biological Expansion of Europe* (1986)

————, "The Past and Present of Environmental History," *American Historical Review* 100 (October 1995), 1177–1190

Jared Diamond, *Guns, Germs, and Steel: The Fates of Human Societies* (1998)

Samuel P. Hays, *Explorations in Environmental History* (1998)

————, Char Miller, Vera Norwood, J. Donald Hughes, and Richard White, "Forum: Environmental History, Retrospect and Prospect," *Pacific Historical Review* 70 (February 2001), 55–101

J. Donald Hughes, "Ecology and Development as Narrative Themes of World History," *Environmental History Review* 19 (Spring 1995), 1–16

Melissa Leach and Cathy Green, "Gender and Environmental History: From Representation of Women and Nature to Gender Analysis of Ecology and Politics," *Environment and History* 3 (1997), 343–370

Barbara Leibhardt, "Interpretation and Causal Analysis: Theories in Environmental History," *Environmental Review* 12 (1988), 23–36

Chris H. Lewis, "Telling Stories About the Future: Environmental History and Apocalyptic Science," *Environmental History Review* 17 (Fall 1993), 43–60

Chris J. Magoc, ed., *So Glorious a Landscape: Nature and the Environment in American History and Culture* (2001)

Carolyn Merchant, *The Columbia Guide to American Environmental History* (2002)

Char Miller and Hal Rothman, eds., *Out of the Woods: Essays in Environmental History* (1997)

Timo Myllyntaus and Mikko Saikku, eds., *Encountering the Past in Nature: Essays in Environmental History* (2001)

Roderick Nash, "American Environmental History: A New Teaching Frontier," *Pacific Historical Review* 41 (1972), 362–372

James O'Connor, "What Is Environmental History? Why Environmental History?" *Capitalism, Nature, Socialism* 8 (June 1997), 1–27

John Opie, "Environmental History: Pitfalls and Opportunities," *Environmental Review* 7 (1983), 8–16

Joseph M. Petulla, *American Environmental History: The Exploitation and Conservation of Natural Resources,* 2nd ed. (1988)

Lawrence Rakestraw, "Conservation History: An Assessment," *Pacific Historical Review* 43 (1972), 271–288

Emily Wyndham Barnett Russell, *People and the Land Through Time: Linking Ecology and History* (1997)

Theodore Steinberg, *Down to Earth: Nature's Role in American History* (2002)

Mart A. Stewart, "Environmental History: Profile of a Developing Field," *History Teacher* 31 (May 1998), 351–368

————, "Southern Environmental History," in John Boles, ed. *A Companion to the American South* (2002)

"Theories of Environmental History," special issue of *Environmental Review* 11 (Winter 1987), 251–305

Louis Warren, *American Environmental History* (2003)

Richard White, "Historiographical Essay, American Environmental History: The Development of a New Field," *Pacific Historical Review* 54 (1985), 297–335

Donald Worster, ed., *The Ends of the Earth* (1989)

————, "History as Natural History: An Essay on Theory and Method," *Pacific Historical Review* 53 (1984), 1–19

————, et al., "A Roundtable: Environmental History," *Journal of American History* 76 (March 1990), 1087–1147

CHAPTER
2

Native American Ecology
and European Contact

☙

Some 14,000 years ago, peoples of Asian origin migrated across the Bering land bridge and then down the North American corridor as glaciers melted. They expanded southward and southeastward into North and South America and subsequently eastward as the ice melted, reaching northeastern Canada about 7,500 years ago. As they moved into different environments, they developed ecologically adapted means of subsistence and unique cultures, including technologies for hunting large mammals; capturing fish, waterfowl, and small mammals; gathering native plants; and cultivating crops. We find three examples of ecological adaptations in the Pueblo Indians of the arid American Southwest, the Micmac Indians of the northeastern forests, and the Plains Indians of the mid-continental grasslands.

When these Native Americans encountered Europeans in the fifteenth century, the Pueblos were living in walled, multistoried pueblos and practicing settled, irrigated agriculture. Their incipient "hydraulic" societies were growing maize, beans, and squash; hunting antelope; and gathering wild desert fruits. The Micmac Indians in the region that is now the Gaspé Peninsula of Canada (just below the mouth of the St. Lawrence River) lived above the latitude at which maize could reliably be harvested and were a nomadic gathering-hunting-fishing people. By contrast, several tribes of Indians living on the borders of the Great Plains became nomadic as a result of a European introduction—the horse—and were able to exploit grassland resources through more efficient hunting.

Encounters between Pueblos and Spanish in the Southwest and between Micmacs and French in the Northeast and the introduction of horses on the Great Plains altered the ecological habitats and cultures of Native Americans. Although the transformation processes in the three cases had similarities, they were also different. Spanish explorers moving north from Mexico into Pueblo territory sought gold, silver, and copper in the mesa lands of the Southwest; European fishers and fur traders extracted fur-bearing animals from the Gaspé region for the European trade; horses created a new way of life on the Great Plains for nomadic Indians, who could now kill game more efficiently, but who lacked the security of sedentary agriculture. European diseases, such as smallpox, measles, diphtheria, and bubonic plague—to which Native Americans had no immunity, the Bering ice fields having long ago filtered *out those disease-bearing microbes—undercut the Indians' ability to reproduce themselves and their cultures, increasing their receptivity to missionary teachings, which in turn undermined their earth-based religions.*

European livestock, such as horses, cattle, goats, and sheep; crops, such as Old World grains, peas, and vegetables; and weeds and varmints altered the native ecology, but also added to Indian subsistence. These three examples of Pueblos, Micmacs, and Plains Indians illustrate different processes of transformation of Indian ways of life by European introductions in three different ecosystems: deserts, forests, and grasslands. (See Maps 2, 4, and 9 in the Appendix.)

℣ D O C U M E N T S

Because Native American cultures were transmitted orally and visually through stories, dance, pottery, baskets, costumes, and masks, the earliest written records of Indian beliefs and ways of life come mainly from European explorers, missionaries, artists, and other observers. The documents in this section reflect the reports, viewpoints, and cultural biases of the Europeans who explored and colonized three different New World environments occupied by Indians: deserts, forests, and grasslands.

Document 1, a report by Hernán Gallegos of a Spanish expedition in 1580 to what is now New Mexico, describes the roles of Pueblo Indian men and women in producing their subsistence—food, clothing, and shelter. Document 2, a narrative by Spanish explorer Antonio de Espejo, a member of the Chamuscado-Rodríguez expedition of 1582, reveals the extent to which Pueblo villages successfully developed and relied on irrigation to create large surpluses of stored foods. Document 3 presents the 1601 testimony of Ginés de Herrera Horta, a twenty-five-year-old legal assessor and auditor who was sent to work for colonizer Don Juan de Oñate. Horta was appearing at an investigation, ordered by the Spanish viceroy, into Oñate's activities in New Mexico. He reports on Oñate's brutality toward the Pueblos and reveals changes in Indian attitudes toward the Spanish since their colonization in 1598.

Documents 4 and 5 were written by French missionaries who lived with the Micmac Indians in the forests of the Gaspé Peninsula. They record not only the Indians' methods and ethics of hunting and food preparation but also the transformation of these methods under the influence of the fur trade. In Document 4, dating from 1672, the Jesuit Nicolas Denys discusses Micmac life before and after the fur trade; Document 5, from 1691, features the recollections of Father Chrestien Le Clercq on the ways in which hunters imitated the habits of their prey, adhered to rituals for disposing of these animals' remains, and respected the power of menstruating women.

Indians on the Great Plains obtained horses from the Pueblo Indians after the Pueblo Revolt of 1680 and utilized them to hunt bison. Document 6 reveals the perceptions of Anglo-American explorers Meriwether Lewis and William Clark concerning the abundance of life on the Great Plains and the Mandan Indians' use of horses and bison during their 1804–1806 expedition to map the Mississippi and Missouri river systems. Another early account of Plains Indians' use of bison and horses is given by the Indians' pictographs drawn on bison hides, as recorded in Document 7 by artist George Catlin in 1844. As a group the documents show how Indians adapted to and used different North American environments and how Europeans changed both the Indians and their landscapes through the introduction of animals, metal weapons, and trade.

1. A Spanish Explorer Views the Pueblos, 1580

The people sustain themselves on corn, beans, and calabashes. They make tortillas and corn-flour gruel (*atole*), have buffalo meat and turkeys—they have large numbers of the latter. There is not an Indian who does not have a corral for his turkeys, each of which holds a flock of one hundred birds. The natives wear Campeche-type cotton blankets, for they have large cotton fields. They raise many small shaggy dogs—which, however, are not like those owned by the Spaniards—and build underground huts in which they keep these animals. . . .

After we took our leave of this people, the Indians led us to a large pueblo of another nation, where the inhabitants received us by making the sign of the cross with their hands in token of peace, as the others had done before. As the news spread, the procedure in this pueblo was followed in the others.

We entered the settlement, where the inhabitants gave us much corn. They showed us many ollas and other earthenware containers, richly painted, and brought quantities of calabashes and beans for us to eat. We took a little, so that they should not think we were greedy nor yet receive the impression that we did not want it; among themselves they consider it disparaging if one does not accept what is offered. One must take what they give, but after taking it may throw it away wherever he wishes. Should one throw it to the ground, they will not pick it up, though it may be something they can utilize. On the contrary, they will sooner let the thing rot where it is discarded. This is their practice. Thus, since we understood their custom, we took something of what they gave us. Moreover, we did this to get them into the habit of giving freely without being asked. Accordingly, they all brought what they could. The supply of corn tortillas, corn-flour gruel, calabashes, and beans which they brought was such that enough was left over every day to feed five hundred men. Part of this the natives carried for us. The women make tortillas similar to those of New Spain, and tortillas of ground beans, too. In these pueblos there are also houses of three and four stories, similar to the ones we had seen before; but the farther one goes into the interior the larger are the pueblos and the houses, and the more numerous the people.

The way they build their houses, which are in blocks, is as follows: they burn the clay, build narrow walls, and make adobes for the doorways. The lumber used is pine or willow; and many rounded beams, ten and twelve feet long, are built into the houses. The natives have ladders by means of which they climb to their quarters. These are movable wooden ladders, for when the Indians retire at night, they pull them up to protect themselves against enemies since they are at war with one another.

These people are handsome and fair-skinned. They are very industrious. Only the men attend to the work in the cornfields. The day hardly breaks before they go about with hoes in their hands. The women busy themselves only in the preparation

Excerpts from "[Hernán Lamero] Gallegos' Relation of the Chamuscado-Rodríguez Expedition," trans. and ed. by George P. Hammond and Agapito Rey, in *The Rediscovery of New Mexico, 1580–1594*. Albuquerque, NM: The University of New Mexico Press, 1966, vol. 3, excerpts from pp. 83–86; originally published in Santa Fe, NM, 1927; translation from original in Archivo General de Indias at Seville. Reprinted by permission of University of New Mexico Press.

of food, and in making and painting their pottery and *chicubites,* in which they prepare their bread. These vessels are so excellent and delicate that the process of manufacture is worth watching; for they equal, and even surpass, the pottery made in Portugal. The women also make earthen jars for carrying and storing water. These are very large, and are covered with lids of the same material. There are millstones on which the natives grind their corn and other foods. These are similar to the millstones in New Spain, except that they are stationary; and the women, if they have daughters, make them do the grinding.

These Indians are very clean people. The men bear burdens, but not the women. The manner of carrying loads, sleeping, eating, and sitting is the same as that of the Mexicans, for both men and women, except that they carry water in a different way. For this the Indians make and place on their heads a cushion of palm leaves, similar to those used in Old Castile, on top of which they place and carry the water jar. It is all very interesting.

The women part their hair in Spanish style. Some have light hair, which is surprising. The girls do not leave their rooms except when permitted by their parents. They are very obedient. They marry early; judging by what we saw, the women are given husbands when seventeen years of age. A man has one wife and no more. The women are the ones who spin, sew, weave and paint. Some of the women, like the men, bathe frequently. Their baths are as good as those of New Spain.

In all their valleys and other lands I have seen, there are one hundred pueblos. We named the region the province of San Felipe and took possession of it in the name of his Majesty by commission of his Excellency, Don Lorenzo Suárez de Mendoza, Count of Coruña, viceroy, governor and captain-general of New Spain.

2. Spanish Explorers Observe Pueblo Irrigation, 1582

They have fields planted with corn, beans, calabashes, and tobacco (*piciete*) in abundance. These crops are seasonal, dependent on rainfall, or they are irrigated by means of good ditches. They are cultivated in Mexican fashion, and in each planted field the worker has a shelter, supported by four pillars, where food is carried to him at noon and he spends the siesta; for usually the workers stay in their fields from morning until night just as do the people of Castile. . . .

We left the province of the Emexes, and after going west for three days, some fifteen leagues, came to a pueblo named Acoma, which we thought had more than six thousand souls. Acoma is built on top of a lofty rock, more than fifty estados high, and out of the rock itself the natives have hewn stairs by which they ascend and descend to and from the pueblo. It is a veritable stronghold, with water cisterns at the top and quantities of provisions stored in the pueblo. Here the Indians gave us many blankets and chamois skins, belts made from strips of buffalo hide that had been dressed like Flanders leather, and abundant supplies of corn and turkeys.

From "Report of Antonio de Espejo," in George P. Hammond and Agapito Rey, *The Rediscovery of New Mexico, 1580–1594.* Albuquerque, N.M.: The University of New Mexico Press, 1966 [1927], vol. 3, pp. 224–225.

These people have their fields two leagues distant from the pueblo, near a medium-sized river, and irrigate their farms by little streams of water diverted from a marsh near the river. Close to the sown plots we found many Castile rosebushes in bloom; and we also found Castile onions, which grow wild in this land without being planted or cultivated. In the adjacent mountains there are indications of mines and other riches, but we did not go to inspect them because the natives there were numerous and warlike.

The mountain dwellers, who are called Querechos, came down to serve the people in the towns, mingling and trading with them, bringing them salt, game (such as deer, rabbits, and hares), dressed chamois skins, and other goods in exchange for cotton blankets and various articles accepted in payment. Their form of government and other characteristics were the same as in the rest of the provinces. They held a solemn ceremonial dance for us, in which the people dressed very gaily and performed juggling tricks, including some with live snakes that were quite elaborate, all of which was most interesting to watch. These Indians presented us with ample provisions of everything they had, and then, after three days, we left their province.

3. A Spaniard Testifies on the Effects of Pueblo Colonization, 1601

In Mexico, July 30, 1601, Factor Don Francisco de Valverde called as witness the bachiller, Ginés de Herrera Horta, a resident of this city, who took his oath in due legal manner and promised to tell the truth. On being questioned the witness stated that he went to the provinces of New Mexico about a year and a half ago, more or less, as chief auditor and legal assessor to Don Juan de Oñate, governor of the said provinces. . . . They reached the pueblo of San Gabriel, New Mexico, which is the place where Don Juan de Oñate has established his headquarters. The whole region is pacified and the natives of that district have rendered obedience to his majesty, all by the efforts of Don Juan de Oñate. . . .

Asked how long he stayed in New Mexico, the witness said that he remained there three or four months, more or less. The reason that he remained only such a short time was that the governor refused to recognize the commission which he brought as auditor and legal assessor. In view of this, the witness asked his permission to return. . . .

Asked what good and bad experiences the Spaniards had encountered, what opposition, what modes of offense or defense the Indians had offered from the time the governor arrived in the province until March 23 of the present year, . . . the witness declared that two days before he started out from the camp, the commissary of the friars, Fray Juan de Escalona, of the seraphic order of Saint Francis, . . . took him to the secrecy of his cell, and told him . . . in detail what had happened to the Indians of a pueblo named Acoma, which is situated on a high rock.

Excerpts from Ginés de Herrera Horta, in George P. Hammond and Agapito Rey, *Don Juan de Oñate, Colonizer of New Mexico, 1595–1628.* Albuquerque, N.M.: The University of New Mexico Press, 1953, pp. 643–656. Reprinted by permission of University of New Mexico Press.

. . . Don Juan de Zaldívar, nephew of the governor, . . . had gone with twelve or fourteen men to explore and seek new things not yet known. . . . They came to the pueblo of Acoma, where they asked the Indians for provisions. The natives furnished them some, and the Spaniards proceeded on their journey about two leagues beyond the pueblo.

Then the maese de campo, Captain Escalante, Diego Núñez, and other men turned back to ask again for provisions, fowl, and blankets, and even to take them by force. When the Indians saw this, they began to resist and to defend themselves. This witness was told that the Spaniards had killed one or two Indians. Then the Indians killed the maese de campo and Diego Núñez and the others with rocks and slabs of stone. When the governor learned of this, he declared war by fire and sword against the Indians of the pueblo. . . . He set out with seventy soldiers to punish the aforesaid Indians. Afraid of what the Spaniards might do, the natives refused to surrender, but defended themselves.

Thus the punishment began, lasting almost two days, during which many Indians were killed. Finally, overcome and exhausted from the struggle, the Indians gave up, offering blankets and fowl to the sargento mayor and his soldiers, who refused to accept them. Instead, the sargento mayor had the Indians arrested and placed in an estufa [hole]. Then he ordered them taken out one by one, and an Indian he had along stabbed them to death and hurled them down the rock. When other Indian men and women, who had taken shelter in other estufas, saw what was going on, they fortified themselves and refused to come out. In view of this, the sargento mayor ordered that wood be brought and fires started and from the smoke many Indian men, women, and children suffocated. This witness was told that some were even burned alive. All of the men, women, and children who survived were brought to the camp as prisoners. The governor ordered the children placed in the care of individuals. The men and women from eighteen to nineteen years of age were declared slaves for twenty years. Others were maimed by having their feet cut off; this witness saw some of them at the said camp. He was told that most of the slaves had run away, that they had tried to reestablish the pueblo, and that the governor neither authorized nor prevented this, but dissimulated, although this witness heard that he wanted to send someone or go himself to see the said pueblo. . . . The reason why the commissary charged this witness on his conscience to tell this story was because he considered the punishment and enslavement of the Indians unjust and that the viceroy should order the prisoners liberated. . . .

The Indians of [Jumanes pueblo] are all orderly, peaceful, and timid, and live in great fear of the Spaniards.

Asked how many Spaniards there were in the said provinces at the time he left, the witness said that there were about one hundred and fifty soldiers, forty-two to fifty of them married.

Asked what cattle there were in those provinces and that Don Juan had at his camp for the service and provisioning of his people, the witness said he thought that there might be one thousand head of sheep and goats, more or less. He saw most of this livestock at a pueblo named Santa Clara, and at San Miguel, in the care of a certain Naranjo. The rest of the animals were at the camp. This witness did not see any mares, but he heard that there were some, though he did not learn how many. He heard that they had taken fifteen hundred horses on the first expedition, of which many were lost; some died and others were found shot with arrows. He heard that altogether, including those taken at first as well as those sent with the reinforcements, there might be five hundred left. As for the cattle, when this witness arrived at the said camp, he noticed that they were not slaughtering or eating beef because the cattle had been consumed. Some told him that they had slaughtered the oxen they had used to pull their carts, and that they were plowing with horses. So he thinks that there may be four hundred head of cattle left, which are those that were taken with the reinforcements. Of these, they have been killing seven animals each week. This provides a very limited supply of meat for each soldier, so they do not eat it throughout the week. This witness understands that the said stock will soon be exhausted, because he heard it said that they do not reproduce very well in that land. On the contrary, the stock will give out, as he has stated. As for oxen, there are no more left than those taken with the carts when the reinforcement was sent, and these number perhaps one hundred and fifty. As to mules, there must be two hundred and fifty or three hundred, including those which came with the carts taken by the friars. . . .

Asked whether the governor had levied any tribute or personal service on the friendly and peaceful Indians under his jurisdiction to work the fields, harvest the crops, or do other necessary labors in his camp, the witness said that all he knows is that every month the soldiers go out by order of the governor to all the pueblos to procure maize. The soldiers go in groups of two or three and come back with the maize for their own sustenance. The Indians part with it with much feeling and weeping and give it of necessity rather than of their own accord, as the soldiers themselves told this witness. If any kernels fall on the ground, the Indians follow and pick them up, one by one. This witness has seen this happen many times. Some of the Indians, men and women, who formerly lived at this pueblo where the camp now is, remained there and bring wood and water for the Spaniards, so that the latter would give them some maize. This witness has seen it himself. He was told that the Indians store their maize for three and four years to provide against the sterility of the land, for it rains very seldom, although there is much snow, which helps to moisten the ground so that they may harvest what they plant.

The tribute which the governor has levied on the Indians requires that each resident give a cotton blanket per year. Those who have no blankets give tanned deerskins and buffalo hides, dressed in their usual manner. The lack of blankets is due to the scarcity of cotton grown there. This witness has seen the cotton next to the maize fields of the Indians. He was assured that, in the pueblos where the soldiers went, if the natives said that they had no blankets to give, the soldiers took them from the backs of the Indian women and left them naked. . . .

As for personal services, this witness does not know that they have been imposed on the natives, except that when there is need to repair a house the Spaniards ask the governor's permission to bring some Indian women to repair it, for, as he has stated, the women are the ones who do this. The Spaniards also employ Indians to help plant the vegetables and cultivate the soil. This witness has seen Spaniards plowing all by themselves, without the assistance of Indians. He has heard that wheat does very well, and that this is because at the camp there is water for irrigation, which is not found elsewhere, and so wheat is grown only there. He does not know nor has he heard that it is planted anywhere else. . . .

The people are also troubled by the sterility of the land, so they will lack provisions for some time to come, and also because the Indians are few and the pueblos more than eighty leagues apart, including those that are said to have more people, as they are at that distance from the camp. For these reasons, this witness does not think that the people could be maintained without great cost to his majesty in provisions, clothing, and other things. Even if his majesty should incur much expense to help them, this witness believes that if the people were free to choose they would prefer to abandon the land and seek their livelihood around here. He never heard a single one say that he was there of his own will, but through force and compulsion. What his excellency, the viceroy of New Spain, should know and remedy is that the orders he transmits to those regions are neither obeyed nor carried out. . . .

So this witness considers the preservation of those provinces very difficult, for the reasons stated. All of this is the truth, under his oath; and he ratified his testimony. He said that he was twenty-five years old, more or less, and that the general questions of the law did not concern him. Signed, DON FRANCISCO DE VALVERDE MERCADO. LICENTIATE GINÉS HERRERA HORTA. Before me, MARCOS LEANDRO, royal notary.

4. Nicolas Denys Describes the Micmac Fur Trade, 1672

The hunting by the Indians in old times was easy for them. They killed animals only in proportion as they had need of them. When they were tired of eating one sort, they killed some of another. If they did not wish longer to eat meat, they caught some fish. They never made an accumulation of skins of Moose, Beaver, Otter, or others, but only so far as they needed them for personal use. They left the remainder where the animals had been killed, not taking the trouble to bring them to their camps. . . .

The Indians to-day practise still their ancient form of burial in every respect, except that they no longer place anything in their graves, for of this they are entirely disabused. They have abandoned also those offerings, so frequent and usual, which they made as homage to their *manitou* [spirit] in passing by places in which there was some risk to be taken or where indeed there had happened some misfortune [or other].

Since they cannot now obtain the things which come from us with such ease as they had in obtaining robes of Marten, of Otter, or of Beaver, [or] bows and arrows, and since they have realised that guns and other things were not found in their woods or in their rivers, they have become less devout. Or, it would be better to say, [they have become] less superstitious since the time when their offerings have cost them so much. But they practise still all the same methods of hunting, with this difference, however, that in place of arming their arrows and spears with the bones of animals,

From Nicolas Denys, *Description Geographical and Historical of the Coasts of North America, With the Natural History of the Country,* trans. and ed. William Ganong. Toronto: The Champlain Society, 1910, originally published Paris, 1672, pp. 399–452.

pointed and sharpened, they arm them to-day with iron, which is made expressly for sale to them. Their spears now are made of a sword fixed at the end of a shaft of seven to eight feet in length. These they use in winter, when there is snow, to spear the Moose, or for fishing Salmon, Trout, and Beaver. They are also furnished with iron harpoons, of the use of which we have spoken before.

The musket is used by them more than all other weapons, in their hunting in spring, summer, and autumn, both for animals and birds. With an arrow they killed only one Wild Goose; but with the shot of a gun they kill five or six of them. With the arrow it was necessary to approach an animal closely: with the gun they kill the animal from a distance with a bullet or two. The axes, the kettles, the knives, and everything that is supplied them, is much more convenient and portable than those which they had in former times, when they were obliged to go to camp near their grotesque kettles, in place of which to-day they are free to go camp where they wish. One can say that in those times the immovable kettles were the chief regulators of their lives, since they were able to live only in places where these were.

With respect to the hunting of the Beaver in winter, they do that the same as they did formerly, though they have nevertheless nowadays a greater advantage with their arrows and harpoons armed with iron than [they had] with the others which they used in old times, and of which they have totally abandoned the use.

But at present, and since they have frequented the fishing vessels, they drink in quite another fashion. They no longer have any regard for wine, and wish nothing but brandy. They do not call it drinking unless they become drunk, and do not think they have been drinking unless they fight and are hurt. However, when they set about drinking, their wives remove from their wigwams the guns, axes, the mounted swords [spears], the bows, the arrows, and [every weapon] even their knives, which the Indians carry hung from the neck. . . .

At the present time, so soon as the Indians come out of the woods in spring, they hide all their best skins, bringing a few to the establishments in order to obtain their right to something to drink, eat, and smoke. They pay a part of that which was lent them in the autumn to support them, without which they would perish of hunger. They insist that this is all their hunting for the winter has produced. As soon as they have departed, they go to recover the skins which they have hidden in the woods, and go to the routes of the fishing ships and keep watch. If they see any vessels, they make great smokes to let it be known that they are there. . . .

A peschipoty is anything which is closed by a string or secured like a purse, provided that the whole does not surpass in size a bag for holding prayer-books. They are made of Marten, of Squirrel, of Muskrat, or other little animals; others are of Moose skin, or of Sealskin. . . . Those made of skins have strings like the purses, and all those peschipotys serve to hold tobacco or lead for hunting. The Indian women fix the price to the fishermen according to the kind of skin and its fantastic ornamentation, which they call *matachiez;* it is made from Porcupine quills, white, red, and violet, and sometimes with their wampum, of which I have already spoken. With these they obtain many things from the sailors.

The women and the older girls also drink much but by stealth, and they go to hide themselves in the woods for that purpose. The sailors know well the rendezvous. It is those who furnish the brandy, and they bring them into so favourable a condition that they can do with them everything they will. All these frequentations of the ships have entirely ruined them, and they care no longer for Religion. . . . Such is the great difference between their present customs and those of the past.

5. A Jesuit Missionary Recalls Micmac Hunting Rituals, 1691

The most ingenious method which our Gaspesians have for taking the Moose is this. The hunters, knowing the place on the river where it is accustomed to resort when in heat, embark at night in a canoe, and, approaching the meadow where it has its retreat, browses, and usually sleeps, one of them imitates the cry of the female, while the other at the same time takes up water in a bark dish, and lets it fall drop by drop, as if it were the female relieving herself of her water. The male approaches, and the Indians who are on the watch kill him with shots from their guns. The same cunning and dexterity they also use with respect to the female, by counterfeiting the cry of the male.

The hunting of the Beaver is as easy in summer as it is laborious in winter, although it is equally pleasing and entertaining in both of these two seasons, because of the pleasure it is to see this animal's natural industry, which transcends the imagination of those who have never seen the surprising evidences thereof. Consequently the Indians say that the Beavers have sense, and form a separate nation; and they say they would cease to make war upon these animals if these would speak, howsoever little, in order that they might learn whether the Beavers are among their friends or their enemies.

The Beaver is of the bigness of a water-spaniel. Its fur is chestnut, black, and rarely white, but always very soft and suitable for the making of hats. It is the great trade of New France. The Gaspesians say that the Beaver is the beloved of the French and of the other Europeans, who seek it greedily; and I have been unable to keep from laughing on overhearing an Indian, who said to me in banter, *Tahoé messet kogoüar pajo ne daoüi dogoüil mkobit.* "In truth, my brother, the Beaver does everything to perfection. He makes for us kettles, axes, swords, knives, and gives us drink and food without the trouble of cultivating the ground." . . .

[The beaver] cuts trees into pieces of different lengths, according to the use it wishes to make of them. It rolls them on the ground or pushes them through the water with its forepaws, in order to build its house and to construct a dam which checks the current of a stream and forms a considerable pond, on the shore of which it usually dwells. There is always a master Beaver, which oversees this work, and which even beats those that do their duty badly. They all cart earth upon their tails, marching upon their hind feet and carrying in their fore-paws the wood which they need to accomplish their work. They mix the earth with the wood, and make a kind of masonry with their tails, very much as do the masons with their trowels. They build causeways and dams of a breadth of two or three feet, a height of twelve or

From Father Chrestien Le Clercq, *New Relation of Gaspesia with the Customs and Religion of the Gaspesian Indians,* trans. and ed. William F. Ganong. Toronto: The Champlain Society, 1910, pp. 276–280, 227–228.

fifteen feet, and a length of twenty or thirty; these are so inconvenient and difficult to break that this is in fact the hardest task in the hunting of the Beaver, which, by means of these dams, makes from a little stream a pond so considerable that they flood very often a large extent of country. They even obstruct the rivers so much that it is often necessary to get into the water in order to lift the canoes over the dams, as has happened several times to myself. . . .

The Beaver does not feed in the water, as some have imagined. It takes its food on land, eating certain barks of trees, which it cuts into fragments and transports to its house for use as provision during the winter. Its flesh is delicate, and very much like that of mutton. The kidneys are sought by apothecaries, and are used with effect in easing women in childbirth, and in mitigating hysterics.

Whenever the Beaver is hunted, whether this be in winter or in summer, it is always needful to break and tear down the house, all the approaches to which our Indians note exactly, in order, with greater assurance of success, to besiege and attack this animal which is entrenched in his little fort.

In Spring and Summer they are taken in traps; when one of these is sprung a large piece of wood falls across their backs and kills them. But there is nothing so interesting as the hunting in the winter, which is, nevertheless, very wearisome and laborious. For the following is necessary; one must break the ice in more than forty or fifty places: must cut the dams: must shatter the houses: and must cause the waters to run off, in order to see and more easily discover the Beavers. These animals make sport of the hunter, scorn him, and very often escape his pursuit by slipping from their pond through a secret outlet, which they have the instinct to leave in their dam in communication with another neighbouring pond. . . .

The bones of the beaver are not given to the dogs, since these would lose, according to the opinion of the Indians, the senses needed for the hunting of the beaver. No more are they thrown into the rivers, because the Indians fear lest the spirit of the bones of this animal would promptly carry the news to the other beavers, which would desert the country in order to escape the same misfortune.

They never burned, further, the bones of the fawn of the moose, nor the carcass of martens; and they also take much precaution against giving the same to the dogs; for they would not be able any longer to capture any of these animals in hunting if the spirits of the martens and of the fawns of the moose were to inform their own kind of the bad treatment they had received among the Indians.

. . . The women and girls, when they suffer the inconveniences usual to their sex, are accounted unclean. At that time they are not permitted to eat with the others, but they must have their separate kettle, and live by themselves. The girls are not allowed, during that time, to eat any beaver, and those who eat of it are reputed bad; for the Indians are convinced, they say, that the beaver, which has sense, would no longer allow itself to be taken by the Indians if it had been eaten by their unclean daughters. Widows never eat of that which has been killed by the young men; it is necessary that a married man, an old man, or a prominent person of the nation shall be the one who hunts or fishes for their support. So scrupulously do they observe this superstitious custom that they still at this day relate with admiration how a Gaspesian widow allowed herself to die of hunger rather than eat moose or beaver which was left in her wigwam even in abundance, because it was killed by young men, and widows were not permitted to eat it. . . .

6. Lewis and Clark Describe the Great Plains, 1804

[From the Vermilion to Teton (Bad) River]

[Lewis]   MONDAY SEPTEMBER 17TH. 1804.

One quarter of a mile in rear of our camp which was situated in a fine open grove of cotton wood [we] passed a grove of plumb trees loaded with fruit and now ripe, observed but little difference betwen this fruit and that of a similar kind common to the Atlantic States. the trees are smaller and more thickly set. this forrest of plumb trees garnish a plain about 20 feet more elivated than that on which we were encamped; this plane extends with the same bredth from the creek below to the distance of near three miles above parrallel with the river, and it is intirely occupied by the burrows of the *barking squiril* [prairie dogs] heretofore described; this anamal appears here in infinite numbers   and the shortness and virdue of grass gave the plain the appearance throughout it's whole extent of beatifull bowling-green in fine order. it's aspect is S. E.   a great number of wolves of the small kind, halks [hawks] and some pole-cats were to be seen. I presume that those anamals feed on this squirril. found the country in every direction for about three miles intersected with deep revenes and steep irregular hills of 100 to 200 feet high; at the tops of these hills the country breakes of as usual into a fine leavel plain extending as far as the eye can reach. from this plane I had an extensive view of the river below, and the irregular hills which border the opposite sides of the river and creek. the surrounding country had been birnt about a month before and young grass had now sprung up to hight of 4 Inches presenting the live green of the spring   to the West a high range of hills, strech across the country from N. to S. and appeared distant about 20 miles; they are not very extensive as I could plainly observe their rise and termination   no rock appeared on them and the sides were covered with virdue similar to that of the plains   this senery already rich pleasing and beatiful was still farther hightened by immence herds of Buffaloe, deer Elk and Antelopes which we saw in every direction feeding on the hills and plains. I do not think I exagerate when I estimate the number of Buffaloe which could be compre[hend]ed at one view to amount to 3000.

[Among the Mandans]

[Clark]   7TH OF DECEMBER FRIDAY 1804—

[T]he Big White Grand Chief of the 1st Village, came and informed us that a large Drove of Buffalow was near and his people was wating for us to join them in a chase   Capt. Lewis took 15 men & went out joined the Indians, who were at the time he got up, Killing the Buffalow on Horseback with arrows which they done with great dexterity,   his party killed 10 Buffalow, *five* of which we got to the fort by the assistance of a horse in addition to what the men Packed on their backs. one cow was killed on the ice after drawing her out of a vacancey in the ice in which She had fallen, and Butchered her at the fort. those we did not get in was

From Bernard DeVoto, ed. *The Journals of Lewis and Clark.* Boston: Houghton Mifflin, 1963, pp. 28–29, 71–72.

taken by the indians under a Custom which is established amongst them i e. any person seeing a buffalow lying without an arrow Sticking in him, or some purticular mark takes possession,   the river Closed opposit the fort last night 1½ inches thick,   The Thermometer Stood this Morning at 1 d. below 0.   three men frost bit badly to day.

7. Plains Indians' Pictographs, Recorded by George Catlin in 1844

In PLATE 308, are *fac-simile* outlines from about one-half of a group on a Pawnee robe, also hanging in the exhibition; representing a procession of doctors or medicine-men, when one of them, the foremost one, is giving freedom to his favourite horse. This is a very curious custom, which I found amongst many of the tribes, and is done by his announcing to all of his fraternity, that on a certain day, he is going to give liberty to his faithful horse that has longest served him, and he expects them all to be present; at the time and place appointed, they all appear on horseback, most fantastically painted, and dressed, as well as armed and equipped; when the owner of the horse leads the procession, and drives before him his emancipated horse, which is curiously painted and branded; which he holds in check with a long laso. When they have arrived at the proper spot on the prairie, the ceremony takes place, of turning it loose, and giving it, it would seem, as a sort of sacrifice to the Great Spirit. This animal after this, takes his range amongst the bands of wild horses; and if caught by the laso, as is often the case, is discharged, under the superstitious belief that it belongs to the Great Spirit, and not with impunity to be appropriated by them. . . .

In PLATE 312, is also a *fac-simile* of a Mandan robe, with a representation of the sun, most wonderfully painted upon it. This curious robe, which was a present from an esteemed friend of mine amongst those unfortunate people, is now in my Collection; where it may speak for itself.

From George Catlin, *Letters and Notes on the Manners, Customs, and Conditions of the North American Indians*. New York: Dover, 1973 [1844], vol. 2, Figs. 308, 311, 312, and pp. 247–248.

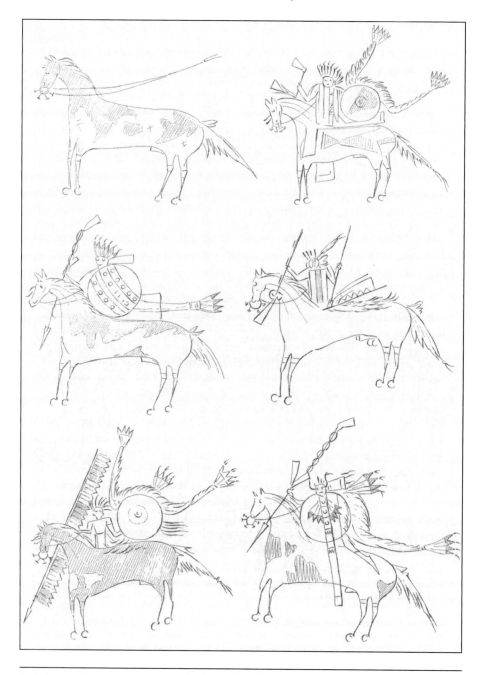

Plate 308. Outlines on a Pawnee robe in Catlin collection.

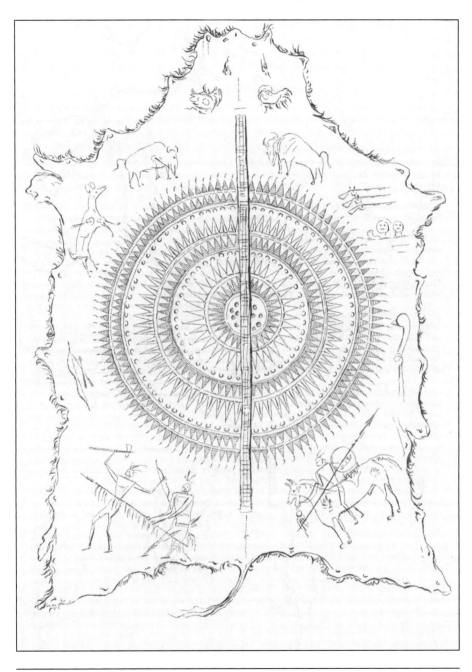

Plate 312. A Mandan robe in Catlin collection.

❧ E S S A Y S

In the first selection, Ramón Gutiérrez, professor of history at the University of California at San Diego, argues that when Jesus came to the society of the Pueblos, the Pueblos' "corn mothers" went away. He relates how the Pueblos' creation stories explain these Indian peoples' emergence from the earth, their belief in the gifts of the corn mothers, and their rituals of corn planting and animal hunting. He discusses how sixteenth-century explorations of the Southwest led ultimately to the breakdown of the Pueblo way of life under Spanish colonizers and Franciscan missionaries, who forcibly took over the Pueblos and installed Catholic churches and belief systems. The Franciscans' domesticated animal herds, crops, and plows offered Indian men and boys new roles, and their "Virgin Mary" rituals accommodated and transformed the native corn-mother rituals. By contrast, Calvin Martin, formerly a professor at Rutgers University, theorizes in the second selection that the Micmac Indians, devastated by diseases that undermined their morale, abandoned their belief in the spiritual power of animals and that, in response to the fur trade, they overharvested their moose herds and beaver colonies. Although the timing of the epidemics in relation to the onset of the fur trade has been questioned, Martin's emphasis is on Indian-animal spiritual relationships and the consequences of European introductions into the Micmac environment. In the third essay, environmental historian Andrew Isenberg argues that the horse, introduced by the Spanish and traded to Plains Indians by Pueblos, transformed the Plains Indians' way of life, creating tribes of mounted nomadic Indians who were able to kill game and bison efficiently. The three historians offer different views on the process of transformation of Indian cultures by Europeans.

Pueblos and Spanish in the Southwest

RAMÓN GUTIÉRREZ

In the beginning two females were born underneath the earth at a place called Shipapu. In total darkness Tsichtinako (Thought Woman) nursed the sisters, taught them language and gave them each a basket that their father Uchtsiti had sent them containing the seeds and fetishes of all the plants and animals that were to exist in the world. Tsichtinako told the sisters to plant the four pine tree seeds they had in their basket and then to use the trees to ascend to the light. One grew so tall that it pushed a hole through the earth. Before the sisters climbed up the tree from the underworld, Thought Woman taught them how to praise the Sun with prayer and song. Every morning as the Sun rose, they would thank him for bringing them to the light by offering with outstretched hands sacred cornmeal and pollen. To the tones of the creation song, they would blow the offering to the sky, asking for long life, happiness, and success in all their endeavors.

When the sisters reached the earth's surface it was soft, spongy, and not yet ripe. So they waited for the Sun to appear. When it rose, the six directions of the cosmos were revealed to them: the four cardinal points, the earth below, and the four skies above. The sisters prayed to the Sun, and as they did, Thought Woman named one

Excerpts reprinted from *When Jesus Came, The Corn Mothers Went Away: Marriage, Sexuality, and Power in New Mexico* by Ramón A. Gutiérrez. Stanford, CA: Stanford University Press, 1991, pp. 3–94.

of the girls Iatiku and made her Mother of the Corn clan; the other she named Nautsiti, Mother of the Sun clan.

"Why were we created?" they asked. Thought Woman answered, "Your father Uchtsiti made the world by throwing a clot of his blood into space, which by his power grew into the earth. He planted you within it so that you would bring to life all the things in your baskets in order that the world be complete for you to rule over it." . . .

After Thought Woman departed, Iatiku took earth from her basket and made the season spirits: Shakako, the ferocious spirit of winter, Morityema, the surly spirit of spring, Maiyochina, the warm spirit of summer, and Shruisthia, the grumpy spirit of fall. Iatiku told the people that if they prayed properly to these spirits they would bring moisture, warmth, ripening, and frost, respectively.

Next Iatiku, their Corn Mother, took dirt from her basket and created the katsina, the Cloud-Spirits or ancestor dead who were to live beneath a lake in the West at Wenimats. Tsitsanits (Big Teeth) was brought to life first as ruler of the katsina, then many other katsina were brought to life. Some looked like birds with long beaks and bulging eyes, others had large animal snouts, and still others were moon creatures with horns sticking out of their heads like lunar crescents. "Your people and my people will be combined," Iatiku told the katsina. "You will give us food from your world and we will give you food from our world. Your people are to represent clouds; you are to bring rain." Iatiku then took cornmeal and opened a road four lengths long so that the katsina could travel to Wenimats and along which they would return when called.

"Now we are going to make houses," said Corn Mother. Suddenly a house made of dirt and trees grew out of the earth resembling in shape the mesa and mountain homes of the season deities. Each of Iatiku's daughters constructed a house for their children and when they were all ready, Iatiku laid them out into a town. "All is well but . . . we have no sacred place, we have no *kaach* [kiva]," Iatiku said. She taught the oldest man of the Oak clan how to build religious houses underneath the earth's surface to resemble Shipapu, the place of emergence.

The people did not have a father of the game animals, so Iatiku appointed a Shaiyaik (Hunt Chief), taught him the songs and prayers of the hunt, gave him an altar, and showed him how to make stone fetishes and prayer sticks to secure the power of the prey animals. . . .

The origin myth of the Acoma Indians just presented likened human life to plant life. Seeds held the potential to generate life. When planted deep within Mother Earth and fertilized by the sky's vivifying rain, seeds germinated, grew into plants, and eventually bore seeds that repeated the cycle of life. Like a sprouting maize shoot rooted in the earth or a child coming forth from its mother's womb, so the Pueblo Indians described their emergence from the underworld.

All of the Pueblos have origin myths that dramatically depict the ideological structure of their world. Myths express the values and ideals that organize and make people's lives meaningful. They explain how the universe was created, its various components, and the tensions and balances that kept it intact. . . . Like the life contained within a seed that sprouts, bears fruit, and dies, only to be reborn again from a seed, so the Pueblo Indians conceived of time and of their historical past.

Gift exchange in Pueblo society created dyadic status relationships between givers and receivers. A gift properly reciprocated with a countergift established the exchanging parties as equals, there being no further claim one could make of the other. If a gift giver initiated an exchange with a highly respected or knowledge-able person to obtain blessings, religious endowments, or ritual knowledge, such as when a parent offered a medicine man gifts so that he would present their child to the rising sun, the obligation created was fulfilled through a proper countergift. But if only one side gave and the other side could not reciprocate, the receiver out of gratitude had to give the presenter unending obedience and respect. . . .

From the moment of their creation the Corn Mothers were indebted to their father for the baskets he had given them. Since they had nothing to give him in return, they did as Tsichtinako instructed, daily singing his praises and offering him food. Humans and animals, just like their mythic ancestors, were bound by these rules of reciprocity in gifting, noted Fray Alonso de Benavides in 1634:

> If they went hunting, they would offer meal to the heads of deer, rabbits, hares, and other dead animals that they had in their houses, believing that this would enable them to catch much game. When they wanted to go fishing, they first offered meal into the river, hoping by this means to obtain a big catch. . . . Whenever they went to war they offered meal and other things to the scalps of the enemy nation which they had brought back as trophies of those they had slain. . . .

The Pueblo Indians viewed the relations between the sexes as relatively bal-anced. Women and men each had their own forms of wealth and power, which created independent but mutually interdependent spheres of action. The corn fetish every child was given at birth and the flint arrowhead with which boys were endowed symbolized these relations and expressed the basic preoccupations of a people living in a semi-arid environment. Corn and flint were food and water, but they were also the cosmic principles of femininity and masculinity. Female and male combined as corn seeds and rain combined to perpetuate life. Corn plants without rain would shrivel and die; water without corn was no life at all. The ear of corn infants received represented the Corn Mothers that had given life to all humans, plants, and animals. At Acoma Pueblo this corn fetish is still called Iatiku, because it contains her heart and breath. For this reason too the Hopi called this corn fetish "mother." "Corn is my heart, it will be to [you] . . . as milk from my breasts," Zia's Corn Mother told her people. Individuals kept this corn fetish throughout their entire lives, for if crops failed its perfect seeds held the promise of a new crop cycle.

If the corn ear represented the feminine generative powers latent in seeds, the earth, and women, the flint arrowhead represented the masculine germinative forces of the sky. Father Sun gave men flint arrowheads to bring forth rain, to harness heat, and to use as a weapon in the hunt. The noise emitted by striking together two pieces of flint resembled the thunder and lightning that accompanied rain. Rain fertilized seeds as men fertilized their women. Without rain or semen life could not continue. The flint arrowhead was the sign of the hunter and warrior. Sun gave his sons, the Twin War Gods, arrowheads with which to give and take away life. From flint too came fire. When men struck flint and created that gift Sun gave them at the beginning of time, they transformed that which was raw into that which was cooked. To the Pueblo Indians flint, rain, semen, and hunting were to male as corn, earth, and childbearing were to female. . . .

Large portions of a woman's day were spent preparing meals for her household. Corn, beans, and squash were the main staples of the diet. Corn was the most important and symbolic of these. It was boiled whole, toasted on the cob, or dried and ground into a fine powder easily cooked as bread or gruel. Every day a woman and her daughters knelt before metates, grinding corn to feed their gods, their fetishes, and their kin. The women worked joyfully at this task, observed Castañeda in 1540. "One crushes the maize, the next grinds it, and the third grinds it finer. While they are grinding, a man sits at the door playing a flageolet, and the women move their stones, keeping time with the music, and all three sing together." . . .

Men's spatial location in village life correlated closely with their roles in the sexual division of labor. Three distinct but overlapping spaces were defined as masculine. The first zone was created through kinship and marriage obligations to women. Sons had to work their mothers' corn plots, brothers those of their sisters, husbands those of their mothers-in-law. "The men attend to the work in the cornfields," observed Gallegos in 1582. "The day hardly breaks before they go about with hoes in their hands." He continued: "The men bear burdens, but not the women." When wood was needed for the construction of a house or to stoke the cooking fires, the household's matriarch dispatched the men to "bring the firewood . . . and stack it up," noted Castañeda in 1540. . . .

The men of every pueblo considered their town to be the center of the universe and placed their main kiva at the vortex of a spatial scheme that extended outward to the four cardinal points, upward to the four skies above, and downward to the underworld. Kivas were usually round (sometimes square) subterranean structures that conjoined space and time to reproduce the sacred time of emergence. Located at the center of the kiva's floor was the *shipapu,* the earth's navel, through which the people emerged from the underworld and through which they would return.

The kiva was circular to resemble the sky. A hole in the center of the roof, the only entrance and source of light, symbolized the opening through which the Corn Mothers climbed onto the earth's surface. The profane space outside and the sacred space within the kiva were connected by a ladder called "rainbow" made of the same pine tree the sisters had used to emerge. The kiva floor had a fire altar that commemorated the gift of fire, and a hollow, dug-out place that represented the door to the house of the Sun, the Moon, and the mountains of the four cardinal points. The walls had altars on which were placed stone fetishes representing all the animals and deities of the world.

Rain was the Pueblo Indians' central preoccupation and the essential ingredient for fecundity. Men recognized that Mother Earth and women had immense capacities to bring forth life, but to realize this potential the sky had to fructify the earth with rain and men their wives with semen. Thus what the people worshipped most, said Hernando de Alarcón in 1540, was "the sun and water." Why did they worship water? According to Coronado it was "because it makes the maize grow and sustains their life, and that the only other reason they know is that their ancestors did so."

The rain chief was one of the most powerful men in every village because he knew how to conjure rain both by calling Horned Water Snake and the katsina. The Pueblos equated serpentine deities with rain. The Horned Water Serpent of the Pueblos united the vertical levels of the cosmos. He lived both upon the earth and below it and so combined the masculine germinative forces of the sky (rain) with the feminine generative power of the earth (seeds). The phallic representations of

Horned Water Snake were cloaked in feathers as a god of lightning and rain. The earliest Pueblo rock drawings depict him as a zigzag line with a horned triangular head and as a lightning snake attached to a cloud burst.

Horned Water Serpent was also feminine and lunar. "Sun is male, Moon is female," maintain the Acoma Indians. The serpent's ability to shed its skin and to be born anew undoubtedly resembled the moon's birth and death every 28 days. In decorative motifs the measured zigzags of the lightning snake and the coiled spiral of the rattlesnake evoked those rhythms governed by the moon: the rains, the agricultural calendar, and a woman's menstrual flow. Water Serpent's horns, too, were lunar. Each horn represented the moon's crescent; with two, the lunar cycle was complete.

Horned Water Serpent, then, provided the Pueblo Indians with fecundity and abundance by joining together the levels of the cosmos (sky/earth, earth/underworld) and social existence (male/female, life/death).

The Pueblo Dead—the katsina—were also potent rain spirits tied to the living in bonds of reciprocity. It was the rain chief who knew how to call the katsina and did so by offering them prayer sticks and gifts, asking them to visit with rain, food, and fertility. Katsina lived at the place of emergence underneath lakes and on mountain tops. Missives to the katsina were dispatched as puffs of smoke, which as mimetic magic beckoned the cloud spirits to visit. At death Puebloans became clouds. That is why to this day the Hopi harangue their dead saying: "You are no longer a Hopi, you are a Cloud. When you get yonder you will tell the chief to hasten the rain clouds hither." . . .

Hunting practices for rabbit, antelope, deer, and buffalo were all very similar. We focus here on deer hunting because deer meat was the most abundant and highly prized, and because men thought of women as two-legged deer. A deer hunt was organized whenever food reserves were low, when a ceremonial was to be staged, or when the katsina were going to visit.

For four days the hunt chief led the hunt society's members in song, prayer, prayer-stick making, and smokes. . . . During these four days, and for four days after the hunt, men were sexually continent. Hunters believed that animals disliked the smell of women and would not allow themselves to be captured by a man so contaminated. To rid himself of such odor, a hunter purified his body with emetic drinks and smokes. If a man was to accomplish his goal, neither his mind nor his heart could be dissipated by the thought of women.

The hunt began on the fourth day. Transformed into the animals they hunted, the hunters donned deerskins with the head and antlers still attached. The hunt chief selected the hunting ground and dispersed the men around its edges, forming a large circle. Slowly the circumference of the circle tightened and the deer became exhausted. Finally the deer were wrestled to the ground and choked. A deer was suffocated so that its breath and spirit would be reborn as more game, and because only the skins of suffocated animals could be used as hunt costumes. . . . The carcass was then carried back to the pueblo, where it was adopted into the hunter's maternal household through ritual intercourse and ritual feeding. "We are glad you have come to our home and have not been ashamed of our people," Acoma's women would tell the deer as they offered it cornmeal. The hunter's relatives rubbed their hands over the deer's body and then across their own faces to obtain its beauty and strength. Finally, the hunter purified himself with juniper smoke so that the deer spirit would not haunt him. The meat was divided between the hunt chief who had taught the boy how to hunt and the hunter's household of affiliation. . . .

In a largely horticultural society women asserted and could prove that they had enormous control and power over seed production, child-rearing, household construction, and the earth's fertility. Men admitted this. But they made a counterclaim that men's ability to communicate with the gods and to control life and death protected the precarious balance in the universe by forestalling village factionalism and dissent. . . .

These, then, were the contours of Pueblo Indian society in the sixteenth century. Each pueblo was an aggregation of sedentary horticulturists living in extended matrilineal households, supplementing their existence through hunting and warfare. Elders controlled the organization of production and, through the distribution of its fruits as gifts and ritual blessings, perpetuated the main inequalities of life; the inequality between juniors and seniors and between successful and unsuccessful seniors. The household and all the activities symbolically related to it belonged to women; the kivas and the pueblo's relationships with its gods was the province of men. That said, we turn . . . to discuss the arrival of the Spanish conquistadores. . . .

From the conquistadores' perspective, the Pueblo Indians were an inferior breed close to savages: "a people without capacity," "stupid," and "of poor intelligence." Marveling at the houses he saw at the Zuñi pueblos in 1540, Coronado's comments are telling: "I do not think that they have the judgment and intelligence needed to be able to build these houses in the way in which they are built, for most of them are entirely naked."

Coronado's troops . . . reconnoitered the Tusayan (Hopi) pueblos of eastern Arizona, the Grand Canyon, and Quivira, a land east of New Mexico, which the Indians said was rich in gold, silver, and silks. The infantry that had been slowly marching north . . . arrived . . . in late November 1540 . . . proceeded to Alcanfor Pueblo in Tiguex province (near Bernalillo) for the winter because it had abundant food.

The intensity of that winter brought exploration temporarily to a halt. The troops huddled at Alcanfor rapidly succumbed to hunger and cold. Coronado's troops extracted blankets and corn from the Tiguex pueblos by force, and when the soldiers satisfied their lust with Indian women but gave nothing in return, the Indian men declared war. The Spaniards retaliated with their own war of blood and fire, ordering "200 stakes be driven into the ground to burn them alive." One hundred warriors were burned at the stake and hundreds more were massacred as they fled the Spaniards.

When the spring thaw arrived, Coronado renewed his search for Quivira (villages of the Wichita Indians, in Kansas), which he beheld in August 1541. But there was no gold!

Throughout the autumn and winter of 1541, Coronado's troops shivered in the cold, hungry and constantly engaged in Indian skirmishes. And so, when news reached Coronado in April 1542 that the Indians of Sonora were in rebellion, he and his forces abandoned New Mexico, bringing to a close the first period of Spanish interest in the area.

From 1581 to 1680, Franciscans provided the impetus for colonization in New Mexico. For most of this period the friars were virtual lords of the land. They organized the Indians into a theocracy that lasted until the Pueblo Revolt in 1680. . . . The

Franciscans organized two expeditions to reconnoiter New Mexico: one, in 1581, was led by Fray Agustín Rodríguez, under the command of Francisco Sánchez Chamuscado; the other, in 1582, was led by Antonio de Espejo, and was ostensibly to rescue two friars who had remained in the Pueblos after the 1581 expedition.

Glowing reports from the Franciscans about New Mexico reached King Philip II, and as a result, license was issued in 1595 to one of New Spain's most illustrious sons, Don Juan de Oñate, for the conquest and colonization of the Kingdom of New Mexico. . . . The mightier, well-fortified towns received the conquistadores as they did other visiting tribes, gifting and hosting them as a sign of goodwill. At "the great pueblo of the Emes [Jémez]," wrote Oñate in his itinerary, "the natives came out to meet us, bringing water and bread." At Acoma "the Indians furnished us liberally with maize, water, and fowls." And at the Hopi Pueblos "the natives came out to welcome us with tortillas, scattering powdered flour over us and our horses as a sign of peace and friendship . . . and gave us a fine reception." . . .

What the Puebloans thought they gave as gifts, the *españoles* thought had been surrendered as tribute. Indeed, the surface calm that had greeted the colonizers erupted violently in December 1598, precisely over the meaning of Indian gifts and how cheerfully they should be surrendered. . . . When a soldier named Vivero stole two turkeys, a bird sacred to the Indians, and violated an Indian maiden, Acoma's warriors attacked, killing Zaldívar and twelve men. A few soldiers survived the fracas by jumping off the edge of Acoma's mesa to the sand dunes below. With the sentinels that had been left watching the horses they retreated to San Juan. Oñate encountered the survivors of Acoma's battle on December 13 as he was returning from Zuñi to San Juan. Immediately, plans were made to punish Acoma. If the colony was to survive, stern and swift action would have to be taken. Oñate reasoned that any hesitation might be interpreted by the Indians as a sign of weakness and might encourage other pueblos to similar rebellions. . . . When the fighting ended, 800 Indian men, women, and children lay dead. Eighty men and 500 women and children were taken as prisoners to Santo Domingo to stand trial. . . .

Acoma's residents were found guilty of murder and failing to surrender willingly the provisions the Spaniards demanded. . . . Oñate informed the viceroy that if the colony was to survive, reinforcements were necessary. On Christmas eve, 1600, 73 men arrived. . . .

. . . The Franciscans established . . . charismatic domination over the Pueblo Indians. . . . They attempted to portray themselves to the Indians as supermen who controlled the forces of nature. . . . One of the first functions the friars assumed was that of potent rain chiefs. Because the Pueblo cosmology was not very different from that of the Indians of central Mexico, the friars were well aware of the symbolic power of rain in the Pueblo belief system. . . . When the[y] . . . entered San Juan Pueblo, they found the earth parched and the crops wilted for lack of rain. The friars constructed a cross, prayed for rain, and ordered the Indians to do likewise. Then, "while the sky was as clear as a diamond, exactly twenty-four hours after the outcry had gone up, it rained . . . so abundantly that the crops recovered." San Juan's inhabitants rejoiced and presented many feathers, corn meal, and other gifts to the crucifix and to the friars. . . .

The friars' animal magic . . . far exceeded anything hunt chiefs could conjure. The only animals the Pueblos had domesticated were the turkey, for its feathers rather than for its meat, and the dog, as a beast of burden. The appearance of friars shepherding enormous flocks of docile animals, their escorts riding atop horses that were stronger, faster, and more obedient than any animal they had ever seen before, was quite astounding. The rapid reproduction of the European herds, which, according to a 1634 account by Fray Alonso de Benavides, nearly doubled every fifteen months, and the introduction of beef, pork, and mutton into the native diet marginalized the role of the hunt chiefs. Here was a permanent, year-round meat supply that, at least for the moment, was not the object of intense competition between neighboring villages and Athapaskan bands, or subject to the vicissitudes of the hunt chiefs' magic.

. . . The padres won female allies by protecting women's rights, by respecting some of the spatial loci of their power, by instructing them that men and women were equal before God, and by allowing them to continue their worship of the Corn Mother, albeit transmogrified as the Blessed Virgin Mary. Throughout the colonial period, when men—Indian or Spanish—engaged in extramarital sex with native women and failed to reciprocate with gifts, it was the friars who protected women's rights, demanding redress from the culprits. Pueblo women, much like their European counterparts, retained control of the household and over the rearing of children, particularly of the girls who were of little import to the friars. Pueblo women were barred from active participation in male rites. So it was also under Christian rule: women served the priests as auxiliaries, cleaned the church and its altar linens, baked the communion bread, prepared food for feasting, and witnessed men's power to communicate with the gods.

The friars posed not only as fathers to their Indian parishioners, but also as mothers, offering them all the religious, social, and economic benefits of maternity: Among the matrilineal Puebloans, the mother provided one's clan name, totemically named household fetishes, care and sustenance through adolescence, and the use of seeds and land on which to cultivate them. The friar as *mater* offered the young very similar gifts, thereby indebting the children to him. At baptism they were given Christian names by the priest. He was the keeper of the Christian fetishes (religious statuary, devotional pictures, relics, and so on). Daily he called them for instruction in the Gospel and the mores of civilization. At the mission boys received wheat and vegetable seeds, fruit trees, plows and hoes to work the land more efficiently, beasts of burden to expand their cultivation, and most important of all, the recognition of land rights vested in men. Pueblo boys had little contact with their fathers before their adolescent katsina initiation into a kiva. The missions presented the children a radically different model of adult male behavior. Here were grown men caring for children. In church the youths saw images of St. Anthony of Padua fondling the infant Christ, of St. Christopher carrying the Christ child on his shoulders, and of St. Joseph holding his foster son in his arms. That the Franciscans poured so much energy into the care and rearing of juveniles must have reinforced the perception that the friars were also mothers, much as Pueblo town chiefs were regarded as the father and mother of all people.

. . . Those Puebloans who most resisted Christianization—the Hopi, the Zuñi, and the Keres at Acoma—remained matrilineal. Among these people we still find a vibrant array of women's fertility societies, spirited ceremonials to vivify the earth, and a host of descendant earth-bound symbols that celebrate femininity. Among the

Puebloans who became most acculturated to European ways—the Tewa and the Keres (except Acoma)—women's fertility societies were suppressed, their dances to awaken men's germinative powers were outlawed as too sinful, and, given the explicit phallic symbolism of the Snake Dance and the "demonic" character of the katsina dances, these elements of Pueblo ceremonialism largely disappeared. The native symbolism that remained was almost totally ascendant and masculine (sun, fire, arrows, and eagles)—symbols that meshed well with those of European patriarchal religion.

. . . The summer solstice celebrated Mother Earth's fecundity and the secret of life the Corn Mothers had given humanity. The prominence of the Mater Dolorosa in the passion plays and the Way of the Cross was certainly one attempt to gloss this seasonal gender disparity, for throughout the Old World and the New, the Blessed Virgin Mary was frequently presented to neophytes as a metamorphosed grain goddess. To accommodate the Indians' summer fertility rituals, Holy Week was followed closely by a time dedicated to Mary, the month of May. By the eighteenth century, Mary and the Corn Mothers had been merged in religious iconography and myth. The Virgin now appeared cloaked in garb decorated with corn ears and stalks with the moon at her feet, surrounded by flowers and butterflies, Indian symbols of fertility. . . .

For Indian residents of small New Mexican pueblos constantly under attack, despoiled of their food, and forced to abandon well-watered spots, the mission fathers offered the semblance of protection. In numbers there was strength, and behind the massive wall of the mission compound there was security. Christianization to these persons meant a reliable meat supply, iron implements of various sorts, and European foods: wheat, legumes, green vegetables, melons, grapes, and a variety of orchard fruits. It does not strain the imagination to envision why such persons, understandably nervous and ambivalent at the arrival of the "Children of the Sun," might have allied themselves as Christians with the new social order.

Micmacs and French in the Northeast

CALVIN MARTIN

Among the first North American Indians to be encountered by Europeans were the Micmacs who occupied present-day Nova Scotia, northern New Brunswick and the Gaspé Peninsula, Prince Edward Island, and Cape Breton Island. According to the Sieur de Dièreville, they also lived along the lower St. John River with the Malecites, who outnumbered them. For our present purposes, the Micmac territory will be considered an ecosystem, and the Micmac occupying it will be regarded as a local population. These designations are not entirely arbitrary, for the Micmac occupied and exploited the area in a systematic way; they had a certain psychological unity or similarity in their ideas about the cosmos; they spoke a language distinct from those of their neighbors; and they generally married within their own population. There were, as might be expected, many external factors impinging on the ecosystem which should also be evaluated, although space permits them only to be mentioned

Abridged from "The European Impact on the Culture of a Northeastern Algonquin Tribe: An Ecological Interpretation," by Calvin Martin. *William and Mary Quarterly,* 31, Jan. 1974, pp. 7–26. Reprinted by permission of the author.

here. Some of these "supralocal" relations involved trade and hostilities with other tribes; the exchange of genetic material and personnel with neighboring tribes through intermarriage and adoption; the exchange of folklore and customs; and the movements of such migratory game as moose and woodland caribou. The Micmac ecosystem thus participated in a regional system, and the Micmac population was part of a regional population.

The hunting, gathering, and fishing Micmac who lived within this Acadian forest, especially along its rivers and by the sea, were omnivores (so to speak) in the trophic system of the community. At the first trophic level, the plants eaten were wild potato tubers, wild fruits and berries, acorns and nuts, and the like. Trees and shrubs provided a wealth of materials used in the fashioning of tools, utensils, and other equipment. At the time of contact, none of the Indians living north of the Saco River cultivated food crops. Although legend credits the Micmac with having grown maize and tobacco "for the space of several years," these cultigens, as well as beans, pumpkins, and wampum (which they greatly prized), were obtained from the New England Algonquians of the Saco River area (Abnakis) and perhaps from other tribes to the south.

Herbivores and carnivores occupy the second and third trophic levels respectively, with top carnivores in the fourth level. The Micmac hunter tapped all three levels in his seasonal hunting and fishing activities, and these sources of food were "to them like fixed rations assigned to every moon." In January, seals were hunted when they bred on islands off the coast; the fat was reduced to oil for food and body grease, and the women made clothing from the fur. The principal hunting season lasted from February till mid-March, since there were enough marine resources, especially fish and mollusks, available during the other three seasons to satisfy most of the Micmacs' dietary needs. For a month and a half, then, the Indians withdrew from the seashore to the banks of rivers and lakes and into the woods to hunt the caribou, moose, black bear, and small furbearers. At no other time of the year were they so dependent on the caprice of the weather: a feast was as likely as a famine. A heavy rain could ruin the beaver and caribou hunt, and a deep, crustless snow would doom the moose hunt.

Since beaver were easier to hunt on the ice than in the water, and since their fur was better during the winter, this was the chief season for taking them. Hunters would work in teams or groups, demolishing the lodge or cutting the dam with stone axes. Dogs were sometimes used to track the beaver which took refuge in air pockets along the edge of the pond, or the beaver might be harpooned at air holes. In the summer hunt, beaver were shot with the bow or trapped in deadfalls using poplar as bait, but the commonest way to take them was to cut the dam in the middle and drain the pond, killing the animals with bows and spears.

Next to fish, moose was the most important item in the Micmac diet, and it was their staple during the winter months when these large mammals were hunted with dogs on the hard-crusted snow. In the summer and spring, moose were tracked, stalked, and shot with the bow; in the fall, during the rutting season, the bull was enticed by a clever imitation of the sound of a female urinating. Another technique was to ensnare the animal with a noose.

Moose was the Micmacs' favorite meat. The entrails, which were considered a great delicacy, and the "most delicious fat" were carried by the triumphant hunter to the campsite, and the women were sent after the carcass. The mistress of the wigwam decided what was to be done with each portion of the body, every part of which was used. Grease was boiled out of the bones and either drunk pure (with "much gusto") or stored as loaves of moose-butter; the leg and thigh bones were crushed and the marrow eaten; the hides were used for robes, leggings, moccasins, and tent coverings; tools, ornaments, and game pieces were made from antlers, teeth, and toe bones, respectively. According to contemporary French observers, the Micmac usually consumed the moose meat immediately, without storing any, although the fact that some of the meat was preserved rather effectively by smoking it on racks, so that it would even last the year, demonstrates that Micmac existence was not as hand-to-mouth as is commonly believed of the northeastern Algonquian. Black bear were also taken during the season from February till mid-March, but such hunting was merely coincidental. If a hunter stumbled upon a hibernating bear, he could count himself lucky.

As the lean months of winter passed into the abundance of spring, the fish began to spawn, swimming up rivers and streams in such numbers that "everything swarms with them." In mid-March came the smelt, and at the end of April the herring. Soon there were sturgeon and salmon, and numerous waterfowl made nests out on the islands—which meant there were eggs to be gathered. Mute evidence from seashore middens and early written testimony reveal that these Indians also relied heavily on various mollusks, which they harvested in great quantity. Fish was a staple for the Micmac, who knew the spawning habits of each type of fish and where it was to be found. Weirs were erected across streams to trap the fish on their way downstream on a falling tide, while larger fish, such as sturgeon and salmon, might be speared or trapped.

The salmon run marked the beginning of summer, when the wild geese shed their plumage. Most wildfowl were hunted at their island rookeries; waterfowl were often hunted by canoe and struck down as they took to flight; others, such as the Canadian geese which grazed in the meadows, were shot with the bow.

In autumn, when the waterfowl migrated southward, the eels spawned up the many small rivers along the coast. From mid-September to October the Micmac left the ocean and followed the eels, "of which they lay in a supply; they are good and fat." Caribou and beaver were hunted during October and November, and with December came the "tom cod" (which were said to have spawned under the ice) and turtles bearing their young. In January the subsistence cycle began again with the seal hunt.

As he surveyed the seasonal cycle of these Indians, Father Pierre Biard was impressed by nature's bounty and Micmac resourcefulness: "These then, but in a still greater number, are the revenues and incomes of our Savages; such, their table and living, all prepared and assigned, everything to its proper place and quarter." Although we have omitted mention of many other types of forest, marine, and aquatic life which were also exploited by the Micmac, those listed above were certainly the most significant in the Micmacs' food quest and ecosystem.

Frank G. Speck, perhaps the foremost student of northeastern Algonquian culture, has emphasized that hunting to the Micmacs was not a "war upon the animals, not a slaughter for food or profit." Denys's observations confirm Speck's point: "Their greatest task was to feed well and to go a hunting. They did not lack animals, which they killed only in proportion as they had need of them." From this, and the above description of their effective hunting techniques, it would appear that the Micmac were not limited by their hunting technology in the taking of game. As Denys pointed out, "the hunting by the Indians in old times was easy for them. . . . When they were tired of eating one sort, they killed some of another. If they did not wish longer to eat meat, they caught some fish. They never made an accumulation of skins of Moose, Beaver, Otter, or others, but only so far as they needed them for personal use. They left the remainder [of the carcass] where the animals had been killed, not taking the trouble to bring them to their camps." Need, not technology, was the ruling factor, and need was determined by the great primal necessities of life and regulated by spiritual considerations. Hunting, as Speck remarks, was "a *holy occupation*"; it was conducted and controlled by spiritual rules.

The bond which united these physical and biological components of the Micmac ecosystem, and indeed gave them definition and comprehensibility, was the world view of the Indian. The foregoing discussion has dealt mainly with the empirical, objective, physical ("operational") environmental model of the observer; what it lacks is the "cognized" model of the Micmac.

Anthropologists regard the pre-Columbian North American Indian as a sensitive member of his environment, who merged sympathetically with its living and nonliving components. The Indian's world was filled with superhuman and magical powers which controlled man's destiny and nature's course of events. Murray Wax explains:

> To those who inhabit it, the magical world is a "society," not a "mechanism," that is, it is composed of "beings" rather than "objects." Whether human or nonhuman, these beings are associated with and related to one another socially and sociably, that is, in the same ways as human beings to one another. These patterns of association and relationship may be structured in terms of kinship, empathy, sympathy, reciprocity, sexuality, dependency, or any other of the ways that human beings interact with and affect or afflict one another. Plants, animals, rocks, and stars are thus seen not as "objects" governed by laws of nature, but as "fellows" with whom the individual or band may have a more or less advantageous relationship.

For the Micmac, together with all the other eastern subarctic Algonquians, the power of these mysterious forces was apprehended as "manitou"—translated "magic power"—much in the same way that we might use the slang word "vibrations" to register the emotional feelings emanating (so we say) from an object, person, or situation.

The world of the Micmac was thus filled with superhuman forces and beings (such as dwarfs, giants, and magicians), and animals that could talk to man and had spirits akin to his own, and the magic of mystical and medicinal herbs—a world where even inanimate objects possessed spirits. Micmac subsistence activities were inextricably bound up within this spiritual matrix, which, we are suggesting, acted as a kind of control mechanism on Micmac land-use, maintaining the environment within an optimum range of conditions.

In order to understand the role of the Micmac in the fur trading enterprise of the colonial period, it is useful to investigate the role of the Micmac hunter in the spiritual world of precontact times. Hunting was governed by spiritual rules and considerations which were manifest to the early French observers in the form of seemingly innumerable taboos. These taboos connoted a sense of cautious reverence for a conscious fellow-member of the same ecosystem who, in the view of the Indian, allowed itself to be taken for food and clothing. The Indian felt that "both he and his victim understood the roles which they played in the hunt; the animal was resigned to its fate."

That such a resignation on the part of the game was not to be interpreted as an unlimited license to kill should be evident from an examination of some of the more prominent taboos. Beaver, for example, were greatly admired by the Micmac for their industry and "abounding genius"; for them, the beaver had "sense" and formed a "separate nation." Hence there were various regulations associated with the disposal of their remains: trapped beaver were drawn in public and made into soup, extreme care being taken to prevent the soup from spilling into the fire; beaver bones were carefully preserved, never being given to the dogs—lest they lose their sense of smell for the animal—or thrown into the fire—lest misfortune come upon "all the nation"—or thrown into rivers—"because the Indians fear lest the spirit of the bones . . . would promptly carry the news to the other beavers, which would desert the country in order to escape the same misfortune." Likewise, menstruating women were forbidden to eat beaver, "for the Indians are convinced, they say, that the beaver, which has sense, would no longer allow itself to be taken by the Indians if it had been eaten by their unclean daughters." The fetus of the beaver, as well as that of the bear, moose, otter, and porcupine, was reserved for the old men, since it was believed that a youth who ate such food would experience intense foot pains while hunting.

Taboos similarly governed the disposal of the remains of the moose—what few there were. The bones of a moose fawn (and of the marten) were never given to the dogs nor were they burned, "for they [the Micmac] would not be able any longer to capture any of these animals in hunting if the spirits of the martens and of the fawns of the moose were to inform their own kind of the bad treatment they had received among the Indians." Fear of such reprisal also prohibited menstruating women from drinking out of the common kettles or bark dishes. Such regulations imply cautious respect for the animal hunted. The moose not only provided food and clothing, but was firmly tied up with the Micmac spirit-world—as were the other game animals. . . .

If taboo was associated with fishing, we have little record of it; the only explicit evidence is a prohibition against the roasting of eels, which, if violated, would prevent the Indians from catching others. From this and from the fact that the Restigouche division of the Micmac wore the figure of a salmon as a totem around their neck, we may surmise that fish, too, shared in the sacred and symbolic world of the Indian.

Control over these supernatural forces and communication with them were the principal functions of the shaman, who served in Micmac society as an intermediary between the spirit realm and the physical. The lives and destinies of the natives were profoundly affected by the ability of the shaman to supplicate, cajole, and otherwise manipulate the magical beings and powers. The seventeenth-century French, who typically labeled the shamans (or *buowin*) frauds and jugglers in league with the devil, were repeatedly amazed at the respect accorded them by the natives. By working himself into a dreamlike state, the shaman would invoke the manitou of his animal helper and so predict future events. He also healed by means of conjuring. The Micmac availed themselves of a rather large pharmacopia of roots and herbs and other plant parts, but when these failed they would summon the healing arts of the most noted shaman in the district. The illness was often diagnosed by the *buowin* as a failure on the patient's part to perform a prescribed ritual; hence an offended supernatural power had visited the offender with sickness. At such times the shaman functioned as a psychotherapist, diagnosing the illness and symbolically (at least) removing its immediate cause from the patient's body.

It is important to understand that an ecosystem is holocoenotic in nature: there are no "walls" between the components of the system, for "the ecosystem reacts as a whole." Such was the case in the Micmac ecosystem of precontact times, where the spiritual served as a link connecting man with all the various subsystems of the environment. Largely through the mediation of the shaman, these spiritual obligations and restrictions acted as a kind of control device to maintain the ecosystem in a well-balanced condition. Under these circumstances the exploitation of game for subsistence appears to have been regulated by the hunter's respect for the continued welfare of his prey—both living and dead—as is evident from the numerous taboos associated with the proper disposal of animal remains. Violation of taboo desecrated the remains of the slain animal and offended its soul-spirit. The offended spirit would then retaliate in either of several ways, depending on the nature of the broken taboo: it could render the guilty hunter's (or the entire band's) means of hunting ineffective, or it could encourage its living fellows to remove themselves from the vicinity. In both cases the end result was the same—the hunt was rendered unsuccessful—and in both it was mediated by the same power—the spirit of the slain animal. Either of these catastrophes could usually be reversed through the magical arts of the shaman. In the Micmac cosmology, the overkill of wildlife would have been resented by the animal kingdom as an act comparable to genocide, and would have been resisted by means of the sanctions outlined above. The threat of retaliation thus had the effect of placing an upper limit on the number of animals slain, while the practical result was the conservation of wildlife.

The injection of European civilization into this balanced system initiated a series of chain reactions which, within a little over a century, resulted in the replacement of the aboriginal ecosystem by another. From at least the beginning of the sixteenth century, and perhaps well before that date, fishing fleets from England, France, and Portugal visited the Grand Banks off Newfoundland every spring for the cod, and hunted whale and walrus in the Gulf of St. Lawrence. Year after year, while other, more flamboyant men were advancing the geopolitical ambitions of their emerging dynastic states as they searched for precious minerals or a passage to the Orient, these unassuming fishermen visited Canada's east coast and made the first effective European contact with the Indians there. For the natives' furs they bartered knives, beads, brass kettles, assorted ship fittings, and the like, thus initiating the subversion and replacement of Micmac material culture by European technology. Far more important, the fishermen unwittingly infected the Indians with European diseases, against which the natives had no immunity. Commenting on what may be called the microbial phase of European conquest, John Witthoft has written:

> All of the microscopic parasites of humans, which had been collected together from all parts of the known world into Europe, were brought to these [American] shores, and new diseases stalked faster than man could walk into the interior of the continent. Typhoid, diphtheria, colds, influenza, measles, chicken pox, whooping cough, tuberculosis, yellow fever, scarlet fever, and other strep infections, gonorrhea, pox (syphilis), and smallpox were diseases that had never been in the New World before. They were new among

populations which had no immunity to them. . . . Great epidemics and pandemics of these diseases are believed to have destroyed whole communities, depopulated whole regions, and vastly decreased the native population everywhere in the yet unexplored interior of the continent. The early pandemics are believed to have run their course prior to 1600 A.D.

Disease did more than decimate the native population; it effectively prepared the way for subsequent phases of European contact by breaking native morale and, perhaps even more significantly, by cracking their spiritual edifice. It is reasonable to suggest that European disease rendered the Indian's (particularly the shaman's) ability to control and otherwise influence the supernatural realm dysfunctional—because his magic and other traditional cures were now ineffective—thereby causing the Indian to apostatize (in effect), which in turn subverted the "retaliation" principle of taboo and opened the way to a corruption of the Indian-land relationship under the influence of the fur trade. . . .

Several . . . observers . . . commented on the new diseases that afflicted the Micmac. In precontact times, declared Denys, "they were not subject to diseases, and knew nothing of fevers." By about 1700, however, Dièreville noted that the Micmac population was in sharp decline. The Indians themselves frequently complained to Father Biard and other Frenchmen that, since contact with the French, they had been dying off in great numbers. "For they assert that, before this association and inter-course [with the French], all their countries were very populous, and they tell how one by one the different coasts, according as they have begun to traffic with us, have been more reduced by disease." The Indians accused the French of trying to poison them or charged that the food supplied by the French was somehow adulterated. Whatever the reasons for the catastrophe, warned Biard, the Indians were very angry about it and "upon the point of breaking with us, and making war upon us."

To the Jesuit fathers, the solution to this sorry state of affairs lay in the civilizing power of the Gospel. To Biard, his mission was clear:

> For, if our Souriquois [Micmac] are few, they may become numerous; if they are savages, it is to domesticate and civilize them that we have come here. . . . We hope in time to make them susceptible of receiving the doctrines of the faith and of the christian and catholic religion, and later, to penetrate further into the regions beyond.

The message was simple and straightforward: the black-robes would enlighten the Indians by ridiculing their animism and related taboos, discrediting their shamans, and urging them to accept the Christian gospel. . . . The priests attacked the Micmac culture with a marvelous fervor and some success. . . .

The result of this Christian onslaught on a decaying Micmac cosmology was, of course, the despiritualization of the material world. Commenting on the process of despiritualization, Denys (who was a spectator to this transformation in the mid-seventeenth century) remarked that it was accomplished with "much difficulty"; for some of the Indians it was achieved by religious means, while others were in-fluenced by the French customs, but nearly all were affected "by the need for the things which come from us, the use of which has become to them an indispensable necessity. They have abandoned all their own utensils, whether because of the trouble they had as well to make as to use them, or because of the facility of obtaining from us, in exchange for skins which cost them almost nothing, the things which seemed

to them invaluable, not so much for their novelty as for the convenience they derived therefrom."

In the early years of the fur trade, before the establishment of permanent posts
among the natives, trading was done with the coastwise fishermen from May to
early fall. In return for skins of beaver, otter, marten, moose, and other furbearers,
the Indians received a variety of fairly cheap commodities, principally tobacco,
liquor, powder and shot (in later years), biscuit, peas, beans, flour, assorted clothing,
wampum, kettles, and hunting tools. The success of this trade in economic terms
must be attributed to pressure exerted on a relatively simple society by a complex
civilization and, perhaps even more importantly, by the tremendous pull of this
simple social organization on the resources of Europe. To the Micmac, who like other
Indians measured the worth of a tool or object by the ease of its construction and use,
the technology of Europe became indispensable. But as has already been shown, this
was not simply an economic issue for the Indian; the Indian was more than just "economically seduced" by the European's trading goods. One must also consider the
metaphysical implications of Indian acceptance of the European material culture.

European technology of the sixteenth and seventeenth centuries was largely
incompatible with the spiritual beliefs of the eastern woodland Indians, despite the
observation made above that the Micmacs readily invested trading goods with spiritual power akin to that possessed by their own implements. As Denys pointed out, the
trade goods which the Micmac so eagerly accepted were accompanied by Christian
religious teachings and French custom, both of which gave definition to these alien
objects. In accepting the European material culture, the natives were impelled to
accept the European abstract culture, especially religion, and so, in effect, their own
spiritual beliefs were subverted as they abandoned their implements for those of the
white man. Native religion lost not only its practical effectiveness, in part owing to
the replacement of the traditional magical and animistic view of nature by the exploitive European view, but it was no longer necessary as a source of definition and
theoretical support for the new Europe-derived material culture. Western technology
made more "sense" if it was accompanied by Western religion.

Under these circumstances in the early contact period, the Micmac's role within
his ecosystem changed radically. No longer was he the sensitive fellow-member of a
symbolic world; under pressure from disease, European trade, and Christianity, he
had apostatized—he had repudiated his role within the ecosystem. Former attitudes
were replaced by a kind of mongrel outlook which combined some native traditions
and beliefs with a European rationale and motivation. . . .

European contact should thus be viewed as a trigger factor, that is, something
which was not present in the Micmac ecosystem before and which initiated a con-
catenation of reactions leading to the replacement of the aboriginal ecosystem by
another. European disease, Christianity, and the fur trade with its accompanying
technology—the three often intermeshed—were responsible for the corruption of
the Indian-land relationship, in which the native had merged sympathetically with
his environment. By a lockstep process European disease rendered the Indian's
control over the supernatural and spiritual realm inoperative, and the disillusioned
Micmac apostatized, debilitating taboo and preparing the way for the destruction of
wildlife which was soon to occur under the stimulation of the fur trade. For those
who believed in it Christianity furnished a new, dualistic world view, which placed

man above nature, as well as spiritual support for the fur trade, and as a result the Micmac became dependent on the European marketplace both spiritually and economically. Within his ecosystem the Indian changed from conservator to exploiter. All of this resulted in the intense exploitation of some game animals and the virtual extermination of others. Unfortunately for the Indian and the land, this grim tale was to be repeated many times along the moving Indian-white frontier. Life for the Micmac had indeed become more convenient, but convenience cost dearly in much material and abstract culture loss or modification.

The historiography of Indian-white relations is rendered more comprehensible when the Indian and the land are considered together: "So intimately is all of Indian life tied up with the land and its utilization that to think of Indians is to think of land. The two are inseparable." American Indian history can be seen, then, as a type of environmental history, and perhaps it is from this perspective that the early period of Indian-white relations can best be understood.

Indians and Bison on the Great Plains

ANDREW ISENBERG

During the Pleistocene epoch, as the ancestors of Native Americans crossed the Bering Strait land bridge from Siberia to Alaska, horses migrated in the opposite direction from America to Asia. Horses flourished in Eurasia but eventually became extinct in the Americas. When semisedentary Native Americans on the fringes of the plains acquired horses in the eighteenth century they began to transform themselves into equestrian nomads. That transformation necessitated an almost total reliance on the bison, a new dependence on trade, and the adoption of a decentralized social structure. . . .

Before the eighteenth century, the Indians of the plains diversified their resource use, relying on the production of the prairie, the forest, and the garden. The village Indians from the Missouri River valley combined corn agriculture with cooperative summer bison hunting. The Indians from the fringes of the plains combined bison hunting in the grasslands with hunting, gathering, and perhaps planting outside of the region. The Indians' resource diversity was a conscious land use strategy, which the environmental historians William Cronon and Richard White have called a system of ecological "safety nets." Economic specialization was dangerous, but Indians who gathered a variety of plants and hunted several species of animals as well as planted crops could survive droughts, the unpredictability of wildlife population dynamics, or agricultural failures. Furthermore, by varying their production the Indians reduced the likelihood that they would overexploit any one resource. The Indians' land use strategy protected them from both random environmental shock and overexploitation.

In the eighteenth century, the societies that would become the nomadic Indians of the western plains abandoned their ecological safety nets in order to concentrate

From Andrew Isenberg. *The Destruction of the Bison.* New York: Cambridge University Press, 2001, pp. 31–33, 39–40, 42–47, 53–62. Reprinted with the permission of Cambridge University Press.

year-round on bison hunting. The catalyst for this change was the horse, which Europeans had introduced to North America in the sixteenth century. Hernando Cortés first brought horses to mainland America in 1519. Aided by a propitious outbreak of smallpox, Cortés's small cavalry unit had conquered Mexico by 1521. Thereafter, European livestock thrived in New Spain. By the third quarter of the sixteenth century, herds of cattle numbering over 100,000 were not uncommon in northern Mexico, and sheep herds of similar size grazed in the central highlands. By the middle of the sixteenth century, the number of horses in Mexico had multiplied into the tens of thousands. Thus in Mexico, livestock populations erupted as Europeans replicated Old World land use strategies. These domesticated ungulates would eventually replace the bison in the western plains.

At the end of the sixteenth century, Spaniards in Mexico initiated the process that eventually brought the horse to the plains. In 1598, Don Juan de Oñate, a Spanish *encomendero* [conquistador], gathered together some soldiers, missionaries, seeds, and livestock, and set out to establish Spanish control over the Pueblo Indians of what is now New Mexico. Oñate stayed in New Mexico until 1607. His colony was distinguished for its cruel treatment of the Pueblos and in 1680, the Indians rebelled. The rebels killed several hundred Spanish settlers, seized their livestock, and forced about 2,000 Spaniards to flee.

By the end of the century, when the Spaniards had reestablished their control over New Mexico, the Pueblos had already opened an intertribal trade in horses. In the first decade of the eighteenth century, the Comanches acquired their first horses from the Pueblos or commercial intermediaries. Given the horse's superiority over the dog for traction and transport, and the greater ease of equestrian over pedestrian bison hunting, horses proliferated throughout the southern plains. Horses were not uncommon along the Red River by 1690, and had reached the Arkansas River by 1719. An equestrian pictograph on a rock wall near the White River in western Arkansas dates from around 1700.

The Navajos to the northwest of the Pueblos also acquired horses in the aftermath of the 1680 revolt. The Navajos initiated an intertribal equestrian trade that spread rapidly along the western slopes of the Rocky Mountains, bringing horses to the Nez Percé and Shoshones in the northern Rocky Mountains in the early eighteenth century. According to David Thompson, the Blackfeet acquired their first horses from the Shoshones in the 1730s. Crow tradition maintains that their first horses came from the Nez Percé around the same time. A Sioux winter count records the acquisition of horses from the Omahas as early as 1708–09. The acquisition of horses from other groups—the Omahas, Assiniboines, Hidatsas, and Pawnees—was regarded as important enough to be recorded in nine winters between 1708–09 and 1766–67. Horses thus diffused into the plains from the southwest and the northwest between 1700 and 1750, reaching the northeastern plains by mid-century. . . .

The acquisition of the horse initiated the long transformation of the Arapahos, Assiniboines, Atsinas, Blackfeet, Cheyennes, Comanches, Crows, Kiowas, and the western divisions of the Sioux from life on the fringes of the plains and partial dependence on the bison for subsistence to nomadism and primary dependence on the bison. The Comanches had staked out their hunting territory in the southern plains by the second decade of the eighteenth century. In the northwestern plains, the Blackfeet and Crows had made the transition to nomadism by the 1730s. The Assiniboines and Atsinas established themselves in the north-central plains by mid-century. The western Sioux reached the Black Hills in the 1770s, and the Cheyennes and Arapahos had migrated to the upper Platte River in the central plains by the 1780s. . . .

The social segmentation of the groups that migrated to the plains was a direct consequence of the nature of mounted bison hunting. In the semi-arid plains, the shortgrasses were thick enough to support large aggregations of bison only during the summer. During the rest of the year, small congregations of bison searched for forage and water in the unpredictable environment. Bison changed their location in response to local conditions of drought, fire, or cold. If they were too densely concentrated, they were apt to overgraze an area and disperse further. The Indians broke into small bands in the winter, mirroring the actions of the herds. . . .

. . . The equestrian nomads mitigated . . . [this] uncertainty by using the horse to adapt their movements to the migrations of the herds. In essence, the horse regularized food procurement in the unpredictable environment of the western plains. This new resource strategy demanded social decentralization, but the diffusion of the horse into the plains made nomadic bison hunting a more secure land-use strategy than the combination of hunting and sedentary horticulture—at least in the short term.

II

According to [Brulé chief] Battiste Good's winter count, the Brulé Sioux first encountered European manufactured articles in 1707. . . . The few guns and kettles the Brulés acquired in 1707 presaged a flood of manufactured goods into the plains in the eighteenth century. This emerging trade network encouraged the nomads to specialize as hunters. Euroamericans were latecomers to trade in the grasslands, where, by the mid-eighteenth century, extensive intertribal exchanges were already centered on the leading edge of the European biotic invasion, the horse. In order to acquire horses and to supplement their reliance on the bison, the nomads developed a widespread intertribal trade network in horses and foodstuffs. Trading—or raiding, when terms were not to their liking—furthered the rise of decentralized bands and kinship groups. When European fur traders came to the plains in the mid-eighteenth century in search of beaver pelts, they found the nomads already socially divided and dependent on hunting and trading. The fur trade in the western plains emerged from the spread of horses and furthered the primacy of hunting among the nomads. . . .

. . . By mid-century, the nomads had abandoned their ecological safety nets to become bison hunters, economic specialists. In order to effect this transformation, they adopted a new technology, the horse. They devised a new gender division of labor: women's primary economic responsibility, once horticulture or gathering or both, became the dressing of meat and the tanning of hides. In order to compensate for the abandonment of their resource diversity, the nomads exchanged the products of the hunt with Missouri River villagers who produced a surplus of corn.

In one sense, the increased importance of intertribal exchange was merely a new form of ecological safety net: the Indians depended on trade rather than on their own labor to insure a diversity of resources. In another sense, the transition to nomadism was a rational economic adjustment: equestrian bison hunting yielded greater wealth at less expense than a combination of hunting, gathering, and planting. At any rate, once the plains nomads had become decentralized bands of economic specialists who produced a surplus for the purpose of intertribal exchange—all elements of the protohistoric transition to nomadism—it was a comparatively small step to commercial exchange with Euroamerican beaver pelt traders. Eighteenth-century European fur traders simply grafted their commerce onto the existing intertribal trade network, centering their activities at or near the villages to which the nomads brought the products of the hunt. . . .

III

In addition to the horse and the fur trade, European diseases helped create the plains nomadic societies in the eighteenth century. Familiar European diseases such as smallpox and measles were particularly devastating to American Indians, who had no acquired immunities to Old World contagion. Native Americans lacked those immunities because, in all probability, their ancestors had migrated to America from Asia through the Arctic environment of the Bering Strait land bridge. Because the microbes that cause smallpox, measles, and other diseases cannot survive long among sparse populations, the Arctic migration acted as a disease filter. Therefore, although pre-Columbian North Americans may have suffered from pinta, yaws, venereal diseases, hepatitis, encephalitis, polio, and some varieties of tuberculosis and intestinal parasites, they were free of smallpox, measles, whooping cough, bubonic plague, typhus, yellow fever, scarlet fever, amoebic dysentery, influenza, and several other deadly Eurasian illnesses. . . .

When hosts carried endemic . . . diseases to remote, previously unexposed populations, . . . the result was a devastating epidemic. Beginning in the sixteenth century, when Old World contagion reached the populations of the New World, millions of Native Americans perished. Such a figure is necessarily an inexact estimate. Much of the difficulty of calculating Indian populations stems from Euroamerican observers' habit of counting the number of lodges and then multiplying by the number of people they believed inhabited an average lodge. In the plains, this factor could vary from five to fifteen. Historians cannot know how many Native Americans died as a result of Old World diseases, but based on the virulence of the diseases and an understanding of how epidemics behave, it appears likely that mortality was extremely high. . . .

The first appearance of Old World contagion in the plains is open to debate. Perhaps smallpox, which the Spanish had unwittingly transmitted with deadly effect to Mexico in 1520, also spread to the grasslands. An unknown disease reached eastern Texas and the southern plains in 1691. Battiste Good's winter count calls 1734–35 the "used-them-up-with-bellyache winter"; oral tradition maintains that fifty Sioux died. In general, affliction followed the paths of commercial interaction between Indians and Euroamericans. In the eighteenth century, contagion devastated the Pueblos of New Mexico and the horticultural villagers of the Missouri River rather than the plains nomads because European fur traders centered their commercial enterprises among the villagers. The densely settled, relatively sedentary villagers were thus more likely to contract diseases than the nomads, who spent much of the year isolated in small, outlying bands. . . .

A devastating epidemic of smallpox, perhaps in combination with other, unknown diseases, struck the plains between 1780 and 1782. . . .

Within months of its first appearance in New Mexico, the epidemic reached the Missouri River villagers to the northeast. Before 1780, a typical Missouri River village consisted of twenty to forty lodges each containing about fifteen people. The relatively densely settled villages were thus acutely liable to Old World contagion. According to [explorer and trader] Jean Baptiste Truteau, smallpox reduced the number of Arikara villages from thirty-two to two. He wrote in 1795, "A few families only, from each of the villages, escaped; these united and formed the two villages now here, which are situated about a half mile apart upon the same land occupied by their ancestors.". . .

Equestrian bison hunting saved the nomads from greater mortality. The nomads were isolated in small populations for much of the year as they pursued bison. . . .

Altogether, between 1780 and 1870, the population of the plains sedentary horticulturalists probably declined by 79 percent. [But d]uring the same period, the population of the nomads likely declined by [only] 45 percent, with most of that loss occurring at the end of the nineteenth century. . . .

The 1780–82 epidemic shifted the balance of power in the plains from the villagers to the nomads. For most of the eighteenth century, the villagers—by virtue of their palisades and their greater numbers—had little to fear from other groups. The villagers' dominance had begun to wane when the Sioux, Comanches, and others acquired horses; the horse gave the nomads the ability to mount quick raids on the villages. The epidemic of 1780–82 left the nomads virtually unchallenged for authority in the plains. . . .

. . . The horse, the fur trade, and epidemic disease together created the nomadic hunters. The emergence of the plains nomads in the eighteenth century was thus largely a reaction to the European conquest of North America.

That conquest was a cooperative enterprise. Horses and smallpox—an Old World animal and an Old World disease—destroyed the dominance of the Missouri River villagers and levered the nomads to power in the grasslands. The ecological and economic forces brought by the Europeans were intertwined. Trade brought the horse to the plains. Smallpox largely affected the villages where Euroamerican fur traders concentrated their activities. Trade in horses, furs, and foodstuffs furthered the specialization of the nomads as bison hunters. . . .

Although nomadic bison hunting ultimately proved to be less sustainable than the reliance on planting, gathering, and hunting in a variety of environments, the transformation of many groups from woodland planter-hunters to grassland bison hunters was not a step backward in human evolution. The semi-arid western plains environment, rich in wildlife but too dry for agriculture, dictated the potentials and limitations of resource use. Indeed, rather than exhibiting backwardness, the nomads—characterized by mobility, social anomie, and economic specialization— anticipated later social and economic developments in the plains. . . .

🌱 *F U R T H E R   R E A D I N G*

Paula Gunn Allen, *The Sacred Hoop: Recovering the Feminine in American Indian Traditions* (1986)

———, *Spider Woman's Granddaughters: Traditional Tales and Contemporary Writing by Native American Women* (1989)

Tom Anderson, *This Fine Piece of Water: An Environmental History of Long Island Sound* (2002)

James Axtell, *The European and the Indian: Essays in the Ethnohistory of Colonial North America* (1981)

Gretchen M. Bataille and Kathleen Mullen Sands, *American Indian Women* (1984)

Robert Boyd, ed., *Indians, Fire, and the Land in the Pacific Northwest* (1999)

J. Baird Callicott and Thomas W. Overholt, *Clothed-in-Fur and Other Tales: An Introduction to an Ojibwa World View* (1982)

Maria Chona (Papago), *Papago Woman,* ed. Ruth Underhill (1936)

Harold Courlander, *The Fourth World of the Hopis* (1971)

Alfred Crosby, *The Columbian Exchange: Biological and Cultural Consequences of 1492* (1972), reprint 2003

Jared Diamond, *Guns, Germs, and Steel: The Fates of Human Societies* (1998)

Richard Erdoes and Alfonso Ortiz, ed., *American Indian Myths and Legends* (1984)

Mona Etienne and Eleanor Leacock, eds., *Women and Colonization* (1980)

Dan L. Flores, "Bison Ecology and Bison Diplomacy: The Southern Plains from 1800 to 1850," *Journal of American History* (1991)

————, *The Natural West: Environmental History in the Great Plains and Rocky Mountains* (2001)

Jack Forbes, *Apache, Navaho, and Spaniard* (1963)

Geronimo (Apache), *Geronimo: His Own Story,* ed. S. M. Barrett (1966)

Donald A. Grinde, *Ecocide of Native America: Environmental Destruction of Indian Lands and Peoples* (1995)

Ramón A. Gutiérrez, *When Jesus Came, The Corn Mothers Went Away: Marriage, Sexuality, and Power in New Mexico* (1991)

Cheryl Harris, "Whiteness as Property," *Harvard Law Review* (1993)

Howard L. Harrod, *The Animals Came Dancing: Native American Sacred Ecology and Animal Kinship* (2000)

J. Donald Hughes, *American Indian Ecology* (1983)

Andew Isenberg, *The Destruction of the Bison* (2001)

Harry C. James, *Pages from Hopi History* (1974)

Calestous Juma, *The Gene Hunters: Biotechnology and the Scramble for Seeds* (1989)

Shepard Krech III, *The Ecological Indian: Myth and History* (1999)

————, ed., *Indians, Animals, and the Fur Trade: A Critique of Keepers of the Game* (1981)

Left Handed (Navajo), *Left Handed, Son of Old Man Hatt: A Navaho Autobiography,* ed. Walter Dyk (1938)

Peter C. Mancall and James H. Merrell, eds., *American Encounters: Natives and Newcomers from European Contact to Indian Removal, 1500–1850* (2000)

Calvin Martin, ed., *The American Indian and the Problem of History* (1987)

————, *Keepers of the Game: Indian-Animal Relationships and the Fur Trade* (1978)

Carolyn Niethammer, *Daughters of the Earth: The Lives and Legends of American Indian Women* (1977)

Alfonso Ortiz, *The Tewa World: Space, Time, Being and Becoming in a Pueblo Society* (1969)

Polingaysi Qoyawayma, *No Turning Back: A Hopi Indian Woman's Struggle to Live in Two Worlds* (1964)

José Rabasa, *Inventing America: Spanish Historiography and the Formation of Eurocentrism* (1993)

Luis N. Rivera, *A Violent Evangelism: The Political and Religious Conquest of the Americas* (1992)

Neal Salisbury, "The Indians' Old World: Native Americans and the Coming of Europeans," *William and Mary Quarterly* (1996)

Helen Sekaquaptewa (Hopi), *Me and Mine: The Life Story of Helen Sekaquaptewa as Told to Louise Udall* (1969)

Leslie Marmon Silko (Laguna), *Storyteller* (1981)

Edward Holland Spicer, *Cycles of Conquest: The Impact of Spain, Mexico, and the United States on the Indians of the Southwest, 1533–1960* (1962)

Don C. Talayesva (Hopi), *Sunchief: The Autobiography of a Hopi Indian* (1974)

John Upton Terrel, *Pueblos, Gods, and Spaniards* (1973)

Christopher Vecsey and Robert W. Venables, eds., *American Indian Environments: Ecological Issues in Native American History* (1980)

Frank Waters, *Book of the Hopi* (1963)

Richard White, "Native Americans and the Environment," in W. R. Swagerty, ed., *Scholars and the Indian Experience* (1984)

————, *The Roots of Dependency: Subsistence, Environment, and Social Change Among the Choctaws, Pawnees, and Navajos* (1983)

Raymond Wilson, "Native American and European Encounters in North America," *Journal of American Ethnic History* (1997)

Alber Yava (Tewa-Hopi), *Big Falling Snow: A Tewa-Hopi Indian's Life and Times and the History and Traditions of His People,* ed. Harold Courlander (1978)

CHAPTER
3

The New England
Forest in the
Seventeenth Century

After several abortive attempts, English settlers established the Plymouth colony
in New England in 1620 and the Massachusetts Bay Colony at Boston in 1629.
Seventeenth-century New England had a resource-extractive economy based on
the four Fs: forests, furs, fish, and farms. England provided investors and manufactures; the colonies, a rich reserve of natural resources.

The southern New England Indians whom the English settlers encountered used
cleared patches in the lowland forests to plant corn, beans, and squash and depended
on the upland forests for hunting the animals they needed for meat and clothing.
They "managed" the forests by burning them to accommodate hunting and travel
and to create grassy pastures for deer. The colonists, in contrast, established settled
agriculture, extracting forest resources for subsistence and trading them for much-
needed manufactured goods and staples—iron tools, kettles, nails, guns, ammunition, clothing, windows, paper, coffee, tea, and sugar. They also introduced new ideas
about nature, grounded in a view of a transcendent God who had chosen them to use
the land and to spread "His word" in the New World.

From the perspectives of the beaver and the white pine tree, each extraction
transformed a forest home. Beaver created complex pond ecosystems in the forests that
left tree stumps and brush for grouse, rabbits, and cavity-nesting birds; watering
spots for deer and moose; and foraging sites for foxes, raccoons, bears, and wildcats.
The spruce-hemlock forests of northern New England and the white pine–oak forests
of the region's southern reaches sustained a variety of tree and bush species, wildflowers, mammals, insects, and birds. The colonists simplified these ecosystems by
trapping beaver for the fur trade and breaking down their dams for tillage and
pasture sites. They converted the forests into farms and extracted pines for masts,
oak for barrel staves, and ash for farm implements.

The colonists also added to the complexity of this ecosystem by introducing
European crops (wheat, barley, oats, and rye), livestock (cows, oxen, sheep, pigs,
goats, and chickens), herbs, weeds, varmints, and diseases. These all affected the

composition of the forest. Colonial settled agriculture, moreover, competed with the Indians' use of forest clearings for horticulture and with the native peoples' meat and clothing reserves. The arrival of Europeans dramatically changed New England's ecology, undercutting the resources that Indians required for subsistence. By the late seventeenth century, the region's Indians, colonists, beaver, and forests had all been transformed. (See Maps 1, 2, 4, and 5 in the Appendix.)

♦ D O C U M E N T S

The documents relate the environmental history of the New England forest from wilderness to marketplace and contrast Indian and colonial uses of the forest. In Document 1, William Bradford, governor and historian of Plymouth colony, captures the Pilgrims' concept of the forest as a vast wilderness and describes its transformation through trade and farming. Bradford also provides graphic evidence of the devastating effects of smallpox on the Indians of the Connecticut River Valley in 1634. The next two documents illuminate the Puritans' use of biblical ideas to justify transforming the forest environment. John Winthrop, governor of the Massachusetts Bay Colony, in Document 2 cites Genesis 1:28 as a mandate for subduing the new lands, replenishing them with English people, and improving them through agriculture and trade. Thomas Morton, in his 1632 *New English Canaan,* excerpted in Document 3, employs the biblical view of Canaan as a promised land, along with the image of nature as female— a virgin whose fruits could be enjoyed when Puritan industry and art transformed the resources of the New World forests. He also describes Indians' burning of the forests for better hunting and traveling.

Document 4 depicts the ways in which Indian women and men used the forest for subsistence. Colonist William Wood's *New England's Prospect,* published in 1634, portrays Indian women's construction of houses and tending of forest garden patches as successful subsistence techniques. Documents 5 and 6, by contrast, reveal colonists' religious perceptions of nature and its usefulness for trade. Anne Bradstreet, New England's first published female poet, writes of the differences between nature and humanity in Document 5, while in Document 6 Edward Johnson, author of *Wonderworking Providence,* describes New England's rapid transformation from wilderness to city in little more than two decades and the ways in which resources could be traded by New England merchants.

The final three documents show both the ways in which forests were used and conserved and the rationale for their human use. Document 7 looks at the New England forest from the perspectives of a wealthy colonial timber merchant. Nicholas Shapleigh's 1682 estate, the subject of the selection, reveals large profits obtained from lumbering, fur trading, and farming. Document 8, by Cotton Mather, one of New England's prominent ministers, presents the received view of his time that a scale of nature (or great chain of being) existed that moved upward from the lowliest stone to human beings to disembodied angels in increasing spiritual closeness to a God who should be glorified through human dominion over nature. In the final excerpt, New Hampshire governor Jonathan Belcher, responding to the timber crisis in England, summarizes the British Broad Arrow policy, reserving white pines for the king's use, and warns the colonists not to exploit New England's timber for their private gain.

1. William Bradford Faces a "Hideous and Desolate Wilderness," 1620–1635

After long beating at sea they fell with that land which is called Cape Cod; the which being made & certainly known to be it, they were not a litle joyful. After some deliberation had amongst themselves & with the master of the ship, they tacked about and resolved to stand for the southward (the wind & weather being fair) to find some place about Hudsons river for their habitation. But after they had sailed that course about half the day, they fell amongst dangerous shoals and roaring breakers, and they were so far intangled there with as they conceived themselves in greater danger; & the wind shrinking upon them withall, they resolved to bear up again for the Cape, and thought themselves happy to get out of those dangers before night overtook them, as by Gods providence they did. And the next day they got into the Cape-harbor where they rode in safety. . . .

Being thus arived in a good harbor and brought saf to land, they fell upon their knees & blessed the God of heaven, who had brought them over the vast & furious ocean, and delivered them from all the perils & miseries thereof, again to set their feet on the firm and stable earth, their proper element. . . . Being thus past the vast ocean, and a sea of troubles before in their preparation (as may be remembered by that which went before), they had now no friends to welcome them, nor inns to entertain or refresh their weatherbeaten bodies, no houses or much less towns to repair to, to seek for succor. It is recorded in scripture as a mercy to the apostle & his shipwrecked company, that the barbarians showed them no small kindness in refreshing them, but these savage barbarians, when they met with them (as after will appear) were readier to fill their sides full of arrows then otherwise. And for the season it was winter, and they that know the winters of that country know them to be sharp & violent, & subject to cruel & fierce storms, dangerous to travel to known places, much more to search an unknown coast. Besides, what could they see but a hideous & desolate wilderness, full of wild beasts & wild men? and what multitudes there might be of them they knew not. Neither could they, as it were, go up to the top of Pisgah, to view from this wilderness a more goodly country to feed their hopes; for which way soever they turned their eyes (save upward to the heavens) they could have litle solace or content in respect of any outward objects. For summer being done, all things stand upon them with a weather-beaten face; and the whole country, full of woods & thickets, represented a wild & savage hue. If they looked behind them, there was the mighty ocean which they had passed, and was now as a main bar & gulf to separate them from all the civil parts of the world. . . . What could now sustain them but the spirit of God & his grace? May not & ought not the children of these fathers, rightly say: *Our fathers were Englishmen which came over this great ocean, and were ready to perish in this wilderness. . . .*

From William Bradford. *Of Plimoth Plantation.* Boston: Wright and Potter, 1901, pp. 93, 94–96, 111, 114–116, 121, 127–130, 387–389.

But that which was most sad & lamentable was, that in 2. or 3. months' time half of their company died, especially in Jan: & February, being the depth of winter, and wanting houses & other comforts; being infected with the scurvy & other diseases, which this long voyage & their inaccommodate condition had brought upon them; so as there died some times 2. or 3. of a day, in the foresaid time; that of 100. & odd persons, scarce 50. remained. And of these in the time of most distress, there was but 6. or 7. sound persons, who, to their great commendations be it spoken, spared no pains, night nor day, but with abundance of toil and hazard of their own health, fetched them wood, made them fires, dressed them meat, made their beds, washed their loathsome clothes, clothed & unclothed them; in a word, did all the homely and necessary offices for them which dainty and queasy stomachs cannot endure to hear named; and all this willingly and cheerfully, without any grudging in the least, showing herein their true love unto their friends and brethren. . . .

All this while the Indians came skulking about them, and would sometimes show themselves aloof of, but when any approached near them, they would run away. And once they stole away their tools where they had been at work, & were gone to dinner. But about the 16. of *March* a certain Indian came boldly amongst them, and spoke to them in broken English, which they could well understand, but marvelled at it. . . . His name was *Samaset;* he told them also of another Indian whose name was *Squanto,* a native of this place, who had been in England & could speak better English then himself. Being, after some time of entertainment & gifts, dismissed, a while after he came again, & 5. more with him, & they brought again all the tools that were stolen away before, and made way for the coming of their great Sachem, called *Massasoyt;* who, about 4. *or* 5. *days after,* came with the chief of his friends & other attendants, with the aforesaid *Squanto.* With whom, after friendly entertainment, & some gifts given him, they made a peace with him (which hath now continued this 24. years). . . . *Squanto* continued with them, and was their interpreter, and was a special instrument sent of God for their good beyond their expectation. He directed them how to set their corn, where to take fish, and to procure other commodities, and was also their pilot to bring them to unknown places for their profit, and never left them till he died. He was a *native of this place,* & scarce any left alive besids himself. He was caried away with divers others by one *Hunt,* a master of a ship, who thought to sell them for slaves in Spain; but he got away for England, and was entertained by a merchant in London, & employed to Newfoundland & other parts, & lastly brought hither into these parts by one Mr. *Dermer,* a gentle-man employed by Sr. Ferdinando Gorges & others, for discovery, & other designs in these parts. . . .

Anno: 1621

[April] Afterwards they (as many as were able) began to plant ther corn, in which service Squanto stood them in great stead, showing them both the manner how to set it, and after how to dress & tend it. Also he told them except they got fish & set with it (in these old grounds) it would come to nothing, and he showed them that in the middle of April they should have store enough come up the brook, by which they began to build, and taught them how to take it, and where to get other provisions necessary for them; all which they found true by trial & experience. Some English seed they sew, as wheat & peas, but it came not to good, either by the badness of the seed, or lateness of the season, or both, or some other defect. . . .

[September] They began now to gather in the small harvest they had, and to fit up their houses and dwellings against winter, being all well recovered in health & strength, and had all things in good plenty; for as some were thus employed in affairs abroad, others were exercised in fishing, about cod, & bass, & other fish, of which they took good store, of which every family had their portion. All the summer there was no want. And now began to come in store of fowl, as winter approached, of which this place did abound when they came first (but afterward decreased by degrees). And besides water fowl, there was great store of wild Turkeys, of which they took many, besides venison, &c. Besides they had about a peck a meal a week to a person, or now since harvest, Indian corn to that proportion. Which made many afterwards write so largely of their plenty here to their friends in England, which were not feigned, but true reports.

In November, about that time twelfth month that themselves came, there came in a small ship to them unexpected or looked for, in which came Mr. Cushman (so much spoken of before) and with him 35. persons to remain & live in the plantation; which did not a little rejoice them. And they when they came a shore and found all well, and saw plenty of victuals in every house, were no less glad. . . . So they were all landed; but there was not so much as biscuit-cake or any other victuals for them, neither had they any bedding, but some sorry things they had in their cabins, not pot, nor pan, to dress any meat in; nor overmany clothes, for many of them had brushed away their coats & cloaks at Plymouth as they came. But there was sent over some burching-lane suits in the ship, out of which they were supplied. The plantation was glad of this addition of strength, but could have wished that many of them had been of better condition, and all of them better furnished with provisions; but that could not now be helped. . . .

This ship (called the Fortune) was speedily dispatched away, being laden with good clapbord as full as she could stow, and 2. hogsheads of beaver and otter skins, which they got with a few trifling commodities brought with them at first, being altogether unprovided for trade; neither was there any amongst them that ever saw a beaver skin till they came here, and were informed by Squanto. The freight was estimated to be worth near 500. pounds. . . .

Anno Dom: 1634

I am now to relate some strange and remarkable passages. There was a company of people lived in the country, up above in the river of Connecticut, a great way from their trading house there, and were enemies to those Indians which lived about them, and of whom they stood in some fear (being a stout people). About a thousand of them had inclosed them selves in a fort, which they had strongly palisaded about. 3. or 4. Dutch men went up in the beginning of winter to live with them, to get their trade, and prevent them for bringing it to the English, or to fall into amity with them; but at spring to bring all down to their place. But their enterprise failed, for it pleased God to visit these Indians with a great sicknes, and such a mortality that of a 1000. above 900. and a half of them died, and many of them did rot above ground for want of burial, and the Dutch men almost starved before they could get away, for ice and snow. But about Feb: they got with much difficulty to their trading house; whom they kindly relieved, being almost spent with hunger and cold. Being thus refreshed by them divers days, they got to their own place, and the Dutch were very thankful for this kindness.

This spring, also, those Indians that lived about their trading house there fell sick of the small pox, and died most miserably; for a sorer disease cannot befall them; they fear it more than the plague; for usually they that have this disease have them in abundance, and for want of bedding & lining and other helps, they fall into a lamentable condition, as they live on their hard mats, the pox breaking and mattering, and running one into another, their skin cleaving (by reason thereof) to the mats they lie on; when they turn them, a whole side will fly of at once, (as it were,) and they will be all of a gore blood, most fearful to behold; and then begin very sore, what with cold and other distempers, they die like rotten sheep. The condition of this people was so lamentable, and they fell down so generally of this disease, as they were (in the end) not able to help one another; no, not to make a fire, nor to fetch a little water to drink, nor any to bury the dead; but would strive as long as they could, and when they could procure no other means to make fire, they would burn the wooden trays & dishes they ate their meat in, and their very bows & arrows; & some would crawl out on all four to get a little water, and some times die by the way, & not be able to get in again. But those of the English house, (though at first they were afraid of the infection,) yet seeing their woeful and sad condition, and hearing their pitifull cries and lamentations, they had compassion of them, and daily fetched them wood & water, and made them fires, got them victuals whilst they lived, and buried them when they died. For very few of them escaped, notwithstanding they did what they could for them, to the hazard of themselves. The chief Sachem him self now died, & almost all his friends & kindred. But by the marvelous goodness & providence of God not one of the English was so much as sick, or in the least measure tainted with this disease, though they daily did these offices for them for many weeks together. And this mercy which they showed them was kindly taken, and thankfully acknowledged of all the Indians that knew or heard of the same; and their masters here did much commend & reward them for the same.

2. John Winthrop Sets Forth the Grounds for Settling in New England, 1629

The grounds of settling a plantation in new England.

[1. Ground.] The propagation of the gospell to the Indians. . . .

2. Ground. Charitie to our neighbors [who are] impoverished by decay of Trade and lefte destitute of hope of imployment in tyme to come, who may comforttably be sustayned by their labors & endeavors in this Country [New England] yeilding

---

From John Winthrop. "Conclusions for the Plantation in New England," in *Old South Leaflets,* no. 50 (1629). Boston: Directors of the Old South Work, 1897, pp. 1–2, 4–5.

them sufficient matter of imployment & meanes of recompence, [such] as, corne[,] both of our kindes [i.e., wheat and rye] which prosper well in those parts & [that] of the country [New England maize] which is farr better for use then ours & maye be sett yearly after our [English] graines are sowne, & consequently without hinderance of our ordinary course of husbandrie.

2dly infinite varietie & store of

Fishes, Sturgion, Salmon, Mullett, Bas, Codd, Lobsters, Eeles.

Fowle, as, Turkie, Feasant, Partridg, Goose, Duck, Teal, and Deare. . . .

3dly The possibility of Breedinge of Kine [cattle] which growe to a farr greater bulke of body in that country then with us, . . . secondly, of Goates which may easily be Transported with small charge. [Thirdly] Swine which breed in great numbers by reason of the abundan*dan*ce of Acornes, groundnutts, . . . Wall-nuts, & clummes, 4ly Trade of Furres which may be Brought out of that Continent. . . . 5ly fishing[,] a knowen & staple Commoditie. 6ly possibilitie of makeinge salt. . . . 7ly plantinge of vines.

8ly makeinge pitch, Tarr, Pottashes & sope ashes.

9ly Cuttinge of masts.

10ly makeing of Iron, what other mines there are we know nott.

11ly some woods fitt for dying, others for Phisicall uses, as, Sarzaperilla Sassafras &c.

12. Silke grass.

13. Hemp & flax for which the soyle is very fitt.

3 *Ground.* The Danger & extremities of the present estate of the Churches. . . .

Reasons to be considered for Justifieing the undertak[ing] of the intended plantation in New England. . . .

First, It wilbe a service [of great consequence] to the Church . . . to carry the Gospell into those parts of the world, to [encourage the conversion] of the [heathens] and to rayse a Bulworke against the kingdome of Antichrist, which the Jesuites labour to [establish] in those parts.

2. All other Churches of Europe are brought to desolation; . . . & who knowes but that god hath provided this place to be a refuge for many whom he meanes to save [from] the generall callamitie. . . .

3. This land [England] growes weary of her Inhabitants, soe as man whoe is the most pretious of all creatures is heer more vile & base then the Earth we Tread uppon. . . .

4. The whole earth is the lords Garden & he hath given it to the sonnes of men, with a generall Condition, Gen: 1, 28. Increase & multiply, replenish the earth & subdue it, which was againe renewed to Noah, . . . that man might injoy the fruites of the earth & god might have his due glory from the creature, why then should we stand hear striveing for places of habitation, (many men [sometimes] spending as much labor & cost to recover or keep . . . a Acre or two of land as would procure them many hundred as good or better in an other country) and in the mean tyme suffer a whole Continent as fruitfull & convenient for the use of man to lie [empty and unimproved].

3. Thomas Morton Praises the New English Canaan, 1632

The Authors Prologue.

If art & industry should doe as much
As Nature hath for Canaan, not such
Another place, for benefit and rest,
In all the universe can be possest,
The more we proove it by discovery,
The more delight each object to the eye
Procures, as if the elements had here
Bin reconcil'd and pleas'd it should appeare,
Like a faire virgin, longing to be sped,
And meete her lover in a Nuptiall bed,
Deck'd in rich ornaments t' advaunce her state
And excellence, being most fortunate,
When most enjoy'd, so would our Canaan be
If well employ'd by art and industry
Whose offspring, now shewes that her fruitfull wombe
Not being enjoy'd, is like a glorious tombe,
Admired things producing which there dye,
And ly fast bound in darck obscurity,
The worth of which in each particuler,
Who list to know, this abstract will declare.

In the Moneth of June, Anno Salutis: 1622. It was my chaunce to arrive in the parts of New England with 30. Servants, and provision of all sorts fit for a plantation: And whiles our howses were building, I did endeavour to take a survey of the Country: The more I looked, the more I liked it.

And when I had more seriously considered of the bewty of the place, with all her faire indowments, I did not thinke that in all the knowne world it could be paralel'd. For so many goodly groues of trees; dainty fine round rising hillucks: delicate faire large plaines, sweete cristall fountaines, and cleare running streames, that twine in fine meanders through the meads, making so sweete a murmering noise to heare, as would even lull the sences with delight a sleepe, so pleasantly doe, they glide upon the pebble stones, jetting most jocundly where they doe meete; and hand in hand runne downe to Neptunes Court, to pay the yearely tribute, which they owe to him as soveraigne Lord of all the springs. Contained within the volume of the Land, Fowles in abundance, Fish in multitude, and discovered besides; Millions of Turtledoves one the greene boughes: which sate pecking, of the full ripe pleasant grapes, that were supported by the lusty trees, whose fruitfull loade did cause the armes to bend, which here and there dispersed (you might see) Lillies and of the Daphnean-tree, which made the Land to mee seeme paradice, for in mine eie, t'was Natures

---

From Thomas Morton, "New English Canaan" in Peter Force, ed., *Tracts and Other Papers.* . . . Washington, D.C., 1838, vol. II, pp. 10, 36–37, 41–42.

Master-peece: Her cheifest Magazine of, all where lives her store: if this Land be not rich, then is the whole world poore. . . .

The Salvages are accustomed, to set fire of the Country in all places where they come; and to burne it, twize a yeare, vixe at the Spring, and the fall of the leafe. The reason that mooves them to doe so, is because it would other wise be so over-growne with underweedes, that it would be all a copice wood, and the people would not be able in any wise to passe through the Country out of a beaten path. . . .

And least their firing of the Country in this manner; should be an occasion of damnifying us, and indaingering our habitations; wee our selves have used care-fully about the same times; to observe the winds and fire the grounds about our owne habitations, to prevent the Dammage that might happen by any neglect thereof, if the fire should come neere those howses in our absence.

For when the fire is once kindled, it dilates and spreads it selfe as well against, as with the winde; burning continually night and day, untill a shower of raine falls to quench it.

And this custome of firing the Country is the meanes to make it passable, and by that meanes the trees growe here, and there as in our parks: and makes the Country very beautifull and commodious.

4. William Wood Portrays Indian Women's Housing and Horticulture, 1634

Of Their Women, Their Dispositions, Employments, Usage by Their Husbands, Their Apparel, and Modesty

[Women's] employments be many: First their building of houses, whose frames are formed like our garden-arbors, something more round, very strong and handsome, covered with close-wrought mats of their own weaving, which deny entrance to any drop of rain, though it come both fierce and long, neither can the piercing North wind find a cranny, through which he can convey his cooling breath, they be warmer than our English houses; at the top is a square hole for the smoke's evacuation, which in rainy weather is covered with a pluver; these be such smoky dwellings, that when there is good fires, they are not able to stand upright, but lie all along under the smoke, never using any stools or chairs, it being as rare to see an Indian sit on a stool at home, as it is strange to see an English man sit on his heeles abroad. Their houses are smaller in the Summer, when their families be dispersed, by reason of heat and occasions. In Winter they make some fifty or threescore foot long, forty or fifty men being inmates under one roof; and as is their husbands' occasion these poor tectonists are often troubled like snails, to carry their houses on their backs sometime to fishing-places, other times to hunting-places, after that to a planting place, where it abides the longest: an other work is their planting of corn, wherein they exceed our English husband-men, keeping it so clear with their Clam shell-hoes, as if it were a garden rather than a corn-field, not suffering a choking weed to advance his audacious head above their infant corn, or an undermining worm to

---

From William Wood, *New England's Prospect.* London: Thomas Cotes, 1634, pp. 99–100.

spoil his spurns. Their corn being ripe, they gather it, and drying it hard in the Sun, convey it to their barns, which be great holes digged in the ground in form of a brass pot, sealed with rinds of trees, wherein they put their corn, covering it from the inquisitive search of their gourmandizing husbands, who would eat up both their allowed portion, and reserved seed, if they knew where to find it. But our hogs having found a way to unhinge their barn doors, and rob their garners, they are glad to implore their husbands' help to roll the bodies of trees over their holes, to prevent those pioneers, whose thievery they as much hate as their flesh.

5. Anne Bradstreet Eulogizes Nature, 1650

"Contemplations" [Verses 18–20]

18

. . . When I behold the heavens as in their prime,
And then the earth (though old) stil clad in green,
The stones and trees, insensible of time,
Nor age nor wrinkle on their front are seen;
If winter come, and greeness then do fade,
A Spring returns, and they more youthfull made;
But Man grows old, lies down, remains where once
he's laid.

[19]

By birth more noble then those creatures all,
Yet seems by nature and by custome curs'd,
No sooner born, but grief and care makes fall
That state obliterate he had at first:
Nor youth, nor strength, nor wisdom spring again
Nor habitations long their names retain,
But in oblivion to the final day remain.

20

Shall I then praise the heavens, the trees, the earth
Because their beauty and their strength last longer
Shall I wish there, or never to had birth,
Because they're bigger, & their bodyes stronger?
Nay, they shall darken, perish, fade and dye,
And when unmade, so ever shall they lye,
But man was made for endless immortality.

From Anne Bradstreet, *The Works of Anne Bradstreet in Prose and Verse*. Ed. John Harvard Ellis. Charlestown: Abram E. Cutter, 1867, p. 376.

6. Edward Johnson Describes the Transformation of the Wilderness, 1654

. . . The chiefe Edifice of this City-like Towne is crowded on the Sea-bankes, and wharfed out with great industry and cost, the buildings beautifull and large, some fairely set forth with Brick, Tile, Stone and Slate, and orderly placed with comly streets, whose continuall inlargement presages some sumptuous City. The wonder of this moderne Age, that a few yeares should bring forth such great matters by so meane a handfull, and they so far from being inriched by the spoiles of other Nations, that the states of many of them have beene spoiled by the Lordly Prelacy, whose Lands must assuredly make Restitutions. But now behold the admirable Acts of Christ; at this his peoples landing, the hideous Thickets in this place were such, that Wolfes and Beares nurst up their young from the eyes of all beholders, in those very places where the streets are full of Girles and Boys sporting up and downe, with a continued concourse of people. Good store of Shipping is here yearly built, and some very faire ones: both Tar and Mastes the Countrey affords from its own soile; also store of Victuall both for their owne and Forreiners-ships, who resort hither for that end: this Town is the very Mart of the Land, French, Portugalls and Dutch come hither for Traffique. . . .

. . . The Lord is pleased also to compleat this Commonwealth abundantly beyond all expectation in all sorts of needful occupations, it being for a long time the great fear of many, and those that were endued with grace from above also, that this would be no place of continued habitation, for want of a staple-commodity, but the Lord, whose promises are large to his Sion, hath blest his peoples provision, and satisfied her poor with bread, in a very little space, every thing in the country proved a staple-commodity, wheat, rye, oats, peas, barley, beef, pork, fish, butter, cheese, timber, mast, tar, sope, plank-board, frames of houses, clabboard, and pipestaves, iron and lead is like to be also; and those who were formerly forced to fetch most of the bread they eat, and beer they drink, a hundred leagues by Sea, are through the blessing of the Lord so encreased, that they have not only fed their Elder Sisters, Virginia, Barbados, and many of the Summer Islands that were prefer'd before her for fruitfulness, but also the Grandmother of us all, even the firtil Isle of Great Britain, beside Portugal hath had many a mouthful of bread and fish from us, in exchange of their Madeara liquor, and also Spain; nor could it be imagined, that this Wilderness should turn a mart for Merchants in so short a space, Holland, France,. Spain, and Portugal coming hither for trade, shipping going on gallantly, till the Seas became so troublesome, and England restrain'd our trade, forbidding it with Barbados, etc. and Portugal stopt and took our ships; many a fair ship had her framing and finishing here, besides lesser vessels, barques, and ketches, many a Master, beside common Seamen, had their first learning in this Colony. Boston, Charles-Town, Salem, and Ipswitch, our Maritan [maritime] Towns began to encrease roundly, especially Boston, the which of a poor country village, in twice seven years is become like unto a small city.

From Edward Johnson, *Johnson's Wonder-working Providence,* ed. J. Franklin Jameson. New York: Barnes & Noble, 1910, pp. 71, 246–247.

7. A Timber Merchant's Estate, 1682

A true Inventory of the Moneys goods Cattle & Chattels belonging & appertaining to the Estate of Major Nicho. Shapleigh, of Kittery in the Province of Maine In New England deceased, taken and apprized by us whose names are here subscribed, this 9th day of May 1682: which are as follows.*

	£	S	D
Inprs† to so much In Cash or ready money	055	17	00
It‡to 70 ounces of plate at 6s p§ oz	021	00	00
It to his wearing apparel thirteen pounds 13s	013	13	00
It to a Parcel of worn Pewter, at 6 pounds 7s	006	07	00
It to a Parcel of New Pewter apprized at	009	03	00
It 68lb of beaver at 5s p lb at Otter skin 5s, a Moose skin 8s	017	00	00
It two hats & a Case 20s, his riding horse & furniture 5: 10: 00	006	10	0
It The home stall, dwelling house out houses orchards grandings pastures fields with all appurtenances hereunto belonging with all other out-lands hereto adjoining, the Timber of the saw Mills only, excepted	500	00	00
It the saw Mill & Grist Mill, and their accommodations at Kittery valued	300	00	00
It William Ellinghams Interest purchased by Major Shapleigh in his life time lying on the North side of the Creek	050	00	00
It about thirty Acres of Marsh lying at Sturgeon Creek	090	00	00
It Ten thousand foot of boards or thereabouts at the Saw Mills	010	00	00
It Three horses apprized at 50s p horse	007	00	00
It eleven oxen 38£: eleven Cows: 27: 10: 00, 3 3 year old Cattle: 7: 10: 00, four two years old at six pounds	079	00	00
It four yearlings 4: 00: 00: 11 sheep & five lambs 4 pounds	008	00	00
It a Parcel of swine at 10£: 4 Negroes 3 men one woman & one little Negro all at ninety pounds	100	00	00
	1273	10	0
It Two Irish boys, one to serve about two years, & one 3 years	010	00	0
It Great Guns & Carriages seven pounds, a great fowling piece that Samson Whitte borrowed 30s, four New Muskets four pounds 4 small guns 40s: a blunderbuss 15s	015	05	0
Two Timber Chains 40s six draft Chains 48s, 6 yokes ready fitted with rings & staples 24s, two plows 16s, two Clevises 5s			
It a Cart & wheels 35s one pair logging Wheels & drags 4: 10: 0	012	18	0
It Two pair of Mast Wheels decayed with Iron work 3 pounds ⎫			
It Two Mast Chains & 1/3 of another Chain at 5 £ ⎬	008	00	0
It 12 old axes, two spades, 1 pair of hand screws, too scythes two drawing knives, Carpenters tools & Turning tools five pounds	005	00	0
It one pair of large steelyards at Mr Richd Waldens	003	00	0
It In the smiths shop one pair of bellows, small Tools & old Iron	002	10	0
It one old lighter, one shallop with old Rigging & furniture at	010	00	0
It 3 great hay Canoes & a Coasting Canoe	005	00	0
It one old Cloak at 35s	001	15	0
	73	08	0

*In the columns, 1 pound (£) equals 20 shillings (s), and 1 shilling (s) equals 12 pence (d).
†Inprs: Probably abbreviation for *in principio,* meaning "in the beginning."
‡It: Abbreviation for *item,* meaning "also," to introduce each article in a list.
§p: Abbreviation for *per.*

From Estate of Major Nicholas Shapleigh of Kittery, Maine. In *York Deeds.* Ed. William M. Sargent. Portland, Me.: Brown Thurston and Co., 1889, Part I, Fol. 15–16. Definitions from *The American Heritage Dictionary of the English Language,* Fourth Edition. Boston: Houghton Mifflin Company, 2002. Copyright © 2000 by Houghton Mifflin Company. Adapted and reproduced by permission from *The American Heritage Dictionary of the English Language,* Fourth Edition.

Definitions

Blunderbuss, n. A short musket of wide bore and flaring muzzle, formerly used to scatter shot at close range. [Alteration of Du. *donderbus : donder,* thunder . . . + *bus,* gun.]

Clevis, n. A U-shaped metal fastening device with holes in each end for a pin or bolt. [Can be used to attach a wagon tongue to a whiffletree.] [< *clevi,* poss. of Scand. orig.; akin to ON *klofi,* cleft.]

Whiffletree, n. The pivoted horizontal crossbar to which the harness traces of a draft animal are attached and which is in turn attached to a vehicle or an implement.

Steelyard, n. A balance consisting of a scaled arm suspended off center, a hook at the shorter end on which to hang the object being weighed, and a counterbalance at the longer end that can be moved to find the weight. [STEEL + YARD, rod.]

Lighter, n. A large flatbottom barge, esp. one used to load and unload cargo ships. [ME, perh. < *lighten,* to make less heavy < OE *līthan.*]

Shallop, n. A small open boat fitted with oars or sails, or both, and used primarily in shallow waters. [Fr. *chaloupe* < Du. *sloep,* sloop.]

8. Cotton Mather Presents the Scale of Nature, 1721

There is a *Scale of Nature,* wherein we pass regularly and proportionably from a *Stone* to a *Man,* the Faculties of the Creatures in their *various Classes* growing still brighter and brighter, and more capacious, till we arrive to those noble ones which are found in the *Soul* of MAN; and yet MAN is, as one [botanist Nehemiah Grew] well expresses it, *but the Equator of the Universe.*

It is a just View which Dr. *Grew* had of *the World,* when he came to this Determination: "As there are several Orders of *animated Body* before we come to *Intellect,* so it must needs be that there are several Orders of *imbodied Intellect* before we come to *pure Mind.*"

It is likely that the Transition from *Human* to *perfect* MIND is made by a *gradual Ascent;* there may be *Angels* whose Faculties may be as much superior to *ours,* as ours may be to those of a *Snail* or a *Worm.*

By and by we may arrive to *Minds* divested of all *Body,* excellent *Minds,* which may enjoy the Knowledge of Things by a more *immediate Intuition,* as well as without any Inclination to any *moral Evil.*

The highest Perfection that any *created Mind* can arise to, is that in the *Soul* of our admirable Saviour, which is indeed *embodied;* but it is the *Soul* of the *Man* who is personally united to the SON of GOD.

Anon we see an infinite GOD; but *canst thou by searching find out GOD? Canst thou find out the Almighty to Perfection?*

It is a good Thought, and well expressed of an honest Writer on *the Knowledge of God from the Works of Creation.* "It is true there are some *Footsteps* of a *Deity* in

From Cotton Mather, *The Christian Philosopher.* Ed. Winton U. Solberg. Urbana: University of Illinois Press, 1994, pp. 306–307.

all the Works of Nature, but we should ascend by these *Footsteps* as by a *Footstool* to the *God* of the World, as *Solomon* by several Steps ascended to his *Throne,* and by the *Scale of Nature* ascend to the *God* of *Nature.*"

This is what we shall now, tho in a more *summary way,* a little more distinctly proceed to.

No *Dominion over the Creatures* can be more acceptably, more delightfully exercised with me than this; for me to *employ them* as often as I please in *leading me to GOD,* and so in serving that which I propose as the chief END for which I *live,* and *move,* and have my *Being;* which is, *to glorify GOD, and acknowledge Him.*

9. A Governor Enforces the King's Forest Policy, 1730

*By His Excellency Jonathan Belcher Esqr Captain
General & Governour in Chief in and over His Maj'ties
Province of New Hampshire in New England—*

A Proclamation to prevent the Destruction or Spoil of His Majesties Woods.—

Forasmuch as the Preservation of His Majesties Woods within this and the neighbouring Provinces is highly necessary for furnishing the Royal Navy, and divers Acts of Parliament have been accordingly from time to time made & pass'd for that end; notwithstanding which and the care of this Governmt to prevent & punish the Destruction and spoil of His Majesties Woods, many evil minded Persons have broke thro' the restraints of the Law in that behalf; and have for their own private gain made great wast of such trees as might be fit for His Majesties service. . . . It is enacted "That from and after the Twenty first day of September one thousand seven hundred & twenty two, no Person or Persons within the Colonys or plantations of Nova Scotia, New Hampshire, the Massachusetts Bay & Province of Mayne, Rhode Island, & Providence Plantations, the Narraganset Countrey, or Kings province, and Connecticut in New England & New York & New Jersey in America, or within any of them do or shall presume to cut, fell or destroy any white pine trees, not growing within any Township or the bounds, lines, or limits thereof in any of the said Colonies or plantations without His Majesties Royal Lycense. . . . And whereas their late Majestys King William & Queen Mary for the better providing & furnishing Masts for the Royal Navy. . . . did reserve to themselves their heirs & successors all Trees of the Diameter of twenty four inches & upwards at twelve inches from the ground growing upon any soil or Tract of Land within the said Province or Territory, not then before granted to any private Person: In order therefore to make the said Reservation more effectual, Be it further Enacted by the Authority aforesaid That no Person or Persons whatsoever within the said Province of the Massachusetts Bay or New England do or shall presume to cut or destroy any white pine trees of

From Jonathan Belcher, "A Proclamation to Prevent the Destruction or Spoil of His Majesties Woods," in State of New Hampshire, *Miscellaneous Provincial and State Papers, 1725–1890,* compiled and ed. Isaac W. Hammond. Manchester, N.H.: John B. Clark, 1890, vol. 18, pp. 32–35.

the Diameter of twenty four inches, or upwards at twelve inches from the ground, not growing within some soil or Tract of Land within the said Province granted to some private person or Persons before the seventh day of October which was in the year 1690 without His Majesties Lycense first had and obtained. . . ."

Dated this thirtieth day of October 1730. . . . GOD SAVE THE KING—

ψ *E S S A Y S*

The essays feature environmental histories written from three different viewpoints. In the first selection, Jim O'Brien, an American historian who has written on the history of the New Left and contributed to the journal *Radical America,* offers a history of North America from the vantage point of the beaver. In considering how the fur trade affected the beaver, O'Brien turns history upside down, suggesting that capitalism transforms everything from fur hats to the enjoyment of nature into commodities. Samuel F. Manning, in the second essay, focuses on the environment from the perspective of the colonists. Manning explores the importance of natural resources to the colonists' livelihood and examines the beginnings of forest legislation in America, as enacted in the British Broad Arrow policy reserving pine trees of specified dimensions for government use rather than entrepreneurial profit. The third essay, by environmental historian Mark Stoll of Texas Technological University, examines the religious motives behind Puritan perceptions of nature as antecedents to both the use of nature for human benefit and the preservation of nature for the contemplation of God's glory in the world. As such, the essays introduce perspectives on nature from both human and nonhuman points of view, stances that characterize the field of environmental history.

A Beaver's Perspective on North American History

JIM O'BRIEN

Robert Benchley was talked out of a diplomatic career after he turned in a college thesis on a certain fishing treaty, written from the point of view of the fish. At the risk of some comparable punishment, it may be interesting to describe the sweep of events on our continent from the vantage point of what beavers have done and what has happened to them. As I hope will be clear, such an exercise when applied to this particular animal gives us a way, not only to gnaw at the limits of our species-centrism, but to comprehend our own history in North America as well.

There are two reasons for thus calling the beavers front and center from the vast ranks of our fellow mammals. One is that they manipulate the physical landscape more than any other animal besides the human. In the course of blocking streams and accumulating a food supply they cut down certain trees, drown others at their roots, raise the water table, check soil erosion and flooding, create a new home for a host of aquatic animals, and (over time, as the pond fills in with silt and organic material) leave rich meadow lands. There is a sense in which it would be fully legitimate to

Excerpts from Jim O'Brien, "The History of North America from the Standpoint of the Beaver," *Free Spirits: Annals of the Insurgent Imagination,* 1982, pp. 45–54. Reprinted by permission of the author.

say that North America was "empty" until the first beavers waddled along and began applying their industry to it.

The second reason for singling out the beaver has nothing whatever to do with the first. By the simple accident of their fur—which has tiny barbs that facilitate a type of hat manufacturing practiced in Europe, and which in the late winter has a rich, smooth texture—the beaver became an irresistible magnet that guided European penetration of the North American interior for nearly three centuries. The "fur trade," it was called. Other animals such as marten, otter, muskrat, bear, wolverine, mink, you name it, were sought, but above all other lures was the beaver. It is Canada's national symbol to this day. In the onrush of the "fur trade," not only was the beaver threatened with extinction but the Indians (who supplied the animals in exchange for the products of European technology) had their traditional cultures severely jarred and their own numbers drastically reduced. Elsewhere, Spaniards sought gold and silver and slaves, but the more advanced capitalist cultures of northern Europe made an even greater impact on the New World by simply setting a high price for the skin of a dead animal. . . .

The beaver has been significant for other species, including our own, and the following outline history will indicate how.

1. *Beginnings.* Unlike humans, who came here fully evolved over the "Siberian land bridge," beavers were here for millions of years, experimenting with different sizes and shapes. The prehistoric giant beaver (*Castoroides ohioensis*) cut a striking figure in the northern lakes, reaching eight feet in length and weighing as much as a black bear. It coexisted with the earliest humans in North America, then became extinct along with other Ice Age behemoths as the climate warmed. Less spectacular but more of a survivor was the dam-building *Castor canadensis,* a close cousin to the European *Castor fiber.* The differences between these two species, which are apparently due to the geographical isolation of North America from the Eurasian land mass after the last Ice Age, are too subtle for the average predator to notice. For the historian, the only difference is that *Castor canadensis* was far more numerous.

. . . [Beavers] live on vegetation, and above all on the bark and young shoots of trees. (That's why they never made it to South America, you see: the dry treeless deserts of northern Mexico stood in their way.) Armed with four big incisors, which stay sharp because they keep growing through a lifetime and wear out faster on one side of the tooth than the other, they collect their delicacies by cutting down the whole tree. And the less edible parts of the tree, along with rocks, mud, old boots, and whatever else is available, go into making dams and lodges. These are necessary because the beaver on land is slow, conspicuous, and a potential meal for the nearest hungry wolf, bear, wolverine, bobcat, or coyote. (Only a potential meal, let us add. Beavers have sharp teeth and hind claws and are built compactly. There are even instances where they've dragged the would-be diner to the water and administered a quick drowning.) It is in the water that the beaver becomes fast and elusive, vulnerable only to the relatively scarce river otter. Hence the dam, which uses a small stream to create a pond. Even the winter freeze can be finessed: with the water level raised, the beaver colony can build a lodge big enough to house an underwater food supply plus above-water compartments with a thick roof; the builders need never leave the lodge except to swim under the ice, and thus they are fully protected from land predators during the winter months.

In a continent filled with trees for millions of square miles, the beaver had free rein. As a beaver colony expands and begins putting pressure on the surrounding food supply—beavers have to stay as close to the water as possible for protection—an instinct is triggered by which parents will expel their older offspring from the colony on pain of injury and even death. The outcasts may be able to set up another dam slightly downstream, or they may have to make the perilous overland trek for a suitable site. On the way, or after finding the stream, each will try to attract a beaver of the opposite sex and thereby found a new colony. Life expectancy is around twelve years, and an offspring may be exiled at age two, so it is easy to guess that a beaver during its lifetime may have descendants who live dozens of miles away. By the time the Europeans came, beavers had long since expanded throughout the area where the lay of the land made it possible.

2. *A human presence.* Of course the Europeans weren't the first people here, though you would never know it from reading the average history book. Anthropologists are now tossing around figures like nine million for the pre-Columbian population of the New World north of Mexico—an extraordinary figure which was not reattained by European immigrants for *more than three centuries.* While any species is important first of all to itself, the advent of humans was important to the beaver as well. Here was that wonder of wonders, horror of horrors, a land animal that could chase the beaver out of the water and kill it when it chose. The technique was crude—it typically involved breaking the ice with axes and setting dogs after the fleeing prey—but adequate. (It was to prevail for well over two centuries after the beginnings of the fur trade in the 1500s.) The human beings could kill the beaver at will.

Here we come to an interesting question of values. Let us make clear at the outset that the Indians did not threaten the beaver as a species. The great naturalist Ernest Thompson Seton estimated toward the end of his career that there were 60 million beaver in North America when the Europeans came. It is hard to imagine how there could have been more even in the absence of the Indians. Now the question is: How do we look on the relationship of two species, one of which hunts, traps, and tries to kill the other? Each individual encounter may be marked by violence and cruelty on the one side, helpless terror on the other. In a stable relationship, though, the predation is often an alternative to starvation and disease.

As Calvin Martin reminds us in *Keepers of the Game: Indian–Animal Relations and the Fur Trade* the primal world view includes a belief that people appropriated animals for their use only, and with, in some sense, the permission of the spirits of those animals. The killing of animals was part of an elaborate and complex culture, full of beliefs which worked to insure that particular kinds of animals would not be overkilled. Woodland Indians enjoyed a stable relationship with nature that an ecologist of today can only look at in envy.

3. *The Europeans.* In the Donald Duck comic book *Tralla La* (May–June 1954), Donald and the three nephews parachute into a remote valley whose inhabitants are blissfully unaware of the outside "civilized" world. By mistake one of the nephews lets a bottle cap fall to the ground; on finding it the natives suddenly go berserk and begin fighting each other for the privilege of offering their most valued possessions for more bottle caps. The whole society has been instantly disrupted. David Wagner ("An Interview with Donald Duck," *Radical America,* January–February, 1973) calls this a brilliant critique of Western imperialism.

In fact, the comic book is backwards history, as we can see from the experience of North America. In that historical instance it was the Europeans who went berserk. They came here first for gold and silver, then for fur for decorative hats, then for drugs (tobacco, sugar, and coffee). Was any of these an intrinsically useful product? The use-value of the products the Indians got in the "fur trade"—cloth, guns, steel axes, metal cooking utensils, the one exception being alcohol—was far higher than the use-value of what the Europeans came here for. At the point of contact it is the European mentality that needs explaining, not that of the Indians.

Of course the Europeans weren't really crazy. They just had a very different social system. As soon as the beaver pelts on the one hand, and the European trade goods on the other hand, are stripped of their practical uses and distilled into European currencies, we see that the disproportion is all the other way. One nineteenth-century student of the trade concluded that the profits had gone as high as 2,000 percent. In England and France—the Dutch were squeezed out fairly early—the buying and selling of beaver fur became an important source of what is disarmingly called an "economic surplus." We can define an economic surplus as a concentration of wealth within a society such that the people who control that wealth have the power to direct the labor of other people in the society—and thereby gain further wealth and further power. A society may have an abundance of everything it needs—for example, a hunting and gathering society in which people have to do only four or five hours a day of what we would call work, and are quite comfortable—but unless the wealth is unequally distributed there is no economic surplus because nobody has power to harness the labor of others for his own purposes. One important effect of the fur trade, as of the production of crops like sugar and tobacco, was to help make northern European society more unequal, and thus further the cause of economic development, alias "progress." . . .

But, to keep the beaver at the center of our concerns, the specific relationship that matters here is that the French, Dutch, and British quickly discovered that *Castor canadensis* had fur very much like that of its almost-extinct cousin *Castor fiber,* and that the Indians knew how to trap it if they were of a mind to do so. The Europeans offered trade goods. More to the point, they offered diseases. Such ills as smallpox, measles, whooping cough, and chicken pox, which had become childhood diseases in Eurasia over the course of centuries, were entirely new to the Americas. Everywhere they had a catastrophic effect. Indian medicine, even though it was at least as good as the European medicine of that age, had no cure; and Indian cultures had no explanation that was not acutely demoralizing. It was this awesome loss of cultural cohesion—not to say loss of life—that led many woodland Indians to abandon their traditional practices and collaborate in the European animal trade.

The results for the beaver were catastrophic. There was a wave of destruction fanning out from the St. Lawrence River, from the Dutch and English colonies on the Atlantic seaboard, later from Hudson's Bay, and still later from John Jacob Astor's fistful of the Oregon coast. In the final stages of expansion, in the Rockies, legendary white "mountain men" like Jim Bridger dispensed with the Indian trade altogether and wrought enormous destruction on their own. And after the trappers came the white settlers, appropriating for their own exclusive use a landscape that had once been home for both humans and an immense array of "wild" animals.

Even as European fashions changed, with less demand for beaver hats, the trapping of the diminished beaver population continued, especially in Canada. Between 1853 and 1877 the Hudson's Bay Company sold almost three million beaver skins on the London market. By 1891 the author of a book on the beaver could write that "progress is no respecter of persons or animals, so we must face the matter squarely and prepare to pay tribute to the loss of the great beaver host which will soon leave us forever." Of the beaver's ultimate extinction, "no possible question can exist."

4. *Back from the Brink.* As any resident of a wooded, hilly countryside today knows, the North American beaver did not disappear as a species. It is hard to sort out the historical causation here, but the fact is that around the turn of the century American states and Canadian provinces began to pass laws strictly controlling the killing of beaver. . . .

In effect, human governmental agencies assumed a managerial role in relation to the beaver. The traditional four-legged predators such as the wolverine ("the beaver eater," it was sometimes called), wolf, bear, bobcat, and fox had been reduced to negligible numbers. The partial check they had once exerted on the beaver's proliferation had been removed, but at the same time vast areas of woodland were destroyed to make way for farms, towns, and cities. Therefore, public agencies have stepped in, and the situations they deal with are complicated. The naturalists Lorus and Margery Milne tell the story of a beaver colony on a remote tributary of the Arkansas River in Colorado which built a series of dams between 1949 and 1955, then outstripped the food supply and migrated *en masse*. In 1957 the untended dams gave way to the spring thaw, and "a wall of muddy water rushed across roads and fields, engulfing human establishments without warning." Having broken into the pre-existing web of life, modern society has had to take control of this particular strand. And it is not easy.

Perhaps it is too bad that Robert Beverley [see Chapter 4] was wrong, that the beaver did not have a king or a superintendent who "walks in State by them all the while, and sees that every one bear his equal share of the burden; while he bites with his Teeth, and lashes with his Tail, those that lag behind, and do not lend all their strength." If they had, the names of these dignitaries might somehow have come down to us today, for our historical records. As it is, you have to be a scientist or a beaver even to tell the males from the females, let alone pick out individuals. All we know about the 4,000-foot-long beaver dam found near Berlin, New Hampshire—that's pretty close to a mile—is that "some beavers" built it. "Some beavers" also built the 750-foot canal that was found near Longs Peak, Colorado, in 1911; canals, often built with locks, are in some ways the beaver's most impressive feat, providing a way to bring distant vegetation to the pond without risking too long a sojourn on dry land. "Some beavers" built a giant lodge housing at least thirty-seven of their number, as described by a Hudson's Bay trader, and felled a tree measuring more than three feet in diameter and 100 feet high in British Columbia. If beavers were like modern human beings, we would not know who actually carried out these exploits but we would at least have a name to attach to them—the name of whoever commissioned the work.

There may be a sense in which the ubiquitous "Warning—I Brake for Animals" bumper stickers are the most encouraging mass phenomenon of recent years. In part they represent a simple concern for highway safety, a plea against tailgating, but they also express a revulsion against the power that modern society holds over the natural world (in this case the power to crush an animal between a heavy machine and a strip of concrete). They are a forceful reminder that, for all we have done to destroy parts of nature and undertake the "management" of what is left, we are after all a *part* of nature. We have, in some profound sense, more in common with the helpless skunk or chicken on the highway than we do with the inanimate object at whose wheel we sit. In an age that tells us otherwise, it is an important insight. . . .

With the elaboration of capitalist civilization, happiness becomes more and more a commodity to be purchased on the one side and profited from on the other. Even the enjoyment of nature becomes a commodity (witness the vital role of the railroads in lobbying for creation of the National Parks system in the early twentieth century). Work is rigidly separated from "leisure," and the latter is defined by "consumption." . . .

The same cultural logic that converted beavers into capital by abstracting the animal and attaching value only to the fur has a similarly limited use for ordinary human beings. In the face of capital accumulation, the fact that we are all human gives us no claim on the mercy of the accumulators. When, as a culture, we lost our kinship with the animals, we lost something profound that has not been replaced.

And this gets us back to the relationship between the beaver and history. It is the *commerce* in beaver that is endlessly documented in the records that are the acceptable grist for historians. The thousands of years in which beavers and humans lived side by side as elements of nature are virtually opaque to us. History, even when it focuses directly on an animal, can treat the animal only as a historical object, not as a subject.

So the world in which the beaver had a spirit is hidden from history. Unless history is augmented with enlightened anthropology, and poetry too, there is no way to understand that world—no way even to glimpse it. And this is not a trivial matter. What is at stake is not simply a way of looking at the past, but the urgent need to find our way out of the cultural logic of capitalism. Human potentiality is much more varied than anyone could realize who knew only the history of the modern age; and this is important for us to grasp. Fighting to understand the past is, after all, part of a bigger struggle to survive the future.

A Colonist's Perspective on the New England Forest

SAMUEL F. MANNING

Settlement, and the Beginnings of New England Trade

New England of 1620 was a wilderness territory offering little incentive for commercial settlement. The fish were already being taken by home vessels without need of any but temporary shore facilities. Furs, obtained by trade with Indians, were slipping into the hands of the Dutch at New Amsterdam as well as to the French by way of the Acadian settlements and the St. Lawrence. Standing timber was too bulky to cut

Excerpts from *New England Masts and the King's Broad Arrow,* by S. F. Manning (Kennebunk, Me.: Tilbury House Publishers, 2000), pp. 23–32, 45–49. Reprinted by permission of the author.

and assemble for shipment without extensive shore establishment, and timber was too expensive to ship transatlantic without preferential duties in the home market. English colonies to the south of New England had commercial advantage due to their gentler climates and longer growing seasons. Virginia and the Carolinas produced foodstuffs, tobacco, rice and indigo in exportable quantities. Further south, the island colonies of Barbados, Nevis, St. Kitts and (later) Jamaica would give up general cropping for a sure-sell specialty in sugar products. For the London merchants a New England venture meant shiploads of colonist supplies and Indian-trade goods risked against return cargoes of whatever raw products could be mustered by settlers taken to that region. Settlement was tried at the mouth of Maine's Kennebec River in 1607 by the Plymouth Company with colonists led by George Popham. Although some furs were returned by trade with the local Indians, winter hardship and the death of its leader doomed the Popham colony to failure. Foothold on Massachusetts Bay was gained thirteen years later by Pilgrim zealots underwritten (for settlement in Virginia) by an association of English merchants headed by Thomas Weston.

Between the Pilgrim arrival in 1620 and the arrival of Admiralty mast ships in 1652 lay three decades of land clearing, hardscrabble farming, and grubbing for return cargoes to pay for supplies sent from England. The 1620's saw returns of furs gained by Pilgrim shrewdness in trading with Indians at truck houses established at the head of navigation on the Kennebec and the Connecticut rivers, and closer to home at the headwaters of Buzzards Bay. Neither the Pilgrims of the 1620's nor the Puritans of the 1630's were versed in seamanship or fishing. A colonial fishing industry got going very slowly due to inexperience and lack of boats. Skilled shipwrights arriving with the flood of Puritan settlers in the 1630's built some shallops for fishing, notably at Salem, but were hampered by lack of capital, nails, cordage, and sailcloth. Lack of money to pay their accustomed wages turned many incoming tradesmen to clearing land for farms. There was some production of hand sawn boards, hand split barrel staves ("clapboards," in older parlance) etc. to send back with the returning immigrant ships, but most incoming trade of the 1630's was the exchange of immigrant possessions for land, cattle, and the materials for new homes. Shipbuilding, to 120 tons, had begun with a few vessels built at Medford, Salem, and on Richmond Island near Casco Bay in Maine. A water-powered sawmill had been established at Berwick, and a tide-powered sawmill at Agamenticus. Pine boards, hand split shingles, and clapboards were added to whatever outbound cargoes of dried codfish or farm produce could be accumulated in surplus. English demand for masts and naval stores was well known to the settlers. Although there was some attempt to grow hemp, flax, and to reduce wood to its naval oils, these products never really took hold as a New England product. There is no doubt that some of the mast cargoes returned to England during this period went back with the discharged immigrant ships. However, loading of masts aboard a regular carrier assumes that the tallest trees of the forest have been cut, moved, hewn and assembled for shipment in a hostile, unpopulated region much further east.

The stream of Puritan immigrants which provided New England settlers with trade goods for nearly a decade closed down in the late years of the 1630's. England was in revolution. Religious and civil reforms begun by the Long Parliament gave English Puritans incentive to stay at home. Economic depression was felt in New England as incoming ships continued to land needed goods without offering immigrant demand for homesteading essentials. However, Boston merchants probing the hemisphere for colonist markets had discovered that oak staves and heading for wet storage containers—pipes, hogsheads, casks, barrels—could be sold to wine producers in the Canary and the Azores islands. In fact there was considerable demand for American white oak which made excellent cooperage for the aging and transport of wine. Staves and heading sent to the wine islands returned wine cargoes to the English market where credits could be offset against goods delivered to New England. This first independent New England export was soon extended to the winemakers of Spain and Portugal who welcomed American dried codfish surplus along with the barrel shooks. Colonial fishing effort had increased and was seeking markets. Shipbuilding industry came to life at Boston and Charlestown, and the first vessels constructed were for carrying shaken casks and dried codfish to the wine islands. Docks everywhere were piled high with staves and heading which departed in large shipments along the wine route. Private speculation in masts and trunnels began with a shipment from Boston to England in 1645. Similar shipments were made during the three years following. In 1650 a new and broader market opened for New England merchants striving to get on their feet: staves and heading of porous red oak, for sugar and molasses casks. The island of Barbados had dropped all other crops and stripped the land of timber in favor of sugar production. Oak for cooperage was needed along with structural timber for rolling machinery, mill buildings, slave quarters, wharves, etc. Dried fish was in demand for feeding slaves and mill hands. The opportunity extended to other Caribbean islands which had also converted to sugar production. Returned sugar, molasses and rum cargoes were saleable just about anywhere. By 1652 New England lumbering, shipbuilding, fishing and overseas trading had made a solid start from primitive beginnings just 30 years before. One can only speculate that if the restrictions and incentives of the oncoming Broad Arrow Policy had been applied to New England when the 1630's Puritan immigration slumped, American appetite for competitive enterprise might have died at birth.

The Broad Arrow Policy

With arrival of mast ships dispatched by the Admiralty in 1652, annual shipment of New England masts to English dockyards began. The mast logging effort was well paid. It sought the best trees in the New England pine forest and required undamaged delivery of the whole tree trunk at specified coastal shipping locations. The work took tremendous skill in the felling and in the overland or water delivery of the logs. Hard money was paid for the labor by the London timber contractors. But gold paid for mast logs could not buy food where planting had been neglected, and many a new settlement of farmer/loggers was to experience winter starvation before the lesson was learned.

New England masts were free enterprise in 1652. The Admiralty's move to get mast logs out of the forest produced the labor force, the woods technology, and the holding facilities to make a business of masts along the growing routes of New England trade. Sawmills followed the loggers and took a growing share of the felled pines for conversion to now-merchantable boards, joists and other structural lumber. Since the Admiralty contracts called for supplying Navy dockyards at Antigua and Jamaica as well as England, an extended mast trade with the French colonies in the sugar islands as well as the needs of Spanish shipbuilders along the wine cask route were not ignored by New England merchants. A sound, dressed log for a great mast was frequently worth more than £100 throughout the whole period discussed. If reduced to wide boards, its delivered lumber was saleable for wooden construction at a figure more easily collected by the woodland entrepreneur. With British pressure for dependable delivery of New England pine masts, a wholesale colonial lumber industry began to flourish. By 1685 colonial merchandising of New England white pines had reached a point where the Admiralty felt that strong measures were needed to protect the remaining mast trees in the settled locations as well as further to the east where lumbering was bound to occur. Accordingly a Surveyor of Pines and Timber in Maine was appointed by the Crown to oversee the Admiralty's mast interests in New England. His commission called for a survey of the Maine woods within 10 miles of any navigable waterway as well as the blazing of all suitable mast pines with the King's mark. Appointment of a Surveyor was the first step in the formation of a colonial forest policy.

England had restored the monarchy under two successive Stuart kings. A war with Spain was concluded in 1660, a second war with the Dutch in 1667, and a third war with the Dutch in 1674. There was continuing need for ships' masts as well as a sudden demand for American lumber of any kind following the great London fire of 1666. As William and Mary ascended the throne in 1689, naval construction was stepped up to meet an oncoming struggle with the French. A new timber crisis developed in the dockyards as the growing hostility of Sweden threatened to close passage to the Baltic. To insure a continuing and dependable supply of masts and naval stores from the American colonies, Parliament moved to commandeer the American pines and to control their destruction by mast entrepreneurs, shingle splitters, and sawmill operators. It was basically a mercantilist move to shift timber emphasis from the Baltic where trade was one-sided, and to force the colonials to focus on export of raw materials rather than develop their own competing finished products. Laws designed to protect the American pines for exclusive use of the Royal Navy became collectively known as the Broad Arrow Policy. Its symbol, the so-called "broad arrow" (a 3-legged letter A without the horizontal bar), was the ancient mark emblazoned on all property of the Royal Navy including prisoners. The Broad Arrow would be cut into every American pine adjudged suitable for a King's mast by the Surveyor of Pines and Timber. Its shadow hung over all pines in most of the American colonies.

Enacted piecemeal between 1691 and 1729, the Broad Arrow Policy governed New England land rights and woodland activity until outbreak of the American Revolution broke its grip in 1775. Carried to Canada with American loyalists, the Broad Arrow Policy continued to supply masts from the Canadian woods until wooden spars were replaced by iron.

Mast Agents and Surveyors

English masts had always come from abroad. Mast timber had been purchased throughout the years from London contractors who retained agents in the Baltic ports where suitable sticks were assembled for export. When North America was turned to for a fresh supply of bigger wood, it was these same mast contractors who obtained license to cut American pines reserved for the King.

Mast agents for the London contractors took up residence in New England. Some of their names became linked with the future of the region: Samuel Waldo, mast agent at Boston; Mark Hunking Wentworth, mast agent at Portsmouth; Thomas Westbrook, to be succeeded by George Tate, mast agent at Falmouth (now Portland); and Edward Parry, at Georgetown (now Bath). Nothing prevented these mast agents from setting up as lumber merchants on their own accounts. Most of them became rich and powerful men in their respective colonies. The mast agents were, in a sense, New England managers of commercial enterprises based in London. They were not King's officers, but licensees of licensees permitted to harvest the Crown timber.

The King's man in New England was the Surveyor of Pines and Timber in Maine. He was given four deputies. Appointments to this post began in 1685. At first the surveys extended ten miles inland from any navigable waterway. Then as the trees disappeared and the need for them continued, the Surveyor and his deputies sought to range the whole of the pine belt from Nova Scotia westward to the St. Lawrence. . . .

The King's Surveyor was hardly popular with the New England colonists. The office was badly paid to begin with, and the area to be covered by this officer and his four deputies was tremendous. It was work enough just to find and mark the trees which tended to disappear when the incisors of the Broad Arrow had passed through. Swamp law governed the future of informers. The colonial courts increasingly sided with the violators as conditions slid toward the Revolution. . . .

Outbreak of the [American] Revolution ended the Broad Arrow Policy in New England. In April, 1775, news of Bunker Hill and Lexington stopped all shipments of masts to the King. Waiting mast cargoes were seized by the colonists at Portsmouth, Falmouth and Georgetown. The load of mast baulks seized by the colonists from the mast ship *Minerva* was reported to be rotting in Portland harbor fifty years later.

Mast logging as a marine trade did not end in New England with eclipse of the Broad Arrow Policy. Pine masts continued to be cut and shipped by Yankee traders to whomever would buy them at the highest price. France was a good customer for New England masts during the Revolution. England continued to import them, although on a commercial basis, after the war had ended. But the King had other trees in North America. Until about 1825, great pines marked with the broad arrow continued to move out of the valleys of the Saint John and the Mirmichi to the King's depot at Halifax.

Puritan Perspectives on the New England Environment

MARK STOLL

No other English colony—for that matter, no other place in the world—was quite like New England. It flourished and grew on some of the poorest soil in the Empire, dissenters ran the established church, and a ministry with little official power dominated lay life. Yet, in that little-regarded corner of the British Empire the inhabitants nursed a fervent and zealous Calvinism. When in the nineteenth century their

From Mark Stoll, *Protestantism, Capitalism, and Nature in America.* Albuquerque, NM: University of New Mexico Press, 1997, pp. 55–66, 69–76. Reprinted by permission of The University of New Mexico Press.

descendants rushed forth across the American continent, they brought with them a mentality molded and fired in a Puritan land. The power of that mentality soon propelled them disproportionately not only into the boardrooms of industry but also into the ranks of reform societies and of nature stewardship and preservation groups. Particularly after the Civil War, New Englanders dominated national economic, intellectual, and cultural life. By then, what the Calvinist and Puritan traditions had to say about nature mattered a great deal.

Europeans first contemplated the wild shores of America much like a painter gazes at a blank canvas. To them, America had no past, no history—it was a continent in future tense. With the colors available to them, how should they paint what they saw? Some filled their canvas with the wilderness of Sinai, where dangers and demons threatened Christian settlers. Others depicted a Canaan flowing with milk and honey, beckoning Europeans away from Egyptian slavery. Was America an Eden where fallen men struggled for redemption? Or were the colonists to follow God's plan and restore the howling wilderness to paradise? Upon this bare canvas poured the visions and dreams (and nightmares) of the European soul.

In the seventeenth century, the English often referred to their new settlements in America and elsewhere not as "colonies" but "plantations." They crossed the seas and "planted" new communities. The Puritans "planted" the Gospel in a heathen wilderness. The English also planted the beliefs, viewpoints, and intellectual traditions that would shape the landscape of the American mind. The first two centuries of English presence on the American continent was a seedtime of ideas and attitudes from European stock. Although European ideas adapted to their new environment, colonial American contributors to the arts and sciences depended upon the Old World for model, style, and conception. Self-conscious of their location on the fringes of Western civilization, educated Americans longed to participate in European learned life.

Of the varieties of attitudes toward nature planted with the first generations of Puritans, three stand out for their lasting influence. The educated elite blended Calvinism with more secular literary and philosophical trends to produce that sense of nature's purity and man's vileness. Most Puritans fixated more narrowly on the Bible, whose concepts and phrases they combined with the Calvinist ethic of work and activity to generate compelling rationales for the transformation of the wilderness into which they had ventured. Finally, many Puritans struggled to overcome their remoteness to keep abreast of European developments, particularly in natural science, to which they made their own contributions in the service of man and God. These three perspectives on nature clearly manifested themselves in the works of Anne Bradstreet, Edward Johnson, and Cotton Mather. . . .

In 1662 Michael Wigglesworth published "God's Controversy with New-England," in which he described America as "A waste and howling wilderness, / Where none inhabited / But hellish fiends, and brutish men / That Devils worshipped." That image of a howling wasteland full of demons and devil-worshippers forms the common portrayal of the attitude of early New England Puritans toward the natural world. Themes of hostility toward and exploitation of nature, grounded in Biblical types and imagery, did dominate such accounts as William Bradford's *Plymouth Plantation,* Edward Johnson's *Wonder-Working Providence of Sions Saviour, in New England,* and Cotton Mather's histories of New England. New Englanders' high literacy rates and intense Protestantism combined with their concentration on the Bible as the source of religious truth meant that the Bible above all else gave their colony meaning and purpose: a persecuted remnant of the righteous driven from Babylon to seek refuge in wilderness where Satan had heretofore ruled unchallenged.

However united in mission and motive, not all New Englanders saw their new land with the same eyes. Deeply impressed with the arguments of natural theology, many found more divinity than deviltry there. Then, too, the unusually large proportion of New Englanders who had received higher education and brought their libraries to this edge of European civilization brought a more cosmopolitan understanding of nature and its relation to God and humanity. These educated Puritans supplemented the biblical and theological conceptions of nature with a third, the nature of Renaissance poetry and philosophy, replete with ideas and conventions drawn from classical antiquity.

From this eclectic mix of sacred and secular learning, seventeenth-century Puritans constructed and bequeathed a powerful, enduring religious understanding of man and nature: paradise lost. Mixing Calvinism, natural theology, and pastoralism, this tradition conceived of mankind as fallen, justly damned except for the chosen few, and of nature as Arcadian, groaning under human sinfulness, yet springing directly from and thus telling of the power and glory of God. While, in England, John Milton produced the classic exemplar of the genre, in America, this cosmopolitan Puritan mixture of Biblicism, natural theology, and classical antiquity found its most eloquent expression in the poetry of Anne Bradstreet. Bradstreet's poetry consistently depicted nature as Edenic if impermanent, and man as fallen but elected for eternity. She best conveyed these themes in two major poems from the beginning and end of her life, the Quaternions and "Contemplations."

When the first Puritans arrived in Massachusetts Bay aboard the *Arbella* in 1630, a newly married woman of about seventeen years was with them. Even though Anne Bradstreet was a dedicated Puritan from a family of dedicated Puritans, she voyaged to the New World with reluctance. As she remembered it from old age, "I . . . came into this Covntry, where I fovnd a new world and new manners at wch my heart rose. But after I was convinced it was ye way of God, I submitted to it & joined to ye chh. at Boston." Soon she helped to found the new "plantacion" of Ipswich, on the sea thirty miles by Indian trails from Boston, where she lived for about a decade. Then again she helped plant a new settlement, this time at Andover, a beautiful inland location on the banks of the Merrimac River. There she raised her eight children and lived out her life, dying in 1672. . . .

. . . Bradstreet challenges the standard understanding of Puritan attitudes toward nature. Almost never did she dwell on nature's negative aspects. This wilderness poet neither hated nature nor feared it nor calculated its value. And certainly Anne Bradstreet was a wilderness poet. Three times she moved with her family to rough new settlements in the forest. Bradstreet unapologetically intermingled Biblical and classical, moral and pastoral, in effective statements of Puritan subjects.

Anne Bradstreet's attitudes were not unusual among Puritans. Prominent Puritans praised her in print during her life and after her death. Edward Taylor owned *The Tenth Muse,* Cotton Mather lauded her, and others attested to her continued popularity. Demand was great enough to produce a third edition of her poems in 1758. Bradstreet was the daughter of a Puritan governor, the wife of a Puritan magistrate, and the mother and mother-in-law of Puritan ministers. The books that inspired her came out of a Puritan's library. She wrote in Puritan New England, was published in

Puritan England, and was read by Puritans for decades. Her pastoral Puritanism was as legitimately Puritan as the familiar "howling wilderness." Bradstreet's poetry is evidence that already the New England elite in its wilderness Jerusalem was thinking in terms of the redemption of fallen man in his wilderness paradise. A future New England elite group, the Transcendentalists, would think along similar lines. . . .

A passionate interpretation of American wilderness and their place in it moved Massachusetts Puritans as a people to transform the natural landscape for the greater glory of God. This dream of a renewed world grew stronger with each new boat-load of godly immigrants, until by 1640 the vision of working in unison to build a literal new Jerusalem fired nearly every soul. This confident faith in the possibility of establishing a godly nation on American soil developed into one of the most enduring elements of the Puritan legacy: the final restoration of Eden and God's kingdom on earth.

Aboard the *Arbella* with Anne Bradstreet in 1630 was Edward Johnson, a 31-year-old joiner. Johnson's heart did not rise when he arrived in America, nor did he ever have to "submit" to the way of the New England churches. Johnson was a dedicated and enthusiastic captain in the Lord's army ready to begin His great work. Johnson went back to England to retrieve his wife and seven children and returned in 1636 to dedicate his energies to the colony. One of the founders of Woburn, he became captain of the militia, town clerk, and deputy to the General Court. . . .

Soon after, Johnson began his own account of God's purpose in New England and compiled the first history of the Puritan settlements, known by its running title, *Wonder-working Providence of Sions Saviour, in New England,* published in London in 1654. . . .

To Johnson, the location of the Puritan colony in the wilderness was rich in Scriptural meaning. Particularly in Book I, the words "wildernesse," "wast[e]," or "desart" appear on practically every page, with various import in different contexts. Wilderness to Johnson first of all provided a refuge for Christ's church from the Antichrist, a gathering and mustering place for his army of saints. Martial metaphor pervaded *Wonder-working Providence.* To be a proper refuge and gathering place, the wilderness must be conquered for Puritan use. The Puritans from the beginning took as part of their purpose to fulfill the command of Genesis to multiply, and replenish and subdue the wilderness, and took pains provisioning their ships, "filling them with the seede of man and beast to sow this yet untilled Wilderness withal. . . ."

Johnson's Puritans saw Biblical wilderness recreated in American wilderness. Puritans used a system called "typology" to recognize in current events an exact re-play of Old Testament episodes. The Hebrews' exodus from Egypt, forty years in the wilderness, and arrival in Canaan, the Promised Land flowing with milk and honey, prefigured the Puritan's progress. Every Biblical parallel they found strengthened their self-conception as the elect of God, his chosen people, and invested "the great straites this Wildernesse people were in" with divine significance. Both Israelite and Puritan fled persecution from unjust rulers, underwent testing and trial in the wilderness, and by the Providence of God arrived in the Promised Land. In the wilderness, both Hebrews and Puritans received the tutelage and correction of God, who would "awaken, rouze up, and quicken them with the rod of his power" if they strayed.

While wilderness formed a sacred setting, nature itself was God's medium for goodness or discipline. Every natural feature or event to Johnson was God's provision for his chosen or providential aid for planting Christ's churches in the wilderness. The beaver trade providentially prepared the country for their presence by attracting early colonists. God dealt with the problem of numerous hostile natives by sending a plague among them which "not onely made roome for his people to plant; but also tamed the hard and cruell hearts of these barbarous *Indians*. . . ." God changed the weather for his people, sending an unusual abundance of rain, which astonished "the Heathen.". . .

Johnson included economic activity as a sign that New Englanders were making a garden of the wilderness and noted that, far from the fears of the first settlers that New England would suffer from lack of a staple commodity, "every thing in the country proved a staple-commodity, wheat, rye, oats, peas, barley, beef, pork, fish, butter, cheese, timber, mast, tar, sope, plank-board frames of houses, clabbord, and pipestaves, iron and lead is like to be also." Colonists who formerly had to import all necessities from England now "have not only fed their Elder Sisters, Virginia, Barbadoes, and many of the Summer Islands that were prefer'd before her for fruitfulness, but also the Grandmother of us all, even the firtil isle of Great Britain" as well as Portugal and Spain. Johnson marveled "that this Wilderness should turn a mart for Merchants in so short a space.". . .

In broader perspective, Johnson's work exemplified the ability of Western Christians of all creeds to justify their global colonization efforts. Clearing land, introducing foreign plants and animals, expanding agriculture, developing trade, and conquering, converting, expelling, or exterminating aborigines—in sum, the wholesale transformation of entire ecosystems—all received blessing as God's work. Yet everywhere as well, the voice of Christian conscience—here in a whisper, there in a shout—limited or shaped European activities. Johnson, for instance, never weakened his demands for continued self-sacrifice and dedication to a higher cause, for stewardship of the earth, and for conversion of the Indians when possible. Christian ideology about nature arrived in the wilderness of the New World as a promise wrapped in a threat. . . .

As an intensely devout, prominent Puritan minister, both son and grandson of prominent Puritan ministers, Cotton Mather assumed the heavy responsibility of carrying the New England Puritan tradition into the eighteenth century. He lived in an era of great change in science, theology, politics, and society—the age of Boyle, Newton, Ray and Derham, and Locke, of the Cambridge Platonists, Deists, and German Pietists, and of the Glorious Revolution. Mather saw decline of ministerial authority and the rise of an increasingly prosperous, materialistic, and religiously liberal colonial upper class. Still, he carried on the old traditions well, and accommodated them to current intellectual trends. Puritans of Mather's day were eagerly accommodating nature in the Bible to the nature of science and philosophy. Extremely proud of both his doctorate in divinity from Calvinist Glasgow University and his election as a fellow of the Royal Society, Mather could write passages of millennialist fervor next to digests of the latest in natural philosophy (science) or natural theology.

Calvinist and Puritan religious intensity derived from the insistent principle that no aspect of life or experience lay outside the realm of religion. In this respect, Mather's universe was identical with Johnson's. However, in language and conception it evolved steadily in new directions. In his early career, Mather's concept of the

Puritans' place in the wilderness echoed the metaphors and world view of Johnson's generation. But by the turn of the century the old terms and concepts were fading from Mather's books, never repudiated but supplanted by the new outlook of an age of rationalism and science. . . .

However much it resembled the world of Edward Johnson or Anne Bradstreet, Mather's universe was different. True, the invisible world still infused the visible: he believed there were devils in the woods and saw angels in his study. Nevertheless, he could be skeptical and insist on proof of supernatural workings. During the Salem witch trials of 1692, he and his father recommended rejection of testimony against witches based solely on "spectral evidence," that is, testimony about spirits who appeared only to the victim. (Unfortunately, their recommendation went unheeded.) Like educated men in England, Mather suspected natural causes were at work in events previously understood to be of supernatural origin. . . .

Cotton Mather and most of his learned peers at home and in Britain welcomed the increasing intrusion of the natural into the realm of the supernatural with ever more confident assertions that science and revelation agreed. Yet, this represented a retreat from the pervasively, relentlessly spiritualized universe of New England's founders. The spell of the supernatural had been broken and the seductively rational and orderly Enlightenment was beginning to entrance the Western mind. Perhaps natural causes and not witchcraft caused cows to die or beer not to ferment. Perhaps microscopic "animalcules" and not God's judgment caused disease. . . . Reason and natural law seemed to fill so much of the universe that it was all churchmen could do to stuff providence into the interstices. While for a century and a half most Protestants like Mather continued to insist upon the harmony of the books of nature and revelation, the increasing number of discordant notes prompted an ever growing number in the eighteenth century to rely upon the book of nature alone.

❦ *F U R T H E R   R E A D I N G*

Bernard Bailyn, *The New England Merchants in the Seventeenth Century* (1955)
———, *The Ordeal of Thomas Hutchinson* (1974)
Paul Boyer and Stephen Nissenbaum, *Salem Possessed* (1974)
Richard L. Bushman, *From Puritan to Yankee* (1967)
Colin G. Calloway, *The Western Abenakis of Vermont, 1600–1800: War, Migration, and the Survival of an Indian People* (1994)
Charles F. Carroll, *The Timber Economy of Puritan New England* (1973)
Peter N. Carroll, *Puritanism and the Wilderness* (1969)
William Cronon, *Changes in the Land: Indians, Colonists, and the Ecology of New England* (1983)
Charles H. W. Foster, ed., *Stepping Back to Look Forward: A History of the Massachusetts Forest* (1998)
David R. Foster, *New England Forests Through Time: Insights from the Harvard Forest Dioramas* (2000)
William A. Haviland and Marjory W. Power, *The Original Vermonters: Native Inhabitants Past and Present* (1981)
Stephen Innes, *Labor in a New Land* (1983)
Lloyd C. Irland, *Wildlands and Woodlots: The Story of New England's Forests* (1982)
Richard W. Judd, Edwin A. Churchill, and Joel W. Eastman, eds., *Maine: The Pine Tree State from Prehistory to the Present* (1995)

Kenneth Lockridge, *A New England Town: The First Hundred Years* (1970)
Calvin Martin, "Fire and Forest Structure in the Aboriginal Eastern Forest," *Indian Historian* 6 (1973)
Robert McCullough, *The Landscape of Community: A History of Communal Forests in New England* (1995)
Carolyn Merchant, *Ecological Revolutions: Nature, Gender, and Science in New England* (1989)
Perry Miller, ed., *The American Puritans: Their Prose and Poetry* (1956)
———, *The New England Mind: The Seventeenth Century* (1939)
Edmund S. Morgan, *The Puritan Dilemma: The Story of John Winthrop* (1958)
Roderick Nash, *Wilderness and the American Mind,* 4th ed. (2001)
Sumner Chilton Powell, *Puritan Village* (1963)
Howard Russell, *Indian New England Before the Mayflower* (1980)
Neal Salisbury, "The Indians' Old World: Native Americans and the Coming of Europeans," *William and Mary Quarterly,* 3rd ser. (53) 3 (July 1996): 435–458
———, *Manitou and Providence: Indians, Europeans, and the Making of New England* (1982)
William Simmons, *Spirit of the New England Tribes* (1986)
Frank Speck, *Penobscot Man* (1940)
John Stilgoe, *Common Landscape of America, 1580–1845* (1982)
Henry David Thoreau, *The Maine Woods* (1877)
Laurel T. Ulrich, *Good Wives: Image and Reality in the Lives of Women in Northern New England, 1650–1750* (1982)
Alden T. Vaughan and Francis J. Bremer, eds., *Puritan New England* (1977)
Michael Williams, *Americans and Their Forests: A Historical Geography* (1989)
Harold F. Wilson, *The Hill Country of Northern New England: Its Social and Economic History, 1790–1830* (1936)
Richard G. Wood, *A History of Lumbering in Maine, 1820–1861* (1935)

CHAPTER
4

Tobacco and Rice in
the Colonial South

☙

If a particle of soil in Virginia could write its own environmental history, it might describe its journey from the Appalachian Mountains down rushing streams to the tidewater lowlands along the Chesapeake Bay or the Atlantic Coast. It would relate meeting and mixing with particles of sand and clay to form a rich, reddish mold as the spring river waters receded; its nourishing of oaks and pines, cypress and sweet-gums, blueberries and huckleberries; and its continual replenishment by squirrel and bird droppings, leaf litter, earthworms, and fungi. For thousands of years, the soil particle existed in this state of flux. Then one day, it was scorched by burning branches and planted with a crop of Indian corn and beans for a few short years, before suddenly being hoed up and planted with tobacco or mingled with tidal waters to nurture a rice crop. Soon, weakened and deprived of its nitrogen, phosphorus, and calcium, it momentarily supported wheat before succumbing—in utter exhaustion—to feeding the roots of sedge, sorrel, and pine seedlings. In this sour and acidic state, surrounded by gullies and hillocks overgrown with weeds, it lay recuperating until one day it was plowed, manured, and limed by an energetic farmer who finally returned its lost nutrients.

This chapter focuses on the use, depletion, and restoration of Chesapeake Bay soils under tobacco cultivation and the use of tidal wetlands to grow rice in the South Carolina lowlands. It examines the use of slaves and slave knowledge to enhance the lifestyles of wealthy southern planters and the perceptions of nature and African Americans in the colonial and revolutionary periods. (See Maps 1, 2, and 5 in the Appendix.)

☙ D O C U M E N T S

Our study of the environmental history of the colonial South begins with pictures and descriptions that reveal the cultural assumptions and lenses through which Europeans saw the New World. Artist John White did numerous sketches and paintings of plants, mammals, and Indian life as a member of a failed 1585–1586 effort to settle Roanoke Island off the coast of North Carolina and subsequently as leader of the 1587 Roanoke "Lost Colony." Realizing that the colony could not subsist on its own, he returned to England on an expedition for supplies; by the time he reached Roanoke again in 1590, it was

95

deserted. The colonists, including his daughter, her husband, and their newly born child Virginia Dare, had left word that they had gone to "Croatoan." White's Indian drawings were engraved by Theodore de Bry and published in 1590 as illustrations to Thomas Harriot's *Briefe and True Report of the New Found Land of Virginia.*

Document 2 relates the discovery by Jamestown settlers Raphe Hamor (1614) and John Rolfe (1616–1617) that tobacco could answer their need for a staple crop that could be traded with England for manufactured items. So successful was "the weed" in producing profits, however, that Sir Thomas Dale, who followed John Smith as governor of the colony, ruled that each colonist must also plant sufficient food to feed his family and servants. In Document 3, William Fitzhugh, a wealthy Chesapeake planter, describes his holdings in a 1686 letter to Dr. Ralph Smith of Bristol, England, for the purpose of arranging an exchange of some of his properties for rural or urban income-producing properties in England. In the early eighteenth century, the American South was considered such an agreeable place to live that planter Robert Beverley could, in Document 4, dating from 1705, describe the land as a garden affording such pleasures as to make the colonists grow lazy and sink, like the Indians, into a childlike harmony with nature.

Documents 5 and 6 focus on methods for growing rice in South Carolina and tobacco in Virginia under slavery. In Document 5, written in 1761, James Glen, governor of South Carolina, describes the environmental requirements for planting, harvesting, and grinding a profitable quantity of rice. In 1775 an anonymous traveler wrote about tobacco management and soil degradation in Virginia and Maryland in a work entitled *American Husbandry,* an excerpt from which appears in Document 6.

Documents 7 and 8 look at racial perceptions and assumptions. In 1787, Thomas Jefferson described American slavery, in Document 7, as the product of such deeply rooted prejudices that it would be impossible to assimilate black people wholly and equally into American culture. Although one of the more enlightened planters and states-men of his time, Jefferson was a slaveholder who believed that "nature" had created real differences that made blacks inferior to whites in reasoning power. Document 8 is drawn from the experiences of Olaudah Equiano, whose autobiography, published in 1791, helped to change white perceptions of blacks. Born in West Africa in 1745, Equiano was enslaved at the age of eleven in his native land. Subsequently brought on a slave ship to Barbados and then to Virginia, Equiano was sold to a planter. After being sold to a British naval officer and educated by a young white seaman, he was finally sold to a Philadelphia merchant, from whom he bought his freedom.

As a group the documents reveal the many levels of symbolic and political meanings used by humans to describe and depict "nature" as the physical world, to define the "natural" conditions necessary for human life, to assert the "nature" of human beings, and to construct a dualism between nature and culture.

1. John White Depicts Indian Planting and Fishing in North Carolina, 1590

The Town of Secota

Their towns that are not enclosed with poles are commonly fairer. Then such as are enclosed, as appeareth in this figure which lively expresseth the town of Secota. For the houses are scattered here and there, and they have gardens expressed by the

From Thomas Harriot, *A Brief and True Report of the New Found Land of Virginia* (1590). With engravings by Theodor de Bry after the drawings of John White. New York: Dover, 1972, pp. 55–56, 68–69.

John White's illustration of the Indian town of Secota, near Roanoke Colony (1585–1586)

Source: Rare Book Division, The New York Public Library, Astor, Lenox and Tilden Foundations.

letter E. wherein grows tobacco, which the inhabitants call Uppowoc. They have also groves wherein they take deer, and fields wherein they sow their corn. In their corn fields they build as it were a scaffolde where on they set a cottage like to a round chair, signified by F. wherein they place one to watch for there are such number of fowls, and beasts, that unless they keep the better watch, they would soon devour all their corn. For which cause the watchman maketh continual cries and noise. They sow their corn with a certain distance noted by H. otherwise one stalk would choke the growth of another and the corn would not come into its ripening G. For the leaves thereof are large, like unto the leaves of great reeds. They have also several broad plots C. where they meet with their neighbours, to celebrate their chief solemn feasts . . . and a place D. where after they have ended their feast they make merry together. Over against this place they have a round plot B. where they assemble themselves to make their solemn prayers. Not far from which place there is a large building A. wherein are the tombs of their kings and princes. . . . Likewise they have garden noted by the letter I. wherein they use to sow pumpkins. Also a place marked with K. wherein they make a fire at their solemn feasts, and hard without the town a river L. from whence they fetch their water. This people therefore void of all covetousness live cheerfully and at their hearts ease. But they solemnize their feasts in the night, and therefore they keep very great fires to avoid darkeness, and to testify their Joy.

The Manner of Making Their Boats

The manner of making their boats in Virginia is very wonderful. For whereas they want instrument of iron, or other like unto ours, yet they know how to make them as handsomely, to sail with where they like in their rivers, and to fish with all, as ours. First, they choose some long, and thick tree, according to the bigness of the boat which they would frame, and make a fire on the ground above the root thereof, kindling the same by little, and little with dry moss of trees, and chips of wood that the flame should not mount up too high, and burn too much of the length of the tree. When it is almost burned through, and ready to fall they make a new fire, which they suffer to burn until the tree falls of its own accord. Then burning of the top, and boughs of the tree in such wise that the body of the same may retain its just length, they raise it upon posts laid over crosswise upon forked posts, at such a reasonable height as they may handsomely work up to it. Then they take off the bark with certain shells; they reserve the innermost part of the length, for the nethermost part of the boat. On the other side they make a fire according to the length of the body of the tree, saving at both the ends. That which they think is sufficiently burned, they quench and scrape away with shells, and making a new fire they burn it again, and so they continue sometimes burning and sometimes scraping, until the boat have sufficient bottoms. This god induces this savage people with sufficient reason to make things necessary to serve their turns.

Their Manner of Fishing in Virginia

They have likewise a notable way to catch fish in their rivers, for whereas they lack both iron and steel, they fasten to their reeds or long rods, the hollow tail of a certain fish like to a sea crab instead of a point, wherewith by night or day they strike fish and take them up into their boats. They also know how to use the prickles and pricks of other fish. They also make wares [weirs], with setting up reeds or twigs in the water, which they so plant one within another, that they grow still narrower, and narrower. . . . There was never seen among us so cunning a way to take fish withal, whereof sundry sorts as they found in the rivers unlike unto ours, which are also of a very good taste. Doubtless it is a pleasant sight to see the people, sometimes wading, and going sometimes sailing in those rivers, which are shallow and not deep, free from all care of heaping up riches for their posterity, content with their state, and living friendly together of those things which god of his bounty hath given unto them, yet without giving him and thanks according to his desert [deserving]. So savage is this people, and deprived of the true knowledge of god. For they have none other than is mentioned before in this work.

John White's illustration of the Indian manner of making boats (1585–1586)

Source: William L. Clements Library, University of Michigan.

2. Virginia Settlers Discover
Tobacco, 1614–1617

Raphe Hamor Extols the Valuable
Commodity Tobacco, 1614

The valuable commodity tobacco, so much prized in England, which every man may plant and tend with a small part of his labor, will earn him both clothing and other necessities. . . . Though none has yet been shipped to England, let no man doubt that it is as good as West Indies Trinidado or Caracus. Having taken up the subject, I must not forget the gentleman, worthy of much commendation, who first took the trouble to try it in 1612, Mr. John Rolfe, partly from the love he has long had for it and partly to develop a profitable commodity to benefit the colonists. . . . My own experience and trial of its goodness persuades me that no country under the sun can or does produce more pleasant, sweet, and strong tobacco than I have tasted there from my own planting. However that was the first year we tried it, and we did not know much about how to cure it and pack it. But there are people there now who learned enough from last year's well observed experience that I have no doubt they will produce and ship this year such tobacco that even England will acknowledge its goodness.

John Rolfe on the Ease of Growing
Tobacco, 1616–1617

Tobacco . . . thrives so well that no doubt, after a bit more experiment and experience in curing it, it will compare with the best in the West Indies. . . . To prevent the people—who are generally inclined to covet profit, especially after they have tasted the sweet results of their labors—from spending too much of their time and labor planting tobacco, which they know can be sold easily in England, and so neglecting their cultivation of grain and not having enough to eat, it is provided by the foresight and care of Sir Thomas Dale that no tenant or other person who must support himself shall plant any tobacco unless he cultivates, plants, and maintains every year for himself and every man servant ten acres of land in grain. . . . Thus they will be supplied with more than enough for their families and can harvest enough tobacco to buy clothing and the other necessities needed by themselves and their households. For an easy-going laborer can maintain and tend two acres of grain and cure a good quantity of tobacco, that being still the principal commodity that the colony produces.

"Raphe Hamor Extols the Valuable Commodity Tobacco, 1614" from Raphe Hamor the younger, *A True Discourse of the Present Estate of Virginia.* London: John Beale for W. Welby, 1615, pp. 24–25, 34–35.
"John Rolfe on the Ease of Growing Tobacco, 1616–1617" from John Rolfe, *A True Relation of the State of Virginia.* New Haven: Yale University Press, 1951, pp. 35–37, 39–40.

3. A Chesapeake Planter Describes His Holdings, 1686

To Doctor Ralph Smith

April 22nd. 1686

Doctr. Ralph Smith

In order to the Exchange you promised to make for me, & I desired you to proceed therein, to say to Exchange an Estate of Inheritance in land there of two or three hundred pound a year, or in houses in any Town of three or four hundred pound a year, I shall be something particular in the relation of my concerns here, that is to go in return thereof. As first the Plantation where I now live contains a thousand Acres, at least 700 Acres of it being rich thicket, the remainder good hearty plantable land, without any waste either by Marshes or great Swamps the Commodiousness, conveniency, & pleasantness yourself well knows, upon it there is three Quarters well furnished, with all necessary houses, ground & fencing, together with a choice crew of Negros at each plantation, most of them this Country born, the remainder as likely as most in Virginia, there being twenty nine in all, with Stocks of cattle & hogs at each Quarter. Upon the same land is my own Dwelling house, furnished with all accommodations for a comfortable & gentle living, as a very good dwelling house, with 13 Rooms in it, four of the best of them hung, nine of them plentifully furnished with all things necessary & convenient, & all houses for use well furnished with brick Chimneys, four good Cellars, a Dairy, Dovecoat, Stable, Barn, Hen house Kitchen & all other conveniences, & all in a manner new, a large Orchard of about 2500 Apple trees most grafted, well fenced with a Locust fence, which is as durable as most brick walls, a Garden a hundred foot square, well pailed in, a Yard wherein is most of the foresaid necessary houses, pallizado'd in with locust Punchens, which is as good as if it were walled in, & more lasting than any of our bricks, together with a good Stock of Cattle hogs horses, Mares, sheep &c, & necessary servants belonging to it, for the supply and support thereof. About a mile & half distance a good water Grist mill, whose tole I find sufficient to find my own family with wheat & Indian corn for our necessitys & occasions. Up the River in this Country three tracts of land more, one of them contains 21996 Acres another 500 acres, & one other 1000 Acres, all good convenient & commodious Seats, & which in a few years will yield a considerable annual Income. A Stock of tobacco with the Crops & good debts lying out of about 250000 lb. besides sufficient of almost all sorts of goods, to supply the families & the Quarter's occasions for two if not three years. Thus I have given you some particulars, which I thus deduce, the yearly Crops of corn & tobacco together with the surplus of meat more than will serve the family's use, will amount annually to 60000 lb. Tobo. which at 10 shillings per Ct. [hundred weight] is 300£ annum, & the Negroes increase being all young, & a considerable parcel of breeders, will keep that Stock good forever. The stock of Tobo. managed with an inland trade, will yearly yield

Excerpts from *William Fitzhugh and His Chesapeake World, 1676–1701*, ed. Richard Beale Davis. Chapel Hill: University of North Carolina Press, 1963. Copyright © 1963 by The University of North Carolina Press. Used by permission.

60000 lb. tobacco without hazard or risk, which will be both clear without charge of housekeeping, or Disbursements for Servants' cloathing. The Orchard in a very few years will yield a large supply to plentiful housekeeping, or if better husbanded, yield at least 15000 lb. tobacco annual Income. What I have not particularly mentioned, your own knowledge in my affairs is able to supply, if any are so desirous to deal for the Estate without the stock of tobacco I shall be ready & willing, but I will make no fractions of that; either all or none at all shall go. I have so fully discoursed you in the affair, that I shall add no farther instructions, but leave it to your prudent & careful management, & would advise that if any Overtures of such a nature should happen, immediately give an account thereof to Mr. Nicholas Hayward Notary public near the Exchange London, both of the person treating, & the place situation, Quantity & quality of the Estate, who will take speedy & effectual care, to give me a full & ready account thereof, which I hope you will . . . [take] all opportunitie do to

Sir Your W. ff. [William Fitzhugh]

4. Robert Beverley Discourses on Indians and Nature in Virginia, 1705

"The Indians of Virginia Are Almost Wasted"

The Indians of Virginia are almost wasted, but such Towns, or People as retain their Names, and live in Bodies, are hereunder set down; All which together can't raise five hundred fighting men. They live poorly, and much in fear of the Neighbouring Indians. Each Town, by the Articles of Peace in 1677. pays 3 Indian Arrows for their Land, and 20 Beaver Skins for protection every year.

In Accomac are 8 Towns, viz.

Matomkin is much decreased of late by the Small Pox, that was carried thither.

Gingoteque. The few remains of this Town are joined with a Nation of the Maryland Indians.

Kiequotank, is reduced to very few Men.

Matchopungo, has a small number yet living.

Occahanock, has a small number yet living.

Pungoteque. Governed by a Queen, but a small Nation.

Oanancock, has but four or five Families.

Chiconessex, has very few, who just keep the name.

Nanduye. A Seat of the Empress. Not above 20 Families, but she hath all the Nations of this Shore under Tribute.

In Northampton. Gangascoe, which is almost as numerous as all the foregoing Nations put together.

From Robert Beverley, "The Indians of Virginia Are Almost Wasted" and "Have You Pleasure in a Garden?" In Robert Beverley, *The History and Present State of Virginia.* London: R. Parker, 1705, pp. 232–233, 296–299.

In Prince George. Wyanoke, is almost wasted, and now gone to live among other Indians.

In Charles City. Appamattox. These Live in Colonel Byrd's Pasture, not being above seven Families.

In Surry. Nottawayes, which are about a hundred Bow men, of late a thriving and increasing People.

By Nansamond. Meheering, has about thirty Bowmen, who keep at a stand.

Nansamond. About thirty Bow-men: They have increased much of late.

In King Williams County, 2. Pamunkie, has about forty Bow-men, who decrease.

Chickahomonie, which had about sixteen Bow-men, but lately increased.

In Essex. Rappahannock, is reduced to a few Families, and live scattered upon the English Seats.

In Richmond. Port-Tabago, has [a]bout five Bow-men, but Wasting.

In Northumberland. Wiccocomoco, has but three men living, which yet keep up their Kingdom, and retain their Fashion; they live by themselves, separate from all other Indians, and from the English.

. . . I have given a succinct account of the Indians; happy, I think, in their simple State of Nature, and in their enjoyment of Plenty, without the Curse of Labour. They have on several accounts reason to lament the arrival of the Europeans, by whose means they seem to have lost their Felicity, as well as their Innocence. The English have taken away great part of their Country, and consequently made every thing less plenty amongst them. They have introduced Drunkenness and Luxury amongst them, which have multiplied their Wants, and put them upon desiring a thousand things, they never dreamed of before. I have been the more concise in my account of this harmless people, because I have inserted several Figures, which I hope have both supplied the defect of Words, and rendered the Descriptions more clear. I shall in the next place proceed to treat of Virginia, as it is now improved, (I should rather say altered,) by the English; and of its present Constitution and Settlement.

"Have You Pleasure in a Garden?"

Of the Temperature of the Climate, and the Inconveniences Attending It

The Natural Temperature of the Inha[bit]ed part of the Country, is hot and moist: though this Moisture I take to be occasioned by the abundance of low Grounds, Marshes, Creeks, and Rivers, which are everywhere among their lower Settlements; but more backward in the Woods, where they are now Seating, and making new Plantations, they have abundance of high and dry Land, where there are only Crystal Streams of Water, which flow gently from their Springs, and divide themselves into innumerable Branches, to moisten and enrich the adjacent Lands.

The Country is in a very happy Situation, between the extremes of Heat and Cold, but inclining rather to the first. Certainly it must be a happy Climate, since it is very near of the same Latitude with the Land of Promise. Besides, As *Judaa* was full of Rivers, and Branches of Rivers; So is *Virginia:* As that was seated upon a great Bay and Sea, wherein were all the conveniences for Shipping and Trade; So is *Virginia.* Had that fertility of Soil? So has *Virginia,* equal to any Land in the known World. In fine, if any one impartially considers all the Advantages of this Country, as Nature made it; he must allow it to be as fine a Place, as any in the Universe; but I confess I am ashamed to say anything of its Improvements, because I must at the same time reproach my Countrymen with a Laziness that is unpardonable. If there be any excuse for them in this Matter, 'tis the exceeding plenty of good things, with which Nature has blest them; for where God Almighty is so Merciful as to work for People, they never work for themselves.

All the Countries in the World, seated in or near the Latitude of *Virginia,* are esteemed the Fruitfulest, and Pleasantest of all Climates. As for Example, *Canaan, Syria, Persia,* great part of *India, China* and *Japan,* the *Morea, Spain, Portugal,* and the coast of *Barbary,* none of which differ many Degrees of Latitude from *Virginia.* These are reckoned the Gardens of the World, while *Virginia* is unjustly neglected by its own Inhabitants, and abused by other People. . . .

. . . If People will be persuaded to be Temperate, and take due care of themselves, I believe it is as healthy a Country, as any under Heaven: but the extraordinary pleasantness of the Weather, and the goodness of the Fruit, lead People into many Temptations. The clearness and brightness of the Sky, add new vigour to their Spirits, and perfectly remove all Splenetic and sullen Thoughts. Here they enjoy all the benefits of a warm Sun, and by their shady Groves, are protected from its Inconvenience. Here all their Senses are entertained with an endless Succession of Native Pleasures. Their Eyes are ravished with the Beauties of naked Nature. Their Ears are Serenaded with the perpetual murmur of Brooks, and the thorow-base [continuo] which the Wind plays, when it wantons through the Trees; the merry Birds too, join their pleasing Notes to this rural Consort, especially the Mockbirds, who love Society so well, that whenever they see Mankind, they will perch upon a Twig very near them, and sing the sweetest wild Airs in the World: But what is most remarkable in these Melodious Animals, they will frequently fly at small distances before a Traveller, warbling out their Notes several Miles an end, and by their Music, make a Man forget the Fatigues of his Journey. Their Taste is regaled with the most delicious Fruits, which without Art, they have in great Variety and Perfection. And then their smell is refreshed with an eternal fragrance of Flowers and Sweets, with which Nature perfumes and adorns the Woods almost the whole year round.

Have you pleasure in a Garden? All things thrive in it, most surprisingly; you can't walk by a Bed of Flowers, but besides the entertainment of their Beauty, your Eyes will be saluted with the charming colours of the Humming Bird, which revels among the Flowers, and licks off the Dew and Honey from their tender Leaves, on which it only feeds. It's size is not half so large as an *English* Wren, and its colour is a glorious shining mixture of Scarlet, Green, and Gold. Colonel *Byrd,* in his Garden, which is the finest in that Country, has a Summer-House set round with the *Indian* Honeysuckle, which all the Summer is continually full of sweet Flowers, in which these Birds delight exceedingly. Upon these Flowers, I have seen ten or a dozen of these Beautiful Creatures together, which sported about me so familiarly, that with their little Wings they often fanned my Face.

5. A Governor Explains South Carolina Rice Production, 1761

The Country abounds every where with large Swamps, which, when cleared, opened, and sweetened by Culture, yield plentiful Crops of *Rice:* along the Banks of our Rivers and Creeks, there are also Swamps and Marshes, fit either for *Rice,* or, by the Hardness of their Bottoms, for Pasturage.

It would open too large a Field, to enter very minutely into the Nature of the Soil; and I think that this will sufficiently appear by the following Account of what the Labour of one *Negroe* employed on our best Lands will annually produce in *Rice, Corn,* and *Indigo.*

The best Land for Rice is a wet, deep, miry Soil; such as is generally to be found in *Cypress* Swamps; or a black greasy Mould with a Clay Foundation; but the very best Lands may be meliorated by laying them under Water at proper Seasons.

Good Crops are produced even the first Year, when the Surface of the Earth appears in some Degree covered with the Trunks and Branches of Trees: The proper Months for sowing *Rice* are *March, April,* and *May;* the Method is, to plant it in Trenches or Rows made with a Hoe, about Three Inches deep; the Land must be kept pretty clear from Weeds; and at the latter End of *August* or the Beginning of *September,* it will be fit to be reaped.

Rice is not the worse for being a little green when cut; they let it remain on the Stubble till dry, which will be in about Two or Three Days, if the Weather be favourable, and then they house or put it in large stacks.

Afterwards it is threshed with a Flail, and then winnowed, which was formerly a very tedious Operation, but it is now performed with great Ease, by a very simple Machine, a Wind-Fan, but lately used here, and a prodigious Improvement.

The next Part of the Process is grinding, which is done in small Mills made of Wood, of about Two Feet in Diameter: it is then winnowed again, and afterwards put into a Mortar made of Wood, sufficient to contain from half a Bushel to a Bushel, where it is beat with a Pestle of a Size suitable to the Mortar and to the Strength of the Person who is to pound it; this is done to free the Rice from a thick Skin, and is the most laborious Part of the Work.

It is then sifted from the Flour and Dust, made by the pounding; and afterwards, by a Wire-Sieve called a Market-Sieve, it is separated from the broken and small Rice, which fits it for the Barrels in which it is carried to Market.

They reckon Thirty *Slaves* a proper Number for a *Rice-Plantation,* and to be tended with one Overseer; these, in favourable Seasons and on good Land, will produce a surprizing Quantity of *Rice;* but that I may not be blamed by those, who being induced to come here upon such favourable Accounts, and may not reap so great a Harvest; and that I may not mislead any Person whatever, I chuse rather to mention the common Computation throughout the Province, *Comunibus Annis;* which is, that each good working Hand employed in a *Rice-Plantation* makes Four Barrels and a Half of Weight neat; besides a sufficient Quantity of Provisions

From James Glen, *A Description of South Carolina.* London: R. and J. Dodsley, 1761, pp. 6–8.

of all Kinds, for the *Slaves, Horses, Cattle,* and *Poultry* of the Planatation, for the ensuing Year.

Rice last Year bore a good Price, being at a Medium about Forty-five *Shillings* of our Currency *per* Hundred Weight; and all this Year it hath been Fifty-five *Shillings* and Three *Pounds;* though not many Years ago it was sold at such low Prices as Ten or Twelve *Shillings per* Hundred.

6. A Traveler Describes Tobacco Cultivation, 1775

This plant [tobacco] is cultivated in all parts of North America, from Quebec to Carolina, and even the West Indies; but, except in Maryland, Virginia, and North Carolina, they plant no more than for private use, making it an object of exportation only in these provinces, where it is of such immense consequence.

It was planted in large quantities by the Indians, when we first came to America, and its use from them brought into Europe; but what their method of culture was is now no longer known, as they plant none, but buy what they want of the English. Tobacco is raised from the seed, which is sown in spring upon a bed of rich mould; when about the height of four or five inches, the planter takes the opportunity of rainy weather to transplant them. The ground which is prepared to receive it, is, if it can be got, a rich black mould; fresh woodlands are best: sometimes it is so badly cleared from the stumps of trees, that they cannot give it any ploughings; but in old cultivated lands they plough it several times, and spread on it what manure they can raise. The negroes then hill it; that is, with hoes and shovels they form hillocks, which lie in the manner of Indian corn, only they are larger, and more carefully raked up: the hills are made in squares, from six to nine feet distance, according to the land; the richer it is the further they are put asunder, as the plants grow higher and spread proportionally. The plants in about a month are a foot high, when they prune and top them; operations, in which they seem to be very wild, and to execute them upon no rational principles; experiments are much wanting on these points, for the planters never go out of the beaten road, but do just as their fathers did, resembling therein the British farmers their brethren. They prune off all the bottom leaves, leaving only seven or eight on a stalk, thinking that such as they leave will be the larger, which is contrary to nature in every instance throughout all vegetation. In six weeks more the tobacco is at its full growth, being then from four and a half to seven feet high: during all this time, the negroes are employed twice a week in pruning off the suckers, clearing the hillocks from weeds, and attending to the worms, which are a great enemy to the plant; when the tobacco changes its colour, turning brown, it is ripe and they then cut it down, and lay it close in heaps in the field to sweat one night: the next day they are carried in bunches by the negroes to a building called the tobacco house, where every plant is hung up separate to dry, which takes a month or five weeks; this house excludes the rain, but is designed for the admission of as much air as possible. They are then laid close in heaps in the tobacco houses

From Anonymous, *American Husbandry.* 2 vols. London: J. Bew, 1775, vol. 1, pp. 222–233, 242, 246–248.

for a week or a fortnight to sweat again, after which it is sorted and packed up in hogsheads; all the operations after the plants are dried must be done in moist or wet weather, which prevents its crumbling to dust. . . .

One of the greatest advantages attending the culture of tobacco is the quick, easy, and certain method of sale. This was effected by the inspection law, which took place in Virginia in the year 1730, but not in Maryland till 1748. The planter, by virtue of this, may go to any place and sell his tobacco, without carrying a sample of it along with him, and the merchant may buy it, though lying a hundred miles, or at any distance from his store, and yet be morally sure both with respect to quantity and quality. For this purpose, upon all the rivers and bays of both provinces, at the distance of about twelve or fourteen miles from each other, are erected warehouses, to which all the tobacco in the country must be brought and there lodged, before the planters can offer it to sale; and inspectors are appointed to examine all the tobacco brought in, receive such as is good and merchantable, condemn and burn what appears damnified or insufficient. The greatest part of the tobacco is prized, or put up into hogsheads by the planters themselves, before it is carried to the warehouses. Each hogshead, by an act of assembly, must be 950 lb. neat [net] or upwards; some of them weigh 14 cwt. and even 18 cwt. and the heavier they are the merchants like them the better; because four hogsheads, whatsoever their weight be, are esteemed a tun, and pay the same freight. The inspectors give notes of receipt for the tobacco, and the merchants take them in payment for their goods, passing current indeed over the whole colonies; a most admirable invention, which operates so greatly that in Virginia they have no paper currency. . . .

Respecting the product of tobacco, they know very little of it themselves by the acre, as they never calculate in that manner, and not many tobacco grounds were ever measured: all their ideas run in the proportion per working hand. Some are hired labourers, but in general they are negroe slaves; and the product, from the best information I have gained, varies from an hogshead and a half to three and an half per head. The hogshead used to be of the value of 5£. but of late years it is 8£. per head, according to the goodness of the lands and other circumstances. But [as for] the planters, none of them depend on tobacco alone, and this is more and more the case since corn has yielded a high price, and since their grounds have begun to be worn out. They all raise corn and provisions enough to support the family and plantation, besides exporting considerable quantities; no wheat in the world exceeds in quality that of Virginia and Maryland. Lumber they also send largely to the West Indies. The whole culture of tobacco is over in the summer months; in the winter the negroes are employed in sawing and butting timber, threshing corn, clearing new land, and preparing for tobacco; so that it is plain, they make a product per head, besides that of tobacco.

Suppose each negroe makes two hogsheads of tobacco, or 16£. and 4£. in corn, provisions, and lumber, besides supporting the plantation, this is a moderate supposition; and if true, the planter's profit may be easily calculated: the negroe costs him 50£. his cloathing, tools, and sundries, 3£.; in this case, the expence of the slave is only the interest of his cost, 2£. 10s. and the total only makes 5£. 10s. a year. To this we must add the interest of the planter's capital, province taxes, &c. which will make some addition, perhaps thirty or forty shillings per head more, there will then remain 12£. 10s. a head profit to the planter. . . .

There is no plant in the world that requires richer land, or more manure than tobacco; it will grow on poorer fields, but not to yield crops that are sufficiently profitable to pay the expences of negroes, &c. The land they found to answer best is fresh woodlands, where many ages have formed a stratum of rich black mould. Such land will, after clearing, bear tobacco many years, without any change, prove more profitable to the planter than the power of dung can do on worse lands: this makes the tobacco planters more solicitous for new land than any other people in America, they wanting it much more. Many of them have very handsome houses, gardens, and improvements about them, which fixes them to one spot; but others, when they have exhausted their grounds, will sell them to new settlers for corn-fields, and move backwards with their negroes, cattle, and tools, to take up fresh land for tobacco; this is common, and will continue so as long as good land is to be had upon navigable rivers: this is the system of business which made some, so long ago as 1750, move over the Alleg[h]any mountains, and settle not far from the Ohio, where their tobacco was to be carried by land some distance, which is a heavy burthen on so bulky a commodity, but answered by the superior crops they gained. . . .

A very considerable tract of land is necessary for a tobacco plantation; first, that the planter may have a sure prospect of increasing his culture on fresh land; secondly, that the lumber may be a winter employment for his slaves and afford casks for his crops. Thirdly, that he may be able to keep vast stocks of cattle for raising provisions in plenty, by ranging in the woods; and where the lands are not fresh, the necessity is yet greater, as they must yield much manure for replenishing the worn-out fields. This want of land is such, that they reckon a planter should have 50 acres of land for every working hand; with less than this they will find themselves distressed for want of room.

But I must observe that great improvements might be made in the culture of this crop; the attention of the planters is to keep their negroes employed on the plants and the small space that the hillocks occupy, being very apt to neglect the intervals; the expence of hoeing them is considerable, and consequently they are apt to be remiss in this work. Here they ought to substitute the horse-hoeing management, which would cost much less, and be an hundred times more effectual.

The tobacco planters live more like country gentlemen of fortune than any other settlers in America; all of them are spread about the country, their labour being mostly by slaves, who are left to overseers; and the masters live in a state of emulation with one another in buildings (many of their houses would make no slight figure in the English counties), furniture, wines, dress, diversions, &c and this to such a degree, that it is rather amazing . . . and in a climate that seems to create rather than check pleasure. . . .

Before I quit these observations on this part of the husbandry of Virginia and Maryland, I should remark that to make a due profit on tobacco, a man should be able to begin with twenty slaves at least, because so many will pay for an overseer: none, or at least very few, can be kept without an overseer, and if fewer than twenty be the number, the expence of the overseer will be too high; for they are seldom to be gained under 25£. a year, and generally from 30 to 50£. But it does not follow from hence, that settlers are precluded from these colonies who cannot buy twenty negroes; every day's experience tells us the contrary of this; the only difference is, that they begin in small; and either have no slaves at all, or no more than what they will submit to take care of themselves; in this case, they may begin with only one or two, and make a profit proportioned to that of the greater number, without the expence of an overseer. . . . Settlers of all kinds fix in these colonies, with advantages as great, if not greater, than any others. The culture of corn and other provisions is as profitable here as any where else; and plantations are every day left by tobacco planters, who quit and sell them at low prices, in order to retire backwards for fresh land, to cultivate tobacco to advantage; besides which, the new country is to be had here, equally with any other province, and upon terms as advantageous.

It is no slight benefit to be able to mix tobacco planting with common husbandry; this is as easily done as can be wished, and is indeed the practice of the greatest planters. A man may be a farmer for corn and provisions, and yet employ a few hands on tobacco, according as his land or manure will allow him. This makes a small business very profitable, and at the same time easy to be attained, nor is any thing more common throughout both Maryland and Virginia.

7. Thomas Jefferson Discusses the "Nature" of Blacks and Worn-Out Soils, 1787

"Deep Rooted Prejudices"

It will probably be asked, Why not retain and incorporate the blacks into the state . . . ? Deep rooted prejudices entertained by the whites; ten thousand recollections, by the blacks, of the injuries they have sustained; new provocations; the real distinctions which nature has made; and many other circumstances, will divide us into parties, and produce convulsions which will probably never end but in the extermination of the one or the other race.—To these objections, which are political, may be added others, which are physical and moral. The first difference which strikes us is that of colour. Whether the black of the negro resides in the reticular membrane between the skin and scarf-skin [epidermis], or in the scarf-skin itself; whether it proceeds from the colour of the blood, the colour of the bile, or from that of some other secretion, the difference is fixed in nature, and is as real as if its seat and cause were better known to us. And is this difference of no importance? Is it not the foundation of a greater or less share of beauty in the two races? . . . Besides those of colour, figure, and hair, there are other physical distinctions proving a difference of race. They have less hair on the face and body. They secrete less by the kidnies, and more by the glands of the skin, which gives them a very strong and disagreeable odour. This greater degree of transpiration renders them more tolerant of heat, and less so of cold, than the whites. . . . They seem to require less sleep. A black, after hard labour through the day, will be induced by the slightest amusements to sit up till midnight, or later, though knowing he must be out with the first dawn of the morning. They are at least as brave, and more adventuresome. But this may perhaps proceed from a want of forethought, which prevents their seeing a danger till it be

From Thomas Jefferson. "Deep-Rooted Prejudices" and "Tobacco Culture Is Fast Declining." In Thomas Jefferson, *Notes on the State of Virginia*. London: J. Stockdale, 1787, query XIV, pp. 229–234, 237–240, query XX, pp. 278–279.

present. . . . In general, their existence appears to participate more of sensation than reflection. To this must be ascribed their disposition to sleep when abstracted from their diversions, and unemployed in labour. An animal whose body is at rest, and who does not reflect, must be disposed to sleep of course. Comparing them by their faculties of memory, reason, and imagination, it appears to me, that in memory they are equal to the whites; in reason much inferior, as I think one could scarcely be found capable of tracing and comprehending the investigations of Euclid; and that in imagination they are dull, tasteless, and anomalous. . . . Many millions of them have been brought to, and born in America. Most of them indeed have been confined to tillage, to their own homes, and their own society: yet many have been so situated, that they might have availed themselves of the conversation of their masters; many have been brought up to the handicraft arts, and from that circumstance have always been associated with the whites. Some have been liberally educated, and all have lived in countries where the arts and sciences are cultivated to a considerable degree, and have had before their eyes samples of the best works from abroad. The Indians, with no advantages of this kind, will often carve figures on their pipes not destitute of design and merit. They will crayon out an animal, a plant, or a country, so as to prove the existence of a germ in their minds which only wants cultivation. They astonish you with strokes of the most sublime oratory; such as prove their reason and sentiment strong, their imagination glowing and elevated. But never yet could I find that a black had uttered a thought above the level of plain narration; never see even an elementary trait of painting or sculpture. In music they are more generally gifted than the whites with accurate ears for tune and time, and they have been found capable of imagining a small catch. Whether they will be equal to the composition of a more extensive run of melody, or of complicated harmony, is yet to be proved. Misery is often the parent of the most affecting touches in poetry.— Among the blacks is misery enough, God knows, but no poetry. Love is the peculiar œstrum of the poet. Their love is ardent, but it kindles the senses only, not the imagination. Religion indeed has produced a Phyllis Whately [Wheatley, see Chapter 6]; but it could not produce a poet. The compositions published under her name are below the dignity of criticism. The heroes of the Dunciad are to her, as Hercules to the author of that poem. . . .

Notwithstanding these considerations which must weaken their respect for the laws of property, we find among them numerous instances of the most rigid integrity, and as many as among their better instructed masters, of benevolence, gratitude, and unshaken fidelity.—The opinion, that they are inferior in the faculties of reason and imagination, must be hazarded with great diffidence. . . . To our reproach it must be said, that though for a century and a half we have had under our eyes the races of black and of red men, they have never yet been viewed by us as subjects of natural history. I advance it therefore as a suspicion only, that the blacks, whether originally a distinct race, or made distinct by time and circumstances, are inferior to the whites in the endowments both of body and mind. . . . This unfortunate difference of colour, and perhaps of faculty, is a powerful obstacle to the emancipation of these people. . . . Among Romans emancipation required but one effort. The slave, when made free, might mix with, without staining the blood of his master. But with us a second is necessary, unknown to history. When freed, he is to be removed beyond the reach of mixture.

"Tobacco Culture Is Fast Declining"

Before the present war we exported . . . according to the best information I can get, nearly as follows:*

In the year 1758 we exported seventy thousand hogsheads of tobacco, which was the greatest quantity ever produced in this country in one year. But its culture was fast declining at the commencement of this war and that of wheat taking its place: and it must continue to decline on the return of peace. I suspect that the change in the temperature of our climate has become sensible to that plant, which, to be good, requires an extraordinary degree of heat. But it requires still more indispensably an uncommon fertility of soil: and the price which it commands at market will not enable the planter to produce this by manure. Was the supply still to depend on Virginia and Maryland alone, as its culture becomes more difficult, the price would rise, so as to enable the planter to surmount those difficulties and to live. But the western country on the Missisipi, and the midlands of Georgia, having fresh and fertile lands in abundance, and a hotter sun, will be able to undersell these two states, and will oblige them to abandon the raising tobacco altogether. And a happy obligation for them it will be. It is a culture productive of infinite wretchedness. Those employed in it are in a continued state of exertion beyond the powers of nature to support. Little food of any kind is raised by them; so that the men and animals on these farms are badly fed, and the earth is rapidly impoverished. The cultivation of wheat is the reverse in every circumstance. Besides cloathing the earth with herbage, and preserving its fertility, it feeds the labourers harvest, raises great numbers of animals for food and service, and diffuses plenty and happiness among the whole. We find it easier to make an hundred bushels of wheat than a thousand weight of tobacco, and they are worth more when made.

8. Olaudah Equiano Describes His Enslavement, 1790

The first object which saluted my eyes when I arrived on the coast [of Nigeria] was the sea, and a slave ship, which was then riding at anchor, and waiting for its cargo. These filled me with astonishment, which was soon converted into terror . . . when I was carried on board. I was immediately handled, and tossed up to see if I were sound, by some of the crew; and I was now persuaded that I had got into a world of bad spirits, and that they were going to kill me. Their complexions too differing so much from ours, their long hair, and the language they spoke (which was very different from any I had ever heard), united to confirm me in this belief.

---

*Jefferson included a table of exports from Virginia listed in order of dollar amounts of revenue as follows: Tobacco; Wheat; Indian corn; Shipping; Masts, planks, skantling, shingles, staves; Tar, pitch, turpentine; Peltry, viz. skins of deer, beavers, otters, muskrats, racoons, foxes; Pork, Flaxseed, hemp, cotton; Pit-coal, pig-iron; Peas; Beef; Sturgeon, whiteshad, herring; Brandy from peaches and apples, and whiskey; Horses.

From Olaudah Equiano. *The Interesting Narrative of the Life of Olaudah Equiano.* London: Printed for and sold by the author, 1790, pp. 46–50, 54–55, 58–64.

Indeed, such were the horrors of my views and fears at the moment, that, if ten thousand worlds had been my own, I would have freely parted with them all to have exchanged my condition with that of the meanest slave in my own country. When I looked round the ship too and saw a large furnace or copper boiling, and a multitude of black people of every description chained together, every one of their countenances expressing dejection and sorrow, I no longer doubted of my fate; and, quite overpowered with horror and anguish, I fell motionless on the deck and fainted.

When I recovered a little I found some black people about me, who I believed were some of those who [had] brought me on board, and had been receiving their pay; they talked to me in order to cheer me, but all in vain. I asked them if [I] were not to be eaten by those white men with horrible looks, red faces, and long hair. They told me I was not: and one of the crew brought me a small portion of spirituous liquor in a wine glass; but, being afraid of him, I would not take it out of his hand. One of the blacks therefore took it from him and gave it to me, and I took a little down my palate, which instead of reviving me, as they thought it would, threw me into the greatest consternation at the strange feeling it produced, having never tasted any such liquor before.

Soon after this, the blacks who brought me on board went off, and left me abandoned to despair. I now saw myself deprived of all chance of returning to my native country, or even the least glimpse of hope of gaining the shore, which I now considered as friendly; and I even wished for my former slavery in preference to my present situation, which was filled with horrors of every kind, still heightened by my ignorance of what I was to undergo.

I was not long suffered to indulge my grief; I was soon put down under the decks, and there I received such a salutation in my nostrils as I had never experienced in my life: so that, with the loathsomeness of the stench, and crying together, I became so sick and low that I was not able to eat, nor had I the least desire to taste anything.

I now wished for the last friend, death, to relieve me; but soon, to my grief, two of the white men offered me eatables; and, on my refusing to eat, one of them held me fast by the hands, and laid me across, I think, the windlass, and tied my feet, while the other flogged me severely.

I had never experienced anything of this kind before; and although not being used to the water, I naturally feared that element the first time I saw it, yet nevertheless, could I have got over the nettings, I would have jumped over the side, but I could not; and, besides, the crew used to watch us very closely who were not chained down to the decks, lest we should leap into the water: and I have seen some of these poor African prisoners most severely cut for attempting to do so, and hourly whipped for not eating. This indeed was often the case with myself.

In a little time after, amongst the poor chained men, I found some of my own nation, which in a small degree gave ease to my mind. I inquired of these what was to be done with us? they gave me to understand we were to be carried to these white people's country to work for them. I then was a little revived, and thought, if it were no worse than working, my situation was not so desperate.

But still I feared I should be put to death, the white people looked and acted, as I thought, in so savage a manner; for I had never seen among any people such instances of brutal cruelty; and this not only shewn towards us blacks, but also to some of the whites themselves. . . .

I asked how the vessel could go? they told me they could not tell; but that there were cloth put upon the masts by the help of the ropes I saw, and then the vessel went on; and the white men had some spell or magic they put in the water when they liked in order to stop the vessel. I was exceedingly amazed at this account, and really thought they were spirits. I therefore wished much to be from amongst them, for I expected they would sacrifice me: but my wishes were vain; for we were so quartered that it was impossible for any of us to make our escape. . . .

During our passage I first saw flying fishes, which surprised me very much: they used frequently to fly across the ship, and many of them fell on the deck. I also now first saw the use of the quadrant; I had often with astonishment seen the mariners make observations with it, and I could not think what it meant. They at last took notice of my surprise: and one of them, willing to increase it, as well as to gratify my curiosity, made me one day look through it. The clouds appeared to me to be land, which disappeared as they passed along. This heightened my wonder; and I was now more persuaded than ever that I was in another world, and that every thing about me was magic.

At last we came in sight of the island of Barbadoes, at which the whites on board gave a great shout, and made many signs of joy to us. We did not know what to think of this; but as the vessel drew nearer we plainly saw the harbour, and other ships of different kinds and sizes; and we soon anchored amongst them off Bridge-Town.

Many merchants and planters now came on board, though it was in the evening. They put us in separate parcels, and examined us attentively.—They also made us jump, and pointed to the land, signifying we were to go there. We thought by this we should be eaten by these ugly men, as they appeared to us; and, when soon after we were all put down under the deck again, there was much dread and trembling. . . .

I stayed in this island for a few days; I believe it could not be above a fortnight; when I and some few more slaves, that were not saleable amongst the rest, from very much fretting, were shipped off in a sloop for North America. On the passage we were better treated than when we were coming from Africa, and we had plenty of rice and fat pork. We were landed up a river a good way from the sea, about Virginia county, where we saw few or none of our native Africans, and not one soul who could talk to me. I was a few weeks weeding grass and gathering stones in a plantation; and at last all my companions were distributed different ways, and only myself was left. I was now exceedingly miserable, and thought myself worse off than any of the rest of my companions; for they could talk to each other, but I had no person to speak to that I could understand. . . .

I had been some time in this miserable, forlorn, and much dejected state, without having any one to talk to, which made my life a burden, when the kind and unknown hand of the Creator . . . now began to appear, to my comfort; for one day the captain of a merchant ship called the Industrious Bee, came on some business to my master's house. This gentleman, whose name was Michael Henry Pascal, was a lieutenant in the royal navy, but now commanded this trading ship, which was somewhere in the confines of the county many miles off. While he was at my master's house it happened that he saw me, and liked me so well that he made a purchase of me. . . . I was carried on board a fine large ship, loaded with tobacco, &c. and just ready to sail for England. . . . A few days after I was on board we sailed for England. . . . There was on board the ship a young lad who had never been at sea before, about four or five years older than myself; his name was Richard Baker. He was a native of America, had received an excellent education, and was of a most amiable temper. Soon after I went on board he shewed me a great deal of partiality and attention, and in return I grew extremely fond of him. . . . [He was] an agreeable companion, and a faithful friend; who, at the age of fifteen, discovered a mind superior to prejudice; and who was not ashamed to notice, to associate with, and to be the friend and instructor of, one who was ignorant, a stranger, of a different complection, and a slave!

❡ E S S A Y S

The essays look at the environmental history of tobacco and rice cultivation in the colonial South. In the first essay, historian Avery O. Craven, formerly of the University of Chicago, describes the environmental conditions that make tobacco cultivation successful and graphically depicts the environmental degradation that follows. Analyzing soil exhaustion in the Tobacco South as the product of both a profit-oriented labor-intensive system of agriculture and a nutrient-devouring crop, he outlines the beginnings of an agricultural-improvement movement aimed at reversing soil degradation. The second essay, by geographer Judith Carney of the University of California at Los Angeles, analyzes the role of African Americans' skill at and deep knowledge of rice cultivation in creating a successful rice economy in the tidelands of South Carolina. The third essay, by historian William Loren Katz, shows how blacks and Native Americans, two oppressed groups, interacted and intermingled to resist degradation as human beings and to make a living from the natural environment. Whether the rise of the colonial South was caused by the slave system of production; the mindset of the planter class; the environmental conditions presented by soils, water, and climate; or some interaction among these factors is the central question posed by this chapter in environmental history.

Tobacco and Soils in the Chesapeake

AVERY O. CRAVEN

The agricultural life of Virginia and Maryland, from earliest colonial days well down to the eve of the Civil War, was carried on under conditions which gave wide play to the destructive forces of [soil] depletion. Physical surroundings were unusually favorable to the direct forces of "exhaustion"; their economic life was begun under frontier conditions; . . . and a whole life was erected upon an exploitive agriculture, that had to be greatly changed before the economic effort which supported it could be altered. "Soil exhaustion" and tobacco cultivation went hand in hand.

The Colonial Period, 1606–1783

Agriculture is fundamentally conditioned by geographic and climatic conditions. Soils, topography, rainfall, etc., not only influence crops but methods as well. . . .

Text by Avery Odelle Craven, Ph.D., *Soil Exhaustion as a Factor in the Agricultural History of Virginia and Maryland, 1606–1860*. Gloucester, MA: Peter Smith, 1965 (1926), pp. 24, 25–35, 82–94, 97, 98, 163. Reprinted by permission of Peter Smith, Publishers, Inc.: Gloucester, MA.

Virginia and Maryland are part of a geographic unit that may be roughly divided into three distinct physical sections:—the Coastal Plain, the Piedmont Plateau, and the Appalachian mountainous region.

The Coastal Plain stretches from the water's edge back to the head of navigation where the older crystalline rocks of the Piedmont break sharply to form a fall line in the rivers, and the flat plains give way to the rolling uplands. It seldom rises over a hundred feet above the sea level and is cut everywhere with bays and inlets, and intersected by broad parallel rivers. The soils have been transported largely from the regions above the fall line and vary greatly in their composition and texture, ranging from pure sand to a sandy loam with occasional areas of silt and clay. . . . Here and there throughout the plain, beds of fossil remains . . . are to be found in the shape of the so called "marl beds," giving a generous supply of calcium carbonate, while near the coast stretches of swamp lands invite drainage and offer large quantities of rich mucks.

The Piedmont Plateau reaches from the fall line on the east to the uncertain border of the Appalachian Mountains on the west. Not more than 30 to 60 miles in width in Maryland, it spreads out across Virginia to a width of some 175 miles at the point where it crosses the North Carolina border. It is a region of variable topography and presents a broad plain-like surface with rolling uplands everywhere cut by narrow river valleys. . . .

The soils of the region are residual, . . . on the whole supplying an abundance of plant food materials. The rocks of the region as a rule are high in potash-bearing minerals and a large amount of iron oxide gives a characteristic reddish hue to the soils in many parts. The fertility is of good average, lower than that of the coastal valleys, but well suited under proper cultivation to the requirements of general farming.

The Appalachian region consists of a line of parallel mountain ridges rising in height to the westward and interspersed with great valleys that open far up into Pennsylvania. In Virginia the region might be further divided into the Blue Ridge, the Great Valley, and the Alleghany Mountains proper, with no sharp division on the east where the Piedmont ridges rise gradually into foothills.

The soils of the Blue Ridge and the Maryland region just north of it, are clay-loams and sandy-loams and closely resemble those of the Piedmont into which they blend. The Valley soils are of all types and a great belt of limestone cuts through it, giving to the loam and clay-loam soils an abundant addition of calcium carbonate debris. It forms a region of high fertility and one well adapted to general farming and grazing. . . .

Originally the larger part of both states was heavily forested and had to be cleared before cultivation could take place—a task so slow and difficult that much of the region was always in timber. Trees grew rapidly and when cultivated lands were abandoned, the forest returned again in a period of a few years. Travelers passing through what appeared to be virgin forest were often surprised to discover the scars of former cultivation and to learn that they were crossing what some twenty years earlier was a tobacco field. Such conditions added much to the problem of labor but afforded some compensation in the form of protection to neglected soils against washing and in the addition of organic materials in the form of falling leaves.

Both Virginia and Maryland are subject to heavy rainfall. The annual precipitation, varying somewhat in different parts, ranges from forty to seventy inches, a third of which comes in concentrated showers during the summer months when cultivation is in progress. This concentrated character of the summer rainfall . . . gives a heavy run-off from the lands. . . .

It is thus apparent that a goodly part of the problem of exhaustion in this region is produced by erosion. . . . Varying in its intensity with the type of agriculture, it nevertheless presented a vital problem in every period and under every system employed. . . .

As frontier regions, the problem of the American Colonies was to find some product for exchange with the old world that would enable them to secure those necessities which a primitive region did not offer. . . . A supply of fish, furs, or timber gave some temporary relief, but the development of a permanent and satisfactory exchange, in the end, depended upon the soil.

Virginia and Maryland early solved this problem with the abundant yields of tobacco which their "lusty soyle" gave forth and by the eagerness with which a ready market absorbed the increasing crops. Within a short period of time a type of life, based on this exchange, was possible that rivaled that of the English gentry and the plantation hospitality and style of living found in the region, filled the less fortunate with envy and the traveller with wonder. "It was merry England transported across the Atlantic, and more merry, light, and joyous than England had ever thought of being." Colonial life came to rest almost completely upon tobacco, and in spite of all efforts at restricting and diversifying production, tobacco became the one object of endeavor. And the very conditions which made it the dominant crop, determined that its production should be at the expense of the soil. The story of colonial tobacco production, therefore, became one of uninterrupted soil depletion.

To begin with, tobacco by its great advantages in exchange excluded all other major crops from the fields and forced an exhausting single-crop type of agriculture upon the soils. Tobacco alone seemed capable of lifting the colonists quickly from the severe conditions of frontier life into the comforts of former days. The European demand for this plant was rapidly increasing and the Spanish supply was far from keeping pace with the growing demands. Prices were so high that in the early days a man's labor in tobacco production yielded him six times as large a return as might be secured from any other crop.

But there were other advantages. The yield of tobacco per acre was high, its keeping qualities good, and its weight, when ready for shipping, comparatively low—advantages great indeed where every acre of land had to be painfully won from the virgin forest, and where markets lay far across a stormy sea. Tobacco alone could stand the long journey, pay the high costs of transportation, and still return a profit to its producer. Furthermore, labor, always scarce, could be concentrated upon a smaller acreage with greater returns from each laborer, and thus also afford a sufficient supply of hands in the winter to clear the new lands needed for future crops. Tobacco growing and land clearing went hand in hand, as we shall see, and so closely did the double task become united that in later years, when tobacco profits had failed, many refused to give it up because they would then have no winter work for their slaves.

Such a course meant soil depletion. The tobacco plant is a heavy consumer of both nitrogen and potash and the removal of the entire growth from the field, as was customary, caused a rapid decline in the available plant food materials at the same time that continued replanting in the soils encouraged toxicity, harmful soil fungi, root rots, and micro-organisms. A superior tobacco could be produced only on fresh land, and after the second crop—usually the best—the quality and quantity began to decline. The planter seldom counted on more than three or four crops from his land before it was abandoned to corn and wheat and then to the pine, sedge, and sorrell growths which usually characterize "sour lands." . . . A constant clearing of the forest was carried on and a constant abandonment of "old fields" followed at the other end. The encroachment upon the forest was so steady that one observer was led to remark that the colonists seemed "to have but one object"—"the plowing up of fresh lands." "He was the cleverest fellow who could show the largest new ground."

As tobacco employed all the labor force and monopolized the best lands, so it also excluded the production of a supply of animal manure by which fertility might have been restored and maintained. This was not a serious matter as long as an abundance of fresh land was available for all, but it produced destructive habits. . . . The building of barns and yards for stock, the laying down of meadows for pasture, and the securing of a supply of winter's food, were out of the question as long as tobacco ruled. . . .

Tobacco from the earliest period was cultivated with the hand and the hoe, the fields being kept clean and the surface soils loose by a continual but shallow stirring at the roots of the plant. Heavy wooden plows were introduced into the colonies around the year 1609, but they were not used in tobacco cultivation because of the constant use of new lands filled with stumps, roots, and other impediments incident to freshly cleared ground. In fact, the plow did not become a factor in the tobacco fields until late in the colonial period, when a check had come to expansion and "old lands" were again brought into use. And even here the cultivation was shallow and the use of the hoe still predominated. The lower reaches of the soil were not touched and turned up to the surface to give new supplies of food materials nor the depth given to the surface soils that would enable them to absorb the rainfall and prevent washing. The whole cultivation thus invited erosion. The clean surface and the constant stirring without piercing the hardpan formed just below, gave added force to the already natural conditions which tended in that direction.

The Post-Revolutionary Period, 1783–1820

The statements of both planters and travelers for the period from 1785 to 1820 bear witness of the continuance of exhausting cultivation, of wasted lands, abandoned fields, neglected stock, and shifting crops. . . . In 1791 George Washington at the request of Arthur Young the noted English agriculturist, made a survey of conditions in northern Virginia and Maryland. . . . His report indicates the widespread continuation of old methods. Summarized, it reveals (1) a steady cropping of lands in tobacco followed by Indian corn with ever lowering yields; (2) the general absence of meadows and stock with only here and there an exceptional farmer making use of manure to prolong the fertility of his lands; (3) and everywhere a tendency to abandon tobacco under the pressure of necessity in favor of wheat. It is of interest to notice that the average yield of wheat is given at little more than ten bushels to the acre, and that in many cases the returns were as low as seven bushels. . . .

The Duc de la Rochefoucauld-Laincourt crossed both Virginia and Maryland in 1795–96 and recorded rather minutely his observations on agricultural methods. Passing along the tidewater he found the farms too large for good cultivation, the cattle "poor and ill favored" and always in the woods; the fields generally planted in corn [and] never manured. . . . In western Maryland where tobacco was "reduced to almost nothing," . . . the ground was never plowed more than two or three inches deep and never manured. As he moved eastward again, conditions became poorer and the old practice existed of planting land in corn the first year, "then wheat for six or seven years without interruption, or as long as the soil will bear any," then fallow while another piece of ground was cleared and "also exhausted in its turn." . . .

Four years after Laincourt had visited Albemarle County, Virginia, a new settler described the country as a "scene of desolation that baffles description—farm after farm . . . worn out, washed and gullied, so that scarcely an acre could be found in a place fit for cultivation." The lands had been "butchered" by the growth of tobacco and even in 1799 there was not a good plough in the entire county. Conditions were so bad that the inhabitants had to make the choice between emigration at once or improvement without delay. . . .

In 1819 both sides of the Chesapeake in Maryland are described as "dreary and miserable in aspect"—"dreary and uncultivated wastes, a barren and exhausted soil, half clothed negroes, lean and hungry stock, a puny race of horses, a scarcity of provender, houses falling to decay, and fences wind shaken and dilapidating," are the terms used by the traveler. A few better farms and farmers were now and then to be found in the region but they stood out against a general background of ruin. . . .

When one turns to the counties in western Maryland, such as Washington, Frederick, and Montgomery, or to certain valleys in the northern portion of the state, he finds decided contrasts. There enough prosperity had come with the foreign demand for wheat and flour to enable leading farmers to begin improvement. . . .

The earliest agencies of the new agricultural life were the owners of great estates. Well back in colonial times a few exceptional planters had carried on experiments and attained some success. The great shift from tobacco to wheat had come about largely from such beginnings. But the great period of effort belongs to the Post-Revolutionary times and was the work of a group already well known in the public life of the new states. Their efforts consisted not only in changes of method and crops but also in the organization of Agricultural Societies and the production of an agricultural literature. Working individually but constantly exchanging ideas by letter or through the press, such men as Washington, Jefferson, Madison, John Taylor, J. M. Garnett, etc., formed what might well be called a school of gentleman farmers who had run counter to the general backward drift. . . .

Washington early established his reputation as a progressive agriculturist. In him the transformation of the planter into the farmer is well exemplified and his efforts at improvement include nearly all of the things attempted in this period. . . . [He] was among the first to understand the importance of good plowing as a means of preserving fertility. In 1769 he tested the value of plowing the earth into ridges as compared with harrowing it out flat as a method of checking the harmful effects of erosion, and during the remainder of his life never ceased his fight against this ever threatening danger. He filled his gullies with old rails, trash and straw, covered them with dirt and manure before planting them with crops. . . .

As early as 1760 at least, he was experimenting with marl as a fertilizer and in that year tested its comparative value with manure and different kinds of mud secured from the river beds on his plantation. He tried out Plaster of Paris (gypsum) and in 1785 sowed his grass seed with carefully measured quantities to ascertain the effects of different amounts upon the yield. The laying down of meadows and the increasing of his manure supply were fundamental in all his efforts at improvement. He planted grasses of different kinds—clover, lucerne, sainfoin, chicory, succory, etc.; he searched out and planted different kinds of cow peas and sowed buckwheat to be turned in as a green manure for the next crop of grain; he constructed sheds for his cattle so that he might "raise manure" and he sought in every way to return to his lands the offal of his barns and pens.

Along with his interest in manure went the effort to increase and improve his stock. "Indifferent" sheep and cattle were culled out from his flocks and better breeds introduced as larger numbers were added. . . .

The work of Washington suggests the threefold lines along which the new movement developed among the great owners: first, the use of better plows and methods in the preparation of the soil for the crops or in the prevention of soil erosion; second, an increased interest in the production of animal manure and the use of artificial fertilizers; and third, the introduction of grass crops for feeding and green dressings as a part of different systems of crop rotation. All were more or less part of a single system of soil improvement but did not always go together and can therefore best be treated separately. . . .

Deep plowing was an essential part of the famous agricultural system now developing in Loudoun County, Virginia, and Montgomery County, Maryland. "The improvement of this valuable machine," (the plow) writes Robert Russell from Loudoun County in 1818, "was the first step we took to improve our lands; we formerly adopted the absurd plan of shallow ploughing leaving the under stratum unbroken which should have been torn up and mixed with the surface; we have constructed our ploughs much larger and stronger, the mould boards are all of cast iron. We seldom break our land with less than three horses to a plough, which enables us to plough our ground deep. . . ."

The addition of animal and vegetable manures to the soil together with the use of artificial fertilizers constitute the second part of the improvement program. . . . It was the first step taken by Jefferson in the recovery of his lands which had been so widely cleared and impoverished during his absence abroad and in the cabinet; Madison considered it absolutely necessary for improvement; it was fundamental in John Taylor's system; Landon Carter, Fielding Lewis, Col. Bosley, Hill Carter, etc., made it a first object and so on down the list from the highest to the lowest who faced the future with a determination to improve their wasted lands.

The value of the liquids from the stable was early realized and drains from each stall were constructed by some farmers so that not a particle would be lost. . . . A few learned the necessity of protecting the manure pile from the rain and weather and more than one man proclaimed the doctrine "that the size of the manure pile is the measure of success in agriculture."

Marl, which was to become so important in the next period through the work of Edmund Ruffin, was tried in various parts of the two states in this period. . . . The early trials are of interest largely because of the later importance of this fertilizer rather than because of any immediate consequences.

The credit for the introduction of Plaster of Paris or gypsum seems to belong to John Alexander Binns of Loudoun County, Virginia, though something can be said for the claims of his neighbor Israel Janney. Binns combined with deep plowing the use of gypsum. . . . The results were marked especially on wheat and he continued his experiments in the following years with other plants. He found gypsum to greatly benefit grass plots and by its use on clover he raised a worn and exhausted farm, on which his neighbors thought he must starve, to a high degree of fertility. So marked were the effects on white clover that many thought he had collected all the manure in the countryside and applied it to the field.

It is hardly necessary to list the different grasses tested by the various improvers. Jefferson, like Washington, tried out lucerne, chicory, succory, sainfoin, and various kinds of clover, and what these leaders did, other men in different parts of the states were doing also. But clover was generally the grass finally selected in all regions where it would grow and clover became the legume in most rotations.

Nor can a list of the different rotations be given. They differed with almost every individual—and most individuals shifted from time to time—and ranged from the simplest three and four field shifts to the more elaborate systems that required from eight to nine years to complete their course.

The system advocated by John Beale Bordley was based upon the Norfolk system of England. It included three crops of clover, and one each of wheat, potatoes, maize, peas, and barley. He advocated a heavy use of manure, rich earth, marl, and ashes and contended that his system would restore exhausted fields to a new degree of fertility. "Grass," wrote Bordley, "is the great basis of Farming products; it gives dung; dung gives vigor to the earth that gives all things." . . .

If capitalistic agriculture wrought greatest ruin it showed an equal capacity for the work of improvement. It was upon the larger plantations, where capital and a careful division of labor could be practiced, that the most rapid recovery took place and the greatest advances were made.

The destructive practices of the Old South were, in fact, in the beginning merely the normal product of frontier conditions. The dependence upon a single crop produced by whatever methods gave largest immediate returns regardless of the waste entailed; the thrusting of the burdens of abnormal production upon land because it was more plentiful than either capital or labor; the placing of an exaggerated value upon the crop which first furnished the surplus by which exchange with the outside world was established—all these were typical frontier practices which have characterized all frontiers.

Rice and Slaves in the Low Country

JUDITH CARNEY

This examination of Carolina rice history and African agency in its diffusion across the Atlantic uses a geographical perspective focused on culture, technology, and environment to support the contention that the origin of rice cultivation in South Carolina is indeed African, and that slaves from West Africa's rice region tutored

From Judith Carney, "Out of Africa: Rice Culture and African Continuities," in *Black Rice: The African Origins of Rice Cultivation in the Americas* (Cambridge, MA: Harvard University Press, Copyright © 2001 by Judith A. Carney), pp. 81–85. Reprinted by permission of the publisher.

planters in growing the crop. In this approach the historical record is reconstructed to elucidate the environments planted to rice in the colonial period. This involves shifting research attention from rice as an export crop grown by slave labor to rice culture, the underlying knowledge system that informed both the cultivation and the milling of rice. Thinking about rice as a knowledge system reveals dynamics of agrarian diffusion, innovation, and the origins of specific agricultural practices that promote historical recovery. This perspective especially underscores the significance of wetland cultivation and how knowledge of growing rice by submersion provided slaves leverage to negotiate and alter some of the terms of their bondage.

The literature on the Columbian Exchange shows how seeds may diffuse independently of the people who domesticated them. Varieties of Asian rice transferred to the Americas long in advance of Asians. But the adoption and establishment of these varieties required the presence of human beings already familiar with rice culture, the knowledge to grow the crop in wetland environments and the means to mill the rice once it had been harvested. The only people in South Carolina possessing this familiarity were Carolina slaves who originated in the rice region of West Africa. To find the origins of rice cultivation one must thus look to Africans, who were among the earliest settlers in the Americas, for adapting the crop to challenging New World conditions.

The crucial period for examining these issues is the first century or so of settlement in South Carolina, from 1670 to the American Revolution, when coastal lowlands were transformed from woodlands and marsh into plantation landscapes based on the cultivation of irrigated rice. The period can be divided into two, with the Stono slave uprising in 1739 providing the demarcation. In the decades preceding Stono, rice emerged as the colony's principal export crop with its cultivation increasingly focused on productive inland swamps. The growing of rice on floodplains was at an incipient stage. In the period immediately following the Stono rebellion, slave imports into the colony declined. When they resumed in the 1750s the cultivation of rice was already shifting to floodplain irrigated systems.

In the initial decades of the Carolina rice economy, the work demand of shaping plantations from the wilderness placed the labor relations between black and white, slave and planter, in flux, because survival and success required mutual interdependence. Blacks' escape to establish maroon settlements in the interior or flight to Indian communities was a real possibility, as were alliances against white rule. As we shall see below, by 1712 conventions between slave and master were already in place over the permissible norms regulating work in the rice economy. Slavery during this early frontier period involved a negotiated relationship.

By the decade of the 1730s, the relationship between black and white had profoundly altered. The Amerindian population had sharply declined due to warfare with colonists, slaving expeditions against them, and the introduction of diseases against which they had no immunity. Their conquest was accompanied by an extension of white land ownership along the coastal lowlands of South Carolina. Slaves of African origin were in demand, and imports grew dramatically from 1720. In the decade preceding the 1739 Stono rebellion, over twenty thousand slaves were imported from Africa, a more than twofold increase over the twelve thousand present in the colony in 1720. The work of clearing swamps for rice cultivation was arduous and accompanied by great loss of life.

White repression increased with the constant flow of new slaves into the colony and labor demands to clear swamps for cultivation, but the pattern of the slave trade in the decade prior to Stono presented new possibilities. Seventy percent of these slaves originated in Angola and its interior, giving the colony's black population a rare degree of cultural and linguistic homogeneity among New World plantation societies. The result was their attempt to throw off the yoke of bondage, known as the Stono rebellion. While the revolt was unsuccessful, fear of what had been attempted resulted in a near ten-year moratorium on further slave imports into the colony. When imports resumed in mid-century, the frontier had vanished and rice cultivation was spreading to Georgia, closing avenues for escape from slavery. The institution of bondage had deepened, diminishing the space for negotiation between slave and master. The first century of black settlement in South Carolina and Georgia, the period that historian Ira Berlin terms the slaves' charter generations, remains crucial for understanding the linkage of rice cultivation to West African slaves.

White and black settlement of South Carolina occurred at the same historical moment. About a hundred slaves accompanied the first settlers arriving in South Carolina from Barbados in 1670; within two years they formed one-fourth of the colony's population, and by 1708 blacks outnumbered whites. From that period on South Carolina became a colony with a black majority. Documentation of rice cultivation appears early in the colonial period. With food supplies limited before 1700, slaves raised their own subsistence crops. A pattern similar to the Cape Verde Islands and South America probably resulted in rice's being grown as a preferential food among blacks in the earliest settlement period. No official document mentions the cultivation of rice before 1690, even though English officials from an early date considered the cereal a potential export crop for South Carolina.

But several facts point to the likelihood that rice was grown from the beginning of the colony's settlement. In 1674 several English indentured servants who ran away to Spanish St. Augustine, Florida, claimed to Spanish officials that "some rice . . . grown on the soil was shipped to Barbados." In 1690 one plantation manager, John Stewart, claimed to have successfully planted rice in twenty-two different locations. His occupation and nationality make it quite unlikely that he, a Scot, literally planted a crop that was not even grown in the country of his birth. His slaves were the ones growing rice. Already present in the colony and among Stewart's slaves were those skilled in rice cultivation who were pioneering its establishment in diverse environments under both rain-fed and wetland conditions. These fragmentary references indicate that the planting of rice in South Carolina was under way by 1690.

But to develop as an export crop, rice would have to be milled before shipment to overseas markets. The consumption of rice depends upon removing the indigestible hull and bran without damaging the grain it encloses. This was not so easily accomplished at the end of the seventeenth century with available forms of European milling. Unlike the cereals known to Europeans, which involve using a millstone to make flour, the objective of rice milling is to keep the grain whole as the husks are removed. Until the advent of machinery around the time of the American Revolution to do this, the only method employed for milling rice was the mortar and pestle used by African women. A report from 1700 suggests the transfer of this knowledge had already taken place by the late 1600s. Edward Randolph, who visited the colony twice in 1697 and 1698, implied the African method of processing rice with a mortar and pestle was being used in South Carolina in his report to the Board of Trade, writing, "They have now found out the true way of raising and husking Rice."

In 1690 John Stewart's correspondence mentioned the demand for Carolina rice in Jamaica, but the first record of its export is in 1695, with the shipment of one and one-fourth barrels to that island. The shift of rice from a subsistence to an export crop over the decades from the 1690s to 1720s was indicative of the cereal's increasing economic importance in the colony. Exports reached 330 tons in 1699, and by the 1720s rice emerged as the colony's leading item of trade. Years later, in 1748, Governor James Glen would underscore the significance of experimentation with rice during the 1690s for the development of the Carolina rice economy.

Although experimentation with growing rice in diverse microenvironments would have revealed the higher yield potential of wetland forms of cultivation, the initial emphasis was on the rain-fed production system. As rice became established as a viable export crop in the early eighteenth century, its cultivation shifted to the higher-yielding inland swamps and from the 1750s, to the even more productive but labor-demanding tidal floodplain system that would dominate Carolina and Georgia rice plantations until the Civil War. The historical record of the crop's development in South Carolina shows a changing economic emphasis on three main production systems over the first century of the colony's rice history, from rain-fed to inland swamp and then to tidal cultivation. While rice was planted in numerous locales during the period when the crop was becoming the leading export, these distinctive forms of production were evident at crucial historical junctures in the evolution of rice as a commodity.

Black Indians in the South

WILLIAM LOREN KATZ

The first Africans introduced into Jamestown's economy in 1619 became indentured servants, not slaves. Upon their release, they became part of the Virginia colony. Some became landowners, and one, Anthony Johnson, ruled an African community of twelve homesteads and two hundred acres in Virginia's Northampton County.

In the 1630s the rules of indenture began to change. It became legal to hold Africans or Indians for more than the usual seven years, even for life. The change began on the English-ruled island of Barbados when the governor announced "that Negroes and Indians . . . should serve for life, unless a contract was made to the contrary." And beginning in 1636, only whites received contracts of indenture.

British America had taken a large step in dividing labor by race and reserving the worst for dark people. More and more white laborers were pouring into the thirteen British colonies, and masters did not want them making common cause with Africans or Native Americans. Masters had probably concluded their profitable labor system would work only as long as whites did not see their condition and fate as identical with nonwhites. . . .

Excerpts from William Loren Katz, *Black Indians: A Hidden Heritage.* New York: Atheneum, 1986, pp. 102–109, 49–52. Reprinted with the permission of Atheneum Books for Young Readers, an imprint of Simon & Schuster Children's Publishing Division. Copyright © Ethrac Publications, Inc.

The first full-scale battle between Native Americans and British colonists took place in Jamestown, Virginia, in 1622. Africans fared a lot better than their owners. According to historian James H. Johnstone "the Indians murdered every white but saved the Negroes." This, noted Johnstone, became a common pattern during wars between colonists and Indians.

British colonial law not only lumped Native American and African people together, but handed both worse punishments than whites. A Virginia law set twenty-five lashes for whites who stole pigs, but increased this to thirty-nine lashes if the accused were a red or black person. Virginia soon declared "Negro, Mulatto and Indian slaves . . . to be real estate."

Beginning slowly in 1670, rules of bondage began to change to permit Native Americans to leave. Virginia began matters that year by stating that Indians were enslaved for only twelve years, Africans for life.

This decision was based on a peculiar legal point that Africans were "imported into this colony by shipping" and Indians came "by land." No mention was made of the fact that Indians did not come by land, but had lived there before English settlers arrived, or that most Africans had been living in Virginia for much longer than most British citizens.

Before Indians were eased out of the slave system, they had lived and married with African slaves, and produced in their offspring a new class of Americans held in chains. When the slave codes talked of "Indian slaves," it probably meant those Black Indians. For example, although New York's Assembly banned Indian bondage in 1679, in 1682 it forbad "Negro or Indian Slaves" from leaving their masters' homes or plantations without permission. The next year the Assembly denied "Negro or Indian Slaves" from meeting anywhere together in groups of four or more or being armed "with guns, Swords, Clubs, Staves or Any Other kind of weapon."

Between 1619 and 1700 labor in North America had become divided by skin color. Liberty itself would remain divisible by skin color through the American Revolution and up to the Civil War and emancipation. . . .

. . . [S]lave labor built the earliest European communities in the south. From 1690 to 1720, Africans cleared land, introduced African rice culture, navigated river vessels, and delivered the mail in the Carolinas. Only the most trustworthy slaves were brought to the frontier, and most stood by their masters. But some fled to the woods and Indians at the first opportunity, giving their owners something more to worry about.

For British subjects the question of bringing slaves so close to the frontier and Native Americans stirred a lively debate. A South Carolina law of 1725 imposed a £200 fine on those who brought their slaves to the frontier. A British colonel urged enforcement "because the Slaves . . . talk good English as well as the Cherokee language and . . . too often tell falsities to the Indians which they are apt to believe." In 1751, another law warned "The carrying of Negroes among the Indians has all along been thought detrimental, as an intimacy ought to be avoided."

But sound racial policies on the frontier clashed with the desire to reap the profits produced by slave labor. Virginia surveyor George Washington, twenty-three, urged the use of "mulattoes and Negroes . . . as pioneers and hatchet men" in the wilderness. An early print shows a young Washington with a black and white surveying team.

British colonists tried to play one dark race against the other on the southern frontier. The Maryland Assembly in 1676 offered Indians rewards for recapturing slave runaways. In South Carolina, in 1708, 5,280 European settlers tried to watch over 2,900 African and 1,400 Indian slaves. Europeans sent slave "cattle hunters" to protect Charleston from Indian raids. In 1740 South Carolina offered Indians £100 for each slave runaway captured alive, £50 for "every scalp of a grown negro slave."

The conflict among the three races on the frontier had each side seeking allies wherever they could be found. During the Yemassee War of 1715, Natchez Indians murdered whites and seized their slaves. When the British ordered one thousand two hundred soldiers against the Natchez, they sent black troops along. And when Governor Charles Craven of South Carolina confronted the Natchez's army he found it also included armed black prisoners.

By 1729 the frontier racial cauldron was boiling over in South Carolina and Louisiana. Slaves rose in rebellion at Stono, South Carolina. Terrified whites turned to Catawbas Indians, noted for their slavehunting skills, to recapture or slay all rebels. . . .

At around this time British colonists in the southern colonies began introducing the practice of African slavery among neighboring Native Americans. They concentrated on the Five Civilized Nations—Cherokees, Chickasaws, Choctaws, Creeks, and Seminoles—as the largest body of Indians present on their borders. Their aim was to make their slave property more secure by making Indians partners in the system. Indians who accepted slavery would not take in runaways fleeing European masters.

Except for the Seminoles, the Five Civilized Nations began to accept the foreign idea of slavery. Even so, their idea of how it should work differed from British practices. Quaker slaveholder John Bartram, botanist to the king of England, visited some Indian owners in 1770. He found their slaves dressed better than the chief, married into the nation easily, and their children were "free, and considered in every respect equal" to other members. After a visit to the Creeks, Bartram wrote:

> I saw in every town in the Nation I visited captives, some extremely aged, who were free and in as good circumstances as their masters; and all slaves have their freedom when they marry, which is permitted and encouraged [and] they and their offspring are in every way upon an equality with their conquerers. . . .

Despite every European effort to keep one dark people from assisting the other, the two races began to blend on a vast scale. Black Indians were apparent everywhere if one bothered to look. Thomas Jefferson, for example, found among the Mattaponies of his Virginia, "more negro than Indian blood in them." Another eyewitness reported Virginia's Gingaskin reservation had become "largely African." Peter Kalm, whose famous diary described a visit to the British colonies in 1750, took note of many Africans living with Indians, with marriage and children the normal result. . . .

British authorities repeatedly tried to convince Native Americans to return the slave fugitives they harbored in their villages. But here they collided with an Indian adoption system that welcomed new members and offered them full protection. When whites argued about the right of private property in owning people and insisted Africans were inferior beings, the Indians usually shrugged "no."

In treaty after treaty southern colonists made native nations promise to return fugitive slaves. In 1721, the Five Civilized Nations solemnly promised a governor of Virginia to deliver slaves, but nothing happened. The British complained bitterly on behalf of their slave owners, the chiefs apologized, and the ex-slaves became a part of Native American life.

When angry slavehunters decided to take matters into their own hands, they met fierce opposition. In 1750 Captain Tobias Fitch sent off a posse of five to retrieve a slave living in the Creek Nation. A Creek chief stood between them and the black man, cut their rope and threw it in a fire. Then he warned them his villagers had as many guns as they did. The posse returned empty-handed but happy to be alive.

African members of Indian Nations often played a vital part in armed resistance to whites. In 1727 Africans and Indians besieged Virginia frontier settlements. During the French and Indian War a British officer, warning about the two races, said "Their mixing is to be prevented as much as possible."

Florida proved unique in U.S. history—a location where large communities of ex-slaves could live hidden from enemy eyes. Escaped slaves living as maroons became Florida's first settlers. Dense jungles, high grass, deadly reptiles, alligators, hordes of insects, and tropical diseases waited for all who entered.

These conditions also protected Africans from European invading forces. Historian Joseph Opala has written: "Politically, Florida was in the hands of its new inhabitants. That it was colored Spanish on the map was largely for the amusement of white men."

Generations before Thomas Jefferson sat down to write the Declaration of Independence, Florida's dark runaways wrote their own. It used no paper or ink and was constructed of spears, arrows, and captured muskets. But it issued a warning of "keep out!" and "leave us alone, or else die." It said "liberty or death." . . .

Around the time African settlers arrived in Florida, refugees from the Creek Nation also settled there. This group called themselves "Seminoles" or runaways, and their Muskogee culture accepted a variety of Indian ethnic groups—Yuchi, Hitchiti, and Alabama. For Seminole people used to admitting those who were different, it was easy to accept Africans.

Africans proved far more familiar with Florida's tropical terrain than Spaniards or Seminoles. They transplanted a rice cultivation method practiced in Senegambia and Sierra Leone. Used to a more moderate climate, Seminoles began to learn how to survive in Florida from these ex-slaves. "From the beginning of Seminole colonization in Florida," writes Opala, "the Indian may have depended upon African farmers for their survival."

The Seminole Nation offered their new friends some valuable gifts in return. Africans and other ethnic groups enjoyed an independent village status. Their only obligation was to pay a small agricultural tax to be used for the common defense. . . .

Black Seminoles tried to live a peaceful life in their towns and around their ceremonial plazas ruled by their own chiefs. While they were shaping a sturdy agricultural community, British officers to the north provided weapons and military advisors for desperadoes ready to raid Florida for slave fugitives. . . .

Black Seminoles played a vital part in the coalition against the slave power to the north. Their knowledge of farming in Florida was second to none. They also brought the kind of information slaves always have about their masters' ways of thinking. One observer described them as "stout and even gigantic . . . the finest looking people I have ever seen." They were almost immune to the malaria and small pox that devastated Indians and Europeans.

. . . Black Seminoles had well-built homes and raised fine crops of corn, sweet potatoes, vegetables, and cotton. They owned herds of livestock and had time for hunting and fishing. They were known for their excellent fighting skills, a major in the Georgia militia calling them the Seminoles' "best soldiers."

By the nineteenth century Black Seminoles had become key advisors and valuable interpreters for the nation. They were familiar with English, Spanish, and the Muskogee or Hitchiti Seminole languages. Not all African runaways from slavery lived among the Seminoles for some had formed their own maroon settlements. Against slaveholders, however, all united.

❦ *F U R T H E R   R E A D I N G*

Hugh H. Bennett, *The Soils and Agriculture of the Southern States* (1921)

Edward L. Bond, *Damned Souls in a Tobacco Colony: Religion in Seventeenth-Century Virginia* (2001)

T. H. Breen, *Tobacco Culture: The Mentality of the Great Tidewater Planters on the Eve of Revolution* (1985)

Jerome Brooks, *Tobacco: Its History Illustrated by the Books & Manuscripts in the Library of George Arents* (1999)

Judith Carney, *Black Rice: The African Origins of Rice Cultivation in the Americas* (2001)

Vincent Carretta, "Olaudah Equiano or Gustavus Vasa? New Light on an Eighteenth Century Question of Identity," *Slavery and Abolition* 20 (December 1999), 96–105

Paul G. E. Clemens, *The Atlantic Economy and Colonial Maryland's Eastern Shore: From Tobacco to Grain* (1980)

Albert E. Cowdrey, *This Land, This South: An Environmental History* (1983)

Avery O. Craven, *Soil Exhaustion as a Factor in the Agricultural History of Virginia and Maryland, 1606–1860* (1925)

Carville Earle, "The Myth of the Southern Soil Miner: Macrohistory, Agricultural Innovation, and Environmental Change," in *The Ends of the Earth,* ed. Donald Worster (1988)

Jack D. Forbes, *Black Africans and Native Americans: Color, Race, and Caste in the Evolution of Red-Black Peoples* (1988)

John Hope Franklin, *The Free Negro in North Carolina, 1790–1860* (1943)

Iain Gately, *Tobacco: A Cultural History of How an Exotic Plant Seduced Civilization* (2003)

Eugene D. Genovese, *The Political Economy of Slavery: Studies in the Economy and Society of the Old South* (1967)

Lewis C. Gray, *History of Agriculture in the Southern United States to 1860* (1958)

Charles Hudson, *The Southeastern Indians* (1976)

Luther P. Jackson, *Free Negro Labor and Property Holding in Virginia, 1830–1860* (1942)

Winthrop Jordan, *White Over Black: American Attitudes Toward the Negro, 1550–1812* (1968)

William Loren Katz, *Black Indians: A Hidden Heritage* (1986)

Frances Anne Kemble, *Journal of a Residence on a Georgian Plantation in 1838–1839* [1863] (1961)

Jeffrey R. Kerr-Ritchie, *Freedpeople in the Tobacco South: Virginia, 1860–1900* (1999)

Allan Kulikoff, *Tobacco and Slaves: The Development of Southern Cultures in the Chesapeake, 1680–1800* (1986)

Karen Kupperman, *Roanoke: The Abandoned Colony* (1984)

———, *Settling with the Indians: The Meeting of English and Indian Cultures in America, 1580–1640* (1980)

Daniel Littlefield, *Africans and Creeks: From the Colonial Period to the Civil War* (1979)

———, *Africans and Seminoles: From Removal to Emancipation* (1977)

———, *The Chickawaw Freedmen: A People Without a Country* (1980)

———, *Rice and Slaves: Ethnicity and the Slave Trade in Colonial South Carolina* (1981)

William M. Matthew, *Edmund Ruffin and the Crisis of Slavery in the Old South* (1988)

Russell R. Menard, "The Tobacco Industry in the Chesapeake Colonies, 1617–1730: An Interpretation," *Research in Economic History* 5 (1980), 109–177

James Merrell, *The Indians' New World: Catawbas and Their Neighbors from European Contact Through the Era of Removal* (1989)

Edmund S. Morgan, *American Slavery, American Freedom: The Ordeal of Colonial Virginia* (1975)

Michael Mullin, *American Negro Slavery: A Documentary History* (1976)

James F. O'Gorman, *Connecticut Valley Vernacular: The Vanishing Landscape and Architecture of the New England Tobacco Fields* (2002)

John Solomon Otto, *The Southern Frontiers, 1607–1860: The Agricultural Evolution of the Colonial and Antebellum South* (1990)

Theda Perdue, *Native Carolinians: The Indians of North Carolina* (1985)

———, *Slavery and the Evolution of Cherokee Society, 1540–1866* (1979)

———, and Michael D. Green, eds. *The Columbia Guide to American Indians of the Southeast* (2001)

Jacob M. Price, *Tobacco in the Atlantic: The Chesapeake, London and Glasgow 1675–1775 (Collected Studies Series , Vol. 513)* (1996)

Eldred E. Prince, *Long Green: The Rise and Fall of Tobacco in South Carolina* (2000)

David B. Quinn and Alison M. Quinn, eds., *The First Colonists: Documents on the Planting of the First English Settlements in North America, 1584–1590* (1982)

Bruce A. Ragsdale, *A Planters' Republic: The Search for Economic Independence in Revolutionary Virginia* (1996)

Helen Rountree, *The Powhatan Indians of Virginia: Their Traditional Culture* (1989)

Parke Rouse, Jr., *Planters and Pioneers: Life in Colonial Virginia* (1968)

Neal Salisbury, "The Indians' Old World: Native Americans and the Coming of Europeans," *William and Mary Quarterly,* 3rd ser. (53) 3 (July 1996): 435–458

Timothy Silver, *A New Face on the Countryside: Indians, Colonists, and Slaves in South Atlantic Forests, 1500–1800* (1990)

Mart Stewart, "Rice, Water, and Power: Landscapes of Domination and Resistance in the Lowcountry, 1790–1880." *Environmental History Review* 15 (1991): 47–64

———, "Southern Environmental History," in John Boles, ed., *A Companion to the American South* (2002)

———, *"What Nature Suffers to Groe": Life, Labor, and Landscape on the Georgia Coast, 1680–1920* (1996)

John Van Willigen, et al., *Tobacco Culture: Farming Kentucky's Burley Belt (Kentucky Remembered)* (1998)

Peter Wood, *Black Majority: Negroes in Colonial South Carolina from 1670 Through the Stono Rebellion* (1974)

CHAPTER
5

Farms and Cities in
the Early Republic

❦

By the turn of the eighteenth century, two economies existed in support of and in
tension with each other. A coastal exporting economy based on trade in staples such
as lumber, tobacco, and rice was centered on cities and their coastal surroundings,
while a rural economy beyond the limits of easy trade flourished in the inland hills
and mountains. This chapter focuses on the environmental issues facing farms and
cities in the late eighteenth century and the transition to industrialization in the
early nineteenth century.

In the eighteenth century, an expanding population moved inland from the
coastal plain and settled in hilly regions above the first falls of the rivers, beyond
easy access to navigable waterways. In New England people founded towns in the
hills on either side of the Connecticut River; in Pennsylvania they moved westward
from Philadelphia into Chester and Lancaster Counties and then southwestward
into the Great Valley of the Appalachians; in Virginia and Maryland they migrated
upcountry into the piedmont; and in the Carolinas they established communities
inland, along the Roanoke, Cape Fear, Peedee, and Santee Rivers. Most of the new
settlers lived in small towns oriented toward agricultural production for subsistence.
They bartered food, clothing, tools, and labor with their neighbors. Their farms
were ecological units that circulated nutrients within the farm boundaries through
crop production, livestock grazing, and forest burning. The farmers interacted with
the outside world by marketing their crops and purchasing goods.

Cities, such as Boston, Newport, New York, Philadelphia, Baltimore, and
Charleston, supported the staple-exporting economy of the coastal plain and housed
growing numbers of artisans, merchants, shipbuilders, and professionals, such as
clergy and lawyers. The inhabitants of these cities depended on market-oriented
farmers on their outskirts for food and on imported and manufactured items from
abroad. Growing populations, craft centers, and early industries, however, also
generated ecological outputs in the form of smoke, sewage, dyes, animal excrement,
and air- and water-borne diseases. With early industrialization, westward expansion
to the Mississippi River, and the development of extensive transportation systems,
the ecological networks joining farms and cities increasingly interacted in both positive and negative ways. Water-powered (and later steam-powered) mills for textiles

and grain brought goods, jobs, and energy sources to rural economies, but the increased economic opportunities also produced air and water pollution for cities downstream. The environmental links and interactions between farms and cities are the topic of this chapter. (See Map 2 in the Appendix.)

❦ D O C U M E N T S

The following documents set out the environmental issues separating and uniting farm and city dwellers in the early republic. Documents 1 and 2 present the idealized subsistence farmer as the backbone of the American economy, although the writers of both documents were members of the propertied elite. J. Hector St. John de Crèvecoeur was a French nobleman who traveled in Pennsylvania, New York, and the Carolinas from 1759 to 1769, after which he married and settled on a farm in New York until 1780. His *Letters from an American Farmer* (1782), excerpted in Document 1, contrast the free, hard-working American "tillers of the earth" with Europe's rich aristocrats and property-less poor, suggesting that cultivating the soil fosters an American purity and contentment unknown in the Old World. Similarly, in Document 2, Thomas Jefferson, a Virginia planter with a large estate at Monticello, in 1787 characterizes ordinary farmers "who labor in the earth" as the "chosen people of God" and recommends that manufacturing, which fosters economic differences, remain in Europe.

In Document 3, Benjamin Rush, doctor, abolitionist, and educator, describes German market farmers in 1789 as frugal and industrious people who grew wheat and vegetables for the city of Philadelphia. Document 4 is excerpted from an almanac diary for 1820 of a farm widow, Anna Howell (1769–1855), of Gloucester County, New Jersey, who at the age of fifty inherited a farm and fisheries on the Delaware River from her husband, Joshua. Her diaries, kept from 1819 to 1839 in interleaved almanacs to improve her farm management, illustrate the opportunities and burdens for women affected by the market economy.

Documents 5 and 6 reveal the transition to industrialization and the ways in which cities responded. In 1798, through the correspondence excerpted in Document 5, Samuel Slater, who had worked in the British textile industry, introduced the first water-powered spinning jenny, reconstructed from memory, to manufacturers William Almy and Moses Brown in Pawtucket, Rhode Island, setting off the American industrial revolution. In Document 6, William Henry Latrobe, who later designed the capitol in Washington, D.C., graphically describes Philadelphia's need for sewers and a clean water supply and advocates the construction of the nation's first water aqueduct.

The final two documents illustrate the expansion of the market and transportation revolutions that created the internal economy of the United States during the early republic. John James Audubon, author of Document 7, describes the way in which the transportation revolution lured settlers westward to the Mississippi River after 1815. Here the seductive power of the market is graphically portrayed as the husbands and sons of family after family raft down the river to New Orleans with produce, returning by steamboat with profits and commodities for their wives and daughters. In Document 8, Calvin Colton, a political essayist and member of the Whig party, in 1844 characterizes America as a "country of self-made men" and the American environment as a source of "inexhaustible wealth." In reality, this worldview applied to white Euramerican males only, not to women, blacks, Indians, or Mexicans. As in the previous chapter, the documents pose probing questions about human nature. Are people "naturally" competitive and entrepreneurial or altruistic and sharing, or are these attributes historically constructed and dependent on environments, economic systems, and cultural characteristics?

1. J. Hector St. John de Crèvecoeur Asks, "What Is an American?" 1782

I wish I could be acquainted with the feelings and thoughts which must agitate the heart and present themselves to the mind of an enlightened Englishman, when he first lands on this continent. He must greatly rejoice that he lived at a time to see this fair country discovered and settled; he must necessarily feel a share of national pride, when he views the chain of settlements which embellishes these extended shores. . . . Here he beholds fair cities, substantial villages, extensive fields, an immense country filled with decent houses, good roads, orchards, meadows, and bridges, where an hundred years ago all was wild, woody, and uncultivated! . . . He is arrived on a new continent; a modern society offers itself to his contemplation, different from what he had hitherto seen. It is not composed, as in Europe, of great lords who possess everything, and of a herd of people who have nothing. Here are no aristocratical families, no courts, no kings, no bishops, no ecclesiastical dominion, no invisible power giving to a few a very visible one; no great manufacturers employing thousands, no great refinements of luxury. The rich and the poor are not so far removed from each other as they are in Europe. Some few towns excepted, we are all tillers of the earth, from Nova Scotia to West Florida. We are a people of cultivators, scattered over an immense territory, communicating with each other by means of good roads and navigable rivers, united by the silken bands of mild government, all respecting the laws, without dreading their power, because they are equitable. We are all animated with the spirit of an industry which is unfettered and unrestrained, because each person works for himself. If he travels through our rural districts he views not the hostile castle, and the haughty mansion, contrasted with the clay-built hut and miserable cabin, where cattle and men help to keep each other warm, and dwell in meanness, smoke, and indigence. A pleasing uniformity of decent competence appears throughout our habitations. The meanest of our log-houses is a dry and comfortable habitation. Lawyer or merchant are the fairest titles our towns afford; that of a farmer is the only appellation of the rural inhabitants of our country. It must take some time ere he can reconcile himself to our dictionary, which is but short in words of dignity, and names of honour. There, on a Sunday, he sees a congregation of respectable farmers and their wives, all clad in neat home-spun, well mounted, or riding in their own humble waggons. There is not among them an esquire, saving the unlettered magistrate. There he sees a parson as simple as his flock, a farmer who does not riot on the labour of others. We have no princes, for whom we toil, starve, and bleed: we are the most perfect society now existing in the world. Here man is free as he ought to be. . . .

The next wish of this traveller will be to know whence came all these people? They are a mixture of English, Scotch, Irish, French, Dutch, Germans, and Swedes. From this promiscuous breed, that race now called Americans have arisen. . . .

What then is the American, this new man? He is either an European, or the descendant of an European, hence that strange mixture of blood, which you will find

From J. Hector St. John de Crèvecoeur, *Letters from an American Farmer.* New York: E. P. Dutton, 1957; originally published London, 1782, pp. 35–37, 39–43, 61.

in no other country. I could point out to you a family whose grandfather was an Englishman, whose wife was Dutch, whose son married a French woman, and whose present four sons have now four wives of different nations. *He* is an American, who leaving behind him all his ancient prejudices and manners, receives new ones from the new mode of life he has embraced, the new government he obeys, and the new rank he holds. He becomes an American by being received in the broad lap of our great *Alma Mater.* Here individuals of all nations are melted into a new race of men, whose labours and posterity will one day cause great changes in the world. Americans are the western pilgrims, who are carrying along with them that great mass of arts, sciences, vigour, and industry which began long since in the east; they will finish the great circle. . . . The American is a new man, who acts upon new principles; he must therefore entertain new ideas, and form new opinions. From involuntary idleness, servile dependence, penury, and useless labour, he has passed to toils of a very different nature, rewarded by ample subsistence—This is an American.

British America is divided into many provinces, forming a large association, scattered along a coast 1500 miles extent and about 200 wide. This society I would fain examine, at least such as it appears in the middle provinces; if it does not afford that variety of tinges and gradations which may be observed in Europe, we have colours peculiar to ourselves. For instance, it is natural to conceive that those who live near the sea, must be very different from those who live in the woods; the intermediate space will afford a separate and distinct class.

Men are like plants; the goodness and flavour of the fruit proceeds from the peculiar soil and exposition in which they grow. We are nothing but what we derive from the air we breathe, the climate we inhabit, the government we obey, the system of religion we profess, and the nature of our employment. . . .

Those who live near the sea, feed more on fish than on flesh, and often encounter that boisterous element. This renders them more bold and enterprising; this leads them to neglect the confined occupations of the land. They see and converse with a variety of people, their intercourse with mankind becomes extensive. The sea inspires them with a love of traffic, a desire of transporting produce from one place to another; and leads them to a variety of resources which supply the place of labour. Those who inhabit the middle settlements, by far the most numerous, must be very different; the simple cultivation of the earth purifies them, but the indulgences of the government, the soft remonstrances of religion, the rank of independent freeholders, must necessarily inspire them with sentiments, very little known in Europe among people of the same class. . . . As citizens it is easy to imagine, that they will carefully read the newspapers, enter into every political disquisition, freely blame or censure governors and others. As farmers they will be careful and anxious to get as much as they can, because what they get is their own. . . . Industry, good living, selfishness, litigiousness, country politics, the pride of freemen, religious indifference, are their characteristics. If you recede still farther from the sea, you will come into more modern settlements; they exhibit the same strong lineaments, in a ruder appearance. Religion seems to have still less influence, and their manners are less improved.

Now we arrive near the great woods, near the last inhabited districts; there men seem to be placed still farther beyond the reach of government, which in some measure leaves them to themselves. How can it pervade every corner; as they were driven there by misfortunes, necessity of beginnings, desire of acquiring large tracts of land, idleness, frequent want of economy, ancient debts; the re-union of such people does not afford a very pleasing spectacle. When discord, want of unity and friendship; when either drunkenness or idleness prevail in such remote districts; contention, inactivity, and wretchedness must ensue. There are not the same remedies to these evils as in a long established community. The few magistrates they have, are in general little better than the rest; they are often in a perfect state of war; that of man against man, sometimes decided by blows, sometimes by means of the law; that of man against every wild inhabitant of these venerable woods, of which they are come to dispossess them. There men appear to be no better than carnivorous animals of a superior rank, living on the flesh of wild animals when they can catch them, and when they are not able, they subsist on grain. He who would wish to see America in its proper light, and have a true idea of its feeble beginnings and barbarous rudiments, must visit our extended line of frontiers where the last settlers dwell, and where he may see the first labours of settlement, the mode of clearing the earth, in all their different appearances; where men are wholly left dependent on their native tempers, and on the spur of uncertain industry, which often fails when not sanctified by the efficacy of a few moral rules. There, remote from the power of example and check of shame, many families exhibit the most hideous parts of our society. They are a kind of forlorn hope, preceding by ten or twelve years the most respectable army of veterans which come after them. In that space, prosperity will polish some, vice and the law will drive off the rest, who uniting again with others like themselves will recede still farther; making room for more industrious people, who will finish their improvements, convert the loghouse into a convenient habitation, and rejoicing that the first heavy labours are finished, will change in a few years that hitherto barbarous country into a fine fertile, well regulated district. Such is our progress, such is the march of the Europeans toward the interior parts of this continent. In all societies there are off-casts; this impure part serves as our precursors or pioneers; my father himself was one of that class, but he came upon honest principles, and was therefore one of the few who held fast; by good conduct and temperance, he transmitted to me his fair inheritance, when not above one in fourteen of his contemporaries had the same good fortune.

Forty years ago this smiling country was thus inhabited; it is now purged, a general decency of manners prevails throughout, and such has been the fate of our best countries. . . .

To examine how the world is gradually settled, how the howling swamp is converted into a pleasing meadow, the rough ridge into a fine field; and to hear the cheerful whistling, the rural song, where there was no sound heard before, save the yell of the savage, the screech of the owl or the hissing of the snake? Here an European, fatigued with luxury, riches, and pleasures, may find a sweet relaxation in a series of interesting scenes, as affecting as they are new. England, which now contains so many domes, so many castles, was once like this; a place woody and marshy; its inhabitants, now the favourite nation for arts and commerce, were once painted like our neighbours. The country will flourish in its turn, and the same observations will be made which I have just delineated. Posterity will look back with avidity and pleasure, to trace, if possible, the era of this or that particular settlement.

2. Thomas Jefferson Extols the Agrarian Ideal, 1787

We never had an interior trade of any importance. Our exterior commerce has suf-fered very much from the beginning of the present contest. During this time we have manufactured within our families the most necessary articles of cloathing. Those of cotton will bear some comparison with the same kinds of manufacture in Europe; but those of wool, flax and hemp are very coarse, unsightly, and unpleasant: and such is our attachment to agriculture, and such our preference for foreign manufactures, that be it wise or unwise, our people will certainly return as soon as they can, to the rais-ing raw materials, and exchanging them for finer manufactures than they are able to execute themselves.

The political œconomists of Europe have established it as a principle that every state should endeavour to manufacture for itself: and this principle, like many others, we transfer to America, without calculating the difference of circumstance which should often produce a difference of result. In Europe the lands are either cultivated, or locked up against the cultivator. Manufacture must therefore be resorted to of necessity not of choice, to support the surplus of their people. But we have an im-mensity of land courting the industry of the husbandman. Is it best then that all our citizens should be employed in its improvement, or that one half should be called off from that to exercise manufactures and handicraft arts for the other? Those who labour in the earth are the chosen people of God, if ever he had a chosen people, whose breasts he has made his peculiar deposit for substantial and genuine virtue. It is the focus in which he keeps alive that sacred fire, which otherwise might escape from the face of the earth. Corruption of morals in the mass of cultivators is a phe-nomenon of which no age nor nation has furnished an example. It is the mark set on those, who not looking up to heaven, to their own soil and industry, as does the husbandman, for their subsistence, depend for it on the casualties and caprice of customers. Dependance begets subservience and venality, suffocates the germ of vir-tue, and prepares fit tools for the designs of ambition. This, the natural progress and consequence of the arts, has sometimes perhaps been retarded by accidental circum-stances: but, generally speaking, the proportion which the aggregate of the other classes of citizens bears in any state to that of its husbandmen, is the proportion of its unsound to its healthy parts, and is a good-enough barometer whereby to meas-ure its degree of corruption. While we have land to labour then, let us never wish to see our citizens occupied at a work-bench, or twirling a distaff. Carpenters, masons, smiths, are wanting in husbandry: but, for the general operations of manufacture, let our work-shops remain in Europe. It is better to carry provisions and materials to workmen there, than bring them to the provisions and materials, and with them their manners and principles. The loss by the transportation of commodities across the Atlantic will be made up in happiness and permanence of government. The mobs of great cities add just so much to the support of pure government, as sores do to the strength of the human body. It is the manners and spirit of a people which preserve a republic in vigour. A degeneracy in these is a canker which soon eats to the heart of its laws and constitution.

From Thomas Jefferson, *Notes on the State of Virginia.* London: J. Stockdale, 1787, query XIX, pp. 276–277.

3. Benjamin Rush Praises the Market
Farmers of Pennsylvania, 1789

1st. In settling a tract of land, . . . [the German Inhabitants of Pennsylvania] always provide large and suitable accommodations for their horses and cattle, before they lay out much money in building a house for themselves. The barn and stables are generally under one roof, and contrived in such manner as to enable them to feed their horses and cattle, and to remove their dung, with as little trouble as possible. The first dwelling house upon this farm is small, and built of logs. It generally lasts the life time of the first settler of a tract of land; and hence they have a saying, that "a son should always begin his improvements where his father left off,"—that is, by building a large and convenient stone house.

2d. They always prefer good land or that land on which there is a large quantity of meadow ground. From an attention to the cultivation of grass, they often double the value of an old farm in a few years, and grow rich on farms, on which their predecessors of whom they purchased them, have nearly starved. They prefer purchasing farms with some improvements to settling a new tract of land.

3d. In clearing new land, they do not girdle the trees simply, and leave them to perish in the ground, as is the custom of their English or Irish neighbors; but they generally cut them down and burn them. In destroying under-wood and bushes, they generally grub them out of the ground; by which means a field is as fit for cultivation the second year after it is cleared, as it is in twenty years afterwards. The advantages of this mode of clearing, consist in the immediate product of the field, and in the greater facility with which it is ploughed, harrowed and reaped. The expense of repairing a plough, which is often broken two or three times in a year by small stumps concealed in the ground, is often greater than the extraordinary expense of grubbing the same field completely, in clearing it.

4th. They feed their horses and cows, of which they keep only a small number, in such a manner, that the former perform twice the labor of those horses, and the latter yield twice the quantity of milk of those cows, that are less plentifully fed. There is great economy in this practice, especially in a country where so much of the labour of a farmer is necessary to support his domestic animals. A German horse is known in every part of the state: indeed he seems to "feel with his lord, the pleasure and the pride" of his extraordinary size or fat.

5th. The fences of a German farm are generally high, and well built; so that his fields seldom suffer from the inroads of his own or his neighbours, horses, cattle, hogs, or sheep.

6th. The German farmers are great economists of their wood. Hence they burn it only in stoves, in which they consume but a 4th or 5th part of what is commonly burnt in ordinary open fire places: besides, their horses are saved by means of this economy, from that immense labour, in hauling wood in the middle of winter, which frequently unfits the horses of their neighbours for the toils of the ensuing spring. Their houses are, moreover, rendered so comfortable, at all times, by large close stoves, that

From Benjamin Rush, *An Account of the Manners of the German Inhabitants of Pennsylvania.* Ed. Theodore E. Schmauk. Lancaster, Pa., 1910, pp. 54–73.

twice the business is done by every branch of the family, in knitting, spinning, and mending farming utensils, that is done in houses where every member of the family crowds near to a common fire-place, or shivers at a distance from it,—with hands and fingers that move, by reason of the cold, with only half their usual quickness.

They discover economy in the preservation and increase of their wood in several other ways. They sometimes defend it, by high fences, from their cattle; by which means the young forest trees are suffered to grow, to replace those that are cut down for the necessary use of the farm. But where this cannot be conveniently done, they surround the stump of that tree which is most useful for fences, viz., the chestnut, with a small triangular fence. From this stump a number of suckers shoot out in a few years, two or three of which in the course of five and twenty years, grow into trees of the same size as the tree from whose roots they derived their origin.

7th. They keep their horses and cattle as warm as possible in winter, by which means they save a great deal of their hay and grain; for those animals when cold, eat much more than when they are in a more comfortable situation.

8th. The German farmers live frugally in their families, with respect to diet, furniture and apparel. They sell their most profitable grain, which is wheat; and eat that which is less profitable, but more nourishing, that is, rye or Indian corn. The profit to a farmer, from this single article of economy, is equal, in the course of a life time, to the price of a farm for one of his children. They eat sparingly of boiled animal food, with large quantities of vegetable, particularly sallad, turnips, onions, and cabbage, the last of which they make into sour crout. They likewise use a large quantity of milk and cheese in their diet. . . .

9th. The German farmers have larger or profitable gardens near their houses. They contain little else but useful vegetables. Pennsylvania is indebted to the Germans for the principal part of her knowledge in horticulture. There was a time when turnips and cabbage were the principal vegetables that were used in diet by the citizens of Philadelphia. . . . Since the settlement of a number of German gardeners in the neighborhood of Philadelphia, the tables of all classes of citizens have been covered with a variety of vegetables, in every season of the year; and to the use of these vegetables, in diet, may be ascribed the general exemption of the citizens of Philadelphia from diseases of the skin.

10th. The Germans seldom hire men to work upon their farms . . . except in harvest. . . . The wives and daughters of the German farmers frequently forsake, for a while, their dairy and spinning-wheel, and join their husbands and brothers in the labour of cutting down, collecting and bringing home the fruits of their fields and orchards. The work of the gardens is generally done by the women of the family.

11th. A large and strong waggon covered with linen cloth, is an essential part of the furniture of a German farm. In this waggon, drawn by four or five large horses of a peculiar breed; they convey to market over the roughest roads, between 2 or 3 thousand pounds weight of the produce of their farms. In the months of September and October, it is no uncommon thing, on the Lancaster and Reading roads, to meet in one day from fifty to an hundred of these waggons, on their way to Philadelphia, most of which belong to German farmers.

12th. The favourable influence of agriculture, as conducted by the Germans in extending human happiness, is manifested by the joy they express upon the birth of a child. No dread of poverty, nor distrust of Providence from an increasing family, depress the spirits of these industrious and frugal people. Upon the birth of a son, they exult in the gift of a ploughman or a waggoner; and upon the birth of a daughter, they rejoice in the addition of another spinster, or milkmaid to their family. . . .

13th. The Germans take great pains to produce, in their children, not only habits of labour, but a love of it. . . . They prefer industrious habits to money itself. . . .

14th. The Germans set a great value upon patrimonial property. This useful principle in human nature prevents much folly and vice in young people. It moreover leads to lasting and extensive advantages, in the improvement of a farm; for what inducement can be stronger in a parent to plant an orchard, to preserve forest trees or to build a commodious and durable house, than the idea, that they will all be possessed by a succession of generations, who shall inherit his blood and name.

15th. The German farmers are very much influenced in planting and pruning trees, also in sowing and reaping, by the age and appearances of the moon. This attention to the state of the moon has been ascribed to superstition; but if the facts related by Mr. Wilson in his observations upon climates are true, part of their success in agriculture must be ascribed to their being so much influenced by it.

16th. From the history that has been given of the German agriculture, it will hardly be necessary to add that a German farm may be distinguished from the farms of the other citizens of the state, by the superior size of their barns; the plain, but compact form of their houses; the height of their inclosures; the extent of their orchards; the fertility of their fields; the luxuriance of their meadows, and a general appearance of plenty and neatness in everything that belongs to them.

4. Anna Howell's Farm Diary, 1820

May

May 1st. Planted cucumbers. The ground as dry as ashes.

3rd. A considerable frost killed the beans in my garden.

6th Planted Water Melons.

16 The wind blowing violently from the N. E. accompanied with a drizzling rain. The weather very cold.

17th Still cold and stormy.

20th There has been one continued storm for the last week. Replanted Nutmeg Melons and cucumbers.

21st Raining nearly all day. The sun has not shone one hour at a time for the last eight days.

22nd Planted sweet potatoes.

24th Replanted Nutmeg Melons. Those that were up being generally kill'd by the wet and cold weather.

26th Began to plant field corn. Replanted water melons.

June

June 1st The weather almost cold enough for frost.

6th Planted a second patch of water and nutmeg melons

12th Planted pumpkins

From Anna Blackwood Howell. Diary, 1820. Manuscript from American Antiquarian Society, Worcester, Mass. Reprinted with permission.

20th Sent a few beans to market

27th of June. Arthur Powel picked cucumbers for market

July

7th The weather distressingly dry. Picked a small basket of cucumbers for market. Finished reaping and trawled my rye into the barn. I had 87 dozen

8th Hawled the rye from the field that D. Ward has 10. the shares 72 dozen We had a refreshing shower to day, after a drought of two weeks

August

5th Sent 6 watermelons to market

11th Sent a basket of Nutmeg melons to market

15th Sowed flat turnips in the new ground

22nd Sowed turnips in the barnyard

24th Picked my geese

November

Produce of Fancy Hill farm of 1820

In the field next to D Ward I had 175 baskets of corn

The very dry weather ruined my buckwheat. I had but 6 bushels

Nov 3rd In the barn field I had 215 baskets of corn. 30 bushels flat turnips in the new ground

I had 100 baskets of corn to my share of the ground tilled by D. Ward. I had 99 bushels of rootabaga turnips

Nov. 11th John Fowler to 2 and half days work To cash paid John Fowler $ 1

12th A violent storm accompanied with hail rain and snow

13th I returned from Tuckahoe the wind blowing a gale from the N W the weather severely cold

15th Still very cold weather

18th John Fowler to cash 1 12

Nov 30th very cold weather

5. Samuel Slater's Proposal on Cotton Spinning, 1789

NEW YORK, December 2d, 1789.

Sir,—A few days ago I was informed that you wanted a manager of *cotton spinning,* &c. in which business I flatter myself that I can give the greatest satisfaction, in making machinery, making good yarn, either for *stockings* or *twist,* as any that is made in England; as I have had opportunity, and an oversight, of Sir Richard Arkwright's works, and in Mr. Strutt's mill upwards of eight years. If you are not provided for, should be glad to serve you; though I am in the New York manufactory, and have

---

From George S. White, *Memoir of Samuel Slater* (Philadelphia, 1836), pp. 72–77.

been for three weeks since I arrived from England. But we have but *one card, two machines,* two spinning jennies, which I think are not worth using. My encouragement is pretty good but should much rather have the care of the perpetual carding and spinning. *My intention* is to erect a *perpetual card and spinning.* (Meaning the Arkwright patents.) If you please to drop a line respecting the amount of encouragement you wish to give, by favour of Captain Brown, you will much oblige, sir, your most obedient humble servant,

SAMUEL SLATER.

N. B.—Please to direct to me at No. 37, Golden Hill, New York.
Mr. Brown, Providence. . . .

PROVIDENCE, 10th 12th month, 1789.

Friend,—I received thine of 2d inst. [this month] and observe its contents. I, or rather Almy & Brown, who has the business in the cotton line, which I began, one being my son-in-law, and the other a kinsman, want the assistance of a person skilled in the frame or water spinning. An experiment has been made, which has failed, no person being acquainted with the business, and the frames imperfect.

We are destitute of a person acquainted with water-frame spinning; thy being already engaged in a factory with many able proprietors, we can hardly suppose we can give the encouragement adequate to leaving thy present employ. As the frame we have is the first attempt of the kind that has been made in America, it is too imperfect to afford much encouragement; we hardly know what to say to thee, but if thou thought thou couldst perfect and conduct them to profit, if thou wilt come and do it, thou shalt have all the profits made of them over and above the interest of the money they cost, and the wear and tear of them. We will find stock and be repaid in yarn as we may agree, for six months. And this we do for the information thou can give, if fully acquainted with the business. After this, if we find the business profitable, we can enlarge it, or before, if sufficient proof of it be had on trial, and can make any further agreement that may appear best or agreeable on all sides. We have secured only a temporary water convenience, but if we find the business profitable, can perpetuate one that is convenient. If thy prospects should be better, and thou should know of any other person unengaged, should be obliged to thee to mention us to him. In the mean time, shall be glad to be informed whether thou come or not. If thy present situation does not come up to what thou wishest, and, from thy knowledge of the business, can be ascertained of the advantages of the mills, so as to induce thee to come and work ours, and have the *credit* as well as advantage of perfecting the first water-mill in America, we should be glad to engage thy care so long as they can be made profitable to both, and we can agree. I am, for myself and Almy & Brown, thy friend,

MOSES BROWN.

Samuel Slater, at 37, Golden Hill, New York.

"The following agreement, made between William Almy and Smith Brown of the one part, and Samuel Slater of the other part,—Witnesseth that the said parties have mutually agreed to be concerned together in, and carry on, the spinning of cotton by water, (of which the said Samuel professes himself a workman, well skilled in all its branches;) upon the following terms, viz:—that the said Almy and Brown, on their part, are to turn in the machinery, which they have already purchased, at the price they cost them, and to furnish materials for the building of two carding machines, viz:—a breaker and a finisher; a drawing and roving frame; and to extend the spinning mills, or frames, to one hundred spindles. And the said Samuel, on his part, covenants and engages, to devote his whole time and service, and to exert his skill according to the best of his abilities, and have the same effected in a workmanlike manner, similar to those used in England, for the like purposes.

And it is mutually agreed between the said parties, that the said Samuel shall be considered an owner and proprietor in one half of the machinery aforesaid, and accountable for one half of the expense that hath arisen, or shall arise, from the building, purchasing, or repairing, of the same, but not to sell, or in any manner dispose of any part, or parcel thereof, to any other person or persons, excepting the said Almy and Brown; neither shall any others be entitled to hold any right, interest, or claim, in any part of the said machinery, by virtue of any right which the said Slater shall or may derive from these presents, unless by an agreement, expressed in writing from the said Almy and Brown, first had and obtained—unless the said Slater has punctually paid one half of the cost of the said machinery with interest thereon; nor then, until he has offered the same to the said Almy and Brown in writing upon the lowest terms; that he will sell or dispose of his part of the said machinery to any other person, and instructed the said Almy and Brown, or some others by them appointed, in the full and perfect knowledge of the use of the machinery, and the art of water spinning.

And it is further agreed, that the said Samuel, as a full and adequate compensation for his whole time and services, both whilst in constructing and making the machinery, and in conducting and executing the spinning, and preparing to spin upon the same, after every expense arising from the business is defrayed, including the usual commissions of two and a half per cent. for purchasing of the stock, and four per cent. for disposing of the yarn, shall receive one half of the profits, which shall be ascertained by settlement from time to time, as occasion may require; and the said Almy and Brown the other half—the said Almy and Brown to be employed in the purchasing of stock, and disposing of the yarn. And it is further covenanted, that this indenture shall make void and supersede the former articles of agreement, made between the said Almy and Brown and the said Slater, and that it shall be considered to commence, and the conditions mentioned in it be binding upon the parties, from the beginning of the business; the said Samuel to be at the expense of his own time and board from thence forward. And it is also agreed that if the said Almy and Brown choose to put in apprentices to the business, that they have liberty so to do. The expense arising from the maintenance of whom, and the advantages derived from their services during the time the said Almy and Brown may think proper to continue them in the business, shall be equally borne and received as is above provided for in the expenses and profits of the business. It is also to be understood, that, whatever is advanced by the said Almy and Brown, either for the said Slater, or to carry on his part of the business, is to be repaid them with interest thereon, for which purpose they are to receive all the yarn that may be made, the one half of which on their own account, and the other half they are to receive and dispose of, on account of the said Slater, the net proceeds of which they are to credit him, towards their advance, and stocking his part of the works, so that the business may go forward.

"In witness whereof the parties to these presents have interchangeably set their hands, this fifth day of the fourth month, seventeen hundred and ninety.

WM. ALMY.
SMITH BROWN.
SAMUEL SLATER

Witnesses—
Oziel Wilkinson, Abraham Wilkinson."

The following letter from Mr. Smith Wilkinson, written at my request, corroborates the above:—

POMFRET, May 30th, 1835.

Mr. Samuel Slater came to Pawtucket early in January 1790, in company with Moses Brown, Wm. Almy, Obadiah Brown, and Smith Brown, who did a small business in Providence, at manufacturing on billies and jennies, driven by men, as also were the carding machines. They wove and finished jeans, fustians, thicksetts, velverets, &c.; the work being mostly performed by Irish emigrants. There was a spinning frame in the building, which used to stand on the south-west abutment of Pawtucket bridge, owned by Ezekiel Carpenter, which was started for trial (after it was built for Andrew Dexter and Lewis Peck) by Joseph and Richard Anthony, who are now living at or near Providence. But the machine was very imperfect, and made very uneven yarn. The cotton for this experiment was carded by hand, and roped on a woollen wheel, by a female.

Mr. Slater entered into contract with Wm. Almy and Smith Brown, and commenced building a water frame of 24 spindles, two carding machines, and the drawing and roping frames necessary to prepare for the spinning, and soon after added a frame of 48 spindles. He commenced some time in the fall of 1790, or in the winter of 1791. I was then in my tenth year, and went to work for him, and began at tending the breaker. The mode of laying the cotton was by hand, taking up a handful, and pulling it apart with both hands, and shifting it all into the right hand, to get the staple of the cotton straight, and fix the handful, so as to hold it firm, and then applying it to the surface of the breaker, moving the hand horizontally across the card to and fro, until the cotton was fully prepared.

6. Benjamin Henry Latrobe on Polluted Water in Philadelphia, 1798

April 29, 1798.

On inspecting the plan of the city of Philadelphia, and observing the numerous wide and straight streets, it will not be easily believed that want of ventilation can be entirely the cause of the yellow fever which has made such dreadful and frequent devastations among the inhabitants. It is true that there are narrow and often

From Benjamin Henry Latrobe, *The Journal of Latrobe: Being the Notes and Sketches of an Architect, Naturalist and Traveler in the United States from 1796 to 1820.* New York: D. Appleton, 1905, pp. 92–98.

very filthy alleys which intersect the interior of the squares bounded by the principal streets and in which the air may stagnate. The back yards of most of the houses are also depositories of filth to a degree which is surprising, if the general cleanly character of the Pennsylvanians be considered. There must be some cause more powerful and more specific. This cause may, I believe, be found in the following circumstance:

The soil between the Delaware and Schuylkill is generally flat, and though not entirely so, yet it has strongly the appearance of being factitious, that is, deposited by the two rivers; or perhaps it was the shallowest part of the bed of the Delaware and Schuylkill united, at the period when the waters of all these North American rivers were elevated between one hundred and two hundred feet above their present levels. At that time, then, the present Delaware and Schuylkill were perhaps two channels only in this immense river. The soil consists of a bed of clay of different depth, from ten to thirty feet. It is excellent brick earth, being very smooth and free beneath the surface from stone or gravel. Below this bed of clay is universally a stratum of sand. In this sand runs a stratum of water, and as it is impossible to dig into it without finding clear and excellent water in an inexhaustible quantity, let the wells and pumps be ever so near to each other, it appears to me not at all extravagant to suppose that the waters of the two rivers unite through this sand stratum, which serves as a filtering bed. The water naturally, therefore, is universally as clear as crystal and tastes as sweet and as free from heterogeneous particles as possible. But this very circumstance, the inexhaustible supply of clear water to be found in every possible spot of ground, and which must have appeared the most tempting inducement to its projector, Penn, to found here a city, is the great cause, in my opinion, of the contagion which appears now to be an annual disease of Philadelphia, the yellow fever. The houses being much crowded, and the situation flat, without subterraneous sewers to carry off the filth, every house has its privy and its drains which lodge their supplies in one boghole sunk into the ground at different depths. Many of them are pierced to the sand, and as those which are sunk thus low never fill up, there is a strong temptation to incur the expense of digging them deep at first to save the trouble and noisomeness of emptying them.

In every street, close to the footpath, is a range of pumps at the distance of about sixty or seventy feet from which all the water which is used for drinking or culinary purposes is drawn. The permeability of the stratum in which the water runs, and which the action of the pump draws to itself from all parts round it, must certainly contaminate the water of every pump in the neighborhood of a sink loaded with the filth of the family, and as the number of these sinks is very superior to that of the pumps, each of them is in a manner surrounded by noxious matter. That this must be the case is evident from these facts: 1. Those who now live in the heart of the town, as in Fifth, Sixth, or Seventh streets, but who can remember when their houses were in the skirts of the city, complain that their water is growing worse since the accumulation of houses beyond them. 2. All the public buildings, which have large open squares around them, as the State House, the penitentiary house, the hospital, etc., have excellent water, and their pumps are resorted to by all their neighborhood. 3. All the houses on the skirts of the town, from Ninth to Eleventh streets, have admirable water as yet. 4. In the rest of the city the water is not to be drunk, and it is worst in the most crowded neighborhoods. It appeared to me to taste as if it contained putrid matter. 5. Before the pumps were furnished with iron ladles, chained to the stocks, for the purpose of drinking at them, those who were desirous of satiating their thirst at the pump—which very frequently happened to the lower class of people in the violent heat of summer—had no other method than to put their mouths to the spout, while they used the handle. It was, therefore, a very common thing that people fell down dead at the pump. This was accounted for by their drinking the cold water while they were heated by exercise. But it appears to me infinitely more probable that the water in the pump, loaded with all kinds of putrid and putrifying animal substances, was in a state of chemical dissolution, and that a noxious gas, containing probably a very large portion of azote, swam, and was confined upon its surface, the top of the pump being closed by an ornamental knob. This gas was, of course, forced into the mouth by the raising of the bucket and inhaled strongly, as everyone who is going to drink at a stream draws in his breath with great force. Instantaneous suspension of life must be the consequence. I have been assured by a very respectable and credible man who lived long in Philadelphia, and was a very active member of the corporation, that to his knowledge no less than thirteen men thus died at the pump in one day, and that no such accident had ever been heard of since the ladles were provided.

Thus, therefore, we have a proof that there does exist in the mode by which the city is supplied with water a very abundant source of disease, independent of the noxious exhalations of the narrow and filthy alleys and lanes. It is true that the inhabitants of Philadelphia drink very little water. It is too bad to be drunk, and that which is used in tea and cookery loses, no doubt, most, if not all, of its noxious quality. But the evil lies in the constant fermentation of the stratum of water and production of mephitic air, to which the pumps are so many chimneys to convey it into the streets and open windows at all times, and from which it is regularly pumped up every time the handle is depressed.

As to the public sewers, there are not very many of them, and I do believe they are productive of much mischief. That in Dock Street is a very great evil, but it spreads over a small extent of the city and through a very few streets, for I believe it produces no noxious vapors excepting when the tide is out.

The great scheme of bringing the water of the Schuylkill to Philadelphia to supply the city is now become an object of immense importance, though it is at present neglected from a failure of funds. The evil, however, which it is intended collaterally to correct is so serious and of such magnitude as to call loudly upon all who are inhabitants of Philadelphia for their utmost exertions to complete it.

7. John James Audubon Depicts the Squatters of the Mississippi, 1808–1834

Although every European traveller who has glided down the Mississippi, at the rate of ten miles an hour, has told his tale of the Squatters, yet none has given any other account of them than that they are "a sallow, sickly-looking sort of miserable beings," living in swamps, and subsisting on pig-nuts, Indian corn and bear's flesh. It

From John James Audubon, *Delineations of American Scenery and Character* (written 1808–1834). New York: G. A. Baker & Co., 1926, pp. 137–142.

is obvious, however, that none but a person acquainted with their history, manners, and condition, can give any real information respecting them.

The individuals who become squatters choose that sort of life of their own free will. They mostly remove from other parts of the United States, after finding that land has become too high in price; and they are persons who, having a family of strong and hardy children, are anxious to enable them to provide for themselves. They have heard from good authorities, that the country extending along the great streams of the West, is of all parts of the Union the richest in its soil, the growth of its timber, and the abundance of its game; that, besides, the Mississippi is the great road to and from all the markets in the world; and that every vessel borne by its waters, affords to settlers some chance of selling their commodities, or of exchanging them for others. To these recommendations is added another, of ever greater weight with persons of the above denomination, namely, the prospect of being able to settle on land, and perhaps to hold it for a number of years, without purchase, rent or tax of any kind. . . .

I shall introduce to you the members of a family from Virginia, first giving you an idea of their condition in that country, previous to their migration to the west. The land which they and their ancestors have possessed for a hundred years, having been constantly forced to produce crops of one kind or other, is now completely worn out. It exhibits only a superficial layer of red clay, cut up by deep ravines, through which much of the soil has been conveyed to some more fortunate neighbour, residing in a yet rich and beautiful valley. Their strenuous efforts to render it productive have failed. They dispose of every thing too cumbrous or expensive for them to remove, retaining only a few horses, a servant or two, and such implements of husbandry and other articles as may be necessary on their journey, or useful when they arrive at the spot of their choice.

I think I see them at this moment harnessing their horses, and attaching them to their waggons, which are already filled with bedding, provisions, and the younger children; while on their outside are fastened spinning-wheels and looms; and a bucket, filled with tar and tallow, swings between the hind wheels. Several axes are secured to the bolster, and the feeding trough of the horses contains pots, kettles, and pans. The servant, now become a driver, rides the near saddled horse, the wife is mounted on another, the worthy husband shoulders his gun, and his sons, clad in plain substantial homespun, drive the cattle ahead, and lead the procession, followed by the hounds and other dogs. Their day's journey is short and not agreeable:—the cattle, stubborn or wild, frequently leave the road for the woods, giving the travellers much trouble; the harness of the horses here and there gives away, and needs immediate repair; a basket, which has accidentally dropped, must be gone after, for nothing that they have can be spared; the roads are bad, and now and then all hands are called to push on the waggon, or prevent it from upsetting. Yet by sunset they have proceeded perhaps twenty miles. Rather fatigued, all assemble round the fire, which has been lighted, supper is prepared, and a camp being erected, there they pass the night.

Days and weeks, nay months, of unremitting toil, pass before they gain the end of their journey. They have crossed both the Carolinas, Georgia, and Alabama. They have been travelling from the beginning of May to that of September, and with heavy hearts they traverse the State of Mississippi. But now, arrived on the banks of the broad stream, they gaze in amazement on the dark deep woods around them. Boats of various kinds they see gliding downwards with the current, while others slowly ascend against it. A few inquiries are made at the nearest dwelling, and, assisted by the inhabitants with their boats and canoes, they at once cross the Mississippi, and select their place of habitation.

The exhalations arising from the swamps and morasses around them, have a powerful effect on these new settlers, but all are intent on preparing for the winter. A small patch of ground is cleared by the axe and the fire, a temporary cabin is erected, to each of the cattle is attached a jingling-bell before it is let loose into the neighbouring canebrake, and the horses remain about the house, where they find sufficient food at that season. The first trading boat that stops at their landing, enables them to provide themselves with some flour, fish-hooks, and ammunition, as well as other commodities. The looms are mounted, the spinning-wheels soon furnish some yarn, and in a few weeks the family throw off their ragged clothes, and array themselves in suits adapted to the climate. The father and sons meanwhile have sown turnips and other vegetables; and from some Kentucky flat boat a supply of live poultry has been procured.

October tinges the leaves of the forest, the morning dews are heavy, the days hot, the nights chill, and the unacclimated family in a few days are attacked with ague. The lingering disease almost prostrates their whole faculties, and one seeing them at such a period might well call them sallow and sickly. Fortunately the unhealthy season soon passes over, and the hoar-frosts make their appearance. Gradually each individual recovers strength. The largest ash trees are felled; their trunks are cut, split, and corded in front of the building; a large fire is lighted under night on the edge of the water, and soon a steamer calls to purchase the wood, and thus add to their comforts during the winter.

This first fruit of their industry imparts new courage to them; their exertions multiply, and when spring returns, the place has a cheerful look. Venison, bear's flesh, wild turkeys, ducks, and geese, with now and then some fish, have served to keep up their strength, and now their enlarged field is planted with corn, potatoes, and pumpkins. Their stock of cattle, too, has augmented; the steamer, which now stops there as if by preference, buys a calf or a pig, together with the whole of their wood. Their store of provisions is renewed, and brighter rays of hope enliven their spirits.

Who is he of the settlers on the Mississippi that cannot realize some profit? Truly none who is industrious. When the autumnal months return, all are better prepared to encounter the ague, which then prevails. Substantial food, suitable clothing, and abundant firing, repel its attacks; and before another twelvemonth has elapsed, the family is naturalized.

The sons by this time have discovered a swamp covered with excellent timber, and as they have seen many great rafts of saw logs, bound for the mills of New Orleans, floating past their dwelling, they resolve to try the success of a little enterprise. Their industry and prudence have already enhanced their credit. A few cross-saws are purchased, and some broad-wheeled "carry-logs" are made by themselves. Log after log is hauled to the bank of the river, and in a short time their first raft is made on the shore, and loaded with cord-wood. When the next freshet sets it afloat, it is secured by long grape-vines or cables, until the proper time being arrived, the husband and sons embark on it, and float down the mighty stream.

After encountering many difficulties, they arrive in safety at New Orleans where they dispose of their stock, the money obtained for which may be said to be all profit;

supply themselves with such articles as may add to their convenience or comfort, and with light hearts, procure a passage on the upper deck of a steamer, at a very cheap rate, on account of the benefit of their labour in taking in wood or otherwise.

And now the vessel approaches their home. See the joyous mother and daughters as they stand on the bank! A store of vegetables lies around them, a large tub of fresh milk is at their feet, and in their hands are plates filled with rolls of butter. As the steamer stops, three broad strawhats are waved from its upper deck; and soon, husband and wife, brothers and sisters, are in each other's embrace. The boat carries off the provisions, for which value has been left, and as the captain issues his orders for putting on the steam, the happy family enter their humble dwelling. The husband gives his bag of dollars to the wife, while the sons present some token of affection to their sisters. Surely, at such a moment, the Squatters are richly repaid for all their labours.

Every successive year has increased their savings. They now possess a large stock of horses, cows, and hogs, with abundance of provisions, and domestic comfort of every kind. The daughters have been married to the sons of neighbouring Squatters, and have gained sisters to themselves by the marriage of their brothers. The government secures to the family the lands, on which, twenty years before, they settled in poverty and sickness. Larger buildings are erected on piles, secure from the inundations; where a single cabin once stood, a neat village is now to be seen; warehouses, stores, and work-shops, increase the importance of the place. The Squatters live respected and in due time die regretted, by all who knew them.

Thus are the vast frontiers of our country peopled, and thus does cultivation, year after year, extend over the western wilds. Time will no doubt be, when the great valley of the Mississippi, still covered with primeval forests, interspersed with swamps, will smile with corn-fields and orchards, while crowded cities will rise at intervals along its banks, and enlightened nations will rejoice in the bounties of Providence.

8. Calvin Colton on Self-Made Men, 1844

Providence has [left] us a rich, productive, and glorious heritage. . . . The wealth of the country is inexhaustible, and the enterprise of the people is unsubdued. . . . Give them a good government, and they can not help going ahead, and outstripping every nation on the globe.

Ours is a country, where men start from an humble origin, and from small beginnings rise gradually in the world, as the reward of merit and industry, and where they can attain to the most elevated positions, or acquire a large amount of wealth, according to the pursuits they elect for themselves. No exclusive privileges of birth, no entailment of estates, no civil or political disqualifications, stand in their path; but one has as good a chance as another, according to his talents, prudence, and personal exertions. This is a country of self-made men, than which nothing better could be said of any state of society.

From Calvin Colton, *The Junius Tracts.* New York: Greeley & McElrath, 1844, No. VII, "Labor and Capital," sec. 36, p. 111.

❦ *E S S A Y S*

The essays explore eighteenth-century farming, the environmental impacts of growing cities, and the transition to the early industrial economy. The first essay, by environmental historian Carolyn Merchant of the University of California at Berkeley, argues that the majority of eighteenth-century farmers lived within a rural, barter-based, subsistence-oriented framework drawing its symbolism and ethic from farmer's almanacs and an organic worldview. With the market and transportation revolutions, this orientation became more mechanistic, and farmers became more commercial and profit-centered. The second essay, by urban environmental historian Martin Melosi of the University of Houston, graphically reviews the growing problem of keeping cities clean and healthy as populations and industries spewed pollutants into the environment. Problems of water use and sanitation became more pronounced as textile mills and other industries developed, first along waterways and then, under steam power, directly in the midst of cities. The third essay, by Theodore Steinberg, professor of history at Case Western Reserve University, shows how a rural New England landscape was transformed as textile mills manipulated nature, water, and people, in fact becoming the very embodiment of "nature incorporated." The three essays as a group reveal the ways in which people in the eighteenth and early nineteenth centuries interacted directly with land, air, and water and responded to the process of development. The authors pose thought-provoking questions about the driving forces of environmental transformation under a developing market economy, a transition still taking place throughout the globe today.

Farms and Subsistence

CAROLYN MERCHANT

By the eighteenth century in America, two types of economies existed in interaction but also independently of each other—a coastal exporting economy along the eastern seaboard and an inland subsistence-oriented economy, where access to transportation and export markets was limited and costly. During the nineteenth century, a dynamic market-oriented economy arose throughout the United States westward to the Mississippi River that integrated the two sectors. This [essay] explores the ways that many inland farmers interacted with the environment in the eighteenth century and the transition to the market economy of the nineteenth century.

The Inland Economy and the Environment

The environmental costs of commercial production did not reach most of America until the nineteenth century. Above the fall line and beyond the reach of coastal markets, retreating Indians were supplanted by Euro-American subsistence farmers attracted by cheap land. Their small farms spread over the hills of upland New England, the woodlands of western Pennsylvania, the southern Piedmont, and the valleys of the Blue Ridge and Appalachian mountains. In these areas, limited production supplied the rude comforts of subsistence, and transportation costs prohibited

From Carolyn Merchant, *The Columbia Guide to American Environmental History.* New York: Columbia University Press, 2002, pp. 59–69. Used by permission of Columbia University Press.

open-ended production for the market. Economic and social relationships were based largely on bartering and cooperation, as opposed to the commercial exchange found along the coast. By the early nineteenth century, this subsistence culture of small farmers comprised the majority of free Americans.

The virtues of this independent and land-owning citizenry were soon being celebrated as an "agrarian ideal" by French immigrant J. Hector St. John de Crèvecoeur and American statesman Thomas Jefferson. Crèvecoeur, a member of the French lesser nobility, came to the American colonies in the mid-eighteenth century. In 1759, after traveling in western Pennsylvania, he settled beside New York's Hudson River, where he wrote *Letters from an American Farmer* (1782). In his letter "What is an American: This New Man," he made a fundamental distinction between hierarchical, aristocratic European society and egalitarian American society. The people of America, he wrote, were simple farmers, "tillers of the soil," and as such typified a new American ideal based on ownership of property and the work ethic. Those willing to live a frugal but comfortable life could obtain title to land held in "fee simple." This agrarian-minded society was supported politically by what Crèvecoeur called the "silken bonds of mild government," a *laissez-faire* economic system untrammeled by government regulations.

The same ideal for America was held up [a few years later] in . . . Jefferson's *Notes on the State of Virginia* (1787). "Those who labor in the earth are the chosen people of God," he asserted. Independent yeoman farmers—those who owned a small piece of land in their own name and controlled their own labor—formed the very foundation of American democracy. In reality, this status applied primarily to white male property-owners, and did not include slaves or women (although some women did own property or were conduits for the passage of inherited property to male heirs of the next generation). Jefferson warned that if manufacturing became established in America, the country's workshops would soon resemble the sweatshops of Europe, destroying the ideals of democracy and farm ownership. He therefore recommended that manufacturing stay in Europe and that the United States remain the home of independent farmers who produced goods and used resources for domestic subsistence.

Environmental historians have debated the extent to which eighteenth-century farmers were involved in the market economy. William Cronon in *Changes in the Land* (1983) states that "land in New England became for the colonists a form of capital, a thing consumed for the express purpose of creating augmented wealth." Carolyn Merchant, on the other hand, sees land as a source of family and community subsistence. In *Ecological Revolutions* (1989), she argues that "between 1700, when the inland towns were being settled, and 1790, when ecological crisis and European markets stimulated agricultural intensification, an economy oriented to subsistence and family preservation flourished in inland-upland New England." Both agree, however, that the market economy did ultimately transform the environment of New England and other eastern states by the nineteenth century.

Land Use in the Inland Economy

The inland economy was based on an ecological system derived from both Europe and Native Americans. After clearing a small patch in the woods, perhaps two to five acres, farmers typically used it two or three years for crops and then five to eight years for pasture before allowing it to revert to woodland. When the soils in the first plot were exhausted of nutrients, they cleared and planted another two-to-five-acre plot. The plot itself was often put through a rotation system (developed in medieval Europe) of three sub-fields, in which Indian corn was grown on one or two acres the first year and a European grain, such as rye or barley, the second year. Each sub-field in succession was then allowed to lie fallow for the third year, to recover its nutrients. This short-term three-field rotation system allowed restoration of the soil, while the long-fallow "swidden" system allowed the regrowth of forests.

Once fields were carved out of the eastern pine and hardwood forests, subsistence ecology prescribed using them, spatially and sequentially, for both crops and animals. While crops were growing, rail fences kept out the pigs and cattle grazing in the woods. Then, after the harvest, cattle were let in to clean up the refuse and, in the process, manure the land for the coming year. Thus soil, water, and light combined with crops and animals to recycle nutrients and maintain crop yields. Meanwhile, the surrounding forest moderated the climate, reduced winds, and provided habitat for beneficial birds and insects.

Farmers also cleared one or two acres of forest a year to obtain fuel for the family, reserving a 40-acre woodlot that would reforest itself over a period of 20 to 30 years. People bartered crops, tools, and labor with neighbors. They used produce as if it were cash, exchanging food for shoes, bricks, or help in building fences and butchering hogs. Women exchanged cheese, eggs, and vegetables with other housewives, sometimes keeping accounts on the pantry door. In these ways, inland farmers formed cooperative communities. Some farmers kept written account books in which money appeared in the debit and credit columns, but no cash actually changed hands. Money, which was scarce in rural areas, was simply a notation for recording the exchange of products and labor between individuals.

Despite the transportation barrier, subsistence farmers found various ways to get enough cash for paying nominal taxes and buying high-utility store goods such as guns, crockery, and metal utensils or farm implements. One farmer might drive cattle to market. Another might burn wood from cleared fields to produce an easily transportable kettle of potash, which fetched a good price as an essential ingredient of glass and fertilizer. Others who lived close enough might haul a cart of firewood or surplus produce to the villages that grew up around country stores. Linking farm to market was the country storekeeper, who, like the miller, was one of the more well-to-do people in the rural community. Coopers, broommakers, and shoemakers (who were also farmers) bartered their wares directly with neighbors or traded them to the storekeeper in exchange for imported wares.

White subsistence farmers pressured the environment differently from Native Americans. Euro-American livestock and three-field short fallows made permanent settlement possible, whereas Indians' long fallows entailed moving their villages to fresh ground every seven or eight years. White farmers' free-ranging cattle trampled the forest floor and their pigs rooted in the soil, creating erosion but also manuring the woods. Whereas Indians' greater reliance on hunting and gathering entailed firing the woods for easier passage and more browse for deer, whites burned only to clear fields. Whites' firearms were more destructive than Indian arrows and spears, and their hunting decimated "pest" species such as bears, wolves, foxes, and hawks; reduced such subsistence prey as squirrels, possums, doves, quail, and grouse; and helped to exterminate passenger pigeons, Carolina parakeets, and heath hens. Their overall effect on the environment eventually exceeded that of Indians, as their populations grew faster and occupied the land more densely. Nevertheless, production for subsistence, whether by Indians or whites, made far lighter drafts on the natural dower than would the impending market economy.

The Inland Economy and the Worldview of Its People

American farmers inherited an organic worldview from their forebears in Renaissance Europe, who likewise drew livelihood directly from the land. Through this prism they saw themselves as interacting with a nature that was alive in all its interconnected parts. Historian Herbert Leventhal describes this perspective in his book entitled *In the Shadow of the Enlightenment: Occultism and Renaissance Science in Eighteenth Century America* (1976). A chain of being, as he explains the organic worldview, linked together all the parts of a living cosmos, from fixed stars and planets and moon down to earth, animals, plants, and even the lowliest stone. "By using the chain of being," Leventhal writes, "man was able to place any entity in its proper place, and determine its relationship to all other beings." God as ultimate creator acted through an animate entity, often characterized as "Mother Nature," who carried out his dictates in the mundane world. People lived out an interactive I-Thou, rather than an instrumental relation with an animate natural order in all its manifestations. Therefore failed harvests, storms, or droughts were interpreted as punishments for improper actions, bountiful harvests as rewards for good behavior. The organic worldview thus contained within it an ethic of reinforcement or retaliation for human actions.

The organic worldview's hold on American subsistence farmers was most evident in their devotion to the almanac. "Except for the Bible," writes historian Charles M. Andrews, "probably no book was held in greater esteem or more widely read in the colonies in the eighteenth century than the almanac." In *Early American Almanacs: The Colonial Weekday Bible* (1977), historian Marion Barber Stowell explains that the almanac comprised mainly "astrological predictions, advice on husbandry and health, and humor," a format dating back to medieval Europe. Based on the idea that the macrocosm, or larger cosmos, influenced the microcosm, or human body, each almanac contained a "man of the signs," a diagram depicting the part of the body influenced by a particular sign of the zodiac. The moon's daily location in a given zodiacal sign rendered the associated part of the body especially vulnerable. Within the organic framework, therefore, possessing an almanac for the farmer's particular location was critical to predicting human health and determining herbal remedies.

Almanacs were also essential for timing agricultural activities. "The waning or declining moon," Leventhal writes, "helped a plant set its roots down in the earth just as the rising moon helped plants grow upward toward the sky." When the moon was full or waxing, it was believed to exert a pull on water and hence on the fluids in plants, an extrapolation from observations of the moon's tidal action on oceans. When the moon was full, farmers planted crops that grew upward, such as corn, rye, and wheat, and when the moon was new, and presumably had the least influence, they planted root crops, such as carrots, turnips, and beets. They bred pigs in the full of the moon, believing that its influence would produce more offspring. They grafted fruit trees or cleared bushes in the "new of the moon" because the sap would bleed less and the graft would heal faster. Such practices were consistent with the microcosm-macrocosm theory that the heavens above influenced the earth below. An organic worldview thus guided the behaviors of farmers and explained their place in the cosmos.

Market Farming

The subsistence culture was ultimately doomed by the growing difficulty of providing viable farms for the sons of traditionally large families. Although many farmers adapted to shrinking land by selling out and moving to larger tracts of cheaper lands farther west, it was becoming clear by the early nineteenth century that cheap land was not as inexhaustible as it had once seemed. In long settled eastern areas—especially New England—where farms had been undergoing subdivision longest and western lands were less accessible, landless sons and daughters resorted to infertile lands, or to putting-out systems of household manufacture such as spinning and weaving, shoemaking, and broommaking, or to wage labor for port cities and the swarm of small manufactories spawned along the fall line by abundant water power and cheap labor.

　　While this agrarian crisis crept inland at the turn of the century, a bonanza galvanized the coastal market economy. Western Europe, disorganized by the wars of the French Revolution and Napoleon, turned to the United States for shipping and foodstuffs. As a commercial boom pushed wheat prices high enough to bear the cost of wagoning from the interior, production of wheat for the market caught up a broad swath of subsistence farmers, stretching from northern Virginia to New York.

　　Leading the shift to market farming were the Pennsylvania "Dutch" (from "Deutsch" or German). Schooled to a painstaking husbandry in Germany, they had migrated to the rich soils of Chester and Lancaster counties outside Philadelphia. As described by Philadelphia physician Benjamin Rush (1745–1813) in his 1789 article, "The German Farmers of Pennsylvania," they constructed substantial barns to protect their animals, built high fences to keep cattle and pigs out of their gardens, and transported wheat and vegetables in large wagons to the city's markets.

　　Inspired by this example, agricultural improvements based on the use of fertilizers spread elsewhere to wealthier farmers with access to an urban market. Only they could afford the additional hired hands required to restore their soils and take up agriculture designed for market profit. To do so, they began raising cattle in order to obtain manure for fertilizing fields and planting higher-yielding crops. They seeded legumes in fallow fields and enriched their soils with fish fertilizers and expensive guano, the dung of seabirds from islands off the coast of Peru. Educated market farmers kept account books, numbered fields, weighed products, and calculated costs and profits for each field, crop, and agricultural practice. Produce was taken to county fairs, where prizes were given for the largest vegetables and heaviest cattle.

　　As pioneers of market farming, the Pennsylvania Dutch had capitalized on the country's first major transportation project—a turnpike, or improved wagon road, financed by tolls, from Philadelphia to Lancaster. Its success inspired a craze for turnpike building, as capital generated by the commercial boom reached out from the great ports and smaller commercial centers to stimulate and engross trade with the countryside. The advent of market farming, based on the dynamic interplay of profit motive, wage labor, and turnpike construction, heralded the interlinked transportation and market revolutions of the early nineteenth century.

The Transportation and Market Revolutions

The commercial boom inspired dreams of a comprehensive national transportation system, and in 1808 Thomas Jefferson's Secretary of the Treasury Albert Gallatin proposed a federally financed network of roads and canals to "shorten the distances into the remote corners of the United States." The War of 1812 and fears of a powerful central government stymied this grandiose plan. But when the war ended in 1815, an outburst of entrepreneurial zeal, technological ingenuity, and financing by state and local governments produced a series of transportation developments that transformed American life.

Leading this transportation revolution was the steamboat, which Robert Fulton had perfected on the Hudson in 1807. After the war, steamboats spread rapidly along the vast network of rivers beyond the Appalachians, where there was no fall line and therefore almost no rapids to impede navigation. Adapted for this purpose with a multi-deck superstructure built on a flat raft and paddlewheels skimming the surface, the western steamboat could navigate up to the shallow headwaters of the Mississippi-Ohio river system and its multitude of tributaries, as well as lesser rivers flowing to the Gulf of Mexico. Transporting bulky commodities upstream as well as downstream far more rapidly and at a fourth of the former cost, steamboats spread market production across the West, from the bustling river ports of Pittsburgh, Cincinnati, St. Louis, Memphis, and the great western entrepôt at New Orleans, to new domains of the Cotton Kingdom on the fertile black loams of Alabama and Mississippi.

New forms of transportation affected the environment not only directly, but also by fostering population growth and production for the market. To supply steamboats with fuel, squatters along the rivers felled great tracts of forests. "Consumption of firewood by steamboats," writes environmental historian Andrew Isenberg, "was probably the primary cause of riparian deforestation in the United States in the first half of the nineteenth century." Traveling the great western rivers in the 1820s, the inspired painter of American birds, John James Audubon (1785–1851), expressed admiration for the industrious squatters along the Mississippi, but amazement at the rapidity of the land's transformation farther upstream on the Ohio. "This grand portion of our Union," he lamented, "instead of being in a state of nature, is now more or less covered with villages, farms, and towns, where the din of hammers and machinery is constantly heard; . . . the woods are fast disappearing under the axe by day, and the fires by night; . . .[and] hundreds of steamboats are gliding to and fro over the whole length of the majestic river, forcing commerce to take root and to prosper at every spot." His *Birds of America* (1827) brilliantly captured the beauty and abundance of American birdlife at a time when much of it was vanishing before axe and rifle.

The rising commodity production fostered by steamboats in the West sharpened competition among East Coast ports to engross western trade by surmounting the Appalachian transport barrier. With state financing in 1817, New York City exploited the unique water-level gap between the Adirondack and Catskill Mountains for the western world's most ambitious engineering project, a canal linking the Hudson and Mohawk rivers with Lake Erie at Buffalo. Generating an amazing flow of commodities upon its completion in 1825, the Erie Canal set off a canal-building mania. Most important were the ambitious systems of Ohio, Indiana, and Illinois connecting the Great Lakes with the Ohio and Mississippi Rivers. By linking the western rivers to the Erie Canal in cheap water transport, they guaranteed the Empire City's dominance as the great American entrepôt.

Rounding out the transportation revolution was a British technological innovation—the railroad. After 1830, railroads reached out to tap interior trade from Charleston, Baltimore, Boston, Philadelphia, and New York. By the 1860s, trunk-line railroads connected the East Coast with St. Louis on the Mississippi and Chicago on Lake Michigan, and 30,000 miles of track brought cheap transport for bulky market commodities within a few days' wagoning of most settled areas. In 1869, the Union Pacific met the Central Pacific at Promontory Point in Utah to complete the first transcontinental railroad.

Railroads cut deep scars through the landscape and made heavy demands on forests and mines for firewood, timber, coal, and iron. They contaminated their routes with noise, smoke, ashes, and threats of fire. William Cronon brings their larger impact to life in *Nature's Metropolis: Chicago and the Great West* (1991), by demonstrating how capital reached out hundreds of miles from the railroad hub of the Midwest to extract lumber, cattle, and wheat from the countryside for the Chicago market.

The railroad fired the mid-century American imagination as nothing else. For Concord's sage, Ralph Waldo Emerson (1803–1882), it was a "work of art which agitates and drives mad the whole people, as music, sculpture, and picture have done in their great days," and it "introduced a multitude of picturesque traits into our pastoral scenery." Emerson waxed most eloquent, however, about the railroad's practical benefits. He exulted over "railroad iron" as a "magician's rod" with "power to awake the sleeping energies of land and water." "A clever fellow," he wrote, "was acquainted with the expansive force of steam; he also saw the wealth of wheat and grass rotting in Michigan. Then he cunningly screws on the steam-pipe to the wheat-crop. Puff now, O Steam! The steam puffs and expands as before, but this time it is dragging all Michigan at its back to hungry New York and hungry England."

Emerson's Concord neighbor and protégé, Henry David Thoreau (1817–1862), was characteristically otherwise-minded. "The whistle of the locomotive penetrates my woods summer and winter," Thoreau complained, ". . . informing me that many restless city merchants are arriving. . . . Here come your groceries, country; your rations, countrymen! Nor is there any man so independent on his farm that he can say them nay. . . . All the Indian huckleberry hills are stripped, all the country meadows are raked into the city."

Both men sensed the historic shift the railroad announced. The transportation revolution was part cause and part effect of a broader market revolution that brought with it a profound transformation of American economy, society, values, and environment. The entire nation was becoming a unified, dynamic market of interdependent sections, each specializing in commodities as advantaged by its natural resources. The South continued to produce tobacco and rice and expanded its cotton and sugar production. The Middle Atlantic states and the Northwest focused on wheat, livestock, iron, and coal. The Northeast, while retaining its dominance of international trade, finance, and commercial services, moved increasingly into the manufacture of textiles, clothing, shoes, and hats.

Tradition-bound farmers did not convert easily to the competitive, get-ahead culture demanded by the market. According to historian Charles Sellers, "Radically new imperatives confronted people when they were lured or pushed from modest subsistence into open-ended market production. By the 1820s rapidly spreading channels of trade were replacing an unpressured security of rude comfort with an insecurity goaded by hope of opulence and fear of failure. Within a generation in every new area the market invaded, competition undermined neighborly cooperation and family equality." Everywhere American society was wrenched in new directions to reshape people for careers of calculation and competitive striving.

The market revolution triumphed politically only after a final struggle that produced the democratic subsistence culture's most lasting legacy. "When market stresses climaxed in the Panic of 1819," Sellers writes, ". . . subsistence farmers and urban workers rose in political rebellion against banks, conventional politicians, and 'aristocrats.'" Seizing on a popular hero scorned by market elites, "the people" elected Andrew Jackson president in 1828 by "the largest popular majority in the nineteenth century." Jacksonian democracy was compromised by its exclusion of women and its racist animus against banished Indians and enslaved blacks, and it eventually bowed to the market's inexorable imperatives. Nevertheless, by attacking banks as engines of capitalist transformation, Jackson mobilized for the first time a mass national electorate and ushered in modern democratic politics. Every American president since has had to run the gauntlet of his popular democracy. "Democracy," Sellers concludes, "arose in resistance to capitalism, not as its natural political expression."

The market revolution threatened the American environment more than any other development in modern history. It threw open land, water, air, and all the life they contained to unrestrained development in the pursuit of wealth and status. It made profit-and-loss the sole criterion for dealing with nature, conceived as inert matter. A mechanistic worldview based on the quantification of matter and energy, interchangeable parts, mathematical prediction, and the control of nature replaced the animate cosmos of the colonial farmer. In its wake lay cut-over forests, smoky air, polluted streams, and endangered wildlife. But the market's triumph evoked the first stirrings of an environmental consciousness that would eventually challenge its excesses through the democratic process.

Pollution and Cities

MARTIN MELOSI

Prior to the 1830s, many American cities faced poor sanitary conditions and suffered the crippling effects of epidemic disease. While some of the earliest citywide water-supply systems appeared at this time, few communities could boast of well-developed technologies of sanitation on the order of those constructed several decades later. Much of the responsibility for sanitation rested in the hands of the individual.

Excerpts from Martin Melosi. *The Sanitary City: Urban Infrastructure in America from Colonial Times to the Present.* Baltimore: Johns Hopkins University Press, 2000, pp. 17–23, 27–30, 39–42. Reprinted with permission of The Johns Hopkins University Press.

As England urbanized and industrialized in the mid- to late eighteenth century, provincial urban communities were only beginning to challenge the rural-dominated landscape of North America. Colonial towns and cities grew in political, social, and economic importance, but only modestly in size and number. Until 1840 almost all population growth derived from natural increase rather than immigration. The first federal census in 1790 showed that city dwellers represented less than 4 percent of the nation's population, and only two cities exceeded 25,000. Philadelphia (42,520) was the largest city in a country with only twenty-four urban places. Between 1790 and 1820 urban growth stagnated, particularly because of threats to trade and commerce due to English discrimination, repercussions of the American Revolution, and wars in Europe associated with the French Revolution and the rise of Napoleon. By the end of the 1820s, however, the urban population had almost doubled, although fewer than 7 out of every 100 Americans lived in cities or towns. . . .

While American urban communities seldom faced sanitation problems on a par with their European counterparts in these years, public and governmental perceptions and reactions were quite similar. Few people had an inkling about the causes of disease and illness. Individuals or private scavengers were usually responsible for disposing of wastes. And the role of government in protecting the community's health, guarding against the ravages of fire, cleaning streets, and providing pure water were often obscure and untested in all but the largest cities. . . .

If American towns fared slightly better in the eighteenth and early nineteenth centuries, it probably had more to do with less crowded conditions than with a more enlightened outlook about sanitation. As public health historian John Duffy observed, "Compared to modern cities, colonial towns were odorous and lacked effective water, sewer, and street cleaning systems." "Yet," he added, "if we compare them with similar British and European towns, the picture is much brighter. Nearly all Europeans visiting the colonies in the eighteenth century commented upon the spaciousness, orderliness, and relative cleanliness of American towns." . . .

Few towns and cities were free of nuisances. And few communities, in their early years at least, showed much resolve to move against the "noxious trades"—soapmakers, tanners, slaughterhouses, butchers, and blubber boilers—especially if they were located in the poorer areas.

Animals resident in urban communities were a part of preindustrial life. Horses for transportation, cattle, hogs, and chickens for food use, and dogs and cats as pets roamed freely through many vacant lots, streets, and alleys. Pigs and turkeys, in particular, were widely accepted as useful scavengers. Manure and dead animals were simply annoyances balanced against the value of sharing space with contributors to the town's welfare.

Epidemic disease was taken much more seriously than sanitation problems because of the obvious threat to life and the uncertainty as to cause. Many colonists feared epidemic disease as the wrath of God. While the relative isolation of North America limited the number of epidemics in colonial towns, they were no less ruinous than those in Europe once they spread.

Trans-Atlantic trade and urban population growth in the seventeenth and eighteenth centuries led to a wide array of infectious disorders, including smallpox, malaria, yellow fever, cholera, typhoid, typhus, tuberculosis, diphtheria, scarlet fever, measles, mumps, and diarrheal disorders. Disruptive events, such as the Revolutionary War, reintroduced widespread epidemics to many major cities and towns.

Smallpox was probably the worst of the early scourges, but while they were less frequent yellow fever and diphtheria were as virulent. Yellow fever first attacked the Atlantic coast in the 1690s, peaked around 1745, subsided through much of the remaining century, and then reappeared savagely in the 1790s in the port cities of Boston and New Orleans. In 1793 yellow fever took 5,000 lives in Philadelphia—one out of every ten residents. In 1798 the dread disease struck New York, killing 1,600–2,000 out of a population of 80,000. By the 1820s yellow fever virtually disappeared in northern states, but remained a chronic problem from Florida to Texas. Not until 1905 did it dissipate with a final outbreak in New Orleans. . . .

Epidemics forced the government to deal with public health, at least from crisis to crisis if not on a permanent basis. Part of the reason for the lack of commitment had to do with limited knowledge about measures necessary to thwart contagious diseases. With little or no understanding about disease vectors, preventative action was baffling, and often futile. Previous experience became the best teacher, whether gained from earlier epidemics in the community, from other communities in North America, or from Europe. . . .

Apart from fleeing the city, quarantining of those who contracted or were suspected of contracting a disease was one of the few proven methods of reducing its spread. Massachusetts Bay Colony set up quarantining regulations as early as 1647 based on concern about the "great mortality" in the West Indies. In 1701, Massachusetts passed a law providing for isolation of smallpox victims and for ship quarantine, particularly in Boston. Other communities lagged behind in passing such laws, and in many cases quarantine regulations were only temporary measures.

Boston is often credited with authorizing the first permanent local board of health in the United States in 1797. The threat of various diseases, especially yellow fever, stimulated some interest in permanent boards of health in other communities, but the few that were established often focused on nuisance abatement. Only limited attention, if any, was given to preventative measures for disease control. Lay persons, especially the mayor and some council members, sat on the boards and rarely exerted much authority. Boston's board was clearly the most effective. Between 1800 and 1830, only five major cities established boards of health, and between the 1790s and 1830 all but Boston's were temporary. . . .

Crude sanitary regulations of some type were common in the American colonies by the late seventeenth century. In 1634 Boston officials prohibited residents from throwing fish or garbage near the common landing, which was possibly the first sanitary ordinance passed before the 1650s. In 1647 an additional regulation was meant to prevent the pollution of Boston Harbor. In 1652, the local government passed other ordinances, including one that dealt with the construction of privies. According to Duffy, privies were a subject "that was to be the source of literally thousands of sanitary laws involving every community in America for the next three hundred years." In 1657 the burghers of New Amsterdam were among the first to pass laws against casting waste into streets.

Some effort was made to regulate the noxious trades by requiring butchers, tanners, and slaughterers to keep their property free of nuisances or, in some cases, by ordering the removal of slaughterhouses from the town limits. Between 1692 and

1708, Boston, Salem, and Charleston passed laws dealing with nuisances and trades deemed offensive or dangerous to the public. In New York City the office of city inspector was established in 1804—the first permanent office concerned specifically with sanitation. Its primary role was gathering information about public nuisances and reporting violations to the city council, but it had no policing power. Erratic enforcement of sanitary laws undermined the effort to protect the public health throughout colonial America and continued to be a problem into the eighteenth and early nineteenth centuries. . . .

For much of the country, dependence on wells or nearby watercourses for water supplies, the use of privy vaults and cesspools for human and household liquid wastes, collection of household and commercial refuse by scavengers, and dumping or burning of garbage, ashes, and rubbish provided adequate, even efficient, sanitary services. In low-density areas, these methods resisted change, obsolescence, or outright replacement. They were labor-intensive and conducted by individual householders and commercial establishments or by private businesses. The practices often were publicly regulated but rarely publicly managed.

As populations increased in the major cities, such approaches to water supply, sewage and drainage, and refuse became less workable. The result was the development of the first technologies of sanitation—"protosystems"—that placed emphasis on more sophisticated technologies, were increasingly capital-intensive, were publicly regulated and often publicly operated, and removed the individual from direct responsibility (other than paying assessments, taxes, and user fees). Prior to the mid-nineteenth century, almost all protosystems in America were devised for water supplies, not for waste disposal.

More than any other sanitary service, an efficient and effective water-supply system was a key factor in the vitality and well-being of urban populations. According to economic historian Letty Anderson, "In the United States, at least until the end of the nineteenth century, the presence of potable water was a major consideration in the location of towns." And limits in the quantity of available pure water could result in "a bottleneck to urban growth." Little wonder that city leaders devoted serious attention to the delivery of water supplies as urban growth accelerated in the early decades of the nineteenth century. The evolving water systems sometimes extended beyond city limits, tapping new supplies and laying claim to new markets for their service. . . .

The fear of fire and epidemics was a great motivator for change. Concentration of humans and structures made the threat of fire serious in burgeoning cities. It was crucial that a water system insure adequate supply and easy access when an emergency arose. The old "bucket brigade" was grossly inadequate when whole blocks of homes and shops were endangered by fire. Prior to the completion of Philadelphia's water-supply system in 1801, it took the bucket brigade fifteen minutes to fill one fire engine with water; after the system was in place it took 1½ minutes.

The hydrant became the modern symbol for fire protection, since its presence meant that water would be immediately available and abundant to fight a major conflagration. New York, one of the cities that took a leadership role in fire protection, did not install hydrants before 1830, however. While hydrants made water quickly available for emergencies, they also increased the use of water, making an abundant supply even more necessary. . . .

Before the turn of the century, most cities and towns depended on a combination of water carriers, wells, and cisterns to meet their needs. Even during the first several decades of the nineteenth century, several larger cities and many smaller towns continued to rely on local sources of supply. Unless they hired water peddlers, each citizen used no more than three to five gallons per day. . . .

While community-wide water-supply systems developed slowly in American cities, in 1801 Philadelphia became the first to complete a waterworks and municipal distribution system sophisticated even by European standards. The necessary health, economic, and technical factors converged to produce what became a model for future systems throughout the country. The Philadelphia waterworks, however, also was something of an anomaly, since it did not spark an immediate nationwide trend. It took several years for other cities to replicate the conditions that allowed Philadelphia to lay claim to its premier status in the field. . . .

In dealing with waste disposal, Americans relied on approaches that had been commonly practiced in Europe for many years—although they had rarely met with complete success in any European country. Before the mid-nineteenth century, few large American cities, or European cities for that matter, constructed drainage systems and refuse-disposal facilities on a par with the great ancient civilizations of Babylon, Mesopotamia, Carthage, or Rome. The ancient societies with the most highly developed sanitary services were large in size and dispensed services through hierarchical authority. As a consequence, service was not equally distributed among the classes.

Americans, instead, adopted Old World methods, focusing on individual responsibility for disposal of wastes as befit the size and circumstances of the country's urban centers prior to 1830. Cesspools, manure pits, and the pail system for removal of waste from privy vaults met local needs in much of Europe until the nineteenth century. The use of sewerage was primarily utilized for drainage rather than carrying wastewater. Sewers, if they existed at all, were mostly open ditches. By 1663 Paris had covered 1.5 miles of its ditches, but five miles of open ditches remained. To meet the needs of sewage disposal, a law had made cesspools in Paris obligatory as early as 1533, leading to the construction of more than 70,000 cesspools within a few years. In addition, dung heaps were centralized into dumps. . . .

Drainage and the disposal of liquid wastes fared similarly in American villages, towns, and cities as they had in Europe. What historian Joel A. Tarr has called the "cesspool–privy vault–scavenger system" dealt adequately with the disposal of human and household liquid wastes in many communities until they experienced rapid growth or seriously altered the disposal system by introducing running water, which inundated the cesspools and privy vaults beyond their capacity to contain the water.

Human waste occasionally was deposited in leaching cesspools, but more often in privy vaults located in cellars or close to the house. The privy vaults were relatively small, and were either covered with dirt when filled and replaced or emptied periodically by the individual or by private scavengers under contract or in the city employ. Most city ordinances required that the vaults be emptied only at night, thus the term "night soil" became a euphemism for human waste. The privy-vault disposal method operated reasonably well for many years, but the vaults were rarely watertight, required regular attention, and produced noxious smells.

Household liquids and wastewater often found their way to on-site cesspools or dry wells in many communities, but too frequently were simply cast on the ground.

Under the best circumstances, the wastes were recycled on farmland or sold to re-processing plants as fertilizers. The record of such uses, especially for night soil, was as erratic in the United States as it had been in England.

More problematic was the impact of wastewater once it left private property and the flow of stormwater through the streets. While the cesspool–privy vault–scavenger system provided rudimentary handling of some residentially derived wastes, existing "sewers" offered increasingly little help in controlling drainage problems, especially as cities grew. As early as the end of the eighteenth century, major urban centers such as New York and Boston had sewers. A "sewer" in this early period was intended to carry off stormwater or to drain stagnant pools rather than to handle wastewater, and was most often a street gutter rather than an underground drain. . . .

Unlike sewerage, street cleaning garnered serious attention because of the many functions that streets performed—transporting goods, providing human and animal traffic, allowing for emergency fire service, and even providing a place for social encounters. Since streets were part of a community's "commons," street cleaning came to be regarded as a municipal responsibility before residential or commercial refuse collection. Individuals, through their own action or via paid scavengers, carried the responsibility of disposing of refuse that they generated around their homes and businesses.

Pioneering sanitary engineer Samuel A. Greeley noted that "the beginnings of city cleaning were undoubtedly in street cleaning." In many towns and cities, citizens frequently lodged complaints about the filthy state of the main thoroughfares, and the neglect of conditions in alleys and on noncommercial streets. As has been noted, it was typical in both Europe and in colonial America for city dwellers to use streets as a dumping ground for all manner of refuse. Horses and other animals contributed their share of wastes to the streets. Beginning with Boston and New Amsterdam, ordinances were passed to prohibit the most egregious practices, but these laws were difficult to enforce and rarely deterred citizens from tossing materials indiscriminately along almost every street and road.

In some of the larger towns and cities, municipally appointed or privately paid scavengers removed clutter from streets and also carted away rubbish and garbage as early as the seventeenth century. By the eighteenth century, almost all major towns relied on scavengers to remove the largest and most obvious discards from the streets, including rubbish and dead animals. Eventually the free-roaming of swine and fowl was curtailed. Charleston officials passed an ordinance in 1700 which prevented hogs from running loose in the streets, but did not hire a scavenger until 1750 to improve street cleanliness.

In hiring scavengers—at least through the early nineteenth century—towns especially with moderate street use could meet the street-cleaning needs of its citizens (and some of its other waste-disposal requirements) in nonresidential areas. Systematic street cleaning with paid crews became increasingly necessary in the mid-nineteenth century when greater vehicular traffic kicked up billows of dust and urban workhorses were more plentiful. At best, attention to many problems associated with liquid and solid wastes were dealt with casually in most towns and only with slightly more determination in larger cities until later in the nineteenth century.

There was little stimulus, internal or external, for American cities to alter their disposal practices prior to 1830. In the case of water supply, however, the fear of fire and epidemics, and eventually the experience of the English, produced some modest changes. The most significant was the construction of the Philadelphia protosystem. Yet, even this achievement was insufficient, in and of itself, to set off a national trend. The English "sanitary idea" and the refining of the miasmatic theory of disease would provide the context in which substantial elaboration in technologies of sanitation would take place in the mid- to late nineteenth century.

Water and Industry

THEODORE STEINBERG

Perched along the shore of the Merrimack [River], and dependent on the river for its livelihood, was a flourishing city of about twenty thousand people. Here [at Lowell, Massachusetts] the river bent sharply north, then south, with a level plain set in the bend—a perfect surface for a city.

Brick buildings hovered over a network of canals that cut the land into angular patches. Arranged neatly in clusters, the buildings looked nearly the same, a sea of uniformity broken occasionally by the bell towers that marked off one complex from the next. Everything here seemed set in motion, the air thick with progress. And water, the flow of the Merrimack, was at the heart of it all.

Water was forced into the canals by a masonry and wood dam that spanned one thousand feet across the Merrimack River. As the water traveled through this complicated system of canals, it was at times diverted into the basements of the brick mill buildings. Concealed below ground were large wheels with buckets attached to their rims; as water filled each bucket, the weight made the wheels turn slowly. The wheels were connected to a system of belts, shafts, and pulleys that dispatched power up several floors and across their ceilings. Belts hanging from the ceiling were linked to machinery that spun cotton yarn and wove cloth from the yarn. The process was simplicity itself: water, gravity, and then power and production.

Twenty-eight mills worked here on several hundred acres of land. Six days a week, the noise of about 150,000 spindles and close to 5,000 looms could be heard across the land. The mills were driven by a massive hydraulic apparatus designed with the single-minded purpose of controlling water for production. The factories employed about eight thousand people—three-fourths of whom were women—and produced roughly 50 million yards of cloth each year, including sheetings, calicoes, broadcloths, carpets, and rugs. . . .

. . . The emergence of industrial capitalism . . . marked a new stage in [a] continuing process, one in which nature has been more thoroughly defined in anthropocentric terms. Industrial expansion involved a profound restructuring of the environment—a far more comprehensive incorporation of nature into the human agenda than ever existed before. At its core, the process entailed a systematic effort to control and master nature, a development that had dramatic implications for both human beings and the environment itself.

Excerpts from Theodore Steinberg, *Nature Incorporated: Industrialization and the Waters of New England.* New York: Cambridge University Press, 1991, pp. 2–3, 12–16, 43–46, 53, 69–70, 76. Reprinted with the permission of Cambridge University Press.

New England's rivers and streams, with their abundance of waterpower, provide an important place to observe this historical process. Carving their way through the land, the region's rivers, with their relatively high average slopes and frequent falls, were perfect for America's early industrial development. . . . The rise of the Waltham–Lowell system began along the Charles River in Waltham [Massachusetts]. As the nineteenth century progressed, the ambitions of the Boston Associates outgrew the modest waterpower of the Charles. The search began for more substantial sources of energy, and before long the well-endowed water resources of the Merrimack River were tapped. The textile cities of the Merrimack valley—Lowell, Lawrence, Nashua, and Manchester—controlled water to an unparalleled degree. . . .

. . . Early New Englanders were amazingly successful at reshaping the natural world to meet their own economic needs, at incorporating nature into their own distinct culture. The thrust then of New England's history in the decades leading up to the nineteenth century tended toward the expansion of natural resource use, toward the more thoroughgoing *commodification of nature*. Simply put, this was a process whereby nature—all things and relations in it—was conceived of, acted upon, and valued primarily for its capacity to be exchanged at market for profit.

Unlike the Indians who preceded them, European settlers brought along a culture that viewed the land, and what was on it, as a source of profit. The Europeans tended, in short, to transform nature into discrete bundles of commodities. This is not to say that the colonists saw only personal gain in the landscape. But when compared to their Indian predecessors, the colonists tended to integrate the natural world into the money economy, into capitalist economic relations. To New England's white settlers, then, the region's fish, fur, and timber often represented commercial opportunity. By the nineteenth century, this early version of capitalism—with its distinct environmental results—was evolving into a more advanced stage. It retained a commitment to markets and private property, but increasingly took the form of class relations and wage labor. This maturation also had environmental import. The relevant question . . . is how rivers and streams fared as capitalism matured into its modern, corporate wage-based form. If capitalism entailed the commodification of nature, how did that commodification change, if at all, as capitalism itself changed?

The colonists were largely successful in sectioning off the land, in setting up stone walls to distinguish one person's property from another. Rivers and lakes, however, could not be fenced off. The New England waterscape, like the waters of the rest of the world, resisted attempts to pin ownership on it. Water, in short, is more difficult to commodify and privatize than land. William Blackstone, the eighteenth-century jurist, believed that a stream's ever-changing physical nature often prevented the recognition of explicit property rights. Water, he explained, "is a moveable, wandering thing, and must of necessity continue common by the law of nature; so that I only have a temporary, transient, usufructuary property therein." By its very nature, water is a common resource—a part of the natural world not easily subject to private ownership. For a society wedded to the institution of private property, water raises troubling questions of control, ownership, and regulation.

Although the colonists had used water for power—to grind grain, saw logs, and full cloth—the history of water use in the nineteenth century marks a break with this past. The advent of large, integrated textile factories with substantial demands for energy transformed the way New England's waters were used. Much of this change forced water to the center of the production process on a new and unheard of scale. The minute, fine-tuned control of water became the hallmark of the Waltham–Lowell mills as they formed and matured throughout New England. The economic development of water, the construction of dams and power canals, created greater quantities of waterpower. And more waterpower meant more water available to be owned, regulated, and sold in the market.

The emergence of industrial capitalism signaled the beginning of a new chapter in New England's ecological history. As the region moved forth into the industrial age, there were all kinds of transformations happening—changes in the workplace, the home, the family, and the church. But few of these changes were as blatant as the effect industrialization had on the environment. The region's river ecology, the natural flow of its streams, its migrating species of fish, all felt the effects of industrial change. Industrialization also produced a radically different human ecology—changes in population density, mortality, water quality, and a new disease environment that all urban dwellers would have to face.

. . . Industrial capitalism is too often conceived in terms of its impact on local communities where factories emerged to transform the fabric of traditional life. It is more properly understood as a phenomenon with enormous geographic reach, with the potential to touch people and places far removed from the actual site of production.

Not only the conflict over the workplace, over wages and hours, but the struggle to control and dominate nature is central to industrialization. The face-to-face relations of power in the factory should be supplemented with a broader vision of conflict going on outside the factory walls. That struggle, at least in part, is over who will control the natural world and to what ends. Industrial capitalism is as much a battle over nature as it is over work, as likely to result in strife involving water or land as wages or hours.

New England ventured down the industrial path, but what a rocky, contested path it was, with conflict over water continually plaguing those who sought control of the region's vast waters. Who was to gain title to the water, who were to be the winners and who the losers? That was a question confronting jurists throughout nineteenth-century New England. . . . The legal rules of water structured the way people responded and behaved toward this resource. Over the course of the nineteenth century, water law developed in a way that suited the growing needs of New England's industrial economy. By midcentury, the law had moved firmly toward an instrumental conception of water use, toward a vision of water and law that sanctioned the maximization of economic growth. . . .

. . . Early American textile mills, such as Samuel Slater's mill at Pawtucket, were perpendicular to the river, in a manner reflecting the small-scale character of industry with limited opportunities for expansion. . . . Indeed, as the historian Barbara Tucker notes, Slater operated his factories somewhat removed from the exigencies of the market. Slater, she explains, "was no cost-conscious factory master who treated friends and laborers as commodities." And his attitude toward nature, we might add, may well have reflected a less ambitious agenda. The owners of the Pawtucket and Waltham mills had different views on their endeavors, although both undoubtedly conceived of nature in instrumental terms. Still, Slater adhered to convention, choosing to look backward to the traditional small factory. What happened in Waltham was entirely different. The BMC [Boston Manufacturing Company] devised a sophisticated system of production that relied on a far more thorough exploitation of waterpower.

Samuel Slater organized his mills as partnerships, shying away from the corporate form of ownership becoming more popular in the early nineteenth century. The BMC, however, secured its charter from the state. Prior to this time, corporations generally had operated as quasi-public agencies. States granted corporate charters to institutions that served a public function such as colleges and libraries. By the early nineteenth century, as the function of the corporation began to shift away from serving the common interest, it became a very attractive form of organization. Between 1800 and 1809, 15 charters were granted to Massachusetts manufacturers; in the next decade the number increased to 133. The changing nature of the corporation and its growing appeal during this period played a vital role in American economic development. This occurred as part of a much broader transformation of the corporation from a public agency to a private one operating in the interests of individual gain—a shift completed during the nineteenth century.

At the founding of the BMC, however, ambiguity surrounded the corporate form of ownership. Caught between a world in which corporations served public functions and one in which they operated on a more self-interested agenda, it was unclear what to expect. Many questions remained unanswered. How much power and authority were corporations to have over their use of the environment? How would corporate ownership and control over land and water mesh with the customs and needs of New England's farmers and small mill owners? How would nature fare when confronted with an institution in which ownership did not necessarily imply the right to manage and control everyday affairs? In 1813, as the ink dried on the BMC's charter, such questions were obscured by the novelty of it all, by the prospect of a water-driven textile factory that some imagined would work for the general good of the community. But as New Englanders quested for further economic growth, the potential for conflict inherent in the corporate form became more apparent. . . .

The [Merrimack] valley's four major textile towns were largely the work of the Boston Associates, a group of men who began as merchants and later turned toward investments in the New England textile industry. [Nathan] Appleton, [Patrick Tracy] Jackson, and Francis Cabot Lowell were well-known members of the group, which by 1845 totaled roughly eighty people. The Boston Associates was not a formal organization but a network of individuals and families joined by bonds of marriage, friendship, and, of course, finance. Textiles were the focus of this complicated financial group, but the people involved did not limit themselves to this one area of investment. They were also prominent in banking, insurance, philanthropy, and politics. By the middle of the century, they had interests in thirty-one textile concerns, controlling about one-fifth of the cotton spindles operating in America. New England's rich supply of water met their manufacturing needs, their factories settling along the Androscoggin, Saco, Salmon Falls, Cocheco, Chicopee, Taunton, Connecticut, and Merrimack rivers. Most of these men were not involved in the daily operation of the textile mills, but the agents and engineers they employed altered New England's waterscape, especially the Merrimack's, to meet the demands of production.

The rise of the Waltham–Lowell system in the Merrimack valley involved a fundamental transformation in the scale, degree, and purpose of water control. This meant a change in behavior, a shift in the way the Associates and those whom they employed made use of the environment. . . .

The Boston Associates succeeded at Lowell in altering nature to meet their ambitions for production. Their vision of the natural world, their understanding of the environment and how it should be used, shaped their efforts to control water. As much as anything, the vast infusion of industry into Chelmsford [Massachusetts] involved a shift in the way nature was perceived. The transition from a world where humankind remains at the mercy of nature to one where this relationship is reversed is surely one of the most powerful pillars on which industrial culture rests. In the modern world, humankind is no longer passive in its relations with nature. Instead, natural constraints are overcome by people intent on exercising their claims to autonomy and independence. Under industrial capitalism, there are many firm believers in human ascendancy, of people set to emancipate their society from ecological dependence, from the restraints of what had once seemed a far more imposing environment.

Historian Arthur Ekirch writes: "The concept that man's progress depended on the fullest use of the natural resources of his environment was a popular idea in the young republic." It was indeed. By the nineteenth century, any fears of subordination to nature were being swiftly overturned by a drive to master it. Industrious Americans were busy chasing progress—diligently improving on what nature bestowed. The Boston Associates were very much a part of this culture, and their thoughts about the natural world are worth noting. Many of them undoubtedly perceived and valued nature as a central component of the process of production. The natural world existed as a reservoir of productive potential awaiting the contriving hand of humanity. And most important, by combining it with labor, its value to humankind rose significantly. Many of them were likely to agree with Nathan Appleton when he invoked David Ricardo's famous maxim: "Labor acts upon materials furnished by Nature; but Nature is gratuitous in her gifts, and it is only when acted on by man that her productions acquire value in his estimation." . . .

The attempt to impose order on the land and waterscape is among the most striking and powerful features of industrial transformation. It is also a vital component of the quest to maximize productive potential, to efficiently capitalize on the earth's natural resources. The control of nature, whether for economic interest or leisure pursuit, underlay the advance of industrial capitalism. This idea united the Associates in their seemingly contrary attitudes toward land—its plants, trees, and flowers—and water.

❦ *F U R T H E R   R E A D I N G*

Joyce Appleby, "Commercial Farming and the 'Agrarian Myth' in the Early Republic," *Journal of American History* 68 (1982), 831–848

Peter Benes, ed., *The Farm* (1988)

Percy Wells Bidwell and John I. Falconer, *History of Agriculture in the Northern United States, 1620–1860* (1941)

Christopher Clark, *The Roots of Rural Capitalism: Western Massachusetts, 1780–1860* (1990)

Hiram M. Drache, *Legacy of the Land: Agriculture's Story to the Present* (1996)

Stephan Hahn and Jonathan Prude, ed. *The Countryside in the Age of Capitalist Transformation* (1985)

James A. Henretta, "Families and Farms in Pre-Industrial America," *William and Mary Quarterly,* 3d. ser. 25 (1978), 3–31

Richard Hofstader, "The Myth of the Happy Yeoman," *American Heritage* 7 (1956), 43–53

R. Douglas Hurt, *American Agriculture: A Brief History* (2002)

William Irwin, *The New Niagara: Tourism, Technology, and the Landscape of Niagara Falls, 1776–1917* (1996)

Kevin D. Kelly, "The Independent Mode of Production," *Review of Radical Political Economics* 11 (1979), 38–48

Alan Kulikoff, "The Transition to Capitalism in Rural America," *William and Mary Quarterly,* 3d ser., 46, no. 1 (1989), 120–144

James Lemon, *The Best Poor Man's Country: A Geographical Study of Early Southeastern Pennsylvania* (1972)

Rodney C. Loehr, "Self-Sufficiency on the Farm," *Agricultural History* 26 (1952), 37–41

Peter D. McClelland, *Sowing Modernity: America's First Agricultural Revolution* (1997)

Sally McMurry, *Transforming Rural Life: Dairying Families and Agricultural Change, 1820–1885* (1995)

Martin Melosi, *The Sanitary City: Urban Infrastructure in America from Colonial Times to the Present* (2000)

Carolyn Merchant, *Ecological Revolutions: Nature, Gender, and Science in New England* (1989)

Michael Merrill, "Cash Is Good to Eat: Self-Sufficiency and Exchange in the Rural Economy of the United States," *Radical History Review* 3 (1977), 42–71

Elizabeth H. Moore and Jack W. Witham, "From Forest to Farm and Back Again: Land Use History as a Dimension of Ecological Research in Coastal Maine," *Environmental History* 1.3 (July 1996), 50–69

Robert E. Mutch, "Yeoman and Merchant in Pre-Industrial America: Eighteenth Century Massachusetts as a Case Study," *Societas* 7 (1977) 279–302

Donald H. Parkerson, *The Agricultural Transition in New York State: Markets and Migration in Mid-Nineteenth-Century America* (1995)

Lawrence N. Powell, *New Masters: Northern Planters During the Civil War and Reconstruction (North's Civil War, No. 9)* (1999)

Bettye Hobbs Pruitt, "Self-sufficiency and the Agricultural Economy of 18th-Century Massachusetts," *William and Mary Quarterly,* 3d. ser., 41 (1984), 333–364

Winifred B. Rothenberg, *From Market-Places to a Market Economy: The Transformation of Rural Massachusetts, 1750–1850* (1992)

———, "The Market and Massachusetts Farmers, 1750–1855," *Journal of Economic History* 41 (1981), 283–314

Howard S. Russell, *A Long Deep Furrow: Three Centuries of Farming in New England* (1976)

John T. Schlebecker, *Whereby We Thrive: A History of American Farming, 1607–1972* (1975)

Max George Schumacher, *The Northern Farmer and His Markets During the Late Colonial Period* (1948)

Carol Shammas, "How Self-sufficient Was Early America?" *Journal of Interdisciplinary History* 13 (1982), 247–272

Fred A. Shannon, *The Farmers' Last Frontier: Agriculture, 1860–1897* (1945)

Carol Sheriff, *The Artificial River: The Erie Canal and the Paradox of Progress, 1817–1862* (1996)

Theodore Steinberg, *Nature Incorporated: Industrialization and the Waters of New England* (1991)

Steven Stoll, *Larding the Lean Earth: Soil and Society in Nineteenth Century America* (2002)

Glenn Trewartha, "Types of Rural Settlement in Colonial America," *Geographical Review* 36 (1946)

Thomas S. Wermuth, *Rip Van Winkle's Neighbors: The Transformation of Rural Society in the Hudson River Valley, 1720–1850* (2001)

CHAPTER 6

Nature and the Market in
the Nineteenth Century

❦

Between the time of Crèvecoeur's Letters from an American Farmer *(1782) and
Henry David Thoreau's* Walden *(1854), the concurrent and mutually stimulated
transportation and market revolutions brought about a dynamic capitalist economy
in the interior of the United States. The military campaigns of the War of 1812
opened up the lands to the Mississippi River for settlement, and settlers flocked west
during the post-1815 economic boom. Turnpikes, canals, and railroads linked textile
and shoe factories in the Northeast, wheat farms in the upper Midwest, coal and iron
production sites in Pennsylvania and Ohio, and rice, sugar, and cotton plantations
in the South. Steamboats on the Mississippi, Ohio, and Hudson river systems and
on the Erie Canal reduced waterway travel times and costs, and railroads provided
land links that joined ports, cities, and the hinterland. The market economy increasingly touched the lives of ordinary people, fostering an ethos of competition, personal
advancement, and accumulation of wealth. Concurrently, the cumulative effects of
environmental deterioration, vanishing wildlife, and forest clearing began to be
apparent to eastern elites. Artists, poets, novelists, essayists, travelers, and explorers
recorded the results of human settlement and development on nonhuman nature
and on non-European humans. Their responses reveal ambivalent feelings about
the benefits of "civilization" and those of "nature." (See Map 2 in the Appendix.)*

❦ D O C U M E N T S

In 1772, Phillis Wheatley, an eighteen-year-old African native who had been purchased
in 1761 in Boston by Susannah Wheatley, was orally examined and certified by eighteen
elite Bostonian citizens as an authentic poet who had studied classical and biblical literature. Published the following year in London, her *Poems on Various Subjects* was the
first book of poetry by a black American woman, and remained the only book of poetry
by a black American until 1829 (when George Moses Horton published a book of poems)
and the only book of literature by a black woman until 1841 (when Ann Plato published
a book of essays). The two Wheatley poems of 1773 that are reprinted in Document 1
concern nature. Using classical references to the nine muses; Aurora, the goddess of

dawn; Calliope, the muse of poetry; and gentle zephyr, or wind, she reveals an appreciation for nature's beauty and for its power as God's agent in the giving and taking of life.

In Document 2, taken from a selection of essays written between 1808 and 1834 by John James Audubon, the famous artist reveals himself not only as a painter whose artwork later awakened a nation to the necessity of preserving bird life from hunters, but as a participant in that very act of hunting, maiming, and killing beautiful birds that preservationists later deplored. In Document 3, excerpted from *The Pioneers* (1823), James Fenimore Cooper similarly writes about shooting birds—specifically, the famous, now extinct passenger pigeons—for sport. Through his spokesperson Natty Bumppo, or Leather-stocking, Cooper powerfully criticizes pioneer wastefulness in response to the apparent abundance of nature.

Document 4 features paintings of the Hudson River school, a group of nineteenth-century artists who appreciated and painted nature for its own sake. Their work captured the beauty of the Hudson River and Catskill areas of New York State, the rivers and mountains of New England, and even the Rocky Mountains and Sierras. Their canvases portray nature as wild, dark, mysterious, and sublime, contrasting it with civilization as light, calm, peaceful, and picturesque. Nature is presented positively, as benign and morally elevating, not as polluted or devastated by industry. Artist George Catlin, the author of Document 5, dating from 1844, revealed an appreciation of the American Indians of the Great Plains through his paintings and writings. These Euramerican artists valued nature and human nature in their "precivilized" forms for their positive qualities.

Documents 6 and 7 are by essayists of the New England Transcendentalist school. Ralph Waldo Emerson, writing in 1844, emphasizes true nature as an ideal, whole, and universal Oversoul—a reality in which the human soul participates as a mind, seeing each natural thing as a mere part of an overarching unity. Applying the mind to nature produces wealth—nature as commodity—and it is the English, Emerson believes, who have produced the science, machines, and economic methods to turn nature into capital. Henry David Thoreau, on the other hand, in excerpts from *Walden* (1854), expresses great skepticism over the disruption of pristine nature by the machine (symbolized by the railroad) and instead infuses subsistence farming (symbolized by his beanfield) with an ethic of preservation.

Finally, Document 8, by novelist Rebecca Harding Davis, alerted Americans to the degrading effects of industrialization on both nature and human nature. Her "Life in the Iron Mills," published in the *Atlantic Monthly* in 1861, portrayed the animal-like existence of Cornish ironworkers in Wheeling, West Virginia, revealing the costs borne by both humans and nature in the American search for "civilization."

1. Phillis Wheatley Eulogizes Nature, 1773

An Hymn to the Morning

Attend my lays, ye ever honour'd nine,
Assist my labours, and my strains refine;
In smoothest numbers pour the notes along,
For bright Aurora now demands my song.
    Aurora, hail, and all the thousand dyes,
Which deck thy progress through the vaulted skies;

From Phillis Wheatley, *Poems on Various Subjects, Religious and Moral.* London: E. Johnson and A. Bell, 1773, pp. 56–59.

The morn awakes, and wide extends her rays,
On ev'ry leaf the gentle zephyr plays;
Harmonious lays the feather'd race resume,
Dart the bright eye, and shake the painted plume.
    Ye shady groves, your verdant gloom display
To shield your poet from the burning day:
Calliope, awake the sacred lyre,
While thy fair sisters fan the pleasing fire:
The bow'rs, the gales, the variegated skies
In all their pleasures in my bosom rise.
    See in the east th' illustrious king of day!
His rising radiance drives the shades away—
But oh! I feel his fervid leaves too strong,
And scarce begun, concludes th' abortive song.

An Hymn to the Evening

Soon as the sun forsook the eastern main
The pealing thunder shook the heav'nly plain;
Majestic grandeur! From the zephyr's wing,
Exhales the incense of the blooming spring,
Soft purl the streams, the birds renew their notes,
And through the air their mingled music floats.
    Through all the heav'ns what beauteous dyes are spread!
But the west glories in the deepest red:
So may our breasts with every virtue glow,
The living temples of our God below!
    Fill'd with the praise of him who gives the light,
And draws the sable curtains of the night,
Let placid slumbers soothe each weary mind,
At morn to wake more heav'nly, more refin'd;
So shall the labors of the day begin
More pure, more guarded from the snares of sin.
    Night's leaden sceptre seals my drowsy eyes,
Then cease, my song, till fair Aurora rise.

2. John James Audubon Describes
Shooting Birds, 1808–1834

As the "Marion" approached the inlet called "Indian Key," which is situated on the eastern coast of the peninsula of Florida, my heart swelled with uncontrollable delight. Our vessel once over the coral reef that every where stretches along the shore like a great wall reared by an army of giants, we found ourselves in safe anchorage,

---

From John James Audubon, *Delineations of American Scenery and Character.* New York: G. A. Baker & Co., 1926, pp. 181–187.

within a few furlongs of the land. The next moment saw the oars of a boat propelling us towards the shore, and in brief time, we stood on the desired beach. With what delightful feelings did we gaze on the objects around us!—the gorgeous flowers, the singular and beautiful plants, the luxuriant trees. The balmy air which we breathed filled us with animation, so pure and salubrious did it seem to be. The birds which we saw were almost all new to us; their lovely forms appeared to be arrayed in more brilliant apparel than I had ever before seen, and as they gambolled in happy playfulness among the bushes, or glided over the light green waters, we longed to form a more intimate acquaintance with them.

Students of nature spend little time in introduction, especially when they present themselves to persons who feel an interest in their pursuits. This was the case with Mr. Thruston, the Deputy Collector of the island, who shook us all heartily by the hand, and in a trice had a boat manned at our service. Accompanied by him, his pilot and fishermen, off we went, and after a short pull landed on a large key. Few minutes had elapsed, when shot after shot might be heard, and down came whirling through the air the objects of our desire. . . .

The pilot, besides being a first-rate shooter, possessed a most intimate acquaintance with the country. . . .

While the young gentlemen who accompanied us were engaged in procuring plants, shells, and small birds, he tapped me on the shoulder, and with a smile said to me, "Come along, I'll shew you something better worth your while." To the boat we betook ourselves, with the Captain and only a pair of tars, for more he said would not answer. The yawl for a while was urged at a great rate, but as we approached a point, the oars were taken in, and the pilot alone "sculling," desired us to make ready, for in a few minutes we should have "rare sport." As we advanced, the more slowly did we move, and the most profound silence was maintained, until suddenly coming almost in contact with a thick shrubbery of mangroves, we beheld, right before us, a multitude of pelicans. A discharge of artillery seldom produced more effect;—the dead, the dying, and the wounded, fell from the trees upon the water, while those unscathed flew screaming through the air in terror and dismay. "There," said he, "did not I tell you so? Is it not rare sport?" The birds, one after another, were lodged under the gunwales, when the pilot desired the captain to order the lads to pull away. Within about half a mile we reached the extremity of the key. "Pull away," cried the pilot, "never mind them on the wing, for those black rascals don't mind a little firing— now, boys, lay her close under the nests." And there we were, with four hundred cormorants' nests over our heads. The birds were sitting, and when we fired, the number that dropped as if dead, and plunged into the water was such, that I thought by some unaccountable means or other we had killed the whole colony. You would have smiled at the loud laugh and curious gestures of the pilot. "Gentlemen," said he, "almost a blank shot!" And so it was, for, on following the birds as one after another peeped up from the water, we found only a few unable to take to wing. "Now," said the pilot, "had you waited until *I had spoken* to the black villains, you might have killed a score or more of them." On inspection, we found that our shots had lodged in the tough dry twigs of which these birds form their nests, and that we had lost the more favourable opportunity of hitting them, by not waiting until they rose. "Never mind," said the pilot, "if you wish it, you may load the *Lady of the Green Mantle* with them in less than a week. Stand still, my lads; and now, gentlemen, in ten minutes you and I will bring down a score of them." And so we did. As we rounded the island, a beautiful bird of the species called Peale's Egret, came up and was shot. We now landed, took in the rest of our party, and returned to Indian Key, where we arrived three hours before sunset.

The sailors and other individuals to whom my name and pursuits had become known, carried our birds to the pilot's house. His good wife had a room ready for me to draw in, and my assistant might have been seen busily engaged in skinning, while George Lehman was making a sketch of the lovely isle.

Time is ever precious to the student of nature. I placed several birds in their natural attitudes, and began to delineate them. A dance had been prepared also, and no sooner was the sun lost to our eye, than males and females, including our captain and others from the vessel, were seen advancing gaily towards the house in full apparel. The birds were skinned, the sketch was on paper, and I told my young men to amuse themselves. As to myself, I could not join in the merriment, for, full of the remembrance of you, reader, and of the patrons of my work both in America and in Europe, I went on "grinding"—not on an organ, like the Lady of Bras d'Or, but on paper, to the finishing, not merely of my outlines, but of my notes respecting the objects seen this day. . . .

It was the end of April, when the nights were short and the days therefore long. Anxious to turn every moment to account, we were on board Mr. Thruston's boat at three next morning. Pursuing our way through the deep and tortuous channels that every where traverse the immense muddy soap-like flats that stretch from the outward Keys to the Main, we proceeded on our voyage of discovery. . . .

Coming under a Key on which multitudes of Frigate Pelicans had begun to form their nests, we shot a good number of them, and observed their habits. The boastings of our pilot were here confirmed by the exploits which he performed with his long gun, and on several occasions he brought down a bird from a height of fully a hundred yards. The poor birds, unaware of the range of our artillery, sailed calmly along, so that it was not difficult for "Long Tom," or rather for his owner, to furnish us with as many as we required. The day was spent in this manner, and towards night we returned, laden with booty, to the hospitable home of the pilot.

The next morning was delightful. The gentle sea-breeze glided over the flowery isle, the horizon was clear, and all was silent save the long breakers that rushed over the distant reefs. As we were proceeding towards some Keys, seldom visited by men, the sun rose from the bosom of the waters with a burst of glory that impressed on my soul the idea of that Power which called into existence so magnificent an object. The moon, thin and pale, as if ashamed to show her feeble light, concealed herself in the dim west. The surface of the waters shone in its tremulous smoothness, and the deep blue of the clear heavens was pure as the world that lies beyond them. The Heron heavily flew towards the land, like the glutton retiring at daybreak, with well-lined paunch, from the house of some wealthy patron of good cheer. The Night Heron and the Owl, fearful of day, with hurried flight sought safety in the recesses of the deepest swamps; while the Gulls and Terns, ever cheerful, gambolled over the water, exulting in the prospect of abundance. I also exulted in hope, my whole frame seemed to expand; and our sturdy crew shewed, by their merry faces, that nature had charms for them too. How much of beauty and joy is lost to them who never view the rising sun, and of whose wakeful existence the best half is nocturnal!

Twenty miles our men had to row before we reached "Sandy Island," and as on its level shores we all leaped, we plainly saw the southernmost cape of the Floridas. The flocks of birds that covered the shelly beaches, and those hovering over head, so astonished us that we could for a while scarcely believe our eyes. The first volley procured a supply of food sufficient for two days' consumption. Such tales, you have already been told, are well enough at a distance from the place to which they refer; but you will doubtless be still more surprised when I tell you that our first fire among the crowd of the Great Godwits laid prostrate sixty-five of these birds. Rose-coloured Curlews stalked gracefully beneath the mangroves; Purple Herons rose at almost every step we took, and each cactus supported the nest of a White Ibis. The air was darkened by whistling wings, while, on the waters, floated Gallinules and other interesting birds. We formed a kind of shed with sticks and grass, the sailor cook commenced his labours, and ere long we supplied the deficiencies of our fatigued frames. The business of the day over, we secured ourself from insects by means of musquito-nets, and were lulled to rest by the cackles of the beautiful Purple Gallinules!

3. James Fenimore Cooper Laments the "Wasty Ways" of Pioneers, 1823

Elizabeth was awakened by the exhilarating sounds of the martins, who were quarreling and chattering around the little boxes that were suspended above her windows, and the cries of Richard, who was calling, in tones as animating as the signs of the season itself—

"Awake! awake! my lady fair! the gulls are hovering over the lake already, and the heavens are alive with the pigeons. You may look an hour before you can find a hole, through which to get a peep at the sun. Awake! awake! lazy ones! Benjamin is overhauling the ammunition, and we only wait for our breakfasts, and away for the mountains and pigeon shooting." . . .

If the heavens were alive with pigeons, the whole village seemed equally in motion, with men, women, and children. Every species of fire-arms, from the French ducking-gun, with its barrel of near six-feet in length, to the common horseman's pistol, was to be seen in the hands of the men and boys; while bows and arrows, some made of the simple stick of a walnut sapling, and others in a rude imitation of the ancient crossbows, were carried by many of the latter. . . .

Among the sportsmen was to be seen the tall, gaunt form of Leather-stocking [Natty Bumppo], who was walking over the field, with his rifle hanging on his arm, his dogs following at his heels, now scenting the dead or wounded birds, that were beginning to tumble from the flocks, and then crouching under the legs of their master, as if they participated in his feelings at this wasteful and unsportsmanlike execution.

The reports of the fire-arms became rapid, whole volleys rising from the plain, as flocks of more than ordinary numbers darted over the opening, covering the field

From James Fenimore Cooper, *The Pioneers* (1823) in *The Works of James Fenimore Cooper.* 25 vols. London: George Routledge & Sons, 1895, vol. 4, Ch. 22, pp. 247–256.

with darkness, like an interposing cloud; and then the light smoke of a single piece would issue from among the leafless bushes on the mountain, as death was hurled on the retreat of the affrighted birds, who were rising from a volley, for many feet into the air, in a vain effort to escape the attacks of man. Arrows, and missiles of every kind, were seen in the midst of the flocks; and so numerous were the birds, and so low did they take their flight, that even long poles, in the hands of those on the sides of the mountain, were used to strike them to earth. . . .

So prodigious was the number of the birds, that the scattering fire of the guns, with the hurling of missiles, and the cries of the boys, had no other effect than to break off small flocks from the immense masses that continued to dart along the valley, as if the whole creation of the feathered tribe were pouring through that one pass. None pretended to collect the game, which lay scattered over the fields in such profusion as to cover the very ground with the fluttering victims.

Leather-stocking was a silent, but uneasy spectator of all these proceedings, but was able to keep his sentiments to himself until he saw the introduction of the swivel into the sports.

"This comes of settling a country!" he said—"here have I known the pigeons to fly for forty long years, and, till you made your clearings, there was nobody to skear or to hurt them. I loved to see them come into the woods, for they were company to a body; hurting nothing; being, as it was, as harmless as a garter-snake. But now it gives me sore thoughts when I hear the frighty things whizzing through the air, for I know its only a motion to bring out all the brats in the village at them. . . ."

Among the sportsmen was Billy Kirby, who, armed with an old musket, was leading, and without even looking into the air, was firing and shouting as his victims fell even on his own person. He heard the speech of Natty, and took upon himself to reply—

"What's that, old Leather-stocking!" he cried, "grumbling at the loss of a few pigeons! If you had to sow your wheat twice, and three times, as I have done, you wouldn't be so massyfully feeling'd to'ards the divils.—Hurrah, boys! Scatter the feathers. This is better than shooting at a turkey's head and neck, old fellow."

"It's better for you, maybe, Billy Kirby," replied the indignant old hunter, "and all them as don't know how to put a ball down a rifle barrel, or how to bring it up ag'n with a true aim; but it's wicked to be shooting into flocks in this wasty manner; and none do it, who know how to knock over a single bird. If a body has a craving for pigeon's flesh, why! it's made the same as all other creater's, for man's eating, but not to kill twenty and eat one. When I want such a thing I go into the woods till I find one to my liking, and then I shoot him off the branches without touching a feather of another, though there might be a hundred on the same tree. But you couldn't do such a thing, Billy Kirby—you couldn't do it if you tried."

"What's that you say, you old dried cornstalk! you sapless stub!" cried the wood-chopper. "You've grown mighty boasting, sin' you killed the turkey; but if you're for a single shot, here goes at that bird which comes on by himself."

. . . A single pigeon . . . was approaching the spot where the disputants stood, darting first from one side, and then to the other, cutting the air with the swiftness of lightning, and making a noise with its wings, not unlike the rushing of a bullet. Unfortunately for the woodchopper, notwithstanding his vaunt, he did not see his bird until it was too late for him to fire as it approached, and he pulled his trigger at the unlucky moment when it was darting immediately over his head. The bird continued its course with incredible velocity.

Natty lowered the rifle from his arm, when the challenge was made, and, waiting a moment, until the terrified victim had got in a line with his eyes, and had dropped near the bank of the lake, he raised it again with uncommon rapidity, and fired. It might have been chance, or it might have been skill, that produced the result; it was probably a union of both; but the pigeon whirled over in the air, and fell into the lake with a broken wing. At the sound of his rifle, both his dogs started from his feet, and in a few minutes the "slut" brought out the bird, still alive.

The wonderful exploit of Leather-stocking was noised through the field with great rapidity, and the sportsmen gathered in to learn the truth of the report.

"What," said young Edwards, "have you really killed a pigeon on the wing, Natty, with a single ball?"

"Haven't I killed loons before now, lad, that dive at the flash?" returned the hunter. "It's much better to kill only such as you want, without wasting your powder and lead, than to be firing into God's creaters in such a wicked manner. But I come out for a bird, and you know the reason why I like small game, Mr. Oliver, and now I have got one I will go home, for I don't relish to see these wasty ways that you are all practysing, as if the least thing wasn't made for use, and not to destroy."

"Thou sayest well, Leather-stocking," cried Marmaduke, "and I begin to think it time to put an end to this work of destruction."

"Put an ind, Judge, to your clearings. An't the woods His work as well as the pigeons? Use, but don't waste. Wasn't the woods made for the beasts and birds to harbour in? And when man wanted their flesh, their skins, or their feathers, there's the place to seek them. But I'll go to the hut with my own game, for I wouldn't touch one of the harmless things that kiver the ground here, looking up with their eyes on me, as if they only wanted tongues to say their thoughts."

With this sentiment in his mouth, Leather-stocking threw his rifle over his arm, and followed by his dogs, stepping across the clearing with great caution, taking care not to tread on one of the wounded birds that lay in his path, he soon entered the bushes on the margin and was hid from view.

4. Hudson River Painters Depict Nature and Civilization, 1836–1849

Kindred Spirits, 1849, by Asher Durand. This painting by the well-known painter of the Hudson River school shows nature poet William Cullen Bryant and nature painter Thomas Cole engaged in conversation in the Catskill Mountains. It commemorates Cole's death in 1848.

View from Mount Holyoke, 1836, by Thomas Cole. This painting contrasts dark wilderness on the left with a bright, pastoral landscape on the right. Note the deforested cuts on the hills and the artist's own umbrella in the lower right.

View from Mount Holyoke, Northampton, Massachusetts, after a Thunderstorm (The Oxbow), 1836, by Thomas Cole. The Metropolitan Museum of Art, NY, Gift of Mrs. Russell Sage, 1908 (0.228).

View of Tarrytown, Looking Towards the Highlands, undated, by John W. Hill (1839–1922).
On one side, a farmer with a horse and a team are transforming the wilderness into a settled
pastoral landscape with a road, farm house, orchard, and open ground, while in the background lies the fully developed community of Tarrytown, north of New York City. In the
foreground a painter and a hiker insert themselves into a landscape readied for recreation
and contemplation.

View of Tarrytown, Looking Towards the Highlands, undated, by John W. Hill (1839–1922), Oil on Canvas,
Gilcrease Museum, Tulsa, OK.

5. George Catlin on Indians, Nature, and Civilization, 1844

I . . . closely applied my hand to the labours of the art [of painting] for several years;
during which time my mind was continually reaching for some branch or enterprise
of the art, on which to devote a whole life-time of enthusiasm; when a delegation of
some ten or fifteen noble and dignified-looking Indians, from the wilds of the "Far
West," suddenly arrived in the city, arrayed and equipped in all their classic beauty,—
with shield and helmet,—with tunic and manteau,—tinted and tasselled off, exactly
for the painter's palette!

In silent and stoic dignity, these lords of the forest strutted about the city for a
few days, wrapped in their pictured robes, with their brows plumed with the quills of
the war-eagle, attracting the gaze and admiration of all who beheld them. After this,

From George Catlin, *North American Indians.* Ed. Peter Matthiessen. New York: Viking, 1989 [London,
1844], pp. 2–8.

they took their leave for Washington City, and I was left to reflect and regret, which I did long and deeply, until I came to the following deductions and conclusions.

Black and blue cloth and civilization are destined, not only to veil, but to obliterate the grace and beauty of Nature. Man, in the simplicity and loftiness of his nature, unrestrained and unfettered by the disguises of art, is surely the most beautiful model for the painter,—and the country from which he hails is unquestionably the best study or school of the arts in the world: such I am sure, from the models I have seen, is the wilderness of North America. And the history and customs of such a people, preserved by pictorial illustrations, are themes worthy the life-time of one man, and nothing short of the loss of my life, shall prevent me from visiting their country, and of becoming their historian.

With these views firmly fixed—armed, equipped, and supplied, I started out in the year 1832, and penetrated the vast and pathless wilds which are familiarly denominated the great "Far West" of the North American Continent, with a light heart, inspired with an enthusiastic hope and reliance that I could meet and overcome all the hazards and privations of a life devoted to the production of a literal and graphic delineation of the living manners, customs, and character of an interesting race of people, who are rapidly passing away from the face of the earth—lending a hand to a dying nation, who have no historians or biographers of their own to portray with fidelity their native looks and history; thus snatching from a hasty oblivion what could be saved for the benefit of posterity, and perpetuating it, as a fair and just monument, to the memory of a truly lofty and noble race. . . .

The Indians (as I shall call them), the savages or red men of the forests and prairies of North America, are at this time a subject of great interest and some importance to the civilized world; rendered more particularly so in this age, from their relative position to, and their rapid declension from, the civilized nations of the earth. A numerous nation of human beings, whose origin is beyond the reach of human investigation,—whose early history is lost—whose term of national existence is nearly expired—three-fourths of whose country has fallen into the possession of civilized man within the short space of 250 years—twelve millions of whose bodies have fattened the soil in the mean time; who have fallen victims to whiskey, the small-pox, and the bayonet; leaving at this time but a meagre proportion to live a short time longer, in the certain apprehension of soon sharing a similar fate. . . .

I am fully convinced, from a long familiarity with these people, that the Indian's misfortune has consisted chiefly in our ignorance of their true native character and disposition, which has always held us at a distrustful distance from them; inducing us to look upon them in no other light than that of a hostile foe, and worthy only of that system of continued warfare and abuse that has been for ever waged against them. . . .

The very use of the word savage, as it is applied in its general sense, I am inclined to believe is an abuse of the word, and the people to whom it is applied. The word, in its true definition, means no more than *wild,* or *wild man;* and a wild man may have been endowed by his Maker with all the humane and noble traits that inhabit the heart of a tame man. Our ignorance and dread or fear of these people, therefore, have given a new definition to the adjective; and nearly the whole civilized world apply the word *savage,* as expressive of the most ferocious, cruel, and murderous character that can be described. . . .

I have roamed about from time to time during seven or eight years, visiting and associating with, some three or four hundred thousand of these people, under an almost infinite variety of circumstances; and from the very many and decided voluntary acts of their hospitality and kindness, I feel bound to pronounce them, by nature, a kind and hospitable people. I have been welcomed generally in their country, and treated to the best that they could give me, without any charges made for my board; they have often escorted me through their enemies' country at some hazard to their own lives, and aided me in passing mountains and rivers with my awkward baggage; and under all of these circumstances of exposure, no Indian ever betrayed me, struck me a blow, or stole from me a shilling's worth of my property that I am aware of.

This is saying a great deal, (and proving it too, if the reader will believe me) in favour of the virtues of these people; when it is borne in mind, as it should be, that there is no law in their land to punish a man for theft—that locks and keys are not known in their country—that the commandments have never been divulged amongst them; nor can any human retribution fall upon the head of a thief, save the disgrace which attaches as a stigma to his character, in the eyes of his people about him. . . .

I cannot help but repeat . . . that the tribes of the red men of North America, as a nation of human beings, are on their wane; that (to use their own very beautiful figure) "they are fast travelling to the shades of their fathers, towards the setting sun;" and that the traveler who would see these people in their native simplicity and beauty, must needs be hastily on his way to the prairies and Rocky Mountains, or he will see them only as they are now seen on the frontiers, as a basket of *dead game,*—harassed, chased, bleeding and dead; with their plumage and colours despoiled; to be gazed amongst in vain for some system or moral, or for some scale by which to estimate their true native character, other than that which has too often recorded them but a dark and unintelligible mass of cruelty and barbarity.

6. Ralph Waldo Emerson Expounds on Nature and Wealth, 1844

The Over-Soul

Man is a stream whose source is hidden. Our being is descending into us from we know not whence. The most exact calculator has no prescience that somewhat incalculable may not balk the very next moment. I am constrained every moment to acknowledge a higher origin for events than the will I call mine.

As with events, so is it with thoughts. When I watch that flowing river, which, out of regions I see not, pours for a season its streams into me, I see that I am a pensioner; not a cause but a surprised spectator of this ethereal water; that I desire and look up and put myself in the attitude of reception, but from some alien energy the visions come.

The Supreme Critic on the errors of the past and the present, and the only prophet of that which must be, is that great nature in which we rest as the earth lies

From Ralph Waldo Emerson, *The Complete Essays and Other Writings of Ralph Waldo Emerson,* ed. Brooks Atkinson. New York: Modern Library, 1940 [originally published 1944], pp. 262, 277–278, 693–697, 715–716.

in the soft arms of the atmosphere; that Unity, that Over-Soul, within which every man's particular being is contained and made one with all other; that common heart of which all sincere conversation is the worship, to which all right action is submission; that overpowering reality which confutes our tricks and talents, and constrains every one to pass for what he is, and to speak from his character and not from his tongue, and which evermore tends to pass into our thought and hand and become wisdom and virtue and power and beauty. We live in succession, in division, in parts, in particles. Meantime within man is the soul of the whole; the wise silence; the universal beauty, to which every part and particle is equally related; the eternal ONE. And this deep power in which we exist and whose beatitude is all accessible to us, is not only self-sufficing and perfect in every hour, but the act of seeing and the thing seen, the seer and the spectacle, the subject and the object, are one. We see the world piece by piece, as the sun, the moon, the animal, the tree; but the whole, of which these are the shining parts, is the soul. . . . The soul gives itself, alone, original and pure, to the Lonely, Original and Pure, who, on that condition, gladly inhabits, leads and speaks through it. Then is it glad, young and nimble. It is not wise, but it sees through all things. It is not called religious, but it is innocent. It calls the light its own, and feels that the grass grows and the stone falls by a law inferior to, and dependent on, its nature. Behold, it saith, I am born into the great, the universal mind. I, the imperfect, adore my own Perfect. I am somehow receptive of the great soul, and thereby I do overlook the sun and the stars and feel them to be the fair accidents and effects which change and pass. More and more the surges of everlasting nature enter into me, and I become public and human in my regards and actions. So come I to live in thoughts and act with energies which are immortal.

Wealth

Every man is a consumer, and ought to be a producer. He fails to make his place good in the world unless he not only pays his debt but also adds something to the common wealth. Nor can he do justice to his genius without making some larger demand on the world than a bare subsistence. He is by constitution expensive, and needs to be rich.

Wealth has its source in applications of the mind to nature, from the rudest strokes of spade and axe up to the last secrets of art. Intimate ties subsist between thought and all production; because a better order is equivalent to vast amounts of brute labor. The forces and the resistances are nature's, but the mind acts in bringing things from where they abound to where they are wanted; in wise combining; in directing the practice of the useful arts, and in the creation of finer values by fine art, by eloquence, by song, or the reproductions of memory. Wealth is in applications of mind to nature; and the art of getting rich consists not in industry, much less in saving, but in a better order, in timeliness, in being at the right spot. One man has stronger arms or longer legs; another sees by the course of streams and growth of markets where land will be wanted, makes a clearing to the river, goes to sleep and wakes up rich. Steam is no stronger now than it was a hundred years ago; but is put to better use. A clever fellow was acquainted with the expansive force of steam; he also saw the wealth of wheat and grass rotting in Michigan. Then he cunningly screws on the steam-pipe to the wheat-crop. Puff now, O Steam! The steam puffs and expands as before, but this time it is dragging all Michigan at its back to hungry New York and hungry England. Coal lay in ledges under the ground since the Flood, until a laborer with pick and windlass brings it to the surface. We may well call it black diamonds. Every basket is power and civilization. For coal is a portable climate. It carries the heat of the tropics to Labrador and the polar circle; and it is the means of transporting itself whithersoever it is wanted. Watt and Stephenson whispered . . . their secret, that *a half-ounce of coal will draw two tons a mile,* and coal carries coal, by rail and by boat, to make Canada as warm as Calcutta; and with its comfort brings its industrial power. . . .

When the farmer's peaches are taken from under the tree and carried into town, they have a new look and a hundredfold value over the fruit which grew on the same bough and lies fulsomely on the ground. The craft of the merchant is this bringing a thing from where it abounds to where it is costly.

Wealth begins in a tight roof that keeps the rain and wind out; in a good pump that yields you plenty of sweet water; in two suits of clothes, so to change your dress when you are wet; in dry sticks to burn, in a good double-wick lamp, and three meals; in a horse or a locomotive to cross the land, in a boat to cross the sea; in tools to work with, in books to read; and so in giving on all sides by tools and auxiliaries the greatest possible extension to our powers; as if it added feet and hands and eyes and blood, length to the day, and knowledge and good will. . . .

Fire, steam, lightning, gravity, ledges of rock, mines of iron, lead, quicksilver, tin and gold; forests of all woods; fruits of all climates; animals of all habits; the powers of tillage; the fabrics of his chemic laboratory; the webs of his loom; the masculine draught of his locomotive; the talismans of the machine-shop; all grand and subtile things, minerals, gases, ethers, passions, war, trade, government—are his natural playmates, and according to the excellence of the machinery in each human being is his attraction for the instruments he is to employ. The world is his tool-chest, and he is successful, or his education is carried on just so far, as is the marriage of his faculties with nature, or the degree in which he takes up things into himself.

The strong race is strong on these terms. The Saxons are the merchants of the world; now, for a thousand years, the leading race, and by nothing more than their quality of personal independence, and in its special modification, pecuniary independence. No reliance for bread and games on the government; no clanship, no patriarchal style of living by the revenues of a chief, no marrying-on, no system of clientship suits them; but every man must pay his scot. The English are prosperous and peaceable, with their habit of considering that every man must take care of himself and has himself to thank if he do not maintain and improve his position in society. . . .

The counting-room maxims liberally expounded are laws of the universe. The merchant's economy is a coarse symbol of the soul's economy. It is to spend for power and not for pleasure. It is to invest income; that is to say, to take up particulars into generals; days into integral eras—literary, emotive, practical—of its life, and still to ascend in its investment. The merchant has but one rule, *absorb and invest;* he is to be capitalist; the scraps and filings must be gathered back into the crucible; the gas and smoke must be burned, and earnings must not go to increase expense, but to capital again. Well, the man must be capitalist. Will he spend his income, or will he invest? His body and every organ is under the same law. His body is a jar in which the liquor of life is stored. Will he spend for pleasure? The way to ruin is short and facile. Will he not spend but hoard for power? It passes through the sacred fermentations, by that law of nature whereby everything climbs to higher platforms, and bodily vigor becomes mental and moral vigor. The bread he eats is first strength and animal spirits; it becomes, in higher laboratories, imagery and thought; and in still higher results, courage and endurance. This is the right compound interest; this is capital doubled, quadrupled, centupled; man raised to his highest power.

The true thrift is always to spend on the higher plane; to invest and invest, with keener avarice, that he may spend in spiritual creation and not in augmenting animal existence. Nor is the man enriched, in repeating the old experiments of animal sensation; nor unless through new powers and ascending pleasures he knows himself by the actual experience of higher good to be already on the way to the highest.

7. Henry David Thoreau on Nature Versus Civilization, 1854

Sounds

My house was on the side of a hill, immediately on the edge of the larger wood, in the midst of a young forest of pitch pines and hickories, and half a dozen rods from the pond, to which a narrow footpath led down the hill. In my front yard grew the strawberry, blackberry, and life-everlasting, johnswort and goldenrod, shrub oaks and sand cherry, blueberry and groundnut. Near the end of May, the sand cherry (*Cerasus pumila*) adorned the sides of the path with its delicate flowers arranged in umbels cylindrically about its short stems, which last, in the fall, weighed down with good-sized and handsome cherries, fell over in wreaths like rays on every side. I tasted them out of compliment to Nature, though they were scarcely palatable. The sumach (*Rhus glabra*) grew luxuriantly about the house, pushing up through the embankment which I had made, and growing five or six feet the first season. Its broad pinnate tropical leaf was pleasant though strange to look on. The large buds, suddenly pushing out late in the spring from dry sticks which had seemed to be dead, developed themselves as by magic into graceful green and tender boughs, an inch in diameter; and sometimes, as I sat at my window, so heedlessly did they grow and tax their weak joints, I heard a fresh and tender bough suddenly fall like a fan to the ground, when there was not a breath of air stirring, broken off by its own weight. In August, the large masses of berries, which, when in flower, had attracted many wild bees, gradually assumed their bright velvety crimson hue, and by their weight again bent down and broke the tender limbs.

As I sit at my window this summer afternoon, hawks are circling about my clearing; the tantivy of wild pigeons, flying by twos and threes athwart my view, or perching restless on the white pine boughs behind my house, gives a voice to the air; a fish hawk dimples the glassy surface of the pond and brings up a fish; a mink steals out of the marsh before my door and seizes a frog by the shore; the sedge is bending under the weight of the reed-birds flitting hither and thither; and for the last

---

From Henry David Thoreau, "Sounds," and "The Beanfield," in *Walden.* Boston: Ticknor and Fields, 1854, pp. 124–126, 168–171, 176.

half-hour I have heard the rattle of railroad cars, now dying away and then reviving like the beat of a partridge, conveying travellers from Boston to the country. For I did not live so out of the world as that boy who, as I hear, was put out to a farmer in the east part of the town, but ere long ran away and came home again, quite down at the heel and homesick. He had never seen such a dull and out-of-the-way place, the folks were all gone off; why, you couldn't even hear the whistle! I doubt if there is such a place in Massachusetts now:—

> In truth, our village has become a butt
> For one of those fleet railroad shafts, and o'er
> Our peaceful plain its soothing sound is—Concord.

The Fitchburg Railroad touches the pond about a hundred rods south of where I dwell. I usually go the village along its causeway, and am, as it were, related to society by this link. The men on the freight trains, who go over the whole length of the road, bow to me as to an old acquaintance, they pass me so often, and apparently they take me for an employee; and so I am. I too would fain be a track-repairer somewhere in the orbit of the earth.

The whistle of the locomotive penetrates my woods summer and winter, sounding like a scream of a hawk sailing over some farmer's yard, informing me that many restless city merchants are arriving within the circle of the town, or adventurous country traders from the other side. As they come under one horizon, they shout their warning to get off the track to the other, heard sometimes through the circles of two towns. Here come your groceries, country; your rations, countrymen! Nor is there any man so independent on his farm that he can say them nay. And here's your pay for them! screams the countryman's whistle; timber like long battering-rams going twenty miles an hour against the city's walls, and chairs enough to seat all the weary and heavy-laden that dwell within them. With such huge and lumbering civility the country hands a chair to the city. All the Indian huckleberry hills are stripped, all the cranberry meadows are raked into the city. Up comes the cotton, down goes the woven cloth; up comes the silk, down goes the woollen; up come the books, but down goes the wit that writes them.

The Beanfield

Meanwhile my beans, the length of whose rows, added together, was seven miles already planted, were impatient to be hoed, for the earliest had grown considerably before the latest were in the ground; indeed they were not easily to be put off. What was the meaning of this so steady and self-respecting, this small Herculean labor, I knew not. I came to love my rows, my beans, though so many more than I wanted. They attached me to the earth, and so I got strength like Antæus. But why should I raise them? Only Heaven knows. This was my curious labor all summer,—to make this portion of the earth's surface, which had yielded only cinquefoil, blackberries, johnswort, and the like, before, sweet wild fruits and pleasant flowers, produce instead this pulse. What shall I learn of beans or beans of me? I cherish them, I hoe them, early and late I have an eye to them; and this is my day's work. It is a fine broad leaf to look on. My auxiliaries are the dews and rains which water this dry soil, and what fertility is in the soil itself, which for the most part is lean and effete. My enemies are worms, cool days, and most of all woodchucks. The last have nibbled for me a quarter of an acre clean. But what right had I to oust johnswort and the rest, and break up their ancient herb garden? Soon, however, the remaining beans will be too tough for them, and go forward to meet new foes.

When I was four years old as I well remember, I was brought from Boston to this my native town, through these very woods and this field, to the pond. It is one of the oldest scenes stamped on my memory. And now to-night my flute has waked the echoes over that very water. The pines still stand here older than I; or, if some have fallen, I have cooked my supper with their stumps, and a new growth is rising all around, preparing another aspect for new infant eyes. Almost the same johnswort springs from the same perennial root in this pasture, and even I have at length helped to clothe that fabulous landscape of my infant dreams, and one of the results of my presence and influence is seen in these bean leaves, corn blades, and potato vines.

I planted about two acres and a half of upland; and as it was only about fifteen years since the land was cleared, and I myself had got out two or three cords of stumps, I did not give it any manure; but in the course of the summer it appeared by the arrowheads which I turned up in hoeing, that an extinct nation had anciently dwelt here and planted corn and beans ere white men came to clear the land, and so, to some extent, had exhausted the soil for this very crop.

Before yet any woodchuck or squirrel had run across the road, or the sun had got above the shrub oaks, while all the dew was on, though the farmers warned me against it,—I would advise you to do all your work if possible while the dew is on,—I began to level the ranks of haughty weeds in my bean-field and throw dust upon their heads. Early in the morning I worked barefooted, dabbling like a plastic artist in the dewy and crumbling sand, but later in the day the sun blistered my feet. There the sun lighted me to hoe beans, pacing slowly backward and forward over that yellow gravelly upland, between the long green rows, fifteen rods, the one end terminating in a shrub oak copse where I could rest in the shade, the other in a blackberry field where the green berries deepened their tints by the time I had made another bout. Removing the weeds, putting fresh soil about the bean stems, and en-couraging this weed which I had sown, making the yellow soil express its summer thought in bean leaves and blossoms rather than in wormwood and piper and millet grass, making the earth say beans instead of grass,—this was my daily work. As I had little aid from horses or cattle, or hired men or boys, or improved implements of husbandry, I was much slower, and became much more intimate with my beans than usual. But labor of the hands, even when pursued to the verge of drudgery, is per-haps never the worst form of idleness. It has a constant and imperishable moral, and to the scholar it yields a classic result. A very *agricola laboriosus* was I to travellers bound westward through Lincoln and Wayland to nobody knows where; they sitting at their ease in gigs, with elbows on knees, and reins loosely hanging in festoons; I the home-staying, laborious native of the soil. But soon my homestead was out of their sight and thought. It was the only open and cultivated field for a great distance on either side of the road, so they made the most of it; and sometimes the man in the field heard more of travellers' gossip and comment than was meant for his ear: "Beans so late! peas so late!"—for I continued to plant when others had begun to hoe,—the ministerial husbandman had not suspected it. "Corn, my boy, for fodder; corn for fodder." "Does he *live* there?" asks the black bonnet of the gray coat; and the hard-featured farmer reins up his grateful dobbin to inquire what you are doing where he sees no manure in the furrow, and recommends a little chip dirt, or any little

waste stuff, or it may be ashes or plaster. But here were two acres and a half of furrows, and only a hoe for cart and two hands to draw it,—there being an aversion to
other carts and horses,—and chip dirt far away. Fellow-travellers as they rattled by
compared it aloud with the fields which they had passed, so that I came to know how
I stood in the agricultural world. This was one field not in Mr. Colman's report. And,
by the way, who estimates the value of the crop which nature yields in the still wilder
fields unimproved by man? The crop of *English* hay is carefully weighed, the moisture calculated, the silicates and the potash; but in all dells and pond-holes in the
woods and pastures and swamps grows a rich and various crop only unreaped by
man. Mine was, as it were, the connecting link between wild and cultivated fields; as
some states are civilized, and others half-civilized, and others savage or barbarous,
so my field was, though not in a bad sense, a half-cultivated field. They were beans
cheerfully returning to their wild and primitive state that I cultivated, and my hoe
played the *Ranz des Vaches* for them. . . .

Those summer days which some of my contemporaries devoted to the fine arts
in Boston or Rome, and others to contemplation in India, and others to trade in
London or New York, I thus, with the other farmers of New England, devoted to
husbandry. Not that I wanted beans to eat, for I am by nature a Pythagorean, so far
as beans are concerned, whether they mean porridge or voting, and exchanged
them for rice; but, perchance, as some must work in fields if only for the sake of
tropes and expression, to serve a parable-maker one day. It was on the whole a rare
amusement, which, continued too long, might have become a dissipation. Though I
gave them no manure, and did not hoe them all once, I hoed them unusually well as
far as I went, and was paid for it in the end, "there being in truth," as [English diarist
John] Evelyn says, "no compost or lætation whatsoever comparable to this continual
motion, repastination, and turning of the mould with the spade." "The earth," he adds
elsewhere, "especially if fresh, has a certain magnetism in it, by which it attracts
the salt, power, or virtue (call it either) which gives it life, and is the logic of all the
labor and stir we keep about it, to sustain us; all dungings and other sordid temper-
ings being but the vicars succedaneous to this improvement." Moreover, this being
one of those "worn-out and exhausted lay fields which enjoy their sabbath," had perchance, as [seventeenth-century scientist] Sir Kenelm Digby thinks likely, attracted
"vital spirits" from the air. I harvested twelve bushels of beans.

8. Rebecca Harding Davis on Pollution and Human Life in the Iron Mills, 1861

> Is this the end?
> O Life, as futile, then, as frail!
> What hope of answer of redress?

A cloudy day: do you know what that is in a town of iron-works? The sky sank
down before dawn, muddy, flat, immovable. The air is thick, clammy with the breath
of crowded human beings. It stifles me. I open the window, and, looking out, can
scarcely see through the rain the grocer's shop opposite, where a crowd of drunken

From Rebecca Harding Davis, "Life in the Iron Mills," *Atlantic Monthly,* April 1861, pp. 430–451.

Irishmen are puffing Lynchburg tobacco in their pipes. I can detect the scent through all the foul smells ranging loose in the air.

The idiosyncrasy of this town is smoke. It rolls sullenly in slow folds from the great chimneys of the iron-foundries, and settles down in black, slimy pools on the muddy streets. Smoke on the wharves, smoke on the dingy boats, on the yellow river,—clinging in a coating of greasy soot to the house-front, the two faded poplars, the faces of the passers-by. The long train of mules, dragging masses of pig-iron through the narrow street, have a foul vapor hanging to their reeking sides. Here, inside, is a little broken figure of an angel pointing upward from the mantel-shelf; but even its wings are covered with smoke, clotted and black. Smoke everywhere! A dirty canary chirps desolately in a cage beside me. Its dream of green fields and sunshine is a very old dream—almost worn out, I think.

From the back-window I can see a narrow brick-yard sloping down to the river-side, strewed with rain-butts and tubs. The river, dull and tawny-colored, (*la belle riviere!*) drags itself sluggishly along, tired of the heavy weight of boats and coal-barges. What wonder? When I was a child, I used to fancy a look of weary, dumb appeal upon the face of the negro-like river slavishly bearing its burden day after day. Something of the same idle notion comes to me today, when from the street-window I look on the slow stream of human life creeping past, night and morning, to the great mills. Masses of men, with dull, besotted faces bent to the ground, sharpened here and there by pain or cunning; skin and muscle and flesh begrimed with smoke and ashes; stooping all night over boiling caldrons of metal, laired by day in dens of drunkenness and infamy; breathing from infancy to death an air saturated with fog and grease and soot, vileness for soul and body. What do you make of a case like that, amateur psychologist? You call it an altogether serious thing to be alive: to these men it is a drunken jest, a joke,—horrible to angels perhaps, to them commonplace enough. My fancy about the river was an idle one: it is no type of such a life. What if it be stagnant and slimy here? It knows that beyond there waits for it odorous sunlight,—quaint old gardens, dusky with soft, green foliage of apple-trees, and flushing crimson with roses,—air, and fields, and mountains. The future of the Welsh puddler passing just now is not so pleasant. To be stowed away, after his grimy work is done, in a hole in the muddy graveyard, and after that,—*not* air, nor green fields, nor curious roses. . . .

If you could go into this mill where Deborah [cousin to a mill worker] lay, and drag out from the hearts of these men the terrible tragedy of their lives, taking it as a symptom of the disease of their class, no ghost Horror would terrify you more. A reality of soul-starvation, of living death, that meets you every day under the besotted faces on the street,—I can paint nothing of this, only give you the outside outlines of a night, a crisis in the life of one man: whatever muddy depth of soul-history lies beneath you can read according to the eyes God has given you.

ψ *E S S A Y S*

The ambivalence expressed in the documents over the value of nature versus the values of market society stems from deeper conflicts within an emerging industrial-capitalist society. More than colonial society, capitalism in the nineteenth century split culture from nature, public from private, reason from emotion, and male from female. The public sphere of production and politics was dominated by men; the private sphere of the home and emotion was culturally assigned to women. Science and technology became instruments of capitalist development; nature, a refuge for spirit and emotion.

The three essays that follow consider the relationships between nature and the market. Michael Heiman, a geographer at Dickinson College, argues in the opening selection that capitalist production was of primary importance to nineteenth-century elites. Nature was secondary to civilization as both a commodity and a refuge for humans. The primary reality of the Hudson Valley lay in its use for commodity production through lumbering, tanning, mining, quarrying, brewing, brick and cement making, and the manufacture of textiles and detachable shirt collars. Those "blemishes" were ignored by artists and tour guides, who instead painted and promoted an ideal nature as a refuge for humans. Both viewpoints had a homocentric orientation: Civilization was the ultimate reality.

The second essay, by historian Robert Kuhn McGregor of Sangamon State University, suggests that a few nineteenth-century Americans recognized the primacy of nature over civilization. Preeminent among them was Henry David Thoreau. Thoreau's biocentric, or life-centered, vision included the activities of mammals, plants, and other organisms as living actors. Humans were part of nature; animals had their own civilizations. To write a biocentric history, McGregor argues, "scholars must discard the notion that human beings are the center of all things." In the long term, nature is the ultimate reality.

In the third essay, Elizabeth Blum, a historian at Troy State University, discusses the complex relationship between slave women and nature. She shows how wilderness was a source of both protection and threat, foods and medicines, material benefits and supernatural beings. Black women thus perceived nature quite differently from the way both the white men of the market economy, who used it for material gain, and the Romantics, who viewed it as an exemplar of God's beneficent presence in the world, perceived it. As a group, therefore, the three essays explore the ways in which nineteenth-century humans assigned value to nature and civilization in the context of an emerging market society.

Civilization over Nature

MICHAEL HEIMAN

The identification of nature as a refuge removed from the negative social and environmental externalities accompanying industrial production is a common feature of American landscape ideology. More specifically, nature, in the form of residential and recreation space, is perceptually and physically appropriated as a subset of personal consumption space. Here, in this defended space, individuals, be they workers or owners, can attempt to escape the rigors of the workplace to consume the hard-earned fruits of their efforts. Nature, however, is also essential for commodity production, furnishing both the raw material as well as the space required for capital accumulation. As such, the defense of nature as residential and recreational consumption space

---

Excerpts from Michael Heiman, "Production Confronts Consumption: Landscape Perception and Social Conflict in the Hudson Valley," *Environment and Planning D: Society and Space* 7 (1989): pp. 165–173. Reprinted by permission of Pion, Ltd.

in the form of wilderness preserves, greenbelts, and even as suburban backyards, presents serious problems for the expansion of capital.

Nature as a Refuge from, and as an Input to, Commodity Production

Although not exclusive to capitalism, the interpretation of nature as a refuge from the workplace is a basic expression of underlying structural contradiction for capitalism. . . . In an expanding economy the conceptual partitioning of space into production zones and consumption zones (or what are perceived as nature zones) is acceptable. This is because the separation, whether conceptual or through the actual practice of land use, permits the development of production zones (and of the resources contained or utilized within) as inputs into commodity production for exchange value, while reserving those areas set aside from commodity production, and defended against the attending environmental degradation and social conflict, as places for biological, psychological, and social rejuvenation. Places for social rejuvenation typically encompass areas where we reside and recreate.

The Hudson Valley . . . since the colonial period . . . was, and continues as, one of the most significant battlegrounds between the forces of production and those seeking protection of leisure and residential consumption amenities. Having given birth and inspiration to artistic, literary, and design schools that dominated nineteenth-century landscape perceptions and continue to inspire contemporary land use battles, the Hudson Valley experience is at once unique yet commonplace and is therefore of value in an examination of capitalist landscape ideology.

Images of Nature in the [Hudson] Valley: The Ideal and the Reality

Today, with the Valley's industries and cities oriented toward onshore transportation routes and away from the river, one can scarcely imagine that the calm waters of the majestic river 150 years ago supported one of the most intensively utilized commercial routes in the nation. With a bed lying below sea level, the broad lower half of the Hudson River could accommodate ocean-going vessels as far as the Albany–Troy area. . . . Here, goods were exchanged for transport on the famous Erie Canal, completed in 1825 through the Mohawk Valley to Buffalo on Lake Erie. Taken together, the Hudson–Mohawk valleys provided the only navigable break through the Appalachian Mountains in the United States.

From the 1780s until the 1830s, travel on the river was dominated by the slow, broad-bottom Hudson River sailing sloop. Averaging 100 tons in capacity, the ships would take from a few days to a week to make the 150-mile run from Albany to New York City, depending upon wind and tides. Every Hudson village had its own fleet, and at the height of sloop use in the 1830s over a hundred could be spotted from a single vantage on the River's broad Tappen Zee section. In 1807, however, Robert Fulton's *Clermont* made the first steam voyage up the Hudson from New York to Albany in just over 32 hours. Soon thereafter steam became the preferred mode of passenger travel, with the sloops reserved for bulk cargo. By 1840 over a hundred steamboats and several hundred sloops were active day and night on the river, and flotillas of up to 50 barges, fastened together and with a steamtug in the middle for propulsion, were beginning to appear.

The Hudson Valley also gave birth and inspiration to the young nation's first indigenous school of painting. Beginning in 1825 with Thomas Cole's arrival in New York City and his initial trip by steamboat up the Hudson, the Hudson River School of Landscape Painting lasted until the 1870s. Impressed by Alexander von Humboldt, Louis Agassiz, and by other naturalists, Cole and his colleagues were pioneering in the exactitude of their geological and botanical depictions. Nonetheless, the popular acceptance of the Hudson River School as portraying a wilderness condition actually found in the Valley and in the adjoining Catskill Mountains was itself mistaken. Thus the Hudson's 'wild shores' already ran through the heart of what was referred to as the 'breadbasket of the nation' from the close of the Revolutionary War until the 1820s, when the Erie Canal provided access to newer wheat-growing regions in western New York and, later, in the Midwest USA. At the peak of the school's influence in the 1830s and 1840s, the intensely settled Valley swarmed with Europeans on the Grand Tour of America's 'wild wonders'. Judging from their diaries as they steamed up the river, most appeared oblivious to intense shoreline resource extraction and to the squalid living conditions of adjoining tenant farmers.

A closer examination of the discrepancy between the ideal, as depicted by nineteenth-century artists and essayists, and the reality, at least as recorded in gazetteers and by more discerning travelers, is enlightening. This is because it illuminates the tension in bourgeois landscape perception as first fashioned in the Valley. Moreover, it underscores the increasing futility of private efforts to maintain a distance between landscapes of production and consumption in the years prior to state assistance for that purpose.

Although tenancy, and the violence of the French, the Indian, and the Revolutionary wars retarded settlement in the Valley, development resumed with the subsequent peace. Production greatly accelerated during the War of 1812, when the Valley emerged as an important manufacturing center to supply the goods no longer available from Britain. Already by 1830 most of the Valley's once-thick forest cover had been cut at least once, and usually several times, to supply the fuel and raw material for the numerous forges, steamboats, and tanneries active in the region. At the scenic Hudson Highlands, straddling the river at West Point 40 miles north of New York City, the forest cover upon Cole's first passage was already greater than it had been 20 years earlier, when the entire area had been cleared to fuel nearby iron foundries. To the north, deforestation was so severe in Rensselaer County that according to one observer the remaining "woodlands [were] . . . worth more than the same quality of land under tolerable cultivation, including buildings, fences and every improvement. . . ."

On the west bank, the Catskill counties were alive by the 1820s with lumbering, tanning, and mining activities. The mountainous terrain had been opened for commercial exploitation through an intricate system of canals and turnpikes. Between 1824 and 1850 the mountain valleys above Cole's studio in the village of Catskill supported the largest tanning industry in the nation. Hides were brought in from as far away as Patagonia. Throughout the Catskills thousands of acres of hemlock were cleared and stripped for the tannin in the bark, and once-pristine mountain streams now ran rancid with hair, grease, acids, and other tanning wastes.

Downriver the west bank areas around Nyack, Haverstraw, and Kingston were already leading quarrying and brick manufacturing centers by the 1820s, supplying much of the material used to pave and build New York City. With the completion of the Delaware and Hudson Canal in 1828, designed to bring in coal from the Pennsylvania fields, the Kingston (Rondout) terminus became a major shipping and manufacturing center. Kingston was also the center of the state's cement production following discovery of deposits through canal construction. Miles of shaft were sunk to quarry Rosendale Cement, world-famous for its capacity to harden under water. By mid-century, 30 miles north of New York City, Haverstraw's brick trade had expanded to cover several miles of waterfront with clay quarries, drying racks, kilns, and shipment wharves. Here labor militancy was a perennial issue, with scabs commonly brought in from Quebec. At about the same time, nearby, at Rockland Lake on a ledge above the Hudson, several thousand people were employed at ice production just to serve the cooling requirements of the city downriver.

With its shallow slope, the eastern bank of the river supported most of the agriculture and even more settlement than the western shore. Here major iron foundries and forges were established at Troy, Hudson, Poughkeepsie, Cold Spring, and Peekskill. On the east bank, 30 miles south of Albany, Hudson was the fourth largest city in the state in 1820 and an international port of trade noted for woollen manufacturing, whaling, and quarrying. Poughkeepsie, 40 miles farther downriver, was also known for its textiles and as an important brewing and limestone center.

Founded by Yankees in the 1780s, Troy was the quintessential manufacturing boom town. In 1827 the wife of a cobbler, fed up with repeated washing of her husband's shirts just to clean the collar, cut off the soiled section and invented the detachable shirt collar. Lasting until the invention of the washing machine in the early twentieth century, the US shirt collar industry at its height employed 15,000 workers in over 20 factories spread throughout the city.

Back on the west bank, Albany, chartered in 1686, was already the state capital and an important brewing and lumber market by the time the Erie Canal opened. The city's 4300-foot-long mooring basin was the principal transshipment center for canal traffic. Already by the mid-1830s, at the height of European fascination with the Valley's natural wonders, the city's dozen steamboats provided daily service to New York City, with 700,000 passengers arriving and departing yearly.

On both banks the river cities and towns were shipment points for densely settled hinterlands. The 10 Valley-counties north of New York City (Westchester, Putnam, Dutchess, Columbia, Rensselaer, Albany, Greene, Ulster, Orange, and Rockland) contained 271,000 inhabitants in 1820. No doubt this was quite low by British standards. The greater London area already had over 1,250,000 people by this period, almost 10 times that of New York City, by then the largest city in the USA. Nonetheless, the Hudson Valley was certainly not the rural semiwilderness depicted by the artists and fancied by itinerant European visitors.

Veiling the disagreeable facts of production in this celebrated landscape required a careful sleight of hand. In their rush to fulfill the growing European and American demand for views of a romantic wilderness, Cole and his contemporaries, including Asher B. Durand, Frederick E. Church, and poet William Cullen Bryant, often overlooked or screened out with vegetation the burnt-over fields, stinking tanneries, polluted streams, clamorous sawmills, and other production intrusions. Deeply religious,

Cole avoided urban scenes because he considered urban social life as lacking in those wholesome qualities which allowed art to be a source of moral inspiration. When they did address human habitation in the valley, Cole and the other artists typically preferred Sunday scenes so as to avoid signs of work and the harsher realities of tenant farming.

The artists were not, however, oblivious to the desecration of their cherished landscape. With patrons actually admonishing him for not putting enough wild nature into his scenes, Cole's lament over the destruction of his favored sketching places in the Catskills was restricted to his prose and, later, to his allegorical canvasses. In a letter of 1836 he complained that the tanneries and a railroad then under construction along Catskill Creek above his studio were "cutting down all of the trees in the beautiful valley on which I have looked so often with a loving eye." "Tell this to [Asher B] Durand—not that I wish to give him a pain, but that I want him to join with me in maledictions on all dollar-godded utilitarians."

Certainly the discord was nowhere near the extent found in Britain, where Manchester's 'satanic mills' and pale of soot had already been used as symbols of fear and apprehension by poets and artists some decades earlier. For many the Hudson region, by comparison, represented a fresh slate, a landscape where wilderness might still give way to a more harmonious and even sublime pattern when viewed from the proper perspective.

The Recreational Escape to Nature

Eagerly sought out by wealthy collectors in New York and London, the Hudson River artists enjoyed an unusual degree of success and exposure. In the Hudson Highlands and along the Catskill escarpment luxurious mountaintop hotels were erected to provide a comfortable experience for the would-be wilderness traveler in search of the scenes made famous by the artists. Many river travelers on the Grand Tour sought out the Catskill Mountain House.

Established in 1823 this fabled resort was one of the nation's first major vacation destinations not tied to medicinal waters. Here, perched 2250 feet above the Valley on the hotel's veranda, the wealthy guests could imagine an idealized rural landscape devoid of social struggle. According to a noted Catskill historian:

> Pilgrims en route to the Mountain House might hold their noses as tanner's wagons passed by or rub their eyes when the smoke of forestfires made the mountain air thick and biting, yet they could console themselves by reflecting that they were in the midst of what the best authorities certified to be a wilderness Garden of Eden into which only the famous Mountain House intruded.

Apparently the charade was too much for one jaded visitor who, upon visiting Katterskill Falls, the most famous cataract in the state after Niagara, astutely recorded the consumption of nature:

> The proprietor of the bar-room is also the genius of the Fall, and drives a trade both with his spirits and his water. In fact, if your romantic nerves can stand the steady truth, the Catskill Fall is *turned on* to accommodate poets and parties of pleasure.
>
> The process of "doing" the sight, for those who are limited in time, is very methodical. You leave the [Mountain House] hotel and drive in a coach to the bar-room. You

"refresh." You step out upon the balcony, and look into the abyss. The proprietor of the Fall informs you that the lower plunge is eighty feet high. It appears to you to be about ten. You laugh incredulously—he smiles in return the smile of a *mens conscia recti.* "Would you step down and have the water turned on?" You do step down a somewhat uneven but very safe staircase. You reach the bottom. "Look! now it comes!" and the proud cascade plunges like a free force into the air and slips, swimming in foam, away from your gaze. . . .

This is ludicrous. But most of us are really only shop-keepers, and natural spectacles are but shopwindows on a grand scale.

Most of the Catskill visitors came for the season to marvel at, and perhaps sketch or record in their diaries, the scenes made famous by the artists. They also came to escape the riots, congestion, heat, malaria, yellow fever, and other environmental and social discomforts of the valley lowlands and the crowded metropolis downriver. Clutching the ubiquitous guidebooks, visitors were advised of exact times and positions when best to view God's creation so as to avoid the disagreeable facts of production owing to tanning, mining, logging, and subsistence farming. In this manner the American literati and bourgeoisie did not so much return to the land, for they rarely had agrarian roots, as they actually turned toward an idealized nature for spiritual inspiration and emotional release.

The escape to nature through recreation in the Hudson Valley was closely related to the social history of New York City. By 1880 over 2 million people lived within a day's travel of the Valley. Nonetheless, insufficient means and overt ethnic discrimination largely limited resort use to wealthy Anglo-Protestants. Beginning in the 1880s, however, union victories in wage and hour demands succeeded in allowing organized labor at least a Sunday outing by steamboat to numerous picnic sites at the foot of the Catskill, Highland, and Palisade cliffs. Here, much to the chagrin of more refined travelers and Sunday prohibitionists, the working-class immigrants feasted and drank to oblivion, attempting as best they could to escape, if only for a few hours. As with the bourgeoisie, nature was also a refuge from production for the workers. However, for the working class nature was less a source of passive contemplation and aesthetic appreciation than it was a resource for active recreational consumption.

Residential Consumption of Nature

During the 1830s and 1840s a new breed of landowner emerged in the Hudson Valley, one whose fortune was derived from industrial and financial activity rather than from land inheritance. The new estate owners were only marginally concerned with Hudson property for rent or for productive investment. Instead, they acquired land for their own residence and leisure consumption.

Many of the larger estates were located atop the more level eastern shore of the River, in Dutchess and Columbia counties. This permitted stunning views across to the rugged Catskill Mountains. The most lavish estates were erected between the 1870s and the 1890s when the Vanderbilts, Harrimans, Rockefellers, and others acquired Hudson property in addition to holdings at Newport (Rhode Island)[,] in the Adirondacks, and at other fashionable resorts.

Famed landscape architect Andrew Jackson Downing was closely identified with the design of the Hudson River estate as a place for residential consumption of nature. Moreover, he was one of the first to publicize the concept of a suburb as a planned community where successful citizens who labored all day in commerce could retire amidst a cultivated, parklike nature. As was evident on his own estate, Highland Gardens, Downing banished all signs of work from the residences. He went so far as to prescribe the placement of pens, portfolios, and other instruments in the library for effect only.

Following completion of the first rail line along the eastern bank of the River in 1851 the lower Hudson, from the Highlands south, fell within the commute shed of New York City, and the suburban dream of Downing became a reality. The very first train up the Hudson to the Greenbush terminal across from Albany completed the run in just under 4 hours, a rate that compares favorably with rail travel today. On the opposite shore a line from Jersey City reached Albany in 1883. On both banks construction had been slow owing to opposition from steamboat lines and from existing estate owners, across whose front lawns the trains would run.

With year-round transit now available, wealthy merchants, bankers, and others whose presence in New York was a daily or weekly requirement moved north from Manhattan abodes to estates clustered along the Westchester and Putnam heights and around Nyack and Cornwall on the western shore. Here they created a privileged landscape, removed from the social turmoil and industrial pollution of their urban workplace, and defended against the intrusion of adjoining production zones.

Nature over Civilization

ROBERT KUHN McGREGOR

On the night of February 5, 1854, two red foxes emerged from the swampy bottom-lands southeast of the Assabet River in the town of Concord, Massachusetts. Moving eastward, the pair crossed open meadows until they reached the skirts of Nut Meadow Brook where they split up. One fox continued east, following the course of the brook through open fields and into a wood. The night was cold, but fortunately only a little snow lay on the ground. White-footed mice, the fox's principal food source, burrow beneath deep snow, making them difficult to catch. Foxes must eat regularly and cache food against the remaining hard days of winter, if possible.

The fox climbed a hillside, momentarily dragging its white-tipped tail in the snow, then struck out across a potato field and into another meadow. Her course intersected the tracks of mice, rabbits, and her chief enemies: dogs and people. South of a bridge, she crossed a road and the brook and came at last to the edge of the Sudbury River. Game seems to have been scarce that night, because she continued on across the river to examine the muskrat houses dotting the marsh on the eastern side. One by one, the fox jumped on the fibrous mounds attempting to frighten out the inhabitants. She urinated on each lodge, marking the site with her strong, musky scent. Thus far she had travelled more than a mile in her search for

From Robert Kuhn McGregor, "Deriving a Biocentric History: Evidence from the Journal of Henry David Thoreau," *Environmental Review*, 12, No. 2 (Summer 1988): 117–124. Reprinted with permission from *Environmental History Review*, © 1988, the American Society for Environmental History.

prey. Because February is the peak of the fox mating season, she needed to build up her food cache in anticipation of the pups, due in six to eight weeks.

Most professionals would deem the nocturnal activities of a fox in the vicinity of the Assabet River in 1854 a matter of little historical concern. Although this incident may have occurred, there seems little reason to attach importance to the journey, or to engage in further research. According to conventional argument, it is not history. The purpose of this essay is to contend that these occurrences are in fact history, and that they are of fundamental importance to the future direction of the discipline. . . . This essay advocates the development of a biocentric history.

To recreate the activities of a historic fox, I employed the familiar methods known to historians, in this case the impeccable *Journal* of Henry David Thoreau. The Concord writer induced the activities of the fox in question by following the animal's foot tracks on the afternoon of February 5, 1854. I supplemented that material with other observations Thoreau made concerning foxes over the course of a dozen years. I turned next to standard technical sources to flesh out my understanding of the habits of the red fox. There is every indication that my description encapsulates a real incident.

In the eyes of colleagues, my history founders on the test of significance. What is so important about a fox? It farmed no soil, practiced no religion, sold no goods, nor did it ever run for Congress. Its journey is a simple occurrence in nature, one that undoubtedly happened countless times in many places.

The first significant point about this fox is the record of its travels. Although it could leave no records of its own, Thoreau believed the fox's activities important enough to enter in his journal. In addition to the movements of foxes, Thoreau recorded the actions of every other creature he encountered, including the behavior of thousands of plants. Those records comprise a wealth of primary material for a history of all the forms of life in Concord during Thoreau's time there. The significance of the fox lies in the role it played in the environmental whole, a part equally important to that of various quadrupeds, insects, birds, fish, and humans. Thoreau generally made daily entries in his journal between 1850 and 1861, recording all the phenomena necessary to understand the nature of life. We might advance our own comprehension by undertaking to write a history of all life in a particular place and time.

To research and develop such a meaningful history, scholars must first discard the notion that human beings are the center of all things. Humans, after all, walk the earth in the company of myriad other creatures, each with its own requirements for survival and well-being. Although humans have exercised tremendous influence on the world's ecologies, they do not control the world, nor do other creatures exist for their benefit. To understand the manner in which life on earth functions, it is necessary to look at things from a holistic point of view; modern ecologists and philosophers have called that intellectual process "biocentrism."

In the biocentric world view all species of life are effectively equal because they depend upon others for survival, for food, shelter, air, and water. The human belief that we live a separate, superior realm of existence is simple anthropocentric self-delusion; humans are, as [ecologist] Aldo Leopold observed, "plain citizens" of the biotic community. . . .

Thoreau recorded a wealth of information concerning the rivers, meadows, woods, hilltops, and bogs of Concord. His journals record in minute detail the activities of the hundreds of living species associated with each landform. He attempted to develop an understanding of the complex relationships and the interdependencies among the living beings of the region. The journals, therefore, provide the basic raw material for a comprehensive history of all species of life in a small town during the nineteenth century. Although his view of that world may have been an involved melding of the transcendental and the scientific, he never wavered in his ultimate determination: to discover truth.

In the late summer of 1846 Thoreau stood atop Mount Katahdin and asked "*Who* are we? *where* are we?" Other scholars have detected a note of despair in the passage, a measured rejection of his earlier commitment to wildness. That is debatable. Those lines are merely agonizingly simple questions posed to himself. He spent the remainder of his life searching for the answers. "The poet says the proper study of mankind is man," Thoreau observed. "I say, study to forget all that; take wider views of the universe." Over time, the scope of his search altered, his methods changed, but the determination to know who and where we are never diminished.

All his life Thoreau considered himself a transcendentalist. He confided a definition of that philosophy to his journal in 1840: transcendentalism was essentially a romantic belief, a rejection of inductive science in favor of self-perceived truth. The material world mattered little, it existed merely as a pale reflection of a higher, spiritual plane. "My thought is a part of the meaning of the world," he stated, "and hence I use part of the world as a symbol to express my thought."

Thoreau did not always express his transcendental belief so clearly. He observed in the spring of 1854 that "the man of most science is the man most alive, whose life is the greatest event." Thoreau employed the scientific method to an extraordinary degree in his search for a sense of place in the universe. By the 1850s, he was a botanist of considerable repute, not merely in identifying species, but in tracking their life cycles through the year. He also recorded the activities of birds, insects, amphibians, reptiles, and fish; and he struggled to understand the manner in which they interacted with one another and with the climate and geography of Concord.

The inherent conflict between transcendental belief and scientific method Thoreau recognized at once: "If you would be wise, learn science and then forget it." At times, especially during winter or during moments of personal tragedy, he heeded that advice, forsaking inductive knowledge to "commune with the spirit of the universe." More often, usually in spring and summer, the lush abundance of nature would overwhelm his spiritual side. Only direct observation and year-to-year record keeping could satisfy his desire to know. For every journal entry expressing transcendental belief, there are a thousand scientific observations of nature at work.

The seeming contradiction between romantic philosophy and inductive science was not an inconsistency on Thoreau's part. "The fact is," he wrote, "I am a mystic, a transcendentalist, and a natural philosopher to boot. . . . I probably stand as near to nature as any of them, and am by constitution as good an observer as most." Thoreau was searching both for the activities that took place in nature and for a sense of the spirit in nature: "There is a civilization going on among brutes as well as men." He believed the forests were sacred and was willing to allow trees the possibility of reaching heaven. Every occurrence in nature, he maintained, "is a parable of the Great Teacher."

More startling to Thoreau was the existence of humanity in nature, "a fact which few have realized." But what exactly was the human place in nature? He readily acknowledged that human beings stood apart from the rest of nature in many ways. His fellow beings were steeped in the exploitive views dominant in Western culture and assumed that God created the world for their benefit. "What is a shrub oak good for?" a neighbor asked him. Often, that narrow self-centered attitude repelled Thoreau. He fumed over government's lack of comprehension or interest in the natural world: "Children are attracted by the beauty of butterflies, but their parents and legislators deem it an idle pursuit."

Thoreau also recognized that most species were suspicious of the humans in their midst: "Birds certainly are afraid of man," he observed. "They [allow virtually] all other creatures—cows, horses, etc. . . . to come near them, but not man. . . . Is he, then, a true lord of creation, whose subjects are afraid of him, and with reason?"

Certainly in Thoreau's view humans had done much to earn the emnity of other creatures. So-called "improvements" had closed the Concord River to several species of fish, and the urge to shoot everything that moved had driven away many birds and mammals. People did not seem to care; they failed to perceive the activities of those creatures still remaining or even to hear the song of the toads in the spring. Humans were far more adept at overuse and misuse of nature's species. "What right has my neighbor to burn ten cords of wood, when I burn only one?" Thoreau demanded. "He who burns the most wood on his hearth is the least warmed by the sight of it growing."

For all that, Thoreau remained convinced that nature's children included human beings. "How plainly we are a part of nature! For we live like the animals around us." He believed that humanity would be far better off living in harmony with nature, rather than attempting to dominate it. "To be serene and successful we must be at one with the universe," he wrote in 1854. "The least conscious and needless injury inflicted on any creature is to its extent a suicide. What peace—or life—can a murderer have?" His belief that "in wildness is the preservation of the world" is well known. People depend upon nature for life itself. To Thoreau, human beings must "live more naturally, and so more safely."

To apply Thoreau's perspective to the writing of history requires a broader point of view, one that encompasses all that goes on in the world, not merely the role that humans play. A biocentric history must include an accounting of all the forces of life pertinent to a specific place and time, and it must place human beings firmly within that context. If people are not separate from the rest of nature, historians should not treat them separately in environmental history. Thoreau's journals provide a few thoughts that might be applied to the process.

The Concord transcendentalist complained in 1857: "How much is written about Nature as somebody has portrayed her, how little about Nature as she is." The task for environmental historians in that context, therefore, is to distance themselves from the habit of examining nature from a solely human perspective. Other species are not merely resources, or impediments, or even objects of beauty; they are each unique individuals, living and attempting to pass life on through their progeny. "Every child should be encouraged to study not man's system of nature, but nature's," Thoreau advised.

A sense of perspective is the place to commence the process of writing such a history. But it is only a beginning, because the problems of source and method still confront those who embark on a project in biocentric history. What is to be the locus of such a story? Necessarily, the initial subjects must be limited in terms of time and space. Researchers who study the lives of common people have adopted a community approach; broadening that perspective to include the rest of nature can only complicate the work. Hence, it will be necessary to focus at first on the microcosm, on a small, biologically inclusive area, concentrating on a limited time span. When scholars have mastered the ability to write histories that see human beings as a part of nature, they may begin the work of synthesis. The problem of sources is perhaps the most difficult challenge to the creation of biocentric history. Although much of the material familiar to historians includes some clues pertinent to the condition of the environment in a particular place, a truly biocentric history requires greater detail than most sources provide. The vast majority of the authors, reporters, correspondents, diarists, and census takers shared the anthropocentric view that is still dominant in the world. Their observations of nature often are little more than background for their genuine interest: the activities of humans.

To create a biocentric version of the past, historians will need an accurate reportage of the myriad activities of a host of species including humans in a given place and time. Only a few sources, however, have demonstrated the breadth of vision sufficient to make a biocentric history possible.

But why do this? Why is it important to create a biocentric history of Concord, Massachusetts, or of anywhere else, for that matter?

The reasons for crafting such a history fall into several categories: the politically immediate, the educational, the scientific, and the metaphysical. A reading of the daily newspapers is enough to drive home the urgent need for such an approach. Greed and the false assumption that the world exists for the exclusive use of humans are rapidly destroying large numbers of species, ruining whole ecosystems, and endangering humanity. A biocentric view will draw attention to the abuse of the earth and the place of humans within its ecosystem. Such histories may serve to educate people to the necessity of considering the needs of other species.

Good biocentric history may also provide perspective for scientific inquiry. Ecological scientists share an inability to conduct effective research and analysis because of the dynamic nature of existing ecosystems. How does one analyze an environment undergoing constant change without treating the system in static terms (and therefore inaccurately)? By studying the actions of previous environments, historians may describe all the interactions of the species resident in a particular place over a period of time, thereby providing scientists a basis for comparison to existing systems.

History is not science, nor should it have such pretensions. Historians stand midway between science and art, commanding a view of both. They are not cold-blooded inductivists, collecting facts with cool rationality; nor are they starry-eyed romantics, ignoring the hard facts in order to paint historical pictures in broad artistic splashes. Yet historians possess the capacity to be a little of each; they have the ability to craft a holistic view of the past that embodies the hard facts. So much of what they create depends entirely on their historical point of view. For that reason, a few of them need to adopt a biocentric approach toward their subject. If the profession truly stands between science and art, it has much to offer to each. Both scientists and artists may profit from a perspective that encompasses the needs of all earth's creatures. Historians can and should assist in that process.

A final word of caution: a biocentric point of view is well outside the mainstream of Western cultural thought. Historians attempting to adopt such an approach will discover that they are walking a very lonely path. Thoreau understood the nature of the problem: "The mind that perceives clearly any natural beauty is in that instant withdrawn from human society. My desire for society is infinitely increased; my fitness for any actual society is diminished."

Thoreau's Aunt Maria looked at the matter from another perspective: "Think of it!" she said. "He stood half an hour to-day to hear the frogs croak, and he wouldn't read the life of Chalmers."

May our condemnations be no worse.

Slave Women and Nature

ELIZABETH D. BLUM

The way people view their surroundings varies greatly by time period, race, class, and gender. Nineteenth century white men in America, according to historians, generally accepted the proposition that nature should be dominated, brought under control, and used for profit. Christianity tended to reinforce this group's view of man as above and separate from nature, justifying the exploitation of natural resources. Native Americans and Africans, on the other hand, recognized that everything, including plants, animals, and humans, had a soul and place in the world. With this outlook, they tended to conserve their resources and demonstrate respect toward their surroundings. These interpretations of each groups' view are overly simplistic, of course. No one group falls into a monolithic view of either complete harmony with nature or complete domination over it.

African-American slave women in the mid-nineteenth century used and conceived of their environment differently than scholars' portrayals of white men or women at the same time. . . . [T]hey found their environment to be both a source of racial and gender power, as well as a source of fear and control by whites.

Enslaved women remain a mysterious group to many historians, due to a lack of both sources and material. With the legal prohibition on education for slaves, these women left behind few written accounts for scholars. . . . Through slave narratives recorded by the Works Progress Administration in the 1930s, African-Americans expressed mixed views of and uses for the wilderness surrounding them. In many ways, these slave women developed a harmonious existence with their surrounding environment, using their knowledge to support and protect their families. As with white women across the country, their interactions with nature provided an avenue of power within both black and white society. Strongly contrasting with elite white women, however, black women were prohibited from engaging in the public realm to any significant degree.

From Elizabeth D. Blum. "Power, Danger, and Control: Slave Women's Perceptions of Wilderness in the Nineteenth Century." *Women's Studies* 31 (2002), pp. 247–258, 260–265. Reprinted with the permission of Thomson Publishing Services.

Just as American women's thoughts about nature flowed from their European heritage, evidence exists that black women's views of their environment contained influences from their African predecessors. Africans had a very functional view of the land, based on their concept of "good use." Considered sacred by many African cultures, land continued relationships among current, previous, and future generations. Africans retained a strong sense of community, even after death, and believed separation from the grave sites of ancestors brought disaster to living family members. Performing certain ceremonies kept the ancestors strong, while the ancestors concurrently promised to keep the land fertile and the community healthy and prosperous. Capture and transportation for slavery broke these important ties to the ancestral land, although Africans refused to allow them to be completely severed. Slave traders reported cases of women swallowing African soil as they left their native land on the perilous journey across the Atlantic. Just as women ingested soil to keep a part of it with them, other Africans also maintained their native "good use" concept of land, while recognizing both benefits and dangers from their new environment.

Slavery affected how blacks thought about the wilderness, altering and melding African beliefs. Slaves maintained some elements of their aesthetic, adapting and changing others to fit their new environment. In many African religions, for example, the wilderness or "bush," far from a place to be feared or avoided, actually was seen as a place of refuge and transformation. Young Africans generally made a sojourn into the bush for an initiation ceremony into adulthood. Parts of this ceremony remained intact in America or melded with European beliefs. In the Gullah culture along the coast of South Carolina and Georgia, for example, blacks used journeys into the wilderness as an integral component of their conversion to Christianity. Others maintained the concept of wilderness as a place of escape. Interestingly, this concept held by slaves mirrored in some ways the view held by white women and transcendentalists of nature as a place of refuge and spirituality. For the slaves, however, the concept of wilderness as a refuge remained a palpable reality, rather than a poet's or scholar's rhetoric.

Importantly, the woods provided a hiding space for many slaves, some escaping from slavery permanently, others seeing the wilderness as a temporary retreat from white supervision and control. For some slaves, escape was a purely individual act. Others either enlisted or obtained the help and support of other slaves. . . .

Female slaves ran away permanently far less often than males, especially if they had small children. Slave women did, however, demonstrate resistance to slavery by acts of "truancy" in the wilderness. Many examples exist of women leaving the plantation for short periods of time, to return when food ran out or homesickness for familiar territory overcame them. "Sometimes de women wouldn't take it an' would run away an' hide in de woods," one slave in Georgia noted, and "Sometimes dey would come back after a short stay an' den again dey would have to put de hounds on dere trail to bring dem back home." Another woman in South Carolina fled to the rattlesnake-infested rice swamps rather than stay on her brutal master's plantation. Women, as well as men, knew of the woods and wilderness as a place of refuge from the horrors and strictures of slave life.

Although recognizing many benefits from their environment, slaves also expressed feelings of fear and danger associated with "the woods." . . . [Slave woman] Vinnie Brunson expressed concern about the education of black children, fearing that they would not be taught about the dangers of the woods. She stated, "De poisonous snakes strike wicked fangs into bare heels, danger hides everywhere in de streams too so we much know how to escape form hit. De wild animals have nimble feet and wings to save dem from de ones dat kill dem but de nigger had to save hisself." In addition, the woods teemed with other wild dangers, including "catamoun," bears and witches at night.

Danger from the wilderness became more than mere threats to children for many slaves who related tales of horror and violence. Panthers and snakes brought out perhaps the most fear in slaves. . . . As a group of women on Jim Abbey's plantation worked to break ground in a new field, they heard a panther scream. Terrified, Tabby stated that "us had to cross a bridge to git home, and dem wimmen jes nacherly like to tore dat bridge down gittin' cross hit to get home but de pant'er didn' ketch none of em."

Snakes evoked similar fears among slaves. Annie Whitley Ware described her mother's reaction to having a six-foot black racer snake chase her. Her mother "run fas' ez she could 'till she git ter a stake an' rider fence an' she clumb up on hit, de snake, he wuz er running' so fas' he jes slid under dat fence 'for he knowed hit. Mammy she clumb er tree dat wuz close ter de fence, an' she stay dar 'till she couldn't see nor hear dat snake. Den she ease down and jes fly home." Because of the persistent danger from poisonous snakes in many wooded areas, some slaves developed sophisticated knowledge of the reptiles, demonstrating an ability to identify many different types of snakes. Winger Van Hook, for example, related stories about close encounters with black racer snakes, copperheads, hoop snakes, knob snakes, and jointed snakes. Both male and female slaves who spent time hunting or playing in the woods probably learned from an early age to identify the dangers associated with various snakes.

Slaves also faced dangers from other humans, both black and white, in the woods. Hattie Jane Brown, a Woodville, Mississippi, slave reportedly born in 1822, described her master taking her to the woods to hang her. His conscience, however, got the better of him, and he spared her life. Anna Baker described the situation leading up to her mother's escape from slavery in Mississippi. Although a black overseer on the plantation had been repeatedly harassing her mother for sexual favors, her mother refused such advances. One day, while working in the fields, the overseer told Baker's mother to "go over to de woods wid him." Feigning agreeability, her mother failed to wait in the designated area, but "just kept a goin' and swam de river and runned away." Just as the wilderness could serve as a hiding place for beneficial aspects of black culture, it could also hide violence against women.

Supernatural forces also seemed to lurk in the wilderness, causing fear for many slaves. When slaves mentioned seeing ghosts or spirits, the encounter often took place in the woods at night. While frightening and perhaps sometimes apocryphal, some of these encounters could take on relatively benign forms. In Mississippi, while walking "through thick woods" to a dance one night, Manda Boggan reported seeing a ghost that looked like a cow, which grew larger and larger until it ultimately ran away.

Natural occurrences, especially shooting stars, also caused fear and alarm in many slaves. Several slaves mentioned the paralyzing fear that overcame many with the onset of meteorite showers, comets or shooting stars, seemingly portending religious catastrophe. Part of the fear surely resulted from the effects these showers could have on the land, setting and spreading dangerous wildfires. . . . The fact that the stars also terrified, and perhaps humbled, the [slaves'] overseer probably brought at least small comfort to many of the slaves he terrorized. The falling stars served as a visible reminder to the slaves of a power greater than that of their master or overseer. . . .

Importantly, Southern white mistresses used stories about the wilderness to maintain control over their slaves, especially children and other women. As a young girl in Texas, Josie Brown remembered being told stories of dangerous wild creatures in the woods. Perhaps to keep the youngster from running away, her white mistress warned her not to play in the woods alone, telling her vivid stories of bald eagles swooping down and taking children the way a hawk preys on chickens. Lou "Granny" Williams enjoyed taking the white children fishing with her, something her mistress expressly forbade. . . . White women used stories of violence and dangerous creatures in the wilderness to keep slaves close to home and under control.

In addition to physical control, Southern white women attempted to use wilderness allegories to maintain control over their slaves' ideas about black people in general. White women frequently adopted the racist stereotype of blacks as animalistic. This image of blacks as similar to animals was, of course, reinforced by whites who sought to keep the slaves thinking of themselves as subhuman, and certainly of lower status than whites. . . .White women used nature stories . . . to reinforce racist images of blacks as closer to animals and therefore less human. These stories also reinforced white women's sense of control and superiority over blacks. Stories of the wilderness served as a powerful mediator between blacks and whites; whites subtly conveyed racist attitudes and control, while blacks relayed veiled threats and warnings against cruel or arrogant behavior.

Slaves recognized many benefits in their surrounding environment, especially regarding medicine, food, and escaping. In dealing with illness, slaves, and especially slave women, frequently used nature for their benefit. Although the wilderness was not exclusively a female domain, older slave women possessed highly detailed medical knowledge about various substances there, including not only how to identify them, but also when to harvest and how to prepare them. For the women who controlled and understood it, this highly specialized knowledge led to power within the slave quarters on the plantation as well as among the white society.

. . . Black slave women's patients included both slaves and whites. In the rural South, doctors were scarce for both races, and often the white owners trusted certain slaves with the medical care of their families. Amos Clark remembered his mother nursing his master's children and that she "allus paid special tension to de medicine." Some slave women even gained respect outside the plantation. Adeline Waldon remembered that her mother "wuz a fair nuss an' dey come ter git her from far an' near." . . .

Nature may have also provided a source of power for slave women over their reproductive lives. Several slaves reported that black women used cotton root to induce abortions, often going to great lengths to procure it. When apprized of the situation, masters attempted to keep cotton root away from slave women. . . . [Such actions perhaps reflected] the widespread nature of the use of the root by women in preventing births and limiting family size. In addition to cotton root, a white Tennessee doctor also listed tansy and rue, pennyroyal, camphor, and cedar berries as substances he suspected slave women of using to produce miscarriages.

In addition to providing sources of medicine for slaves, the wilderness also provided an important food source, namely protein. Many slaves' diets, controlled and provided by their masters, were generally very poor, even by the standards of the day. Most slaves received little more than an allowance of corn meal and occasional pork fat. Some masters allowed slaves a small plot of land to cultivate a vegetable garden, but in general, slave diets lacked adequate sources of many vitamins and nutrients. With such a poor diet, wildlife provided vital sources of protein and other food necessary for the slave's health. In addition, providing food for their families also could be seen as a source of pride, independence from the master, and control over their own lives. . . .

Although men generally performed hunting duties as adults, the uncertainties of slave life necessitated that women be able to hunt if required. Granny Williams remembered combining her hunting with her nursemaid duties. She took the master's children down to the river, watching them while she fished. Baalam Lyles remembered fishing on his master's plantation with his mother when he was small. Another former slave noted that "My Mamma could hunt as good as any man. She'd have 'coon hides n' deer, n' mink, n' beavers, laud." In addition to sharing hunting duties, black women also generally had the responsibility of preparing the animals for consumption.

. . . The woods also provided additional variety to the slave diet with sources other than protein. Slaves located fresh honey in bee hives, while women made preserves or jelly from the wild grapes, dewberries, cherries, yellow plums, blackberries or other wild fruit. Slaves also gathered nuts when available to supplement their diet or as treats. . . .

With so little research conducted in the area of nineteenth-century black women's conceptions of the environment, any generalizations must be considered tentative at best. However, evidence exists that, contrary to scholars' description of Euro-American men as uniformly hostile and fearful of wilderness areas at this time, slave women expressed mixed feelings about "the woods." They frequently saw wilderness areas as beneficial and as sources of power. Wooded or wilderness areas provided sources for herbs and other ingredients for medicine as a first line of defense for sickness among slaves. Often controlled by women, this knowledge included not only which ingredients to use, but also when to harvest them and the methods of preparation. In addition, the woods yielded substantial amounts of food, enriching slaves' diets considerably with additional sources of protein. Wilderness areas also provided a safe haven for both men and women. Slaves ran away to the woods, or hid for short periods of time in rebellion from the harshness and drudgery of slavery. Whether or not a slave personally escaped his bonds, each seemed cognizant of the concept of wilderness areas as a place of escape. Ironically, this conception of the wilderness as a source of freedom and renewal linked far more closely with transcendentalist views of nature than the dominant white male ethos.

In addition to these beneficial uses for wilderness, slaves expressed fear and concerns over the danger associated with the woods. Woods often housed the supernatural, including ghosts and spirits that materialized to terrify the living. In addition, the seclusion of the woods, which offered haven as escape, also offered cover for various nefarious dealings, including rape, murder, and other acts of terrorism.

The surrounding wilderness also became a means of mediating the relationships between slaves and their masters. Using allegorical or apocryphal tales, both blacks and whites expressed ideas about the power structure under slavery.

Overall, slaves realized the natural world yielded benefits, and yet needed to be treated with respect, fear, and knowledge to avoid harm. Some black slave women also realized not insignificant levels of power within their society from their interactions with the environment—through knowledge of medicines, talismans, abortifacients, and wildlife. . . . [B]lack slave women linked their well-being and sources of community power to their environment.

❦ F U R T H E R   R E A D I N G

Catherine Albanese, *Nature Religion in America: From the Algonkian Indians to the New Age* (1990)

Daniel Botkin, *No Man's Garden: Thoreau and a New Vision for Civilization and Nature* (2001)

Lawrence Buel, *The Environmental Imagination: Thoreau, Nature Writing, and the Formation of American Culture* (1995)

James F. Cooper, *Knights of the Brush: The Hudson River School and the Moral Landscape* (1999)

William Cronon, "Telling Tales on Canvas," in Jules David Prown, et al., *Discovered Lands, Invented Pasts* (1992)

Everett Dick, *The Lure of the Land: A Social History of the Public Lands from the Articles of Confederation to the New Deal* (1970)

Arthur A. Ekirch, Jr., *Man and Nature in America* (1963)

Robert Gangewere, ed., *The Exploited Eden: Literature on the American Environment* (1972)

Sam D. Gill, *Mother Earth: An American Story* (1987)

William H. Goetzmann, *New Lands, New Men: America and the Second Great Age of Discovery* (1986)

E. Richard Hart, ed., *That Awesome Space: Human Interaction with the Intermountain Landscape* (1981)

William L. Howarth, *The Book of Concord: Thoreau's Life as a Writer* (1982)

John K. Howat, ed., *American Paradise: The World of the Hudson River School* (1988)

———, *The Hudson River and Its Painters* (1972)

Hildegard Binder Johnson, *Order upon the Land: The U.S. Rectangular Land Survey and the Upper Mississippi Country* (1976)

Annette Kolodny, *The Lay of the Land* (1975)

David Kowalewski, *Deep Power: The Political Ecology of Wilderness and Civilization* (2000)

Paula Mitchell Marks, *In a Barren Land: American Indian Dispossession and Survival* (1998)

Leo Marx, *The Machine in the Garden: Technology and the Pastoral Ideal in America* (1964)

James McIntosh, *Thoreau as Romantic Naturalist: His Shifting Stance Toward Nature* (1974)

Lee Clark Mitchell, *Witnesses to a Vanishing America: The Nineteenth-Century Response* (1981)

Roderick Nash, *The Rights of Nature: A History of Environmental Ethics* (1989)

———, *Wilderness and the American Mind,* 3d ed. (1982)

Barbara Novak, *American Painting of the Nineteenth Century: Realism, Idealism and the American Experience* (1969)

———, *Nature and Culture: American Landscape and Painting, 1825–1875* (1980)

Raymond J. O'Brien, *American Sublime: Landscape and Scenery of the Lower Hudson Valley* (1981)

Roy M. Robbins, *Our Landed Heritage: The Public Domain, 1776–1970,* 2d ed. (1970)

Peter J. Schmitt, *Back to Nature: The Arcadian Myth in Urban America* (1969)
Henry Nash Smith, *Virgin Land* (1950)
Theodore Steinberg, *Nature Incorporated: Industrialization and the Waters of New England* (1991)
Alan S. Taylor, *William Cooper's Town: Power and Persuasion on the Frontier of the Early American Republic* (1995)
Henry David Thoreau, *In the Woods and Fields of Concord* (1982)
———, *The Natural History Essays* (1980)
Cecelia Tichi, *New World, New Earth: Environmental Reform in American Literature From the Puritans Through Whitman* (1979)
Frederick Turner, *Beyond Geography: The Western Spirit Against the Wilderness* (1980)
Philip Weeks, *Farewell, My Nation: The American Indian and the United States in the Nineteenth Century* (2000)
David Scofield Wilson, *In the Presence of Nature* (1978)
Donald Worster, *Nature's Economy: A History of Ecological Ideas* (1977)
———, *The Wealth of Nature: Environmental History and the Ecological Imagination* (1993)

CHAPTER
7

The Cotton South Before
and After the Civil War

❦

This chapter explores the environmental history of the Cotton South as an interaction between its climate, soil, pests, and fertilizers on the one hand and the capitalist system of slave agriculture on the other hand.

In the late eighteenth and early nineteenth centuries, textile-production technologies (spinning mills, power looms, and steam engines) introduced in England and New England combined with Eli Whitney's invention of the cotton gin (1793) to make cotton culture profitable. Sea Island cotton, with its long fibers and smooth, easily removed seeds, had grown well along the coast of Georgia and South Carolina during the colonial era, but the upland long- and short-staple cotton varieties, with their shorter fibers and sticky seeds, were well adapted to the inland valleys and the Gulf coastal plain. The cotton gin (which separated seeds from lint), the growth and spread of slavery, and expanding markets made the mass production of these upland varieties feasible. Cotton, which requires a 200-day frost-free growing season and 50 to 60 inches of rainfall a year, could be raised as far north as Virginia, Tennessee, and northern Arkansas and Oklahoma and in eastern Texas as well. Georgia, Alabama, and Mississippi experienced cotton booms in the 1830s, as did Louisiana and Texas in the 1850s, when people migrated west, pushing Native Americans off the Gulf lands. By 1860 the South was producing 7 million bales of cotton a year, along with other staple crops—sugar, corn, rice, and tobacco. Unlike the North, the region remained largely rural and heavily forested throughout the nineteenth century, with plantations often separated by a day's travel along poor roads.

The environmental history of the South before the Civil War was shaped by the interaction between a labor-intensive system of agriculture based on slavery and the resultant soil degradation. In 1860 only 25 percent of the South's white population owned slaves (about 10,000 families), and 88 percent of these had fewer than twenty slaves. Two-thirds of the whites were independent, non-slave-owning farmers who farmed and herded in the hills and woods. Free blacks and mulattoes made up the remainder of the southern population. Slaves typically worked in the cotton fields in gangs, hoeing, plowing, planting, weeding, and picking, and as house servants, cooks, and child caretakers. They were often whipped for failure to perform.

The intensity of southern agricultural production resulted in degraded, exhausted soils—a deterioration only partially mitigated by corn-cotton rotations, the practice of grazing livestock in the harvested fields, and labor-intensive methods of weed and pest control (to remove the cotton bollworm, a moth larva).

The years following the Civil War saw the rise of sharecropping, in which land-owners furnished land, tools, mules, seed, a cabin, and food in return for a share of the crop; tenant farming, in which farmers owned their own tools and mules but rented the land by returning a percentage of the crop; and the crop-lien system, in which farmers borrowed supplies from a merchant at interest in return for a por-tion of the forthcoming crop. One-third of all farmers, usually blacks and poor whites, were sharecroppers or tenants in 1880, and two-thirds were sharecroppers by 1920. The northward migration of the cotton boll weevil (a beetle) from Mexico after 1893 severely damaged cotton-crop yields and led to the expansion of the U.S. Agricultural Extension Service to assist farmers with methods of controlling the weevil and improving soil fertility. (See Maps 1, 2, 3, 4, and 6 in the Appendix.)

❦ D O C U M E N T S

The documents in this chapter look at the ways in which planters and slaves used the lands of the Lower South in the nineteenth and early twentieth centuries to produce marketable crops. Frances Anne Kemble, the author of Document 1, was an English actress who married the Philadelphian Pierce Butler, the heir to a Georgia plantation that began producing Sea Island cotton in the late eighteenth century. In this document, taken from a journal of letters written in 1838–1839 to her friend Elizabeth Dwight Sedgwick of Massachusetts, Kemble describes her visit to her husband's holdings and her revulsion against the slave system of cotton production in which, by virtue of her marriage, she participated. Her horror at the treatment of slaves contrasts sharply with her joy at the beauties of nature in the South. In Document 2, Georgia planter John B. Lamar, in letters written in 1847 to his brother-in-law Howell Cobb, a member of Con-gress, discusses his acquisition of fertile cotton lands in newly settled Sumpter County, about sixty miles southwest of his headquarters in Macon, and his excitement at the prospect of huge cotton profits.

Document 3 comes from the travel accounts of New York landscape architect Frederick Law Olmsted, who traveled through the South in 1856. Olmsted covered several thousand miles in the southern states over fourteen months. This document includes his portrayal of a well-managed cotton plantation and of abandoned plantations and exhausted soils in Mississippi. Document 4 contains sharecroppers' contracts made after the Civil War between landowner A. T. Mial of Wake County, North Carolina, and croppers A. Robert Medlin in 1876 and Fenner Powell in 1886. Mial furnished Medlin, who owned his own land, the goods and provisions to grow his crops (a crop-lien contract), whereas Powell also received the land (a sharecropper's contract).

The techniques of cotton planting, pest control, harvesting, and ginning are seen through the eyes of ex-slave Louis Hughes in Document 5, excerpted from his book *Thirty Years a Slave* (1897). Prior to the use of pesticides, slave labor was used to control the cotton bollworm, a moth larva that destroyed cotton plants. The boll weevil, a beetle, invaded the Cotton South from Mexico beginning in 1892 and moved north-ward in waves, affecting Texas, Louisiana, Mississippi, Arkansas, and Oklahoma. In Document 6, dating from 1903, the Louisiana Boll Weevil Convention raises the alarm and advocates methods for arresting the weevil's progress, most of them ultimately to no avail. Despite the destructiveness of the weevil and the reduction of yields by as much as 50 percent, cotton remained profitable in the Lower South into the early twentieth century.

During the Great Depression of the 1930s, the Federal Writers' Project of the WPA (Works Progress Administration) funded the interviewing of former slaves concerning their life experiences. In Document 7, published in 1937, freed slaves Monroe Brackins, Andy J. Anderson, and Ellen Payne of Texas and Sarah Felder, Della Buckley, and John Belcher of Mississippi describe their reliance on fishing, hunting, poultry raising, and gardening to supplement their daily rations. In Document 8, part of the Folklore edition of the Federal Writers' Project, published in 1945, an anonymous ex-slave proposes an alternative "ecological" explanation of why the boll weevil came.

The documents as a whole suggest that the environmental history of the Cotton South could be told from several different perspectives: from that of a cotton planter, a slave, a particle of soil—or even a boll weevil!

1. Frances Anne Kemble Discusses Slavery and Nature in Georgia, 1838–1839

[Philadelphia. December, 1838]

My dear E[lizabeth],

I return you Mr. _____'s letter. I do not think it answers any of the questions debated in our last conversation at all satisfactorily: the *right* one man has to enslave another, he has not the hardihood to assert; but in the reasons he adduces to defend that act of injustice, the contradictory statements he makes appear to me to refute each other. He says, that to the Continental European protesting against the abstract iniquity of slavery, his answer would be, "the slaves are infinitely better off than half the Continental peasantry"; to the Englishman, "they are happy compared with the miserable Irish." But supposing that this answered the question of original injustice, which it does not, it is not a true reply. Though the Negroes are fed, clothed, and housed, and though the Irish peasant is starved, naked, and roofless, the bare name of freemen—the lordship over his own person, the power to choose and will— are blessings beyond food, raiment, or shelter; possessing which, the want of every comfort of life is yet more tolerable than their fullest enjoyment without them. . . .

Mr. _____, and many others, speak as if there were a natural repugnance in all whites to any alliance with the black race; and yet it is notorious, that almost every Southern planter has a family more or less numerous of illegitimate colored children. Most certainly, few people would like to assert that such connections are formed because it is the *interest* of these planters to increase the number of their human property, and that they add to their revenue by the closest intimacy with creatures that they loathe, in order to reckon among their wealth the children of their body. . . . Now it appears very evident that there is no law in the white man's nature which prevents him from making a colored woman the mother of his children, but

From Frances Anne Kemble, *Journal of a Residence on a Georgian Plantation in 1838–1839.* Ed. John A. Scott. New York: Alfred A. Knopf, 1961 [originally published New York: Harper & Brothers, 1863], pp. 3–4, 10–11, 202–203, 215–216.

there *is* a law on his statute books forbidding him to make her his wife. . . . It seems almost as curious that laws should be enacted to prevent men marrying women toward whom they have an invincible natural repugnance, as that education should by law be prohibited to creatures [presumed] incapable of receiving it.

As for the exhortation with which Mr. _____ closes his letter, that I will not "go down to my husband's plantation prejudiced against what I am to find there," I know not well how to answer it. Assuredly I *am* going prejudiced against slavery, for I am an Englishwoman, in whom the absence of such a prejudice would be disgraceful. Nevertheless, I go prepared to find many mitigations in the practice to the general injustice and cruelty of the system—much kindness on the part of the masters, much content on that of the slaves; and I feel very sure that you may rely upon the carefulness of my observation, and the accuracy of my report, of every detail of the working of the thing that comes under my notice; and certainly, on the plantation to which I am going, it will be more likely that I should some things extenuate, than set down aught in malice.

St. Simons Island, [Georgia]
[Feburary 18, 1839]

Dearest E[lizabeth],

The cotton crop [here] is no longer by any means as paramount in value as it used to be, and the climate, soil, and labor of St. Simons are better adapted to old, young and feeble cultivators than the swamp fields of the rice island. I wonder if I ever told you of the enormous decrease in value of this same famous sea-island, long-staple cotton. When Major [Butler], Mr. [Butler]'s grandfather, first sent the produce of this plantation where we now are to England, it was of so fine a quality that it used to be quoted by itself in the Liverpool cotton market, and was then worth half a guinea a pound; it is now not worth a shilling a pound. This was told me by the gentleman in Liverpool who has been factor for this estate for thirty years. Such a decrease as this in the value of one's crop, and the steady increase at the same time of a slave population, now numbering between seven hundred and eight hundred bodies to clothe and house, mouths to feed, while the land is being exhausted by the careless and wasteful nature of the agriculture itself, suggests a pretty serious prospect of declining prosperity; and, indeed, unless these Georgia cotton planters can command more land, or lay abundant capital (which they have not, being almost all of them over head and ears in debt) upon that which has already spent its virgin vigor, it is a very obvious thing that they must all very soon be eaten up by their own property. The rice plantations are a great thing to fall back upon under these circumstances, and the rice crop is now quite as valuable, if not more so, than the cotton one on Mr. [Butler]'s estates, once so famous and prosperous through the latter.

[February 28–March 2, 1839]

Dear E[lizabeth],

[Today] I detained Louisa, whom I had never seen but in the presence of her old grandmother, whose version of the poor child's escape to, and hiding in the woods, I had a desire to compare with the heroine's own story.

She told it very simply, and it was most pathetic. She had not finished her task one day, when she said she felt ill, and unable to do so, and had been severely flogged by driver Bran, in whose "gang" she then was. The next day, in spite of this encouragement to labor, she had again been unable to complete her appointed work; and Bran having told her that he'd tie her up and flog her if she did not get it done, she had left the field and run into the swamp.

"Tie you up, Louisa!" said I; "what is that?"

She then described to me that they were fastened up by their wrists to a beam or a branch of a tree, their feet barely touching the ground, so as to allow them no purchase for resistance or evasion of the lash, their clothes turned over their heads, and their backs scored with a leather thong, either by the driver himself, or, if he pleases to inflict their punishment by deputy, any of the men he may choose to summon to the office; it might be father, brother, husband, or lover, if the overseer so ordered it. I turned sick, and my blood curdled listening to these details from the slender young slip of a lassie, with her poor piteous face and murmuring, pleading voice.

"Oh," said I, "Louisa; but the rattlesnakes—the dreadful rattlesnakes in the swamps; were you not afraid of those horrible creatures?"

"Oh, missis," said the poor child, "me no tink of dem; me forget all 'bout dem for de fretting."

"Why did you come home at last?"

"Oh, missis, me starve with hunger, me most dead with hunger before me come back."

"And were you flogged, Louisa?" said I, with a shudder at what the answer might be.

"No, missis, me go to hospital; me almost dead and sick so long, 'spec driver Bran him forgot 'bout de flogging."

I am getting perfectly savage over all these doings, E[lizabeth], and really think I should consider my own throat and those of my children well cut if some night the people were to take it into their heads to clear off scores in that fashion. . . .

I am helped to bear all that is so very painful to me here by my constant enjoyment of the strange, wild scenery in the midst of which I live, and which my resumption of my equestrian habits gives me almost daily opportunity of observing. I rode today to some new-cleared and plowed ground that was being prepared for the precious cotton crop. I crossed a salt marsh upon a raised causeway that was perfectly alive with land crabs, whose desperately active endeavors to avoid my horse's hoofs were so ludicrous that I literally laughed alone and aloud at them. The sides of this road across the swamp were covered with a thick and close embroidery of creeping moss, or rather lichens of the most vivid green and red: the latter made my horse's path look as if it was edged with an exquisite pattern of coral; it was like a thing in a fairy tale, and delighted me extremely.

I suppose, E[lizabeth], one secret of my being able to suffer as acutely as I do, without being made either ill or absolutely miserable, is the childish excitability of my temperament, and the sort of ecstasy which any beautiful thing gives me. No day, almost no hour, passes without some enjoyment of the sort this coral-bordered road gave me, which not only charms my senses completely at the time, but returns again and again before my memory, delighting my fancy, and stimulating my imagination. . . .

After my crab and coral causeway I came to the most exquisite thickets of evergreen shrubbery you can imagine. If I wanted to paint Paradise I would copy this undergrowth, passing through which I went on to the settlement at St. Annie's, traversing another swamp on another raised causeway. The thickets through which I next rode were perfectly draped with the beautiful wild jasmine of these woods. Of all the parasitical plants I ever saw, I do think it is the most exquisite in form and color, and its perfume is like the most delicate heliotrope.

I stopped for some time before a thicket of glittering evergreens, over which hung, in every direction, streaming garlands of these fragrant golden cups, fit for Oberon's banqueting service. These beautiful shrubberies were resounding with the songs of mockingbirds. I sat there on my horse in a sort of dream of enchantment, looking, listening, and inhaling the delicious atmosphere of those flowers.

2. A Georgia Planter Tells Why Cotton Pays, 1847

To Howell Cobb

Macon [Georgia], Jan. 10, 1847

. . . I have established a large planting interest in Sumpter, having purchased 2500 acres. Of this I have paid for one place 5500 $ already & have 1 & 2 years to pay 4000 for the other. Now you see at one extremity of this land & joining the first place I bought, I have a neighbor owning 600 acres of most superior land, which I shall buy to add to my last purchase, which will make me one place of unequalled fertility. And at the other extremity I have a chance of buying from an estate 1200 acres, joining the second purchase, which added to it will make a plantation scarcely inferior to the above named. All put together will make an investment of 24,000 $. I have already paid 5500 $. I shall be able to pay say 5000 $ out of the crop of this year. And then I shall have 14,000 $ to pay in one & two years. This is pretty extensive business for one so scary as I am about pecuniary responsibility. But I have ciphered it out and it can be done without risk. With the arable land I already have and what is on the two places to be purchased, considering the quality, for it is all fresh & rich as river bottoms, I can pay through easy. I have made my calculations safely. I have estimated my crops at 1/3rd less than an average & calculated on 6 cents per pound for cotton, & I can pay out & have a surplus. After this recital you see I shall be too heavy laden to take on the Baker place for the Trust estate until I get through with Sumpter.

Lord, Lord, Howell you and I have been too used to poor land to know what crops people are making in the rich lands of the new counties. I am just getting my eyes open to the golden view. On those good lands, when cotton is down to such a price as would starve us out, they can make money. I have moved 1/3rd of my force to Sumpter. I shall move another 1/3rd this fall or winter, leaving the remaining 1/3rd to cultivate the best lands on my Bibb place. This year I shall do better than I ever have done, & next year I shall do better than I ever expected to do. This year

From John B. Lamar to Howell Cobb, January 10, 1847, in John R. Commons et al., eds., *Documentary History of American Industrial Society.* New York: Russell & Russell Publishers, 1958, vol. I, pp. 176–181.

I shall cultivate very little poor land & next year I shall not waste labour on a foot of unprofitable soil. All will be of the 1st quality. When I work through I will try & help you onward to the promised land. But for 2 years after the present one, I shall be up to my chin in responsibility. I hate responsibility, but I have figured it out, that unless I take some as other prudent folks do I shall be like John Grier of Chack farm cultivating poor land all my life, which I am resolved not to do.

[John B. Lamar]

3. Frederick Law Olmsted Describes Cotton Production and Environmental Deterioration, 1861

A Well-Managed Cotton Plantation

We had a good breakfast in the morning, and immediately afterward mounted and rode to a very large cotton-field, where the whole field-force of the plantation was engaged.

It was a first-rate plantation. On the highest ground stood a large and handsome mansion, but it had not been occupied for several years, and it was more than two years since the overseer had seen the owner. He lived several hundred miles away, and the overseer would not believe that I did not know him, for he was a rich man and an honorable, and had several times been where I came from—New York.

The whole plantation, including the swamp land around it, and owned with it, covered several square miles. It was four miles from the settlement to the nearest neighbor's house. There were between thirteen and fourteen hundred acres under cultivation with cotton, corn, and other hoed crops, and two hundred hogs running at large in the swamp. It was the intention that corn and pork enough should be raised to keep the slaves and cattle. This year, however, it has been found necessary to purchase largely, and such was probably usually the case, though the overseer intimated the owner had been displeased, and he "did not mean to be caught so bad again."

There were 135 slaves, big and little, of which 67 went to field regularly—equal, the overseer thought, to 60 able-bodied hands. Beside the field-hands, there were 3 mechanics (blacksmith, carpenter and wheelwright), 2 seamstresses, 1 cook, 1 stable servant, 1 cattle-tender, 1 hog-tender, 1 teamster, 1 house servant (overseer's cook), and one midwife and nurse. These were all first-class hands; most of them would be worth more, if they were for sale, the overseer said, than the best of field-hands. There was also a driver of a hoe-gang who did not labor personally, and a foreman of the plow-gang. These two acted as petty officers in the field, and alternately in the quarters.

There was a nursery for sucklings at the quarters, and twenty women at this time who left their work four times each day, for half an hour, to nurse their young ones, and whom the overseer counted as half-hands—that is, expected to do half an ordinary day's work.

From Frederick Law Olmsted, "A Well-Managed Cotton Plantation" and "Abandoned Plantations" in *The Slave States.* New York: G.P. Putnam's Sons, 1959, pp. 180–181, 200–201. [Originally published as *Journeys and Explorations in the Cotton Kingdom: A Traveller's Observations on Cotton and Slavery in the American Slave States.* London: S. Low, Son, & Co., 1861.]

Abandoned Plantations

I passed during the day four or five large plantations, the hill-sides gullied like ice-bergs, stables and negro quarters all abandoned, and given up to decay.

The virgin soil is in its natural state as rich as possible. At first it is expected to bear a bale and a half of cotton to the acre, making eight or ten bales for each able field-hand. But from the cause described its productiveness rapidly decreases.

Originally, much of this country was covered by a natural growth of cane, and by various nutritious grasses. A good northern farmer would deem it a crying shame and sin to attempt to grow any crops upon such steep slopes, except grasses or shrubs which do not require tillage. The waste of soil which attends the practice is much greater than it would be at the North, and, notwithstanding the unappeasable demand of the world for cotton, its bad economy, considering the subject nationally, can not be doubted.

If these slopes were thrown into permanent terraces, with surfed or stone-faced escarpments, the fertility of the soil might be preserved, even with constant tillage. In this way the hills would continue for ages to produce annual crops of greater value than those which are at present obtained from them at such destructive expense—from ten to twenty crops of cotton rendering them absolute deserts. But with negroes at $1000 a head and fresh land in Texas at $1 an acre, nothing of this sort can be thought of. The time will probably come when the soil now washing into the adjoining swamps will be brought back by our descendants, perhaps on their heads, in pots and baskets, in the manner Huc describes in China, which may be seen also in the Rhenish vineyards, to be relaid on the sunny slopes, to grow the luxurious cotton in.

4. Sharecroppers' Contracts, 1876–1886

STATE OF NORTH CAROLINA, Wake County

Articles of Agreement, Between *Alonzo T. Mial* of said County and State, of the first part, and *A. Robert Medlin* of the County and State aforesaid, of the second part, to secure an Agricultural Lien according to an Act of General Assembly of North Carolina, entitled "An Act to secure advances for Agricultural purposes":

Whereas, the said *A. R. Medlin* being engaged in the cultivation of the soil, and being without the necessary means to cultivate his crop, *The Said A. T Mial* has agreed to furnish goods and supplies to the said *A. R. Medlin* to an amount not to exceed *One Hundred and fifty* Dollars, to enable him to cultivate and harvest his crops for the year 1876.

And in consideration thereof, the said *A. R. Medlin* doth hereby give and convey to the said *A. T. Mial* a LIEN upon all of his crops grown in said County in said year, on the lands described as follows: *The land of A. R. Medlin adjoining the lands of Nelson D. Pain Samuel Bunch & others.*

And further, in Consideration thereof, the said *A. R. Medlin* for One Dollar in hand paid, the receipt of which is hereby acknowledged, have bargained and

From Roger Ransom and Richard Sutch, *One Kind of Freedom.* New York: Cambridge University Press, 1977, pp. 91, 124.

sold, and by these presents do bargain, sell and convey unto the said *A. T. Mial his* heirs and assigns forever, the following described Real and Personal Property to-wit: *All of his Stock horses, Cattle Sheep and Hogs—Carts and Wagons House hold and kitchen furnishings.* To Have and to Hold the above described premises, together with the appurtenances thereof, and the above described personal property, to the said *A. T. Mial his* heirs and assigns.

The above to be null and void should the amount found to be due on account of said advancements be discharged on or before the *1st* day of *November* 1876: otherwise the said *A. T. Mial* his executors, administrators or assigns, are hereby authorized and empowered to seize the crops and Personal Property aforesaid, and sell the same, together with the above Real Estate, for cash, after first advertising the same for fifteen days, and the proceeds thereof apply to the discharge of this Lien, together with the cost and expenses of making such sale, and the surplus to be paid to the said *A. R. Medlin,* or his legal representatives.

IN WITNESS WHEREOF, The said parties have hereunto set their hands and seals this *29th* day of *February,* 1876.

his
A. Robert × *Medlin,* [seal]

mark

Witness: *L. D. Goodloe* [signed]   A. T. Mial [signed], [seal]

This contract made and entered into between A. T. Mial of one part and Fenner Powell of the other part both of the County of Wake and State of North Carolina—

Witnesseth—That the Said Fenner Powell hath barganed and agreed with the Said Mial to work as a cropper for the year 1886 on Said Mial's land on the land now occupied by Said Powell on the west Side of Poplar Creek and a point on the east Side of Said Creek and both South and North of the Mial road, leading to Raleigh, That the Said Fenner Powell agrees to work faithfully and dilligently without any unnecessary loss of time, to do all manner of work on Said farm as may be directed by Said Mial, And to be respectful in manners and deportment to Said Mial. And the Said Mial agrees on his part to furnish mule and feed for the same and all plantation tools and Seed to plant the crop free of charge, and to give the Said Powell One half of all crops raised and housed by Said Powell on Said land except the cotton seed. The Said Mial agrees to advance as provisions to Said Powell fifty pound of bacon and two sacks of meal pr month and occationally Some flour to be paid out of his the Said Powell's part of the crop or from any other advance that may be made to Said Powell by Said Mial. As witness our hands and seals this the 16th day of January A.D. 1886

A. T. Mial [signed] [Seal]

his
Fenner × *Powell* [Seal]
mark

Witness

W. S. Mial [signed]

5. Freed Slave Louis Hughes Describes Cotton Raising and Cotton Worms, 1897

Cotton Raising

After the selection of the soil most suitable for cotton, the preparation of it was of vital importance. The land was deeply plowed, long enough before the time for planting to allow the spring rains to settle it. Then it was thrown into beds or ridges by turning furrows both ways toward a given center. The seed was planted at the rate of one hundred pounds per acre. The plant made its appearance in about ten days after planting, if the weather was favorable. Early planting, however, followed by cold, stormy weather frequently caused the seed to rot. As soon as the third leaf appeared the process of scraping commenced, which consisted of cleaning the ridge with hoes of all superfluous plants and all weeds and grass. After this a narrow plow known as a "bull tongue," was used to turn the loose earth around the plant and cover up any grass not totally destroyed by the hoes. If the surface was very rough the hoes followed, instead of preceding, the plow to unearth those plants that may have been partially covered. The slaves often acquired great skill in these operations, running plows within two inches of the stalks, and striking down weeds within half an inch with their hoes, rarely touching a leaf of the cotton. Subsequent plowing, alternating with hoeing, usually occurred once in twenty days. There was danger in deep plowing of injuring the roots, and this was avoided, except in the middle of rows in wet seasons when it was necessary to bury and more effectually kill the grass. The implements used in the culture of cotton were shovels, hoes, sweeps, cultivators, harrows and two kinds of plows. It required four months, under the most favorable circumstances, for cotton to attain its full growth. It was usually planted about the 1st of April, or from March 20th to April 10th, bloomed about the 1st of June and the first balls opened about August 15th, when picking commenced. The blooms come out in the morning and are fully developed by noon, when they are a pure white. Soon after meridian they begin to exhibit reddish streaks, and next morning are a clear pink. They fall off by noon of the second day.

The Cotton Worm

A cut worm was troublesome sometimes; but the plants were watched very carefully, and as soon as any signs of worms were seen work for their destruction was commenced. The majority of the eggs were laid upon the calyx and involucre. The worm, after gnawing through its enclosed shell, makes its first meal upon the part of the plant upon which the egg was laid, be it leaf, stem or involucre. If it were laid upon the leaf, as was usually the case, it might be three days before the worm reached the boll; but were the eggs laid upon the involucre the worm pierced through within twenty-four hours after hatching. The newly hatched boll worm walks like a geometrical larva or looper, a measuring worm as it was called. This is easily explained

---

From Louis Hughes, *Thirty Years a Slave: From Bondage to Freedom.* New York: Negro Universities Press, 1969; originally published n.p.: South Side Printing Co., 1897, pp. 27–37.

by the fact that while in the full grown worm the abdominal legs, or pro legs, are nearly equal in length, in the newly hatched worm the second pair are slightly shorter than the third, and the first pair are shorter and slenderer than the second—a state of things approaching that in the full grown cotton worm, though the difference in size in the former case is not nearly so marked as in the latter. This method of walking is lost with the first or second molt. There is nothing remarkable about these young larvæ. They seem to be thicker in proportion to their length than the young cotton worms, and they have not so delicate and transparent an appearance. Their heads are black and their bodies seem already to have begun to vary in color. The body above is furnished with sparse, stiff hairs, each arising from a tubercle. I have often watched the newly hatched boll while in the cotton fields. When hatched from an egg which had been deposited upon a leaf, they invariably made their first meal on the substance of the leaf, and then wandered about for a longer or shorter space of time, evidently seeking a boll or flower bud. It was always interesting to watch this seemingly aimless search of the young worm, crawling first down the leaf stem and then back, then dropping a few inches by a silken thread and then painfully working its way back again, until, at last, it found the object of its search, or fell to the ground where it was destroyed by ants. As the boll worms increase in size a most wonderful diversity of color and marking becomes apparent. In color different worms will vary from a brilliant green to a deep pink or dark brown, exhibiting almost every conceivable intermediate stage from an immaculate, unstriped specimen to one with regular spots and many stripes. The green worms were more common than those of any other color—a common variety was a very light green. When these worms put in an appearance it raised a great excitement among the planters. We did not use any poison to destroy them, as I learn is the method now employed.

The Cotton Harvest

The cotton harvest, or picking season, began about the latter part of August or first of September, and lasted till Christmas or after, but in the latter part of July picking commenced for "the first bale" to go into the market at Memphis. This picking was done by children from nine to twelve years of age and by women who were known as "suckers," that is, women with infants. The pickers would pass through the rows getting very little, as the cotton was not yet in full bloom. From the lower part of the stalk where it opened first is where they got the first pickings. The season of first picking was always a great time, for the planter who brought the first bale of cotton into market at Memphis was presented with a basket of champagne by the commission merchants. This was a custom established throughout Mississippi. After the first pickings were secured the cotton developed very fast, continuing to bud and bloom all over the stalk until the frost falls. The season of picking was exciting to all planters, every one was zealous in pushing his slaves in order that he might reap the greatest possible harvest. The planters talked about their prospects, discussed the cotton markets, just as the farmers of the north discuss the markets for their products. I often saw Boss so excited and nervous during the season he scarcely ate. The daily task of each able-bodied slave during the cotton picking season was 250 pounds or more, and all those who did not come up to the required amount would get a whipping. When the planter wanted more cotton picked than usual, the overseer would arrange a race. The slaves would be divided into two parties, with a leader for each party. The first leader would choose a slave for his side, then the second leader one for his, and so on alternately until all were chosen. Each leader tried to get the best on his side. They would all work like good fellows for the prize, which was a tin cup of sugar for each slave on the winning side. The contest was kept up for three days whenever the planter desired an extra amount picked. The slaves were just as interested in the races as if they were going to get a five dollar bill.

Preparing Cotton for Market

The gin-house was situated about four hundred yards from "the great house" on the main road. It was a large shed built upon square timbers, and was similar to a barn, only it stood some six feet from the ground, and underneath was located the machinery for running the gin. The cotton was put into the loft after it was dried, ready for ginning. In this process the cotton was dropped from the loft to the man who fed the machine. As it was ginned the lint would go into the lint room, and the seed would drop at the feeder's feet. The baskets used for holding lint were twice as large as those used in the picking process, and they were never taken from the gin house. These lint baskets were used in removing the lint from the lint room to the place where the cotton was baled. A bale contained 250 pounds, and the man who did the treading of the cotton into the bales would not vary ten pounds in the bale, so accustomed was he to the packing. Generally from fourteen to fifteen bales of cotton were in the lint room at a time.

Other Farm Products

Cotton was the chief product of the Mississippi farms and nothing else was raised to sell. Wheat, oats and rye were raised in limited quantities, but only for the slaves and the stock. All the fine flour for the master's family was bought in St. Louis. Corn was raised in abundance, as it was a staple article of food for the slaves. It was planted about the 1st of March, or about a month earlier than the cotton. It was, therefore, up and partially worked before the cotton was planted and fully tilled before the cotton was ready for cultivation. Peas were planted between the rows of corn, and hundreds of bushels were raised. These peas after being harvested, dried and beaten out of the shell, were of a reddish brown tint, not like those raised for the master's family, but they were considered a wholesome and nutritious food for the slaves. Cabbage and yams, a large sweet potato, coarser than the kind generally used by the whites and not so delicate in flavor, were also raised for the servants in liberal quantities. No hay was raised, but the leaves of the corn, stripped from the stalks while yet green, cured and bound in bundles, were used as a substitute for it in feeding horses.

Farm Implements

Almost all the implements used on the plantation were made by the slaves. Very few things were bought. Boss had a skilled blacksmith, uncle Ben, for whom he paid $1,800, and there were slaves who were carpenters and workers in wood who could turn their hands to almost anything. Wagons, plows, harrows, grubbing hoes, hames, collars, baskets, bridle bits and hoe handles were all made on the farm and from the material which it produced, except the iron. The timber used in these implements was generally white or red oak, and was cut and thoroughly seasoned long before it was needed. The articles thus manufactured were not fine in form or finish, but they were durable, and answered the purposes of a rude method of agriculture. Horse collars were made from corn husks and from poplar bark which was stripped from the tree, in the spring, when the sap was up and it was soft and pliable, and separated into narrow strips which were plaited together. These collars were easy for the horse, and served the purpose of the more costly leather collar. Every season at least 200 cotton baskets were made. One man usually worked at this all the year round, but in the spring he had three assistants. The baskets were made from oak timber, grown in the home forests and prepared by the slaves. It was no small part of the work of the blacksmith and his assistant to keep the farm implements in good repair, and much of this work was done at night. All the plank used was sawed by hand from timber grown on the master's land, as there were no saw mills in that region. Almost the only things not made on the farm which were in general use there were axes, trace chains and the hoes used in cultivating the cotton.

The Clearing of New Land

When additional land was required for cultivation the first step was to go into the forest in summer and "deaden" or girdle the trees in a given tract. This was cutting through the bark all around the trunk about thirty inches from the ground. The trees so treated soon died and in a year or two were in condition to be removed. The season selected for clearing the land was winter, beginning with January. The trees, except the larger ones, were cut down, cut into lengths convenient for handling and piled into great heaps, called "log heaps," and burned. The undergrowth was grubbed out and also piled and burned. The burning was done at night and the sight was often weird and grand. The chopping was done by the men slaves and the grubbing by women. All the trees that blew down during the summer were left as they fell till winter when they were removed. This went on, year after year, until all the trees were cleared out. The first year after the new land was cleared corn was put in, the next season cotton. As a rule corn and cotton were planted alternately, especially if the land was poor, if not, cotton would be continued year after year on the same land. Old corn stalks were always plowed under for the next year's crop and they served as an excellent fertilizer. Cotton was seldom planted on newly cleared land, as the roots and stumps rendered it difficult to cultivate the land without injury to the growing plant.

I never saw women put to the hard work of grubbing until I went to McGee's and I greatly wondered at it. Such work was not done by women slaves in Virginia. Children were required to do some work, it mattered not how many grown people were working. There were always tasks set for the boys and girls ranging in age from nine to thirteen years, beyond these ages they worked with the older slaves. After I had been in Pontotoc [Mississippi] two years I had to help plant and hoe, and work in the cotton during the seasons, and soon learned to do everything pertaining to the farm.

6. A Louisiana Convention Declares War on the Boll Weevil, 1903

At noon on the 30th Nov., the Convention was called to order in the Odd Fellows Hall, in the City of New Orleans, by the temporary chairman, Abe Brittin, President of the N. O. Cotton Exchange, who spoke as follows:

"I bring you

GREETINGS FROM THE COTTON EXCHANGE

which extends you its privileges while you are in the city, and will co-operate with you in any movement for the extermination of the Mexican cotton boll weevil.

"You are called upon to consider ways and means for arresting the further progress of the pest. More than this, you are expected to devise means to permanently exterminate the weevil. It is folly to say that this cannot be accomplished. It can be accomplished; it must be accomplished; it will be accomplished. When the vineyards of France were threatened, France produced her Pasteur, and the vineyards were saved. America will produce her Pasteur, and the cotton fields will be saved.

"Last September I said that the most momentous peril involved in the cotton outlook was the Mexican cotton boll weevil. The evil is spreading, and eventually it will spread from Texas to other States. The seriousness of the situation should be brought to the attention of the Government.

"With the increased acreage, improved fertilizers and methods of culture, we are to-day five years away from the production of a maximum crop. This has not occurred in twenty-five years, and, if we except the period of the Civil War, it has never occurred in the history of the South. Production is not keeping pace with consumption, and if this condition be not relieved, some other section of the world will produce the cotton needed. This should not be. This may be a time for the States to hedge the weevil in or out, but the paramount responsibility rests upon the National Government. And we need not go to Congress as mendicants, but, with heads erect, present the situation, and say that if it would protect the industry, a remedy must be found. . . ."

At the conclusion of his remarks, Mr. Brittin introduced the permanent Chairman,

HON. CHAS. SCHULER,

who spoke as follows:

"Gentlemen of the Convention and Brother Farmers Interested in the Culture of Cotton: This Convention has been called by His Excellency, the Governor of this State, with a view to consulting with the people most interested in the welfare of the State and the cotton industry, to see whether it is necessary to call an extra session of the Legislature to take steps and pass laws by which to check the progress of the insect that is threatening the welfare not only of the State, but of the country.

From *Proceedings of the Boll Weevil Convention,* New Orleans, La., 1903, pp. 5–7, 12–15.

"The State of Louisiana is threatened on the west by an insect known as the Mexican cotton-boll weevil. It has been a mystery to me that the great State of Texas, with its immense territory from west to east, would permit an insect to destroy millions of its property without any effort, so far as I know, on the part of the State to check its course. How was it that the veterans who sacrificed their property and their lives to drive back the human vermin that infested their State would suffer this insect to overwhelm them? If we consider the amount of money that is in circulation; if we consider the number of people that live upon the production and handlings of this staple, we can realize the immense importance of the crop.

VALUE OF COTTON

during the month of October, in this last year—one month, no more—amounted to $60,000,000. Does any individual, knowing this, think that the National Government could afford to keep hands off and not render help in this crisis? Some of us who are old enough remember the effect on the National Treasury when the exportation of cotton was prohibited by blockade.

"Sometimes we hear of men saying that it will be a blessing in disguise; that we cotton planters ought to learn to plant lettuce, cabbage, onions, etc., in order to make a profit. Now, every cotton planter here present knows how absolutely foolish this is. Others say that it will prove a blessing in disguise, because we can get 50 cents a pound for cotton. But they forget that the balance of the world is making heroic efforts to grow this very staple in other portions of the world. . . ."

The next speaker was

PROF. H. A. MORGAN,

Station Entomologist. He said:

HOW TO PROTECT LOUISIANA AGAINST THE INVASION OF THE BOLL WEEVIL.

We are confronted to-day with a problem of very difficult solution. To successfully overcome, or even to retard for a few years, the entrance of the Mexican boll weevil into Louisiana will require the united efforts of every one interested in Louisiana's future.

All effective preventive and remedial measures used against the injurious insects of the world are the outcome of careful investigation and study of life-cycles and habits and of the conditions peculiar to the locality where these remedies are put into operation. Unless the work against the weevil is based upon all the known facts of its habits and development, and upon the conditions peculiar to the section of country where the warfare is to be carried on, the results will be disappointing and harmful. . . .

The weevil belongs to that division of insects which have complete metamorphoses—i.e., there are four stages in the existence of each weevil, viz: the egg, the grub or worm stage, the pupa, sometimes called "the kicker," stage, and finally the adult or sexually mature form—the weevil. The adults, or weevils, live through the winter among material of various kinds. Grass, leaves, bark of trees and trash of any kind in the cotton field or in close proximity to it, offer suitable hibernating quarters. That weevils do not migrate far is clearly indicated in the great saving to a cotton crop where fall plowing of all infected cotton fields is practiced after the cotton stalks and other trash have been raked up and thoroughly burned. The weevils that survive the hibernating period emerge from winter quarters in the spring and feed upon volunteer or planted cotton. In the forms or squares eggs (one in each square) are deposited. The eggs hatch in a day or two into the worms (grubs or larvae), which feed upon the contents of the squares for from eight to twenty days, depending upon the temperature. The grubs at the end of the existence of this stage assume the pupa or kicker condition, and in from five to twelve days the weevils emerge from the pupae and are soon ready to lay eggs. Two facts must be here emphasized, viz: that the entire early life is completely concealed in the square or boll, and that the length of the cycle of development depends upon food and temperature conditions. In early and late summer thirty or more days may be consumed in the transformation from egg to weevil, while in midsummer only fifteen to twenty are required.

During winter the weevil does not require food, but in spring, summer and fall, when life's functions are active, food is essential.

COTTON IS THE ONLY KNOWN FOOD PLANT

In the . . . absence of cotton the weevils die in summer. . . .

When squares are punctured and eggs deposited in them they invariably fall to the ground, where, in the shade of the plant, the weevil goes on developing until its life cycle is completed. The sun's heat frequently dries up fallen squares before the weevils are mature, and hence the value of planting cotton in wide rows and plenty of distance between the plants in the row in weevil-infected cotton lands.

In the presence of sufficient food the boll weevil does not range extensively, and hence cultural methods that will limit the number of weevils during the active breeding season is of the utmost importance in checking the migration of the weevil to other fields and States. It therefore seems plain that the wide distribution of the weevil each year is not due so much to the ranging or migratory habits of the weevil itself, but to the distribution of material such as cotton, cottonseed, hay and other products from infected lands, in and upon which the weevil may be resting or hibernating. The cotton gin is a focal point for weevils, which are gathered in seed cotton, and the cottonseed a distributing medium, especially in the spring of the year.

Among the suggestions as to how best to protect Louisiana against the invasion of the boll weevil, none seem more important than the one whereby every planter in the State shall become conversant with all the known facts associated with the life and habits of the weevil in order that he may scrupulously avoid its importation and understand the very best means of eradicating it, should isolated outbreaks appear. For a number of years the United States Department of Agriculture and the Experiment Station authorities of Texas have been earnestly at work to develop methods of successfully combatting the weevil. The result of these investigations have so far established that insecticides are useless, and that the clean culture of early varieties of cotton make it possible to grow a profitable crop. The number of weevils in infected fields is limited by these cultural methods until the cotton plants have had time to mature their fruit. When these cultural methods are adopted the natural range or overflow of the weevil is minimized, but, unfortunately for Texas, and to the great regret of the planters of Louisiana, these suggestions have not been universally put into practice, and the consequent increase of the infected area has become alarming. The weevil area of Texas has spread until it is only a few miles from the western border of our State, and from this time out it behooves us to guard zealously our borders, quarantine against infected products and to adopt reasonable methods of preventing the natural and general spread of this pest throughout Louisiana.

A NON-INFECTED COTTON ZONE

lies between the borders of Louisiana and the weevil fields of Texas. This zone will protect us in a very great measure from gross infection next year, provided the utmost care is exercised in preventing infected products, particularly cotton seed, hulls, hay and corn, from entering our State. The most serious impediment to the prosecution of preventive measures is the indifference of many of our farmers and planters as to the seriousness and extreme gravity of the situation, and hence I wish again to emphasize the great need of an educational campaign along the western border of our State that will arouse every man to the necessity of intelligent, uniform and immediate action.

Should the weevil appear next spring and summer in isolated fields of the western border of this State, such fields should be immediately quarantined, and all infected plants destroyed. The adult weevils may be gathered from a few trap plants left for this purpose. Upon this area and on adjacent fields no cotton should be grown the following year, in order to completely starve out any forms that may have escaped.

7. Ex-Slaves Describe Their Means of Subsistence, 1937

Monroe Brackins

We had possums and coons to eat sometimes. My father, he generally cooked the coons; he would dress them and stew them and then bake them. My mother would eat them. There were plenty of rabbits, too. Sometimes when they had taters, they cooked them with them. I remember one time they had just a little patch of blackhead sugar cane. After the freedom, my mother had a kind of garden, and she planted snap beans and watermelons pretty much every year.

The master fed us tolerably well. Everything was wild; beef was free, just had to bring one in and kill it. Once in a while, on a Sunday morning, we'd get biscuit flour bread to eat. It was a treat to us. They measured the flour out, and it had to pan out just like they measured. He gave us a little something every Christmas and something good to eat. I heard my people say coffee was high, at times, and I know we didn't get

Excerpts from Ronnie C. Tyler and Lawrence R. Murphy, eds., *The Slave Narratives of Texas.* Austin: Encino Press, 1974, pp. 46–47, 51. Excerpts from George P. Rawick, ed., *The American Slave: A Composite Autobiography,* vols. 6, 7 of *Mississippi Narratives* (Westport, Ct.: Greenwood Publishing Group, Inc., 1977), pp. 110–113, 300–302, 722–723.

no flour, only Sunday morning. We lived on cornbread, mostly, and beef and game out of the woods. That was during the [Civil] war and after the war, too.

Andy J. Anderson

I'm going to explain how it was managed on Master Haley's plantation. It was sort of like a little town, because everything we used was made right there. There was the shoemaker, and he was the tanner and made the leather from the hides. Master had about a thousand sheep, and he got the wool, and the niggers carded and spinned, and wove it, and that made all the clothes. Then master had cattle and such to provide the milk and the butter and beef meat for eating. Then he had the turkeys and chickens and the hogs and the bees. With all that, we never were hungry.

The plantation was planted in cotton, mostly, with the corn and wheat a little, because master didn't need much of them. He never sold anything but the cotton.

Ellen Payne

I mostly minded the calves and chickens and turkeys. Massa Evans used an overseer, but he didn't allow him to cut and slash his niggers, and we didn't have a hard taskmaster. There were about thirty slaves on the farm, but I am the only one living now. I loved all my white folks, and they were sweet to us.

The hands worked from sun to sun and had a task at night. Some spun or made baskets or chair bottoms or knitted socks. Some of the young ones courted and some just rambled around most all night.

There was always plenty to eat, and one nigger didn't do anything but raise gardens. They hunted coon and possum and rabbits with dogs, and the white folks killed deer and big game like that. My daddy always had some money because he made baskets and chair bottoms and sold them, and massa Evans gave every slave a patch to work, and they could sell what it produced and keep the money.

Sarah Felder

I allus planted my garden in de moon, an' iffen you plant beans or cucumbers when de sign is in de arm yer will allus hev big bunches of beans ter cum at one time, cause dat is when de sign means twins.

Iffen you want good luck ter cum ter you, when you see er white mule, jes stamp him, by wettin' yer finger an' hittin de palm uf yer hand an' yer will hev good luck fur dat day; an' iffen yer see a bussard dat same day yer will hev good luck all dat week.

When we wus chulluns old Mandy uster mek 'teas an' give us ter keep us well, an' I larnt how ter doctor my chaps dat same way, an' dat beats eny doctor you ebery seed. Iffen dar is whoopin' cough in de neighborhood, jes tie er lil' l 'asfiddy' in er rag an' tie it round yer neck an' yer wont hev whoppin' cough.

I am old now an' de young folks doan think we old folks hev eny sense, but dar is er lotter things I culd tell dem iffen I wuld, but when dey git sick dey hev ter buy store bought medicine.

I am not able ter wurk now, but I hev seed de time when I culd beat eny uf de niggers wurkin' in de fiel' an' doin' all my wurk at de house, an' tendin' ter de chaps as well. None uf dese young one can do dat now.

We allus walked whar eber we wint an' dese young folks say dey cant walk now er day, an' de want er fine car an' go in debt fur it ter git it.

Della Buckley

I aint never studied 'bout how old I is; that's sumpen I aint never paid any 'tention to. I was bornd in Montgomery on the East'ley plantation, kinder out in the country, you know. The lady I nuss'd fer was all time travelin' back an' fofe ter Mer-*ree*-dian ter see her husband; he worked in an' outer there; an' finely she 'come on' ter Mer-*ree*-dian fer good an' I come with her.

When I was 'bout grown, I started cookin' but I learned ter cook good befo' I started workin' fer Boss Williams an' Ol' Miss. I 'speck I was 'bout thirty-five then. I mar'ied right here in my own house in they backyard, mar'ied Pretty. Yas'm, that's what they calls him, 'cause he's so ugly, I reckon. I been had fo' chullen but they all dead.

They do say I cooks right good, must er been cookin' fer 'em might 'nigh forty years. They all time havin' comp'ny. When Boss's gent'mun friends comes from New York an' Baltimore, they brags right smart on my spoonbread an' sech. But they aint but one sho' 'nough way ter cook a possum. I'll tell you jes how I does it.

Firs', you gits the boy ter clean him fer you, scrape him twell he git white. Then you soaks him all night in salten water; take him out in the mornin' an' *dreen* him an' wipe him off nice an' dry; then you par-boils him a while. Then you takes him out an' grease him all over with butter an' rub flour all over him an' rub pepper in with it. Then you bas'e him with some er the juice what you par-boiled him in. Then you puts him in the stove an' lets him bake. Ever' time you opens the stove do', you bas'es him with he gravy. Peel yo sweet pertaters an' bake along with him twell they is nice an' sof' an' brown like the possum hisse'f. Sprinkle in flour ter thicken yo gravy jes' like you was makin' reg'lar chicken gravy. When he's nice an' brown, you puts a pertater in he mouf an' one on each side, an' yo possum is ready ter eat.

Yas'm, I been sailin' right high all my life. When you comin' ter dinner with us again?

John Belcher

I fishes wid a pole and line all together. I got no license but I sells all I cotch. I jes walks up an down de river bank an fishes. Once I cotch a 59 pound cat fish. I wuz livin on a farm, on Mr. Duncan McCloud's place, bout ten years ago. I had set my pole and gone back to de house fer supper. 'fore goin to bed I sent one of de boys down to see effen dere wuz any thing on de line and after a while hearin' so much fuss down dar I lit de lamp and went down to see bout it. I shore wuz 'sprised; we did'n know, for sho, what wux on dat line. I got a boat and 'tween us we bringed dat fish in. It took us two hours to land him as he weighed 59 pounds. We et fish fer three or four days and give all de folks roun fish, too.

Fer catchin' Buffalo now I uses flour dough an a little corn meal, mixed wid a little cotton worked in it, fer bait. Durin de time I'm not fishin I puts two or three "Draws" out in different places on de river. To make dese "Draws" I puts chops, corn meal, or bread, in a crocker sack making a roll bout 12 inches long by 10 inches wide. I attach a wire to dis and anchor de wire to a stob long de river bank. I leaves dis here fer bout 8 days to toll de fish to dis spot. When I gits ready to fish dere I partly draws dis wire in den drap in my line and I really catches dem buffaloe.

In de spring an summer I uses earth worms and chicken entrails fer bait. But the best trick of all, I doan want no one to know dis trick, Mis is dis. Git ten cents worth of olive oil, mix wid a pint of waste oil from a filling station, mix wid about 1/2 pint of coal oil. Put all dis in a big fruit jar and shake rale good. Drap yo fish line and hooks in dis den put a little bait on yo hook and when de fish smells dis dey sho come.

Yas'm I used to hunt lots. De way I cotch wild turkeys I'd roost him at night, you know when you hears em settlin on a limb, sorta rustlin dere wings, I'd spot him and git dere fore he left nex mornin and shoot him, fore day light.

I use to set traps fer deer. You take a stick 'bout 3 feet long sharpen it at one end and put it in de ground leanin toward a rail fence. One stick on the inside and one on the outside. When de deer jumped over dat fence the stob snagged him. I'se cot several dat way. A old Indian taught me dat trick when I lived in Florida. I fergits de name of dat swamp but dere wuz lots of Indians dere and Deer, too.

We use to cotch seven or eight possums a night. We used dogs, to tree em den we'd shake em out on de ground and de dogs would catch em. Effen one uf us had to clamb a tree we'd allus leave one man on de ground to catch em. Sometimes we'd git mixed up wid a coon and a coon can whip two or three good dogs.

One wild cat could run a set (4) of dogs down any time. We used to take after a cat and as fast as one would run one set of dogs down we'd set another set on him. It took bout twelve hours to run a cat down. After the dogs would bay him den we'd shoot him or kill him some way. Once a wild cat runned a white lady, school teacher, and most scared her to death. He wuz a big one and we had a time catchin him. Dis wuz in Monroe County, Alabama.

In Clark County, Alabam between the Alabama and Tombigbee Rivers Mr. Allan Holder used to set his double barrel shot gun, lay it in a way and setting the trigger wid a string tied to it. He'd load dat gun wid 12 or 18 buck shot and some powder, in each barrel. He killed bear dis way. Dat bear would trip over de string and de gun would go off an kill him. I'se helped him bring in, sometimes, two and three a week dat he killed dis way.

8. A Freed Slave Explains
"Why That Boll Weevil Done Come," 1945

I knows why that boll weevil done come. They say he come from Mexico, but I think he always been here. Away back yonder a spider live in the country, 'specially in the bottoms. He live on the cotton leaves and stalks, but he don't hurt it. These spiders kept the insects eat up. They don't plow deep then, and plants cotton in February, so it made 'fore the insects git bad.

Then they gits to plowing deep, and it am colder 'cause the trees all cut, and they plows up all the spiders and the cold kill them. They plants later, and there ain't no spiders left to eat up the boll weevil.

From "Why That Boll Weevil Done Come," in B. A. Botkin, ed., *A Folk History of Slavery.* Chicago: University of Chicago Press, 1945, p. 13.

✹ E S S A Y S

The essays for this chapter emphasize different aspects of Cotton South agriculture, soil utilization, and crop pests. In the first essay, Albert Cowdrey, an environmental historian of the South from the U.S. Army Center of Military History, discusses the soils and environmental conditions of the Lower South that made cotton production feasible, as well as the row-crop monocultures of corn and cotton that resulted in soil erosion and toxicity, parasites, and pest outbreaks. Whereas Cowdrey associates soil degradation with the technological characteristics of row-crop cultivation, Eugene Genovese, a historian at the University Center of Georgia, in the second essay ascribes it to the slave system of production. "Slavery and the plantation system," he argues, "led to agricultural methods that depleted the soil." Slavery was not conducive to the care and attention that the application of fertilizers required, and the use of cotton-corn rotations alone did not return sufficient fertility to the soil. Yet ending slavery did not lead to the restoration of soil fertility, as historian Theodore Steinberg, professor of history at Case Western Reserve University, shows in the third essay. The application of fertilizers to increase yields was countered by the advent of the boll weevil in 1893, which devastated cotton crops. Sharecropping in the post-Civil War era was especially hard on blacks and poor whites: Many of them had traditionally used the woods, open fields, and common lands to hunt, gather foods, and graze cattle. But hard times and new restrictive laws pushed those who could leave to migrate north to industrial cities. The essays thus reveal the complexities of life in the South for those at all levels of society as environmental actors interacted with human actors.

Soils Used

ALBERT COWDREY

The expansion of the South across the Appalachians and the Mississippi River to the fringes of the high plains was one of the great American folk wanderings. Motivated by the longing for fresh and cheap land, and by obscurer urges, such as simple restlessness and the large human capacity for dissatisfaction, southerners completed their occupation of a region as large as western Europe. Despite the variety of the land—which contained regions of pine barrens and prairies, of hardwood forests and limey plateaus, of some of the world's oldest mountains and a considerable part of its third longest river—and the variety of the societies from which they came, the settlers of the Southwest had certain broad similarities. They might be farmers large or small, but most farmed or lived by serving the needs of farmers. Their way of dealing with the wild assumed each man's right to use beasts and timber as he saw fit. Not all owned or ever would own slaves, but most accepted slavery as a mode of holding and creating wealth. Throughout the Southwest a burgeoning democracy amplified the folk voice for both good and ill. . . .

In 1803 the Louisiana Purchase added to the South a new city, a new culture, and a new physiographic region. Indeed, several regions, for beyond the western escarpment of the alluvial valley stretched forested hills giving way to treeless plains which were to mark for the white and black South, as they had for the red, an indefinite yet enduring cultural boundary.

Excerpts from Albert E. Cowdrey, "The Row Crop Empire," in *This Land, This South: An Environmental History,* Lexington, KY: The University Press of Kentucky, 1983, pp. 65–80. Reprinted by permission of the University Press of Kentucky.

Dominating the immediate area of settlement was the Mississippi, which had created the alluvial valley. From Missouri's Commerce Hills to the sea 600 miles to the south, the river expanded during floodtime to cover vast areas of bottomland, precipitating its heavier alluvium to form natural levees, and carrying finely-divided clays back into the swamps. Human settlement gravitated to these natural levees to be safe from floods, to exploit their fertility, and to use the river for transport. The Franco-Spanish Creole culture of the valley showed in this respect certain similarities to the Mississippian Indian culture, whose remnants it encountered among the Natchez and helped to destroy.

The settlers grew rice because the land behind the levees was easily flooded, and maize, which as usual established itself as the food of the poor. A modest tobacco industry grew up, and indigo, as well, until destroyed in the 1790s by Asian competition and local insects. Experiments began with sugar cane, a much-travelled plant, which had been carried from India to Spain by the Muslims, by the Spanish to the New World, and by the French from Haiti to Louisiana. . . .

Across much of the new territory south and east of the Appalachians rose the phenomenon of the Cotton Kingdom. The development in the late eighteenth century of an efficient gin for separating the lint and seeds of short-staple cotton is a justly famous example of the impact of technology on culture. It is also true that the culture was in search of the technology. To fuel an expansion of the character and speed that occurred between 1790 and 1837, the South needed some commercial crop adapted to the climate, demanded by the overseas market, and suitable for production in circumstances ranging from the frontier farm to the great plantation. The fact that the English textile industry was already mechanizing made this crop particularly timely. Cotton as a great staple was invented as much as grown, made to order for the place and time. Early in the nineteenth century Mexican cotton was introduced, because its "large wide-open bolls" facilitated picking and greatly increased the amount that a worker could gather in a day. . . .

Like the crop itself, the boundaries of the Cotton Kingdom were determined by tacit agreement between [humans] and nature. Antebellum opinion sometimes held that, roughly speaking, the southern border of Pennsylvania, extended west, marked the limit of profitable production. With few exceptions, however, the actual dimensions of the region were smaller. A better boundary was the 77°F summer isotherm. This line runs roughly from the northeastern border of North Carolina, dipping south of the Appalachian massif, and rising to the northwestern border of Tennessee. West of the Mississippi it skirts the Ozark highlands and rises again to north-central Oklahoma. On occasion cotton was grown commercially north of this line in response to high prices—notably in southern Virginia and the Nashville basin. Noncommercial production for household use was also common. But in general terms, this was the boundary of the Cotton Kingdom. Northward, cotton grew well enough in mild years but poorly in cool ones; in short, it was not a money crop that could be depended upon. The line was a limit defined partly by the human need for consistency in a commercial undertaking, partly by the nature of the plant itself. . . .

Between 1800 and 1860 Georgia's white population increased about nine times, Louisiana's and Tennessee's about ten times, Mississippi's about one hundred times, Arkansas's over four hundred times, and Alabama's about one thousand times. (Such figures of course indicate not only the rapidity of settlement but the initial lack of a white populace in the middle Gulf region.) . . .

The Cotton Kingdom made rapid conquests, not only in the middle Gulf region, but along the lower Mississippi River and its tributaries. Prior to the War of 1812 cotton production in Louisiana had been comparatively small (two million pounds estimated for 1811). But the fiber was already being grown in the Natchez area, and between 1810 and 1820 it made rapid progress in Louisiana, as well, spreading into the Attakapas and Opelousas regions and up the Red River. Soon settlers, led by squatters and harassed by federal troops trying to protect Indian lands, were entering the region where Louisiana, Arkansas, and Texas later met. . . .

As long as prices held and erosion was a process only beginning, the Cotton Kingdom throve. Acreage, production, and yield all grew, and would continue to do so until 1890 or so. Especially during the 1850s the mood of the cotton planters was ebullient, as reflected in their journals. Profits were good and "slavery itself was generally returning high profits to those who invested in that peculiar institution." The question of whether the antebellum South was able, in the face of its commercial commitments, to feed itself remains in doubt. A complex of many subregions, the South defies summary on this point; by and large it probably did so, though considerable food was imported from the West, as well.

Triumphant agriculture took out heavy liens against the natural dower. Row crops bared the soil, the rows made watercourses for the rains, which were heavy, and the colonial practice of plowing straight up and down hills was by no means extirpated. Further, any system which covers too many fields with the same plant falls afoul of the ecological principle which states that the simplest systems are apt to be the most unstable. Natural systems, almost always complex, contain multitudes of checks which prevent any single event from threatening the whole with destruction. In any great center of monoculture, soil toxins develop and parasites of many sorts are encouraged to multiply explosively. The South was not unique in planting great areas to a few basic plants, but no more than the Ireland of the 1840s was it exempt from the dangers inherent in such dependence.

Few can view without sympathy the extraordinary achievements of the black and white pioneers and settlers who created the row-crop empire in a few generations of prodigious effort. To make a living from the land without injuring it is nowhere easy, and in much of the South probably harder than elsewhere in America. It does appear, however, that the westward movement had imposed a burden on the southern environment which neither wisdom nor good will would be able to lighten significantly for generations to come.

Soils Abused

EUGENE GENOVESE

Soil Exhaustion as a Historical Problem

The South, considered as a civilization, found itself locked in an unequal, no-quarter struggle with the more modern and powerful capitalist civilization of the free states. The concentration of wealth in the hands of an aristocratic ruling class retarded the

Excerpt from Eugene Genovese, "Soil Exhaustion as a Historical Problem," in *The Political Economy of Slavery.* Middletown, CT: Wesleyan University Press, 1989, pp. 85, 88–97. Reprinted with permission from Wesleyan University Press.

accumulation of capital and the evolution of a home market and thereby spelled defeat for the South's efforts at matching the North's industrial progress. Paradoxically, the agrarian South could not keep pace with the North in agricultural advancement, and the attempt to break the pattern of one-crop farming and colonial dependence on the export trade largely ended as a failure. The South's inability to combat soil exhaustion effectively proved one of the most serious economic features of its general crisis. . . .

The essence of soil exhaustion is not the total exhaustion of the land, nor merely "the progressive reduction of crop yields from cultivated lands," for the reduction may be arrested at a level high enough to meet local needs. An acceptable general theory of the social effects of soil exhaustion must be sufficiently flexible to account for the requirements of different historical epochs. The rise of capitalism requires a theory that includes the inability of the soil to recover sufficient productivity to maintain a competitive position. The main problem lies in the reaction of social institutions, rather than in the natural deterioration of the soil. The Old South, specifically, had to compete in economic development with the exploding capitalist power of the North, but its basic institution, slavery, rendered futile its attempts to fight the advance of soil exhaustion and economic decline.

The Role of Slavery

Although the land of the Black Belt ranked among the finest in the world and although cotton was not an especially exhausting crop, the depletion of Southern soil proceeded with a rapidity that frightened and stirred to action some of the best minds in the South. Many of the principles of soil science have only recently come to be understood, and many misleading ideas prevailed during the nineteenth century. Several important points had nevertheless been settled by the mid-1850s: that crops require phosphates and salts of alkalis; that nonleguminous crops require a supply of nitrogenous compounds; that artificial manures may maintain soil fertility for long periods; and that fallowing permits an increase in the available nitrogen compounds in the soil. Southern reformers, especially the talented Edmund Ruffin, had discovered these things for themselves and were particularly concerned with counteracting soil acidity. Southern agricultural periodicals and state geological surveys repeatedly stressed the need for deep plowing, crop rotation, the use of legumes, manuring, and so forth.

Although the results of the agricultural reform movement were uneven at best and although John Taylor of Caroline, the South's first great agricultural reformer, had called slavery "a misfortune to agriculture incapable of palliation," later agronomists denied that slavery contributed to the deterioration of the soil. Ruffin, for example, attributed soil exhaustion to the normal evolution of agriculture in a frontier community and assumed that economic pressures would eventually force farmers and planters to adopt new ways. Ruffin's attitude has been resurrected and supported by many historians, who have held that slavery did not prevent the adoption of better methods and that the Civil War interrupted a general agricultural reformation. . . .

Slavery contributed to soil exhaustion by preventing the South from dealing with the problem after the frontier conditions had disappeared. [William Chandler] Bagley [Jr.] argues that "the slaveowner cannot because of slavery escape wearing out the soil," but the greater weakness lay in the slaveholders' inability to restore lands to competitive levels after they had become exhausted naturally in a country with a moving frontier. The one-crop system perpetuated by slavery prevented crop rotation; the dearth of liquid capital made the purchase of fertilizer difficult; the poor quality of the implements that planters could entrust to slaves interfered with the proper use of available manures; and the carelessness of slaves made all attempts at soil reclamation or improved tillage of doubtful outcome.

The Use of Fertilizers

The direct and indirect effects of slavery greatly restricted the use of fertilizers. For cotton and corn the application of fertilizers to hills or rows is far superior to spreading it broadcast, and considerable care must be taken if the labor is not to be wasted. The planter had to guarantee maximum supervision to obtain minimum results. Planters did not have the equipment to bury fertilizers by deep plowing, and the large estates, which inevitably grew out of the slave economy, made fertilization almost a physical and economic impossibility. In certain parts of the Upper South planters solved the problem by selling some of their slaves and transforming them into liquid capital with which to buy commercial fertilizers. The smaller slave force made possible greater supervision and smaller units. This process depended upon the profitable sale of slaves to the Lower South and was therefore applicable only to a small part of the slave region. In the Southeast the use of fertilizers proceeded, as did reform in general, slowly and painfully. Despite the pleas of the reformers, the reports of state geologists, and the efforts of local or state agricultural societies, county after county reported to the federal Patent Office, which was then responsible for agricultural affairs, that little fertilization of any kind was taking place.

Many planters used cottonseed, which was most effective in the cornfields, as fertilizer in the 1850s, but the cotton fields had to depend largely on barnyard manure. This dependence need not have been bad, for barnyard manure probably supplies plants with needed iron, but planters did not keep sufficient livestock and did not feed their animals well enough to do much good. To be of use barnyard manure requires considerable care in storage and application, and even today much of it is lost. In 1938 experts in the Department of Agriculture estimated that one-half was dropped on uncultivated land and that the valuable liquid portion of the remainder was often lost. Improper application rendered much of the rest useless, for manure must be applied at the right time according to soil conditions and climate. This fertilizer requires all the time, care, supervision, and interest that farmers can provide and that slaves cannot or will not. Overseers or even planters themselves hardly had the desire to watch their laborers with the unrelenting vigilance that was needed. . . .

The difficulties in accumulating barnyard manure stirred a growing interest in marl, which Ruffin recommended so highly as an agent capable of counteracting soil acidity and of "deepening the soil" by lowering the level of good earth. In 1853 he claimed that properly marled land in Virginia had increased in value by 200 per cent. . . .

Yet by 1860 few in Mississippi used either guano or marl. Perhaps in time more of these fertilizers would have been used, but not many planters could possibly have borne the cost of transporting enough marl for their huge estates, much less the cost of buying and transporting enough guano. Planters and farmers in Alabama and

Georgia used little marl before 1850, and there is no evidence of an appreciable improvement in the fifties. When they did use marl, they generally had it applied so badly that Ruffin despaired of ever teaching them to do it properly. To make matters worse, errant planters only succeeded in convincing themselves that Ruffin was, after all, only a "book farmer."

Peruvian guano emerged as the great hope of planters and farmers with ex-hausted lands. The desire for guano reached notable proportions during the 1840s and 1850s: whereas less than 1,000 tons were imported from Peru during 1847–1848, more than 163,000 tons were imported during 1853–1854. . . .

Guano, like other fertilizers, required considerable care in application; if not used intelligently, it could damage the land. The less expensive American guano required more attention than the Peruvian, especially since it contained hard lumps that had to be thoroughly pulverized.

When guano did come into use in the Lower South indications are that wealthy coastal planters applied it to their badly exhausted fields. . . .

According to the *Report on Agriculture* submitted by the Commissioner of Patents in 1854, about 300 pounds of Peruvian guano had to be applied to fertilize an acre of exhausted land, with a second dressing of 100 to 200 pounds recommended for land planted to Southern staples. That is, cotton land required about 450 pounds of guano per acre. Although the American Guano Company claimed that 200 to 350 pounds of its brand would do, the more objective De Bow's *Industrial Resources* insisted on 900 pounds of this inferior but adequate guano. At forty dollars per ton a planter with 250 acres would have had to spend somewhere between $500 and $2,500 for this second-rate guano; and since its effects were not lasting he would have had to spend it regularly. Whatever the advantages of the relatively inexpensive American variety, it required more cash than all but a few planters had. . . .

When one considers the size of the plantations of the Cotton Belt and the care-less, wasteful way in which the slaves worked, planters cannot be blamed for ignoring the results of neat experiments conducted by a few unusual men like David Dickson of Georgia or Noah B. Cloud of Alabama. James S. Peacocke of Redwood, Louisiana, summed up some of the planters' problems:

> In respect to our worn out lands, it is almost useless for anyone to waste paper and ink to write the Southern planter telling him to manure. It is well enough for Northern farmers to talk; they can well afford to fertilize their little spots of ten or a dozen acres; but a Southern plantation of 500 or 600 acres in cultivation would require all the manure in the parish and all the force to do it justice . . . Again, we have no time to haul the large quantities of manure to the field, for it generally takes until January to get all our cotton, and we have to rush it then, to get time to make repairs before we go to plowing for our next crop.

Peacocke was writing about barnyard manure, but all that he needed to add to account for other fertilizers was that few planters, and fewer farmers, could afford to buy them.

Crop Rotation

Rotation of staple crops with alfalfa, clover, and other legumes might have protected and restored Southern soils. Rotation helps counteract the effects of leaching and erosion, and green manure, although probably less useful than barnyard manure, increases the supply of nitrogen in the soil. Ebenezer Emmons, state geologist of North Carolina, pointed out that marl could be harmful if too much was applied and that proper crop rotation and plowing under the peas could offset the danger of excessive lime.

The South is not the best grass country, although in recent years its share of the nation's grassland has risen remarkably. There was no natural obstacle to the production of more alfalfa, oats, rye, cowpeas, clover, hairy vetch, and other soil-improving crops. Although nitrogenous manuring for cereals tends to encourage the growth of straw relative to grain, the reverse is true for cotton and corn. . . . The cotton-corn-cowpea sequence did not return enough elements to the soil to prevent a steady decline of fertility.

Exceptions to the no-rotation rule appeared only here and there. Ruffin used a fine six-field system, and a fellow Virginian, Colonel Tulley, rotated his wheat with clover and got excellent results. Most planters, especially in the Cotton Belt, were unwilling and more often economically unable to take land away from their cash crop. . . . In 1860, Eugene W. Hilgard, Mississippi state geologist, wrote that the only rotation practiced on a large scale was that of cotton and corn, and similar reports came from throughout the Lower South.

The Exhaustion of the Soils of the Lower South

Daniel Lee, editor of the *Southern Cultivator,* estimated in 1858 that 40 per cent of the South's cotton land was already exhausted, and he was given considerable support by other competent observers. . . . As early as 1842 the *Southern Planter* had reported worn-out lands across the interior of Mississippi, and the soil deteriorated steadily thereafter. . . .

Fertilizers absorbed more than 7 per cent of the South's farm income, compared with 1 per cent for the rest of the country, although only fifteen bushels of corn were produced per acre, compared with forty-three bushels in New England and thirty-six in the Middle Atlantic states. Parts of South Carolina in 1920 required about 1,000 pounds of fertilizer per acre of cotton land, and the general requirements of Mississippi ranged from 200 to 1,000 pounds. The South still grows cotton only because of tremendous expenditures for the fertilizers with which to strengthen its exhausted soils.

Slavery and the plantation system led to agricultural methods that depleted the soil. In this respect the results did not differ much from those experienced on the Northern frontier, but slavery forced the South into continued dependence on exploitative methods after the frontier had passed. Worse, it prevented the reclamation of the greater part of the worn-out land. The planters had too much land under cultivation; they lacked the necessary livestock; they could practice crop rotation only with difficulty; and they had to rely on a labor force of poor quality. Under such circumstances, notwithstanding successes in some areas, the system could not reform itself. When reforms did come to Maryland, Virginia, and certain counties of the Lower South, it was either at the expense of slavery altogether or by a reduction in the size of slaveholdings and the transformation of the surplus slaves into liquid capital. The South faced a dilemma of which the problem of soil exhaustion formed only a part. On the one hand, it needed to develop its economy to keep pace with that of the free states, or the proud slaveholding class could no longer expect to retain its hegemony. On the other hand, successful reform meant the end of slavery and of the basis for the very power the planters were trying to preserve.

Soils Extracted

THEODORE STEINBERG

The South emerged from the [Civil] war—its fields and livestock plundered, its forests cut down for firewood and barrack timber—as an economically crippled region and persisted that way for at least the next half century. The cotton mono-culture, which had gained a strong foothold in the region during the antebellum period, advanced across the landscape at a pace that would have challenged even the most accomplished Confederate cavalryman. In its wake, it left the land scarred, its people, black and white farmers alike, destitute and more dependent on outside sources of food as well as capital. As the region descended into poverty, people from outside the region—northern capitalists, midwestern lumbermen, and British financiers—siphoned off its natural wealth, especially its forests and minerals. The ecological origins of the New South that grew up on the ashes of war centered squarely on the extraction of resources for the benefit of the greater national economy. Blacks were set free in a region enslaved.

Fast Food Farming

King Cotton emerged from the war more imperious and despotic than ever before. As the single most important cash crop in the postbellum South, the staple soared in importance, turning autumn in the stretch from South Carolina to east Texas into a sea of white that drifted off toward the horizon. Like addicts unable to control themselves, Southern farmers grew so much cotton that they continued to undercut their ability to feed themselves. By 1880, per capita corn and hog production in the Deep South plummeted to nearly half of 1860 levels, forcing farmers to import food from the Midwest. Wisconsin flour, Chicago bacon, Indiana hay—all flowed in to shore up the region's food deficit, when in fact, as one observer noted, these items could have been grown in Dixie "at nothing a ton."

At one level, the attraction of cotton is easy to understand. The economic profit from planting was simply far greater than for any other grain crop. With its acid soil conditions and heavy rainfall, the South, unlike the temperate northern states, was not well suited to raising grains and grasses. Add to this the animal parasites that dragged down livestock prospects, and the magnetism of cotton becomes easier to comprehend.

Of course favorable market conditions and this same ecological context had existed in the antebellum South. And yet, despite the extraordinary importance of cotton in the prewar South, it came nowhere near rivaling the crop's incredible dominance in the postbellum era. What happened? Two main factors—the rise of

From Theodore Steinberg. *Down to Earth: Nature's Role in American History.* New York: Oxford University Press, 2002, pp. 99–110. Used by permission of Oxford University Press, Inc.

sharecropping and the growing commercialization of farming—explain cotton's eventual chokehold on the region.

Sharecropping developed as blacks were denied the right to own land in the aftermath of the Civil War. By 1868, the same white planter class that controlled the land in the antebellum period continued to retain its title to the region's most valuable resource, only now the slaves had been set free and planters could no longer count on their labor. This proved especially problematic for those who raised cotton because the crop must be picked in a timely way or it can be seriously damaged by rainfall. Freed from their chains, blacks were known to leave planters in the lurch, moving on smack in the middle of the cotton-picking season. Sharecropping helped to resolve this problem by tying laborers to the land for a specified period of time. Planters divided their plantations into 30- to 50-acre farms and rented them out to freedmen, providing tenants with land, seed, and the necessary tools and, in return, taking half the share of the crop at harvest. The arrangement appealed to planters and also to freedmen who, unable to buy land on their own, found that sharecropping at least gave them an opportunity to get out from under the thumb of white supervision. Landlords, however, did reserve the right to dictate the crop mix to tenants; with their own personal fortunes tied to what the sharecropper raised, logic led them to choose cotton because it was more profitable per acre than any other crop.

Sharecropping and the cotton monoculture went hand in hand with the increasing commercialization of farming, spurred by the spread of railroads and merchants. In the 1870s, railroads began laying track in the Georgia Up Country, tying this region more closely to markets in the North. With the railroads in place, merchants, who bought locally grown cotton and sold goods on credit, were not far behind. Under crop lien laws, passed in the 1870s, merchants loaned farmers money with a future crop as collateral. For obvious reasons, they insisted that farmers plant cotton. "If I say 'plant cotton' they plant cotton," one merchant was reputed to have said. With the system stacked in cotton's favor, sharecroppers tripped over each other as they trundled off to their fields to plant more. But the more they planted, the less food they produced on their own. Hence the more they had to turn to stores for supplies, drawing them into a vicious cycle of indebtedness.

Nothing was more critical to cotton growing under the sharecropping system than fertilizer. Landlords and renters alike had little incentive to invest in the long-term health of their land and thus little interest in crop rotation or manuring, practices designed to ward off soil depletion. Current yields were what mattered most to them, with the land simply a vehicle for raising cotton for cash. Such present-mindedness encouraged farmers to mine the soil for all that it was worth, using fertilizer to pump up yields in the short run.

Beginning in 1867, with the establishment of large phosphate mines in South Carolina, commercial fertilizer use boomed. Much of the soil in Georgia and South Carolina suffered from a natural deficiency in phosphorous, a problem the fertilizer addressed with a great deal of initial success. Cotton yields soared as this powerful chemical input bolstered the fertility of the soil. Fertilizer also sped up crop growth, causing cotton to mature more quickly and uniformly. The speedup shortened the cotton harvest to as little as five weeks and lowered the threat posed by rain or frost. Given the virtues of fertilizer and its pivotal role in the cotton monoculture under the sharecropping system, it is perhaps not surprising to find that the South consumed a larger percentage of it (on a per acre basis) than any other region in the nation.

A mix of inorganic chemicals was pumped into ecosystems across the South, ratcheting up what the soil would yield. No longer self-contained entities sustained by their own nutrient cycle, southern farms increasingly became receptacles for various outside inputs in the quest for more cotton. For a time, phosphorous-based fertilizer worked, but what the cotton crop needed most was nitrogen, a chemical not yet incorporated into plant food mixtures. Worse still, as sharecroppers fell further into debt, they bought greater amounts of commercial fertilizer from merchants on credit in an effort to boost output and generate the cash to pay off their loans—a self-defeating process that pushed the soil to its ultimate limit. "Who said fertilizer? Well, that's just it. Every farmer says it, every tenant says it, every merchant says it, and even the bankers must speak of it at times," one observer noted. "The trouble is that in times past the easy purchase and use of fertilizer has seemed to many of our Southern farmers a short cut to prosperity, a royal road to good crops of cotton year after year. The result has been that their lands have been cultivated clean year after year, their fertility has been exhausted." While some areas turned to more ecologically stable crop rotation practices, much of Georgia and South Carolina, as well as portions of Alabama and Mississippi, fell prey to the fertilizer craze. The trend made the late nineteenth century the worst period for soil erosion in the South's entire history.

Single-crop farming is always a perilous enterprise, a point that became apparent when farmers found their soil woes compounded by the arrival of an insect with a taste for cotton. In 1892, the boll weevil, a small insect whose larva fed on the cotton boll, made its way out of Mexico into Texas. Eastward it marched, reaching Louisiana in 1904, crossing the Mississippi five years later, and arriving in South Carolina by 1917. The pest left destruction in its wake, dramatically reducing cotton yields just about everywhere it went. In Greene County, Georgia, farmers picked 11,854 bales of cotton in 1916, the year the boll weevil first arrived. Six years later, the county produced a minuscule 333 bales.

The weevil may well have played a role in the great exodus of blacks to the North that began in 1910—one of the largest migrations in the history of the world. Between 1910 and 1920, it is estimated that as many as 500,000 African Americans left the South for northern cities. Many factors were at work to entice blacks to leave their rural homes, including the higher wages that came with the tightening of the labor market during World War I as well as the South's failure to provide blacks with the social and political equality they deserved. But changes in the land also drove blacks North. In the early 1910s, one woman from Mississippi spoke of a "general belief [among blacks] that God had cursed the land." The boll weevil was especially devastating for black tenant farmers. Under the thumb of creditors who demanded cotton, black tenants had little say over the mix of crops they planted. But more than just the weevil caused blacks to wonder whether God was speaking up. Devastating flooding along the lower Mississippi River in 1912, made worse by the policy of building levees, broke records on nearly all of the river gauges set up to measure water heights between Cairo, Illinois, and the Gulf of Mexico. It seems fair to say that the pull of higher northern wages combined then with various setbacks on the land and inequality to cause blacks to flee.

Whatever the weevil's role in African American history, it had at least two other consequences. First, it drove farmers to use even more fertilizer to help the cotton crop mature before the weevil attacked it, solidifying the shift away from organic farming. And second, the insect caused cotton yields to decline precipitously.

The number of acres devoted to cotton in the Deep South (Louisiana, Mississippi, Alabama, Georgia, and South Carolina) declined an average of 27 percent when figures are compiled for the four years immediately before and after the infestation. The weevil broke cotton's grip on the region, heralding the move to a more diversified form of agriculture centered on corn, peanuts, and hogs. Some farmers even went so far as to thank the weevil for creating a way out of one-crop farming. Citizens in Enterprise, Alabama, actually erected a statue in honor of the bug, one of the more curious national monuments to dot the American landscape, a symbol for what it took—outright calamity—to force southerners to abandon their single-minded and ill-fated relationship with the land.

Blacks too sometimes welcomed the weevil as a way of breaking the grip that cotton and financial dependence on merchants had on their lives. Blues singers immortalized the insect, most famously in this song by Huddie Ledbetter (Ledbelly), who was born in 1888 in Shiloh, Louisiana.

> First time I seen the boll weevil, he was sitting on a square.
> Next time I seen a boll weevil, he had his whole family there.
> He's a looking for a home.
> He's a looking for a home.
>
> The old lady said to the old man, "I've been trying my level best
> Keep these boll weevils out of my brand new cotton dress.
> It's full of holes.
> And it's full of holes."
>
> The old man said to the old lady, "What do you think of that?
> I got one of the boll weevils out of my brand new Stetson hat,
> And it's full of holes.
> And it's full of holes."
>
> Now the farmer said to the merchant, "I never made but one bale.
> Before I let you have that last one, I will suffer and die in jail.
> And I will have a home.
> And I will have a home."

Open and Shut Range

If cotton's stranglehold impoverished the ecology of the South, it also helped to drive many people deeper into poverty as well. In the postbellum period, rural population densities, backed by relatively high fertility rates, rose to the point where in 1930 the region was twice as thickly settled as the North. Farm size, meanwhile, continued a relentless downward trend. Rural southerners sunk deeper into poverty as small farm size combined with low production levels to push them to the edge of financial calamity. In 1880, federal census takers described black farmers as "sometimes without bread for their families." "Many are in a worse [economic] condition than they were during slavery." As their diet declined, poor southerners, both black and white, did what they had long been accustomed to doing: They turned to the region's common lands—unenclosed woods and pastures—taking game, fishing, and turning out whatever few hogs and cattle they had to find forage. Only now with pressure on the

South's common resources more intense than ever—the product of increased sport and market hunting—many white landlords, merchants, and planters, with the law as their weapon, sought to prohibit the free taking of game by sealing off the range.

In the antebellum period, slaves, especially those on tidewater plantations, headed for rivers and forests to procure food and supplement their rations. "My old daddy," Louisa Adams of North Carolina recollected, "partly raised his chilluns on game. He caught rabbits, coons an' possums. He would work all day and hunt at night." Slaves also hunted and fished for the sport of it, these being among the few recreational activities afforded them. In the woods of the South Carolina Low Country, slaves hunted deer, rabbits, squirrels, opossums, bears, ducks, turkeys, pigeons, and other animals. "Possum and squirrel all we could get," recalled one slave. "Wild turkey, possum. Don't bother with no coon much." In 1831, a visitor from the North observed, "The blacks are never better pleased than when they are hunting in the woods; and it is seldom that they have not in the larder the flesh of a raccoon or opossum." In the Georgia Low Country almost half of the slaves' meat, it is estimated, came from game and fish.

Slaves also counted on the woods as a source of fodder for their livestock. Curious as it may sound, although themselves owned by others, slaves possessed property, including animals like cattle and hogs. One slave, described by a white planter as "more like a free man than any slave," claimed in the mid-nineteenth century to have had 26 pigs, 16 sheep, and 8 cows.

It was to the pine forests and patches of cane commonly found along streams that slaves and whites alike went to run their hogs and cattle. "We raise our hogs by allowing them to range in our woods, where they get fat in the autumn on acorns," explained one resident of the South Carolina Piedmont. Cattle were raised "with so little care, that it would be a shame to charge anything for their keep up to three years old." The open range thrived in the South in large part because the mild winters allowed herders to leave their stock on the range all year round (in the North, farmers had to bring in the animals to prevent them from freezing to death and thus barn size limited the number of animals that could be left free to roam the common lands). . . .

With emancipation, however, things began to change. Planters wondered how they would ever make a living growing cotton if their labor force continued to roam the countryside exercising their customary right to game. In 1866, one Virginia newspaper bemoaned the fact that planters "suffer great annoyance and serious pecuniary loss from the trespasses of predacious negroes and low pot hunters, who with dogs and guns, live in the fields . . . as if the whole country belonged to them." Slowly, planters called for making private property more private and less open to customary hunting and fishing by commoners. "The right to hunt wild animals is held by the great body of the people, whether landholders or otherwise, as one of their franchises," lamented the wealthy South Carolina planter and sportsman William Elliott. One observer who toured the South in the 1870s found that blacks "are fond of the same pleasures which their late masters gave them so freely—hunting, fishing, and lounging; pastimes which the superb forests, the noble streams, the charming climate minister to very strongly." . . .

By the late nineteenth century the southern commons was in turmoil. Market and sport hunters descended in search of game, while cattle and pigs overran it in the quest for forage. Few animals inspired more resentment than the hog, described by one Mississippian, in a fit of anger, as an "old, pirating, fence-breaking, corn-destroying, long-snouted, big boned and leather-bellied" beast. Apart from planters, railroads also suffered from the effects of allowing livestock to roam the range. Under the law, the roads were liable if animals became injured on their tracks. The legal nicety may have driven some stockowners—eager to collect damages—to apply salt to the rails so as to lure the hapless creatures into oncoming trains. . . .

. . . By the 1890s, a new set of fence laws, often called stock laws, were on the books in counties across the South (although it would take decades, in some places until the 1970s, before the range was fully closed). The laws required farmers and stockmen to pen in their livestock, making them legally responsible if the animals somehow escaped and caused damage to someone's property. The stock laws penalized those—poor whites and blacks—who had formerly relied on the unenclosed stretches of land. People with power and money used the law to preserve the sanctity of their property and make it more private. Those who had once counted on such land had to turn to other means of subsistence.

The stock laws had ecological and biological consequences to match their social ones. Animals formerly allowed to run loose in the woods now became true domesticates. Penned up in barnyards and no longer free to roam the land, the animals were either fattened on feed or forced to graze on self-contained pastures, where overuse, especially on hillsides, may have contributed to the South's already intense erosion problem. The closing of the range also helped to limit the spread of the cattle tick, carrier of the parasitic infection babesiosis (eventually named Texas fever by midwesterners who feared the Lone Star state's infected livestock). In the early twentieth century, the federal government introduced a program for eradicating the tick, now that the animals could no longer roam the landscape and infect one another at will; the move greatly benefited large commercial stock raisers. Tragically, the high capital costs involved in purchasing the technology to eliminate the cattle tick, plus the huge expense of fencing in livestock, combined to further disadvantage southern yeomen who raised just a few cattle for household use. The stock laws, a social development, brought about a biological shift (a less congenial environment for the tick) that led to still more social changes—unfavorable ones, at least from the standpoint of struggling farmers.

The domestication of people and animals, it would seem, went hand in hand, but with one critical difference: The poor people put out by the enclosure of the commons could protest their woes. The fencing controversy, which ultimately worked its way as far west as Texas, figured prominently in the rise of the late-nineteenth-century agrarian protest movement known as Populism. The Populists formed a third political party, the People's party, opposed to the business-dominated organizations run by the Democrats and Republicans. But their critique of American society stemmed in part from changes in the land. For it was there that the yeoman farmer's earlier subsistence lifestyle, resting on corn, some cotton, and the pasturing of hogs in woods and bottomlands, gave way to the single-minded pursuit of cotton alone by the 1880s. Now the logic of distant markets in New York, St. Louis, and Liverpool, not the dietary needs of families, combined with the enclosure of the commons to force such farmers deeper into poverty. Driven from a safer and more ecologically sound form of farming to embrace the monoculture, small farmers became victims of those who sought an end to the open range.

ψ F U R T H E R   R E A D I N G

Charles S. Aiken, *The Cotton Plantation South Since the Civil War* (1998)

William Andrews, *Six Women's Slave Narratives* (1988)

Hugh Hammond Bennett, *The Soils and Agriculture of the Southern States* (1921)

John W. Blassingame, *The Slave Community: Plantation Life in the Antebellum South* (1979)

W. J. Cash, *The Mind of the South* (1941)

Albert E. Cowdrey, *This Land, This South: An Environmental History* (1983)

Pete Daniel, *Breaking the Land: The Transformation of Cotton, Tobacco, and Rice Cultures Since 1880* (1985)

Elizabeth Fox-Genovese, *Within the Plantation Household: Black and White Women of the Old South* (1989)

Eugene D. Genovese, *The Political Economy of Slavery* (1965)

———, *Roll, Jordan Roll: The World the Slaves Made* (1972)

Dianne D. Glave, "The African American Cooperative Extension Service: A Folk Tradition in Conservation and Nature Appreciation in the Early Twentieth Century," *The International Journal of Africana Studies* 6, no. 1 (Fall 2000): 85–100.

———, "'A Garden So Brilliant with Colors, So Original in Its Design': Rural African American Women, Gardening, Progressive Reform, and the Foundation of an African American Environmental Perspective," *Environmental History* 8, no. 3 (July 2003): 395–411.

Lewis Cecil Gray, *History of Agriculture in the Southern United States to 1860* (1958)

Deborah Gray White, *Ar'n't I a Woman?* (1985)

Frances Anne Kemble, *Journal of a Residence on a Georgian Plantation in 1838–1839* [1863], (1961)

John Hebron Moore, *The Emergence of the Cotton Kingdom in the Old Southwest: Mississippi, 1770–1860* (1987)

Frederick Law Olmsted, *The Slave States* (1959)

John Solomon Otto, *The Southern Frontiers, 1607–1860: The Agricultural Evolution of the Colonial and Antebellum South* (1989)

Theda Perdue and Michael D. Green, eds., *The Columbia Guide to American Indians of the Southeast* (2001)

Ulrich B. Phillips, *Life and Labor in the Old South* (1956)

George P. Rawick, ed., *The American Slave: A Composite Autobiography* (1977)

Joseph P. Reidy, *From Slavery to Agrarian Capitalism in the Cotton Plantation South: Central Georgia, 1800–1880* (1992)

Theodore Rosengarten, *All God's Dangers: The Life of Nate Shaw* (1974)

———, *Tombee: Portrait of a Cotton Planter* (1986)

Edmund Ruffin, *Agriculture, Geology, and Society in Antebellum South Carolina: The Private Diary of Edmund Ruffin, 1843,* William M. Mathew, ed. (1999)

Susan Dabney Smedes, *Memorials of a Southern Planter* (1965)

Kenneth Stampp, *The Peculiar Institution: Slavery in the Ante-Bellum South* (1956)

Theodore Steinberg, *Down to Earth: Nature's Role in American History* (2002)

Mart A. Stewart, "Southern Environmental History," in John Boles, ed., *A Companion to the American South* (2002)

William L. Van Deburg, *The Slave Drivers: Black Agricultural Labor Supervisors in the Antebellum South (Contributions in Afro-American and African Studies, No. 43)* (1997)

Rupert Bayless Vance, *Human Factors in Cotton Culture: A Study in the Social Geography of the American South* (1929)

Charles Reagan Wilson and William Ferris, *Encyclopedia of Southern Culture* (1989)

D.A. Wolfenbarger, L. D. Hatfield, and E. V. Gage, eds., *The Tobacco Budworm and Bollworm in Cotton in the Mid-South, Southwestern United States and Mexico* (1991)

C. Vann Woodward, *American Counterpoint: Slavery and Racism in the North-South Dialogue* (1964)

Gavin Wright, *The Political Economy of the Cotton South* (1978)

CHAPTER
8

Extracting the Far West in the Nineteenth Century

❦

West Coast development reflected a different set of international, racial, and ethnic issues and affected different natural resources than did East Coast settlement. Indian tribes experienced the advent of Spanish and Mexican explorers and missionaries from the south, followed by Russians and Aleuts from the north, New England traders and whalers by sea from the west, and finally Europeans, Americans, Asians, Mexicans, Chileans, and other ethnicities by sailing east and around the world during the Gold Rush of the last half of the nineteenth century. This chapter focuses on ocean and river waters, on the otters and salmon that became global commodities, and on the impact of water use during the era of hydraulic mining.

Among the earliest commodities to be extracted from the northern Pacific for trade were the pelts of sea otters ("soft gold") and sea lions, which were prized by Chinese and traded by Russians. In 1841 the Danish sea captain Vitus Bering, in the service of the Russian Navy, set out on his second voyage to explore the region east of Siberia, discovering America from the east. Although Bering and others died of scurvy following a shipwreck on the journey back, the survivors returned to Russia with valuable sea otter pelts, setting off the Russian-American-Chinese otter trade. The sea otter and sea lion trade flourished for almost a century, bringing Russian settlement to Alaska and as far south as the California coast. Although the Russians and their Aleut servants were resisted in Alaska by the Tlingit and in California by the Spanish, the trade resulted in the near extinction of the otters. By 1842, the Russian trade in California ended, just a few scant years before the 1846 settlement of Oregon and the 1849 Gold Rush to California.

The Gold Rush dramatically changed the land and rivers of California. Miners' use of "white gold," or water, in extracting the yellow gold metal conflicted with farmers' needs for that same water for their "green gold" crops. Racial composition too was altered. The Gold Rush brought Americans (including Indians and blacks), Europeans, Canadians, Chinese, Mexicans, and other immigrants who carried a variety of cultural traditions and beliefs to the gold fields, mining towns, farms, and incipient cities of northern and central California. White society cast aside its egalitarian dreams, succumbing to class-based realities as the mining of gold and other minerals required ever more costly and sophisticated hydraulic nozzles and hoses, iron-stamp mills, grinders, and amalgamation techniques for exploiting river bottoms, gravel deposits, and quartz rock formations. Mining had severe environmental reper-cussions. Miners' camps polluted the water and air. Hydraulic mining with giant nozzles washed so much debris into the Sacramento River and San Francisco Bay that valley farmers brought suit against mountain miners and successfully halted hydraulic mining in 1884. Fishing and spawning were affected not only by the debris but also by the mercury used as an amalgam to capture gold and silver in the sluice boxes. Soils suffered from runoff, flooding, and erosion.

Salmon, or "pink gold," were among the organisms most affected by hydraulic mining and Gold Rush debris, pushing California salmon fishers and processors northward to the Columbia River system, where they competed with Indians for fishing locations and developed ever more sophisticated technologies for netting and processing fish catches. Dams obstructed the passage of spawning salmon, fish wheels scooped up vast numbers of fish during their upstream migrations, and hatcheries were developed to restock supplies. Fishing came to be regulated by state and federal fish commissions, Indian agents and lawyers defended Indians' rights to fish in their "usual and accustomed places," and gillnetters banded together in organizations, creating ever more complex sets of interests and relationships. This chapter explores the global ecological and human networks that developed on the Pacific coast of North America during the nineteenth century. (See Maps 1, 2, 3, 4, 8, and 10 in the Appendix.)

❦ D O C U M E N T S

The documents in this chapter view the Far West from a variety of perspectives, illustrat-ing the impacts of the sea otter trade, mining, and fishing on the natural environment and on the lives of and relationships among a diversity of peoples. The selections raise questions about the possible connections between a healthy natural environment and a healthy social environment.

In Document 1, published in 1813, Russian sailor and artist Louis Choris, who sailed on a voyage around the world, described the Russian sea otter trade, which extended south from Sitka and Kodiak Island, Alaska, to the Russian settlement thirty miles north of San Francisco Bay. Document 2 is an account by Kiril Khlebnikov of the Russian Alexander Baranov's management of the Russian-American trade out of Kodiak and Sitka, Alaska; Baranov's use of the Aleuts and their baidarkas (two-person kayaks) to capture sea otters; and his temporary defeat by the Tlingit Indians of Sitka.

During the 1840s, Euramerican society leapfrogged across the Great Plains to settle Oregon Territory (which the United States officially acquired in 1846 after the settlement of disputes with Great Britain located the northern U.S. border at the 49th parallel) and California (which the nation acquired in 1848, at the end of the Mexican War). Docu-ment 3 is a speech made by Missouri senator Thomas Hart Benton to Congress in 1846 in which he urges the U.S. settlement of Oregon and justifies settlement of the Pacific lands on grounds of the superiority of the "white" race over the "red, yellow, black, and brown" races.

The one hundred thousand Indians who lived in California in 1849 were reduced to fifteen thousand by 1900 through disease, massacre, and loss of subsistence resources. Document 4 is an 1853 letter from a federal agent to his superintendent in the San Fran-cisco Bureau of Indian Affairs describing the impact of the gold mines on Indian rivers and on their fish, wildlife, and acorn supplies. In Document 5, excerpted from an 1857 article for *California Magazine,* James Marshall recalls his 1848 discovery of gold near Sutter's Fort outside Sacramento. News of the discovery spread like wildfire around the world, sparking the 1849 Gold Rush. Document 6 focuses on the fate of the gold country around Mount Shasta. Taken from Joaquin Miller's 1890 book *Life Amongst the Modocs,* the passages reveal the simultaneous demise of the Indians and deterioration of their environment under the impact of mining.

The salmon canneries of northern California also suffered from the impact of hydraulic mining and moved north to Oregon and Washington in the 1860s. Document 7 is the assessment by Fish Commissioner Livingston Stone in 1885 of the decline of salmon on the Columbia River between Oregon and Washington during the twenty years since the advent of canneries. In Document 8, entrepreneur R. D. Hume discusses his canning and hatchery enterprises on Oregon's Rogue River.

Document 9 is the voice of an Indian woman, Kate Luckie, in 1925, speaking on behalf of water and telling how it may take its revenge on the whites who destroyed the land. Her voice poignantly depicts the ways in which water is an actor that links all life together and winds its way through the themes of the chapter.

1. A Russian Sailor Depicts the Sea Otter Trade, 1813

Sea-otters abound in the harbour [of San Francisco] and in the neighbouring waters. Their fur is too valuable for them to be overlooked by the Spaniards. An otter skin of good size and of the best quality is worth $35 in China. The best grade of skins must be large, of a rich colour, and should contain plenty of hairs with whitish ends that give a silvery sheen to the surface of the fur.

Russians from Sitka (Norfolk Sound), the headquarters of the Russian-American colony, are established at Bodega Bay, thirty miles north of San Francisco. Their chief in this new settlement is M[onsieur I. A.] Kuskof, an expert fur-trader [and assistant to Russian American Company's Alaskan manager, Alexander Baranov]. They are thirty in number and they have fifteen Kadiaks with them. They have built a small fort which is equipped with a dozen cannon. The harbour will admit only vessels that draw eight or nine feet of water. This was formerly a point for the selling of smuggled goods to the Spaniards. M. Kuskof actually has in his settlement horses, cows, sheep, and everything else that can be raised in this beautiful and splendid country. It was with great difficulty that we obtained a pair of each species from the Spaniards because the government had strictly forbidden that any be disposed of.

M. Kuskof, assisted by the small number of men with him, catches almost two thousand otters every year without trouble. . . . The otter skins are usually sold to American fur-traders. When these fail of a full cargo, they go to Sitka where they obtain skins in exchange for sugar, rum, cloth, and Chinese cotton stuff. The Russian company, not having a sufficient number of ships, sends its own skins to China (or only as far as [the Russian port] Okhotsk) as freight on American ships.

Two hundred and fifty American ships, from Boston, New York, and elsewhere, come to the coast every year. Half of them engage in smuggling with enormous profit. No point for landing goods along the entire Spanish-American coast bathed

From Louis Choris, *Voyage pittoresque autour du monde . . .* , trans. Porter Garnett, in *San Francisco One Hundred Years Ago* (San Francisco: A. M. Robertson, 1913), pp. 16–20.

by the Pacific Ocean, from Chili to California, is neglected. It often happens that Spanish warships give chase to American vessels, but these, being equipped with much sail, having large crews, and having, moreover, arms with which to defend themselves, are rarely caught.

The commodities most acceptable to the Indians of the coast of Northwest America are guns, powder, bullets, and lead for their manufacture, knives, coarse woolen blankets, and mother-of-pearl from the Pacific which they use to make ornaments for the head and neck.

Ships are often attacked with the very arms that they themselves sold, and even on the same day that they were delivered. Most of them, however, carrying from eight to fourteen guns, are able to defend themselves. Such occurrences are frequently turned to profit, for, should they carry off one of the chiefs, they are certain to get a great deal of merchandise as ransom, and gain greater facilities for trading.

2. A Manager Describes the Russian American Company, 1835

On April 24, 1801, the first United States trading ship, the *Enterprise,* arrived in Kad'iak [Kodiak, Alaska] from New York. Her Captain, James Scott, brought [Russian American Company manager Aleksandr Andreevich] Baranov a message from the manager at Sitka, and proposed that he exchange part of his cargo for furs. Baranov had to accept this proposal because of pressing needs, but it caused him great difficulties since under the trading rules at that time all pelts had to be divided between the Company and the hunters; consequently the exchange with foreigners for general wares broke these conditions. On the other hand the complete lack of goods throughout the colonies, for clothing and for paying the Russian employees, and for paying Aleuts for hunting, forced a change in the previous system. Necessity alters laws. The [earlier] loss of the *Phoenix* had removed the possibility of supplies from [the Russian port] Okhotsk, and there was no news of the party sent to Unalashka [Unalaska] for supplies in July of the previous year. In this extremity Baranov decided to trade with the foreigners, but as the Captain offered low prices for pelts, only 2,000 black and red fox furs were exchanged. From these visitors Baranov learnt of the continuing war all over Europe; they frightened him with tales that Spain, acting in concert with France, intended to arm frigates and send them to our colonies. If this happened, for want of official information he might accept the enemies as allies and vice-versa. Thus Baranov was informed by his deputy Larionov, whom he asked to forward him news as it came from Russia.

In May, as the Americans were leaving, Potorochin arrived from Unalashka by baidarka [two-person kayak], having left there on September 29. Storms had delayed his journey all through the winter. This reveals how unreliable and dangerous was communication between the islands in small leather craft and how precious and irreplaceable was the time lost in this way. . . .

Excerpts from Kiril Khlebnikov. *Baranov, Chief Manager of the Russian Colonies in America* [St. Petersburg, 1835]. Trans. Colin Bearne. Ed. Richard A. Pierce. Kingston, ON: Limestone Press, 1973, pp. 35–43, 46–50.

. . . [In September], the brig *Ekaterina* delivered from Sitka [Alaska] all the pelts caught by [Baranov's assistant I. A.] Kuskov's party and gained by barter at the settlement in all, nearly 5,000 skins. Kuskov, who had returned on the same vessel, reported that with his party, he had gone round Sitka Island and found a great many sea otter on the shores: he had everywhere made the Koloshes [Tlingits] gifts, and they had not hindered the hunting.

In April of the following year (1802) Baranov again sent Kuskov off with a party of Aleuts on the same journey. . . .

On the 24th of [June] the English ship *Unicorn* arrived at Kad'iak. Her Captain, Barber, delivered three Russians, two Aleuts and 18 Kad'iak women who had been rescued from the Kolosh, after the latter had destroyed the fort on Sitka. Baranov was then on a journey to Afognak and some of the other islands, but when he received this news he quickly returned.

Those who witnessed these unfortunate and terrible events related that a great force of Kolosh had attacked the fort at mid-day; they had given the Russians an agonising death: they had plundered the sea otter pelts in the storehouses and had reduced the settlement and a boat which was under construction to ashes.

Barber did not put the former prisoners ashore, but displayed 20 cannon and armed his men. He informed Baranov that although he belonged to a nation at war with Russia he had out of humanity ransomed these people from the hands of savages, clothed and fed them. He had had to break off his trading operations to bring them to Baranov. In recompense for all this, he demanded 50,000 rubles in cash or in furs at a price which he would determine. But Baranov discovered that on the contrary, Barber had not only paid no ransom for them, but according to the evidence of the prisoners, he had seized the ringleaders responsible for the destruction—the toens Skautlelt and his nephew Kotleian—had clapped them in irons and threatened to hang them from the yard arm. In this way the sympathetic Barber forced them to cede him many of the sea otter pelts plundered from the settlement and his expenses had merely been to clothe and feed the prisoners during less than a month's journey.

The incompatibility of such demands with obligations, and the warlike threats put Baranov in a tight corner. Yet, unafraid, he steadfastly rejected the Briton's shameless demands and took what defensive measures his strength allowed to repulse any attack. Meanwhile he and Barber continued their talks, and finally agreed on a ransom of 10,000 rubles worth of furs. When these were delivered to the Captain, with a receipt, he released the prisoners.

The vessel *Ekaterina* arrived in Kad'iak on September 5 from Yakutat, where Kuskov had been with the hunting party. He had repulsed an attack by the Kolosh on the way to Sitka, and had reached a point near Sitka when he learnt that the Kolosh intended to destroy the settlement there. He halted and sent ahead several baidarkas to warn the fort, but when his Aleuts arrived in the night they found that the new settlement had been plundered, burnt, and left empty. They hurried back to Kuskov with this sorry news, and then they all returned to Yakutat together. Several days later they were joined there by Urbanov, the leader of another expedition. He and some Aleuts had been sent from Sitka to hunt and they had thereby survived the destruction of the fort.

Their arrival in Kad'iak in no way eased Baranov's desperate position. He had earlier been tormented by not knowing the fate of the expeditions sent from Sitka and Kad'iak, but in all this he thanked God and considered it especially fortunate that the settlement at Yakutat had remained intact, and that his assistant Kuskov and his party had returned without loss—unsuccessfully, but safely.

Baranov was extremely depressed by the loss of the settlement at Sitka. It was a harrowing experience for him; he realized that this misfortune had greatly hampered his original plan to occupy places beyond Sitka. Weighing the impact of the loss, he resolved firmly to reoccupy the settlements, at the first opportunity. He desired to preserve the Nation's fame in the eyes of the foreign traders, to keep the trust placed in him by the Government and the Company, and, by expanding trade and hunting, to make them yield profits, and thus render new service to the Fatherland. . . .

The Company directors gave just honor and respect to Baranov by appointing him Chief Manager of the colonies in America, in charge of Unalashka and the other districts, authorizing him to establish offices in them, to combine all Company possessions and to put everything on the same footing. Thus all the previously issued furs should go to the Company at a uniform rate and be paid for in money. This new system was more profitable to the Company than to the promyshlenniks and met with stiff opposition. This cost Baranov much time and worry and several years correspondence with the Directors. . . .

In April, 1803, Baranov, on assuming the administration of all the colonies, sent Banner on the galley *Olga* to Unalashka with written instructions for the administrator there. He was to send to Kad'iak the ship *Petr i Pavel* with men and whatever goods and supplies were available in the storehouses there. He was to select the best fur seals and temporarily suspend their unprofitable hunting on Paul and George Islands; as they had not been shipped out, a stock of 800,000 pelts had built up, and through lack of warehouses to protect them from damp and other influences, they had spoiled. Baranov also asked that the hunters agree to the new conditions sent by the Main Office, and gave other minor instructions, for Banner and the Unalashka manager to fulfill.

In June Khvostov set out for Okhotsk on the brig *Elisaveta* with a very valuable cargo; there were more than 17,000 sea otter pelts, and with all other furs this cargo was valued at 1,200,000 rubles.

Baranov set out for Yakutat in the galley *Olga.* There he found both his vessels and Kuskov, who had returned with a party of Aleuts and a meager catch of sea otters. Baranov then planned to proceed to Sitka, reoccupy the lost site, and show the Kolosh that whereas during the alliance the Russians had been their true friends, they would now find that because of their, the Kolosh', treachery and theft the Russians could be merciless avengers. However, he respected Kuskov's sensible advice that in this late season the baidarkas might founder in a storm and an unsuccessful expedition could only encourage the Kolosh. Thus the journey to Sitka was postponed. Meantime, in order to strengthen their fleet, instructions were given to build two small sailing boats at Yakutat. Kuskov and shipwrights were placed in charge of this, while Baranov himself returned to Kad'iak on October 14. Here he found the American ship *O'Cain* under Captain O'Cain, who two years earlier had been boatswain on the *Enterprise,* and exchanged a goods cargo for 10,000 rubles. O'Cain suggested that he be supplied with Aleuts and baidarkas so he could hunt sea otters off the California coast and then return to Kad'iak where the whole catch would be divided. The trouble Baranov now faced as to sea otter hunting with his own forces had deprived him of the prospect of a profitable haul; for along the coast around Sitka every sea otter had to be fought for with fierce enemies until permanent settlements could be established there with strong mutual support. Therefore he decided, when he had received from O'Cain most of the goods to maintain the party, to give him 20 baidarkas under the supervision of his trusted and sensible employee Shvetsov, whom he instructed to inspect all the places on the coast where they should put in. In this way Baranov hoped to receive reliable information about places where sea otters were still to be found. He also wished to acquaint himself with the inhabitants of California, at that period known only through confused tales of foreigners. He wished to know what products originated there and, finally, what measures the Americans were taking for trading with the Californians and the savages inhabiting the Northwest Coast of America. He also wanted information on whether, what, and how much they paid them for local produce, and so forth.

On October 26 they set sail from Kad'iak, called at the port of San Diego and thence went to San Quentin Bay where they hunted sea otter until March 1. When the pelt take reached 1,100, as arranged they returned to Kad'iak. Shvetsov informed Baranov of the produce of those places they had visited and that O'Cain had used his own goods in San Diego and San Quentin to barter for furs from the missionaries and soldiers. In this way he had gained up to 700 sea otter pelts at three to four plasters a pelt.

On March 23 1804, Navigator Bubnov arrived by baidarka from Unalashka. He had been sent from Okhotsk to Kad'iak in the previous year on the transport ship *Dimitrii,* but the ship had been wrecked near Umnak Island. However, all the cargo, crew, and passengers had been saved. With Bubnov's arrival Baranov learned that thanks to the recommendation of the Main Office of the Company, for services rendered and duties performed, the Emperor had most graciously conferred upon him the rank of Collegiate Assessor.

Then, shedding tears of gratitude for the beneficence of the Monarch, who appreciated these services in such far off parts, he cried with fervor, "I have been rewarded, but Sitka is lost! No! I cannot live! I shall go—and I shall either die or make it another of the territories of my most August Patron!" . . .

. . . [In July 1804], Baranov asked Captain Lisianskii [of the *Neva,* which had arrived in Kad'iak on July 1] to help him to persuade the Kolosh to return the places they had taken from the Russians, and if they refused, to help him compel them by force of arms. They conferred, and deciding on a course of action, on the 17th left Krestov Harbor [near Sitka] with all the ships, and the party of Aleuts. Towards evening they stood at anchor off the Sitka settlement, opposite the Kekur, (a high rock) where, however they found all the huts empty. . . . In order to clear the surrounding shore they fired several balls to see if anyone was waiting in ambush for them to disembark from the vessels. After this, Baranov landed and occupied the high and steep Kekur, raised the flag as a sign of the authority of the Russan state, and proclaimed it once again Novo-Arkhangel'sk fort. On the Kekur they sited and manned the cannon, and the Aleuts occupied all the surrounding countryside. . . .

. . . [B]ut the Kolosh gathered all their forces together and opened a heavy fire from their fort. At that very moment when the fort should have been smashed and set on fire, Baranov was wounded in the right arm. . . .

On the 21st Baranov, in pain from his wound . . . begged Captain Lisianskii to take complete command and to act as he should see fit. Lisianskii ordered the ships to keep up heavy cannon fire on the fort. This eventually produced the desired result. . . .

On the 22nd the Kolosh hung out a white flag on the fort. . . .

The first building [the Russians] put up near the site of the fort was one needed for storage. Almost a thousand trees were felled to make a stockade, and a small plank cabin was built for the Manager. A belltower and watchtower were built with surrounds of sharpened spikes, protecting the fort from hostile onslaughts by the Kolosh. . . .

All winter the Kolosh toens [chiefs] never appeared at the fort, though from time to time they sent small scouting bands to spy on the Russians, who meantime worked zealously. The Aleuts fished all the time.

On June 10 1805, the *Neva* arrived from Kad'iak. Captain-Lieutenant Lisianskii, when he saw the solid buildings and the many articles of husbandry, was amazed at Baranov's unceasing efforts and unexpected successes. . . .

The *Neva* was loaded with 3,000 beavers, 150,000 seals and many other goods to the sum, according to prices then current in the colonies, of around 450,000 rubles. With this valuable cargo Captain Lisianskii left Sitka on August 20, and sailed direct to Canton.

3. Senator Thomas Hart Benton Explains Manifest Destiny, 1846

It would seem that the White race alone received the divine command, to subdue and replenish the earth: for it is the only race that has obeyed it—the only race that hunts out new and distant lands, and even a New World, to subdue and replenish. . . .

The Red race has disappeared from the Atlantic coast; the tribes that resisted civilization met extinction. This is a cause of lamentation with many. For my part, I cannot murmur at what seems to be the effect of divine law. I cannot repine that this Capitol has replaced the wigwam—this Christian people, replaced the savages— white matrons, the red squaws. . . . Civilization, or extinction, has been the fate of all people who have found themselves in the trace of the advancing Whites, and civilization, always the preference of the Whites, has been pressed as an object, while extinction has followed as a consequence of its resistance. . . .

The van of the Caucasian race now top the Rocky Mountains, and spread down on the shores of the Pacific. In a few years a great population will grow up there, luminous with the accumulated lights of European and American civilization. Their presence in such a position cannot be without its influence upon eastern Asia. . . .

The Mongolian, or Yellow race is there, four hundred millions in number spreading almost to Europe; a race once the foremost of the human family in the arts of civilization, but torpid and stationary for thousands of years. It is a race far above

From *Congressional Globe,* 29, no. 1 (1846): 917–918.

the Ethiopian, or Black—above the Malay, or Brown, (if we admit five races)—and above the American Indians, or Red; it is a race far above all these, but still far below the White and like all the rest, must receive an impression from the superior race whenever they come in contact. . . .

The sun of civilization must shine across the sea; socially and commercially the van of the Caucasians, and the rear of the Mongolians, must intermix. They must talk together, and trade together, and marry together. . . . Moral and intellectual superiority will do the rest; the White race will take the ascendant, elevating what is susceptible of improvement—wearing out what is not. . . . And thus the youngest people, and the newest land, will become the reviver and the regenerator of the oldest. . . .

It is in this point of view, and as acting upon the social, political, and religious condition of Asia, and giving a new point of departure to her ancient civilization, that I look upon the settlement of the Columbia river by the van of the Caucasian race as the most momentous human event in the history of man since his dispersion over the face of the earth.

4. A Federal Agent Assesses Mining's Impact on the Indians, 1853

Diamond Springs
El Dorado County
December 31st 1853

The Indians in this portion of the State are wretchedly poor, having no horses, cattle or other property. They formerly subsisted on game, fish, acorns, etc., but it is now impossible for them to make a living by hunting or fishing, for nearly all the game has been driven from the mining region or has been killed by the thousands of our people who now occupy the once quiet home of these children of the forest. The rivers or tributaries of the Sacramento formerly were clear as crystal and abounded with the finest salmon and other fish. I saw them at Salmon Falls on the American river in the year 1851, and also the Indians taking barrels of these beautiful fish and drying them for winter. But the miners have turned the streams from their beds and conveyed the water to the dry diggings and after being used until it is so thick with mud that it will scarcely run it returns to its natural channel and with it the soil from a thousand hills, which has driven almost every kind of fish to seek new places of resort where they can enjoy a purer and more natural element. And to prove the old adage that misfortunes never come singly the oaks have for the last three years refused to furnish the acorn, which formed one of the chief articles of Indian food. They have often told me that the white man had killed all their game, had driven the fish from the rivers, had cut down and destroyed the trees and that what were now standing were worthless for they bore no acorns. In their superstitious imaginations they believe that the White man's presence among them has caused the trees (that

From a letter from E. A. Stevenson, Special Indian Agent, to Hon. Thomas J. Henley, Supt. of Indian Affairs, San Francisco, in Robert F. Heizer, ed., *The Destruction of the California Indians.* Salt Lake City: Peregrine Smith, 1974, pp. 15–16.

formerly bore plentifully) to now be worthless and barren. In concluding this brief report I deem it my duty to recommend to your favorable consideration the early establishment of a suitable reservation and the removal of these Indians thereto, where they can receive medical aid and assistance which at the present time they so much require.

All of which is very respectfully submitted.

E. A. Stevenson
Spec. Indian Agent

Hon. Thos. J. Henley
Supt. of Indian Affairs
San Francisco Cal.

5. James Marshall Tells How He Discovered Gold, 1857

While we were in the habit at night of turning the water through the tail race we had dug for the purpose of widening and deepening the race, I used to go down in the morning to see what had been done by the water through the night; and about half past seven o'clock on or about the 19th of January—I am not quite certain to a day, but it was between the 18th and 20th of that month—1848, l went down as usual, and after shutting off the water from the race, I stepped into it, near the lower end, and there, upon the rock, about six inches beneath the surface of the water, I discovered the gold. I was entirely alone at the time. I picked up one or two pieces and examined them attentively; and having some general knowledge of minerals, I could not call to mind more than two which in any way resembled this—*sulphuret of iron,* very bright and brittle; and *gold,* bright, yet malleable; I then tried it between two rocks, and found that it could be beaten into a different shape, but not broken. I then collected four or five pieces and went up to Mr. Scott (who was working at the carpenter's bench making the mill wheel) with the pieces and said, "I have found it."

"What is it?" inquired Scott.

"Gold," I answered.

"Oh! no," returned Scott, "that can't be."

I replied positively—"I know it to be nothing else."

Mr. Scott was the second person who saw the gold. W. J. Johnston, A. Stephens, H. Bigler, and J. Brown, who were also working in the mill yard, were then called up to see it. Peter L. Wimmer, Mrs. Jane Wimmer, C. Bennet, and I. Smith, were at the house; the latter two of whom were sick; E. Persons and John Wimmer, (a son of P. L. Wimmer), were out hunting oxen at the same time. About 10 o'clock the same morning, P. L. Wimmer came down from the house, and was very much surprised at the discovery, when the metal was shown him; and which he took home to show his wife, who, the next day, made some experiments upon it by boiling it in strong lye, and saleratus; and Mr. Bennet by my directions beat it very thin.

Four days afterwards, I went to the Fort for provisions, and carried with me about three ounces of the gold, which Capt. Sutter and I tested with *nitric acid.* I then

---

From *Hutchings' California Magazine,* 2 (1857): 199–201.

tried it in Sutter's presence by taking three silver dollars and balancing them by the dust in the air, then immersed both in water, and the superior weight of the gold satisfied us both of its nature and value.

6. Joaquin Miller Reveals the Environmental Deterioration in the Gold Country, 1890

As lone as God, and white as a winter moon, Mount Shasta starts up sudden and solitary from the heart of the great black forests of Northern California.

You would hardly call Mount Shasta a part of the Sierras; you would say rather that it is the great white tower of some ancient and eternal wall, with nearly all the white walls overthrown. . . .

Ascend this mountain, stand against the snow above the upper belt of pines, and take a glance below. Toward the sea nothing but the black and unbroken forest. Mountains, it is true, dip and divide and break the monotony as the waves break up the sea; yet it is still the sea, still the unbroken forest, black and magnificent. To the south the landscape sinks and declines gradually, but still maintains its column of dark-plumed grenadiers, till the Sacramento Valley is reached, nearly a hundred miles away. Silver rivers run here, the sweetest in the world. They wind and wind among the rocks and mossy roots, with California lilies, and the yew with scarlet berries dipping in the water, and trout idling in the eddies and cool places by the basketful. On the east, the forest still keeps up unbroken rank till the Pitt River Valley is reached; and even there it surrounds the valley, and locks it up tight in its black embrace. To the north, it is true, Shasta Valley makes quite a dimple in the sable sea, and men plow there, and Mexicans drive mules or herd their mustang ponies on the open plain. But the valley is limited, surrounded by the forest, confined and imprisoned.

Look intently down among the black and rolling hills, forty miles away to the west, and here and there you will see a haze of cloud or smoke hung up above the trees; or, driven by the wind that is coming from the sea, it may drag and creep along as if tangled in the tops.

These are mining camps. Men are there, down in these dreadful cañons, out of sight of the sun, swallowed up, buried in the impenetrable gloom of the forest, toiling for gold. Each one of these camps is a world of itself. History, romance, tragedy, poetry, in every one of them. They are connected together, and reach the outer world only by a narrow little pack trail, stretching through the timber, stringing round the mountains, barely wide enough to admit of footmen and little Mexican mules, with their apparajos, to pass in single file.

But now the natives of these forests. I lived with them for years. You do not see the smoke of their wigwams through the trees. They do not smite the mountain rocks for gold, nor fell the pines, nor roil up the waters and ruin them for the fishermen. All this magnificent forest is their estate. The Great Spirit made this mountain first of all, and gave it to them, they say, and they have possessed it ever since. They preserve the forest, keep out the fires, for it is the park for their deer.

From Joaquin Miller, *Life Amongst the Modocs.* Chicago: Morril, Higgins & Co., 1892 [1890], pp. 18–22, 54–55.

This narrative, while the thread of it is necessarily spun around a few years of my early life, is not of myself, but of this race of people that has lived centuries of history and never yet had a historian; that has suffered nearly four hundred years of wrong, and never yet had an advocate.

Yet I must write of myself, because I was among these people of whom I write, though often in the background, giving place to the inner and actual lives of a silent and mysterious people, a race of prophets, poets without the gift of expression—a race that has been often, almost always, mistreated, and never understood—a race that is moving noiselessly from the face of the earth; dreamers that sometimes waken from their mysteriousness and simplicity, and then, blood, brutality, and all the ferocity that marks a man of maddened passions, women without mercy, men without reason, brand them with the appropriate name of savages.

I have a word to say for the Indian. I saw him as he was, not as he is. In one little spot of our land, I saw him as he was centuries ago in every part of it perhaps, a Druid and a dreamer—the mildest and tamest of beings. I saw him as no man can see him now. I saw him as no man ever saw him who had the desire and patience to observe, the sympathy to understand, and the intelligence to communicate his observations to those who would really like to understand him. He is truly "the gentle savage;" the worst and the best of men, the tamest and the fiercest of beings. The world cannot understand the combination of these two qualities. For want of truer comparison let us liken him to a woman—a sort of Parisian woman, now made desperate by a long siege and an endless war.

A singular combination of circumstances laid his life bare to me. I was a child, and he was a child. He permitted me to enter his heart. . . .

All this city [Sacramento] had been built, all this country opened up, in less than two years. Twenty months before, only the Indian inhabited here; he was lord absolute of the land. But gold had been found on this spot by a party of roving mountaineers; the news had gone abroad, and people poured in and had taken possession in a day, without question and without ceremony.

And the Indians? They were pushed aside. At first they were glad to make the strangers welcome; but, when they saw where it would all lead, they grew sullen and concerned. . . .

I hurried on a mile or so to the foot-hills, and stood in the heart of the placer mines. Now the smoke from the low chimneys of the log cabins began to rise and curl through the cool, clear air on every hand, and the miners to come out at the low doors; great hairy, bearded, six-foot giants, hatless, and half-dressed.

They stretched themselves in the sweet, frosty air, shouted to each other in a sort of savage banter, washed their hands and faces in the gold-pans that stood by the door, and then entered their cabins again, to partake of the eternal beans and bacon and coffee, and coffee and bacon and beans.

The whole face of the earth was perforated with holes; shafts sunk and being sunk by these men in search of gold, down to the bed-rock. Windlasses stretched across these shafts, where great buckets swung, in which men hoisted the earth to the light of the sun by sheer force of muscle.

The sun came softly down, and shone brightly on the hillside where I stood. I lifted my hands to Shasta, above the butte and town, for he looked like an old acquaintance, and again was glad.

7. A Fish Commissioner Explains the Need for Salmon Protection, 1885

Twenty years ago, before the business of canning salmon on the Columbia was inaugurated, salmon literally swarmed up all the small creeks and little tributaries of the main river in such immense quantities that several million eggs could, without doubt, have been easily collected from the spawning fish at the head of comparatively insignificant streams; but that day has gone by, probably forever. The vast number of nets that are being continually dragged through the water at the canneries on the main river during the fishing season catch millions of full-grown salmon on their way up the river to spawn, and of course reduce to a corresponding extent the number of parent fish that reach the spawning-grounds. The comparatively few that succeed in running the gauntlet of the innumerable nets in the main river would, if they could be gathered together at one spot, still be enough to supply a great many million eggs; but those which ascend the river above the nets, instead of all going to one place, separate and divide up among the hundreds of tributaries, large and small, that help to form the great Columbia. Consequently a very small percentage, indeed, of the few salmon that get by the nets are to be found in any one manageable stream, unless some peculiar natural causes exist at some specified place to make that point an exception to the general rule. It is accordingly useless to look now to small streams which are subject to ordinary conditions for a large supply of salmon eggs, however abundant the salmon used to be in them in the former and better days of these salmon rivers. . . .

I wish to add, however, that if Washington Territory and the State of Oregon, between which the lower Columbia flows, could agree upon a code of good protective laws for the salmon, the Clackamas River would again teem with salmon as before, and in that event perhaps the best point for a breeding station would be on that river where the station of the Oregon and Washington Fish Propagating Company was built in 1877. Before the times of canneries and excessive netting of the salmon in the lower Columbia, the Clackamas in Oregon was as good a salmon river as the McCloud in California, and if the salmon should ever be allowed to reach it, it might be again.

8. A Capitalist Advocates Salmon Hatcheries, 1893

The Salmon of the Pacific Coast

1. Their Influence upon the Industries and Share in the Development of the Northwest

TO GIVE the reader a clear idea of the salmon industry of the Pacific Coast, and the influence it has had in the development of the Northwest, it will be necessary to give a brief history of the salmon canning business, the advent of which practically

---

Document 7 is from Livingston Stone, *Explorations on the Columbia River from the Head of Clarke's Fork to the Pacific Ocean, Made in the Summer of 1883, with Reference to the Selection of a Suitable Place for Establishing a Salmon-breeding Station* (Washington, D.C.: Government Printing Office, 1885), 241–243, 254.

Document 8 is from R. D. Hume, *Salmon of the Pacific Coast* (San Francisco: Schmidt Label and Lithographic, 1893).

begins the salmon fishing era of the Pacific Coast; although prior to that time the taking of salmon had been done to considerable extent to supply the market with fresh fish, and a moderate quantity had been salted. But in comparison with the canning business, the quantity taken for these purposes was of little importance.

The business of canning salmon on the Pacific Coast was begun in the spring of 1864, at the town of Washington, Yolo county, California, on the banks of the Sacramento river, opposite the foot of K street, Sacramento city, by the firm of Hapgood, Hume & Co., the firm consisting of Andrew S. Hapgood, George W. and William Hume, with the writer as "sub" under small pay, but with large expectations of a partnership interest, to be realized whenever the business should prove the success anticipated. The pack of the first year amounted to about 2,000 cases, and the trials and difficulties attending their production are almost impossible to realize and describe, after the lapse of twenty-nine years, considering the improved methods of to-day. . . .

In the next two years the amount packed per annum was not much increased, on account of the scarcity of salmon in the Sacramento, and in the spring of 1866 William Hume went to the Columbia to see what could be done. Upon his return with favorable reports, G. W. Hume also went to the Columbia, for the purpose of selecting a site and building a cannery and other necessary buildings, that should be ready for the reception of the others, who went there some time in October of that year. The point selected by him was at Eagle Cliff in Wahkiakum county, Washington, and part of the cannery now owned and operated there by Wm. Hume is the original building erected by him. During the winter of 1866-67 we put our machines in order and made the nets and cans for the spring season of 1867, at which time we packed 4,000 cases of 48 cans each. . . .

In a lapse of ten years, what a change! Portland has by this time become a city of importance, and Astoria has stretched itself along three miles of water front; while instead of four small landings along the main Columbia, between Astoria and Portland the number has increased to more than forty, and instead of one small steamer making tri-weekly trips, we have four elegant steamers running between these places daily, besides about a dozen running in the fish carrying trade for the use of the canneries, and in place of a product of 4,000 cases of 48 tins each, we have a product of 450,000 cases, of the same number of tins, and we have our wheezy and dilapidated old mills running night and day to supply the demand for lumber to build new canneries, and where desolation ruled before we find signs of the greatest activity. We find all trades and professions plunging to get a whack at this new El Dorado, all seeking a fortune to be made from the capture of the scaly beauties. What a mine of wealth, that even all who might plunge might be enriched. But all good things which nature has furnished have a capacity beyond which they cannot be strained, and the year 1883 brings Columbia its maximum, when the vast quantity of 630,000 cases was reached; and from this time begins the decline of the salmon product of that wonderful stream. . . .

What a contrast between the years 1867 and 1892, as regards the industry. At the first date one cannery, with its small product, having great difficulty in obtaining sufficient employees to prosecute the business, while in 1892, in addition to the large number of canneries in British Columbia and on the Columbia river, which were employing thousands of people, there was not a stream putting into the ocean along the Oregon and California coast, which can be entered even by the lightest draught vessels, that has not one or more canneries located on its banks. . . .

The salmon industry of the Pacific coast has furnished lucrative employment to thousands, and has been both directly and indirectly the means by which very many have made fortunes, and who without its benefits would perhaps find themselves out of employment and lighter in pocket.

In view of the great importance of this industry, it would seem the imperative duty of all engaged or in anywise interested in the business to protect and preserve, so far as is possible, the source from which the essential factor springs, namely, the salmon of the Pacific coast; and the best efforts of the minds of those who are in any manner familiar with the conditions which are favorable to that end should be turned in that direction. . . .

2. Their Value as a Food Product and the Proper Methods for their Protection. . . .

The Sacramento river, prior to the introduction of hydraulic mining in 1853 was, during the running season, so plentifully stocked with salmon that no use could be made of but a moiety of the supply, and we have an illustration of the destructive force of this new agent when we consider the fact that eleven years after its introduction the Sacramento river was practically rendered useless for commercial purposes as a salmon stream.

The Klamath river furnishes another illustration of the destructive action of hydraulic mining upon the salmon streams of the coast. In 1850 in this river during the running seasons, salmon were so plentiful, according to the reports of the early settlers, that in fording the stream it was with difficulty that they could induce their horses to make the attempt, on account of the river being alive with the finny tribe. At the present time the main run, which were the spring salmon, are practically extinct, not enough being taken to warrant the prosecution of business in any form. The river has remained in a primitive state, with the exception of the influence which mining has had, no salmon of the spring run having been taken except a few by Indians, as a reservation by the government has been maintained, until within a few years, and no fishing has been allowed on the lower river by white men; and yet the spring run has almost disappeared, and the fall run reduced to very small proportions, the pack never exceeding 6,000 cases, and in 1892 the river producing only 1,047 cases.

The next and most important river on the coast to receive consideration is the Columbia, and this, though not yet exhausted, has shrunken its output since 1883, in the number of cases produced, more than one-third, and according to good authorities the product of 1892 was but little more than 150,000 cases of true adult Chinook salmon, the balance of the pack being steel-heads, bluebacks, and a small salmon of a variety which will later receive attention. This, if true, would show a fearful decrease in the past nine years, amounting to more than three-quarters of the supply of the quality packed when at its best; and from both packers and fishermen comes the cry that, although the demand for the article is good, they are unable to make living profits from the prosecution of the business. A contemplation of this proposition leads one to inquire what have been the conditions that have brought about such a result, when since 1883 the number of canneries on that river have decreased considerably, and during the time a hatchery has been in operation, which has turned out millions of young salmon every year.

Prior to 1879 traps and fish wheels cut a small figure in the methods of taking salmon on the Columbia river, the few traps in operation being mostly in the vicinity of Oak Point, the lower river about Astoria being free from their influence. Since 1883, however, the number of traps at Astoria and fish wheels on the upper river have rapidly increased, with a corresponding decrease in both the quality and quantity of the salmon packed on that stream, as well as a rapid falling off of the profits of the business. The question will naturally be asked, in view of the difficulties surrounding the proposition, can the supply be maintained in such a manner as to protect the industry? This I answer in the affirmative, if the operations toward stocking the rivers are maintained in a proper manner, and the right sort of legislation is had upon the question of taking the product of the rivers. . . .

A careful attention on the part of the fish commission of the State regarding obstructions which prevent the salmon from reaching the natural spawning grounds, such as dams and traps, placed entirely across the streams, would be a powerful factor toward the preservation of the species; and the passage of a law which would make it a crime for taking or having a gravid or spawning salmon in possession, except for spawning purposes, . . . assisted by the operation of such hatcheries as the importance of the business seems to justify, would enable the industry to remain as permanent a branch as that of agriculture.

3. A Short Treatise upon the Commercial Varieties and their Habits. . . .

I contend that without reasonable exertion for the erection and operation of hatcheries, and the exercise of wise laws for the protection of the spawning grounds, and regulating the size of fish to be taken, the States of Oregon and Washington, which now enjoy a monopoly of the finest quality of salmon in the world, will have soon lost their heritage. The lack of interest manifested by those engaged in the salmon canning business on the Columbia, in the matter of their propagation, is surprising, when very many are aware how simple and inexpensive is the process of merely hatching the eggs—in fact, so simple that any cannery could have a small hatchery, and by obtaining eggs in which the eye spots were formed could finish the process, and when the fish were well developed distribute them with little trouble in the fresh water branches nearest their location. They could also procure eggs, if by concerted action they would establish ripening ponds at the mouths of some of the small streams that put into the lower river. . . .

4. The Art of Salmon Culture. The Apparatus Necessary for Propagation.

In order that any readers who may be stimulated by what is herein contained to undertake the propagation of salmon, may avoid the mistakes and difficulties which were made and encountered by the writer in his early attempts, and the very considerable expense consequent thereto, a short history of the early part of the undertaking may prove useful. . . .

Hearing that salmon of a fine quality were very plentiful at the Rogue river, I purchased a location and built a cannery there the latter part of 1876, and in the spring of 1877, much to my surprise, packed only 3197 cases, which was all that could be obtained by the utmost exertion, which proved that the reports, except as to quality, were but echoes of the past; and thus I was furnished with the necessity as well as the opportunity to put into practice those crude ideas which had long been forming in my mind. As soon as I realized how few salmon the stream afforded, operations were begun towards stocking by excavating a pond for holding and ripening the adult fish, on a little spring branch which afforded about one thousand gallons per hour, during the dry season, that put into the river about a mile from the bar or entrance, and a small hatching house was built close by the pond. After completing the pond and house I stocked the pond with one hundred adult female salmon and fifty of the male species of the finest specimens that could be selected. After this was accomplished I made a trip overland to the hatchery on the McCloud river. . . . I engaged [hatchery manager] Mr. [Kirby B.] Pratt, and we at once made our way to Rogue river, when Mr. Pratt took charge, and against all difficulties with which he had to contend, in spite of the fact that he had previously had no experience with fish that had been kept in retaining ponds for the purpose of ripening, from one hundred females, in the following spring succeeded in turning out three hundred and fifty thousand healthy salmon. . . .

. . . When the [next] season had arrived we placed a fine lot of salmon in the pond, but much to my surprise in a short time they began to swim about near the surface of the water, showing white patches in various parts of their bodies, which kept growing worse until they were covered by a growth of fungus, their eyes blinded, and finally nearly all died, leaving only enough to give us about fifty thousand eggs. At this result of what I had considered would enable me to surpass any previous efforts, I was much disheartened. . . .

The evidence of the value of propagation being so forcibly brought to my mind made me very anxious to succeed, and I would spend hours on the point above looking at the poor creatures paddling about the surface of the pond, and worry myself sick in the effort to discover a remedy. One day while occupied in this manner I began to reflect upon the propositon [*sic*], and asked myself the question, under what conditions was the greatest success of this undertaking made? And the recitals of conditions came in this order: a little pond, a little water, a great deal of mud, and so much brush and trees that the place never got the sun. "Eureka!" I cried, "*I've got it!* That is what has been the trouble![*"*] I at once began the construction of a building over the pond that would close out the light, and when completed put in a new lot of salmon, with the result that they showed no signs of the previous trouble. When the building was closed the place became so dark that the fish remained perfectly quiet, probably having the idea that they were in a deep pool, while previously they were bruising themselves badly in their attempts to find an outlet. . . .

5. The Art of Salmon Culture. Propagating the Fish. . . .

. . . It would seem that in view of the simplicity of the methods and certainty of success of salmon cultivation . . . together with the showing made by the writer, whose work has increased the supply of spring salmon in Rogue river nearly four fold, in spite of very adverse circumstances, the record showing that it is the only river in the world where fishing has been done steadily each season that has shown such an increase, while the fall run in the same river, which has not been propagated, has fallen off in as great a proportion, should satisfy any reasonable mind as to the value of salmon culture, and stimulate not only those engaged in the business of canning, but the State and general government, to assist and encourage in every way possible the cultivation of this excellent fish.

9. An Indian Woman Deplores the Soreness of the Land, Recorded in 1925

Maybe this child [pointing to her eldest child] will see something, but this world will stay as long as Indians live. When the Indians all die, then God will let the water come down from the north. Everyone will drown. That is because the white people never cared for land or deer or bear. When we Indians kill meat, we eat it all up. When we dig roots, we make little holes. When we build houses, we make little holes. When we burn grass for grasshoppers, we don't ruin things. We shake down acorns and pine nuts. We don't chop down the trees. We only use dead wood. But the white people plow up the ground, pull up the trees, kill everything. The trees say, "Don't. I am sore. Don't hurt me." But they chop it down and cut it up. The spirit of the land hates them. They blast out trees and stir it up to its depths. They saw up the trees. That hurts them. The Indians never hurt anything, but the white people destroy all. They blast rocks and scatter them on the earth. The rock says, "Don't! You are hurting me." But the white people pay no attention. When the Indians use rocks, they take little round ones for their cooking. The white people dig deep long tunnels. They make roads. They dig as much as they wish. They don't care how much the ground cries out. How can the spirit of the earth like the white man? That is why God will upset the world—because it is sore all over. Everywhere the white man has touched it, it is sore. It looks sick. So it gets even by killing him when he blasts. But eventually the water will come.

  This water, it can't be hurt. The white people go to the river and turn it into dry land. The water says: "I don't care. I am water. You can use me all you wish. I am always the same. I can't be used up. Use me. I am water. You can't hurt me." The white people use the water of sacred springs in their houses. The water says: "That is all right. You can use me, but you can't overcome me." All that is water says this. "Wherever you put me, I'll be in my home. I am awfully smart. Lead me out of my springs, lead me from my rivers, but I came from the ocean and I shall go back into the ocean. You can dig a ditch and put me in it, but I go only so far and I am out of sight. I am awfully smart. When I am out of sight I am on my way home."

ψ *E S S A Y S*

The essays in this chapter explore the contributions of and conflicts among people of diverse cultures who used the waters of the West Coast for trade and economic gain during the nineteenth century. The first, by James Gibson, describes the Russian American Company's activities in Alaska and the Pacific Northwest and Russian interaction

From Kate Luckie (Wintu) in Cora DuBois, *Wintu Ethnography*. Berkeley, Calif.: University of California Press, 1935, pp. 75–76.

with Native American peoples from the time of Vitus Bering's 1741 voyage to the decline of Russian influence in the 1830s. The second essay, by Robert Kelley, formerly a historian at the University of California, Santa Barbara, depicts the environmental deterioration in California resulting from the hydraulic mining of the 1860s and 1870s and analyzes the ensuing legal battle between farmers defending their property from debris and miners defending their right to engage in hydraulic mining. In the third essay, environmental historian Richard White of Stanford University analyzes the use of human bodily labor by Indians and white gillnetters who extracted salmon from the Columbia River in the late nineteenth and early twentieth centuries. As a group, the essays spotlight some different ways in which environmental actors such as otter and salmon came into conflict with people of diverse cultures who extracted resources from the aquatic environments of the Far West and transformed its ecology.

Otters versus Russians in Alaska

JAMES GIBSON

From the middle 1780s, when Russian galiots [galleys] penetrated the Gulf of Alaska and British snows (brigs) reached Nootka Sound, the fur trade was the dominant economic activity on the Northwest Coast, a well-known but loosely defined stretch of the damp, rugged Pacific shore of North America between, say, glacier-ringed Icy Bay [Alaska] and redwood-studded Cape Mendocino [California]. For more than half a century the Tlingit, Haida, Tsimshian, Nootka (or West Coast, or Nuu-chah-nulth), Salish, and Chinook Indians in particular spent much of their time hunting fur bearers and trading their pelts, especially the "black skins" of sea otters, to Russian, British, and—above all—American shipmasters for metals, firearms, textiles, and foodstuffs. The Yankee Nor'westmen dealt the skins at Canton for teas, silks, and porcelains, which they then took for sale to European and American customers. More and more land furs were traded on the Northwest Coast from the mid-1810s until the early 1840s, by which time the depletion of all of the fur bearers by over-hunting, the depression of the fur markets by civil strife or changing fashion, and the depopulation of the Indians themselves by disease and warfare had reduced the Northwest trade to insignificance. The history of this far-flung and many-sided enterprise deserves to be told, not only because of its inherent interest but also because of its wide-ranging and far-reaching impact; the Northwest Coast itself and the Hawaiian Islands were particularly affected, both physically and culturally. . . .

The Northwest Coast was peculiar in that it was able to support a large Indian population with a high level of cultural development without the benefit of farming—"complex" hunters-fishers in the taxonomy of anthropologists. The pre-contact population likely approached 200,000, making the coast one of the most densely peopled non-agricultural parts of the world. The sole domesticated animal was a basenji-like dog, which was kept in large numbers for deer running (especially on the northern coast in winter) and sometimes eating; about 1800 each Haida family owned nearly

From James Gibson, *Otter Skins, Boston Ships, and China Goods: The Maritime Fur Trade of the Northwest Coast, 1785–1841*. Seattle: University of Washington Press, 1992, pp. xi, 4–8, 12–14, 17–18. Reprinted by permission of the University of Washington Press.

a dozen, and in 1791 an American sailor noted "the multiplicity of dogs" among the Nootkas. . . .

. . . The Northwest Coast's rugged terrain and thin soil (save the sedimentated Puget Sound shore and Fraser River delta in particular), and the dearth of sunshine towards the north, did not favour agriculture; indeed this fact was to prove advantageous to the Indians with the coming of white settlers, for their largely unarable ancestral lands were generally shunned by agrarian intruders, although their fishing grounds and timber stands were often usurped. Fortunately, nature was otherwise generous, as well as majestic. The rushing rivers and long "canals" (inlets) teemed with edible fish, including five species of salmon as well as herring, halibut, cod, and "small fish" (oolachen). (Salmon was the most prized food of the Nootkas, and it was one of the few articles that they usually refused to trade, and only very dearly when they consented.) Shellfish (clams, mussels, crabs) and various sea animals (hair seals, sea lions, sea otters, fur seals, porpoises, whales) likewise abounded, and the Pacific flyway afforded numerous waterfowl. Not to be outdone, the abutting mountains, higher and more angular to the north and lower and more rounded to the south but everywhere seldom breached by transverse rivers, offered magnificent forests of workable timber, red and yellow cedar above all, as well as various berries and other food plants. The ubiquitous conifers outcompeted grasses, so big game in the form of ungulates was not plentiful on the coast, except at the southern end (elk and deer in the Willamette valley) and in the northern part (Sitka blacktailed deer in the Alaskan panhandle and Alexander Archipelago). . . .

Not all Northwest Coast Indians, however, had access to sea otters, which were the mainstay of the maritime fur trade. *Enhydra lutris* is the largest member of the weasel family but the smallest marine mammal. . . . Lacking an insulating layer of body fat, its fur coat is exceptionally dense (60,000 hairs per square inch) in order to lend both warmth and buoyancy. The thick, dark, lustrous pelt became by far the most valuable fur on the world market. "Other furs bear no proportion, in value, to those of the sea otter," asserted the owners of one of the earliest British trading voyages. In 1829 it took more than ten beaver pelts, the pillar of the continental fur trade of North America, to equal the value of a single sea-otter skin. . . .

Hundreds of thousands of these playful creatures frequented the protective kelp beds of the North Pacific littoral from the Sea of Japan to the Sea of Cortez, feeding on sea urchins, mollusks, and starfish. But there were gaps in this range, especially between Cape Flattery and Trinidad Bay and even in Puget Sound and the Strait of Georgia. Around the mouth of the Columbia River, too, sea otters were not plentiful, although they were large in size and high in quality, so that the Natives set a "great value" on them. . . .

Although not all of the coastal Natives had an opportunity to hunt the sea otter, all of them did prize its resplendent coat. Robes of sea-otter fur, like those of mountain-goat "wool" (hair) and whistling-marmot fur, were esteemed as objects of beauty, wealth, and prestige, as well as comfort. Among the Nootkas, only chiefs and nobles hunted sea otters and wore their pelts, which were considered their finest clothing. The animal's flesh was eaten, too. According to Captain John Meares, one of the earliest British traders, sea-otter hunting was even more troublesome and more hazardous for the Nootkas than whaling, for the otter was wary and cunning, an excellent swimmer, and ferocious in defense of its young. Yet "scarce a day passes," he noted, "but numbers are eagerly employed in the pursuit of it." Thus, with the advent of Euroamerican traders the Indians did not have to initiate an untried activity in order to meet white demands; rather, they had simply to intensify a traditional occupation. Hunting singly with harpoon and bow and arrow was replaced by hunting severally via the sweep-and-surround method. And the gun was adopted as a hunting weapon, although as late as 1801 the Haidas, who had been introduced to firearms a decade earlier, were still killing sea otters with "a long dart, barbed like an arrow."

Furthermore, the first Euroamerican coasters certainly did not have to introduce the Indians to commerce, for they already had a strong tradition of barter among themselves and with interior groups. Trade was well suited to Northwest Coast Indian society, for one of its main values and goals was the accumulation, display, and redistribution of material goods. . . .

The Russians were the first Euroamericans to make contact with the Northwest Coast Indians, although technically speaking they were not the first to enter the coast *trade,* owing in part to their preference for hunting to trading. In 1741, after eight years of arduous and costly preparation, the Vitus Bering–Aleksey Chirikov expedition finally left Kamchatka [Russia] in two small ships to probe the "big land" across the Bering Sea. Chirikov's party made two landfalls on the Alexander Archipelago, where fifteen well-armed crewmen disappeared; they were likely seized by wary Tlingits—an omen of the future uneasy state of Russian-Tlingit relations. The expedition returned to Petropavlovsk in 1742 without its Danish-born commander [Bering], who was fatally shipwrecked, but with hundreds of sea-otter skins instead. They were found to bring handsome prices in north China, whose large and affluent Manchu upper class valued sea-otter fur as both fancy trim and snug garb in winter. "The skin of a sea-otter is preferred in China to every other, but is used only by the opulent," noted a Russian observer. Russian promyshlenniks (freelance entrepreneurs in general and fur traders in particular) launched a fur rush down the Kurile Islands to Yezo (Hokkaido) and across the Aleutian Islands to the Gulf of Alaska in search of what they called "sea beavers." From 1743 to 1800 one hundred ventures obtained more than 8,000,000 silver rubles worth of "soft gold." In 1799, alarmed by the violent competition among the several Russian companies and by the prospect of international entanglement on the Northwest Coast, the tsarist government chartered a joint-stock monopoly, the RAC [Russian-American Company] (modelled upon the British East India Company . . .), to administer and develop Russian America.

Thus the Muscovites enjoyed a lead in the maritime fur trade of nearly half a century, rival Euroamericans not entering the contest until the middle 1780s. This advantage was compounded by Russian control of the habitats of the most valuable grades of sea otters: Kurilian-Kamchatkan and Aleutian; their fur was blacker, thicker, and glossier than that of the Northwest Coast and Californian otters. The British Captain George Dixon, for example, asserted that the sea otters to the south of the Alexander Archipelago were of a "very inferior quality." It was not until the superior varieties were exhausted that the Russians advanced to the Northwest Coast in 1788, whereupon they engaged other Euroamerican traders in a competition that was eventually to exterminate the local strain (it has only recently been reintroduced from the Aleutians). Until 1795, however, few Russian ships made the coast because of a shortage of both vessels and sailors. In 1794–95 three new ships were built in the Gulf of Alaska and two more arrived from Okhotsk, then Russia's chief Pacific port, and the number of tsar's men more than doubled. In 1794 the reinforced Russians reached Yakutat Bay (Captain Cook's Bering Bay), getting 2,000 sea otters in the process and founding the settlement of Slavorossiya there the following year.

Meanwhile, an expedition under the command of James Shields, a British employee of the Golikov-Shelikhov Company, reconnoitered the coast as far south as the Queen Charlotte Islands and sighted numerous sea otters. In January 1795 Alexander Baranov, the company's colonial manager, sailed in the *Olga* to Sitka Sound, raised a cross on shore, and named the waters Cross Bay. In July of the following year Shields and a party of Aleuts from Kodiak arrived on the *Oryol* and bagged 1,847 sea otters; two years later another party of Kodiak Aleuts killed up to 1,000 otters. Finally, in June 1799 Baranov returned on the *Oryol* with 550 kayaks of Aleuts to hunt, and in late July he established the settlement of Arkhangelsk. (It was destroyed by the Tlingits in July 1802 but re-established on a nearby *kekur* [rocky promontory] in September 1804 as Novoarkhangelsk [New Archangel], whose population as the colonial capital at the beginning of 1810 numbered 621, including 199 Russians, 411 Konyagas [Kodiak Eskimos], and 11 Tlingit hostages.)

By 1800 three-quarters of the RAC's sea-otter skins were coming from the vicinity of Sitka Sound; here Aleut hunting parties killed more than 2,000 otter in July 1800 and up to 4,000 in June 1801. Here, too, the Russians finally encountered their American rivals, who were likewise seeking fresh sources of sea otters (this imperialist overlap was reflected in the area's dual toponomy: the Alexander Archipelago and Sitka Sound to the Russians but the King George Archipelago and Norfolk Sound to the Americans and British). . . . In late April 1799 the American ship *Hancock* met "Canoes coming from all parts of the Sound appearing to have many Skins," and in two weeks of trading some 250 pelts were taken from the Tlingits; at the end of spring the *Hancock* was joined by the *Caroline* and the *Despatch,* and they hailed a Russian brig, the *Oryol,* whose commander said that its owners had 1,300 Aleut and Kodiak hunters "out after Otters." At the end of 1805 the Russian navy's *Neva,* which was accompanying the *Nadezhda* on the first Russian voyage around the world and which had helped the Russians recapture New Archangel, or Sitka, left the port for Canton with 442,819 rubles worth of furs, including 151,000 fur seals, 9,288 foxes, and 4,220 sea otters.

The Russians enjoyed additional advantages, such as the financial and political backing of the tsarist government. Some of its highest officials, including the emperor himself, owned shares in the concern. Another advantage was the existence of permanent bases on the coast: Slavorossiya (1796–1805) on Yakutat Bay, the colonial capital of New Archangel, or Sitka (1799–1802, 1804–) on Sitka Sound, and St. Dionysius Redoubt (1834–40) at the mouth of the Stikine River. They were not matched by American or Spanish settlements; Fort Clatsop (1805–06) and Astoria (1811–12), both at the mouth of the Columbia, were shortlived and insubstantial, as were Santa Cruz de Nutka (1789–95) on Vancouver Island and Nuñez Gaona (1792) on the Olympic Peninsula. The British did not have a coastal post until 1812—Fort George, formerly Astoria; the larger establishments of Forts Vancouver and Langley were not founded until the middle 1820s, and neither was located right on the coast.

Moreover, the RAC benefited from the use or, more correctly, enserfment of the Aleuts and Kodiaks, the world's best hunters of sea otters. In fact, Russian participation in the Northwest Coast trade amounted more to hunting than trading, with their ships serving to transport and protect hunting parties of kayakers. . . . The company told the Aleuts and Kodiaks beforehand how many kayaks would be needed, and in December the Native elders made duty rosters. . . . The kayaks set out in March or April—usually up to 150 [miles] from Kodiak, up to 100 from Unalaska, and about 50 from Atka, and even some from Kenai (Cook) Inlet and Chugach (Prince William) Sound, each party under a Russian or Aleut foreman. They proceeded to assigned stations along the mainland and island coasts and stayed until August or September. Upon their return they submitted their catch, receiving 30 rubles per first-grade sea-otter skin, 15 per second-grade skin, and 3 per third-grade skin, minus any expenses for outfitting.

    . . . The RAC [was] able to get skins in return for paltry Aleut and Kodiak wages in kind. Consequently, . . . the Russians incurred lower costs than British or American traders in the procurement of skins. The former likewise benefitted from access to more than one market on the Chinese frontier. . . .

    Russian trading voyages . . . remained infrequent . . . [, however, on] the "straits," the maze of often narrow and shallow channels dividing the islands of the Alexander Archipelago, in the face of Tlingit hostility. . . .

    . . . [T]he Tlingits were militarily formidable, employing orderly battle formations, wearing hide and slat cuirasses (which could stop musket shot), gorgets, and bone helmets, and eventually wielding firearms, including cannons. They destroyed Sitka itself in 1802 and threatened it as late as 1855, and periodically they killed unwary Aleut and Kodiak hunters; in the spring of 1818, for example, twenty-three Aleuts were killed and twelve wounded by Tlingit gunfire on Prince of Wales Island. The American trader William Sturgis described the Tlingits in 1799 as the most "daring and insolent" Indians on the Northwest Coast, while the Tongass Tlingits were rated "the bravest people, as well as the best hunters, on the coast" in the middle 1820s by Dr John Scouler, a British surgeon-botanist. The Koloshes, as the Russians called the Tlingits (from the Russian word for "labret"), were never completely pacified by the Muscovites, whose warships could seldom reach the main Indian villages far up the narrow, tortuous inlets.

    Thus Russian participation in the maritime fur trade did not extend south of the "straits," and it remained marginal figuratively as well as literally. . . . [After] 1839, [it] . . . was further restricted to the Alexander Archipelago.

Miners versus Farmers in California

ROBERT KELLEY

The floor of the Sacramento Valley is flat, almost featureless, and quite close to sea level. Meandering rivers cross it to empty into the cluster of bays which center upon San Francisco. The longest and deepest of these rivers is the Sacramento, which emerges from the high country at Redding and flows down the middle of the 150-mile long valley, swinging past the city of Sacramento and then losing itself in the complex of islands and channels in the delta lands. To the west of the valley are

---

Text from Robert Kelley, *Gold vs. Grain: The Hydraulic Mining Controversy in California's Sacramento Valley,* Glendale, CA: Arthur H. Clark, 1959, pp. 21–28, 57–82, 229–242. Reprinted by permission of Arthur H. Clark Co.

the lumpy hills and low eminences of the coast ranges; to the north Mount Shasta dominates a vast complex of uplands, and to the east is the Sierra Nevada, the most imposing single geographic feature of California. For four hundred miles it stands as a great, shaggy barrier between the fertile Sacramento and San Joaquin valleys and the Nevada deserts. . . .

Down the long western slope of the northern Sierra Nevada rush four rivers: the Feather, the Yuba, the Bear, and the American. They do not drop from such great heights as those in the southern reaches of the Sierra, but they are powerful, torrential streams, especially in the spring when the great snow pack above them melts. They have trenched themselves in deep canyons, and flow far below the horizon formed by the gently sloping strata which form the Sierra Nevada. The farthest north and longest of these rivers is the Feather, whose forks rise in the remote wilds of Plumas County. . . .

About midway in its course from Oroville to the Sacramento, the Feather receives the waters of the second of the four northern rivers, the Yuba. Its forks, whose wide watersheds of conifer forest in the mountains encompass most of Nevada and Sierra counties, join just before leaving the foothills at Smartville. A vigorous, swiftly-moving stream, the Yuba hurries out of the mountains, . . . joining the Feather where Marysville sits within its great levees. . . . The Feather receives the third of these rivers; the Bear. . . .

The last of the four rivers is the long, winding American, a stream heavy with history. In its south fork James Marshall, in 1848, found the dull flakes which set off the rush to the golden Sierra. The broad ridge paralleling its north fork has borne, in turn, the argonauts who came in search of wealth, the Chinese building the first railroad to vault the Sierra, and now the endless flow of immigration which coasts down this long ridge on the major transcontinental highway. It was where the American joins the Sacramento that John Sutter decided to build the fort which grew into California's capital city. . . .

When the gravel hills were first discovered at Nevada City, miners left the stream bed with a rush. Rising and falling picks glinted all over the valley as miners planted claims on the hillside and attacked it vigorously. They tore up the underbrush, stripped off overburden, and even uprooted soaring pines in their search for gold. . . .

. . . Men came flocking to the new diggings from all over the Sierra, for stream placers were giving out and river towns were dying. Several thousand men were soon digging and washing pay dirt on the hill above Nevada City. Pick and shovel tore up the entire valley, yet few claims paid enough to warrant all the toil. The technical problem was apparently insoluble. But in the spring of 1852, a miner named Anthony Chabot, who was working a claim on the side of Buckeye Hill above Nevada City, devised a tolerable solution. He built a set of inclined wooden penstocks, strengthened by iron clamps so that they could hold a fifty-foot column, or "head" of water without bursting. To this he attached a four-inch canvas hose which he laid upon his claim. The water gushing out of it created an artificial stream strong enough to tear up the soil. It soon excavated a ditch into which Chabot fed pay dirt by breaking the ground on either side and shoveling it into the water. He periodically shut off the water to recover the gold which had collected on the bed of the ditch. This process, called "ground-sluicing," was much more efficient than older methods, and spread rapidly as a step to an economical system for working Tertiary gravels.

Early the following year, in March of 1853, Edward E. Matteson began mining on American Hill, just north of Nevada City. . . . He suggested to his partners that they try breaking down the bank of a cut they had made into the hillside not by pick, but by a stream of water. . . . Chabot, a sail-maker by trade, constructed a hose for them, and Eli Miller, Matteson's partner and a tinsmith, made a tapered nozzle of sheet iron. Hose and nozzle were attached to a barrel on top of the bank to regulate the head of water which was carried to it by Chabot's wooden penstocks. . . .

To their delight, the jet of water turned the bank into sliding mud and washed it into and through their sluice. The gold, being much heavier than gravel and dirt, settled behind riffle boards in the bottom of the sluice. Given water, ground, drainage, and the proper equipment, one man could do in a day what dozens could hardly do in weeks. They had revolutionized gold mining and invented a process which was eventually to spread all over the world.

The results were immediate and profound. An entirely new industry was born. Wherever Tertiary gravels were being worked, rudimentary water systems were hastily enlarged, claims were fitted up with hoses and nozzles, and the roar of hurtling water filled the air. . . .

The northern Sierra boomed with prosperity. During the 1870's, Nevada City grew from a town of roughly four thousand people to one of fifty-four hundred. The townships along the Ridge and in the upper Bear watershed all increased in the same proportion, while Grass Valley, the quartz mining town, dropped a few hundred from its population of a bit over seven thousand in 1870. . . .

But though the mines were prosperous, they were in deep trouble. Down in the Sacramento Valley, where the rivers draining the mines crossed broad, flatland counties, the farms and cities had been bitterly complaining for years about what the miners were doing. The Yuba and its sister streams, as they rushed down their mountain canyons to the Valley floor, carried enormous quantities of mining debris. In their beds lay vast heaps of tailings which slowly moved downstream as the torrential rivers sought to scour out their beds. Abruptly levelling out on the flatlands, the rivers dropped their silt, thereby laying down rapidly-growing fan deposits of tailings. . . .

When the boom swept the mountains in the late sixties and great companies began dumping debris directly into the canyons instead of into slow-moving upland creeks where most of the tailings remained fairly permanently lodged, concern mounted again. Farmers talked of how the rivers were filling, how each small rise in the water produced flood, how hundreds of acres of fruit orchard along the rivers were dying as debris spread slowly, imperceptibly, out into the valley. Their problem was the more ominous because the rivers were undiked and untended. At no level of government was there any agency charged with controlling the Sacramento and its tributaries, or for that matter any other river in the state. River management was completely in the hands of private individuals, and this could only produce chaos, for the rivers overwhelmed the pathetic efforts of isolated individuals to protect themselves. As channels filled with debris and rivers were forced out of their beds, the Sacramento Valley entered a protracted state of siege.

The towns of Marysville and Yuba City were in an especially dangerous situation. Sitting on either side of the Feather where it is joined by the Yuba, they were assaulted not only by the debris coming down from the mines near Oroville, but also by the great flow coming out of the upper Yuba basin. By 1868, the beds of the two

rivers were higher than Marysville's streets, and in that year the town began building the levees which eventually encircled the city as high as the housetops. Within
the next decade Marysville was to spend hundreds of thousands of dollars on these
great walls; their cost eventually soared well over a million dollars. . . .

In early January of 1875 a storm moved in over the valley and deluged mountains and flatlands for a week with snow, rain, thunder and lightning. By the morning
of the nineteenth the swollen brown waters of the Yuba were rushing along near the
top of Marysville's levees. With the fire house bell ringing in their ears, men rushed
out of their homes and flung themselves into a nightmare struggle to save the city.
Near the cemetery, despite frantic efforts, the river began slipping over the levee
and pouring down into town. By nightfall people were rushing wildly for safety; at
eight o'clock the levee broke near the hospital, and a torrent of water rushed into
the streets. In wild confusion women and children were rescued, barns, sheds and
frame houses began floating about, and a little boy drowned. By the following
noon the city had filled like a bowl. Not until the evening of the twenty-first did the
cold and hungry citizens of Marysville get aid, with the steamer "Flora" breasting
the flood from Sacramento. . . .

By [the] time the legislature was beginning its 1876 session, a cloud of resolutions, bills, and sundry proposals of all sorts descended upon it. . . . On the eighth
of January, 1876, Campbell Berry, Sutter County's assemblyman, added to these
proposals a recommended concurrent resolution which he hoped the legislature
would send to Congress. It condemned the hydraulic mining industry in terms by
then familiar, and asked that Congress do two things: prevent the opening of any
more hydraulic claims until the operators took steps to impound their debris; and
send out an engineering team to examine the situation and make recommendations
to Congress. . . .

Miners fought desperately in their attempt to convince a people in transition
that gold production was essential to the state's prosperity, and at all costs must be
protected. The report of the Committee on Mines and Mining pointed out that agriculture was called into existence in California by the needs of the mining population,
and insisted that one-fifth of the farmers' customers still lived in the mountains. Indeed, an excessive concentration on farming would be inimical, for "It is a well-
known historical fact, that every country which has largely exported its cereals for
many consecutive years, has, in the end, impoverished itself, and finally fallen into
decay." Above all, a local market should be fostered and this could best be done by
increasing the hydraulic mining industry, not decreasing it. Anything undertaken to
cripple hydraulic mining would injure the farmer, not help him.

The Committee on Agriculture submitted a . . . brief recommendation. No man
should use his property, it insisted, so as to damage that of others, yet this had been
done for years in spite of the fact that the gold yield was steadily declining and the
mines were less valuable to the state at large. Where "once stood fine mansions,
pleasant homes, rich orchards, and fields smiling with golden grain, is now to be seen
only barrenness and desolation." Furthermore, hydraulic mining was only in its
infancy, and devastation of farm lands would become far worse in the near future.
The farms faced utter destruction, as did also the city of Marysville. Farm production
far exceeded in value the gold extracted even in the best years of the mines; on
"agriculture, and its kindred pursuits, . . . the wealth and strength of states and

nations are founded; it is our great reliance in the future." Moreover, navigable streams were filling, and the state would be delivered completely into the greedy hands of the railroads. The Bay of San Francisco would shoal, its entrance would fill, and San Francisco's prosperity would be ruined. . . .

The mines continued to operate at peak capacity despite all that had gone on previously and the farmers resolved to carry their fight further. . . .They decided to take the controversy into the federal courts, on the supposition that their great power and prestige would be adequate to enforce any injunctions which might be issued.

On the nineteenth of September, 1882, Edwards Woodruff, a citizen of New York state and a property owner in Marysville and its surrounding countryside, entered the Ninth United States Circuit Court in San Francisco and filed suit against the North Bloomfield and all other mines along the Yuba, asking for a perpetual injunction. Judge Lorenzo Sawyer notified the defendants that they must show cause why a temporary injunction to be effective during the suit should not be issued, basing his action on affidavits submitted by Woodruff's attorney, George Cadwalader.

The Woodruff case extended over the better part of a year and a half; not until January of 1884 did Sawyer render his decision. In the meantime, the case remained close to the center of public interest. . . .

On several occasions, Judge Sawyer made trips up the rivers, over the farms, and into the mines. These trips were usually made by steamer so that he could see for himself how the rivers had changed since he had tramped along them thirty years earlier. . . .

On Thursday, January 6, 1884, word came to Marysville that the decision would be given the next day. The townspeople, tremendously excited, rushed about preparing for a celebration. . . .

At 11:00 A.M. the following morning in San Francisco, Judge Sawyer entered his courtroom, which was packed by a large audience of attorneys and interested parties, and began reading his decision. He described at great length the injurious effect of mining debris, pointing out that two state-built dams, costing about $500,000, proved utterly ineffective and were eventually destroyed. Those dams which the miners themselves constructed had rapidly filled with debris, breached, and become ineffective. Since mining debris was doing such widespread damage, he held that unless dumping tailings into the rivers was authorized by law it constituted a general, far-reaching and most destructive public and private nuisance in both common and statutory law. Furthermore, the generality of action by one against the other was justified, since the suits were actually between the mining and valley counties interested. As proof, he pointed to the formation of organizations on both sides which paid all expenses.

Three and a half hours after he had started reading his decision, which covered two hundred and twenty-five pages, Sawyer stated that the defendant companies were "perpetually enjoined and restrained from discharging or dumping into the Yuba river . . . [or its tributaries] any of the tailings, bowlders [*sic*], cobble stones, gravel, sand, clay, debris or refuse matter. . . ." Furthermore, the companies enjoined, who owned most of the ditches and dams in the Yuba basin, were enjoined from allowing anyone to use their water supplies for hydraulic mining. No longer could they look the other way while their workmen engaged in clandestine operations. Every possible legal loophole had been closed. The miners were absolutely forbidden to allow any of their tailings to get into the rivers. . . .

The mining counties received the news as they would a death sentence. Smartville was sunk in gloom; Grass Valley reported a general feeling of "profound sorrow;" in Nevada City there was "universal dissatisfaction and regret;" a Dutch Flat resident laconically remarked, "Most of us will pack our gripsacks."

In San Francisco, the *Bulletin* expressed what might well have been a majority view when it remarked that, after all, the mines were no longer the mainstay of California. This distinction had shifted to agriculture: "The wheat field produces year after year, and wine and oil and wool are perennial." California's values were passing through a crucial transition. The farmer was taking the place of eminence long held by the miner.

Salmon versus Fishers in the Northwest

RICHARD WHITE

The world is in motion. Tectonic plates drift across a spinning planet. Mountains are lifted up and eroded to the sea. Glaciers advance and retreat. All natural features move, but few natural features move so obviously as rivers. Our metaphors for rivers are all metaphors of movement: they run and roll and flow.

Like us, rivers work. They absorb and emit energy; they rearrange the world. The Columbia has been working for millennia. During the Miocene, volcanic eruptions deposited layers of basalt across the Columbia Plain. The upper Columbia cut a gutter through which it ran along the margins of the basaltic flow. At Wenatchee the rise of the Horse Heaven anticline caused the river to cut into the basalt; it drained into the Pasco basin, the lowest point on its route east of the Cascades, and emerged from the basin at the Wallula Gap. During the Pleistocene the collapse of an ice dam holding glacial Lake Missoula created the largest known freshwater flood in the earth's history. It was an afternoon's work for one of the Missoula floods to create the Grand Coulee and other rock channels of the Channeled Scablands. In those few hours it accomplished work that it would have taken the Mississippi three hundred years at full flood to duplicate. The flood rushed into the Columbia channel and finally slowed enough to create the "Portland Delta" of the Willamette lowlands. Since then ice dams have blocked the Columbia's bed, temporarily spilling the river into the Grand Coulee; mountains have slid into it, and humans have dammed it. All these changes have left work for the river to do.

For much of human history, work and energy have linked humans and rivers, humans and nature. But today, except when disaster strikes, when a hurricane hits, or earthquakes topple our creations, or when a river unexpectedly rises and sweeps away the results of our effort and labor, we forget the awesome power—the energy—of nature. There is little in our day-to-day life to preserve the connection. Machines do most of our work; we disparage physical labor and laborers. The link between our work and nature's work has weakened. We no longer understand the world through labor. Once the energy of the Columbia River was felt in human

Excerpts from Chapter 1 and excerpt from Chapter 2 of Richard White, *The Organic Machine: The Remaking of the Columbia River.* New York: Hill and Wang, 1995, pp. 3–4, 15–20, 40–43. Copyright © 1995 by Richard White. Reprinted by permission of Hill & Wang, a division of Farrar, Straus and Giroux, LLC.

bones and sinews; human beings knew the river through the work the river demanded of them.

Early-nineteenth-century accounts of the Columbia can be read in many ways, but they are certainly all accounts of work, sweat, exhaustion, and fear. The men of the early nineteenth century who wrote the Lewis and Clark journals and the accounts of the Astorian trading post, the North West Company and Hudson's Bay Company, knew the energy of the river. They had to expend their own energy to move up, down, and across it. Alexander Ross's marvelous *Adventures of the First Settlers on the Oregon or Columbia River,* a narrative of the arrival of the Astorians and the establishment of the fur-trading outpost of Astoria in 1811, can serve as a primer on the Columbia as an energy system during a time when human beings— Indian and white—had only the wind and the strength of their own muscles to match against the powerful currents of the river.

"The mouth of the Columbia River," Ross wrote, "is remarkable for its sand bars and high surf at all seasons, but more particularly in the spring and fall, during the equinoctial gales." The shoals and sandbars at the Columbia's mouth are relicts of its work and energy. In areas without strong tidal action a river deposits the load it carries to its mouth as a delta, but the Columbia emerges into the Pacific in an area of strong tides and persistent storms. . . .

Examining how humans moved on the river provides one angle of vision on the rapids and falls of the Columbia; examining how salmon moved up and down the river provides a second, equally revealing, perspective. It was, after all, the salmon that brought thousands of Indians to the Cascades, to the Dalles and Celilo Falls, to Priest Rapids and Kettle Falls.

As much as wind, wave, and current, salmon were part of the energy system of the Columbia. Salmon are anadromous fish: they live most of their adult life in the ocean but return to the stream of their birth to spawn since the Columbia does not provide sufficient food to support the salmon born in its tributaries. The precise timing of the movement of young salmon to the sea depends on the species, but eventually all except the kokanee (a form of sockeye which, although nonanadromous, retains the genetic potential to become so) make their way to the ocean. During their time at sea Columbia salmon harvest the far greater solar energy available in the Pacific's food chain and, on their return, make part of that energy available in the river. By intercepting the salmon and eating them, other species, including humans, in effect capture solar energy from the ocean. Salmon thus are a virtually free gift to the energy ledger of the Columbia. They bring energy garnered from outside the river back to the river.

For salmon the rapids and the falls represent obstacles that force them to expend energy, but to the Indians the combination of salmon and rapids and falls seemed providential. In 1811 Gabriel Franchère traveled with one of the sons of Concomly, the leading Chinook chief on the lower Columbia. He told Franchère that in perfecting creation Ekanunum (Coyote) had "caused rocks to fall in the river so as to obstruct it and bring the fish together in one spot in order that they might be caught in sufficient quantities." On the Columbia, where the river was the most turbulent the fishing was best. Rapids and waterfalls forced fish into narrow channels; they forced salmon toward the surface. And as the fish became concentrated and visible, they became more vulnerable to capture.

At the rapids human art and technology altered the river to increase the difficulties for fish. At low water in early May, for example, the Nespelems and Sanpoils built weirs to deflect fish toward artificial channels cleared at certain points in the rapids. The bottoms of the channels were lined with white quartz to make the fish more visible. On smaller tributaries, the Indians built weirs to block the fish until their harvest was complete. At Kettle Falls the Indians fixed timber frames in the rocks of the falls and from them they hung huge willow baskets, ten feet in diameter and twelve feet deep. Leaping salmon would strike the frames and fall into the baskets, where waiting fishermen clubbed and removed them. A single such basket could supposedly yield five thousand pounds of fish a day at the height of the runs.

Robert Stuart described how, at the Dalles, Cathlakaheckits and Cathlathalas built scaffoldings which extended out over the water. "The places chosen are always a point where the water is strongest, and if possible a mass of rock near the projection between which and the shore the Salmon are sure to pass, to avoid the greater body of the current." From the platforms fishermen extended dip nets, and during the peak of the run "the operator hardly ever dips his nett without taking one and sometimes two Salmon, so that I call it speaking within bounds when I say that an experienced hand would by assiduity catch at least 500 daily."

The human energy expended to obtain salmon did not dependably yield a proportionate return of caloric energy from the fish. Salmon do not bestow their gift of energy evenly. Salmon cease feeding when they enter freshwater and live off the fat they have formed while feeding in the ocean. Because salmon burn stored calories to progress against the current, they lose caloric value as they proceed upstream. Early travelers along the river noted the changing quality of the salmon. Descending the river, David Thompson did not find fat salmon until he was near present-day Pasco. Thompson found the Indians taking salmon as high up as the Arrow Lakes, but "they were very poor, necessity made them eatable."

Thompson was not being an epicure. His own body, needing calories to provide energy to do the work the Columbia demanded, craved fat salmon for a reason and rightly gauged its quality. A salmon caught at the mouth had 100 percent of its original caloric value. A salmon caught by the Wishrams at the Dalles had roughly 88 percent. A salmon caught by the Nez Percés near the Snake River had 52 percent. A salmon caught by the Kutenais on the Kootenay River at Nelson or Windemere, British Columbia, had only 25 percent.

The gifts salmon gave varied temporally as well as spatially. The extraordinary yields at the fisheries Stuart mentioned were fleeting. There was a seasonality to the river flow and fish runs that neither art nor knowledge could overcome. During spring flood in late May and June, many sites at the rapids could not be fished at all. The salmon set other limits. Four species of salmon (*Oncorhynchus*), as well as the steelhead trout (*Oncorhynchus mykiss*), spawn in the Columbia and its tributaries, and there is some evidence that a fifth species, pink salmon, once did so. Before their late-nineteenth- and twentieth-century decline, they returned to the Columbia in astonishing numbers, but they did not go everywhere nor did they come evenly. All species passed through the lower river, but at each tributary some spawners separated from the main run; the size of a run decreased as it proceeded up the Columbia.

The largest salmon species was the chinook or king salmon, and it was the chinook that came up the river in the greatest numbers. They actually came in three separate runs: spring, summer, and fall. Each run differed not only in its timing but in its combination of spawning areas, size of fish, and life history. Originally, the spring chinook run was the largest and, for most Indians, the most critical. The first fish might enter the river in February, but the Chinook Indians told Lewis and Clark that they arrived in significant numbers in April. Robert Stuart said spring chinooks reached the Dalles in mid-May, with the greatest numbers coming over the next two months.

Subsequent runs shaded into each other. The spring run of chinook (*O. tshawytscha*) merged into the summer run and the summer into the fall. Sockeye or blueback (*O. nerka*), which spawn in lakes, come in late summer and early fall, and the coho or silver (*O. kisutch*) arrive in the fall. The chum or dog salmon (*O. keta*), the least desirable species, first enters the river in October and spawns largely in the lower tributaries below the Dalles. The steelhead (*O. mykiss*), an oceangoing trout which spawns and returns to the sea, has a summer and winter run. The size of each of these runs fluctuates from year to year.

The seasonality of salmon and the geography of energy that concentrated fishing sites meant that during a relatively short span of time a single place provided a sizable portion of the total annual caloric intake of Indian peoples on the Columbia. At the Dalles the Wishrams and Wascos derived between 30 and 40 percent of their annual energy requirements from salmon; at the other extreme, farther upriver, the Kutenais, Flatheads, and Coeur d'Alenes obtained 5 percent or less.

Taking so many salmon in so short a time, however, meant that the salmon were worthless unless preserved. Preserving fish on the Columbia meant drying them, and this demanded a second convergence of labor and energy. Women's work preserved the fish men caught. On the lower river fish often had to be smoked to be dried, but at the Dalles and above Indians could rely on solar energy—the direct heat of the sun—to dry the fish they split and set out on racks.

As the salmon dwindle and environmental crises deepen, there is an understandable tendency to romanticize and even invent pasts in which the planet was nurturing and humans simply accepting and grateful. And the Columbia, with the annual passage of millions of fish, invites such images. Salmon have sustained culturally rich human communities whose way of life stretches back over five thousand years.

But the people who awaited the salmon were not simple fisherfolk gratefully taking the bounty of their mother earth. Culturally, they made no assumptions about the inevitability of the salmon's return. Their rituals, their social practices, their stories all recognized the possibility that the fish would fail to appear. They waited for salmon not with faith but with anxiety. Depending on how long Indian cultural memories extended, they had good reason to worry. When Table Mountain slid into the river eight hundred years ago and formed a huge lake, it almost certainly cut off all the people upriver from the salmon runs until the river broke through.

In the myths of the river there is a recurring motif of a time when sisters imprisoned the salmon—sometimes within a lake or pond, sometimes behind a dam—and how they are freed by Coyote, the lecherous and often foolish culture hero. Coyote, who defecates so he can consult his feces whenever he needs advice, often uses either the wisdom of women or the tools of women—digging sticks—to take the salmon from the sisters. Indians usually put the site of this dam near the Cascades.

In these stories the women who prevent the coming of the salmon are identified with birds. They are often *wi'dwid*, a Sahaptin word usually translated as swallows, but which also can refer to water snipes or wild ducks. Sometimes it is eagle people who imprison the salmon. Sometimes it is the sandpipers. But as the Wishram story makes explicit, the connection is with a bird whose migration coincides with the spring arrival of the chinook, or as among the Sanpoils, with birds who live by the water and eat fish. In another Wishram myth Dove is Salmon's wife. "Whenever the salmon comes, they kill him at Wishram, and then the dove cries."

This connection between women, birds, salmon, and a time when the salmon did not come was ritually reenacted each year along the river. When the salmon ran and the birds returned, the activities of women became circumscribed. Space reflected and structured power as men controlled access to the fish. Among the Sanpoils and Nespelems men prohibited women not only from visiting fish traps but also from crossing or using trails that led to them. Women could not take water from a stream that contained a fish trap. They had to remain several paces away from the distributing center which contained the common catch. The taboos affected all women, but their prime object was menstruating women, whose contact with water or salmon could cause the run to cease.

The blood of menstruating women was not unique in its power to offend salmon. Any bone had the same effect. So did internal organs. So, too, did the death of a fisherman. David Thompson, watching the fishing at Kettle Falls, reported that neither the scales nor the bowels of cleaned fish were thrown back into the water. If a speared fish escaped, fishing was done for the day. When the spear of one fisherman came too close to the skull of a dead dog, it was polluted and fishing ceases until spear and spearman were ritually purified. Thompson himself was inclined to dismiss all this as superstition, but when one of Thompson's Canadians threw the bone of a dead horse into the river, he reported that the fish vanished. An Indian had to dive down and retrieve the bone. A few hours later the salmon returned.

But the fishery in actual practice was about doing everything that the taboos prohibited: it was about shedding blood; it was about taking what was inside living things—blood, bone, and organs—and putting it outside. It was about the death necessary to sustain life. And the rituals acknowledged this and compensated for it by treating with reverence and respect, in a controlled ceremonial context, those things which, if uncontrolled, could cause the salmon to disappear.

When the salmon first appeared, Indians shed its blood ritually; they consumed it ritually; they preserved the bones. Sometimes the ritually treated blood and bones were restored to the river. To catch salmon, the Astorians had to observe ritual prohibitions. They could not cut salmon crosswise, and if cooked, the salmon had to be consumed before sundown.

The rituals along the Columbia took the biological necessity of obtaining the caloric energy needed to live and elaborated it into a web of social meaning and power that took on consequences of its own. Both men and women caught and ate salmon, but not equally. Ritual restricted the movements and actions of women far more than those of men. The rituals connected the taking of fish with the privileged position of men over women and reinforced that position. They gave men the credit for bringing salmon to the people and placed most of the burden of the failure of the salmon runs on women. . . .

. . . Gillnetters controlled access to particular drifts: stretches of the river where they cast their nets and floated downstream. Fixed-gear men with their pound nets commandeered space on the river. Their very equipment fenced out others. Fish wheels took over old Indian fishing sites and pushed aside the Indians, despite the treaty rights which promised them a particular share of the commons.

Gillnetters were at the center of the struggle for the river commons because they were the largest group of fishermen. In the nineteenth century the canneries rented boats and nets to immigrants accustomed to the water. The counts were never exact, but there were at least 1,700 gillnetters in 1883, with the number dipping to a low of 1,224 in 1890. The number peaked at 2,596 in 1904.

In the late nineteenth century the mosquito fleet (as the boats of the gillnetters were called) covered the river below Portland from May to August. Their nets formed a vast floating barrier to salmon—545 miles long by the late 1880s if connected and stretched end to end—but the daily catch of any individual boat was small. In 1891 and 1892, George and Barker, one of the Astoria canneries, kept track of the gillnetters' average daily catch. Early in the runs the boats averaged only three fish a day. When the runs grew stronger at the end of May and early June and again in July, the boats might average ten to twelve fish. At the peak of the run, they brought in eighteen or twenty fish a day. During the heyday of the runs, the aggregate of these catches was more than the canneries could handle. In the early twentieth century the canneries had to institute limits of 800 pounds per boat for several days around the Fourth of July. Anything above that was waste. Twenty fish could amount to more than 800 pounds, since among them were the big spring chinooks, locally called hogs. These fish ran fifty or sixty pounds or more. Kipling saw them. We never will. They no longer exist.

Although they operated in a world of steam, gillnetters continued to rely on wind and human muscle to harvest fish. A distinctive Columbia River fishing vessel evolved in the Astoria boatyards. The vessels were small (twenty-five feet long), single-masted, and equipped with oars. They were open, only partially decked, and took two men, the captain and the puller, to sail and operate. The men could rig the sail as a tent and sleep under it.

To catch fish the gillnetters had to control a three-dimensional space which extended across and beneath the surface of the river. This space was a drift—a two- to five-mile section of the river through which the tide pulled the boat and its net. All gill nets work on a simple principle: fish swim into them but cannot fit through their mesh. In trying to extricate themselves, they get caught by the gills and drown. The art of gillnetting involved disguising the net so fish could neither see it nor avoid it. Thus gillnetters fished at night or when the river was muddy. They altered the design of the nets to keep fish from swimming underneath them or above them. By introducing layers of different-size mesh, they could take both large and small fish, enmeshing the big ones, catching the small ones by the gills. Their nets and their methods of using them embodied a working knowledge of nature.

But gillnetters modified as well as knew nature and the river. Floating nets dominated the river from Point Ellice to the mouth, but above Tongue Point by 1900 gillnetters turned to diver nets. The cork line at the top of the diver net was just buoyant enough to keep the net vertical in the river while the lead line sank down to touch bottom. The gillnetters could not use the net where the bottom was littered with snags or debris, for they would tear the net. They needed to clear the bottom, and to do so the fishermen on particular drifts created snag unions. By virtue of their labor, members of a snag union claimed exclusive fishing rights on that drift.

To watch gillnetters at work was to witness an elaborately choreographed dance of fish, river, and men. The habits of fish, the hydraulics of the river, and the organized labor of men all intersected. Labor and nature merged. No element, no movement could be separated from the other; each, to some degree, shaped the other. On a summer's dawn with the sails against the blue sky and green forest, with the fish silver in the net, the result was a thing of brutal beauty. When the canneries had disappeared, when the fishing fleet on the Columbia had shrunk nearly to the vanishing point, when Astoria lived on memories of fish, what stuck in human memories were flashes of color, of movement, of bodies, both fish and human, that seemed too vivid and elemental to have been so transitory. Edward Beard, who rose to become a partner in a cannery, could at the end of his life remember no more beautiful sight than the mosquito fleet sailing out of Astoria on a Sunday evening against the setting sun.

But the beauty was brutal because fish died in astonishing numbers and because men died in chilling numbers. Cleaning the river's bottom, dividing and allocating its space did not domesticate the river. Gillnetting was dangerous; its practitioners "hardy and brave." There was a constant temptation to prolong the net's drift, but if the fishing boat came too close to the bar, its breakers could ensnare both nets and boat. In the 1880s an estimated twenty to sixty fishermen died annually on the Columbia bar. And when storms surprised the fleet, as the gale of May 7, 1880, did, the toll was terrible. That storm hit the fleet with many boats drifting, "hanging on their nets," as the gillnetters said. Desperately, the fishermen cut their nets and fled. The winds capsized some, and ripped apart the sails of others, driving them onto Chinook Point. Even many who reached their anchorages foundered there. The storm claimed eighty boats and forty-five fishermen.

But gillnetters also died because they competed against other fishermen for space on the river. The Columbia fishery was not a homogeneous space. Fish were much more reliably found in some areas than others, and mechanical devices secured those areas for particular owners. Fish traps—originally wooden traps of piles and slats—grew with the canning industry, but by 1890 they had yielded to more sophisticated and expensive pound nets introduced by fishermen from the Great Lakes. Steam pile drivers drove in permanent piles to which nets were attached that extended out from the riverbank. Salmon meeting the barrier followed it away from the shore to a heart-shaped container which, in turn, steered them into smaller webbed areas, first a "pot," then a "spiller," from which they were removed. By 1889 there were 121 traps in Baker Bay alone. In all, there were nearly 400 fish traps and pound nets in operation. Gillnetters who tried to fish the bay risked snaring their own nets on the traps and endangering their own lives.

By the turn of the century the chinooks that escaped the gill nets and pound nets had also to evade seine nets operated from shore before facing more than forty fish wheels between the Cascades and Celilo Falls. These devices, either fixed on shore or mounted on scows with artificial leads to guide fish, first appeared on the Columbia in 1879 at the same sites prized by Indian dipnetters where the water was swift and the fish in their migration upstream were forced into narrow channels. Fish wheels never took more than 7 percent of the total catch, but their efficiency, as Major W. A. Jones reported to the U.S. Fisheries Commission in 1887, was "painful." They literally pumped fish out of the river. During the height of the runs their individual output was tremendous, with each taking an average of 20,000 pounds of fish a day. The record, set in the 1880s, was 50,000 pounds in a day.

By the early twentieth century there were not enough salmon for all who sought them. The runs of spring and summer chinook had been visibly declining since the 1880s. Major Jones noted that between April and August it was "a sort of a miracle that any fish escape to go up the river, except the small Blue backs, Steelheads, and the precocious St. Jacob's Chinook which can pass through the 4½ inch mesh of the gillnets." By 1890 salmon were growing scarce at the Indian fishery of Kettle Falls. On the Yakima, overfishing weakened the runs; irrigation depleted the river and nearly killed them. Based on anecdotal evidence, there had been a dramatic decline in the runs of chinook on the Snake and its tributaries by the 1890s.

Preserving salmon was, however, as much a social and cultural matter as a biological or economic one. On the river humans struggled to turn space into property and salmon into a commodity, but this was only part of the transformation of nature taking place. In their dying, salmon revealed constellations of competing social values. Understanding the fate of salmon involves understanding complicated and particular social struggles and not some universal human nature at work in an undifferentiated commons.

❦ *F U R T H E R   R E A D I N G*

Jean S. Aigner et al., eds., *Interior Alaska: A Journey Through Time* (1986)

M. A. Baumhoff, *Ecological Determinants of Aboriginal California Populations* (1963)

Lydia Black, *Russians in Alaska (1741–1867)* (2002)

Sucheng Chan, *The Bittersweet Soil: The Chinese in California Agriculture, 1860–1910* (1986)

Jack Chen, *The Chinese of America: From the Beginnings to the Present* (1981)

Joseph Cone and Sandy Ridlington, eds., *The Northwest Salmon Crisis: A Documentary History* (1996)

William Cronon, "Kennecott Journey: The Paths out of Town," in William Cronon, George Miles, and Jay Gitlin, eds., *Under an Open Sky: Rethinking America's Western Past* (1992)

Douglas Henry Daniels, *Pioneer Urbanites: A Social and Cultural History of Black San Francisco* (1980)

Raymond F. Dasmann, *California's Changing Environment* (1988)

James R. Gibson, *Farming the Frontier: The Agricultural Opening of the Oregon Country, 1786–1846* (1985)

William H. Goetzmann, *Army Exploration in the American West, 1803–1863* (1959)

Marion S. Goldman, *Gold Diggers and Silver Miners: Prostitution and Social Life on the Comstock Lode* (1981)

LeRoy R. Hafen, ed., *Mountain Men and Fur Traders of the Far West* (1965)

Robert F. Heizer and Albert B. Elsasser, *The Natural World of the California Indians* (1980)

———— and M. A. Whipple, *The California Indians: A Source Book,* 2nd ed. (1971)

J. S. Holliday, *Rush for Riches: Gold Fever and the Making of California* (1999)

————, *The World Rushed In: The California Gold Rush Experience (2002)*

Albert L. Hurtado, "Sex, Gender, Culture, and a Great Event: The California Gold Rush," *Pacific Historical Review* 68 (November 1999), 1–20

John C. Jackson, *Children of the Fur Trade: Forgotten Metis of the Pacific Northwest* (1995)

Amy Kaplan, "Manifest Domesticity," *American Literature* 70(3), (1998), 581–606

Robert Kelley, *Battling the Inland Sea; American Political Culture, Public Policy, and the Sacramento Valley, 1850–1986* (1989)

————, *Gold vs. Grain: The Hydraulic Mining Controversy in California's Sacramento Valley* (1959)

William Robert Kenny, "Mexican-American Conflict on the Mining Frontier, 1848–1852," *Journal of the West* 6 (October 1967): 582–592

Ruth S. Lamb, *Mexican Americans: Sons of the Southwest* (1970)

Rudolph Lapp, *Blacks in Gold Rush California* (1977)

Henry T. Lewis, *Patterns of Indian Burning in California: Ecology and Ethnohistory* (1973)

Jim Lichatowich, *Salmon Without Rivers: A History of the Pacific Salmon Crisis* (2000)

Patricia Nelson Limerick, *The Legacy of Conquest: The Unbroken Past of the American West* (1988)

Mary Malloy, *"Boston Men" on the Northwest Coast: The American Maritime Fur Trade 1788–1844* (1998)

Malcolm Margolin, *The Ohlone Way: Indian Life in the Monterray-San Francisco Bay Area* (1978)

———, ed., *The Way We Lived: California Indian Reminiscences, Stories, and Songs* (1981)

Paula M. Marks, *Precious Dust: The America Gold Rush Era, 1848–1900* (1994)

Jessica Maxwell, "Swimming with Salmon," *Natural History* 104 (September 1995), 26–39

Carolyn Merchant, ed., *Green Versus Gold: Sources in California's Environmental History* (1998)

Samuel Eliot Morison, *The European Discovery of America: The Northern Voyages, A.D. 500–1600* (1971)

Ruth B. Moynihan, et al., eds., *So Much to Be Done: Women Settlers on the Mining and Ranching Frontier* (1990)

Adele Ogden, *The California Sea Otter Trade, 1784–1848* (1941)

Joshua Paddison, ed., *A World Transformed: Firsthand Accounts of California Before the Gold Rush* (1999)

George H. Phillips, *The Enduring Struggle: Indians in California History* (1981)

Milo Milton Quaife, *Pictures of Gold Rush California* (1949)

James J. Rawls and Richard J. Orsi, eds., *A Golden State: Mining and Economic Development in Gold Rush California* (1999)

T. A. Rickard, *A History of American Mining* (1932)

Fayette Robinson and Franklin Street, *The Gold Mines of California: Two Guidebooks* (rpt. 1974)

Alexander Ross and Kenneth A. Spaulding, *The Fur Hunters of the Far West* (2001)

Sarah Royce, *A Frontier Lady: Recollections of the Gold Rush and Early California* (1977)

Carl P. Russell, Firearms, *Traps, and Tools of the Mountain Men* (1967)

Mari Sandoz, *The Beaver Men* (1964)

Morgan Sherwood, *Alaska and Its History* (1967)

———, *Big Game in Alaska: A History of Wildlife and People* (1981)

———, *The Exploration of Alaska* (1965)

Duane Smith, *Colorado Mining: A Photographic History* (1977)

———, *Mining America: The Industry and the Environment, 1800–1980* (1987)

Steven Stoll, *The Fruits of Natural Advantage: Making the Industrial Countryside in California* (1998)

Joseph E. Taylor, *Making Salmon: An Environmental History of the Northwest Fishing Crisis* (1999)

Mark Twain, *Roughing It* (1902)

Jack R. Wagner, *Gold Mines of California* (1970)

Ralph T. Wattenburger, *The Redwood Lumbering Industry on the Northern California Coast, 1850–1900* (1931)

Richard White, *"It's Your Misfortune and None of My Own": A New History of the American West* (1993)

——— and John M. Findlay, eds., *Power and Place in the North American West* (1999)

Otis E. Young, Jr., *Western Mining* (1970)

CHAPTER 9

Great Plains
Grasslands Exploited

𝜓

As you travel west from the oak openings and tall-grass prairies of Illinois to the short-grass plains of western Kansas and Nebraska, to the sagebrush deserts of Nevada, you travel from a land of plentiful rain to a land of little rain. As you move forward through time from an era of waving seas of perennial grama grasses, thundering herds of buffalo, and horse-mounted Indians to a time of acres of introduced cheatgrass, stockyards of steers, and chapped and spurred cowboys, you move through a century of changing grassland history. The story of the Great Plains can be told as a tale of human progress and technological triumph over buffalo, Indians, and drought (from desert to garden) or as a saga of human decline and ecological deterioration (from garden to desert). Each version of the story reveals the perspectives of the storyteller, the perspectives of the listener, and the time of telling. Each leaves out some of the facts and some of the actors to create a particular plot for a particular audience.

The Kiowa Indians tell the story of the grasslands from a unique viewpoint— that of the buffalo. "There was war between the buffalo and the white men. . . . The white men hired hunters to do nothing but kill the buffalo. Up and down the plains those men ranged, shooting sometimes as many as a hundred buffalo a day. . . . The buffalo saw that their day was over. . . . Sadly, the last remnant of the great herd gathered in council, and decided what they would do. . . . Straight to Mount Scott the leader of the herd walked. Behind him came the cows and their calves, and the few young males who had survived. . . . The face of the mountain opened. Inside Mount Scott the world was green and fresh. . . . The rivers ran clear, not red. The wild plums were in blossom, chasing the redbuds up the inside slopes. Into this world of beauty the buffalo walked, never to be seen again."*

---

*Richard Erdoes and Alfonso Ortiz, eds., *American Indian Myths and Legends* (New York: Pantheon, 1984), pp. 490–491.

274

What story do the documents and essays of this chapter suggest to you? What is its plot? Who are the actors? Whom have you left out? What alternative stories can you tell? (See Maps 1, 2, 3, 4, and 8 in the Appendix.)

ψ D O C U M E N T S

The documents in this chapter reveal the changing perceptions and uses of the Great Plains during a century of development. The speakers and writers provide elements for a number of possible stories of the grasslands' environmental history.

Although sometimes stereotyped as reluctant pioneers, women were often eager settlers, as well as astute observers and chroniclers of life on the plains. Document 1 features some women pioneers' perceptions of the grasslands environment and its challenges during the settlement of Kansas in the period from 1860 to 1886. The Homestead Act of 1862, excerpted in Document 2, did not restrict homestead entry—possession through settlement—to men. Although land speculators often abused the law's provisions, any single person over twenty-one years of age, any head of a household, or any immigrant intending to become a citizen could file for entry and make final proof of his or her claim after five years of living on and improving 160 acres of land. Single, divorced, widowed, and even married women (who illegally filed in their maiden names) became landowners through the Homestead Act.

The short-grass plains west of the hundredth meridian, a region where rainfall usually did not reach the twenty inches a year necessary for reliable farming, were ideal for cattle ranching. Until they were depleted by overgrazing, perennial grasses provided nutritious forage for herds of Texas longhorned and eastern shorthorned cattle. Eventually, the open range became a realm of fenced ranches watered by wells and seeded with annual grasses that supported far fewer head per acre than the native perennials. Document 3 is excerpted from the autobiography of entrepreneur Joseph McCoy, founder of the first cowtown in Abilene, Kansas, in 1866. He describes the cattle drives northward along the Chisholm Trail that brought steers directly to the newly completed east-west Kansas Pacific Railroad for shipment to midwestern slaughterhouses.

Document 4 presents excerpts from historian Frederick Jackson Turner's famous essay of 1893 on the significance of the frontier in American history. In this progressive story, Turner argued that the region's frontier conditions produced rugged individualism and democracy. Plentiful furs, nutritious grasses, and rich soils lured successive waves of trappers, ranchers, and farmers westward who wrested civilization from the wilderness. The environment thus formed American character and social institutions, Turner maintained. In Document 5 John Steinbeck tells a very different story—one of the decline of the grasslands and of humanity as drought leads to the dust bowl of the 1930s and the land itself withers and dies. Despite strong human character and desire to succeed, an arid environment fosters failure.

Just as cattle competed with buffalo for grassland nourishment, white settlers competed with Indians for claims to the land. Whites' unchecked slaughter of buffalo for their hides, which were used in such products as machine belts and robes, released the grasslands for cattle grazing and reduced the Indians' sources of subsistence. As Crow Indian chief Plenty-Coups tells it in Document 6, recounted in 1950, the Indian way of life passed away with the passing of the buffalo. What was a tragic story for Indians and bison, however, was a triumph for European Americans, as is emphasized in Document 7, a 1979 newspaper editorial.

1. Pioneer Women Portray the Plains Environment, 1860–1886

Matilda Steele

My father, Rev. John Armstrong Steele, and my mother, Catherine Hampton Steele, came to Topeka with their family of eight children in 1860 from Illinois. . . . There was not a tree nor shrub nor fence. Our house seemed to be in the open prairie and around it was that yellow clay soil so noticeable to strangers and so well remembered by old settlers. No spear of grass grew there. No shade, no fruit, no flowers, and worst of all, no rain, for this was the year of the great drouth in Kansas. It needs no descriptive adjectives, and no dates to make any old Kansan know what it meant. Since then dry spells have destroyed this crop and that, some-times at one end of the season and sometimes at the other, but the drouth of 1860 swept the calendar.

Aura St. John

I had a puncheon floor, . . . and I think but few of you know what that is. They would take a section of saw log about four feet long and split off slabs as thin as they could, from one to four inches thick, and they made a much better floor than dirt. I scrubbed them with a splint broom made from a piece of hickory and they would look so bright and grateful after it. This broom was made by shaving fine splints from the bottom up about eight or ten inches, removing the very center, then shaving from the same distance above down near these at the bottom, turning these down and tying them.

Mrs. F. M. Pearl

Oh, what flavor and fragrance! . . . Blackberries were plentiful over in Doniphan County along Missions Bluff, also some wonderful plums. Supposition was that rov-ing Indians brought them from the east and dropped the seed at one of their camps, for they were by no means wild. One variety in size, shape and color was that of a small lemon, another very large red and all told were several distinct varieties.

There were also wild gooseberries, wild grapes, chokeberries, pawpaws, wild crab apples, hazel nuts, and hickory nuts, if you went far enough to get them, but the one lone fruit on the prairie was the globe apple, which was made into preserves and was very much appreciated on account of the scarcity of fruit.

Some of the other necessary things gathered was the Mullen plant to be made into candy to ward off winter colds, also horsemint and catnip for teas.

Sarah Hammond White

Many years ago, . . . the resources of this new country were Buffalo, Deer, Wild Turkey and Antelope, Prairie Chicken, Quail and many fur-bearing animals. The

From Joanna L. Stratton, *Pioneer Women: Voices from the Kansas Frontier.* New York: Simon and Schuster, 1981, pp. 51, 64–65, 99–103. Copyright ©1981 by Joanna L. Stratton. Reprinted by permission of Simon & Schuster.

settlers subsisted on wild game for meat, particularly Buffalo and Prairie Chicken. The Buffalo roamed at will in western Kansas and woe to the travelers who encountered a herd of them when they decided to go south in the fall of the year as was their custom. In the fall the men usually went west and killed our winter supply. Some of it was dried and hung up to be used as we needed it, and the best parts of the animals were allowed to freeze and put away for winter use. We needed no expensive butcher shops at this time as each family was provided with this buffalo meat, and the prairie chicken was an agreeable change. I can still hear that peculiar noise the prairie chicken made when they went forth in the early morning for their morning meal. But the prairie chicken, like the buffalo, were ruthlessly slain and it is no wonder that after sixty-five years have elapsed they are almost extinct.

Susan Proffitt

I remember driving over to the [Groves] ranch one beautiful day in early spring. . . . The great acres gave promise of an unusual harvest of feed for the thousands of white-faced cattle grazing contentedly in the pastures. A more beautiful scene I never saw.

Spring gave into summer, and in August at the close of a hot day when the grasses seemed to wither and the cattle bunched up near the creek and well and no air seemed to stir the leaves on the trees, all nature seemed still with an ominous stillness. A mass of black clouds loomed up in the west, distant thunder rumbled, the clouds gathered fast, taking on a greenish hue, thunder boomed and lightning streaked the sky and cut through the landscape and then with a rush and roar came the hail, devastating everything.

Mary Lyon

August 1, 1874, . . . is a day that will always be remembered by the then inhabitants of Kansas. . . . For several days there had been quite a few hoppers around, but this day there was a haze in the air and the sun was veiled almost like Indian summer. They began, toward night, dropping to earth, and it seemed as if we were in a big snowstorm where the air was filled with enormous-size flakes. . . .

They devoured every green thing but the prairie grass. . . . They ate the leaves and young twigs off our young fruit trees, and seemed to relish the green peaches on the trees, but left the pit hanging. They went from the corn fields as though they were in a great hurry, and there was nothing left but the toughest parts of the bare stalks. Our potatoes had to be dug and marketed to save them.

I thought to save some of my garden by covering it with gunny sacks, but the hoppers regarded that as a huge joke, and enjoyed the awning thus provided, or if they could not get under, they ate their way through. The cabbage and lettuce disappeared the first afternoon; by the next day they had eaten the onions. They had a neat way of eating onions. They devoured the tops, and then ate all of the onion from the inside, leaving the outer shell.

The garden was soon devoured, and when all of these delicacies were gone, they ate the leaves from the fruit trees. They invaded our homes, and if our baking was not well guarded by being enclosed in wood or metal, we would find ourselves minus the substantial part of our meals; and on retiring to bed, we had to shake them out of the bedding, and were fortunate if we did not have to make a second raid before morning.

2. The Homestead Act, 1862

An Act to secure Homesteads to actual Settlers on the Public Domain.

Be it enacted by the Senate and House of Representatives of the United States of America in Congress assembled, That any person who is the head of a family, or who has arrived at the age of twenty-one years, and is a citizen of the United States, or who shall have filed his declaration of intention to become such, as required by the naturalization laws of the United States, and who has never borne arms against the United States Government or given aid and comfort to its enemies, shall, from and after the first January, eighteen hundred and sixty-three, be entitled to enter one quarter section or a less quantity of unappropriated public lands, . . . *Provided,* That any person owning and residing on land may, under the provisions of this act, enter other land lying contiguous to his or her said land, which shall not, with the land so already owned and occupied, exceed in the aggregate one hundred and sixty acres.

Sec. 2. *And be it further enacted,* That the person applying for the benefit of this act shall, upon application to the register of the land office in which he or she is about to make such entry, make affidavit before the said register or receiver that he or she is the head of a family, or is twenty-one years or more of age, or shall have performed service in the army or navy of the United States, and that he has never borne arms against the Government of the United States or given aid and comfort to its enemies, and that such application is made for his or her exclusive use and benefit, and that said entry is made for the purpose of actual settlement and cultivation, and not either directly or indirectly for the use or benefit of any other person or persons whomsoever; and upon filing the said affidavit with the register or receiver, and on payment of ten dollars, he or she shall thereupon be permitted to enter the quantity of land specified: *Provided, however,* That no certificate shall be given or patent issued therefor until the expiration of five years from the date of such entry; and if, at the expiration of such time, or at any time within two years thereafter, the person making such entry; or, if he be dead, his widow; or in case of her death, his heirs or devisee; or in case of a widow making such entry, her heirs or devisee, in case of her death; shall prove by two credible witnesses that he, she, or they have resided upon or cultivated the same for the term of five years immediately succeeding the time of filing the affidavit aforesaid, and shall make affidavit that no part of said land has been alienated, and that he has borne true allegiance to the Government of the United States.

From George P. Sanger, ed. *The Statutes at Large, Treaties, and Proclamations of the United States of America From December 5, 1895 to March 3, 1863.* Boston: Little Brown & Co., 1865, vol. 12, pp. 392–393, excerpts.

3. Joseph G. McCoy Describes the Chisholm Trail and Abilene Stockyards, 1874

We left the herd fairly started upon the trail for the northern market. Of these trails there are several: one leading to Baxter Springs and Chetopa; another called the "Old Shawnee trail," leaving Red river and running eastward, crossing the Arkansas not far above Fort Gibson, thence bending westward up the Arkansas river. But the principal trail now traveled is more direct and is known as "Chisholm trail," so named from a semicivilized Indian who is said to have traveled it first. It is more direct, has more prairie, less timber, more small streams and less large ones, and altogether better grass and fewer flies (no civilized Indian tax or wild Indian disturbances) than any other route yet driven over, and is also much shorter in distance because direct from Red river to Kansas. Twenty-five to thirty-five days is the usual time required to bring a drove from Red river to the southern line of Kansas, a distance of between two hundred and fifty and three hundred miles and an excellent country to drive over. So many cattle have been driven over the trail in the last few years that a broad highway is tread out, looking much like a national highway; so plain, a fool could not fail to keep in it.

One remarkable feature is observable as being worthy of note, and that is how completely the herd becomes broken to follow the trail. Certain cattle will take the lead, and others will select certain places in the line, and certain ones bring up the rear; and the same cattle can be seen at their post, marching along like a column of soldiers, every day during the entire journey, unless they become lame, when they will fall back to the rear. A herd of one thousand cattle will stretch out from one to two miles whilst traveling on the trail, and is a very beautiful sight, inspiring the drover with enthusiasm akin to that enkindled in the breast of the military hero by the sight of marching columns of men. Certain cowboys are appointed to ride beside the leaders and so control the herd, whilst others ride beside and behind, keeping everything in its place and moving on, the camp wagon and caviyard bringing up the rear.

Few occupations are more cheerful, lively, and pleasant than that of the cowboy on a fine day or night; but when the storm comes, then is his manhood and often his skill and bravery put to test. When the night is inky dark and the lurid lightning flashes its zigzag course athwart the heavens, and the coarse thunder jars the earth, the winds moan fresh and lively over the prairie, the electric balls dance from tip to tip of the cattle's horns—then the position of the cowboy on duty is trying, far more than romantic. When the storm breaks over his head, the least occurrence unusual, such as the breaking of a dry weed or stick, or a sudden and near flash of lightning, will start the herd as if by magic, all at an instant, upon a wild rush, and woe to the horse or man or camp that may be in their path. The only possible show for safety is to mount and ride with them until you can get outside the stampeding column. It is customary to train cattle to listen to the noise of the herder, who sings in a voice more sonorous than musical a lullaby consisting of a few short monosyllables. A stranger to the business of stock driving will scarce credit the statement

Excerpts from *Historic Sketches of the Cattle Trade of the West and Southwest,* by Joseph G. McCoy (Glendale, Calif.: Arthur H. Clark, 1940 [1874]), pp. 162–168, 173–177.

that the wildest herd will not run, so long as they can hear distinctly the voice of the herder above the din of the storm.

But if by any mishap the herd gets off on a real stampede, it is by bold, dashing, reckless riding in the darkest of nights, and by adroit, skillful management that it is checked and brought under control. The moment the herd is off, the cowboy turns his horse at full speed down the retreating column and seeks to get up beside the leaders, which he does not attempt to stop suddenly, for such an effort would be futile, but turns them to the left or right hand and gradually curves them into a circle, the circumference of which is narrowed down as fast as possible until the whole herd is rushing wildly round and round on as small a piece of ground as possible for them to occupy. Then the cowboy begins his lullaby note in a loud voice, which has a great effect in quieting the herd. When all is still and the herd well over its scare, they are returned to their bed ground, or held where stopped until daylight. . . .

After a drive of twenty-five to one hundred days the herd arrives in western Kansas, whither, in advance, its owner has come, and decided what point at which he will make his headquarters. Straightway a good herding place is sought out, and the herd, upon its arrival, placed thereon, to remain until a buyer is found, who is diligently sought after; but if not found as soon as the cattle are fat, they are shipped to market. . . .

Of the 35,000 cattle that arrived in 1867 at Abilene, about 3,000 head were bought and shipped to Chicago by the parties owning the stockyards; of the balance, much the larger portion was sent to Chicago and either sold on the market or packed for the account of the drovers. The latter proved more [un]fortunate for the drover. The cattle were thin in flesh and made only the lower grades of beef, for which there was but little demand at ruinously low figures. Those who sold on the market did better than those who packed, yet they lost money heavily. . . . Had the drovers of 1867 gone into winter quarters and kept their stock until the following season, a fine profit instead of a loss would have been realized. But it was upon the tongue of nearly everyone that the cattle would not stand the rigors of a northern winter, and inasmuch as there was no precedent by which to be governed, it was thought best to sell and pack them as before described. . . .

But we will close this chapter with [a] brief sketch of [a] widely known and universally liked [drover] and [trader], . . . J. D. Reed, a resident of Texas for twenty-three years but an Alabamian by birth. Upon entering Texas, he went straightway on a stock ranch of his own selection on the frontier of his adopted state. Notwithstanding he devotes much of his time and attention to driving and trading in cattle, he keeps up his stocks in Texas. Of cattle he has about ten thousand head, and of horses a stock sufficiently large to keep good the supply of saddle ponies with which to care for his cattle stocks. Although his ranch consists of fully one thousand acres of land, his stock ranges over an immense area of country, mostly belonging to the state of Texas. . . . In 1871 he changed his plans of operation and turned his herds toward western Kansas. Each year since has witnessed on an average fully thirty-five hundred head of beeves en route for western Kansas driven by Mr. Reed's cowboys. Whatever frontier cattle town can secure his patronage and influence, regards him a host in its behalf. He drives none but good beeves, and is, upon arrival, ready to sell out all or in part; or if prices do not suit him to sell, he will turn about and buy. He is not particular which he does, so he is doing something, for he is a man of fine energy and great perseverance; a man who is familiar with all phases of life and is always in to see, know, and learn everything that may be going on, among the highest to the lowest, where he may be stopping. He is one of that type of men that makes friends in all spheres of life, and few there are who have a larger list of warm admirers than J. D. Reed, of Goliad, Texas.

4. Frederick Jackson Turner Explains the Significance of the Frontier in American History, 1893

In a recent bulletin of the Superintendent of the Census for 1890 appear these sig-nificant words: "Up to and including 1880 the country had a frontier of settlement, but at present the unsettled area has been so broken into by isolated bodies of settle-ment that there can hardly be said to be a frontier line. In the discussion of its extent, its westward movement, etc., it can not therefore, any longer have a place in the census reports." This brief official statement marks the closing of a great historic movement. Up to our own day American history has been in a large degree the his-tory of the colonization of the Great West. The existence of an area of free land, its continuous recession, and the advance of American settlement westward, explain American development.

Behind institutions, behind constitutional forms and modifications, lie the vital forces that call these organs into life and shape them to meet changing conditions. The peculiarity of American institutions is, the fact that they have been compelled to adapt themselves to the changes of an expanding people—to the changes involved in crossing a continent, in winning a wilderness, and in developing at each area of this progress out of the primitive economic and political conditions of the frontier into the complexity of city life. . . . American social development has been con-tinually beginning over again on the frontier. This perennial rebirth, this fluidity of American life, this expansion westward with its new opportunities, its continuous touch with the simplicity of primitive society, furnish the forces dominating Ameri-can character. The true point of view in the history of this nation is not the Atlantic coast, it is the great West. . . .

The frontier is the line of most rapid and effective Americanization. The wilder-ness masters the colonist. It finds him a European in dress, industries, tools, modes of travel, and thought. It takes him from the railroad car and puts him in the birch canoe. It strips off the garments of civilization and arrays him in the hunting shirt and the moccasin. It puts him in the log cabin of the Cherokee and Iroquois and runs an In-dian palisade around him. Before long he has gone to planting Indian corn and plow-ing with a sharp stick; he shouts the war cry and takes the scalp in orthodox Indian fashion. In short, at the frontier the environment is at first too strong for the man. He must accept the conditions which it furnishes, or perish, and so he fits himself into the Indian clearings and follows the Indian trails. Little by little he transforms the wilderness, but the outcome is not the old Europe, not simply the development of

From American Historical Association, *Annual Report for the Year 1893*. Washington, D.C., 1894, pp. 199–227, excerpts.

Germanic germs, any more than the first phenomenon was a case of reversion to the Germanic mark. The fact is, that here is a new product that is American. At first, the frontier was the Atlantic coast. It was the frontier of Europe in a very real sense. Moving westward, the frontier became more and more American. . . .

In these successive frontiers we find natural boundary lines which have served to mark and to affect the characteristics of the frontiers, namely: The "fall line"; the Alleghany Mountains; the Mississippi; the Missouri, where its direction approximates north and south; the line of the arid lands, approximately the ninety-ninth meridian; and the Rocky Mountains. The fall line marked the frontier of the seventeenth century; the Alleghanies that of the eighteenth; the Mississippi that of the first quarter of the nineteenth; the Missouri that of the middle of this century (omitting the California movement); and the belt of the Rocky Mountains and the arid tract, the present frontier. Each was won by a series of Indian wars. . . .

The Atlantic frontier was compounded of fisherman, fur-trader, miner, cattle-raiser, and farmer. Excepting the fisherman, each type of industry was on the march toward the West, impelled by an irresistible attraction. Each passed in successive waves across the continent. Stand at Cumberland Gap and watch the procession of civilization, marching single file—the buffalo following the trail to the salt springs, the Indian, the fur-trader and hunter, the cattle-raiser, the pioneer farmer—and the frontier has passed by. Stand at South Pass in the Rockies a century later and see the same procession with wider intervals between. The unequal rate of advance compels us to distinguish the frontier into the trader's frontier, the rancher's frontier, or the miner's frontier, and the farmer's frontier. . . .

The exploitation of the beasts took hunter and trader to the west, the exploitation of the grasses took the rancher west, and the exploitation of the virgin soil of the river valleys and prairies attracted the farmer. Good soils have been the most continuous attraction to the farmer's frontier. . . .

But the most important effect of the frontier has been in the promotion of democracy. . . . The frontier is productive of individualism. Complex society is precipitated by the wilderness into a kind of primitive organization based on the family. The tendency is anti-social. It produces antipathy to control, and particularly to any direct control. The tax gatherer is viewed as a representative of oppression. . . . The frontier individualism has from the beginning promoted democracy. . . .

So long as free land exists, the opportunity for a competency exists, and economic power secures political power. But the democracy born of free land, strong in selfishness and individualism, intolerant of administrative experience and education, and pressing individual liberty beyond its proper bounds, has its dangers as well as its benefits. Individualism in America has allowed a laxity in regard to governmental affairs. . . . [But] . . . steadily the frontier of settlement advanced and carried with it individualism, democracy, and nationalism, and powerfully affected the East and the Old World. . . .

Never again will such gifts of free land offer themselves. For a moment, at the frontier, the bonds of custom are broken and unrestraint is triumphant. There is not *tabula rasa*. The stubborn American environment is there with its imperious summons to accept its conditions; the inherited ways of doing things are also there; and yet, in spite of environment, and in spite of custom, each frontier did indeed furnish a new field of opportunity. . . . And now, four centuries from the discovery of America, at the end of a hundred years of life under the Constitution, the frontier has gone, and with its going has closed the first period of American history.

5. John Steinbeck Depicts the Dust Bowl, 1939

To the red country and part of the gray country of Oklahoma, the last rains came gently, and they did not cut the scarred earth. The plows crossed and recrossed the rivulet marks. The last rains lifted the corn quickly and scattered weed colonies and grass along the sides of the roads so that the gray country and the dark red country began to disappear under a green cover. In the last part of May the sky grew pale and the clouds that had hung in high puffs for so long in the spring were dissipated. The sun flared down on the growing corn day after day until a line of brown spread along the edge of each green bayonet. The clouds appeared, and went away, and in a while they did not try any more. The weeds grew darker green to protect them- selves, and they did not spread any more. The surface of the earth crusted, a thin hard crust, and as the sky became pale, so the earth became pale, pink in the red country and white in the gray country.

In the water-cut gullies the earth dusted down in dry little streams. Gophers and ant lions started small avalanches. And as the sharp sun struck day after day, the leaves of the young corn became less stiff and erect; they bent in a curve at first, and then, as the central ribs of strength grew weak, each leaf tilted downward. Then it was June, and the sun shone more fiercely. The brown lines on the corn leaves widened and moved in on the central ribs. The weeds frayed and edged back toward their roots. The air was thin and the sky more pale; and every day the earth paled.

In the roads where the teams moved, where the wheels milled the ground and the hooves of the horses beat the ground, the dirt crust broke and the dust formed. Every moving thing lifted the dust into the air: a walking man lifted a thin layer as high as his waist, and a wagon lifted the dust as high as the fence tops, and an auto- mobile boiled a cloud behind it. The dust was long in settling back again.

When June was half gone, the big clouds moved up out of Texas and the Gulf, high heavy clouds, rain-heads. The men in the fields looked up at the clouds and sniffed at them and held wet fingers up to sense the wind. And the horses were ner- vous while the clouds were up. The rain-heads dropped a little spattering and hur- ried on to some other country. Behind them the sky was pale again and the sun flared. In the dust there were drop craters where the rain had fallen, and there were clean splashes on the corn, and that was all.

A gentle wind followed the rain clouds, driving them on northward, a wind that softly clashed the drying corn. A day went by and the wind increased, steady, unbroken by gusts. The dust from the roads fluffed up and spread out and fell on the weeds beside the fields, and fell into the fields a little way. Now the wind grew strong and hard and it worked at the rain crust in the corn fields. Little by little the sky was darkened by the mixing dust, and the wind felt over the earth, loosened the dust, and carried it away. The wind grew stronger. The rain crust broke and the dust lifted up out of the fields and drove gray plumes into the air like sluggish smoke. The corn threshed the wind and made a dry, rushing sound. The finest dust did not settle back to earth now, but disappeared into the darkening sky.

The wind grew stronger, whisked under stones, carried up straws and old leaves, and even little clods, marking its course as it sailed across the fields. The air and the sky darkened and through them the sun shone redly, and there was a raw sting in the air. During a night the wind raced faster over the land, dug cunningly among the rootlets of the corn, and the corn fought the wind with its weakened leaves until the roots were freed by the prying wind and then each stalk settled wearily sideways toward the earth and pointed the direction of the wind.

The dawn came, but no day. In the gray sky a red sun appeared, a dim red circle that gave a little light, like dusk; and as that day advanced, the dusk slipped back toward darkness, and the wind cried and whimpered over the fallen corn.

Men and women huddled in their houses, and they tied handkerchiefs over their noses when they went out, and wore goggles to protect their eyes.

When the night came again it was black night, for the stars could not pierce the dust to get down, and the window lights could not even spread beyond their own yards. Now the dust was evenly mixed with the air, an emulsion of dust and air. Houses were shut tight, and cloth wedged around doors and windows, but the dust came in so thinly that it could not be seen in the air, and it settled like pollen on the chairs and tables, on the dishes. The people brushed it from their shoulders. Little lines of dust lay at the door sills.

In the middle of that night the wind passed on and left the land quiet. The dust-filled air muffled sound more completely than fog does. The people, lying in their beds, heard the wind stop. They awakened when the rushing wind was gone. They lay quietly and listened deep into the stillness. Then the roosters crowed, and their voices were muffled, and the people stirred restlessly in their beds and wanted the morning. They knew it would take a long time for the dust to settle out of the air. In the morning the dust hung like fog, and the sun was as red as ripe new blood. All day the dust sifted down from the sky, and the next day it sifted down. An even blanket covered the earth. It settled on the corn, piled up on the tops of the fence posts, piled up on the wires; it settled on roofs, blanketed the weeds and trees.

The people came out of their houses and smelled the hot stinging air and covered their noses from it. And the children came out of the houses, but they did not run or shout as they would have done after a rain. Men stood by their fences and looked at the ruined corn, drying fast now, only a little green showing through the film of dust. The men were silent and they did not move often. And the women came out of the houses to stand beside their men—to feel whether this time the men would break. The women studied the men's faces secretly, for the corn could go, as long as something else remained. The children stood near by, drawing figures in the dust with bare toes, and the children sent exploring senses out to see whether men and women would break. The children peeked at the faces of the men and women, and then drew careful lines in the dust with their toes. Horses came to the watering troughs and nuzzled the water to clear the surface dust. After a while the faces of the watching men lost their bemused perplexity and became hard and angry and resistant. Then the women knew that they were safe and that there was no break. Then they asked, What'll we do? And the men replied, I don't know. But it was all right. The women knew it was all right, and the watching children knew it was all right. Women and children knew deep in themselves that no misfortune was too great to bear if their men were whole. The women went into the houses to their work, and the children began to play, but cautiously at first. As the day went forward the sun became less red. It flared down on the dust-blanketed land. The men sat in the doorways of their houses; their hands were busy with sticks and little rocks. The men sat still—thinking—figuring.

6. Plenty-coups Mourns the Vanishing Buffalo, Recorded in 1950

"Our country is the most beautiful of all. Its rivers and plains, its mountains and timber lands, where there was always plenty of meat and berries, attracted other tribes, and they wished to possess it for their own.

"To keep peace our chiefs sent out clans to the north, east, south, and west. They were to tell any who wished to come into our country that they were welcome. They were told to say, 'You may hunt and may gather berries and plums in our country, but when you have all you can carry you must go back to your own lands. If you do this all will be well. But if you remain overlong, we will warn you to depart. If you are foolish and do not listen, your horses will be stolen; and if even this does not start you homeward, we will attack you and drive you out.'"

The country belonging to the Crows was not only beautiful, but it was the very heart of the buffalo range of the Northwest. It embraced endless plains, high mountains, and great rivers, fed by streams clear as crystal. No other section could compare with the Crow country, especially when it was untouched by white men. Its wealth in all kinds of game, grass, roots, and berries made enemies for the Crows, who, often outnumbered, were obliged continually to defend it against surrounding tribes.

"These clans did not go to the other people, but camped near the boundaries of our domain so that they might speak to any visitor coming from any direction and give him the message from our chiefs. But little heed was paid to what we said. There was almost continual war with those who coveted our country.

"The Lacota [Sioux], Striped-feathered-arrows [Cheyennes], and Tattooed-breasts [Arapahoes] kept pushing us back, away from the Black Hills, until finally when I was a young man we were mostly in the country of the Bighorn and Little Bighorn rivers. These tribes, like the Pecunies [Piegans], Bloods, and Blackfeet [all Blackfeet], had many guns which they had obtained from white traders, while we had almost no guns in the tribe. The northern tribes could easily trade with the Hudson's Bay people, while the tribes eastward of us traded furs and robes to the American Fur Company for guns, powder, and lead.

Excerpts from Frank B. Linderman, *American: The Life Story of a Great Indian,* New York: John Day, 1950, pp. 29–31, 48–49, 55–57, HarperCollins Publishers, Inc. Copyright 1930 by Frank B. Linderman. Copyright © renewed 1957 by Norma Linderman Waller, Verne Linderman, and Wilda Linderman. Reprinted by permission of HarperCollins Publishers, Inc.

"There is no better weapon than the bow for running buffalo, but in war the gun is often the best. All tribes were against us, the Blackfeet north and west, the Cheyennes and Sioux east, the Shoshones and Arapahoes on the south; and besides these there was often war with the Flatheads, Assinniboines, and Hairy-Noses [Gros Ventres of the prairies]." . . .

To count coup a warrior had to strike an armed and fighting enemy with his coup-stick, quirt, or bow before otherwise harming him, or take his weapons while he was yet alive, or strike the first enemy falling in battle, no matter who killed him, or strike the enemy's breastworks while under fire, or steal a horse tied to a lodge in an enemy's camp, etc. The first named was the most honorable, and to strike such a coup a warrior would often display great bravery. An eagle's feather worn in the hair was a mark of distinction and told the world that the wearer had counted coup. He might wear one for each coup he counted "if he was that kind of man," Plenty-coups said. But if a warrior was wounded in counting coup, the feather he wore to mark the event must be painted red to show that he bled. Strangely enough from our point of view, this was not considered so great an honor as escaping unharmed. After a battle, or exploit, by one or more individuals there ensued the ceremony of counting coup, relating adventures. This is the custom that led the white man to declare the Indian a born boaster. Some of the tribes of the Northwest added an eagle's feather to their individual coup-stick for each coup counted. But the Crows did not follow this custom.

"We feasted there," said Plenty-coups. "Fat meat of bighorn, deer, and elk was plentiful. The hunters had killed many of these animals because they knew there would soon be a very large village to feed. Besides, light skins were always needed for shirts and leggings. Even the dogs found more than they could eat near that village, and our horses, nearly always feasting on rich grass, enjoyed the change the mountains gave them. All night the drums were beating, and in the light of fires that smelled sweet the people danced until they were tired."

Author's [Frank B. Linderman] Note

Plenty-coups refused to speak of his life after the passing of the buffalo, so that his story seems to have been broken off, leaving many years unaccounted for. "I have not told you half that happened when I was young," he said, when urged to go on. "I can think back and tell you much more of war and horse stealing. But when the buffalo went away the hearts of my people fell to the ground, and they could not lift them up again. After this nothing happened. There was little singing anywhere. Besides," he added sorrowfully, "you know that part of my life as well as I do. You saw what happened to us when the buffalo went away."

I do know that part of his life's story, and that part of the lives of all the Indians of the Northwestern plains; and I did see what happened to these sturdy, warlike people when the last of the buffalo was finally slaughtered and left to decay on the plains by skin-hunting white men.

The Indian's food supply was now gone; so too were the materials for his clothes and sheltering home. Pitched so suddenly from plenty into poverty, the Indian lost his poise and could not believe the truth.

7. An Editor Bids Good Riddance to Buffalo, 1979

Gone are the millions of American buffalo. Their wanton slaughter brought temporary profit and sport. But their departure opened the North American continent for human development.

The bison known as the plains buffalo in America well could serve as a national symbol for the concept that human progress requires environmental alterations, whether in mining ore, building factories, plowing ground or controlling wild beasts.

From vast crops in the heartlands of the United States and Canada, the modern farmer produces enough food and fiber for his needs and 55 other persons, making ours the richest agricultural area of the world. Thundering herds of buffalo no longer exist to trample down the seas of grain.

Domestic animals bred to highest qualities of dinner-plate tastes and cost-efficiency graze in peace across America without fear of attack from stampeding buffalo. A hiker can stroll unafraid of buffalo assault in any urban area from Atlanta to Butte to Grand Forks.

The buffalo have almost disappeared as a result of one of the remarkable wild-animal eradication programs recorded in human history. The benefit is mankind's. Few should weep over buffalo. America never would have blossomed to its current status in world leadership unless buffalo were removed from the land.

The oxlike grazing animal of family Bovidae weighs a ton or more when mature. Long-lived, agile, fast and unpredictable, an estimated 60 million buffalo were roaming over North America when the white man arrived. Unimpeded by sentimental environmentalists having short-range vision, early settlers found that buffalo were commercially worthless when compared with domestic animals.

As the white civilization pushed westward from the Allegheny Mountains, vast herds of buffalo were slaughtered purposely to permit farms to be created, railroads to be built, housewives to pluck carrots without being trampled. Short term profits from buffalo slaughter came from tough meat, hides and sport. The beasts existed for private enterprise to consume, to clear the land for superior breeds, crops, cities, human growth and progress.

William F. Cody (Buffalo Bill) among others was renowned for the number of bison he killed. Around 1900, as buffalo neared extinction, action by cattlemen and conservationists led to their protection on government preserves in fortified paddocks.

By coincidence, a thriving buffalo herd today thunders about a heavily fenced mountain ranch at Cody, Wyo., as a tourist tribute to Buffalo Bill Cody. Other Western buffalo paddocks are in Colorado, Oregon and at Banff, Canada. There are a few buffalo on private ranches in Washington.

With some 60 million of the awesome beasts virtually wiped from the face of North America, human ingenuity and hard work rapidly converted the Great Plains and rolling hills into modern miracles of agricultural production, thriving cities, hearty commerce and vigorous Americans.

From *The Daily Chronicle*, Centralia–Chehalis, Washington, September 10, 1979. Reprinted by permission of *The Daily Chronicle*.

When we pat the nose of a precious animal, we are thankful it's a Polled Hereford or a brown-eyed Jersey instead of horned buffalo defying domestication. Gone are the millions of American buffalo, thanks to visionary settlers of the 18th and 19th Centuries.

ψ *E S S A Y S*

Like the documents, the essays tell different stories about the grasslands. In the first essay, Walter Prescott Webb, an eminent historian of the Great Plains, constructs his history as a triumph of white settlers and their technologies over a formidable arid environment and fierce, horse-mounted Indian tribes. Donald Worster, an environmental historian at the University of Kansas, in the second selection, presents the region's history as a tragedy of environmental deterioration at the hands of capitalist ranchers. Finally, in the third essay, William Cronon, an environmental historian at the University of Wisconsin, Madison, analyzes the characteristics of storytelling, showing how histories are stories of the past with a beginning, a middle, and an end. Progressive histories often depict what might be considered human triumphs, such as Europeans' conquest of the American wilderness, with an upward or ascending plot. Conversely, environmental histories often have downward or declining plots that portray nature as being destroyed by humans. These ascensionist and declensionist plots are ways in which humans inevitably impose order on the world. There may be alternative stories with other plots, actors, and settings, but human cognition, and even science itself, necessarily takes the form of storytelling.

Great Plains Ecology

WALTER PRESCOTT WEBB

The Great Plains area, as the term will be used in this [selection], does not conform in its boundaries to those commonly given by geographers and historians. The Great Plains comprise a much greater area than is usually designated,—an area which may best be defined in terms of topography, vegetation, and rainfall.

A plains environment, such as that found in the western United States, presents three distinguishing characteristics:

1. It exhibits a comparatively level surface of great extent.
2. It is a treeless land, an unforested area.
3. It is a region where rainfall is insufficient for the ordinary intensive agriculture common to lands of a humid climate. The climate is sub-humid.

In the region west of the Mississippi River, the region under consideration here, these three characteristics of a plains environment are not coextensive or coterminal. The three are not found in conjunction except in a portion of what is commonly called the Central Great Plains; that is, in the High Plains, or the Plains proper. In

---

the High Plains the land is relatively level and unscored, it is barren of timber, and the climate is sub-humid, semi-arid, or arid. The High Plains constitute the heart of what may be called the Great Plains, and exemplify to the highest degree the features of a plane surface, a treeless region, and a sub-humid one. . . .

This area, with its three dominant characteristics, affected the various peoples, nations as well as individuals, who came to take and occupy it, and was affected by them. . . . The historical truth that becomes apparent in the end is that the Great Plains have bent and molded Anglo-American life, have destroyed traditions, and have influenced institutions in a most singular manner.

The Great Plains offered such a contrast to the region east of the ninety-eighth meridian, the region with which American civilization had been familiar until about 1840, as to bring about a marked change in the ways of pioneering and living. For two centuries American pioneers had been working out a technique for the utilization of the humid regions east of the Mississippi River. They had found solutions for their problems and were conquering the frontier at a steadily accelerating rate. Then in the early nineteenth century they crossed the Mississippi and came out on the Great Plains, an environment with which they had had no experience. The result was a complete though temporary breakdown of the machinery and ways of pioneering. They began to make adjustments. . . .

As one contrasts the civilization of the Great Plains with that of the eastern timberland, one sees what may be called an institutional *fault* (comparable to a geological fault) running from middle Texas to Illinois or Dakota, roughly following the ninety-eighth meridian. At this *fault* the ways of life and of living changed. Practically every institution that was carried across it was either broken and remade or else greatly altered. The ways of travel, the weapons, the method of tilling the soil, the plows and other agricultural implements, and even the laws themselves were modified. When people first crossed this line they did not immediately realize the imperceptible change that had taken place in their environment, nor, more is the tragedy, did they foresee the full consequences which that change was to bring in their own characters and in their modes of life. In the new region—level, timberless, and semi-arid—they were thrown by Mother Necessity into the clutch of new circumstances. Their plight has been stated in this way: east of the Mississippi civilization stood on three legs—land, water, and timber; west of the Mississippi not one but two of these legs were withdrawn,—water and timber,—and civilization was left on one leg—land. It is small wonder that it toppled over in temporary failure. . . .

The distinguishing climatic characteristic of the Great Plains environment from the ninety-eighth meridian to the Pacific slope is a deficiency in the most essential climatic element—water. Within this area there are humid spots due to local causes of elevation, but there is a deficiency in the average amount of rainfall for the entire region. This deficiency accounts for many of the peculiar ways of life in the West. It conditions plant life, animal life, and human life and institutions. In this deficiency is found the key to what may be called the Plains civilization. It is the feature that makes the whole aspect of life west of the ninety-eighth meridian such a contrast to life east of that line. . . . The line representing twenty inches of annual precipitation follows approximately the hundredth meridian. In no appreciable area between that line and the Pacific slopes does the rainfall run far above twenty inches. Over great stretches it falls below twenty to fifteen, to ten, and, in the true desert, to five inches.

It is generally agreed that wherever precipitation is less than twenty inches the climate is deficient. This means, or has come to mean, that the land in such areas cannot be utilized under the same methods that are employed in the region where precipitation is more than twenty inches. . . .

Five weather phenomena—hot winds and chinooks, northers, blizzards, and hailstorms—are all localized in the Great Plains country. . . . They are a significant part of the unusual conditions which civilization had to meet and overcome in the Great Plains. . . .

The ninety-eighth meridian separates the vegetation of the East from that of the West. In its primeval state practically the entire region east of this line was heavily timbered, truly a forest land. West of the line (excepting the northern Pacific slope and the islands in the mountains) there is a scarcity or a complete absence of timber. . . . The non-forested area, the Great Plains environment, falls into three subdivisions: the tall grass, or prairie; the short grass, or Plains; and the desert shrub. . . .

In the prairie country the tall grass falls into three subdivisions, or communities: the blue-stem sod, the blue-stem bunch grass, and the needle grass and slender wheat grass. The blue-stem sod is found in Illinois, Iowa, eastern Kansas, in parts of Missouri, Oklahoma, and Texas, and in western Minnesota, eastern North Dakota, South Dakota, and Nebraska. The whole region is rich, and the central portion forms what is known as the corn belt.

The short, or Plains, grasses are the grama, galleta, buffalo, and mesquite. All these types occur west of the ninety-eighth meridian.

West of the grasslands lies the desert-shrub area, the intermountain region. This vegetation belongs to three general types: sagebrush, or northern-desert shrub; creosote bush, or southern-desert shrub; greasewood, or salt-desert shrub. In all this region the desert type of vegetation prevails over the grassland. . . .

The Plains animals exhibit certain common characteristics:

1. All, save the coyote and the wolf, are grass-eaters.
2. Two types, the antelope and the jack rabbit, are noted for their speed, and both stick to the open country, depending primarily on speed for safety.
3. All can get along with little or no actual water supply. The prairie dog and the jack rabbit need none. The antelope exhibits great ingenuity in finding water and, by virtue of its speed, can travel far for its supply.
4. All these animals are extremely shy, and must be hunted with long-range guns, a fact that had a marked influence on the development of weapons in the United States. . . .

The buffalo had few qualities, save massive size and gregariousness, that fitted it to the Plains. It is described by all observers, from [George] Catlin on, as a stupid animal, the easiest victim to the hunter, whether the redman with bow and arrow or the white man with his long-range buffalo gun. The buffalo was slow of gait, clumsy in movement, and had relatively poor eyesight and little fear of sound. Though it had a fairly keen sense of smell, this sense was useless to it when it was approached from down the wind.

Historically the buffalo had more influence on man than all other Plains animals combined. It was life, food, raiment, and shelter to the Indians. The buffalo and the Plains Indians lived together, and together passed away. The year 1876 marks practically the end of both. . . .

Within the Plains area dwelt thirty-one tribes of Indians. Eleven of these are typical Plains tribes, possessing in common, in the highest degree, the characteristic Plains culture. These eleven tribes are the Assiniboin, Arapaho, Blackfoot, Cheyenne, Comanche, Crow, Gros Ventre, Kiowa, Kiowa-Apache, Sarsi, and Teton-Dakota. They occupied the region from southern Canada to Mexico. The . . . tribes to the east and west possessed many characteristics of the Plains culture, but they exhibited also characteristics of the non-Plains tribes; that is to say, they represented a transition from one culture to another, a transition found in both vegetation and animal life. . . . The following are the significant facts:

1. The Plains Indians were nomadic and nonagricultural.
2. They depended for their existence on the wild cattle or buffalo, and were often called buffalo Indians. The buffalo furnished them with all the necessities and luxuries of life.
3. They used weapons especially adapted to the hunting of big game, particularly the buffalo.
4. They used beasts of burden for transportation, an indication of their nomadic character. They were the only Indians in North America occupying land in a temperate climate who used a beast of burden. First they used the dog and later the horse.
5. They adopted the horse long before white civilization came in contact with them, and their use of the horse effected a far-reaching revolution in their ways of life. The Plains Indians became the horse Indians, and the Plains area might then well have been called the horse area of America. . . .

Fossil remains indicate that horses roamed over both North America and South America, to disappear before Columbus came and probably before the Indians themselves arrived. . . . The association of man and horse apparently arose in an environment very similar to the Great Plains; that is, in the steppes of Asia.

[The] . . . horsemen of the steppes extended their forays in every direction. The Huns came west into Europe; other tribes passed eastward into China, compelling the Chinese to erect the Great Wall on their northern border. . . .

To put the matter briefly, there arose in Europe two traditions of horsemanship, or horse culture—the one that of a settled people with whom horses were but one of the incidents of life, and the other the tradition of the nomadic people to whom horses were vital. Both traditions found their way to America, and each found its appropriate environment. . . . [W]e know that the Kiowa and Missouri Indians were mounted by 1682; the Pawnee, by 1700; the Comanche, by 1714; the Plains Cree and Arikara, by 1738; the Assiniboin, Crow, Mandan, Snake, and Teton, by 1742; and the most northern tribe, the Sarsi, by 1784. How much earlier these Indians rode horses we do not know; but we can say that the dispersion of horses which began in 1541 was completed over the Plains area by 1784. . . .

The horsemanship of the Plains Indian aroused the wonder and admiration of all who observed it. The following account of the prairie warrior's equestrian skill is by Captain Marcy.

> His only ambition consists in being able to cope successfully with his enemy in war and in managing his steed with unfailing adroitness. He is in the saddle from boyhood to old age, and his favorite horse is his constant companion. It is when mounted that the prairie warrior exhibits himself to the best advantage; here he is at home, and his skill

in various manœuvres which he makes available in battle—such as throwing himself entirely upon one side of his horse and discharging his arrows with great rapidity toward the opposite side from beneath the animal's neck while he is at full speed—is truly astonishing. Many of the women are equally expert, as equestrians, with the men. . . .

Of the horsemanship of the Comanches, Catlin says:

> Amongst their feats of riding, there is one that has astonished me more than anything of the kind I have ever seen, or expect to see, in my life:—a stratagem of war, learned and practiced by every young man in the tribe; by which he is able to drop his body upon the side of his horse at the instant he is passing, effectually screened from his enemies' weapons as he [lies] in a horizontal position behind the body of his horse, with his heel hanging over the horse's back; by which he has the power of throwing himself up again, and changing to the other side of the horse if necessary. In this wonderful condition, he will hang whilst his horse is at fullest speed, carrying with him his bow and his shield, and also his long lance of fourteen feet in length, all or either of which he will wield upon his enemy as he passes; rising and throwing his arrows over the horse's back, or with ease and equal success under the horse's neck. . . .

It should be pointed out here that Catlin was accompanied by a cavalry troop whose members should have been familiar with all the feats of horsemanship that are known to military science or to the people of the Eastern states. It was a case of the two horse cultures coming into contact in the West. . . .

Thus armed, equipped, and mounted the Plains Indians made both picturesque and dangerous warriors. . . . They were far better equipped for successful warfare in their own country than the white men who came against them, and presented to the European or American conqueror problems different from those found elsewhere on the continent. . . .

Let us visualize the American approach to the Great Plains by imagining ourselves standing on the dividing line between the timber and plain, say at the point where the ninety-eighth meridian cuts the thirty-first parallel. As we gaze northward we see on the right side the forested and well-watered country and on the left side the arid, treeless plain. On the right we see a nation of people coming slowly but persistently through the forests, felling trees, building cabins, making rail fences, digging shallow wells, or drinking from the numerous springs and perennial streams, advancing shoulder to shoulder, pushing the natives westward toward the open country. They are nearing the Plains. Then, in the first half of the nineteenth century, we see the advance guard of this moving host of forest homemakers emerge into the new environment, where there are no forests, no logs for cabins, no rails for fences, few springs and running streams. Before them is a wide land infested by a fierce breed of Indians, mounted, ferocious, unconquerable, terrible in their mercilessness. They see a natural barrier made more formidable by a human barrier of untamed savagery. Upon this barrier of the Great Plains the pioneers threw themselves, armed and equipped with the weapons, tools, ideas, and institutions which had served them so long and so well in the woods that now lay behind them. Inevitably they failed in their first efforts, and they continued to fail until they worked out a technique of pioneering adapted to the Plains rather than to the woodland. . . . Their effort constitutes a gigantic human experiment with an environment. . . .

Undoubtedly the Texans needed a new weapon, something with a reserve power and capable of "continuous" action—a weapon more rapid than the Indian's arrows, of longer reach than his spear, and, above all, one adapted to use on horseback. The man who supplied the weapon that fulfilled all these necessities was a Connecticut Yankee by the name of Samuel Colt. . . . Those who went into the West went on horseback with [Colt] six-shooters in their belts. . . . It should be borne in mind that [the six-shooter's] introduction, rapid spread, and popularity throughout the Plains area, the Indian and cattle country, were in response to a genuine need for a horseman's weapon. Whatever sins the six-shooter may have to answer for, it stands as the first mechanical adaptation made by the American people when they emerged from the timber and met a set of new needs in the open country of the Great Plains. It enabled the white man to fight the Plains Indian on horseback. . . .

New inventions and discoveries had to be made before the pioneer farmer could go into the Great Plains and establish himself. . . . In the interval of awaiting the Industrial Revolution there arose in the Plains country the cattle kingdom.

The cattle kingdom was a world within itself, with a culture all its own, which, though of brief duration, was complete and self-satisfying. . . .

The cattle kingdom had its origin in Texas before the Civil War. After the war it expanded, and by 1876 it had spread over the entire Plains area. The physical basis of the cattle kingdom was grass, and it extended itself over all the grassland not occupied by farms. Within a period of ten years it had spread over western Texas, Oklahoma, Kansas, Nebraska, North and South Dakota, Montana, Wyoming, Nevada, Utah, Colorado, and New Mexico; that is, over all or a part of twelve states. For rapidity of expansion there is perhaps not a parallel to this movement in American history.

After the [economic] panic of 1873 the range cattle industry began to struggle upward once more, though the drives from Texas were less frequent owing to the approaching saturation of the range and the fact that the railroads were extending into the West and diverting the cattle from the trails. . . .

By 1876 the cattle industry was recovering from the panic of three years before, and there was a steady demand for cattle, with a rising market—premonitory symptom of the cattle boom of the eighties. During the last four years of the seventies (1876–1880) the cattle business expanded on a steady or rising market. In the last year two million head were marketed. A well-matured Northwestern ranger would bring about $60 in the Northern markets, and a Texan steer about $50. Grass was still free, the range was open, and the farmer was far away. Again, it could not last.

Then came the great boom of the early eighties. "It was a time of golden visions in a blaze of glory that led on to riotous feastings on the rim of the crater of ruin—a brief era of wild extravagance in theories and in practices." There were many contributing factors to explain the boom; and, given the boom, the collapse was inevitable. . . .

Analyzing the situation about 1885 we find the following factors present. . . .

1. Several railroads had by this time crossed the Plains or had gone far out on them.
2. These railroad companies were laying out and booming towns, doing all they could to get settlers into the region out of which they hoped to obtain a revenue both from the use of the road and from the sale of the bounty lands.
3. Money was plentiful in the country as a whole and was seeking an outlet for investment.

4. The eastern part of the United States was becoming more crowded, and farmers were pushing farther and farther into the cattle country. . . .
5. The Indians had all been reduced, and people were no longer held back from the Plains by fear of the scalping knife and the tomahawk.
6. Some of the ranges were being fenced, and this alarmed those who had hoped that the free range would last, causing them to grab for more land.

We have noted that the agricultural frontier came to a standstill about 1850, and that for a generation it made but little advance into the sub-humid region of the Great Plains. It was barbed wire and not the railroads or the homestead law that made it possible for the farmers to resume, or at least accelerate, their march across the prairies and onto the Plains. . . .

The invention of barbed wire revolutionized land values and opened up to the homesteader the fertile Prairie Plains, now the most valuable agricultural land in the United States. With cheap fencing the farmers were enabled to stake out their free homesteads, and the agricultural frontier moved rapidly across the prairie to the margin of the dry plains, where the farmers were again checked until further adaptations could be made. The homestead law was not a success in the High Plains and the more arid country, as will be shown later; but it served as an effective bait which lured the farmers on beyond the tall-grass country, where agriculture could be carried on successfully, into the short-grass country, where the occupation was extremely hazardous. In the wet years the farmers pushed across the dead line into the Plains country and took up homesteads which they could now fence. In this way they encroached on the cattlemen and forced all land under fence. Without barbed wire the Plains homestead could never have been protected from the grazing herds and therefore could not have been possible as an agricultural unit.

Th[e] first inroad of farmers synchronized with the cattle boom of the eighties and the general conditions of prosperity at that time, and was accompanied or preceded by the deceptive wet years which led the people to conclude that the rainfall would increase.

It was . . . experiences growing out of the droughts that led the men who remained in the Plains country to enter upon countless hundreds of experiments with the windmill. . . . It was the acre or two of ground irrigated by the windmill that enabled the homesteader to hold on when all others had to leave.

The effects of the windmill in Nebraska, which may be considered typical for most of the Great Plains, are set forth eloquently by [Erwin Hinckley] Barbour [Professor at the University of Nebraska, 1898]:

> What a contrast may be presented by two farms—one with cattle crowding around the well, waiting for some thoughtless farm hand to pump them their scanty allowance of water, the other where the cattle are grazing and the tanks and troughs are full and running over. . . .

Thus did the West carry on its search for water by means of the windmill. Extravagant hopes were entertained—hopes which could never be realized; but still the whirling wheel made life on the Great Plains possible in hitherto untenable places. It was an important agent in transforming the so-called Great American Desert into a land of homes.

Cowboy Ecology

DONALD WORSTER

Ask almost any group of people in the world, from Peoria to Perth, and they will say that the American West is about the cowboy and his life of chasing cows on the range. They may add, without much encouragement, that that West has come to symbolize the national identity of the United States. Instead of seeing in that response a measure of truth, historians have tended to dismiss it as popular myth-making, a fashion of mass culture, essentially false and insignificant. . . .

The low status of ranching history, and with it western history, strikes one with special force when compared to the status of the plantation history of the American South. Even at this late point in the twentieth century, after so much urbanization and economic growth, the plantation still stands at the very center of southern studies. Moreover, unlike the ranch, it occupies a distinctly prominent place in the textbooks. Yet the ranch and the plantation were alike spawned by the capitalist revolution in agriculture. Each institution has been a powerful determinant of a regional identity. The critical difference between them lies, of course, in the fact that the plantation practiced an especially heinous form of labor exploitation, which has left an enduring mark on race relations, not only in the United States but in a number of other societies, mainly in the warmer latitudes where Europeans came to force nonwhites to raise exotic foods and fiber for them on a large scale. The plantation has been a critical instrument in the European conquest of people of color, and historians seeking to understand that long story of racial conquest, exploitation, and injustice have rightly given it careful attention.

But out on the western range, human relations have always seemed a lot more open, sunny, unrepressive, and therefore forgettable. True, every ranch involved, somewhere in the past, a dispossession of native peoples. And on the typical ranch there was a poorly paid work crew and it was partly nonwhite: Indian, Mexican, African-American, and if one includes the Hawaiian range, even Asian and Polynesian. The European languages spoken out West included Spanish, German, Danish, and the Gaelic dialects; far more often than the southern plantation, the range was a microcosmic league of nations under white hegemony. We have tended, through the influence of too many John Wayne movies, to assume otherwise; the full history of the diverse racial and ethnic relations on the range has yet to be written. All the same, compared to chattel slavery, the work relationships there seem to be pretty ordinary and even benign, more egalitarian than exploitative. The system was one of wage laborers' selling their services freely, sometimes for only a season or two, then moving on. With the job necessarily went a lot of autonomy. Since chasing after steers often took one far away from the scrutiny of a foreman, since the work in fact required a great deal of self-directedness and initiative, and since hired men were allowed to ride big horses and carry big guns across a big space, there was relatively more personal freedom for workers in the ranching industry than in, say,

From the book *Under Western Skies: Nature and History in the American West* by Donald Worster (New York: Oxford University Press, 1992). Reprinted by permission of the author.

the eastern textile factory or the cotton field. Consequently, the idea of a "cowboy proletariat" is a seed that has been sown a few times by historians but always fallen on stony ground.

However, if labor and racial exploitation did not occur on the range to the same terrible degree they did on the plantation, there is another aspect that stands out as distinctive, compelling, and historically significant. This is an issue that is absolutely crucial to the course of western American development. It is one that has much to teach the rest of the nation. And, above all, it is an issue that is vital to much of today's world, particularly the developing nations of Asia, Africa, and Latin America. I mean the question of how we are to get a living from a fragile, vulnerable earth without destroying it—or put otherwise, how we are to lead a sustainable life that does not deplete the natural environment or ourselves. For this issue the West, because so much of it is ecologically marginal for many human purposes, has represented one of the preeminent laboratories on the planet. It is, as Walter Prescott Webb once noted, a semidesert with a desert at its heart. Compared to the North and South, the western environment did not yield easily to agriculture or urban growth, and only in recent decades, with the aid of modern, sophisticated technology to pump the water and cool the air, has the region acquired much population. Such is also the condition of much of the Third World: they too face the challenge of marginal lands—lands that are too hot, too cold, too dry, too mountainous—lands that defy human ambitions; but lands that today, under the pressure of explosive population growth, are being brought under cultivation or husbandry and being settled.

Compounding those environmental challenges is the question of what form of tenure or property rights will best ensure a sustainable future: individual or communal, private or bureaucratic? Here again, the history of ranching in the American West offers a relevant experience, for it has been wracked from its earliest days by debate over the question.

But in order to be useful in these ways western history has to be presented more forcefully than it has in terms of comparative human ecology, emphasizing the relation of people to other animals, of animals to vegetation, and of vegetation to patterns of tenure. In the rest of this brief essay I want to sketch that alternative approach and suggest lines of research that can bring the region's significance home to scholars from all over the world. We ought to begin by getting outside our regional provincialisms, overcoming our insistence on American uniqueness, and try to situate the cowboy and his ranch in the broad panorama of human adaptation to the earth.

Except in California, where everything is a ranch (avocado ranches, tomato ranches, golf ranches, retired president ranches), a ranch is an extensive farm that specializes in raising cows, sheep, goats, or horses. But it is also a modern reworking of an ancient pastoral way of life, and we need to understand what it replaced in order to comprehend fully what it has been and what it is becoming.

Pastoralism, an adaptation involving the herding of livestock, seems to have begun as a variant on agriculture, with its mixed economy of plants and animals. Possibly it appeared in response to the pressure of a growing population on a limited space; some people may have been excluded from farming, by whatever method of selection, and forced to find a living in more marginal lands—that is, they were forced out of river valleys onto broad uplands or high mountains or steppes, often where only scrub brush grew and the rainfall was scanty and erratic. Here they had to abandon much of their old life, limiting their subsistence base mainly to various ruminants. Apparently, the earliest people to be, so to speak, thrown out into the wasteland were the nomads of the Middle East, the children of Ishmael, who took to roaming the deserts with their camels, goats, and sheep, though maintaining a mutualistic relationship with the agrarian settlements, now trading with them, now raiding them, maintaining that uncertain relationship well down into recent times. . . .

Generally, nomads show little interest in resource conservation or pasture improvement, though they are incredibly knowledgeable about the lands they exploit. They have to know where there will be grass in the months ahead, how many head of animals it will support, where there will be waterholes, when to expect drought. As they deplete their supplies locally, they go looking for more, sometimes entering upon the territory of others, where they use diplomacy if they can to gain access but take by arms if they must. Eventually, when the abandoned pastures have recovered, they bring their stock back to chew it all up again. So long as their human numbers remain limited by war and disease and their herd sizes are regularly culled by drought, hunger, predation, theft, and infertility, they manage to stay within the carrying capacity of their range, the vegetation evolving toward resilience and tenacity.

In other cases, however, the history of pastoralism took an altogether different direction; the strategy of survival was not one of wandering impermanently from one site to another, in an endless cycle of nomadism, but of learning to stay in one place and adjusting to its limits. The circumalpine environment of Europe furnishes many examples of this more intensive, sedentary form of pastoralism. There the herders traditionally spent a part of the year grazing their animals in nearby alpine meadows—practicing a kind of vertical and partial nomadism called transhumance. At summer's end they trailed their stock down to established villages, where they fed them through the winter on stored hay; thus, they lived much of the year like other farmers, but harvested milk and cheese rather than grain. The high summer pastures of this region have been used since Neolithic times, and since the Middle Ages there has "gradually evolved what would appear to be the most stable and finely balanced form of peasant society and culture in the European area." Similar patterns of settled village life, limited pastoral movement, and cautious environmental control can be found in the Andean region of South America and in the Himalayas. . . .

One could travel on and on around the world examining . . . pastoral ways of life. . . . [T]he student of the American West has a vast history to become at least passingly familiar with and has a wealth of possibilities for comparative analysis. The cowboy in an important sense belongs to this greater world of human ecology, not merely to Wyoming.

The North American ranch began to emerge as an institution in the southern part of Texas during the 1860s, and its history belongs completely to the post–Civil War era of the nation. Though it adopted terms, tools, and animal lore going back into the dim past, drawing on Iberian and Celtic pastoral antecedents, the ranch was unmistakably a modern capitalist institution. It specialized in raising cattle or other animals to sell in the marketplace, furnishing meat, hides, and wool to the growing metropolises in the East and their armies of laborers. Livestock became a form of capital in this innovative system, and that capital was made to earn a profit and increase itself many times over, without limit. But the animals were only one part of the capital—a mere mechanism for processing the more essential capital, the western grasslands, into a form suitable for human consumption; the cattle carried the grass, as it were, to the Chicago or Kansas City stockyards, where they were slaughtered by the millions and carved into beefsteak. From the beginning, the scale of this industry was continental, growing up as it did with the national railroad lines; and, then following the invention of the refrigerated ship in 1879, it became transoceanic and global.

In the place of the Swiss and the Maasai cowherd, the Berber and Baluchistan shepherd, the Peruvian llama, and Yemeni camel tender, the American cowboy steps forth, a brand-new figure in the long tradition. But like his predecessors, he must confront the fundamental questions: What is his relationship to the land to be, and how long can he sustain himself in comparison with the others?

The first quarter-century of American livestock ranching was, according to every historian who has written on the subject, an unmitigated disaster—colorful, exciting, fabulous, yes, but a disaster all the same. From Texas to the Canadian plains and all the way westward to the Pacific, thousands of entrepreneurs assembled their herds and drove them onto the public lands, millions of acres lying open to enterprise. They had no tribal headmen to guide them, no ancient parchments to spell out their rights and responsibilities, little or no knowledge of the landscapes they were invading, and no willingness to wait for any of these to appear. The range belonged to no one, they claimed; therefore, it belonged to everyone. The first individuals to arrive simply appropriated what they wanted and, without legal title, began to take off the grass. Others soon arrived and claimed the same right. Then there was a multitude, some of them individuals, some of them corporations, not a few of them cowboys living in Edinburgh or London. Let one of the most prominent of these newfangled pastoralists, Granville Stuart, describe the frenzied scene in Montana in the boom years:

> In 1880, the country was practically uninhabited. One could travel for miles without seeing so much as a traveler's bivouac. Thousands of buffalo darkened the rolling plains. There were deer, elk, wolves and coyotes on every hill and in every ravine and thicket. . . .
>
> In the fall of 1883, there was not a buffalo remaining on the range, and the antelope, elk, and deer were indeed scarce. In 1880 no one had heard tell of a cowboy in "this niche of the woods" and Charlie Russell had made no pictures of them; but in the fall of 1883, there were 600,000 head of cattle on the range. The cowboy . . . had become an institution.

But a mere five years later, in 1888, he might have added, much of the western ranching industry was lying in ruins, the victim of severe overgrazing and desperately cold winters. Many thousands of animals were lying dead all over the range, starved and frozen; others were riding in boxcars to the stockyards for rapid liquidation by their owners. Even faster than it had boomed, the new American pastoralism busted. It would take decades for it to recover.

That collapse—or what we might call the "tragedy of the laissez-faire commons" —was one of the greatest in the entire history of pastoralism, as measured in the loss of animal life. It has been told many times in western history courses, and probably forgotten as often, for Americans do not like to remember that they once failed abysmally in a form of husbandry where illiterate African tribesmen have succeeded. My purpose in recalling it here, though, is not to emphasize the failure of our early cowboy capitalists but rather to draw out of it the difficult predicament it left us with in the United States. We had acquired a vast public domain, and a large part of it would never be suitable for agriculture; it was as marginal as they come. What it offered was a pasture of considerable potential for livestock, a pasture covering several hundred million acres. But who would own it? Who would manage it? Was there any safe, permanent, humane way to turn the grass and the poor, dumb, hoofed animals on that acreage into modern dreams of unlimited personal wealth?

For a hundred years now there have been two competing answers to that set of questions, and neither has so far managed to make its case convincing enough to settle the matter once and for all. I should add that neither answer has much continuity with that long tradition of Old World pastoralism; indeed, they are both based on a rejection of tradition, on a confidence in the new, and perhaps it is that fact which has made neither of them quite an acceptable solution.

One of the answers that came quickly out of the debacle of the 1880s was predictable in a nation devoted to the principles of free enterprise: turn the whole public domain over to the ranchers as their private property and let them manage it without hindrance. If farmers could get free homesteads of 160 acres, why should the stockmen not get free ranches of 1,600 or 16,000 acres, get whatever they needed to raise their herds and flocks? . . . Privatizing the range, it was argued, would give the western grazier a real incentive to manage the land better and avoid the kind of irresponsible free-for-all of the 1880s. With a fee simple title in hand, he would be more likely to invest his capital in long-term improvements, especially fencing. The fences were all important: a set of fences, it was said, would provide a far greater return from the land, for they would allow the stockman to bring in a better grade of animal, free of the fear that they would breed uncontrollably with lesser stock. Fences would also make possible a system of pasture rotations, confining the animals to areas where the vegetation was in good shape, keeping them off areas that needed to recover. There would be less erosion, depletion, and weed invasion. Under a program of privatization the range could be made to yield a higher economic return while, simultaneously, remaining a more healthy and productive environment. . . .

The other, opposing answer came from conservationists and government officials, along with a number of scientists. The great western pastures had been acquired at the price of considerable blood and money by the federal government on behalf of all the American people, it was argued, and they should stay public. Though almost everything else had been disposed of into private hands, these lands ought to continue in a state of federal ownership. Here again there was a moral dimension to the argument, an appeal to social democratic ideals of equality and commonwealth. There was also an effort to refute the claim that only privatization could produce the greatest economic return; on the contrary, it was insisted, public ownership would ensure the greatest return to the greatest number of people. But perhaps the most effective part of the argument, though it was never put too starkly, was that the private entrepreneur simply could not be trusted to look out for the long-term ecological health of the range resource. He would tend to exploit rather than conserve it; making the pastures private would not be a reliable way to protect them for posterity. A much better solution would be to create a centralized bureaucracy of disinterested, scientifically trained professionals to oversee the public range.

In 1934 Congress, leaning toward this second proposal, passed the Taylor Grazing Act, which for the first time established a significant measure of control over the unappropriated public domain. The declared purpose of the act was "to stop injury to the public grazing lands by preventing overgrazing and soil deterioration, to provide for their orderly use, improvement, and development, to stabilize the livestock industry dependent upon the public range, and for other purposes." The legislation set up a National Grazing Service to carry out those purposes through a scheme of leasing acreage for a fee; together with the Forest Service, which administers grazing leases within the national forest system, the Grazing Service (later the Bureau of Land Management) would supervise ranchers over a domain encompassing the largest part of the rural West. Some stockmen would have their entire ranch on the public lands, but the average lessee would mix private holdings with public leases in about a 4:6 ratio. The leases were almost but not quite a rancher's private property. They could be traded in the market, could serve as bank collateral, and could be fenced. But always, in the corner of the rancher's eye, there would be standing a federal bureaucrat with a mandate to protect the public's interest in the land. During the 1960s and 1970s, after a long era of benign neglect and under rising pressure from conservationists, the bureaucrats began to assert their mandate in modest but galling ways. They contended that many leases were badly overgrazed and stock would have to be removed. In the eyes of many rancher-lessees that ever-present bureaucracy was from the beginning, but particularly has become in recent years, an unacceptable infringement on their freedom and a threat to their security of tenure.

The long contest between these two rivals in modern pastoralism has given much of the American West a peculiar set of property and managerial arrangements: a hybrid of capitalist and bureaucratic regimes, each assuming it knows what is best for the nation's pocketbook and for nature. The significance of the struggle is immense. In a century where land everywhere has been put under more and more intensive use, the West speaks directly to the issue of where we can find the ideal manager. Is it the man or woman dressed in Stetson hat and boots, claiming to belong to the land and to know it intimately but speaking the language of private property, business, and profit maximization? Or is it the government official, also likely to be dressed in the traditional western garb, as much a local resident as the other but trained in the discourse of biology or range management? Does the self-interest of the capitalist really lead to rational land use, as many claim, or is it destructive of self, society, and the land? Can those who have no immediate economic stake in the land be trusted to make better decisions about its use? Has either the capitalist or the bureaucrat the capacity to match the Old World pastoralists' ability to sustain themselves on the margins of the good earth? The West offers millions of acres and decades of experience in which to find answers for those questions.

. . . What is needed is a full ecological history of the western range that will examine comparatively the condition of the range under private and public (or quasi-public) ownership, that will explore the impact of rangeland science on management, that will test the claims made by the rival parties and help resolve the old debate, and that will frame such an inquiry in terms of a broad world of people, animals, and arid lands.

. . . [I]t is historians, familiar with the hundred years of ranching in the West, familiar with the much longer span of pastoral life on the planet, who can help resolve the unsettled question of how we are most likely to find a sustainable future.

Telling Stories About Ecology*

WILLIAM CRONON

In 1979, two books were published about the long drought that struck the Great Plains during the 1930s. The two had nearly identical titles: one, by Paul Bonnifield, was called *The Dust Bowl;* the other, by Donald Worster, *Dust Bowl.* The two authors dealt with virtually the same subject, had researched many of the same documents, and agreed on most of their facts, and yet their conclusions could hardly have been more different.

Bonnifield's closing argument runs like this:

> The story of the dust bowl was the story of people, people with ability and talent, people with resourcefulness, fortitude, and courage. . . . The people of the dust bowl were not defeated, poverty-ridden people without hope. They were builders for tomorrow.

Worster, on the other hand, paints a bleaker picture:

> The Dust Bowl was the darkest moment in the twentieth-century life of the southern plains, . . . one of the three worst ecological blunders in history. . . . It cannot be blamed on illiteracy or overpopulation or social disorder. It came about because the culture was operating in precisely the way it was supposed to. . . . The Dust Bowl . . . was the inevitable outcome of a culture that deliberately, self-consciously, set itself [the] task of dominating and exploiting the land for all it was worth.

For Bonnifield, the dust storms of the 1930s were mainly a natural disaster; when the rains gave out, people had to struggle for their farms, their homes, their very survival. Their success in that struggle was a triumph of individual and community spirit: nature made a mess, and human beings cleaned it up. Worster's version differs dramatically. Although the rains did fail during the 1930s, their disappearance expressed the cyclical climate of a semiarid environment. The story of the Dust Bowl is less about the failures of nature than about the failures of human beings to accommodate themselves to nature. . . .

Whichever of these interpretations we are inclined to follow, they pose a dilemma for scholars who study past environmental change—indeed, a dilemma for all historians. As often happens in history, they make us wonder how two competent authors looking at identical materials drawn from the same past can reach such divergent

Excerpts from William Cronon, "A Place for Stories: Nature, History, and Narrative," *Journal of American History,* 78 (March 1992), 1347–1376. Reprinted by permission of the Organization of American Historians.

*This essay is an abridged version of the original article. Readers interested in the history of Great Plains narratives and postmodern criticism are urged to read the longer version.

conclusions. But it is not merely their *conclusions* that differ. Although both narrate the same broad series of events with an essentially similar cast of characters, they tell two entirely different *stories*. In both texts, the story is inextricably bound to its conclusion, and the historical analysis derives much of its force from the upward or downward sweep of the plot. So we must eventually ask a more basic question: where did these stories come from?

The question is trickier than it seems, for it transports us into the much contested terrain between traditional social science and postmodernist critical theory. As an environmental historian who tries to blend the analytical traditions of history with those of ecology, economics, anthropology, and other fields, I cannot help feeling uneasy about the shifting theoretical ground we all now seem to occupy. On the one hand, a fundamental premise of my field is that human acts occur within a network of relationships, processes, and systems that are as ecological as they are cultural. To such basic historical categories as gender, class, and race, environmental historians would add a theoretical vocabulary in which plants, animals, soils, climates, and other nonhuman entities become the coactors and codeterminants of a history not just of people but of the earth itself. . . .

And yet scholars of environmental history also maintain a powerful commitment to narrative form. When we describe human activities within an ecosystem, we seem always to tell *stories* about them. Like all historians, we configure the events of the past into causal sequences—stories—that order and simplify those events to give them new meanings. We do so because narrative is the chief literary form that tries to find meaning in an overwhelmingly crowded and disordered chronological reality. When we choose a plot to order our environmental histories, we give them a unity that neither nature nor the past possesses so clearly. In so doing, we move well beyond nature into the intensely human realm of value. There, we cannot avoid encountering the postmodernist assault on narrative, which calls into question not just the stories we tell but the deeper purpose that motivated us in the first place: trying to make sense of nature's place in the human past. . . .

If we consider the Plains in the half millennium since Christopher Columbus crossed the Atlantic, certain events seem likely to stand out in any long-term history of the region. If I were to try to write these not as a *story* but as a simple *list* . . . the resulting chronicle might run something like this.

Five centuries ago, people traveled west across the Atlantic Ocean. So did some plants and animals. One of these—the horse—appeared on the Plains. Native peoples used horses to hunt bison. Human migrants from across the Atlantic eventually appeared on the Plains as well. People fought a lot. The bison herds disappeared. Native peoples moved to reservations. The new immigrants built homes for themselves. Herds of cattle increased. Settlers plowed the prairie grasses, raising corn, wheat, and other grains. Railroads moved people and other things into and out of the region. Crops sometimes failed for lack of rain. Some people abandoned their farms and moved elsewhere; other people stayed. During the 1930s, there was a particularly bad drought, with many dust storms. Then the drought ended. A lot of people began to pump water out of the ground for use on their fields and in their towns. Today, Plains farmers continue to raise crops and herds of animals. Some have trouble making ends meet. Many Indians live on reservations. It will be interesting to see what happens next. . . .

How do we discover a story that will turn the facts of Great Plains history into something more easily recognized and understood? The repertoire of historical plots we might apply to the events I've just chronicled is endless and could be drawn not just from history but from all of literature and myth. To simplify the range of choices, let me start by offering two large groups of possible plots. On the one hand, we can narrate Plains history as a story of improvement, in which the plot line gradually ascends toward an ending that is somehow more positive—happier, richer, freer, better—than the beginning. On the other hand, we can tell stories in which the plot line eventually falls toward an ending that is more negative—sadder, poorer, less free, worse—than the place where the story began. The one group of plots might be called "progressive," given their historical dependence on eighteenth-century Enlightenment notions of progress; the other might be called "tragic" or "declensionist," tracing their historical roots to romantic and antimodernist reactions against progress.

If we look at the ways historians have actually written about the changing environment of the Great Plains, the upward and downward lines of progress and declension are everywhere apparent. The very ease with which we recognize them constitutes a warning about the terrain we are entering. However compelling these stories may be as depictions of environmental change, their narrative form has less to do with nature than with human discourse. . . .

Take, for instance, the historians who narrate Great Plains history as a tale of frontier progress. The most famous of those who embraced this basic plot was of course Frederick Jackson Turner, for whom the story of the nation recapitulated the ascending stages of European civilization to produce a uniquely democratic and egalitarian community. Turner saw the transformation of the American landscape from wilderness to trading post to farm to boomtown as the central saga of the nation. If ever there was a narrative that achieved its end by erasing its true subject, Turner's frontier was it: the heroic encounter between pioneers and "free land" could only become plausible by obscuring the conquest that traded one people's freedom for another's. By making Indians the foil for its story of progress, the frontier plot made their conquest seem natural, commonsensical, inevitable. But to say this is only to affirm the narrative's power. . . . In its ability to turn ordinary people into heroes and to present a conflict-ridden invasion as an epic march toward enlightened democratic nationhood, it perfectly fulfilled the ideological needs of its late-nineteenth-century moment. . . .

The Great Plains would eventually prove less tractable to frontier progress than many other parts of the nation. . . . One of Dakota Territory's leading missionaries, Bishop William Robert Hare, prophesied in the 1880s that the plot of Dakota settlement would follow an upward line of migration, struggle, and triumph:

> You may stand ankle deep in the short burnt grass of an uninhabited wilderness—next month a mixed train will glide over the waste and stop at some point where the railroad has decided to locate a town. Men, women and children will jump out of the cars. . . . The courage and faith of these pioneers are something extraordinary. Their spirit seems to rise above all obstacles.

For Hare, this vision of progress was ongoing and prospective, a prophecy of future growth, but the same pattern could just as easily be applied to retrospective visions. . . .

Ordinary people saw such descriptions as the fulfillment of a grand story that had unfolded during the course of their own lifetimes. As one Kansas townswoman, Josephine Middlekauf, concluded,

> After sixty years of pioneering in Hays, I could write volumes telling of its growth and progress. . . . I have been singularly privileged to have seen it develop from the raw materials into the almost finished product in comfortable homes, churches, schools, paved streets, trees, fruits and flowers.

Consider these small narratives more abstractly. They tell a story of . . . linear progress, in which people struggle to transform a relatively responsive environment. There may be moderate setbacks along the way, but their narrative role is to play foil to the heroes who overcome them. Communities rapidly succeed in becoming ever more civilized and comfortable. The time frame of the stories is brief, limited to the lifespan of a single generation, . . . just after invading settlers first occupied Indian lands. Our attention as readers is focused on local events. . . . All of these framing devices . . . compel us toward the conclusion that this is basically a happy story.

If the story these narrators tell is about the drama of settlement and the courage of pioneers, it is just as much about the changing stage on which the drama plays itself out. The transformation of a Kansas town is revealed not just by its new buildings but by its shade trees, apple orchards, and gardens. . . . As the literary critic Kenneth Burke long ago suggested, the scene of a story is as fundamental to what happens in it as the actions that comprise its more visible plot. Indeed, Burke argues that a story's actions are almost invariably consistent with its scene. . . .

If the way a narrator constructs a scene is directly related to the story that narrator tells, then this has deep implications for environmental history, which after all takes scenes of past nature as its primary object of study. If the history of the Great Plains is a progressive story about how grasslands were turned into ranches, farms, and gardens, then the end of the story requires a particular kind of scene for the ascending plot line to reach its necessary fulfillment. Just as important, the closing scene has to be different from the opening one. If the story ends in a wheatfield that is the happy conclusion of a struggle to transform the landscape, then the most basic requirement of the story is that the earlier form of that landscape must either be neutral or negative in value. It must *deserve* to be transformed.

It is thus no accident that these storytellers begin their narratives in the midst of landscapes that have few redeeming features. Bishop Hare's Dakota Territory begins as "an uninhabited wilderness," and his railroad carries future settlers across a "waste." . . . Josephine Middlekauf perceived the unplowed Kansas grasslands chiefly as "raw materials." Even so seemingly neutral a phrase as this last one—"raw materials"—is freighted with narrative meaning. Indeed, it contains buried within it the entire story of progressive development in which the environment is transformed from "raw materials" to "finished product." In just this way, story and scene become entangled—with each other, and with the politics of invasion and civilized progress—as we try to understand the Plains environment and its history.

Now in fact, these optimistic stories about Great Plains settlement are by no means typical of historical writing in the twentieth century. The problems of settling a semiarid environment were simply too great for the frontier story to proceed without multiple setbacks and crises. Even narrators who prefer an ascending plot line in their stories of regional environmental change must therefore tell a more complicated tale of failure, struggle, and accommodation in the face of a resistant if not hostile landscape.

Among the most important writers who adopt this narrative strategy are Walter Prescott Webb and James Malin. . . . For Webb, the Plains were radically different from the more benign environments that Anglo-American settlers had encountered in the East. Having no trees and little water, the region posed an almost insurmountable obstacle to the westward march of civilization. After describing the scene in this way, Webb sets his story in motion with a revealing passage:

> In the new region—level, timberless, and semi-arid—[settlers] were thrown by Mother Necessity into the clutch of new circumstances. Their plight has been stated in this way: east of the Mississippi civilization stood on three legs—land, water, and timber; west of the Mississippi not one but two of these legs were withdrawn,—water and timber,— and civilization was left on one leg—land. It is small wonder that it toppled over in temporary failure.

It is easy to anticipate the narrative that will flow from this beginning: Webb will tell us how civilization fell over, then built itself new legs and regained its footing to continue its triumphant ascent. The central agency that solves these problems and drives the story forward is human invention. Unlike the simpler frontier narratives, Webb's history traces a dialectic between a resistant landscape and the technological innovations that will finally succeed in transforming it. Although his book is over five hundred pages long and is marvelously intricate in its arguments, certain great inventions mark the turning points of Webb's plot. Because water was so scarce, settlers had to obtain it from the only reliable source, underground aquifers, so they invented the humble but revolutionary windmill. Because so little wood was available to build fences that would keep cattle out of cornfields, barbed wire was invented in 1874 and rapidly spread throughout the grasslands. These and other inventions— railroads, irrigation, new legal systems for allocating water rights, even six-shooter revolvers—eventually destroyed the bison herds, created a vast cattle kingdom, and broke the prairie sod for farming.

Webb closes his story by characterizing the Plains as "a land of survival where nature has most stubbornly resisted the efforts of man. Nature's very stubbornness has driven man to the innovations which he has made." Given the scenic requirements of Webb's narrative, his Plains landscape must look rather different from that of earlier frontier narrators. For Webb, the semiarid environment is neither a wilderness nor a waste, but itself a worthy antagonist of civilization. It is a landscape the very resistance of which is the necessary spur urging human ingenuity to new levels of achievement. Webb thus spends much more time than earlier storytellers describing the climate, terrain, and ecology of the Great Plains so as to extol the features that made the region unique in American experience. . . . In the struggle to make homes for themselves in this difficult land, the people of the Plains not only proved their inventiveness but built a regional culture beautifully adapted to the challenges of their regional environment. . . .

Webb's story of struggle against a resistant environment has formed the core of most subsequent environmental histories of the Plains. We have already encountered one version of it in Paul Bonnifield's *The Dust Bowl*. It can also be discovered in the more ecologically sophisticated studies of James C. Malin, in which the evolution of "forest man" to "grass man" becomes the central plot of Great Plains history. Malin's prose is far less story-like in outward appearance than Webb's, but it nonetheless narrates an encounter between a resistant environment and human ingenuity. Malin's human agents begin as struggling immigrants who have no conception of how to live in a treeless landscape; by the end, they have become "grass men" who have brought their culture "into conformity with the requirements of maintaining rather than disrupting environmental equilibrium." . . . Human inhabitants have become one with an environment that only a few decades before had almost destroyed them. . . .

. . . For Webb and Malin, the Great Plains gain significance from their ties to a world-historical plot, Darwinian in shape, that encompasses the entire sweep of human history. The ascending plot line we detect in these stories is in fact connected to a much longer plot line with the same rising characteristics. Whether that longer plot is expressed as the Making of the American Nation, the Rise of Western Civilization, or the Ascent of Man, it still lends its grand scale to Great Plains histories that outwardly appear much more limited in form. . . .

But there is another way to tell this history, one in which the plot ultimately falls rather than rises. The first examples of what we might call a "declensionist" or "tragic" Great Plains history began to appear during the Dust Bowl calamity of the 1930s. The dominant New Deal interpretation of what had gone wrong on the Plains was that settlers had been fooled by a climate that was sometimes perfectly adequate for farming and at other times disastrously inadequate. Settlement had expanded during "good" years when rainfall was abundant, and the perennial optimism of the frontier had prevented farmers from acknowledging that drought was a permanent fact of life on the Plains. In this version, Great Plains history becomes a tale of self-deluding hubris and refusal to accept reality. Only strong government action, planned by enlightened scientific experts to encourage cooperation among Plains farmers, could prevent future agricultural expansion and a return of the dust storms. . . .

. . . [James] Malin wrote in the wake of the New Deal and was a staunch conservative opponent of everything it represented. His narratives of regional adaptation expressed his own horror of collectivism by resisting the New Deal story at virtually every turn. The planners, he said, had exaggerated the severity of the Dust Bowl to serve their own statist ends and had ignored the fact that dust storms had been a natural part of the Plains environment as far back as anyone remembered. . . . Ecosystems were dynamic, and so was the human story of technological progress: to assert that nature set insurmountable limits to human ingenuity was to deny the whole upward sweep of civilized history. . . .

It is James Malin's anti–New Deal narrative that informs Paul Bonnifield's *The Dust Bowl.* Writing in the late 1970s, at a time when conservative critiques of the welfare state were becoming a dominant feature of American political discourse, Bonnifield argues less urgently and polemically than Malin, but he tells essentially the same story. . . . When the Dust Bowl hit, it was the people who lived there, not government scientists, who invented new land-use practices that solved earlier problems. New Deal planners understood little about the region and were so caught up in their own ideology that they compounded its problems by trying to impose their vision of a planned society. . . . In fact, Bonnifield argues, the Plains contained some of the best farming soil in the world. The landscape was difficult but ultimately benign for people who could learn to thrive upon it. Their chief problem was less a hostile nature than a hostile government. The narrative echoes Malin's scenic landscape but gains a different kind of ideological force when placed at the historical moment of its narration—in the waning years of the Carter administration just prior to Ronald Reagan's triumphant election as president. Bonnifield's is a tale of ordinary folk needing nothing so much as to get government off their backs.

If Bonnifield elaborates the optimistic Dust Bowl narrative of a conservative critic of the New Deal, Donald Worster returns to the New Deal plot and deepens its tragic possibilities. Worster, who is with Webb the most powerful narrator among these writers, accepts the basic framework of Roosevelt's planners—the refusal of linear-minded Americans to recognize and accept cyclical environmental constraints—but he shears away its statist bias and considerably expands its cultural boundaries. . . . Worster . . . argues instead that the Plains were actually a paradigmatic case in a larger story that might be called "the rise and fall of capitalism."

For Worster, the refusal to recognize natural limits is one of the defining characteristics of a capitalist ethos and economy. He is therefore drawn to a narrative in which the same facts that betokened progress for Webb and Malin become signs of declension and of the compounding contradictions of capitalist expansion. The scene of the story is world historical only this time the plot leads toward catastrophe:

> That the thirties were a time of great crisis in American, indeed, in world, capitalism has long been an obvious fact. The Dust Bowl, I believe, was part of that same crisis. It came about because the expansionary energy of the United States had finally encountered a volatile, marginal land, destroying the delicate ecological balance that had evolved there. We speak of farmers and plows on the plains and the damage they did, but the language is inadequate. What brought them to the region was a social system, a set of values, an economic order. There is no word that so fully sums up those elements as "capitalism." . . . Capitalism, it is my contention, has been the decisive factor in this nation's use of nature.

By this reading, the chief agent of the story is not "the pioneers" or "civilization" or "man"; it is capitalism. The plot leads from the origins of that economic system, through a series of crises, toward the future environmental cataclysm when the system will finally collapse. The tale of Worster's Dust Bowl thus concerns an intermediate crisis that foreshadows other crises yet to come; in this, it proclaims an apocalyptic prophecy that inverts the prophecy of progress found in earlier frontier narratives. Worster's inversion of the frontier story is deeply ironic, for it implies that the increasing technological "control" represented by Webb's and Malin's human ingenuity leads only toward an escalating spiral of disasters. He also breaks rank with the New Dealers at this point, for in his view their efforts at solving the problems of the Dust Bowl did nothing to address the basic contradictions of capitalism itself. For Worster, the planners "propped up an agricultural economy that had proved itself to be socially and ecologically erosive."

Given how much his basic plot differs from Webb's and Malin's, the scene Worster constructs for his narrative must differ just as dramatically. Since Worster's story concerns the destruction of an entire ecosystem, it must end where the frontier story began: in a wasteland. His plot must move downward toward an ecological disaster called the Dust Bowl. Whereas the frontier narratives begin in a negatively valued landscape and end in a positive one, Worster begins his tale in a place whose narrative value is entirely good. . . . Delicate and beautiful, the Plains were an eco-system living always on the edge of drought, and their survival depended on an intricate web of plants and animals that capitalism was incapable of valuing by any standard other than that of the marketplace. From this beginning, the story moves down a slope that ends in the dust storms whose narrative role is to stand as the most vivid possible symbol of human alienation from nature.

The very different scenes that progressive and declensionist narrators choose as the settings for their Great Plains histories bring us to another key observation about narrative itself: where one chooses to begin and end a story profoundly alters its shape and meaning. . . . If we shift time frames to encompass the Indian past, we suddenly encounter a new set of narratives, equally tragic in their sense of crisis and declension, but strikingly different in plot and scene. As such, they offer further proof of the narrative power to reframe the past so as to include certain events and people, exclude others, and redefine the meaning of landscape accordingly.

[For example], Plenty Coups, a Crow Indian chief, tells in his 1930 autobiogra-phy of a boyhood vision sent him by his animal Helper, the Chickadee. In the dream, a great storm blown by the Four Winds destroyed a vast forest, leaving standing only the single tree in which the Chickadee—smallest but shrewdest of animals—made its lodge. The tribal elders interpreted this to mean that white settlers would eventually destroy not only the buffalo but also all tribes who resisted the American onslaught. On the basis of this prophetic dream, the Crows decided to ally themselves with the United States, and so they managed to preserve a portion of their homelands. Saving their land did not spare them from the destruction of the bison herds, however, and so they shared with other Plains tribes the loss of subsistence and spiritual commun-ion that had previously been integral to the hunt. As Plenty Coups remarks at the end of his story, "when the buffalo went away the hearts of my people fell to the ground, and they could not lift them up again. After this nothing happened."

Few remarks more powerfully capture the importance of narrative to history than this last of Plenty Coups: "After this nothing happened." For the Crows as for other Plains tribes, the universe revolved around the bison herds, and life made sense only so long as the hunt continued. When the scene shifted—when the bison herds "went away"—that universe collapsed and history ended. Although the Crows con-tinued to live on their reservation and although their identity as a people has never ceased, for Plenty Coups their subsequent life is all part of a different story. The story he loved best ended with the buffalo. Everything that has happened since is part of some other plot, and there is neither sense nor joy in telling it. . . .

And just what *is* a narrative? As the evidence of my Great Plains chronicle would imply, it is not merely a sequence of events. To shift from chronicle to narra-tive, a tale of environmental change must be structured so that, as Aristotle said, it "has beginning, middle, and end." What distinguishes stories from other forms of discourse is that they describe an action that begins, continues over a well-defined period of time, and finally draws to a definite close, with consequences that become meaningful because of their placement within the narrative. Completed action gives a story its unity and allows us to evaluate and judge an act by its results. The moral of a story is defined by its ending: as Aristotle remarked, "the end is every-where the chief thing."

Narrative is a peculiarly human way of organizing reality, and this has important implications for the way we approach the history of environmental change. . . . Many natural events lack [a] linear structure. Some are cyclical: the motions of the planets, the seasons, or the rhythms of biological fertility and reproduction. Others are random: climate shifts, earthquakes, genetic mutations, and other events the causes of which remain hidden from us. One does not automatically describe such things with narrative plots, and yet environmental histories, which purport to set the human past in its natural context, all have plots. Nature and the universe do not tell stories; we do. . . .

The stories we tell about the past do not exist in a vacuum, and our storytelling practice is bounded in at least three ways that limit its power. First, our stories cannot contravene known facts about the past. This is so much a truism of traditional historical method that we rarely bother even to state it; but it is crucial if we wish to deny that all narratives do an equally good job of representing the past. At the most basic level, we judge a work bad history if it contradicts evidence we know to be accurate and true. Good history does not knowingly lie. A history of the Great Plains that narrated a story of continuous progress without once mentioning the Dust Bowl would instantly be suspect, as would a history of the Nazi treatment of Jews that failed to mention the concentration camps. Historical narratives are bounded at every turn by the evidence they can and cannot muster in their own support.

Environmental historians embrace a second set of narrative constraints: given our faith that the natural world ultimately transcends our narrative power, our stories must make ecological sense. You can't put dust in the air—or tell stories about putting dust in the air—if the dust isn't there. Even though environmental histories transform ecosystems into the scenes of human narratives, the biological and geological processes of the earth set fundamental limits to what constitutes a plausible narrative. The dust storms of the 1930s are not just historical facts but natural ones: they reflect the complex response of an entire ecosystem—its soils, its vegetation, its animals, its climate—to human actions. . . .

Finally, historical narratives are constrained in a third important way as well. Historians do not tell stories by themselves. We write as members of communities, and we cannot help but take those communities into account as we do our work. Being American, being male, being white, being an upper-middle-class academic, being an environmentalist, I write in particular ways that are not all of my own choosing, and my biases are reflected in my work. But being a scholar, I write also for a community of other scholars—some very different from me in their backgrounds and biases—who know nearly as much about my subject as I do. They are in a position instantly to remind me of the excluded facts and wrongheaded interpretations that my own bias, self-delusion, and lack of diligence have kept me from acknowledging. . . .

Historians and prophets share a common commitment to finding the meaning of endings. However much we understand that an ecosystem transcends mere humanity, we cannot escape the valuing process that defines our relationship to it. To see how much this is so, one has only to consider the various labels Americans have attached to the Great Plains since 1800: the Land of the Buffalo; the Great American Desert; the Great Plains; the Wheat Belt; the Dust Bowl; the Breadbasket of the World; the Land Where the Sky Begins. These are not simply names or descriptive phrases.

Each implies a different possible *narrative* for environmental histories of the region, and different possible endings for each of those stories. Narrative is thus inescapably bound to the very names we give the world. Rather than evade it—which is in any event impossible—we must learn to use it consciously, responsibly, self-critically. To try to escape the value judgments that accompany storytelling is to miss the point of history itself, for the stories we tell, like the questions we ask, are all finally about value. So it is with questions that I will end:

What do people care most about in the world they inhabit?

How do they use and assign meaning to that world?

How does the earth respond to their actions and desires?

What sort of communities do people, plants, and animals create together?

How do people struggle with each other for control of the earth, its creatures, and its meanings?

And on the grandest scale: what is the mutual fate of humanity and the earth?

Good questions all, and starting points for many a story.

ψ *F U R T H E R   R E A D I N G*

Larry Barsness, *Heads, Hides and Horns: The Compleat Buffalo Book* (1985)

Theodore Binnema, *Common and Contested Ground: A Human and Environmental History of the Northwestern Plains* (2001)

Black Elk (Oglala Lakota), *Black Elk Speaks,* ed. John Neihardt (1932)

Allan G. Bogue, *From Prairie to Corn Belt: Farming on the Illinois and Iowa Prairies in the Nineteenth Century* (1963)

Paul Bonnifield, *The Dust Bowl: Men, Dirt, and Depression* (1979)

David F. Costello, *The Prairie World* (1969)

Bernard DeVoto, ed., *The Journals of Lewis and Clark* (1953)

Philip Durham and Everett L. Jones, *The Negro Cowboy* (1965)

Clinton L. Evans, *The War on Weeds in the Prairie West: An Environmental History* (2002)

John Mack Faragher, *Women and Men on the Overland Trail* (1979)

Eugene D. Fleharty, *Wild Animals and Settlers on the Great Plains* (1995)

Dan L. Flores, "Bison Ecology and Bison Diplomacy: The Southern Plains from 1800 to 1850," *Journal of American History* 78 (September 1991), 465–485

——, *The Natural West: Environmental History in the Great Plains and Rocky Mountains* (2001)

Arlen L. Fowler, *The Black Infantry in the West, 1869–1891* (1971)

Josiah Gregg, *The Commerce of the Prairies* [1926] (1967)

Mary Wilma M. Hargreaves, *Dry Farming in the Northern Great Plains, 1900–1925* (1957)

R. Douglas Hurt, *The Dust Bowl: An Agricultural and Social History* (1981)

Andrew C. Isenberg, *The Destruction of the Bison: An Environmental History, 1750–1920* (2000)

William Loren Katz, *The Black West* (1987)

Annette Kolodny, *The Land Before Her: Fantasy and Experience of the American Frontiers, 1630–1860* (1984)

John (Fire) Lame Deer, *Lame Deer: Seeker of Visions,* ed. Richard Erdoes (1972)

Brad D. Lookingbill, *Dust Bowl, USA: Depression America and the Ecological Imagination, 1929–1941* (2001)

James C. Malin, *The Grassland of North America: Prolegomena to Its History,* 4th ed. (1967)

——, *History and Ecology: Studies of the Grassland,* ed. Robert Swierenga (1984)

Richard Manning, *Grasslands: The History, Biology, Politics, and Promise of the American Prairie* (1995)

Tom McHugh, *The Time of the Buffalo* (1972)

Russell McKee, *The Last West: A History of the Great Plains in North America* (1974)

John S. Milloy, *The Plains Cree: Trade, Diplomacy and War, 1790 to 1870* (1988)

Sandra L. Myres, *Westering Women and the Frontier Experience, 1800–1915* (1982)

Daniel Nelson, *Farm and Factory: Workers in the Midwest 1880–1990* (Midwestern History and Culture) (1995)

Paula Nelson, *The Prairie Winnows Out Its Own: The West River Country of South Dakota in the Years of Depression and Dust* (1996)

Francis Parkman, *The Oregon Trail* (1950)

Sheryll Patterson-Black, "Women Homesteaders on the Great Plains Frontier," *Frontiers* 1, 2 (Spring 1976), 67–88

———— and Gene Patterson-Black, *Western Women in History and Literature* (1978)

Sarah T. Phillips, "Lessons from the Dust Bowl: Dryland Agriculture and Soil Erosion in the United States and South Africa, 1900–1950," *Environmental History* 4, no. 2 (April 1999), 245–266

Plenty-Coups (Crow), *Plenty-Coups: Chief of the Crows,* ed. Frank B. Linderman (1962)

Pretty-Shield (Crow), *Pretty-Shield, Medicine Woman of the Crows,* ed. Frank B. Linderman (1974)

John F. Reiger, *The Passing of the Great West* (1972)

Osborne Russell, *Journal of a Trapper, 1834–1843* (1955)

Sherman W. Savage, *Blacks in the West* (1976)

Lillian Schlissel, *Women's Diaries of the Westward Journey* (1982)

James C. Shaw, *North from Texas* (1952)

Luther Standing Bear (Sioux), *Land of the Spotted Eagle,* ed. E. A. Brininstool (1933)

Joanna L. Stratton, *Pioneer Women: Voices from the Kansas Frontier* (1981)

Frederick Jackson Turner, "The Significance of the Frontier in American History" (1893)

Walter Prescott Webb, *The Great Plains* (1931)

Richard White, *The Middle Ground: Indians, Empires, and Republics in the Great Lakes Region, 1650–1850* (1991)

————, *The Roots of Dependency: Subsistence, Environment, and Social Change among the Choctaws, Pawnees, and Navajos* (1983)

Jim Whitewolf (Kiowa Apache), *Jim Whitewolf: The Life of a Kiowa Apache Indian,* ed. Charles S. Brant (1969)

David Wishart, *The Fur Trade of the American West, 1807–1840* (1979)

Donald Worster, *Dust Bowl: The Southern Plains in the 1930s* (1979)

CHAPTER
10

Resource Conservation in
the Twentieth Century

❦

By the late nineteenth century, most of the land composing the contiguous United
States had been settled. The 1890 census announced the closing of the frontier
and the declining availability of free land. As scientists, writers, and politicians
drew attention to the decreasing stocks of the natural resources needed for an
industrializing society, a conservation consciousness arose. Laissez-faire capitalism, which had left resource development to individuals and private enterprise,
was challenged by a Progressive Era politics of natural-resource conservation
through government regulation. An egocentric (individualistic) ethic centered
on the notion that what was good for the individual was good for society as a
whole was challenged by a homocentric (utilitarian) ethic based on the greatest
good for the greatest number of people. Politics and political institutions thus
responded to a perception of limited renewable and nonrenewable resources in
an era of closing frontier opportunities and expanding industrialization. Spawned
by the demand for reliable sources of water in the arid western states, by deteriorating rangelands, and by the rapid depletion of forests, a nationwide movement
to preserve watersheds, build dams, replant trees, and reseed grasslands took
shape. During the first decade of the twentieth century, under the presidency of
Theodore Roosevelt, the disparate strands of the movement were united under the
term conservation, defined as "the use of natural resources for the greatest good
of the greatest number for the longest time."
    During the New Deal era, the administration of President Franklin Delano
Roosevelt, which ran from 1933 to 1945, promoted forest preservation, the building
of large dams and irrigation works, soil conservation, the Civilian Conservation
Corps (CCC), and other public works programs. Throughout the Great Depression
and World War II, Roosevelt ardently supported farmers and workers and spiritedly
lectured on behalf of conservation. After World War II, public consciousness shifted
away from efficiency and large government conservation programs toward concerns
for quality of life, human and environmental health, and recreational amenities.
This chapter probes government policies and public responses to concerns over natural resources and the environment from the conservation movement of the early
twentieth century to the 1950s. (See Map 7 in the Appendix.)

ψ D O C U M E N T S

The documents in this chapter convey the growing awareness of the depletion of natural resources in the United States by the late nineteenth century and detail government and public support for the conservation of natural resources from the early to the mid-twentieth century. They feature proposals for government development and regulation of water, rangelands, forests, and soils.

When Vermont statesman George Perkins Marsh published *Man and Nature* in 1864, no one predicted that within a decade the book would be an international classic. In exhaustive detail, Marsh wrote a history of human despoliation of nature from the ancient civilizations of the Mediterranean world to the nineteenth century, with abundant comparisons between Europe and the United States. Document 1 includes passages from this environmental classic, in which Marsh depicts nature in the female gender, strong and stable when left alone but vulnerable and transformable by "man" and "his" technologies. Humans' proper ethical role, Marsh argues, is to cooperate with nature to repair the damage and restore lost harmonies through forest conservation and restoration. The establishment of the Forest Reserves in 1891 set aside forests on public land as public reservations.

Water management was another key component of conservation. In 1878 John Wesley Powell, a one-armed Civil War veteran, explorer, and ethnographer, published his *Report on the Lands of the Arid Region of the United States,* excerpted in Document 2, a classic analysis of water availability in the arid West. Following a hair-raising expedition down the Colorado River in four wooden boats, including ascents up some of the region's most hazardous peaks, Powell put forward in his *Report* a radical, democratic plan for developing the arid West within the constraints set by the environment. Lowlands around streams could be irrigated through cooperative labor and farmed, the forested mountain highlands could be used for watershed and timber, and the rangelands between could be developed as communal pasturage for cattle. In 1902, the federal government implemented some of Powell's recommendations when it passed the Reclamation Act, as shown in Document 3. This law established a reclamation fund for the construction of dams and irrigation works in the arid western states. Individuals could receive water from federal projects to irrigate a maximum of 160 acres, provided that they lived on or near the land. Like the acreage restrictions of the 1862 Homestead Act, however, the limits specified by the Reclamation Act were never strictly enforced, a lapse that allowed land and water speculators to thwart the law's democratic intentions.

Efforts to develop and use water, range, and forest resources more wisely and frugally were brought together under the concept of conservation in 1908. Launched at a White House conference of governors through a speech by President Theodore Roosevelt, excerpted in Document 4, the movement to conserve natural resources soon became a national cause célèbre. However, the Roosevelt administration's program was opposed by laissez-faire capitalists, as is illustrated by Document 5, taken from a 1910 article by George L. Knapp, published in the prestigious, conservative *North American Review.* Women's groups, such as the General Federation of Women's Clubs (GFWC) and the Daughters of the American Revolution (DAR), enthusiastically promoted conservation, as Document 6, a speech by Mrs. Marion Crocker of the GFWC at the Fourth National Conservation Congress in 1912, reveals.

During the 1930s and 1940s, President Franklin Delano Roosevelt's "New Deal" program extended government support for large-scale water projects (see Chapter 14), forest management, and soil conservation. Conservation activist Bob Marshall served the administration in the Bureau of Indian Affairs and the National Forest Service and helped to found the Wilderness Society in 1935. Document 7 is an excerpt from Marshall's book *The People's Forests* (1933), advocating nationalization of the forests as the only way to preserve the remaining timber from devastation by private interests. Document 8, from a 1947 article by Hugh Bennett, head of the Soil Conservation Service in the U.S. Department of Agriculture, points to the irreversibility of soil erosion and the possibility of preventing it through democratically run soil-conservation districts organized by local farmers and ranchers. In the last document, forest administrator Gifford Pinchot, one of the primary architects of the conservation movement, recalls the birth of the term *conservation.* The documents as a whole show increasing public recognition of the importance of conserving natural resources in an industrial society that was dependent on both renewable and nonrenewable resources for its economic growth and well-being.

1. George Perkins Marsh Discusses the Relationship of Man and Nature, 1864

Stability of Nature

Nature, left undisturbed, so fashions her territory as to give it almost unchanging permanence of form, outline, and proportion, except when shattered by geologic convulsions; and in these comparatively rare cases of derangement, she sets herself at once to repair the superficial damage, and to restore, as nearly as practicable, the former aspect of her dominion. In new countries, the natural inclination of the ground, the self-formed slopes and levels, are generally such as best secure the stability of the soil. They have been graded and lowered or elevated by frost and chemical forces and gravitation and the flow of water and vegetable deposit and the action of the winds, until, by a general compensation of conflicting forces, a condition of equilibrium has been reached which, without the action of man, would remain, with little fluctuation, for countless ages. . . .

Two natural causes, destructive in character, were, indeed, in operation in the primitive American forests, though, in the Northern colonies, at least, there were sufficient compensations; for we do not discover that any considerable permanent change was produced by them. I refer to the action of beavers and of fallen trees in producing bogs, and of smaller animals, insects, and birds, in destroying the woods. . . .

I am disposed to think that more bogs in the Northern States owe their origin to beavers than to accidental obstructions of rivulets by wind-fallen or naturally decayed trees; for there are few swamps in those States, at the outlets of which we may not, by careful search, find the remains of a beaver dam. . . . I do not know that we have any evidence of the destruction or serious injury of American forests by insects, before or even soon after the period of colonization; but since the white man has laid bare a vast proportion of the earth's surface, and thereby produced changes favorable, perhaps, to the multiplication of these pests, they have greatly increased in numbers, and, apparently, in voracity also.

In countries untrodden by man, the proportions and relative positions of land and water, the atmospheric precipitation and evaporation, the thermometric mean, and the distribution of vegetable and animal life, are subject to change only from geological influences so slow in their operation that the geographical conditions may

From George Perkins Marsh, *Man and Nature.* New York: Charles Scribner's Sons, 1864, pp. 29–37.

be regarded as constant and immutable. These arrangements of nature it is, in most cases, highly desirable substantially to maintain, when such regions become the seat of organized commonwealths. It is, therefore, a matter of the first importance, that, in commencing the process of fitting them for permanent civilized occupation, the transforming operations should be so conducted as not unnecessarily to derange and destroy what, in too many cases, it is beyond the power of man to rectify or restore.

Restoration of Disturbed Harmonies

In reclaiming and reoccupying lands laid waste by human improvidence or malice, and abandoned by man, or occupied only by a nomade or thinly scattered population, the task of the pioneer settler is of a very different character. He is to become a co-worker with nature in the reconstruction of the damaged fabric which the negligence or the wantonness of former lodgers has rendered untenantable. He must aid her in reclothing the mountain slopes with forests and vegetable mould, thereby restoring the fountains which she provided to water them; in checking the devastating fury of torrents, and bringing back the surface drainage to its primitive narrow channels; and in drying deadly morasses by opening the natural sluices which have been choked up, and cutting new canals for drawing off their stagnant waters. He must thus, on the one hand, create new reservoirs, and, on the other, remove mischievous accumulations of moisture, thereby equalizing and regulating the sources of atmospheric humidity and of flowing water, both which are so essential to all vegetable growth, and, of course, to human and lower animal life.

Destructiveness of Man

Man has too long forgotten that the earth was given to him for usufruct alone, not for consumption, still less for profligate waste. Nature has provided against the absolute destruction of any of her elementary matter, the raw material of her works; the thunderbolt and the tornado, the most convulsive throes of even the volcano and the earthquake, being only phenomena of decomposition and recomposition. But she has left it within the power of man irreparably to derange the combinations of inorganic matter and of organic life, which through the night of æons she had been proportioning and balancing, to prepare the earth for his habitation, when, in the fulness of time, his Creator should call him forth to enter into its possession.

Apart from the hostile influence of man, the organic and the inorganic world are, as I have remarked, bound together by such mutual relations and adaptations as secure, if not the absolute permanence and equilibrium of both, a long continuance of the established conditions of each at any given time and place, or at least, a very slow and gradual succession of changes in those conditions. But man is everywhere a disturbing agent. Wherever he plants his foot, the harmonies of nature are turned to discords. The proportions and accommodations which insured the stability of existing arrangements are overthrown. Indigenous vegetable and animal species are extirpated, and supplanted by others of foreign origin, spontaneous production is forbidden or restricted, and the face of the earth is either laid bare or covered with a new and reluctant growth of vegetable forms, and with alien tribes of animal life. These intentional changes and substitutions constitute, indeed, great revolutions; but vast as is their magnitude and importance, they are . . . insignificant in comparison with the contingent and unsought results which have flowed from them.

The fact that, of all organic beings, man alone is to be regarded as essentially a destructive power, and that he wields energies to resist which, nature—that nature whom all material life and all inorganic substance obey—is wholly impotent, tends to prove that, though living in physical nature, he is not of her, that he is of more exalted parentage, and belongs to a higher order of existences than those born of her womb and submissive to her dictates. . . .

The earth was not, in its natural condition, completely adapted to the use of man, but only to the sustenance of wild animals and wild vegetation. These live, multiply their kind in just proportion, and attain their perfect measure of strength and beauty, without producing or requiring any change in the natural arrangements of surface, or in each other's spontaneous tendencies, except such mutual repression of excessive increase as may prevent the extirpation of one species by the encroachments of another. In short, without man, lower animal and spontaneous vegetable life would have been constant in type, distribution, and proportion, and the physical geography of the earth would have remained undisturbed for indefinite periods, and been subject to revolution only from possible, unknown cosmical causes, or from geological action. . . .

Purely untutored humanity, it is true, interferes comparatively little with the arrangements of nature, and the destructive agency of man becomes more and more energetic and unsparing as he advances in civilization, until the impoverishment, with which his exhaustion of the natural resources of the soil is threatening him, at last awakens him to the necessity of preserving what is left, if not of restoring what has been wantonly wasted.

2. John Wesley Powell Advocates Reclamation, 1878

The Arid Region is the great Rocky Mountain Region of the United States, and it embraces something more than four-tenths of the whole country, excluding Alaska. In all this region the mean annual rainfall is insufficient for agriculture, but in certain seasons some localities, now here, now there, receive more than their average supply. . . .

Irrigable Lands

Within the Arid Region only a small portion of the country is irrigable. These irrigable tracts are lowlands lying along the streams. On the mountains and high plateaus forests are found at elevations so great that frequent summer frosts forbid the cultivation of the soil. Here are the natural timber lands of the Arid Region—an upper region set apart by nature for the growth of timber necessary to the mining, manufacturing, and agricultural industries of the country. Between the low irrigable lands and the elevated forest lands there are valleys, mesas, hills, and mountain slopes bearing

From John Wesley Powell, *Report on the Arid Lands of the United States.* Ed. Wallace Stegner. Cambridge, Mass.: Harvard University Press, 1962 [1878], pp. 15–16, 20–34.

grasses of greater or less value for pasturage purposes. . . . In discussing the lands of the Arid Region, three great classes are recognized—the irrigable lands below, the forest lands above, and the pasturage lands between.

Advantages of Irrigation.   There are two considerations that make irrigation attractive to the agriculturist. Crops thus cultivated are not subject to the vicissitudes of rainfall; the farmer fears no droughts; his labors are seldom interrupted and his crops rarely injured by storms. This immunity from drought and storm renders agricultural operations much more certain than in regions of greater humidity. Again, the water comes down from the mountains and plateaus freighted with fertilizing materials derived from the decaying vegetation and soils of the upper regions, which are spread by the flowing water over the cultivated lands. . . . It may be anticipated that all the lands redeemed by irrigation in the Arid Region will be highly cultivated and abundantly productive, and agriculture will be but slightly subject to the vicissitudes of scant and excessive rainfall.

Coöperative Labor or Capital Necessary for the Development of Irrigation.   Small streams can be taken out and distributed by individual enterprise, but coöperative labor or aggregated capital must be employed in taking out the larger streams.

The diversion of a large stream from its channel into a system of canals demands a large outlay of labor and material. To repay this all the waters so taken out must be used, and large tracts of land thus become dependent upon a single canal. It is manifest that a farmer depending upon his own labor cannot undertake this task. . . . When farming is dependent upon larger streams such men are barred from these enterprises until coöperative labor can be organized or capital induced to assist. . . .

In Utah Territory coöperative labor, under ecclesiastical organization, has been very successful. Outside of Utah there are but few instances where it has been tried; but at Greeley, in the State of Colorado, this system has been eminently successful. . . .

Timber Lands

Throughout the Arid Region timber of value is found growing spontaneously on the higher plateaus and mountains. These timber regions are bounded above and below by lines which are very irregular, due to local conditions. Above the upper line no timber grows because of the rigor of the climate, and below no timber grows because of aridity. Both the upper and lower lines descend in passing from south to north; that is, the timber districts are found at a lower altitude in the northern portion of the Arid Region than in the southern. The forests are chiefly of pine, spruce, and fir, but the pines are of principal value. Below these timber regions, on the lower slopes of mountains, on the mesas and hills, low, scattered forests are often found, composed mainly of dwarfed piñon pines and cedars. . . . The protection of the forests of the entire Arid Region of the United States is reduced to one single problem—Can these forests be saved from fire? . . .

In the main these fires are set by Indians. Driven from the lowlands by advancing civilization, they resort to the higher regions until they are forced back by the deep snows of winter. Want, caused by the restricted area to which they resort for food; the desire for luxuries to which they were strangers in their primitive condition, and especially the desire for personal adornment, together with a supply of more effective instruments for hunting and trapping, have in late years, during the rapid settlement of the country since the discovery of gold and the building of railroads, greatly stimulated the pursuit of animals for their furs—the wealth and currency of the savage. On their hunting excursions they systematically set fire to forests for the purpose of driving the game. This is a fact well known to all mountaineers. Only the white hunters of the region properly understand why these fires are set, it being usually attributed to a wanton desire on the part of the Indians to destroy that which is of value to the white man. The fires can, then, be very greatly curtailed by the removal of the Indians. . . .

Lumbermen and woodmen will furnish to the people [in the lands] below their supply of building and fencing material and fuel. In some cases it will be practicable for the farmers to own their timber lands, but in general the timber will be too remote, and from necessity such a division of labor will ensue.

Pasturage Lands

The irrigable lands and timber lands constitute but a small fraction of the Arid Region. Between the lowlands on the one hand and the highlands on the other is found a great body of valley, mesa, hill, and low mountain lands. To what extent, and under what conditions can they be utilized? Usually they bear a scanty growth of grasses. These grasses are nutritious and valuable both for summer and winter pasturage. Their value depends upon peculiar climatic conditions; the grasses grow to a great extent in scattered bunches, and mature seeds in larger proportion perhaps than the grasses of the more humid regions. . . .

The Farm Unit for Pasturage Lands.   The grass is so scanty that the herdsman must have a large area for the support of his stock. In general a quarter section of land alone is of no value to him; the pasturage it affords is entirely inadequate to the wants of a herd that the poorest man needs for his support.

Four square miles may be considered as the minimum amount necessary for a pasturage farm, and a still greater amount is necessary for the larger part of the lands; that is, pasturage farms, to be of any practicable value, must be of at least 2,560 acres, and in many districts they must be much larger.

Farm Residences Should Be Grouped.   These lands will maintain but a scanty population. The homes must necessarily be widely scattered from the fact that the farm unit must be large. That the inhabitants of these districts may have the benefits of the local social organizations of civilization—as schools, churches, etc., and the benefits of coöperation in the construction of roads, bridges, and other local improvements, it is essential that the residences should be grouped to the greatest possible extent. This may be practically accomplished by making the pasturage farms conform to topographic features in such manner as to give the greatest possible number of water fronts.

The great areas over which stock must roam to obtain subsistence usually prevents the practicability of fencing the lands. It will not pay to fence the pasturage fields, hence in many cases the lands must be occupied by herds roaming in common; for poor men coöperative pasturage is necessary, or communal regulations for the occupancy of the ground and for the division of the increase of the herds. Such communal regulations have already been devised in many parts of the country.

3. The Reclamation Act, 1902

An Act Appropriating the receipts from the sale and disposal of public lands in certain States and Territories to the construction of irrigation works for the reclamation of arid lands.

Be it enacted by the Senate and House of Representatives of the United States of America in Congress assembled, That all moneys received from the sale and disposal of public lands in Arizona, California, Colorado, Idaho, Kansas, Montana, Nebraska, Nevada, New Mexico, North Dakota, Oklahoma, Oregon, South Dakota, Utah, Washington, and Wyoming . . . shall be, and the same are hereby, reserved, set aside, and appropriated as a special fund in the Treasury to be known as the "reclamation fund," to be used in the examination and survey for and the construction and maintenance of irrigation works for the storage, diversion, and development of waters for the reclamation of arid and semiarid lands in the said States and Territories, and for the payment of all other expenditures provided for in this Act: . . .

SEC 3 . . . that public lands which it is proposed to irrigate by means of any contemplated works shall be subject to entry only under the provisions of the homestead laws in tracts of not less than forty nor more than one hundred and sixty acres, . . .

SEC. 5. That the entryman upon lands to be irrigated by such works shall, in addition to compliance with the homestead laws, reclaim at least one-half of the total irrigable area of his entry for agricultural purposes, and before receiving patent for the lands covered by his entry shall pay to the Government the charges apportioned against such tract, as provided in section four. No right to the use of water for land in private ownership shall be sold for a tract exceeding one hundred and sixty acres to any one landowner, and no such sale shall be made to any landowner unless he be an actual bona fide resident on such land, or occupant thereof residing in the neighborhood of said land, and no such right shall permanently attach until all payments therefor are made.

4. Theodore Roosevelt Publicizes Conservation, 1908

Governors of the several States; and Gentlemen:

I welcome you to this Conference at the White House. You have come hither at my request, so that we may join together to consider the question of the conservation and use of the great fundamental sources of wealth of this Nation. . . .

Document 3 is from The Reclamation Act, 1902, *The Statutes at Large of the United States of America From December 1901 to March 1903.* Washington, D.C.: Government Printing Office, 1903, vol. 32, part 1, pp. 388–390.

Document 4 is from Theodore Roosevelt, "Opening Address by the President," *Proceedings of a Conference of Governors in the White House,* ed. Newton C. Blanchard. Washington, D.C.: Government Printing Office, 1909, pp. 3, 5–10, 12.

This Conference on the conservation of natural resources is in effect a meeting of the representatives of all the people of the United States called to consider the weightiest problem now before the Nation; and the occasion for the meeting lies in the fact that the natural resources of our country are in danger of exhaustion if we permit the old wasteful methods of exploiting them longer to continue.

With the rise of peoples from savagery to civilization, and with the consequent growth in the extent and variety of the needs of the average man, there comes a steadily increasing growth of the amount demanded by this average man from the actual resources of the country. And yet, rather curiously, at the same time that there comes that increase in what the average man demands from the resources, he is apt to grow to lose the sense of his dependence upon nature. He lives in big cities. He deals in industries that do not bring him in close touch with nature. He does not realize the demands he is making upon nature. . . .

In [George] Washington's time anthracite coal was known only as a useless black stone; and the great fields of bituminous coal were undiscovered. As steam was unknown, the use of coal for power production was undreamed of. Water was practically the only source of power, save the labor of men and animals; and this power was used only in the most primitive fashion. But a few small iron deposits had been found in this country, and the use of iron by our countrymen was very small. Wood was practically the only fuel, and what lumber was sawed was consumed locally, while the forests were regarded chiefly as obstructions to settlement and cultivation. The man who cut down a tree was held to have conferred a service upon his fellows. . . .

Since then our knowledge and use of the resources of the present territory of the United States have increased a hundred-fold. Indeed, the growth of this Nation by leaps and bounds makes one of the most striking and important chapters in the history of the world. Its growth has been due to the rapid development, and alas that it should be said! to the rapid destruction, of our natural resources. Nature has supplied to us in the United States, and still supplies to us, more kinds of resources in a more lavish degree than has ever been the case at any other time or with any other people. Our position in the world has been attained by the extent and thoroughness of the control we have achieved over nature; but we are more, and not less, dependent upon what she furnishes than at any previous time of history since the days of primitive man. . . .

The wise use of all of our natural resources, which are our national resources as well, is the great material question of today. I have asked you to come together now because the enormous consumption of these resources, and the threat of imminent exhaustion of some of them, due to reckless and wasteful use, . . . calls for common effort, common action.

We want to take action that will prevent the advent of a woodless age, and defer as long as possible the advent of an ironless age. . . .

Natural resources . . . can be divided into two sharply distinguished classes accordingly as they are or are not capable of renewal. Mines if used must necessarily be exhausted. The minerals do not and can not renew themselves. Therefore in dealing with the coal, the oil, the gas, the iron, the metals generally, all that we can do is to try to see that they are wisely used. The exhaustion is certain to come in time. We can trust that it will be deferred long enough to enable the extraordinarily inventive genius of our people to devise means and methods for more or less adequately replacing what is lost; but the exhaustion is sure to come.

The second class of resources consists of those which can not only be used in such manner as to leave them undiminished for our children, but can actually be improved by wise use. The soil, the forests, the waterways come in this category. Every one knows that a really good farmer leaves his farm more valuable at the end of his life than it was when he first took hold of it. So with the waterways. So with the forests. In dealing with mineral resources, man is able to improve on nature only by putting the resources to a beneficial use which in the end exhausts them; but in dealing with the soil and its products man can improve on nature by compelling the resources to renew and even reconstruct themselves in such manner as to serve increasingly beneficial uses—while the living waters can be so controlled as to multiply their benefits. . . .

. . . .The time has come for a change [from unrestricted individualism]. As a people we have the right and the duty, second to none other but the right and duty of obeying the moral law, of requiring and doing justice, to protect ourselves and our children against the wasteful development of our natural resources, whether that waste is caused by the actual destruction of such resources or by making them impossible of development hereafter.

Finally, let us remember that the conservation of our natural resources, though the gravest problem of today, is yet but part of another and greater problem to which this Nation is not yet awake, but to which it will awake in time, and with which it must hereafter grapple if it is to live—the problem of national efficiency, the patriotic duty of insuring the safety and continuance of the Nation. [Applause.] When the People of the United States consciously undertake to raise themselves as citizens, and the Nation and the States in their several spheres, to the highest pitch of excellence in private, State, and national life, and to do this because it is the first of all the duties of true patriotism, then and not till then the future of this Nation, in quality and in time, will be assured. [Great applause]

5. George L. Knapp Opposes Conservation, 1910

For some years past, the reading public has been treated to fervid and extended eulogies of a policy which the eulogists call the "conservation of our natural resources." In behalf of this so-called "conservation," the finest press bureau in the world has labored with a zeal quite unhampered by any considerations of fact or logic; and has shown its understanding of practical psychology by appealing, not to popular reason, but to popular fears. We are told by this press bureau that our natural resources are being wasted in the most wanton and criminal style; wasted, apparently, for the sheer joy of wasting. We are told that our forests are being cut at a rate which will soon leave us a land without trees; and Nineveh, and Tyre, and any other place

From George L. Knapp, "The Other Side of Conservation," *North American Review* 191 (1910): pp. 465–481.

far enough away are cited to prove that a land without trees is foredoomed to be a land without civilization. We are told that our coal-mines would be exhausted within a century; that our iron ores are going to the blast-furnace at a rate which will send us back to the stone age within the lifetime of men who read the fearsome prophecy. In short, we are assured that every resource capable of exhaustion is being exhausted; and that the resource which cannot be exhausted is being monopolized. . . .

I propose to speak for those exiles in sin who hold that a large part of the present "conservation" movement is unadulterated humbug. That the modern Jeremiahs are as sincere as was the older one, I do not question. But I count their prophecies to be baseless vaporings, and their vaunted remedy worse than the fancied disease. I am one who can see no warrant of law, of justice, nor of necessity for that wholesale reversal of our traditional policy which the advocates of "conservation" demand. I am one who does not shiver for the future at the sight of a load of coal, nor view a steel-mill as the arch-robber of posterity. I am one who does not believe in a power trust, past, present or to come; and who, if he were a capitalist seeking to form such a trust, would ask nothing better than just the present conservation scheme to help him. I believe that a government bureau is the worst imaginable landlord; and that its essential nature is not changed by giving it a high-sounding name, and decking it with home-made haloes. I hold that the present forest policy ceases to be a nuisance only when it becomes a curse. . . .

The terrors from which "conservation" is to save us are phantoms. The evils which "conservation" brings us are very real. Mining discouraged, homesteading brought to a practical standstill, power development fined as criminal, and, worst of all, a Federal bureaucracy arrogantly meddling with every public question in a dozen great States—these are some of the things which result from the efforts of a few well-meaning zealots to install themselves as official prophets and saviors of the future, and from that exalted station to regulate the course of evolution.

It is no more a part of the Federal Government's business to enter upon the commercial production of lumber than to enter upon the commercial production of wheat, or breakfast bacon, or hand-saws. . . .

Our natural resources have been used, not wasted. Waste in one sense there has been, to be sure; in that a given resource has not always been put to its best use as we now see that use. But from Eden down, knowledge has been the costliest thing that man could covet; and the knowledge of how to make the earth best serve him seems well-nigh the most expensive of all. But I think we have made a fair start at the lesson; and considering how well we have already done for ourselves, the intrusion of a Government schoolmaster at this stage seems scarcely needed. The pine woods of Michigan have vanished to make the homes of Kansas; the coal and iron which we have failed—thank Heaven!—to "conserve" have carried meat and wheat to the hungry hives of men and gladdened life with an abundance which no previous age could know. We have turned forests into villages, mines into ships and sky-scrapers, scenery into work. Our success in doing the things already accomplished has been exactly proportioned to our freedom from governmental "guidance," and I know no reason to believe that a different formula will hold good in the tasks that lie before. If we can stop the governmental encouragement of destruction, conservation will take care of itself. . . . There is just one heritage which I am anxious to transmit to my children and to their children's children—the heritage of personal liberty, of free individual action, of "leave to live by no man's leave underneath the law." And I know of no way to secure that heritage save to sharply challenge and relentlessly fight every bureaucratic invasion of local and individual rights, no matter how friendly the mottoes on the invading banners.

6. Mrs. Marion Crocker Argues for the Conservation Imperative, 1912

Madam Chairman, and Mr. President and Members of the Convention: Conservation is a term so apt that it has been borrowed and made to fit almost all lines of public work, but Conservation as applied to that department bearing its name in the General Federation [of Women's Clubs] means conservation of natural resources only. . . . If we do not follow the most scientific approved methods, the most modern discoveries of how to conserve and propagate and renew wherever possible those resources which Nature in her providence has given to man for his use but not abuse, the time will come when the world will not be able to support life, and then we shall have no need of conservation of health, strength or vital force, because we must have the things to support life or else everything else is useless.

We will begin with the forests, because in our natural conservation we consider that the foundation of the fundamental principle of the conservation of natural resources. And what does the forest for us? What is the purpose of the forest? Why must we have them? Well, the forest makes soil in a way; that is, it makes humus matter, which is so large a portion of the soil that it may well be termed the soil. The forest is the only crop that grows that gives to the soil more than it takes from the soil. It also conserves the mineral in the soil that it takes Nature ages to produce by its slow processes of disintegration, and at the same time prevents the filling up of reservoirs, lakes and streams, and to that extent prevents the pollution of the waters. The forest is a great health resort, and why? Because it actually purifies the air. Its action is just the reverse of animals. It gives the air what we need and takes from it that which is detrimental to our health.

We must look a little into plant life and see what nature does that we may fully appreciate that point. I cannot take time tonight because of the late hour to go into the whole life of the tree, but I will say that its principal constituent is carbon, and it takes from the air the carbonic acid gas which is so detrimental to human beings and to all animals. It has a way of converting it into its own life blood in combination with the sap taken up from the roots, by the marvelous process in the leaves, by this little understood substance called chlorophyll, that has the power of converting this poisonous substance for us into the life of the tree, and then taking so much from it and giving it to the soil. That is a most important factor which is so often overlooked.

Then the forest is valuable as a wind shield for crops. And for the wood supply. Wood is demanded in all the industries or the arts, for almost all things we use.

From Mrs. Marion Crocker, *Proceedings of the Fourth Conservation Congress.* Indianapolis: National Conservation Congress, 1912, pp. 258–262.

These are the fundamental things the forest does for us. Are we not working for conservation of strength and health and human life when we are working for the forest?

While the General Federation takes up many phases of water Conservation, perhaps I may just say that we have irrigation, drainage, waterways, the deep canals for transportation, we have water power, which is the coming thing. This is something to be conserved, and which conserves our coal, which conserves the purity of our atmosphere by not having all the gases turned into it by the burning of the coal.

And then the very last and most vital is the pure continuous supply of water, which all human beings and which all animals demand. It is, next to the air we breathe, the most important factor in animal existence. . . .

The soil is indirectly our staff of life. From it does not come our bread? Must not this seed fall into the ground, spring from the earth and be protected until it reaches maturity, and we have food? Many other instances might I bring forward had I time.

Then the animal kingdom is much more nearly related to human existence than we would think at the outset; but when we come to look more deeply into it we find this close relationship.

I so often come up against the saying, "Oh, I am so much interested in human life. I have no time, no thought, no desire to give to the animal kingdom. It is all right enough for you sentimentalists, but I am not interested." Yes, but even from a selfish point of view, if we do not care at all for any suffering, or anything which may come to the animal kingdom beside ourselves, it is of economic value to us.

I will choose but one example of the animal kingdom, and that is the birds, because it is said that all vegetation from the earth would cease if the birds existed no longer. . . .

This very conservation of bird life is one of the things that is the great new problem of conservation of natural resources, and one in which you women take a hand and have the real control. I know you have heard so much about that I am not going to give you statistics as to what the birds do for agriculture. I am going to ask you a personal favor: that this fall when you choose your fall millinery, will you not think of your Chairman of your Conservation Department of the General Federation, and I beg you choose some other decoration for your hats. This is not sentiment. It is pure economics. You have no idea what you do when you wear these feathers, until you think really deeply into it. . . .

Now, I want to say just a few words about the way to go to work to do some of these things. I will not go into the larger fields of forestry, or even into shade trees, except to emphasize the fact that while the shade tree is a very important one, and especially in the cities, we must never lose sight of the larger fact that after all it is not forestry, it does not stand for that, and that our arbor day, where we plant the one tree, should extend far beyond that. . . . There is a great work to be done with the children, in making the school garden, and then the home garden; to teach the children to know what the soil is made of and how it should be treated, to make them love the growing flower and to make them respect the property of others. There we are laying the foundation of things for the next generation. . . .

I am going to tell you a little story of how I became interested in these things. It was before I was out of school myself, although pretty nearly so. It was when the welfare work began of taking the children out in the country from the slums in the north end. I was personally acquainted with one of the teachers, who was among the first to take the children out in the fresh air to breathe and see the grass and flowers and trees that they had never seen before. One little boy, after he had looked around in amazement—it was in the fall of the year—saw the bright red apples on the trees, and he looked up and said, "Apples on trees, by God!" ...

I will say to you this one message, while you are working for this thing of prime importance, the conservation of life, for which this Congress has stood at this fall meeting, do not forget that the conservation of life itself must be built on the solid foundation of conservation of natural resources, or it will be a house built upon the sands that will be washed away. It will not be lasting. I thank you. (Great applause.)

7. Robert Marshall Advocates the People's Forests, 1933

Under their present management the American forests are drifting into constantly expanding ruin. Year by year the area of devastated land keeps mounting, until today it has reached the appalling total of 83 million acres, to which nearly a million acres are being added annually. Even more serious than the devastation is the grave deterioration which has occurred on at least 200 million additional acres. Between devastation and deterioration the American forests and all the social values which they represent are indeed in a tragic condition.

The major cause of this sorry plight is the mismanagement of privately owned forests. Fire damage, erosion, devastation, and destruction of scenic values are many times more severe on private than on public forests. This hopeless insufficiency of private ownership has obtained even though the government has carried five sixths of the burden of fire protection. When this miserable failure is contrasted with the splendid record of public forest management the moral seems inescapable. Public ownership is the only basis on which we can hope to protect the incalculable values of the forests for wood resources, for soil and water conservation, and for recreation. It is urged, therefore, that the public should acquire at least 562 million acres out of the 670 million acres of potential forest land.

Regardless of whether it might be desirable, it is impossible under our existing form of government to confiscate the private forests into public ownership. We cannot afford to delay their nationalization until the form of government changes, because if we do the forests will be so deteriorated as to be scarcely worth owning. Consequently, it will be necessary to acquire them by purchase. This purchase program cannot be consummated all at once. Pending the change from private to public ownership it will be necessary to regulate the private use of forests so that they are not too severely gutted by the time the government takes over their management. In spite of this genuine value of public regulation, it will only be an incidental to the main solution of our forest problem. This main solution, as has been stated, is public ownership. But public ownership is not a panacea. It must be backed by careful land planning, protection of the rights of those who labor on the forests, reorganization of rural government and redistribution of rural population, safeguarding of recreational values from commercial exploitation, and a great increase in the knowledge of the forest through an ambitious program of research. . . .

At present it is generally recognized that the government must provide relief for a large share of the 12 million unemployed. It seems to be a serious problem to find enough useful work for these people to do. If the government were to take over the majority of forest lands there would be enough work to keep several million people busy for many years. . . .

It is also important to consider that every year which we delay spending money to rehabilitate our forests will mean a greatly increased ultimate cost. The deterioration of the forest is proceeding at a geometric ratio, so the sooner we put an end to it, the less we shall have to pay. Since the cost will be higher later, the only sensible way is to protect sooner, regardless of the amount which past mismanagement now demands that we must spend. . . .

In order to carry out the program of public ownership and administration which has been recommended, certain specific legislation will be needed. The following is of major importance:

1. Congress and the state legislatures should first grant authority and the appropriate funds for the purchase of the 240 million acres which have been recommended.
2. Congress and the state legislatures should make the necessary appropriations for the adequate administration of the 562 million acres of proposed public forests.
3. Congress should add to the National Forest system the 22 million acres of public domain forest lands. The government's mismanagement of these unadministered acres is the only blot on its otherwise excellent record of forest protection.
4. Laws should be passed by the federal government and the states which would automatically make tax-delinquent lands a part of the state forests if the states desire to administer them and otherwise a part of the federal forests.
5. Congress should increase the appropriations for federal research by about 1½ million dollars.
6. For those forest lands which will remain in private ownership, the federal government should pass laws giving itself the right to control fire and stop logging and grazing practice which leads to devastation.

There are two possibilities which stare us in the face with exceptional clarity. We can continue our present policy of being more solicitous of the rights of private timber owners than of the welfare of the public. There can only be one result of such a policy, the hopeless deterioration of our vitally needed forests. On the other hand, we can spend the large sums of money necessary to acquire and administer the public forests for the benefit of all the citizens. This policy will, in the long run, save us vast amounts of money, and it will preserve the unassessable value of the forest for timber production, for water and soil conservation, and for recreation. The time has come when we must discard the unsocial view that our woods are the lumbermen's and substitute the broader ideal that every acre of woodland in the country is rightly a part of the people's forests.

8. Hugh Bennett Presses for Soil Conservation, 1947

Productive land is unlike any other natural resource. It is characterized by the element of life placed by Nature in the thin mantle of fruitful soil occurring over a limited portion of the earth's surface. It is this life-producing quality that makes some lands productive, and it is the absence of this quality that makes some barren.

Productive land is further differentiated from other natural resources in that it must be maintained and used simultaneously; that is, it must be kept intact while in use. All other natural resources, with very few exceptions, must be taken from the earth—separated from it—in order to be used by man. The exceptions are certain forms of wildlife and those natural areas which, because of their aesthetic values, are kept in their original state.

Productive land is much more limited than commonly has been supposed. It occurs only on the surface of the earth, and only on part of this surface. It is not permanent. Once the fertile topsoil is washed or blown away, it cannot be restored or replaced in any practical way for generations. And what is left—subsoil—usually is far less productive, or sterile, and less stable. There are no undiscovered reserves of productive land of any substantial area.

We cannot dig deeper into the earth and find new productive soil. We cannot pump it from wells, plant it with seeds, or dig it from mines. We must keep what we have or do without. Assorted residues of sand and gravel left stranded along streamways are of small value.

Productive land is the only natural resource without which we cannot live. We are completely dependent on it for the food we eat, except fish. We also depend on it for a very large share of our clothing and shelter. We cannot get enough to feed ourselves or provide our clothing from the oceans. On any large scale, hydroponics would be utterly impractical. We might conceivably turn sometime to some form of synthetic food, as pills, plus a roughage, but this appears to be a fantastic extreme, still far away, and likely, if it ever comes, it will be decidedly unpopular.

There is no doubt about the need for protecting productive land. Year after year, for generations, man has been steadily engaged in ruining millions and millions of acres of this basic resource. Every hard rain falling on unprotected, cultivated, or overgrazed sloping land washes additional tons of soil downslope, downstream, into the rivers, reservoirs, and oceans. There is no practical way of bringing this back. And every hard wind, blowing across bare, dry soil, whether sloping or level, adds to the damage. Wind lifts the fine soil particles into the air and often develops huge dust storms that destructively scatter the substance of the land. What is left behind,

---

Excerpts from H. H. Bennett, "Development of Natural Resource: The Coming Technological Revolution on the Land," *Science,* 105 (January–June 1947), pp. 1–3. Copyright 1947 by the American Association for the Advancement of Science.

frequently, is infertile, shifting sand that smothers out vegetation on neighboring good land. . . .

In the United States, land technology is spreading through a new democratic device known as the soil conservation district. The district is a subdivision of State government, brought into being by a process of referendum among the land-owners and operators involved. In practical application it is a legal organization of landowners and operators within a designated area for the purpose of developing and carrying forward a mutually desirable program of soil and water conserva-tion. Its principal advantages are in the encouragement of local initiative and in the greater strength that comes with organized numbers—farmers and ranchers working together.

In soil conservation districts the farmers themselves decide what they want to do to improve their land and water resources and how they want to go about doing it. Then they proceed along this course, working together, and utilizing all the available facilities and services they can command. In almost every instance, districts are ob-taining technical guidance from the Soil Conservation Service.

On August 15 there were more than 1,670 districts in the United States, volun-tarily voted into existence by the farmers themselves. These districts encompassed more than 900,000,000 acres and approximately 4,000,000 farms. Farmers are con-tinuing to organize districts at the rate of approximately 25 per month. . . .

In the long run, the overwhelming urge of mankind for survival will dictate that every remaining productive acre be handled in such a way that it will continue to pro-duce indefinitely. In the meantime, other factors are combining to speed up the appli-cation of technology to the land. From the standpoint of the individual and the nation alike, the development and application of soil and water conservation technology (the tool of soil conservation science) is good business. It results in greater yields and greater returns per acre for the capital and labor expended. Moreover, it maintains or improves the basic strength and self-sufficiency of individual and nation. It probably can prevent at least half the potential famines of the future.

9. Gifford Pinchot Recalls the Origins of the Conservation Movement, 1947

It was my great good luck that I had more to do with the work of more bureaus than any other man in Washington. This was partly because the Forest Service was deal-ing not only with trees but with public lands, mining, agriculture, irrigation, stream flow, soil erosion, fish, game, animal industry, and a host of other matters with which other bureaus also were concerned. The main reason, however, was that much of T.R.'s [Theodore Roosevelt's] business with the natural resources bureaus was con-ducted through me.

It was therefore the most natural thing in the world that the relations of forests, waters, lands, and minerals, each to each, should be brought strongly to my mind.

From *Breaking New Ground,* by Gifford Pinchot (Washington, D.C.: Island Press, 1947), pp. 322–323, 326. Reprinted by permission of Island Press.

But for a long time my mind stopped there. Then at last I woke up. And this is how it happened:

In the gathering gloom of an expiring day, in the moody month of February, some forty years ago, a solitary horseman might have been observed pursuing his silent way above a precipitous gorge in the vicinity of the capital city of America. Or so an early Victorian three-volume novelist might have expressed it.

In plain words, a man by the name of Pinchot was riding a horse by the name of Jim on the Ridge Road in Rock Creek Park near Washington. And while he rode, he thought. He was a forester, and he was taking his problems with him, on that winter's day of 1907, when he meant to leave them behind.

The forest and its relation to streams and inland navigation, to water power and flood control; to the soil and its erosion; to coal and oil and other minerals; to fish and game; and many another possible use or waste of natural resources—these questions would not let him be. What had all these to do with Forestry? And what had Forestry to do with them?

Here were not isolated and separate problems. My work had brought me into touch with all of them. But what was the basic link between them?

Suddenly the idea flashed through my head that there was a unity in this complication—that the relation of one resource to another was not the end of the story. Here were no longer a lot of different, independent, and often antagonistic questions, each on its own separate little island, as we had been in the habit of thinking. In place of them, here was one single question with many parts. Seen in this new light, all these separate questions fitted into and made up the one great central problem of the use of the earth for the good of man.

To me it was a good deal like coming out of a dark tunnel. I had been seeing one spot of light ahead. Here, all of a sudden, was a whole landscape. Or it was like lifting the curtain on a great new stage.

There was too much of it for me to take it all in at once. As always, my mind worked slowly. From the first I thought I had stumbled on something really worth while, but that day in Rock Creek Park I was far from grasping the full reach and swing of the new idea.

It took time for me to appreciate that here were the makings of a new policy, not merely nationwide but world-wide in its scope—fundamentally important because it involved not only the welfare but the very existence of men on the earth. I did see, however, that something ought to be done about it. . . .

The first man I carried it to was Overton Price. Within a few days I told him the story as we rode our horses together on the Virginia side of the Potomac, and asked what he thought of it. He saw it as I did. I was glad of that, for my reliance on his judgment was very great.

After Overton, I discussed my brain child not only with my Father and Mother, whose interest in my work never flagged, but with geologist and philosopher WJ McGee, [U.S. Geological Survey Chief, Frederick] Newell, . . . and others. It was McGee who grasped it best. He sensed its full implication even more quickly than I had done, and saw its future more clearly.

McGee became the scientific brains of the new movement. With his wide general knowledge and highly original mind we developed, as I never could have done alone, the breadth and depth of meaning which lay in the new idea. McGee had constructive imagination.

It was McGee, for example, who defined the new policy as the use of the natural resources for the greatest good of the greatest number for the longest time. It was McGee who made me see, at long last and after much argument, that monopoly of natural resources was only less dangerous to the public welfare than their actual destruction.

Very soon after my own mind was clear enough to state my proposition with confidence, I took it to T.R. And T.R., as I expected, understood, accepted, and adopted it without the smallest hesitation. It was directly in line with everything he had been thinking and doing. It became the heart of his Administration.

Launching the Conservation movement was the most significant achievement of the T.R. Administration, as he himself believed. It seems altogether probable that it will also be the achievement for which he will be longest and most gratefully remembered.

Having just been born, the new arrival was still without a name. There had to be a name to call it by before we could even attempt to make it known, much less give it a permanent place in the public mind. What should we call it?

Both Overton and I knew that large organized areas of Government forest lands in British India were named Conservancies, and the foresters in charge of them Conservators. After many other suggestions and long discussions, either Price or I (I'm not sure which and it doesn't matter) proposed that we apply a new meaning to a word already in the dictionary, and christen the new policy Conservation.

During one of our rides I put that name up to T.R., and he approved it instantly. So the child was named, and that bridge was behind us.

Today, when it would be hard to find an intelligent man in the United States who hasn't at least some conception of what Conservation means, it seems incredible that the very word, in the sense in which we use it now, was unknown less than forty years ago.

❦ E S S A Y S

The essays in this chapter focus on the politics and institutions that provided both cohesion and tension in the conservation movement during the early to mid-twentieth century and the transition to the post–World War II environmental movement. In the first essay, Samuel Hays, one of the foremost historians of the conservation movement, discusses the origins of conservation among scientists and engineers who promoted efficiency in resource use and shows how the early conservation movement's goals and policies differed from those of the later environmental movement. The second essay, by the late journalist Marc Reisner, depicts conservation as a movement that attempted to promote the democratic distribution of resources, particularly water, in the arid West. Finally, Carolyn Merchant, an environmental historian at the University of California, Berkeley, argues in the third selection that conservation as a popular movement owed much of its inspiration and major accomplishments to women and shows why they ultimately broke ranks with Theodore Roosevelt and Gifford Pinchot over conflicts between the goals of conservation and those of preservation.

From Conservation to Environment

SAMUEL P. HAYS

Conservation neither arose from a broad popular outcry, nor centered its fire primarily upon the private corporation. Moreover, corporations often supported conservation policies, while the "people" just as frequently opposed them. In fact, it becomes clear that one must discard completely the struggle against corporations as the setting in which to understand conservation history, and permit an entirely new frame of reference to arise from the evidence itself.

Conservation, above all, was a scientific movement, and its role in history arises from the implications of science and technology in modern society. Conservation leaders sprang from such fields as hydrology, forestry, agrostology, geology, and anthropology. Vigorously active in professional circles in the national capital, these leaders brought the ideals and practices of their crafts into federal resource policy. Loyalty to these professional ideals, not close association with the grass-roots public, set the tone of the Theodore Roosevelt conservation movement. Its essence was rational planning to promote efficient development and use of all natural resources. The idea of efficiency drew these federal scientists from one resource task to another, from specific programs to comprehensive concepts. It molded the policies which they proposed, their administrative techniques, and their relations with Congress and the public. It is from the vantage point of applied science, rather than of democratic protest, that one must understand the historic role of the conservation movement.

The new realms of science and technology, appearing to open up unlimited opportunities for human achievement, filled conservation leaders with intense optimism. They emphasized expansion, not retrenchment; possibilities, not limitations. True, they expressed some fear that diminishing resources would create critical shortages in the future. But they were not Malthusian prophets of despair and gloom. The popular view that in a fit of pessimism they withdrew vast areas of the public lands from present use for future development does not stand examination. In fact, they bitterly opposed those who sought to withdraw resources from commercial development. They displayed that deep sense of hope which pervaded all those at the turn of the century for whom science and technology were revealing visions of an abundant future.

The political implications of conservation, it is particularly important to observe, grew out of the political implications of applied science rather than from conflict over the distribution of wealth. Who should decide the course of resource development? Who should determine the goals and methods of federal resource programs? The correct answer to these questions lay at the heart of the conservation idea. Since resource matters were basically technical in nature, conservationists

Excerpt from *Conservation and the Gospel of Efficiency: The Progressive Conservation Movement, 1800–1920* by Samuel P. Hays, Cambridge, Mass.: Harvard University Press, Copyright 1959 by the President and Fellows of Harvard College. Courtesy of Harvard University. And excerpts from Samuel P. Hays, "From Conservation to Environment: Environmental Politics in the United States Since World War II," in *Explorations in Environmental History* (University of Pittsburgh Press, 1998). Originally appeared in *Environmental Review* 6, no. 2 (Fall 1982), pp. 14–29.

argued, technicians, rather than legislators, should deal with them. Foresters should determine the desirable annual timber cut; hydraulic engineers should establish the feasible extent of multiple-purpose river development and the specific location of reservoirs; agronomists should decide which forage areas could remain open for grazing without undue damage to water supplies. Conflicts between competing resource users, especially, should not be dealt with through the normal processes of politics. Pressure group action, logrolling in Congress, or partisan debate could not guarantee rational and scientific decisions. Amid such jockeying for advantage with the resulting compromise, concern for efficiency would disappear. Conservationists envisaged, even though they did not realize their aims, a political system guided by the ideal of efficiency and dominated by the technicians who could best determine how to achieve it. . . .

The Conservation and Environmental Impulses

Prior to World War II, . . . the dominant theme in conservation emphasized physical resources, their more efficient use and development. The range of emphasis evolved from water and forests in the late 19th and early 20th centuries, to grass and soils and game in the 1930's. In all these fields of endeavor there was a common concern for the loss of physical productivity represented by waste. The threat to the future which that "misuse" implied could be corrected through "sound" or efficient management. Hence in each field there arose a management system which emphasized a balancing of immediate in favor of more long-run production, the coordination of factors of production under central management schemes for the greatest efficiency. All this is a chapter in the history of production rather than of consumption, and of the way in which managers organized production rather than the way in which consumers evolved ideas and action amid the general public.

. . . After World War I, the concern about soil erosion, from both rain and wind . . . lay in warnings about the loss of agricultural productivity. What had taken years to build up over geologic time now was threatened with destruction by short-term practices. The soil conservation program inaugurated in 1933 gave rise to a full-scale attack on erosion problems which was carried out amid almost inspired religious fervor. In the Taylor Grazing Act of 1934 the nation's grazing lands in the West were singled out as a special case of deteriorating productivity; it set in motion a long-term drive to reduce stocking levels and thereby permit recovery of the range. Also during the 1930's, scientific game management came into its own with the Pittman-Robertson Act of 1936 which provided funds. This involved concepts much akin to those in forestry, in which production and consumption of game would be balanced in such a fashion so as not to outrun food resources and hence sustain a continuous yield. . . .

State departments of "natural resources" emerged, such as in Michigan, Wisconsin and Minnesota, and some university departments of forestry became departments of natural resources—all this as the new emphasis on soils and game were added to the older ones on forests and waters. By the time of World War II a complex of professionals had come into being, with a strong focus on management as their common task, on the organization of applied knowledge about physical resources so as to sustain output for given investments of input under centralized management direction. This entailed a common conception of "conservation" and a common focus on "renewable resources," often within the rubric of advocating "wise use" under the direction of professional experts. . . . Those concerned with national parks and the later wilderness activities often used the term "conservation" to describe what they were about. In the Sierra Club the "conservation committees" took up the organization's political action in contrast with its outings. And those who formed the National Parks Association and later the Wilderness Society could readily think of themselves as conservationists, struggling to define the term quite differently than did those in the realm of efficient management. . . . [Yet] the theme of management efficiency in physical resource development dominated the scene prior to World War II and natural environment programs continued to play a subordinate role.

After the War a massive turnabout of historical forces took place. The complex of specialized fields of efficient management of physical resources increasingly came under attack amid a new "environmental" thrust. It contained varied components. One was the further elaboration of the outdoor recreation and natural environment movements of pre-War, as reflected in the Wilderness Act of 1964, the Wild and Scenic Rivers Act of 1968, and the National Trails Act of the same year, and further legislation and administrative action on through the 1970's. But there were other strands even less rooted in the past. The most extensive was the concern for environmental pollution, or "environmental protection" as it came to be called in technical and managerial circles. While smoldering in varied and diverse ways in this or that setting from many years before, this concern burst forth to national prominence in the mid-1960's and especially in air and water pollution. And there was the decentralist thrust, the search for technologies of smaller and more human scale which complement rather than dwarf the more immediate human setting. One can find decentralist ideologies and even affirmations of smaller-scale technologies in earlier years, such as that inspired by Ralph Borsodi not long before World War II. But the intensity and direction of the drive of the 1970's was of a vastly different order. The search for a "sense of place," for a context that is more manageable intellectually and emotionally amid the escalating pace of size and scale had not made its mark in earlier years as it did in the 1970's to shape broad patterns of human thought and action.

One of the most striking differences between these post-War environmental activities, in contrast with the earlier conservation affairs, was their social roots. Earlier one can find little in the way of broad popular support for the substantive objectives of conservation, little "movement" organization, and scanty evidence of broadly shared conservation values. The drive came from the top down, from technical and managerial leaders. In the 1930's one can detect a more extensive social base for soil conservation, and especially for new game management programs. But, in sharp contrast, the Environmental Era displayed demands from the grassroots, demands that are well charted by the innumerable citizen organizations and studies of public attitudes. One of the major themes of these later years, in fact, was the tension that evolved between the environmental public and the environmental managers, as impulses arising from the public clashed with impulses arising from management. This was not a new stage of public activity per se, but of new values as well. The widespread expression of social values in environmental action marks off the environmental era from the conservation years.

It is useful to think about this as the interaction between two sets of historical forces, one older that was associated with large-scale management and technology, and the other newer that reflected new types of public values and demands. . . . Conflicts between older "conservation" and newer "environment" help to identify the nature of the change.

One set of episodes in this tension concerned the rejection of multiple-purpose river structures in favor of free flowing rivers; here was a direct case of irreconcilable objectives, one stemming from the conservation era, and another inherent in the new environmental era. There were cases galore. But perhaps the most dramatic one, which pinpoints the watershed between the old and the new, involved Hell's Canyon on the Snake River in Idaho. For many years that dispute had taken the old and honorable shape of public versus private power. Should there be one high dam, constructed with federal funds by the Bureau of Reclamation, or three lower dams to be built by the Idaho Power Company? These were the issues of the 1930's, the Truman years and the Eisenhower administrations. But when the Supreme Court reviewed a ruling of the Federal Power Commission on the issue in 1968, it pointed out in a decision written by Justice [William O.] Douglas that another option had not been considered—no dam at all. Perhaps the river was more valuable as an undeveloped, free flowing stream. The decision was unexpected both to the immediate parties to the dispute, and also to "conservationists" in Idaho and the Pacific Northwest. In fact, those conservationists had to be persuaded to become environmentalists. But turn about they did. The decision seemed to focus a perspective which had long lain dormant, implicit in the circumstances but not yet articulated, and reflected a rather profound transformation in values which had already taken place.

There were other realms of difference between the old and the new. There was, for example, the changing public conception of the role and meaning of forests. The U.S. Forest Service, and the entire community of professional foresters, continued to elaborate the details of scientific management of wood production; it took the form of increasing input for higher yields, and came to emphasize especially even-aged management. But an increasing number of Americans thought of forests as environments for home, work and play, as an environmental rather than as a commodity resource, and hence to be protected from incompatible crop-oriented strategies. Many of them bought woodlands for their environmental rather than their wood production potential. But the forestry profession did not seem to be able to accept the new values. The Forest Service was never able to "get on top" of the wilderness movement to incorporate it in "leading edge" fashion into its own strategies. . . . The diverging trends became sharper with the steadily accumulating environmental interest in amenity goals in harvesting strategies and the expanding ecological emphases on more varied plant and animal life within the forest.

There were also divergent tendencies arising from the soil conservation arena. In the early 1950's, the opposition of farmers to the high-dam strategies of the U.S. Army Corps of Engineers led to a new program under the jurisdiction of the Soil Conservation Service, known as PL 566, which emphasized the construction of smaller headwater dams to "hold the water where it falls." This put the SCS in the business of rural land and water development, and it quickly took up the challenge of planning a host of such "multiple-use" projects which combined small flood control reservoirs with flat-water recreation and channelization with wetland drainage. By the time this program came into operation, however, in the 1960's, a considerable interest had arisen in the natural habitats of headwater streams, for example for trout fishing, and wetlands for both fish and wildlife. A head-on collision on this score turned an agency which had long been thought of as riding the lead wave of conservation affairs into one which appeared to environmentalists to be no better than the Corps—development minded and at serious odds with newer natural environment objectives.

There was one notable exception to these almost irreconcilable tensions between the old and the new in which a far smoother transition occurred—the realm of wildlife. In this case the old emphasis on game was faced with a new one on nature observation or what came to be called a "non-game" or "appreciative" use of wildlife. Between these two impulses there were many potential arenas for deep controversy. But there was also common ground in their joint interest in wildlife habitat. The same forest which served as a place for hunting also served as a place for nature observation. In fact, as these different users began to be identified and counted it was found that even on lands acquired exclusively for game management the great majority of users were non-game observers. As a result of this shared interest in wildlife habitat it was relatively easy for many "game managers" to shift in their self-conceptions to become "wildlife managers." Many a state agency changed its name from "game" to "wildlife" and an earlier document, "American Game Policy, 1930," which guided the profession for many years, became "The North American Wildlife Policy, 1973."

If we examine the values and ideas, then, the activities and programs, the directions of impulses in the political arena, we can observe a marked transition from the pre–World War II conservation themes of efficient management of physical resources, to the post–World War environmental themes of environmental amenities, environmental protection, and human scale technology. Something new was happening in American society, arising out of the social changes and transformation in human values in the post-War years. These were associated more with the advanced consumer society of those years than with the industrial manufacturing society of the late 19th and the first half of the 20th centuries. . . .

The Evolution of Environmental Action

Emerging environmental values did not make themselves felt all in the same way or at the same time. Within the context of our concern here for patterns of historical change, therefore, it might be well to secure some sense of stages of development within the post–World War II years. The most prevalent notion is to identify Earth Day in 1970 as the dividing line. There are other candidate events, such as the publication of Rachel Carson's *Silent Spring* in 1962, and the Santa Barbara oil blowout in 1969. But in any event definition of change in these matters seems to be inadequate. Earth Day was as much a result as a cause. It came after a decade or more of underlying evolution in attitudes and action without which it would not have been possible. Many environmental organizations, established earlier, experienced considerable growth in membership during the 1960's, reflecting an expanding concern. . . .

The legislative results were manifold. Air pollution was the subject of new laws in 1967 and 1970; water pollution in 1965, 1970 and 1972. The evolving concern about pesticides led to revision of the existing law in the Pesticides Act of 1972. The growing public interest in natural environment values in the coastal zone, and threats to them by dredging and filling, industrial siting and offshore oil development first made its mark on Congress in 1965 and over the next few years shaped the course of legislation which finally emerged in the Coastal Zone Management Act of 1972. Earth Day in the spring of 1970 lay in the middle of this phase of historical development, both a result of the previous half-decade of activity and concern and a new influence to accelerate action. The outline of these various phases of environmental activity, however, can be observed only by evidence and actions far beyond the events of Earth Day. Such more broad-based evidence identifies the years 1965 to 1972 as a well-defined phase of historical development in terms of issues, emphasizing the reaction against the adverse effects of industrial growth as distinct from the earlier emergence of natural environment issues. . . .

Environmental impulses [thus] served as a major influence in shaping the newer, more "modern," economy. They brought to the fore new demand factors which in turn generated new types of production to fill them; they placed increasing pressure on greater technological efficiency in production to reduce harmful residuals and resource waste. In many aspects of the economy one can distinguish between older and newer forms of demand and supply, institutions and modes of economic analysis. The transition represents a shift from the older manufacturing to the newer advanced consumer economy. In this transition environmental influences were an integral part of the emerging economy that was struggling for a larger role in America amid more established economic institutions.

Conservation as Reclamation

MARC REISNER

One hundred and sixty acres. If anything unifies the story of the American West— its past and its present, its successes and its dreadful mistakes—it is this mythical allotment of land. Its origins are found in the original Homestead Act of 1862, which settled on such an amount—a half-mile square, more often referred to as a quarter section—as the ideal acreage for a Jeffersonian utopia of small farmers. The idea was to carve millions of quarter sections out of the public domain, sell them cheaply to restless Americans and arriving immigrants, and, by letting them try to scratch a living out of them, develop the nation's resources and build up its character.

In the West, the Homestead Act had several later incarnations. The Desert Lands Act, the Timber Culture Act, and the Timber and Stone Act were the principal ones. Neither Congress nor the General Land Office, which was responsible for administering the acts, could ever comprehend that the relative success of the land program east of the Mississippi River had less to do with the perseverance of the settlers or the wisdom of the legislation than with the forgiving nature of the climate. In the East, virtually every acre received enough rainfall, except during years of extraordinary

Excerpts from Marc P. Reisner, *Cadillac Desert: The American West and Its Disappearing Water.* Revised and updated by Marc P. Reisner. Copyright © 1986, 1993 by Marc P. Reisner. Used by permission of Viking Penguin, a division of Penguin Group (USA) Inc.

drought, to grow most anything that didn't mind the soil and the temperature. (Unlike much of the West, which suffers through months of habitual drought, the East gets precipitation year-round; in the spring and early summer, when crops need water most, much of the East is exceptionally wet.) Since the growing season, except in the extreme north, was at least five months long, even an ignorant or lazy farmer could raise *some* kind of crop.

In the West, even if you believed that the rainfall was magically increasing, you still had to contend with high altitudes (the western plains, the Snake River Valley, and most of the irrigable lands in the Great Basin would float over the tops of all but the highest Appalachian Mountains) and, as a result, chronic frost danger even in May and September. Then there were the relentless winds, hailstones bigger than oranges, tornadoes, and breathtaking thunderstorms. There were sandy lands that would not retain moisture and poorly drained lands that retained too much; there were alkaline lands that poisoned crops.

The General Land Office bureaucrats sat in Washington pretending that such conditions did not exist. Their job, as they perceived it, was to fill little squares with people. They extended no credit, provided no water, offered no services. And the permutations of the Homestead Act [1862] that found their way into the western versions of the law sometimes *added* to the farmers' burdens. Under the Timber Culture Act [1873], for example, you had to plant one-quarter of your quarter section with trees, a stipulation inserted because it was thought that trees increased the rainfall. In West Texas, where, meteorologically speaking, all that is predictable is the wind, you would have to spend most of your time replanting your fallen-down trees. Under the Desert Lands Act, which applied to land so arid even the government realized that farming was hopeless without irrigation, you had to demonstrate "proof of irrigation" before you could own the land. Unless you owned reasonably flat land immediately adjacent to a relatively constant stream which did not, as most western rivers do for much of their length, flow in a canyon, complying with the Desert Lands Act [1877] was almost out of the question. A mutual irrigation effort by the inhabitants of a valley was, perhaps, a possibility. That was what the Mormons had done, but they were a close-knit society linked by a common faith and a history of persecution.

The members of Congress who wrote the legislation, the land office agents who doled out land, and the newspaper editors who celebrated the settlers' heroism had, in a great many cases, never laid eyes on the land or the region that enclosed it. They were unaware that in Utah, Wyoming, and Montana—to pick three of the colder and drier states—there was not a single quarter section on which a farmer could subsist, even with luck, without irrigation, because an unirrigated quarter section was enough land for about five cows. The Indians accepted things as they were; that is why they were mostly nomadic, wandering toward greener grass and fuller herds and flowing water. If whites were going to insist on living there—fixed, settled, mortgaged, fenced—the best they could do with the land was graze it. But in those three states, an economical grazing unit was, say, twenty-five hundred to five thousand acres, depending on the circumstances. To amass that much land you had to cheat—on a magnificent scale. If you didn't, you had to overgraze the land and ruin it, and many millions of acres were damaged or ruined in exactly this way. Many settlers were tasting property ownership for the first time in their lives, and all they had in common was greed.

Speculation. Water monopoly. Land monopoly. Erosion. Corruption. Catastrophe. By 1876, after several trips across the plains and through the Rocky Mountain states, [explorer] John Wesley Powell was pretty well convinced that those would be the fruits of a western land policy based on wishful thinking, willfulness, and lousy science. And by then everything he predicted was happening, especially land monopoly, water monopoly, graft, and fraud.

Homesteads fronting on streams went like oranges aboard a scurvy-ridden ship. The doctrine of riparian rights, which had been unthinkingly imported from the East, made it possible to monopolize the water in a stream if you owned the land alongside it. But if the stream was anything larger than a creek, only the person who owned land upstream, where it was still small, could manage to build a dam or barrage to guarantee a summer flow; then he could divert all he wanted, leaving his downstream neighbors with a bed of dry rocks. Riparian doctrine alone, therefore, made it possible for a tiny handful of landowners to monopolize the few manageable rivers of the West. When their neighbors saw their predicament and sold out, they could monopolize the best land, too.

As for the [1877] Desert Land[s] Act and the [1878] Timber and Stone Act, they could not have promoted land monopoly and corruption more efficiently if they had been expressly designed for that purpose. A typical irrigation scene under the Desert Land Act went as follows: A beneficiary hauled a hogshead of water and a witness to his barren land, dumped the water on the land, paid the witness $20, and brought him to the land office, where the witness swore he had seen the land irrigated. Then, with borrowed identification and different names, another land application was filed, and the scene was repeated. If you could pull it off six or seven times, you had yourself a ranch. Foreign sailors arriving in San Francisco were offered a few dollars, a jug of whiskey, and an evening in a whorehouse in exchange for filing a land claim under the Timber and Stone Act. Before shipping out, the sailors abdicated title; there were no restrictions on transfer of ownership. Whole redwood forests were acquired in such a manner.

Then there was the Swamplands Act [1850], or Swamp and Overflow Act—a Desert Lands Act of the bulrushes. If there was federal land that overflowed enough so that you could traverse it at times in a flat-bottomed boat, and you promised to reclaim it (which is to say, dike and drain it), it was yours. Henry Miller, a mythical figure in the history of California land fraud, acquired a large part of his 1,090,000-acre empire under this Act. According to legend, he bought himself a boat, hired some witnesses, put the boat and witnesses in a wagon, hitched some horses to it, and hauled the boat and witnesses over county-size tracts near the San Joaquin River where it rains, on the average, about eight or nine inches a year. The land became his. The sanitized version of the story, the one told by Miller's descendants, has him benefiting more from luck than from ruse. During the winter of 1861 and 1862, most of California got three times its normal precipitation, and the usually semiarid Central Valley became a shallow sea the size of Lake Ontario. But the only difference in this version is that Miller didn't need a wagon for his boat; he still had no business acquiring hundreds of thousands of acres of the public domain, yet he managed it with ease.

One of the unforeseen results of the homestead legislation was a high rate of employment among builders of birdhouses. In most instances, you were required to display an "erected domicile" on your land. The Congress, after all, was much too smart to give people land without requiring them to live on it. In a number of instances, the erected domicile was a birdhouse, put there to satisfy a paid witness with a tender conscience. It is quite possible that the greatest opportunity offered by the homestead legislation in the West was the opportunity to earn a little honest graft. By conservative estimates, 95 percent of the final proofs under the Desert Land[s] Act were fraudulent. "Whole townships have been entered under this law in the interest of one person or firm," thundered Binger Hermann, a commissioner of the General Land Office, about the Timber and Stone Act. Not long afterward, Hermann himself was fired for allowing unrestricted fraud.

Mark Twain might have written it off to the human condition, but [John Wesley] Powell, who subscribed to a more benevolent view of humanity, wrote it off to the conditions of the desert and the failure to understand them. Americans were making a Procrustean effort to turn half a continent into something they were used to. It was a doomed effort. Even worse, it was unscientific.

The document that Powell hoped would bring the country to its senses was called *A Report on the Lands of the Arid Region of the United States, with a More Detailed Account of the Lands of Utah.* Published in 187[8], the volume was seven years in preparation—though Powell took time out for a second expedition down the Colorado, in 1871, and for his usual plethora of intermittent pursuits. Powell's *Report* is remarkably brief, a scant two hundred pages in all. Unlike many of his rivals, such as the bombastic Ferdinand V. Hayden, Powell was more interested in being right than in being long. But his portrait of the American West has revolutionary implications even today.

At the beginning, Powell reconfirmed his view, which he had already submitted to an unbelieving Congress, that two-fifths of the United States has a climate that generally cannot support farming without irrigation. On top of that, irrigation could reclaim only a fraction of it. "When all the waters running in the streams found in this region are conducted on the land," Powell said, "there will be but a small portion of the country redeemed, varying in the different territories perhaps from *one to three percent*" (emphasis added). Powell regarded the theory that increased rainfall accompanied human settlement as bunk, but, typically, he disposed of it in a sympathetic and felicitous way: "If it be true that increase of the water supply is due to increase in precipitation, as many have supposed, the fact is not cheering to the agriculturalist of the arid region. . . . Any sudden great change [in climate] is ephemeral, and usually such changes go in cycles, and the opposite or compensating change may reasonably be anticipated. . . . [W]e shall have to expect a speedy return to extreme aridity, in which case a large portion of the agricultural industries of these now growing up would be destroyed."

The whole problem with the Homestead Acts, Powell went on, was that they were blind to reality. In the West, a 160-acre *irrigated* farm was too *large,* while a 160-acre *unirrigated* farm was too *small.* Most western valley soil was fertile, and a good crop was a near certainty once irrigation water was applied; in the milder regions the growing season was very long and two crops were possible, so one could often subsist on eighty irrigated acres or less. That, in fact, was about all the irrigated land one family could be expected to work. Remove the irrigation water, however, and things were drastically different. Then even a whole section was too small a piece of land. Under most circumstances, Powell claimed, no one could make a living through dryland ranching on fewer than 2,560 acres—four full sections. And even with that much land, a settler's prospects would be dicey in times of drought, because the land might lie utterly bare. Therefore, every pasturage farm should ideally have a water right sufficient to irrigate twenty acres or so during emergencies.

Having thrown over the preeminent myths about agriculture in the American West, Powell went on to the truly revolutionary part of his report. Under riparian water law, to give everyone a water right for twenty irrigated acres was impossible if you gave everyone a neat little square of land. Some squares would contain much greater stream footage than others, and their owners would have too much water compared with the others. The property boundaries would therefore have to be gerrymandered to give everyone a sufficient piece of the stream. That was one way you could help avert the monopolization of water. Another way was to insist that people *use* their water rights, not hold on to them in the hope that cities would grow up and one could make a killing someday selling water to them. An unused water right should revert—let us say after five years—to the public trust so someone else could claim it.

Doing all this, Powell reasoned, might help assure that water would be used equitably, but not necessarily efficiently. Ideally, to get through drier months and times of drought, you needed a reservoir in a good location—at a low altitude, and on the main branch of a stream. That way you could get more efficient storage of water—a dam only twice as large, but lower down, might capture five times as much water as a smaller one upstream. Also, you could then irrigate the lower valley lands, which usually have better soil and a longer growing season. In any event, an on-stream storage reservoir was, from the point of view of irrigation, preferable to small shallow ponds filled with diverted streamwater, the typical irrigation reservoirs of his day; the ponds evaporated much greater amounts of water and displaced valuable cropland.

But who, Powell asked, was building on-stream reservoirs? Practically no one. . . . Sooner or later, the federal government would have to get into the irrigation business or watch its efforts to settle the West degenerate into failure and chaos. Once it realized that, it would have to undertake a careful survey of the soil characteristics so as not to waste a lot of money irrigating inferior land with drainage problems. . . .

Having gone this far, Powell figured he might as well go the whole route. Fences, for example, bothered him. What was the sense of every rancher enclosing his land with a barbed-wire fence? Fenced lands tended to be unevenly grazed, and fences were obvious hazards to cattle in winter storms. Fencing was also a waste of time and money, especially in a region where rainfall could skid from twenty to six inches in successive years and someone was lucky to survive at all, let alone survive while constantly repairing and replacing fences. Individually fenced lands were a waste of resources, too; it takes a lot more tin, Powell reasoned, to make five eight-ounce cans than to make one forty-ounce can. The sensible thing was for farms to be clustered together and the individually owned lands treated as a commons, an *ejido,* with a single fence around the perimeter.

States bothered Powell, too. Their borders were too often nonsensical. They followed rivers for convenience, then struck out in a straight line, bisecting mountain ranges, cutting watersheds in half. Boxing out landscapes, sneering at natural reality, they were wholly arbitrary and, therefore, stupid. In the West, where the one thing that really mattered was water, states should logically be formed around watersheds. Each major river, from the glacial drip at its headwaters to the delta at its mouth, should be a state or semistate. The great state of Upper Platte River. Will the Senator from the state of Rio Grande yield? To divide the West any other way was to sow the future with rivalries, jealousies, and bitter squabbles whose fruits would contribute solely to the nourishment of lawyers.

While Powell knew that his plan for settling the American West would be considered revolutionary, he saw a precedent. After all, what was the difference between a cooperative irrigation district and a New England barn-raising? One was informal, the other organized and legalized, but otherwise they were the same thing. Communal pasturelands might be a gross affront to America's preoccupation with private property rights, but they were common in Europe. In the East, where inland navigation was as important as irrigation was in the West, you already had a strong federal presence in the Corps of Engineers. If anything was revolutionary, it was trying to graft English common law and the principles and habits of wet-zone agriculture onto a desert landscape. There was not a desert civilization in the world where that had been tried—and most of those civilizations had withered even after following sensible rules.

Powell was advocating cooperation, reason, science, an equitable sharing of the natural wealth, and—implicitly if not explicitly—a return to the Jeffersonian ideal. He wanted the West settled slowly, cautiously, in a manner that would work. If it was done intelligently instead of in a mad, unplanned rush, the settlement of the West could help defuse the dangerous conditions building in the squalid industrial cities of the East. If it was done wrong, the migration west might go right into reverse.

The nation at large, however, was in no mood for any such thing. It was avid for imperial expansion, and the majority of its citizens wanted to get rich. New immigrants were arriving, dozens of boatloads a day, with that motive burning in their brains. To them America was not so much a democratic utopia as a gold mine. . . .

The unpeopled West, naturally, was where a great many immigrants hoped to find their fortunes. They didn't want to hear that the West was dry. Few had ever seen a desert, and the East was so much like Europe that they imagined the West would be, too. A tiny bit semiarid, perhaps, like Italy. But a desert? Never! They didn't want to hear of communal pasturelands—they had left those behind, in Europe, in order that they could become the emperors of Wyoming. They didn't want the federal government parceling out water and otherwise meddling in their affairs; that was another European tradition they had left an ocean away. . . .

The result, in the end, was that Powell got some money to conduct his Irrigation Survey for a couple of years—far less than he wanted, and needed—and then found himself frozen permanently out of the appropriations bills. The excuse was that he was moving too slowly, too deliberately; the truth was that he was forming opinions the West couldn't bear to hear. There was inexhaustible land but far too little water, and what little water there was might, in many cases, be too expensive to move. Having said this, held to it, and suffered for it, Powell spent his last years in a kind of ignominy. Unable to participate in the settlement of the West, he retreated into the Bureau of Ethnology, where his efforts, ironically, helped prevent the culture of the West's original inhabitants from being utterly trampled and eradicated by that same settlement. On September 23, 1902, he died at the family compound near Haven, Maine, about as far from the arid West as he could get. . . .

The passage of the Reclamation Act of 1902 was such a sharp left turn in the course of American politics that historians still gather and argue over why it was passed. To some, it was America's first flirtation with socialism, an outgrowth of the Populist and Progressive movements of the time. To others, it was a disguised reactionary measure, an effort to relieve the mobbed and riotous conditions of the eastern industrial cities—an act to save heartless capitalism from itself. To some, its roots were in Manifest Destiny, whose incantations still held people in their sway; to others, it was a military ploy to protect and populate America's western flank against the ascendant Orient.

What seems beyond question is that the Reclamation Act, or some variation of it, was by the end of the nineteenth century, inevitable. To resist a federal reclamation program was to block all further migration to the West and to ensure disaster for those who were already there—or for those who were on their way. . . . No matter what the government did, short of erecting a wall at the hundredth meridian, the settlement of the West was going to continue. The only way to prevent more cycles of disaster was to build a civilization based on irrigated farming.

As soon as Roosevelt was in the White House, [Nevada Representative Francis] Newlands introduced a bill creating a federal program along the lines suggested by Powell. But the bitterness he felt over huge financial loss[es] was so strong that he described his bill in language almost calculated to infuriate his western colleagues, who were clinging to the myth that the hostile natural forces of the West could be overcome by individual initiative. In a long speech on the floor of the Congress, Newlands said outright that the legislation he was introducing would "nationalize the works of irrigation"—which was like saying today that one intended to nationalize the automobile industry. Then he launched into a long harangue about the failures of state reclamation programs, blaming them on "the ignorance, the improvidence, and the dishonesty of local legislatures"—even though many of his listeners had recently graduated from such legislatures themselves. . . . Newlands['] bill . . . ran into immediate opposition . . . [and] Roosevelt intervened. . . . On June 17, 1902, the Reclamation Act became law.

Women and Conservation

CAROLYN MERCHANT

In his book *The Fight For Conservation* (1910), Gifford Pinchot praised the women of the progressive era for their substantial contributions to conservation. He cited the conservation committee of the Daughters of the American Revolution (chaired by his mother), the Pennsylvania Forestry Association, "founded by ladies," which carried out some of the earliest work done in that state, the National Forests preserved by Minnesota women, and the Calaveras Big Trees set aside by the women of California after a nine year fight.

From Carolyn Merchant, "The Women of the Progressive Conservation Crusade, 1900–1915," in Kendall E. Bailes, ed., *Environmental History: Critical Issues in Comparative Perspective* (Lanham, MD: University Press of America, 1985), pp. 153–170. Reprinted by permission of University Press of America.

Writing his definitive history of the progressive conservation campaign in 1959, Samuel Hays also acknowledged the enthusiasm of women's organizations for conservation and their staunch support, until 1913, for Pinchot as leader of the movement. Historians Robert Welker and Stephen Fox amplified other female contributions, especially to the Audubon movement and the hiking clubs, while admitting that much remains to be learned regarding women's role in conservation.

Who were the women of the conservation crusade? What were their accomplishments, objectives, and ideals? How did they interact with the men who promoted conservation? What ideological framework did they bring to the crusade and to the conflicts that developed within it?

In the nineteenth century, women had developed interests and organizations that paved the way for their work in the conservation and reform movements of the progressive era. Literary clubs oriented toward culture drew women together for mutual improvement and shared experiences, while the women's rights and abolition movements exposed them to the political process and the public arena. Leisure time had afforded middle and upper-class women opportunities for botanizing, gardening, birdlore, and camping. Women visited the National Parks and scenic wonderlands of the West or, sometimes casting off skirts and donning Turkish pants, joined the Appalachian Mountain Club (founded in 1876) or the Sierra Club (founded in 1892).

Propelled by a growing consciousness of the panacea of bucolic scenery and wilderness, coupled with the need for reform of the slums and squalor of the cities, women burst vividly into the public arena in the early twentieth century as a force in the progressive conservation crusade. Behind the brief tributes by historians to their substantial contributions lies an untold story of immense energy, achievement, and dedication by thousands of women to the cause of conservation. Although only the most prominent women appear in the archives of history, without the input of women in nearly every locale in the country, conservation gains in the early decades of the century would have been fewer and far less spectacular.

Feminist Conservation: The General Federation of Women's Clubs

In 1900, Mrs. Lovell White of San Francisco, the brilliant, dynamic, and resourceful founder and president of the California Club, took up the cause of forestry. Founded at the home of Mrs. White on a cold rainy evening in 1897 in the wake of the first and abortive California suffrage campaign—a campaign "brilliant, rich in experiences" with "a spirit of wholesome comradeship,"—the California Club merged in January of 1900 with women's clubs throughout the state to form the California Federation of Women's Clubs. With Mrs. Robert Burdette of Pasadena as president and Mrs. White as vice-president at large, the first meeting was steeped in conservation ideals.

"The preservation of the forests of this state is a matter that should appeal to women," declared Mrs. Burdette in her opening address. "While the women of New Jersey are saving the Palisades of the Hudson from utter destruction by men to whose greedy souls Mount Sinai is only a stone quarry, and the women of Colorado are saving the cliff dwellings and pueblo ruins of their state from vandal destruction, the word comes to the women of California that men whose souls are gang-saws are meditating the turning of our world-famous Sequoias into planks and fencing worth so many dollars." The forests of the state, she went on, were the source of the state's waters and together they made possible the homes and health of the people of California. "Better one living tree in California, than fifty acres of lumber-yard. Preserve and replant them and the State will be blessed a thousandfold in the development of its natural resources. . . ."

Nationally, the General Federation of Women's Clubs (G.F.W.C.), founded in 1890, had been active in forestry since the turn of the century as part of women's civic obligation to become informed on the most urgent political, economic, and social issues of the day. Selecting women in each state who were familiar with the principles of forestry to head the clubs' forestry committees, local members first conducted cosmetic campaigns to save waste paper and clean up their towns and cities. They formed coalitions with civic organizations which engaged in the beautification of yards, vacant lots, school yards, and public buildings through planting trees and shrubs. Following the example of German women, with whom they corresponded, they planted avenues of shade trees. They also worked toward the acquisition and preservation of wooded tracts of land wherein "Nature should be left unrestrained." . . .

In addition to keeping 800,000 members informed of the conservation policies and achievements of Roosevelt and Pinchot, the General Federation's Forestry Committee played an influential role in the passage of legislation to protect forests, waters, and birdlife. Under the direction of Mrs. Lydia Phillips Williams (for 1904–6), an enthusiastic conservationist who had learned forestry at the family's Peterson Nursery in Chicago and on her numerous excursions to forests in Norway, Sweden, and Germany; Mrs. F. W. Gerard (1908–10) from Connecticut, and Mrs. Lovell White (1910–1912), who had established a national reputation in saving the Calaveras Big Trees of California, the committee coordinated efforts to support such projects as the creation of national forest reserves in New Hampshire and the Southern Appalachians and passage of the Weeks Bill for protection of the watersheds of navigable streams. . . .

During the period 1907–1912, women contributed notices, news items, reports, and articles to *Forestry and Irrigation,* the journal of the American Forestry Association. They pointed out women's work to save forests in places such as Colorado, Vermont, Maine, and New York, printed lengthy summaries of progress in conservation as reported at the Federation's biennial meetings, and announced protest actions such as that taken by Mrs. D. M. Osborne of Auburn, New York who, outraged by telephone pole workers who had mercilessly trimmed her trees without permission, "drove off the workmen and cut down the poles."

Mrs. Lydia Adams-Williams, a self-styled feminist conservation writer and member of the Women's National Press Association was particularly vociferous in her efforts to popularize women's accomplishments. Her article "Conservation—Women's Work" (1908), in which she characterized herself as the first woman lecturer and writer on conservation, complained that "man has been too busy building railroads, constructing ships, engineering great projects, and exploiting vast commercial enterprises" to consider the future. Man the moneymaker had left it to woman the moneysaver to preserve resources. She placed women's roles in conservation squarely in the context of feminist history:

> To the intuition of Isabella of Spain, to her tenacious grasp of a great idea, to her foresight and her divine sympathy the world is indebted for the discovery of a great continent, for the civilization we enjoy today and for the great wealth of resources. . . . And as

it was the intuitive foresight of a woman which brought the light of civilization to a great continent, so in great measure, will it fall to woman in her power to educate public sentiment to save from rapacious waste and complete exhaustion the resources upon which depend the welfare of the home, the children, and the children's children.

In "A Million Women for Conservation" (1908), again taking liberal notice of her own accomplishments, Mrs. Adams-Williams discussed the resolutions passed by the women's clubs in support of the conservation efforts of Roosevelt, Pinchot, the Inland Waterways Commission, the Forest Service, the Geological Survey, and the American Mining Congress. The Federation in Washington, D.C., of which she was a member, was the first to pass these resolutions followed by four other national women's organizations the combined membership of which totalled one million.

By 1908, the General Federation had begun to play an important role in the national conservation movement. Mrs. Philip N. Moore, president of the Federation from 1908–1910, was a member of the executive committee of the National Conservation Congress during its first four years, was a presiding officer in 1912, and became its vice-president in 1913. Tribute was paid by the president of the Congress to her "rare ability" to organize and preside over large numbers of enthusiastic women. Mrs. Moore of St. Louis, Missouri, a leader in educational and philanthropic work, was born in Rockford, Illinois, graduated from Vassar College, and later became one of its trustees. She had been active for many years at the local, state, and national levels of the Federation. The voice[s] of Mrs. Moore and dozens of other women were heard loudly and forcefully at the National Conservation Congresses held from 1909–1912.

Women's National Rivers and Harbors Congress.   In 1908, seven women in Shreveport, Louisiana, banded together to form the Women's National Rivers and Harbors Congress that would cooperate with the National Rivers and Harbors Congress then headed by Joseph E. Ransdell. Within fourteen months, under the leadership of its president, Mrs. Hoyle Tomkies, it had grown to 20,000 members and had held a national congress in Washington, D.C. at which twenty states were represented. As Mrs. Tomkies expressed it, "Our work is mainly to educate upon the subject. . . . We are putting forth all the energy and influence we can muster for the cause, lest the enemy come while we are sleeping and sow in the peoples' minds the tares of 'individualism' and non-conservation."

The Daughters of the American Revolution.   In 1909 Mrs. Matthew T. Scott was elected President General of the 77,000 member Daughters of the American Revolution. A representative of the more liberal wing of the D.A.R. who had recently defeated the conservatives in a national election, Mrs. Scott was an enthusiastic conservationist who encouraged the maintenance of a conservation committee consisting of 100 members representing every state. The chair of this committee was Mrs. James Pinchot, mother of Gifford Pinchot, who by that token as well as her conservation efforts was said to have "done more for the cause of conservation than any other woman." . . .

. . . [C]onservation efforts of the D.A.R. were directed toward the preservation of the Appalachian watersheds, the Palisades, and Niagara Falls (then threatened by over usage of water by power companies). In fact, as Mrs. Carl Vrooman pointed out to the National Conservation Congress of 1911, "these 77,000 women do indeed represent a perfect Niagara of splendid ability and force—enough, if intelligently directed, to furnish the motive power to keep revolving all the wheels of progress in this country." In 1905–6 women nationwide had responded to Horace MacFarland of the American Civic Association whose editorials in the *Ladies' Home Journal* on the preservation of Niagara Falls had produced tens of thousands of letters to Congress.

The Audubon Movement.   The post–Civil War resurgence of high fashion for ladies had, by the end of the century, taken an immense toll on American bird-life in the creation of exotic styles in millinery. Bird feathers and whole birds nestled atop the heads of society's upper and middle-class women. The first Audubon societies, organized in 1886, protested the "abominable" habit of wearing feather fashions. Women who sought to educate their sisters to the peril of birds formed Audubon clubs, such as the one at Smith College where two young female students developed a plan to protect plume birds.

In 1898 "a score of ladies met in Fairfield," Connecticut, to form the Audubon society of the State of Connecticut, electing as president Mrs. Mabel Osgood Wright. With the publication in 1899, of the first issue of the Audubon Societies' official journal, *Bird Lore,* Mrs. Wright took on the task of editing the magazine's Audubon section and of reporting the latest developments in the politics of bird preservation. She requested that the secretaries of the initial nineteen state societies, all but one of whom were women, send news and notes to broaden and strengthen the movement.

In 1905 the Audubon Society appealed to the National Federation of Women's Clubs for help: "The club women of America with their powerful influence should take a strong stand against the use of wild birds' plumage, and especially against the use of the Aigrette. . . . A close affiliation between this Association and the National Federation of Women's clubs would be mutually helpful." . . .

In cooperation with the request made by the Audubon Society, Mrs. Gerard, Chair of the General Federation of Women's Clubs' Forestry Committee appealed to women at the Federation's 1910 Biennial Convention: "Our work for the Audubon Society is not as active as it should be. Can we logically work for conservation and expect to be listened to, while we still continue to encourage the destruction of the song birds by following the hideous fashion of wearing song birds and egrets upon our hats?"

And speaking to the 1912 Conservation Congress, Mrs. Crocker of the GFWC's Conservation Committee asked a personal favor of the women present: "This fall when you choose your fall millinery . . . I beg you to choose some other decoration for your hats. . . ."

After a long campaign, in October 1913, a new Tariff Act was passed that outlawed the importing of wild bird feathers into the United States. It was so vigorously enforced that newspapers were filled with accounts of "the words and actions of indignant ladies who found it necessary to give up their aigrettes, paradise plumes, and other feathers upon arriving from Europe." Two days after the new law went into effect, Audubon Save the Birds Hats were being advertised in New York for $15 to $45 apiece. Congratulations poured in from all over the world for the Audubon Society's great victory. . . .

So rare as to be on the verge of extermination a few years before, by 1915 egrets in guarded rookeries in the southern United States, numbered 10,580 along with 50,000 Little Blue Herons, and an equal number of Ibis. Owing to the combined efforts of the Audubon Societies and the women's clubs, public opinion had shifted so far toward bird protection that far fewer "bad bird-laws" were being introduced into state legislatures. The work of a decade and a half had begun to show results. . . .

Conservation Ideology

The Conservation Trilogy.   Although the women of the organizations represented at the National Conservation Congresses were public activists in their local communities, they nevertheless accepted the traditional sex roles assigned to them by late nineteenth century American society as caretakers of the nation's homes, husbands, and offspring, supporting rather than challenging the two spheres ideology of the nineteenth century.

At the National Congresses, women repeatedly called on the traditions assigned them by society in justifying the public demands they were making. Unwilling and unable to break out of these social roles, and supported by the men of the Congresses, they drew on a trilogy of slogans—conservation of womanhood, the home, and the child.

The Conservation of True Womanhood.   The "conservation of true womanhood" was a subject repeatedly stressed by women at the Conservation Congresses. Mrs. Scott of the D.A.R. pleaded "as the representative of a great National organization of the women of the land, for the exalting, for the lifting up in special honor, of the Holy Grail of Womanhood." Just as the agricultural college prepared prospective farmers, so schools of domestic science would produce prospective housewives.

Speaking to the Conservation Congress of 1909, Mrs. Overton Ellis of the General Federation of Women's Clubs, called conservation "the surest weapon with which women might win success." Centuries of turning last night's roast into hash, remaking last year's dress and controlling the home's resources had given women a heightened sense of the power of the conservation idea in creating true womanhood. "Conservation in its material and ethical sense is the basic principle in the life of woman. . . ."

In her presidential address to the General Federation's Tenth Biennial Meeting in 1910, Mrs. Philip N. Moore set conservation in its context for women as "no new word, no new idea," but a unifying theme for the contributions of women to society as the conservors of life. "There is a 'new woman,' the product of evolution the result of social and commercial changes. She rebels, however, when she sees woman spelled with capital letters or harnessed to the word 'Career.'" . . .

The Conservation of the Home.   The home as the domain of true womanhood became the second theme in the conservation trilogy. The National Congress of Mothers, represented by Mrs. Orville Bright of Chicago, dedicated itself to the conservation of natural resources for "the use, comfort, and benefit of the homes of the people." "Life, health and character all depend on the home and its efficiency." Mrs. Bright adopted the utilitarian philosophy of the progressives in stressing that conservation primarily benefitted human life rather than that of other organisms,

since the fate of forests, land, waters, minerals, or food would be of little consequence were there "no men, women, and children to use and enjoy them."

Margaret Russell Knudsen of Hawaii, of the Women's National Rivers and
Harbors Congress argued (at the 1909 Conservation Congress) that the conservation of the home was the special mission of woman. The "mark of civilization was
the arrival of woman on the scene. . . . In no national movement has there been
such a spontaneous and universal response from women as in this great question
of conservation. Women from Maine to the most Western shore of the Hawaiian
Islands are alive to the situation, because the home is woman's domain. She is the
conserver of the race."

Conservation of the Child.   Third in the trilogy was the link between the conservation of natural resources and the conservation of the children and future generations of the United States. According to Mrs. John Walker, a member of the
Kansas City chapter of Daughters of the American Revolution, woman's role in
conservation was dedicated to the preservation of life, while man's role was
the conservation of material needs. "Woman, the transmitter of life" must therefore care for the product of life—future generations. The children of the nation
should not be sacrificed to "factories, mills, and mines," but must be allowed "to
enjoy the freedom of the bird and the butterfly . . . and all that the sweet breast of
Nature offers so freely."

Mrs. Overton Ellis of the General Federation of Women's Clubs promoted the
conservation of children's lives at the 1909 Congress: "Women's supreme function
as mother of the race gives her special claim to protection not so much individually as
for unborn generations." . . .

Denouement.   The Fifth National Conservation Congress opened in Washington,
D.C., on November 18, 1913, and proceeded for three days. Its vice-president,
Mrs. Philip N. Moore of the General Federation of Women's Clubs, did not speak.
Nor did any other woman from the Federation, the D.A.R., the Country Women's
Clubs or the Women's National Rivers and Harbors Congress. The sole female voice
heard was Miss Mabel Boardman from the American Red Cross who lectured on
"Conservation of Life in the Lumber Camps."

American Forestry (the new name of the journal of the American Forestry Association) carried a full report on the meeting in its November issue. Descriptions
of the activities of the Congress were accompanied by the portraits of fifty men
who had chaired or worked on the committees. A photograph taken the night of the
Forestry Banquet on November 19 showed some 160 men seated at round tables
before a speaker's platform. Mrs. Philip N. Moore was not among them.

A brief note in the Forestry Committee's report to the Congress seems to provide the explanation for the absence of women:

> The desirability of . . . an organization [to represent the mutual forestry and lumbering
> interests] was emphasized by the presence at [the Fourth National Congress in] Indianapo-
> lis [1912] of a number of men who were no longer in need of the general educational
> propaganda relative to the conservation of natural resources, but attended the Congress
> for the purpose of meeting progressive men in their own and related lines and securing
> specific information helpful in the solution of their own problems.

Conservation and forestry had come of age as technical professions. As such they were no longer accessible to women. After 1912 the American Forestry Association ceased to print articles or news items on the work of women in forestry. Lydia Adams-Williams disappeared from the scene.

A second explanation for the disappearance of women also seems plausible. That same year the popular nationwide struggle for the preservation of Hetch Hetchy Valley, a part of California's Yosemite National Park, reached its conclusion. With the passage of the Raker Act by Congress in 1913, the City of San Francisco won its long battle for a public water supply. The women of the conservation crusade had worked hard to preserve the valley as an integral part of the park.

Gifford Pinchot, the women's early inspiration and supporter in conservation efforts, had taken the opposing side, recommending at the congressional hearings that a dam be constructed across the valley to serve the interests of thousands of city people rather than accommodate the needs of the few who camped and hiked in the area.

Soon after a City of San Francisco referendum in November 1903 favored construction of the dam, John Muir had taken the Hetch Hetchy issue to the nation. Preservationists rallied to support its retention in the park through letters and telegrams to the House Committee on Public Lands which held hearings in January 1909. Among them were women who had camped in the valley, who were members of the Sierra Club or Appalachian Mountain Club, or who were opposed to the commercial use of such a scenic wonderland. . . .

In 1913, the National Committee for the Preservation of Yosemite National Park headed by Robert Underwood Johnson, editor of *The Century,* and Charles Eliot, president of the First Conservation Congress, circulated brochures on "The Hetch Hetchy Grab" and "The Invasion of Yosemite National Park" documenting opposition from over 100 newspapers. Among the prominent citizens listed as preservationists for the park were Mrs. Emmons Crocker, chair of the Conservation Committee of the General Federation of Women's Clubs. On the committee, which represented most of the states of the union were twenty-five women, some of whom, like Mrs. Philip N. Moore, were General Federation leaders now openly opposed to Pinchot.

Although preservationists lost the battle over Hetch Hetchy in December 1913, they had aroused the nation. The passage of the National Parks Act in 1916 that established an administration in the Department of the Interior for the numerous parks created since 1862, gave them some compensation for its loss. . . .

During the decade and a half that introduced the century, women's organizations had helped the nation to achieve enormous gains in the conservation of natural resources and the preservation of scenic landscapes. Yet the platform for promoting these objectives had been a mixed one. Working closely with the men of the movement, women frequently saw themselves as ideologically opposed to what they perceived as commercial and material values. Feminist and progressive in their role as activists for the public interest, they were nevertheless predominantly conservative in their desire to uphold traditional values and middle-class life styles rooted in these same material interests. These contradictions within the women's conservation movement, however, were in reality manifestations of the similar mixture of progressive and conservative tendencies that characterized the Progressive Era itself.

❦ *F U R T H E R   R E A D I N G*

Jeanne Nienaber Clarke and Hanna J. Cortner, *The State and Nature: Voices Heard, Voices Unheard in America's Environmental Dialogue* (2002)

Kendrick A. Clements, "Engineers and Conservationists in the Progressive Era," *California History* 58 (1979–80), 282–303

Henry E. Clepper, *Crusade for Conservation: The Centennial History of the American Forestry Association* (1975)

Samuel Dana and Sally Fairfax, *Forest and Range Policy, Its Development in the U.S.* (1980)

Edward Dolnick, *Down the Great Unknown: John Wesley Powell's 1869 Journey of Discovery and Tragedy Through the Grand Canyon* (2002)

Arthur A. Ekirch, *Man and Nature in America* (1963)

Susan L. Flader, ed., *The Great Lakes Forest: An Environmental and Social History* (1983)

Emanuel Fritz, *The Development of Industrial Forestry in California* (1960)

Michael Frome, *Whose Woods These Are: The Story of the National Forests* (1962)

Samuel P. Hays, *Beauty, Health, and Permanence: Environmental Politics in the United States, 1955–1985* (1987)

———, *Conservation and the Gospel of Efficiency: The Progressive Conservation Movement, 1890–1920* (1959)

———, *A History of Environmental Politics Since 1945* (2000)

Karl Jacoby, *Crimes Against Nature: Squatters, Poachers, Thieves, and the Hidden History of American Conservation* (2001)

Ronald F. Lockmann, *Guarding the Forests of Southern California: Evolving Attitudes Toward Conservation of Watershed, Woodlands, and Wilderness* (1981)

George Michael McCarthy, *Hour of Trial: The Conservation Conflict in Colorado and the West, 1891–1907* (1977)

Char Miller, *Gifford Pinchot and the Making of Modern Environmentalism* (2001)

———, Rebecca Staebler, James E. Coufal, and William H. Banzhaf, eds., *The Greatest Good: 100 Years of Forestry in America* (1999)

Carl H. Moneyhon, "The Environmental Crisis and American Politics, 1860–1920," in Lester J. Bilsky, ed., *Historical Ecology: Essays on Environment and Social Change* (1980)

Roderick Nash, ed., *The American Environment: Readings in the History of Conservation* (1976)

———, "John Muir, William Kent, and the Conservation Schism," *Pacific Historical Review* 36 (1967), 423–433

James Penick, Jr., *Progressive Politics and Conservation* (1968)

Gifford Pinchot, *The Use of the National Forests* (1907)

John Wesley Powell, *The Exploration of the Colorado River and Its Canyons,* introduction by Wallace Stegner (1997)

Steven Pyne, *How the Canyon Became Grand: A Short History* (1998)

Lawrence Rakestraw, *A History of the United States Forest Service in Alaska* (2002)

John F. Reiger, *American Sportsmen and the Origins of Conservation,* 3rd ed. (2001)

Elmo R. Richardson, *The Politics of Conservation: Crusades and Controversies, 1897–1913* (1962)

William G. Robbins, *Lumberjacks and Legislators: Political Economy of the U.S. Lumber Industry, 1890–1941* (1982)

Glen O. Robinson, *The Forest Service: A Study in Land Management* (1975)

Theodore Roosevelt, *Wilderness Writings* (1986)

William D. Rowley, *U.S. Forest Service Grazing and Rangelands: A History* (1985)

Harold K. Steen, *The U.S. Forest Service: A History* (1976)

Wallace Stegner, *Beyond the Hundredth Meridian: John Wesley Powell and the Second Opening of the West* (1954)

Donald C. Swain, *Federal Conservation Policy, 1921–1933* (1963)

James A. Tober, *Who Owns the Wildlife: The Political Economy of Conservation in Nineteenth Century America* (1981)

John Walton, *Western Times and Water Wars: State, Culture, and Rebellion in California* (1992)

Louis S. Warren, *The Hunter's Game: Poachers and Conservationists in Twentieth Century America* (1997)

Richard White, *The Organic Machine* (1996)

James Whorton, *Before Silent Spring: Pesticides and Public Health in Pre-DDT America* (1974)

Peter Wild, *Pioneer Conservationists of Western America* (1979)

Dennis C. Williams, *God's Wilds: John Muir's Vision of Nature* (2002)

Donald Worster, *A River Running West: The Life of John Wesley Powell* (2001)

———, ed., *American Environmentalism: The Formative Period, 1860–1915* (1973)

William K. Wynant, *Westward in Eden: The Public Lands and the Conservation Movement* (1982)

CHAPTER

11

Wilderness Preservation
in the Twentieth Century

❦

Burgeoning cities, steep population growth, a flood of immigration, and brisk industrialization had changed Americans' perception of wilderness by the early twentieth century. As easy access to open land and forests receded from urban areas, wilderness took on a positive value as a source of the rugged pioneer spirit that had built America. As cities became polluted by soot, garbage, and noise, and as their working-class neighborhoods mushroomed, they took on a negative value. The inspiration to save wild nature grew out of romantic and Transcendentalist art and literature, middle-class desires to seek solace in the countryside, and male needs to recapture pioneer vigor. The politics of wilderness preservation emerged from the interests of Congress and the railroads in establishing parks for tourists; of city planners in creating safe, "moral" spaces for both elites and working classes; and of politicians and the public in reclaiming wild areas devoid of human habitation. The wilderness preservation movement sprang from opposition to a proposal by the city of San Francisco to dam Hetch Hetchy Valley in Yosemite National Park, a plan that Congress approved in 1913. Three years later, in 1916, the National Parks Act was passed, a victory for preservationists. In 1935 the Wilderness Society was founded, and in 1964 Congress passed the Wilderness Act to preserve pristine areas in their "natural condition" for future generations. This chapter looks at the political and class interests that are at stake in the movement to preserve wilderness, what wilderness is, and why wilderness is important to humanity. (See Maps 4, 7, and 9 in the Appendix.)

❦ D O C U M E N T S

Wilderness preservation is one of the most emotionally charged issues of the twentieth century. What wilderness is, what values it provides to humanity, and which areas should be preserved as wilderness (from mountains and forests to deserts, tundra, and the snow-swept Antarctic) are among the fundamental issues that have faced Americans in the past and continue to face them in the present and future. Women were prominent among the early nature preservationists. In Document 1, Florence Merriam Bailey, an

Audubon Society activist and one of the country's foremost popular writers on bird life, reveals some techniques that women used to preserve bird life and to dissuade other women from purchasing hats decorated with the feathers of endangered bird species. Mary Austin, author of Document 2, was one of the earliest nature writers to depict the western deserts and their Native American inhabitants sympathetically. The vastness, stark beauty, and climatic extremes of the desert humbled humans and dwarfed individual significance.

The differing rationales of utilitarian conservation and aesthetic preservation came to a head in the nationwide controversy over damming California's Hetch Hetchy Valley as a water supply for San Francisco. John Muir's arguments, presented in Document 3, written in 1912, popularized the preservationists' reasons for saving the valley, whereas Gifford Pinchot's utilitarian arguments for water conservation ultimately persuaded Theodore Roosevelt to side with San Francisco. Although the 1913 Raker Act authorizing the dam temporarily defeated Muir, it led to the passage of the National Parks Act in 1916. This act, excerpted in Document 4, created the National Park Service within the Department of the Interior to administer the separately created national parks. It represented a notable victory for the preservationists.

In the seventeenth century, William Bradford had described New England as a place filled with "wild beasts and wild men." By the twentieth century, European Americans had redefined wilderness as a place without Indians. But to Native Americans, as Chief Luther Standing Bear points out in Document 5, the land had never been a wilderness—only a home. Wilderness was an ethnocentric idea, a European creation. When the Wilderness Act, excerpted in Document 6, was passed in 1964, it defined wilderness as an area "where the earth and its community of life are untrammeled by man, where man himself is a visitor who does not remain," a definition that did not seem to acknowledge the many ways in which those very areas had been shaped by Native Americans or the gender issues involved in the use of the term "man." By the 1960s, areas that had seemed initially to have the qualities of wilderness, and that were preserved in national parks and monuments, were laced with paved roads, permanent accommodations, automobiles, and tourists. Document 7, by former park ranger Edward Abbey, excoriates the National Park Service for promoting "industrial tourism" and advocates leaving much of the park system undeveloped.

1. Florence Merriam Bailey Recalls the Early Audubon Women, 1900

As far back as 1886, when the Audubon movement was just beginning, the Smith College girls took to 'birding.' Before the birding began, however, behind the scenes, the two amateur ornithologists of the student body had laid deep, wily schemes. "Go to," said they; "we will start an Audubon Society. The birds must be protected; we must persuade the girls not to wear feathers on their hats." "We won't say too much about hats, though," these plotters went on. "We'll take the girls afield, and let them get acquainted with the birds. Then, of inborn necessity, they will wear feathers never more." So these guileful persons, having formally organized a Smith College Audubon Society for the Protection of Birds, put on their sunhats and called, "Come on, girls!" This they did with glee in their hearts, for it irked them

From Florence Merriam Bailey, *Bird Lore* 2, no. 3 (June 1900): 83–84.

to proclaim, "Behold, see, meditate upon this monster evil," while it gave them joy to say, "Come out under the sun-filled heavens and open your soul to the song of the Lark."

This, then, was the inspiration of the bird work that started up and spread so surprisingly, and was carried on with such eager enthusiasm in those early days at Smith. And this must be the inspiration of all successful field work, wherever it is done. A list of species is good to have, but without a knowledge of the birds themselves, it is like Emerson's Sparrow brought home without the river and sky. The true naturalist, like Audubon, will ever go to nature with open heart as well as mind.

Feeling this, the organizers of the Smith work persuaded John Burroughs to come to give it an impetus. When he took the girls to the woods at five o'clock in the morning, so many went that the bird had often flown before the rear guard arrived, but the fine enthusiasm of the man's spirit could not be missed. No one could come in touch with it without realizing that there was something in nature unguessed before, and worth attending to. And when the philosopher stood calmly beside a stump in the rain, naming unerringly each bird that crossed the sky, the lesson in observation, impressive as it was, was not merely one in keenness of vision. His attitude of stillness under the heavens made each one feel that 'by lowly listening' she too might hear the right word—the message nature holds for each human heart.

2. Mary Austin Describes the Wonders of the Desert, 1903

East away from the Sierra, south from Panamint and Amargosa, east and south many an uncounted mile, is the Country of Lost Borders.

Ute, Paiute, Mojave, and Shoshone inhabit its frontiers, and as far into the heart of it as man dare go. Not the law, but the land sets the limit. Desert is the name it wears upon the maps, but the Indian's is the better word. Desert is a loose term to indicate land that supports no man; whether the land can be bitted and broken to that purpose is not proven. Void of life it never is, however dry the air and villainous the soil.

This is the nature of that country. There are hills, rounded, blunt, burned, squeezed up out of chaos, chrome and vermilion painted, aspiring to the snowline. Between the hills lie high level-looking plains full of intolerable sun glare, or narrow valleys drowned in blue haze. . . .

The sculpture of the hills here is more wind than water work, though the quick storms do sometimes scar them past many a year's redeeming. In all the Western desert edges there are essays in miniature at the famed, terrible Grand Canyon, to which, if you keep on long enough in this country, you will come at last.

Since this is a hill country one expects to find springs, but not to depend upon them; for when found they are often brackish and unwholesome, or maddening, slow dribbles in a thirsty soil. Here you find the hot sink of Death Valley, or high rolling districts where the air has always a tang of frost. Here are the long heavy winds and breathless calms on the tilted mesas where dust devils dance, whirling up into a wide, pale sky. Here you have no rain when all the earth cries for it, or quick downpours

From Mary Austin, *Land of Little Rain.* Boston: Houghton Mifflin, 1950 [1903], pp. 1–8.

called cloudbursts for violence. A land of lost rivers, with little in it to love; yet a land that once visited must be come back to inevitably. If it were not so there would be little told of it.

This is the country of three seasons. From June on to November it lies hot, still, and unbearable, sick with violent unrelieving storms; then on until April, chill, quiescent, drinking its scant rain and scanter snows; from April to the hot season again, blossoming, radiant, and seductive. These months are only approximate; later or earlier the rain-laden wind may drift up the water gate of the Colorado from the Gulf, and the land sets its seasons by the rain. . . .

If you have any doubt about it, know that the desert begins with the creosote. This immortal shrub spreads down into Death Valley and up to the lower timber-line, odorous and medicinal as you might guess from the name, wandlike, with shining fretted foliage. . . .

Nothing the desert produces expresses it better than the unhappy growth of the tree yuccas. Tormented, thin forests of it stalk drearily in the high mesas, particularly in that triangular slip that fans out eastward from the meeting of the Sierras and coastwise hills where the first swings across the southern end of the San Joaquin Valley. The yucca bristles with bayonet-pointed leaves, dull green, growing shaggy with age, tipped with panicles of fetid, greenish bloom. . . .

Above the lower tree-line, which is also the snow-line, mapped out abruptly by the sun, one finds spreading growth of piñon, juniper, branched nearly to the ground, lilac and sage, and scattering white pines. . . .

Go as far as you dare in the heart of a lonely land, you cannot go so far that life and death are not before you. Painted lizards slip in and out of rock crevices, and pant on the white hot sands. Birds, hummingbirds even, nest in the cactus scrub; wood-peckers befriend the demoniac yuccas; out of the stark, treeless waste rings the music of the night-singing mockingbird. If it be summer and the sun well down, there will be a burrowing owl to call. . . .

If one is inclined to wonder at first how so many dwellers came to be in the loneliest land that ever came out of God's hands, what they do there and why stay, one does not wonder so much after having lived there. None other than this long brown land lays such a hold on the affections. The rainbow hills, the tender bluish mists, the luminous radiance of the spring, have the lotus charm. They trick the sense of time, so that once inhabiting there you always mean to go away without quite real-izing that you have not done it. Men who have lived there, miners and cattle-men, will tell you this, not so fluently, but emphatically, cursing the land and going back to it. For one thing there is the divinest, cleanest air to be breathed anywhere in God's world. Some day the world will understand that, and the little oases on the windy tops of hills will harbor for healing its ailing, house-weary broods. . . .

For all the toll the desert takes of a man it gives compensations, deep breaths, deep sleep, and the communion of the stars. It comes upon one with new force in the pauses of the night that the Chaldeans were a desert-bred people. It is hard to escape the sense of mastery as the stars move in the wide clear heavens to risings and set-tings unobscured. They look large and near and palpitant; as if they moved on some stately service not needful to declare. Wheeling to their stations in the sky, they make the poor world-fret of no account. Of no account you who lie out there watching, nor the lean coyote that stands off in the scrub from you and howls and howls.

3. John Muir Advocates Wilderness Preservation, 1912

Yosemite is so wonderful that we are apt to regard it as an exceptional creation, the only valley of its kind in the world; but Nature is not so poor as to have only one of anything. Several other yosemites have been discovered in the Sierra that occupy the same relative positions on the Range and were formed by the same forces in the same kind of granite. One of these, the Hetch Hetchy Valley, is in the Yosemite National Park about twenty miles from Yosemite and is easily accessible to all sorts of travelers by a road and trail that leaves the Big Oak Flat road at Bronson Meadows a few miles below Crane Flat, and to mountaineers by way of Yosemite Creek basin and the head of the middle fork of the Tuolumne.

It is said to have been discovered by Joseph Screech, a hunter, in 1850, a year before the discovery of the great Yosemite. After my first visit to it in the autumn of 1871, I have always called it the "Tuolumne Yosemite," for it is a wonderfully exact counterpart of the Merced Yosemite, not only in its sublime rocks and waterfalls but in the gardens, groves and meadows of its flowery park-like floor. The floor of Yosemite is about 4000 feet above the sea; the Hetch Hetchy floor about 3700 feet. And as the Merced River flows through Yosemite, so does the Tuolumne through Hetch Hetchy. The walls of both are of gray granite, rise abruptly from the floor, are sculptured in the same style and in both every rock is a glacier monument.

Standing boldly out from the south wall is a strikingly picturesque rock called by the Indians, Kolana, the outermost of a group 2300 feet high, corresponding with the Cathedral rocks of Yosemite both in relative position and form. On the opposite side of the Valley, facing Kolana, there is a counterpart of the El Capitan that rises sheer and plain to a height of 1800 feet, and over its massive brow flows a stream which makes the most graceful fall I have ever seen. From the edge of the cliff to the top of an earthquake talus it is perfectly free in the air for a thousand feet before it is broken into cascades among talus boulders. It is in all its glory in June, when the snow is melting fast, but fades and vanishes toward the end of summer. The only fall I know with which it may fairly be compared is the Yosemite Bridal Veil; but it excels even that favorite fall both in height and airy-fairy beauty and behavior. . . .

Hetch Hetchy Valley, far from being a plain, common, rock-bound meadow, as many who have not seen it seem to suppose, is a grand landscape garden, one of Nature's rarest and most precious mountain temples. As in Yosemite, the sublime rocks of its walls seem to glow with life, whether leaning back in repose or standing erect in thoughtful attitudes, giving welcome to storms and calms alike, their brows in the sky, their feet set in the groves and gay flowery meadows, while birds, bees, and butterflies help the river and waterfalls to stir all the air into music—things frail and fleeting and types of permanence meeting here and blending, just as they do in Yosemite, to draw her lovers into close and confiding communion with her.

Sad to say, this most precious and sublime feature of the Yosemite National Park, one of the greatest of all our natural resources for the uplifting joy and peace and health of the people, is in danger of being dammed and made into a reservoir to

From John Muir, *The Yosemite*. New York: Century, 1912, pp. 249–262.

help supply San Francisco with water and light, thus flooding it from wall to wall and burying its gardens and groves one or two hundred feet deep. This grossly destructive commercial scheme has long been planned and urged (though water as pure and abundant can be got from sources outside of the people's park, in a dozen different places), because of the comparative cheapness of the dam and of the territory which it is sought to divert from the great uses to which it was dedicated in the Act of 1890 establishing the Yosemite National Park. . . .

The first application to the Government by the San Francisco Supervisors for the commercial use of Lake Eleanor and the Hetch Hetchy Valley was made in 1903, and on December 22nd of that year it was denied by the Secretary of the Interior, Mr. [Ethan] Hitchcock, who truthfully said:

> Presumably the Yosemite National Park was created such by law because of the natural objects of varying degrees of scenic importance located within its boundaries, inclusive alike of its beautiful small lakes, like Eleanor, and its majestic wonders, like Hetch Hetchy and Yosemite Valley. It is the aggregation of such natural scenic features that makes the Yosemite Park a wonderland which the Congress of the United States sought by law to reserve for all coming time as nearly as practicable in the condition fashioned by the hand of the Creator—a worthy object of National pride and a source of healthful pleasure and rest for the thousands of people who may annually sojourn there during the heated months. . . .

In 1907 when Mr. [James] Garfield became Secretary of the Interior the application was renewed and granted; but under his successor, Mr. [Walter] Fisher, the matter has been referred to a Commission, which as this volume goes to press still has it under consideration.

That any one would try to destroy such a place seems incredible; but sad experience shows that there are people good enough and bad enough for anything. The proponents of the dam scheme bring forward a lot of bad arguments to prove that the only righteous thing to do with the people's parks is to destroy them bit by bit as they are able. Their arguments are curiously like those of the devil, devised for the destruction of the first garden—so much of the very best Eden fruit going to waste; so much of the best Tuolumne water and Tuolumne scenery going to waste. Few of their statements are even partly true, and all are misleading.

Thus, Hetch Hetchy, they say, is a "low-lying meadow." On the contrary, it is a high-lying natural landscape garden. . . .

"It is a common minor feature, like thousands of others." On the contrary it is a very uncommon feature; after Yosemite, the rarest and in many ways the most important in the National Park.

"Damming and submerging it 175 feet deep would enhance its beauty by forming a crystal-clear lake." Landscape gardens, places of recreation and worship, are never made beautiful by destroying and burying them. The beautiful sham lake, forsooth, would be only an eyesore, a dismal blot on the landscape, like many others to be seen in the Sierra. For, instead of keeping it at the same level all the year, allowing Nature centuries of time to make new shores, it would, of course, be full only a month or two in the spring, when the snow is melting fast; then it would be gradually drained, exposing the slimy sides of the basin and shallower parts of the bottom, with the gathered drift and waste, death and decay of the upper basins, caught here instead of being swept on to decent natural burial along the banks of the river or in the sea.

Thus the Hetch Hetchy dam-lake would be only a rough imitation of a natural lake for a few of the spring months, an open sepulcher for the others.

"Hetch Hetchy water is the purest of all to be found in the Sierra, unpolluted, and forever unpollutable." On the contrary, excepting that of the Merced below Yosemite, it is less pure than that of most of the other Sierra streams, because of the sewerage of camp grounds draining into it, especially of the Big Tuolumne Meadows camp ground, occupied by hundreds of tourists and mountaineers, with their animals, for months every summer, soon to be followed by thousands from all over the world.

These temple destroyers, devotees of ravaging commercialism, seem to have a perfect contempt for Nature, and, instead of lifting their eyes to the God of the mountains, lift them to the Almighty Dollar.

Dam Hetch Hetchy! As well dam for water-tanks the people's cathedrals and churches, for no holier temple has ever been consecrated by the heart of man.

4. The National Parks Act, 1916

August 25, 1916. [H. R. 15522.]

An Act To Establish a National Park Service

Be it enacted by the Senate and House of Representatives of the United States of America in Congress assembled, That there is hereby created in the Department of the Interior a service to be called the National Park Service, which shall be under the charge of a director, who shall be appointed by the Secretary. . . . The service thus established shall promote and regulate the use of the Federal areas known as national parks, monuments, and reservations hereinafter specified by such means and measures as conform to the fundamental purpose of the said parks, monuments, and reservations, which purpose is to conserve the scenery and the natural and historic objects and the wild life therein and to provide for the enjoyment of the same in such manner and by such means as will leave them unimpaired for the enjoyment of future generations. . . .

SEC. 3. That the Secretary of the Interior shall make and publish such rules and regulations as he may deem necessary or proper for the use and management of the parks, monuments, and reservations under the jurisdiction of the National Park Service. . . . He may also, upon terms and conditions to be fixed by him, sell or dispose of timber in those cases where in his judgment the cutting of such timber is required in order to control the attacks of insects or diseases or otherwise conserve the scenery or the natural or historic objects in any such park, monument, or reservation. He may also provide in his discretion for the destruction of such animals and of such plant life as may be detrimental to the use of any of said parks, monuments, or reservations. He may also grant privileges, leases, and permits for the use of land for the accommodation of visitors in the various parks, monuments, or other reservations herein provided for, but for periods not exceeding twenty years;

From The National Parks Act, *The Statutes at Large of the United States of America from December 1915 to March 1917.* Washington, D.C.: Government Printing Office, 1917, vol. 39, part 1, pp. 535–536.

and no natural curiosities, wonders, or objects of interest shall be leased, rented, or granted to anyone on such terms as to interfere with free access to them by the public: *Provided, however,* That the Secretary of the Interior may, under such rules and regulations and on such terms as he may prescribe, grant the privilege to graze live stock within any national park, monument, or reservation herein referred to when in his judgment such use is not detrimental to the primary purpose for which such park, monument, or reservation was created, except that this provision shall not apply to the Yellowstone National Park.

5. Chief Luther Standing Bear Gives an Indian View of Wilderness, Recorded in 1933

"We did not think of the great open plains, the beautiful rolling hills, and winding streams with tangled growth, as 'wild.' Only to the white man was nature a 'wilderness' and only to him was the land 'infested' with 'wild' animals and 'savage' people. To us it was tame. Earth was bountiful and we were surrounded with the blessings of the Great Mystery. Not until the hairy man from the east came and with brutal frenzy heaped injustices upon us and the families we loved was it 'wild' for us. When the very animals of the forest began fleeing from his approach, then it was that for us the 'Wild West' began."

6. The Wilderness Act, 1964

AN ACT

To establish a National Wilderness Preservation System for the permanent good of the whole people, and for other purposes.

Be it enacted by the Senate and House of Representatives of the United States of America in Congress assembled,

Short Title

Section I. This Act may be cited as the "Wilderness Act".

Wilderness System Established Statement of Policy

Sec. 2. (a) In order to assure that an increasing population, accompanied by expanding settlement and growing mechanization, does not occupy and modify all areas within the United States and its possessions, leaving no lands designated for preservation and protection in their natural condition, it is hereby declared to be the policy of the Congress to secure for the American people of present and future generations

---

Document 5 is from Chief Standing Bear, *Land of the Spotted Eagle*. Boston: Houghton Mifflin, 1933, p. xix.

Document 6 is from The Wilderness Act, Public Law 88-577, 88th Congress, S.4, September 3, 1964.

the benefits of an enduring resource of wilderness. For this purpose there is hereby established a National Wilderness Preservation System to be composed of federally owned areas designated by Congress as "wilderness areas", and these shall be administered for the use and enjoyment of the American people in such manner as will leave them unimpaired for future use and enjoyment as wilderness; and no Federal lands shall be designated as "wilderness areas" except as provided for in this Act or by a subsequent Act.

(b) The inclusion of an area in the National Wilderness Preservation System notwithstanding, the area shall continue to be managed by the Department and agency having jurisdiction thereover immediately before its inclusion in the national Wilderness Preservation System unless otherwise provided by Act of Congress. No appropriation shall be available for the payment of expenses or salaries for the administration of the national Wilderness Preservation System as a separate unit nor shall any appropriations be available for additional personnel stated as being required solely for the purpose of managing or administering areas solely because they are included within the National Wilderness Preservation System.

Definition of Wilderness

(c) A wilderness, in contrast with those areas where man and his own works dominate the landscape, is hereby recognized as an area where the earth and its community of life are untrammeled by man, where man himself is a visitor who does not remain. An area of wilderness is further defined to mean in this Act an area of undeveloped Federal land retaining its primeval character and influence, without permanent improvements or human habitation, which is protected and managed so as to preserve its natural conditions and which (1) generally appears to have been affected primarily by the forces of nature, with the imprint of man's work substantially unnoticeable; (2) has outstanding opportunities for solitude or a primitive and unconfined type of recreation; (3) has at least five thousand acres of land or is of sufficient size as to make practicable its preservation and use in an unimpaired condition; and (4) may also contain ecological, geological, or other features of scientific, educational, scenic, or historical value.

7. Edward Abbey on Industrial Tourism in the National Parks, 1968

I was sitting out back on my 33,000-acre terrace, shoeless and shirtless, scratching my toes in the sand and sipping on a tall iced drink, watching the flow of evening over the desert. Prime time: the sun very low in the west, the birds coming back to life, the shadows rolling for miles over rock and sand to the very base of the brilliant mountains. I had a small fire going near the table—not for heat or light but for the fragrance of the juniper and the ritual appeal of the clear flames. For symbolic reasons. For ceremony. When I heard a faint sound over my shoulder I looked and saw a file of deer watching from fifty yards away, three does and a velvet-horned buck, all dark against the sundown sky. They began to move. I whistled and they stopped again, staring at me. "Come on over," I said, "have a drink." They declined, moving off with casual, unhurried grace, quiet as phantoms, and disappeared beyond the rise. Smiling, thoroughly at peace, I turned back to my drink, the little fire, the subtle transformations of the immense landscape before me. On the program: rise of the full moon.

It was then I heard the discordant note, the snarling whine of a jeep in low range and four-wheel-drive, coming from an unexpected direction, from the vicinity of the old foot and horse trail that leads from Balanced Rock down toward Courthouse Wash and on to park headquarters near Moab. The jeep came in sight from beyond some bluffs, turned onto the dirt road, and came up the hill toward the entrance station. Now operating a motor vehicle of any kind on the trails of a national park is strictly forbidden, a nasty bureaucratic regulation which I heartily support. My bosom swelled with the righteous indignation of a cop: by God, I thought, I'm going to write these sons of bitches a ticket. I put down the drink and strode to the house trailer to get my badge.

Long before I could find the shirt with the badge on it, however, or the ticket book, or my shoes or my park ranger hat, the jeep turned in at my driveway and came right up to the door of the trailer. It was a gray jeep with a U.S. Government decal on the side—Bureau of Public Roads—and covered with dust. Two empty water bags flapped at the bumper. Inside were three sunburned men in twill britches and engineering boots, and a pile of equipment: transit case, tripod, survey rod, bundles of wooden stakes. (*Oh no!*) The men got out, dripping with dust, and the driver grinned at me, pointing to his parched open mouth and making horrible gasping noises deep in his throat.

"Okay," I said, "come on in."

It was even hotter inside the trailer than outside but I opened the refrigerator and left it open and took out a pitcher filled with ice cubes and water. As they passed the pitcher back and forth I got the full and terrible story, confirming the worst of my fears. They were a survey crew, laying out a new road into the Arches. . . .

As I type these words, several years after the little episode of the gray jeep and the thirsty engineers, . . . Arches National Monument has been developed. The Master Plan has been fulfilled. Where once a few adventurous people came on weekends to camp for a night or two and enjoy a taste of the primitive and remote, you will now find serpentine streams of baroque automobiles pouring in and out, all through the spring and summer, in numbers that would have seemed fantastic when I worked there: from 3,000 to 30,000 to 300,000 per year, the "visitation," as they call it, mounts ever upward. The little campgrounds where I used to putter around reading three-day-old newspapers full of lies and watermelon seeds have now been consolidated into one master campground that looks, during the busy season, like a suburban village: elaborate housetrailers of quilted aluminum crowd upon gigantic camper-trucks of Fiberglas and molded plastic; through their windows you will see the blue glow of television and hear the studio laughter of Los Angeles; knobby-kneed oldsters in plaid Bermudas buzz up and down the quaintly curving asphalt road on motorbikes; quarrels break out between campsite neighbors while others gather around their burning charcoal briquettes (ground campfires no longer permitted — not enough wood) to compare electric toothbrushes. The Comfort

Stations are there, too, all lit up with electricity, fully equipped inside, though the generator breaks down now and then and the lights go out, or the sewage backs up in the plumbing system (drain fields were laid out in sand over a solid bed of sandstone), and the water supply sometimes fails, since the 3000-foot well can only produce about 5gpm—not always enough to meet the demand. Down at the beginning of the new road, at park headquarters, is the new entrance station and visitor center, where admission fees are collected and where the rangers are going quietly nuts answering the same three basic questions five hundred times a day: (1) Where's the john? (2) How long's it take to see this place? (3) Where's the Coke machine?

Progress has come at last to the Arches, after a million years of neglect. Industrial Tourism has arrived.

What happened to Arches Natural Money-mint is, of course, an old story in the Park Service. All the famous national parks have the same problems on a far grander scale, as everyone knows, and many other problems as yet unknown to a little subordinate unit of the system in a backward part of southeastern Utah. And the same kind of development that has so transformed Arches is under way, planned or completed in many more national parks and national monuments. I will mention only a few examples with which I am personally familiar:

The newly established Canyonlands National Park. Most of the major points of interest in this park are presently accessible, over passable dirt roads, by car—Grandview Point, Upheaval Dome, part of the White Rim, Cave Spring, Squaw Spring campground and Elephant Hill. The more difficult places, such as Angel Arch or Druid Arch, can be reached by jeep, on horseback or in a one- or two-day hike. Nevertheless the Park Service had drawn up the usual Master Plan calling for modern paved highways to most of the places named and some not named.

Grand Canyon National Park. Most of the south rim of this park is now closely followed by a conventional high-speed highway and interrupted at numerous places by large asphalt parking lots. It is no longer easy, on the South Rim, to get away from the roar of motor traffic, except by descending into the canyon.

Navajo National Monument. A small, fragile, hidden place containing two of the most beautiful cliff dwellings in the Southwest—Keet Seel and Betatakin. This park will be difficult to protect under heavy visitation, and for years it was understood that it would be preserved in a primitive way so as to screen out those tourists unwilling to drive their cars over some twenty miles of dirt road. No longer so: the road has been paved, the campground enlarged and "modernized," and the old magic destroyed.

Natural Bridges National Monument. Another small gem in the park system, a group of three adjacent natural bridges tucked away in the canyon country of southern Utah. Formerly you could drive your car (over dirt roads, of course) to within sight of and easy walking distance—a hundred yards?—of the most spectacular of the three bridges. From there it was only a few hours walking time to the other two. All three could easily be seen in a single day. But this was not good enough for the developers. They have now constructed a paved road into the heart of the area, between the two biggest bridges.

Zion National Park. The northwestern part of this park, known as the Kolob area, has until recently been saved as almost virgin wilderness. But a broad highway, with banked curves, deep cuts and heavy fills, that will invade this splendid region, is already under construction.

Capitol Reef National Monument. Grand and colorful scenery in a rugged land—south-central Utah. The most beautiful portion of that park was the canyon of the Fremont River, a great place for hiking, camping, exploring. And what did the authorities do? They built a state highway through it.

Lee's Ferry. Until a few years ago a simple, quiet, primitive place on the shores of the Colorado, Lee's Ferry has now fallen under the protection of the Park Service. And who can protect it against the Park Service? Powerlines now bisect the scene, a 100-foot pink water tower looms against the red cliffs; tract-style houses are built to house the "protectors"; natural campsites along the river are closed off while all campers are now herded into an artificial steel-and-asphalt "campground" in the hottest, windiest spot in the area; historic buildings are razed by bulldozers to save the expense of maintaining them while at the same time hundreds of thousands of dollars are spent on an unneeded paved entrance road. And the administrators complain of *vandalism.*

I could easily cite ten more examples of unnecessary or destructive development for every one I've named so far. What has happened in these particular areas, which I chance to know a little and love too much, has happened, is happening, or will soon happen to the majority of our national parks and national forests, despite the illusory protection of the Wilderness Preservation Act, unless a great many citizens rear up on their hind legs and make vigorous political gestures demanding implementation of the Act. . . .

The Park Service, established by Congress in 1916, was directed not only to administer the parks but also to "provide for the enjoyment of same in such manner and by such means as will leave them unimpaired for the enjoyment of future generations." This appropriately ambiguous language, employed long before the onslaught of the automobile, has been understood in various and often opposing ways ever since. The Park Service, like any other big organization, includes factions and factions. The Developers, the dominant faction, place their emphasis on the words *"provide for the enjoyment."* The Preservers, a minority but also strong, emphasize the words *"leave them unimpaired."* It is apparent, then, that we cannot decide the question of development versus preservation by a simple referral to holy writ or an attempt to guess the intention of the founding fathers; we must make up our own minds and decide for ourselves what the national parks should be and what purpose they should serve.

The first issue that appears when we get into this matter, the most important issue and perhaps the only issue, is the one called *accessibility.* The Developers insist that the parks must be made fully accessible not only to people but also to their machines, that is, to automobiles, motorboats, etc. The Preservers argue, in principle at least, that wilderness and motors are incompatible and that the former can best be experienced, understood, and enjoyed when the machines are left behind where they belong—on the superhighways and in the parking lots, on the reservoirs and in the marinas.

What does accessibility mean? Is there any spot on earth that men have not proved accessible by the simplest means—feet and legs and heart? Even Mt. McKinley, even Everest, have been surmounted by men on foot. (Some of them, incidentally, rank amateurs, to the horror and indignation of the professional mountaineers.) The interior of the Grand Canyon, a fiercely hot and hostile abyss, is visited each summer by thousands and thousands of tourists of the most banal and unadventurous type, many of them on foot—self-propelled, so to speak—and the others on the backs of mules. Thousands climb each summer to the summit of Mt. Whitney, highest point in the forty-eight United States, while multitudes of others wander on foot or on horseback through the ranges of the Sierras, the Rockies, the Big Smokies, the Cascades and the mountains of New England. Still more hundreds and thousands float or paddle each year down the currents of the Salmon, the Snake, the Allagash, the Yampa, the Green, the Rio Grande, the Ozark, the St. Croix and those portions of the Colorado which have not yet been destroyed by the dam builders. And most significant, these hordes of nonmotorized tourists, hungry for a taste of the difficult, the original, the real, do not consist solely of people young and athletic but also of old folks, fat folks, pale-faced office clerks who don't know a rucksack from a haversack, and even children. The one thing they all have in common is the refusal to live always like sardines in a can—they are determined to get outside of their motorcars for at least a few weeks each year. . . .

Industrial Tourism is a threat to the national parks. But the chief victims of the system are the motorized tourists. They are being robbed and robbing themselves. So long as they are unwilling to crawl out of their cars they will not discover the treasures of the national parks and will never escape the stress and turmoil of the urban-suburban complexes which they had hoped, presumably, to leave behind for a while.

How to pry the tourists out of their automobiles, out of their back-breaking up-holstered mechanized wheelchairs and onto their feet, onto the strange warmth and solidity of Mother Earth again? This is the problem which the Park Service should confront directly, not evasively, and which it cannot resolve by simply submitting and conforming to the automobile habit. The automobile, which began as a trans-portation convenience, has become a bloody tyrant (50,000 lives a year), and it is the responsibility of the Park Service, as well as that of everyone else concerned with preserving both wilderness and civilization, to begin a campaign of resistance. The automotive combine has almost succeeded in strangling our cities; we need not let it also destroy our national parks.

❧ E S S A Y S

The essays in this chapter examine wilderness values from a range of perspectives. In the first selection, Roderick Nash, an environmental historian formerly at the University of California at Santa Barbara, argues that wilderness preservation emerged primarily from the concerns of eastern urbanites, and he delineates eight reasons why wilderness should be saved. In the second essay, historian and Native American advocate Philip Burnham shows how American Indians were removed from or excluded from newly created national parks, including areas where they had seasonally gathered, hunted, and fished for millennia, or alternatively were allowed to remain as tourist attractions, issues that are still contested today. In the third essay, University of Wisconsin environ-mental historian William Cronon asks probing questions about the rationale for creating wilderness and argues that it is a human construct influenced by historical circumstances such as the ending of the frontier and a romantic appreciation for the sublime. Rather than focusing exclusively on an awe of remote places, thereby creating a dualism be-tween nature and humanity, Cronon argues, we should also appreciate and care for our home places and the nature found therein, for these are the places in which we actually dwell. As a whole the essays explore the history of the movement to appreciate and save natural areas; the class, race, and gender issues that are at stake when nonhuman nature is defined and preserved as wilderness; and the meaning of wild areas and their importance to human well-being.

The Value of Wilderness

RODERICK NASH

Historians believe that one of the most distinguishing characteristics of American culture is the fact that it emerged from a wilderness in less than four centuries. The Europeans who migrated to North America in the seventeenth century settled in a wilderness. The so-called Indians, who had occupied the region for some 20,000 years, were unfortunately regarded as wild animals. The pioneers, as they were called, were principally concerned with transforming wilderness into civilization. They were the vanguard of a westward-moving empire, and they referred to the continually moving line at which their civilization abutted the wilderness as the "frontier." Clearly this term signifies in the United States something quite different from in Europe, where a "frontier" is taken to be the boundary between nations. The American frontier was the boundary between the wild and the civilized. It existed in the United States as recently as 1890. In that year the federal census published a report showing that settlement of the continent had proceeded to such an extent that the term frontier no longer had meaning. Significantly, 1890 was also the year of the last major war of Indian resistance in the American West. The white man's control of the continent and its aboriginal occupants was complete.

The early American attitude toward wilderness was highly unfavorable. Wild country was the enemy. The pioneer saw as his mission the destruction of wilderness. Protecting it for its scenic and recreational values was the last thing frontiersmen desired. The problem was too much raw nature rather than too little. Wild land had to be battled as a physical obstacle to comfort and even to survival. The country had to be "cleared" of trees; Indians had to be "removed;" wild animals had to be exterminated. National pride arose from transforming wilderness into civilization, not preserving it for public enjoyment. But by 1872, the year of the creation of Yellowstone National Park, the world's first, the attitude of some Americans toward undeveloped land had sufficiently shifted to permit the beginnings of appreciation. So Yellowstone National Park was designated on March 1, 1872 as "a public park or pleasuring ground" in which all the features of this 3,000 square-mile wilderness in northwestern Wyoming would be left "in their natural condition." . . .

The appreciation of wilderness . . . appeared first in the minds of sophisticated Americans living in the more civilized East. George Catlin, American painter of Indians and landscapes, and the father in 1832 of the idea of a national park, made the point clearly and succinctly. "The further we become separated from pristine

From Roderick Nash, "The Value of Wilderness," *Environmental Review* 3 (1977), pp. 14–25. Reprinted with permission from *Environmental History Review,* © 1977, the American Society for Environmental History.

wildness and beauty, the more pleasure does the mind of enlightened man feel in recurring to those scenes." Catlin was himself an example. He lived in Philadelphia, an Eastern city in one of the original thirteen states, Pennsylvania. Catlin was civilized enough to appreciate wilderness. Living in a city, he did not have to battle wild country on a day-to-day basis like a pioneer. For him it was a novelty and a place for a vacation. Indeed Catlin looked forward each summer in the 1830's to escaping from his Eastern artist's studio to the wilderness along the upper Missouri River.

All the nineteenth-century champions of wilderness appreciation and national parks in the United States were products of either urban Eastern situations or of one of the West's most sophisticated cities, such as San Francisco. Lumbermen, miners, and professional hunters did not, as a rule, advocate scenic and recreational conservation. They lived too close to nature to appreciate it for other than its economic value as raw material. Let one additional example suffice to make the point. Henry David Thoreau, American nature philosopher, went to Harvard University and lived near Boston in the highly civilized Eastern seaboard state of Massachusetts. Thoreau believed that a certain amount of wildness (which he regarded as synonymous with freedom, vigor, and creativity) was essential to the success of a society as well as an individual. Neither a person nor a culture should, in Thoreau's opinion, become totally civilized. For this reason Thoreau advocated national parks as reservoirs of physical and intellectual nourishment. "Why should not we . . . have our national preserves," he wondered in 1858, ". . . not for idle sport or food, but for inspiration and our own true recreation?" Of course Thoreau approved of the idea of large national parks in the West, although he did not live to see the concept realized, but he also advocated reserving wild places in settled areas. Every Massachusetts town or village, he argued in 1859, "should have a park, or rather a primitive forest, of five hundred or a thousand acres." The public would own such places, according to Thoreau's plan, and they would be guarded against economic exploitation of any kind. With natural landscapes disappearing rapidly from the environment of the eastern portions of the United States, arguments like those of Thoreau made increasing sense. The special American relationship to wilderness—having it, being shaped by it, and then almost eliminating it—was working to create the most persuasive case for Yellowstone and the other national parks that followed. . . .

The first legal preservation for public use of an area with scenic and recreational values occurred in 1864 when the federal government granted the Yosemite Valley to the state of California "for public use, resort and recreation." Technically, the Yosemite grant of 1864 was not the first federal act. In 1832 some hot springs in the state of Arkansas were set aside as a national reservation. The area was tiny, however, heavily developed, hardly scenic, and very much in the tradition of public spas and baths common, for example, in Europe. Carved by glaciers and the Merced River into the western slope of a mountain range in California called the Sierra, Yosemite ranks among the world's most spectacular scenic wonders. It was discovered by white men less than two decades before the act of 1864. The area reserved was only the valley floor, about ten square miles. The larger national park that also bears the name "Yosemite" did not exist until 1891.

The landscape architect Frederick Law Olmsted proved most perceptive in understanding the principles which justified the 1864 reservation of Yosemite Valley as a state park. Olmsted's 1865 report also illustrates how social ownership of scenic and recreational resources could be enthusiastically supported in a nation that, especially in the late nineteenth century, valued private property and a minimum of govern-ment interference with the development of natural resources by an unrestrained cap-italist economy. Olmsted began by observing that exceptional natural environments, such as Yosemite Valley, should not become private property. He explained that it was the duty of a democratic government "to provide means of protection for all its citizens in the pursuit of happiness against the obstacles . . . which the selfishness of individuals or combinations of individuals is liable to interpose to that pursuit." Until the 1860's, few political philosophers had understood this protective function of government to extend beyond economic, military, and educational consideration to those involving the enjoyment of nature. Nowhere in the documents and com-mentary associated with the establishment of the United States in 1776 and 1787 did the concept of "pursuit of happiness" appear to include the provision by the gov-ernment of opportunities to enjoy natural scenery and outdoor recreation. Olmsted, however, argued that this was a justifiable extension of the central principle of the democratic-republican theory on which the nation stood. . . .

Besides a favorable attitude toward undeveloped nature and a democratic politi-cal tradition, the final factor explaining the American invention of national parks was simply affluence. The wealth of the United States subsidized national parks. We were and have remained rich enough to afford the luxury of setting aside some land for its non-material values. Had the United States been struggling at the subsistence level, scenic and recreational conservation would have, at the least, demanded a much harder decision. Probably they would not have occurred at all. Ironically, American success in exploiting the environment increased the likelihood of its protection. The axiom seems to hold that nature protection is a full-stomach phenomenon.

Since the time of Catlin, Thoreau, and Olmsted, American thinkers have sub-stantially expanded the justification for scenic and recreational conservation. They have been aided considerably by changing circumstances. To a far greater extent than in 1864 and 1872, when the Yosemite and Yellowstone reservations were made, the United States is urbanized and industrialized. About 75 per cent of the population lives in cities. The amount of wilderness (both protected and unprotected and not counting the state of Alaska) is, by generous reckoning, about 180,000 square miles out of three million, or 6 per cent of the forty-eight contiguous states. Close to the same amount of land is *paved!*

In this context, so new to Americans who once believed the wilderness beyond the frontier to be endless, several arguments have emerged to become the staples in the contemporary defense of nature protection in the United States. While they are presented here in terms of wilderness, such as exists in the larger national parks like Yellowstone and Yosemite, they may be applied in slightly altered form to any open space or nature reserve. They might also be applied, with appropriate alteration, to Italy or any other nation. The summary that follows is in outline form.

Argument 1: Wilderness as a Reservoir of Normal Ecological Processes

Aldo Leopold, wildlife manager and philosopher whose efforts led in 1924 to creation of the first reserved wilderness on National Forest land in the United States, once said that wilderness reveals "what the land was, what it is, and what it ought to be." He added that nature reserves conceivably had more importance for science than they did for recreation. What Leopold meant was that wilderness is a model of healthy, ecologically balanced land. At a time when so much of the environment is disturbed by technological man, wilderness has vital importance as a criterion against which to measure the impact of civilization. Without it we have no way of knowing how the land mechanism functions under normal conditions. The science of ecology needs nature reserves as medical science needs healthy people.

Argument 2: Wilderness as a Sustainer of Biological Diversity

It is axiomatic in the biological sciences that there is strength in diversity. The whole evolutionary miracle is based on the presence over time of an almost infinite diversity of life forms. Maintenance of the full evolutionary capacity that produced life as we know it and, we may suppose, will continue to shape life on earth, means that the size of the gene pool should be maximized. But with his agriculture and urban growth, modern man has made extensive inroads on biological diversity. Some of the changes, to be sure, have been desirable. But many are carried too far. More species have been exterminated in the last three hundred years than in the previous three million. Many other species, including some of the most awesome life forms on earth, are threatened. The whales fall into this category. The problem is that man in his shortsighted pursuit of what he believes to be his self-interest has branded some forms of life as "useless" and therefore expendable. The creative processes that produced these life forms in the first place did not regard them as such. Modern man frequently appears to be a clumsy mechanic, pounding on a delicate and complex machine with a sledgehammer. . . .

Argument 3: Wilderness as Formative Influence on American National Character

It was not until the census report of 1890 pronounced the frontier era ended that many Americans began to ponder the significance of wilderness in shaping them as individuals and as a society. The link between American character or identity, and wilderness, was forged, as historian Frederick Jackson Turner argued so persuasively in 1893, during three centuries of pioneering. Independence and individualism were two heritages; a democratic social and political theory and the concept of equal opportunity were other frontier traits. So was the penchant for practical achievement that marks the American character so distinctly.

If wilderness shaped our national values and institutions, it follows that one of the most important roles of nature reserves is keeping those values and institutions alive. Theodore Roosevelt, President of the United States from 1901 to 1909 and the leader of the first period of great achievement in conservation, was keenly aware of this relationship. "Under the hard conditions of life in the wilderness," Roosevelt wrote, those who migrated to the New World "lost all remembrance of Europe" and became new men "in dress, in customs, and in mode of life." But the United States by 1900 was becoming increasingly like the more civilized and longer settled parts of the world. Consequently Roosevelt declared that "as our civilization grows older and more complex, we need a greater and not a less development of the fundamental frontier virtues." The Boy Scouts of America was just one of the responses of Roosevelt's contemporaries to the problem he described. Without wilderness areas in which successive generations can relearn the values of their pioneer ancestors, the American culture will surely change. Perhaps it should, but many remain concerned about cutting off the roots of their national character. And merely from the standpoint of safeguarding an historical document, a part of the national past, we should save wilderness. Once all America was wild; without remnants to refresh our memories we run the risk of cultural amnesia.

Argument 4: Wilderness as Nourisher of American Arts and Letters

Time and again in the course of history the native land has been the inspiration for great works of music, painting, and literature. What the American painter, Alan Gussow, calls "a sense of place" is as vital to the artistic endeavor as it is to patriotism and national pride. And "place," it should be clear, has to do with the natural setting. Subdivisions, factories, and used car lots rarely inspire artistic excellence. Nature commonly does. Parks and reserves, as reservoirs of scenic beauty that touches the soul of man, have a crucial role in the quality of a nation's culture.

Certainly the United States would have a poorer artistic heritage without the existence of wild places of inspiring beauty. James Fenimore Cooper in literature, Thomas Cole and Albert Bierstadt in painting, and, to take a recent example, John Denver in music, have based their art on wilderness. In the case of the United States, wilderness had a special relationship to culture. It was the one attribute the young nation had in abundance, the characteristic that set it apart from Old World countries. Ralph Waldo Emerson and Henry David Thoreau were among the many who, by the mid-nineteenth century, called on America to attain cultural self-reliance by basing its art on the native landscape. Nature, for these philosophers, was intellectual fertilizer. Blended in the proper proportion with civilization, it produced cultural greatness. Thoreau was fond of pointing out that the grandeur that was Rome at its zenith had its beginnings in the rearing of Romulus and Remus by that symbol of the wild, a wolf. When these wild roots became buried beneath too much civilization, Rome declined and fell. The conquerers, significantly, were wilder people—barbarians from the forests and the steppes. . . .

Cole's [1836 five panel painting, "The] Course of Empire" contained a clear lesson for the United States. If it was to avoid the cyclical pattern of rise and fall, the inspiring qualities of nature had best be made a permanent part of the American environment. The point was to avoid becoming *over* civilized and decadent. One means to that end, Cole advised his countrymen, was to preserve parts of the American wilderness while civilization grew up around them. Cultural greatness, indeed cultural survival, depended on this blending of environments.

Argument 5: Wilderness as a Church

With the aid of churches and religions, people attempt to find solutions to, or at least live with, the weightiest mental and emotional problems of human existence. One value of wilderness for some people is its significance as a setting for what is, essentially, religious activity. In nature, as in a church, they attempt to bring meaning and tranquility to their lives. They seek a sense of oneness, of harmony, with all things. Wilderness appeals as a place to knot together the unity that civilization tends to fragment. Contact with the natural world shows man his place in systems that transcend civilization and inculcates reverence for those systems. The result is peace.

The Transcendental philosophers, Ralph Waldo Emerson and Henry David Thoreau, were among the first Americans to emphasize the religious importance of nature. Moral and aesthetic truths seemed to them to be more easily observed in wild places than in regions where civilization interposed a layer of artificiality between man and nature. John Muir, a leading force in the preservation of Yosemite National Park and first president of the Sierra Club, also believed that to be closer to nature was to be closer to God. The wild Sierra that he explored and lived in was simply a "window opening into heaven, a mirror reflecting the Creator." Leaves, rocks, and lakes were "sparks of the Divine Soul." Muir spent little time in a building called a church, but his enjoyment of wilderness was religious in every sense of the word.

Argument 6: Wilderness as a Guardian of Mental Health

Sigurd Olson, veteran guide and interpreter of the canoe country extending northward from Lake Superior, noted in 1946 that "civilization has not changed emotional needs that were ours long before it arose." Sigmund Freud had the same idea when he said that civilization bred "discontents" in the form of repressions and frustrations. One of the most distressing for modern man is the bewildering complexity of events and ideas with which civilization obliges him to deal. The price of failing to cope with the new "wilderness" of people and paper is psychological problems. The value of wilderness and outdoor recreation is the opportunity it extends to civilized man to slip back, occasionally, into what Olson calls "the grooves of ancestral experience." The leading advocate of wilderness protection in the 1930's, Robert Marshall, spoke of the "psychological necessity" for occasional escape to "the freedom of the wilderness."

Olson and Marshall were referring to the fact that wild country offers people an alternative to civilization. The wilderness is different. For one thing, it simplifies. It reduces the life of those who enter it to finding basic human needs and satisfactions, such as unmechanized transportation, water, food, and shelter. Civilization does not commonly permit us this kind of self-sufficiency and its dividend, self-confidence. A hike of ten miles has more meaning in this respect than a flight of ten thousand. Wilderness also reacquaints civilized people with pain and fear. Surprising to some, these are ancient energizing forces—springboards to achievement long before monetary success and status were even conceived. The gut-level fears associated with survival drove the wheels of evolution. At times, of course, they hurt and even killed, but we pay a price in achievement for entering the promised land of safety and comfort. For many it is horribly dull. They turn to crime or drugs or war to fill their needs for risk and challenge. Others find beds in mental institutions the only recourse. Wilderness recreation is a better alternative.

Argument 7: Wilderness as a Sustainer of Human Diversity

Just as it promotes biological diversity (see Argument 2), the preservation of wilderness helps to preserve human dignity and social diversity. Civilization means control, organization, homogenization. Wilderness offers relief from these dehumanizing tendencies; it encourages individuality. Wild country is an arena where man can experiment, deviate, discover, and improve. Was not this the whole meaning of the New World wilderness for those settlers who migrated to it from Europe? Wilderness meant freedom. Aldo Leopold put it this way: "of what avail are forty freedoms without a blank spot on the map?" For novelist Wallace Stegner wild country was "a place of perpetual beginnings." . . .

There is another sense in which wilderness preservation joins hands with the perpetuation of human diversity. The very existence of wilderness is evidence of respect for minority rights. Only a fraction, although a rapidly growing one, of the American people seek scenic beauty and wilderness recreation. Only a fraction care about horse racing or opera or libraries. The fact that these things can exist is a tribute to nations that cherish and defend minority interests as part of their political ideology. Robert Marshall of the United States Forest Service made it plain in the 1930's that protection of minority rights is one of the hallmarks of a successful democracy. The majority may rule, said Marshall, but that does not mean it can impose its values universally. Otherwise art galleries (a minority interest) would be converted into hamburger stands and amusement parks. The need was for a fair division—of land, for instance—to accommodate a variety of tastes and values.

Argument 8: Wilderness as an Educational Asset in Developing Environmental Responsibility

To experience wilderness is to discover natural processes and man's dependency upon them. It is to discover man's vulnerability and, through this realization, to attain humility. Life in civilization tends to promote antipodal qualities: arrogance and a sense of mastery. Not only children believe that milk comes from bottles and heat from radiators. "Civilization," Aldo Leopold wrote, "has so cluttered [the] elemental man-earth relation with gadgets and middlemen that awareness of it is growing dim. We fancy that industry supports us, forgetting what supports industry." Contact with wilderness is a corrective that modern man desperately needs if he is to achieve long-term harmony between himself and his environment.

Wilderness can also instruct man that he is a member, not the master, of a community that extends to the limits of life and the earth itself. Because wild country is beyond man's control, because it exists apart from human needs and interests, it suggests that man's welfare is not the primary reason for or purpose of the existence of the earth. This seemingly simple truth is not easily understood in a technological civilization whose basis is control and exploitation. In wilderness we appreciate other powers and interests because we find our own limited.

A final contribution of wilderness to the cause of environmental responsibility is a heightened appreciation of the meaning and importance of restraint. When we establish a wilderness reserve or national park we say, in effect, thus far, and no farther to development. We establish a limit. For Americans self-limitation does not come easily. Growth has been our national religion. But to maintain an area as wilderness is to put other considerations before material growth. It is to respect the rights of non-human life to habitat. It is to challenge the wisdom and moral legitimacy of man's conquest and transformation of the entire earth. This acceptance of restraint is fundamental if people are to live within the limits of the earth.

The United States developed its present system of scenic and recreational conservation because of public acceptance of the eight arguments just presented. So it is that attitudes and values can shape a nation's environment just as do bulldozers and chain saws. Nature reserves exist and will continue to exist under republican forms of government only because they are valued by society.

Indians and Wilderness

PHILIP BURNHAM

When the artist George Catlin wrote in the 1830s of "a *magnificent park,* where the world could see for ages to come, the native Indian in his classic attire, galloping his wild horse, with sinewy bow, and shield and lance, amid the fleeting herds of elks and buffaloes," he envisioned a national park that would never be. Regarded as one of the founders of the national park idea, Catlin's image of an Indian chasing buffalo before an adoring crowd was not only misguided but, as it turned out, unthinkable. . . . During the fifty years that followed the founding of these parks, Indians were assumed, at best, to be useful as advertising icons or as a source of cheap labor and entertainment. Though Catlin foresaw, as early as the 1830s, the demise of the buffalo and feared a similar fate would befall Indians, he could not have predicted that native people would one day be banned from Yellowstone park: a true repudiation of his dream. . . .

Catlin's vision, however exhilarating, today seems hopelessly doomed: "I would ask no other monument to my memory," he wrote, "nor any other enrolment of my name amongst the famous dead, than the reputation of having been the founder of such an institution." Even as he made his celebrated travels across the West in the 1830s, painting images of Mandan villages and Sioux buffalo hunts that today are ethnographic treasures, settlement patterns were bringing pressure to bear on his noble subjects. The reason was the existence of an American commodity made all the more affordable by its abundance: land. To understand how national parks and Native Americans came to be antagonists at all, it's necessary to consider nineteenth-century attitudes toward the land—most of it in the West held by Washington under the protective status of "public domain."

Land in public domain belonged to the federal government by right of discovery, purchase, conquest, or treaty. After the Ordinance of 1785 established an extensive system of land surveys, the government began auctioning public domain to speculators and small landowners. The revenues from such sales were important, for some of the money went to pay off the national debt incurred from the Revolutionary War. By 1860, most of the public land remaining in the United States was west of the Mississippi River—thanks to the Louisiana Purchase of 1803, the 1846 treaty with Great Britain that put the Northwest under federal control, and the huge expanse of the Southwest gained in the aftermath of the Mexican-American War in 1848. Most land on the eastern seaboard was in private hands long before the Constitution; in

From Philip Burnham, *Indian Country, God's Country: Native Americans and the National Parks.* Washington, D.C.: Island Press, 2000, pp. 15–22, 23, 39, 45–49, 51–53, 55–58. Reprinted by permission of Island Press.

the West, however, the federal government was in a position, however tenuous, to monitor the sale and distribution of landed property.

"Public domain" wasn't as public as it sounded. In fact, much of the "public" land was already home to American Indians who claimed the right of prior occupancy. In European thinking, however, the rights of "nomadic" peoples were severely limited. The French and Spanish, for example, claimed to own Indian lands in the Americas by simple "right of discovery." By contrast, the United States inherited a long-standing British policy of negotiating with Indian tribes as sovereign entities and compensating them for ceded lands. However "sovereign" tribes may have been in theory, their status was often compromised when settlement pressures made the acquisition of Indian land highly desirable. . . .

By the standards of an industrializing nation, Indian people were not fully "civilized." Though tribes like the Cherokee were successfully agrarian, the image of Indians roaming as aimless nomads across the continent became central in the public consciousness. In fact, people asserted, Indian tribes wandered over much more territory than they would need to support themselves as farmers, especially in the West. It thus became a civilized "duty" to convert the Indian from a nomadic way of life that was wasteful and inefficient to a settled—and more predictable—existence on a circumspect plot of land.

"When [Indians] withdraw themselves to the culture of a small piece of land," wrote Thomas Jefferson in 1803, the same year he purchased the Louisiana Territory from France, "they will perceive how useless to them are the extensive forests, and will be willing to pare them off from time to time in exchange for necessaries for their farms and families." This thinking was typical of Jefferson's belief that an economy of small landowners was America's best hope for democracy. Even the Indian might be made to fit Jefferson's prescription of the yeoman farmer—the utilitarian and democratic figure at the center of his agrarian dream. Though the president did not know it, he had written the very script by which many lands were destined to become national parks. . . .

In 1862, Congress passed the Homestead Act, a benchmark law in American democracy that provided claimants with "free" land. The act awarded 160 acres of public domain to anyone who would make improvements on it and pay a nominal filing fee. Native Americans, not considered citizens at the time, were denied the benefits of the act. When they did gain the legislative right to a homestead in 1875, it was with the provision that they sunder their tribal affiliations and take out a land patent in an individual name. Most Indians, however, did not have the cash to pay even a "nominal" filing fee. Ignorant of the laws regarding filing deadlines after the survey of lands, they frequently saw their homesteads preempted by white settlers. But the Plains tribes were soon to have yet another, still more powerful, rival to contend with. By the time the Civil War was over, a different ethic of land management was about to resist the private rush for land, further endangering Indian title on the Plains. . . .

The national parks were born from the irony that much of the West was inhospitable to white settlers. After all, homesteads weren't feasible everywhere across the dry and mountainous area known as "the Great American Desert." By the 1860s, many people were coming to believe there might be compelling reasons to reserve some of the public domain for purposes other than settlement or economic gain. Their concern was not for ecology, however, a science that wouldn't become a basis for park establishment until the 1930s. Nor did the role of recreation figure large in their thinking. As historian Alfred Runte has noted, our first parks were intended as a "cultural repository" of America whose monuments, in fact, were crafted by nature. Conceived at a time when the frontier was being claimed by settlers and ranchers, parks were established as a permanent way to preserve the grandeur of the American experience. . . .

The movement to create the parks began during the Civil War. Abraham Lincoln signed an act of Congress creating Yosemite state park in California in 1864, setting aside public domain that would "be held for public use, resort, and recreation . . . inalienable for all time." But the Yosemite area was far from uninhabited. In fact, the 1864 act meant the continuation of trouble for the Indians of the Yosemite Valley, soon to become the first native people to experience the mixed blessings of park tourism. The Yosemite people were a blend of several cultural and linguistic groups in the Sierra Nevada mountains—a mixture of the Miwok and Mono Paiute—and had populated the area for several centuries before being forced to compete with white settlers over land and other scarce resources during the two decades following the California gold rush.

The new park offered the Yosemite people the promise of work. Tribal members came to guide tourists (more than two thousand by 1874), supply fishing parties, chop wood, and harvest hay in the early years of the state park, for the popular Yosemite Valley was not under federal jurisdiction until 1906. The scarcity of local labor and the romantic appeal of Indians made the Yosemite people, at first, useful neighbors. By the 1880s, the tribe was weaving tourist baskets, dancing in public for fees, and charging visitors for the privilege of taking photographs. Thought by many to be "vanishing" at the turn of the century, native people, or their fleeting image, made an impressive souvenir. The Yosemite people were tolerated in the park and even enjoyed.

Not everyone found their presence so compelling. Environmentalist John Muir, instrumental in making the park a federal preserve and a later founder of the Sierra Club, found the Yosemite people dirty and indolent during a park visit in 1869, remarking with distaste on their fondness for imbibing ant and fly larvae. In his search for the pristine, there was little room for hunter-gatherers who "seemed sadly unlike Nature's neat well-dressed animals." Noted Muir: "From no point of view that I have found are such debased fellow beings a whit more natural than the glaring tailored tourists we saw that frightened the birds and squirrels." Acknowledging only a passing familiarity with the Yosemite people, Muir decided that "the worst thing about them is their uncleanliness," adding that, to his way of thinking, "nothing truly wild is unclean." Author Helen Hunt Jackson found the Yosemite "filthy" during a park excursion in the 1870s—a fact that did not bode well for the tribe, coming as it did from a woman whose book, *A Century of Dishonor* (1881), was about to make her the most famous Indian advocate of the nineteenth century.

The Yosemite people had some gripes of their own. Increased travel to the area forced tribal headmen, in an undated petition to the U.S. president from about 1890, to complain of ranchers and hoteliers who "have come into the valley to make money only." Complained the petitioning group of Yosemite, Mono, and Paiute chiefs and headmen: "Yosemite is no longer a State or National Park but merely a hay-farm and cattle range. . . . The People's Park is a thing of the past. It has now resolved itself into a private institution." Seeking an indemnity of $1 million for the loss of their homeland, the chiefs lamented further that "it will only be a short time before they will tell the Indians that they must go away and not come back any more." Through federal neglect, lack of employment, and a steep Park Service rent increase on resident Indians, the prophecy would be borne out some eighty years later. By that time the Indian village within the park had been razed.

The Yosemite people were tolerated in California for a time because they were useful. With the creation of Yellowstone in 1872—commonly regarded as our first national park—the local inhabitants were not so lucky. A tribe called the Sheepeater Shoshone had arrived in the Yellowstone area about 1800, migrating northeast from the Great Basin. A few hundred strong, they hunted bighorn sheep as their main food source, were renowned for tanning sheepskins, and crafted composite bows from animal horn so powerful they could drive an arrow entirely through a buffalo. In 1835, Captain Benjamin Bonneville described the tribe as "a kind of hermit race, scanty in number, that inhabit the highest and most inaccessible fastness."

As white expeditions penetrated the Yellowstone area in the 1860s, the Sheepeaters moved from being a curiosity to a nuisance to an impediment. In 1879, the tribe was removed from the park area by dint of a never-ratified treaty from 1868; some were taken in by Chief Washakie and the Eastern Shoshone at the Wind River Reservation, others removed to Idaho. Not long after removal, this small branch of the Shoshone would seem like an ancient relic. Philetus W. Norris, a Civil War veteran and Michigan real estate broker before being appointed Yellowstone superintendent, described the Sheepeaters in 1880 as a "pigmy tribe of three or four hundred timid and harmless" souls.

The tribe's one moment of fame was the so-called Sheepeater War of 1879, when fifty-one of them were brought to heel by the U.S. Army in Idaho after a three-month search for an enemy consisting mainly of women and children with fewer than a dozen firearms. This is the only time the Sheepeaters appear in our history books—and then with the dubious honor of lending their name (or one given them by a rival) to a war that they didn't win and may not have started in the first place. Three years after the war, General Philip Sheridan, leading a scouting expedition through the park, remarked how his Sheepeater guides, now confined to a reservation, "were greatly excited in getting back to their old country." . . .

Many other tribes hunted and used the Yellowstone Plateau, among them the Crow, Bannock, Blackfeet, and Nez Perce. Though the Shoshone were recent inhabitants of the area, Sheridan added in his report, they had "never visited the Geyser Basin and knew nothing about it," a fact that astonished him. Superintendent Norris went to great lengths to impress visitors that the geysers kept the naturally superstitious Indians out of the park, reassuring them that Yellowstone was a safe place for tourists to camp and hike. . . .

In 1880, Superintendent Norris negotiated a banishment of Indians from most of Yellowstone proper. Though tribes like the Bannock continued hunting in the backcountry until late in the century, it was not Indians that posed the gravest threat to the park: the bulk of poachers were white. In the 1880s, Yellowstone asked the government for help in enforcing regulations against hunters and squatters. Just as they had [earlier], the U.S. Army rode to the rescue. It can fairly be said—and has been said many times—that the army saved Yellowstone during its early decades from the plunder of squatters, souvenir collectors, and poachers. But for the tribes who had hunted the Yellowstone Plateau for centuries, the presence of the army was a reminder that Indians no longer belonged in a place the 1872 legislation declared would be "dedicated and set apart as a public park or pleasuring-ground for the benefit and enjoyment of the people." . . . By century's end, the park system had expanded across the West. Sequoia, General Grant, and Yosemite became federal parks in 1890; Mount Rainier followed within a decade. Indeed, one of the biggest prizes in the park system quietly entered the federal domain before the century was out. The acquisition of what would become the eastern half of Glacier National Park, in fact, was achieved by a strategy similar to the one employed [earlier]: isolate the Indians, remind them of their dependence on government "largesse," and tender a cash bid for territory that, given the depth of poverty on the reservation, could only be embraced.

Situated near the Canadian border, the Piegan people (a branch of the Blackfeet Confederacy) were vulnerable not only to harsh northern winters but also to the land commissions that seemed to emanate from Washington with the regularity of migrating elk. The Piegan, archaeological evidence shows, have dwelled in the vicinity of Glacier and worshiped in its mountain environs at sacred sites, with some interruptions, for over a thousand years—contrary to earlier scholarship that dated their arrival in the area to the mid-eighteenth century. At the eastern base of the Rocky Mountains they corralled buffalo and hunted abundant herds of deer and elk. Not until the eighteenth century did they meet white men, taking horses, guns, and metal tools in the exchange—and smallpox, too, surviving several devastating epidemics. The Piegan, perhaps the least aggressive of the Blackfeet people, were recognized by a treaty of 1855 to control a domain including much of present-day Montana from the Continental Divide to the Missouri River. . . .

. . . In 1882, General Philip Sheridan, following a trip through Yellowstone park, offered a modest proposal that, if not already stated policy, was a de facto description of the federal stratagem. Washington should buy Indian land on the cheap, advised Sheridan in his expedition report, purchase bonds with the money gained from public land sales, and set up a permanent interest-bearing fund for the tribes. But that was only half the story. "It would also be a good bargain for the Government," added Sheridan, "as the purchased land could be sold to actual settlers for an advance, and be occupied by people paying taxes, to say nothing of the opening up of the country." The liquidation of the reservations would do more than pay for itself.

But the theory didn't hold at Glacier. . . . In fact, it was soon decided that this region fit, if any did, the concept of "worthless lands." By 1897, . . . the government designated much of the ceded section a forest reserve. As mining claims proved unprofitable, a peculiar alliance developed with the intent of making the Glacier area a national park. The strange bedfellows included adventurers like [Audubon Society founder George Bird] Grinnell, conservation groups such as the Sierra Club, and the Great Northern Railway, which entered the Glacier region in 1892 and completed its transcontinental route the following year.

Respected government commissioners like . . . Grinnell played a major role in making the parks possible. Such men subscribed to the letter of democracy—organizing referendums and parleys to approve Indian land cessions—only to violate its spirit. . . . A secret ballot wasn't advisable—people might be swayed by leaders if given the luxury of voting unseen. Those supporting the cessions were usually asked to "touch the pen" in broad daylight—surely a convincing example to people with strong communal sentiments. Preach and pout as the doubters might, the reluctant ones were typically given time to change their minds. The result was ironic: the first experience many tribes had with "democracy" was the act of selling away their land. . . .

. . . The Blackfeet had sold [their homeland] Chief Mountain, one might say politely, "of their own accord." But given the misunderstandings and strong-armed elocution of the negotiations, the problems over Glacier were just beginning. The tribe had reserved to itself the right to practice subsistence activities like hunting, gathering, and cutting timber in the land they had sold—a concession that Washington frequently made in ceded Indian land. After the park was established in 1910 (a smaller part of the ceded strip continued in forest preserve status), the tribe pointed to the hunting rights the 1895 agreement reserved them in the ceded land. They were bluntly informed of their mistake: the status of a national park was, the solicitor general ruled, no longer "public domain" in the usual sense.

As a result, there would be no Indian hunting in Glacier. That a treaty or agreement could simply be cast aside seemed unconscionable to the Blackfeet, but in 1903 Congress had been awarded just such a right. In that year the Supreme Court had recognized the plenary power of Congress in its famous decision, *Lone Wolf v. Hitchcock*. In *Lone Wolf,* a suit that alleged the failure of the government to live up to treaty obligations to the Kiowa and Comanche tribes, the court decided that Congress had the power to unilaterally overturn a treaty if such an act was in the best interests of the Indians in question. The foundation of the right to subsist on the east slope of the Rockies had caved in like rotten timber. Suddenly the Piegan had become poachers on the crown of the continent. . . .

Within ten years of the Blackfeet deal, the park system was in the thick of Indian Country. In 1902, Washington purchased mineral springs from the Chickasaw and Choctaw tribes in Oklahoma Territory for what became, in 1906, Platt National Park, now part of the Chickasaw National Recreation Area. More important, in 1906, Congress passed an act enabling the president to unilaterally protect lands that were of historical significance or endangered by the burgeoning illegal trade in Indian antiquities. The so-called Antiquities Act gave the president arbitrary authority to withdraw land from public sale—a landmark step in the history of federal preservation. . . .

The Antiquities Act boded ill for many Indian people. First, it gave the president the unilateral right to seize "lands owned or controlled by the Government of the United States"— a provision that threatened ceded treaty land on which tribal hunting rights were often retained and Indian trust land itself. The upshot of the law for Native Americans was that the democratic ploddings of Congress were no longer necessary to rubber-stamp Indian land cessions, even the best-intentioned of them. As always, the rationale for intervention was that the government would be "protecting" Indian cultures—in this case, ancient ones.

Yet the turn-of-the-century fascination with Indian antiquities had an ironic side. While the government had outlawed pagan rituals like the sun dance on Plains reservations, shards of ancient Indian pottery from the Southwest were celebrated on Capitol Hill as the artifacts of a great civilization. A main objective of the Antiquities Act was to protect Indian relics. Of course, it was *ancient* Indian peoples, not contemporary ones, who were being esteemed. Under President Roosevelt and his successors, the long-ago Anasazi of the Southwest, ancestors of the Pueblo peoples, were going to be safer from the depredations of trespassers than were the modern

Ute who occupied some of their land. There was an unstated but unavoidable assumption: value the relic above the Indian. . . .

There was only one obstacle to developing most of the Mesa Verde ruins [now Mesa Verde National Park in southwestern Colorado]: they were owned, in trust, by the Southern Ute. The Ute were a seminomadic tribe of hunter-gatherers whose aboriginal territory covered much of Colorado, about 130,000 square miles by the 1830s. The Utes hunted and fished at communally owned sites, using pitfalls and poison arrows to bring down big game; their diet included deer, elk, antelope, ants, rattlesnakes, and lizards. . . .

. . . In 1890, the Utah legislative assembly entered a memorial in Congress asking that the Southern Utes remain in Colorado. The next year, the Colorado assembly returned the favor, announcing support of a bill establishing a Cliff Dwellers park that would require the Southern Utes to vacate the southwestern corner of the state—thus preventing "a constant menace to the safety, happiness, and prosperity of the white settlers, whose well-cultivated districts completely inclose the Indian reservation, which is entirely devoid of game or other natural sources of food supply." Private parties were donating thousands of dollars in political money, pleasantly called "the lubricating system," to promote removal. But removal where?

Finally pushed by the Indian Rights Association, a national watchdog group, the government decided to keep the Ute on or near the La Plata River in southern Colorado where they had been for years. By 1896, the government had allotted 72,000 acres to Southern Ute tribal members. Three years later, the government opened the reservation "surplus lands" to homesteaders. The western part of the land—today known as the Ute Mountain Reservation—remained unallotted to be held in common by members of the Weeminuche band. As a result, the Southern Ute lands were fractured in two. But some sections of Ute Mountain were still endangered. "It will be easier to reserve these lands now while they are part of an Indian Reservation," commented a General Land Office agent in 1900 on the subject of a Mesa Verde park, "than later when they may become public land open to settlement." . . .

Washington tried for years to reason with the Ute. The Mesa Verde legislation of 1906, it turned out, had included no ruins within the new park boundaries, merely instituting federal "custodianship" over all ancient sites within 5 miles of the park—a lack of federal title that would have to be rectified. During the new Progressive Era, however, politicians prided themselves on handling Indian affairs with more honor than had their rough-and-ready frontier predecessors. This time, the government pledged, the Ute would be handsomely compensated. And this time, money wasn't to be the item of exchange. The Ute land where the important ruins lay, it was believed, was not readily accessible and worth little to the tribe as pasture. And Washington had just the deal for taking it off Indian hands. Mesa Verde was going to be a case of historic preservation by fiat. . . .

In the end, the tribe held out for 30,000 acres on Sleeping Ute Mountain in exchange for the 14,000 acres on the mesa. It was better, the tribe believed, than the two smaller tracts Washington first offered—a fact the commissioners doubted—but still not as much land as the Ute wanted. The selling point seemed to be that Washington was willing to part with more land than it was getting: "The government is willing to give you three ponies for two ponies," [assistant commissioner of Indian affairs and chief federal negotiator, Frederick H.] Abbott volunteered in what he thought was the local idiom, anxious to communicate in a place where concepts like mile and acre were still foreign, "but it don't want to give you thirty." In fact, the federal lands in nearby Montezuma National Forest were at least said to promise good grazing and easy access to the tribe. . . .

Having been pressed into a corner of Colorado and an adjoining section of New Mexico, 65 Ute males (out of a reservation total of 108) finally consented. A two-for-one deal, after all, was a rare bargain in Indian Country. . . . In 1913 the tribal council agreed to cede some 14,000 acres to the government in return for 30,000 more on Sleeping Ute Mountain, and the deal was closed. . . .

Indian treaty making [had come] to an end in 1871; the following year, Congress established Yellowstone park. While one event didn't cause the other, their proximity is no coincidence. At almost the same time that tribes were stripped of sovereign status in negotiations, the national park idea was born. The differences between park and Indian reservation were plain: the parks showed the grandeur of the American outback while the reservations trailed behind like a poor government relation, a holding place for defeated enemies (and friends), many living in abject poverty. Then, too, reservation and park were founded on contrary principles: tourists were going to be encouraged to visit Yosemite and Glacier, whereas Indians were forbidden in 1873 from leaving their reservations without a pass. The parks, moreover, were a monument to perpetuity; reservations were regarded by their creators as temporary solutions to the chronic "Indian problem." . . .

For all their obvious differences, however, park and reservation also bore a striking resemblance. They were born of the same era; were both established as havens from unscrupulous private development; and were administered by the swelling bureaucracy ensconced in the Department of Interior. Together they competed for scarce federal resources, coexisting along shared boundaries in Montana, Colorado, Arizona, New Mexico, and South Dakota. The relationship, however, was far from congenial. Treaty land was ideal for incorporation in the parks since it was already federally controlled and could be ceded in enormous parcels. Not only that, but Indian Country in the West was marginal by definition—exactly the kind of "worthless" terrain that Washington sought to include in the park system. The tribal reservation and the "pleasuring ground" like Yellowstone were like a set of fraternal twins. They came of age in a country where profound questions of ownership remained long after the blood of the Indian Wars had dried.

The Trouble with Wilderness

WILLIAM CRONON

The time has come to rethink wildnerness.

This will seem a heretical claim to many environmentalists, since the idea of wilderness has for decades been a fundamental tenet—indeed, a passion—of the environmental movement, especially in the United States. For many Americans wilderness stands as the last remaining place where civilization, that all too human disease, has not fully infected the earth. It is an island in the polluted sea of urban-industrial

From William Cronon, "The Trouble with Wilderness" in William Cronon, ed., *Uncommon Ground: Rethinking the Human Place in Nature*. New York: Norton, 1995, pp. 69–73, 75–82, 86–90. Copyright © 1995 by William Cronon. Reprinted by permission of W. W. Norton & Company, Inc.

modernity, the one place we can turn for escape from our own too-muchness. Seen in this way, wilderness presents itself as the best antidote to our human selves, a refuge we must somehow recover if we hope to save the planet. As Henry David Thoreau once famously declared, "In Wildness is the preservation of the World."

But is it? The more one knows of its peculiar history, the more one realizes that wilderness is not quite what it seems. Far from being the one place on earth that stands apart from humanity, it is quite profoundly a human creation—indeed, the creation of very particular human cultures at very particular moments in human history. It is not a pristine sanctuary where the last remnant of an untouched, endangered, but still transcendent nature can for at least a little while longer be encountered without the contaminating taint of civilization. Instead, it is a product of that civilization, and could hardly be contaminated by the very stuff of which it is made. Wilderness hides its unnaturalness behind a mask that is all the more beguiling because it seems so natural. As we gaze into the mirror it holds up for us, we too easily imagine that what we behold is Nature when in fact we see the reflection of our own unexamined longings and desires. For this reason, we mistake ourselves when we suppose that wilderness can be the solution to our culture's problematic relationships with the nonhuman world, for wilderness is itself no small part of the problem.

To assert the unnaturalness of so natural a place will no doubt seem absurd or even perverse to many readers, so let me hasten to add that the nonhuman world we encounter in wilderness is far from being merely our own invention. I celebrate with others who love wilderness the beauty and power of the things it contains. Each of us who has spent time there can conjure images and sensations that seem all the more hauntingly real for having engraved themselves so indelibly on our memories. Such memories may be uniquely our own, but they are also familiar enough to be instantly recognizable to others. Remember this? The torrents of mist shoot out from the base of a great waterfall in the depths of a Sierra canyon, the tiny droplets cooling your face as you listen to the roar of the water and gaze up toward the sky through a rainbow that hovers just out of reach. Remember this too: looking out across a desert canyon in the evening air, the only sound a lone raven calling in the distance, the rock walls dropping away into a chasm so deep that its bottom all but vanishes as you squint into the amber light of the setting sun. And this: the moment beside the trail as you sit on a sandstone ledge, your boots damp with the morning dew while you take in the rich smell of the pines, and the small red fox—or maybe for you it was a raccoon or a coyote or a deer—that suddenly ambles across your path, stopping for a long moment to gaze in your direction with cautious indifference before continuing on its way. Remember the feelings of such moments, and you will know as well as I do that you were in the presence of something irreducibly nonhuman, something profoundly Other than yourself. Wilderness is made of that too.

And yet: what brought each of us to the places where such memories became possible is entirely a cultural invention. Go back 250 years in American and European history, and you do not find nearly so many people wandering around remote corners of the planet looking for what today we would call "the wilderness experience." As late as the eighteenth century, the most common usage of the word "wilderness" in the English language referred to landscapes that generally carried adjectives far different from the ones they attract today. To be a wilderness then was to be "deserted," "savage," "desolate," "barren"— in short, a "waste," the word's nearest synonym. Its connotations were anything but positive, and the emotion one was most likely to feel in its presence was "bewilderment"— or terror.

Many of the word's strongest associations then were biblical, for it is used over and over again in the King James Version to refer to places on the margins of civilization where it is all too easy to lose oneself in moral confusion and despair. The wilderness was where Moses had wandered with his people for forty years, and where they had nearly abandoned their God to worship a golden idol. "For Pharoah will say of the Children of Israel," we read in Exodus, "They are entangled in the land, the wilderness hath shut them in." The wilderness was where Christ had struggled with the devil and endured his temptations: "And immediately the Spirit driveth him into the wilderness. And he was there in the wilderness for forty days tempted of Satan; and was with the wild beasts; and the angels ministered unto him." The "delicious Paradise" of John Milton's Eden was surrounded by "a steep wilderness, whose hairy sides / Access denied" to all who sought entry. When Adam and Eve were driven from that garden, the world they entered was a wilderness that only their labor and pain could redeem. Wilderness, in short, was a place to which one came only against one's will, and always in fear and trembling. Whatever value it might have arose solely from the possibility that it might be "reclaimed" and turned toward human ends—planted as a garden, say, or a city upon a hill. In its raw state, it had little or nothing to offer civilized men and women.

But by the end of the nineteenth century, all this had changed. The wastelands that had once seemed worthless had for some people come to seem almost beyond price. That Thoreau in 1862 could declare wildness to be the preservation of the world suggests the sea change that was going on. Wilderness had once been the antithesis of all that was orderly and good—it had been the darkness, one might say, on the far side of the garden wall—and yet now it was frequently likened to Eden itself. When John Muir arrived in the Sierra Nevada in 1869, he would declare, "No description of Heaven that I have ever heard or read of seems half so fine." He was hardly alone in expressing such emotions. One by one, various corners of the American map came to be designated as sites whose wild beauty was so spectacular that a growing number of citizens had to visit and see them for themselves. Niagara Falls was the first to undergo this transformation, but it was soon followed by the Catskills, the Adirondacks, Yosemite, Yellowstone, and others. Yosemite was deeded by the U.S. government to the state of California in 1864 as the nation's first wildland park, and Yellowstone became the first true national park in 1872.

By the first decade of the twentieth century, in the single most famous episode in American conservation history, a national debate had exploded over whether the city of San Francisco should be permitted to augment its water supply by damming the Tuolumne River in Hetch Hetchy valley, well within the boundaries of Yosemite National Park. The dam was eventually built, but what today seems no less significant is that so many people fought to prevent its completion. Even as the fight was being lost, Hetch Hetchy became the battle cry of an emerging movement to preserve wilderness. Fifty years earlier, such opposition would have been unthinkable. Few would have questioned the merits of "reclaiming" a wasteland like this in order to put it to human use. Now the defenders of Hetch Hetchy attracted widespread national attention by portraying such an act not as improvement or progress but as desecration and vandalism. Lest one doubt that the old biblical metaphors had been turned completely on their heads, listen to John Muir attack the dam's defenders. "Their arguments," he wrote, "are curiously like those of the devil, devised for the destruction of the first garden—so much of the very best Eden fruit going to waste; so much of the best Tuolumne water and Tuolumne scenery going to waste." For Muir and the growing number of Americans who shared his views, Satan's home had become God's own temple.

The sources of this rather astonishing transformation were many, but for the purposes of this essay they can be gathered under two broad headings: the sublime and the frontier. Of the two, the sublime is the older and more pervasive cultural construct, being one of the most important expressions of that broad transatlantic movement we today label as romanticism; the frontier is more peculiarly American, though it too had its European antecedents and parallels. The two converged to remake wilderness in their own image, freighting it with moral values and cultural symbols that it carries to this day. Indeed, it is not too much to say that the modern environmental movement is itself a grandchild of romanticism and post-frontier ideology, which is why it is no accident that so much environmentalist discourse takes its bearings from the wilderness these intellectual movements helped create. Although wilderness may today seem to be just one environmental concern among many, it in fact serves as the foundation for a long list of other such concerns that on their face seem quite remote from it. That is why its influence is so pervasive and, potentially, so insidious.

To gain such remarkable influence, the concept of wilderness had to become loaded with some of the deepest core values of the culture that created and idealized it: it had to become sacred. This possibility had been present in wilderness even in the days when it had been a place of spiritual danger and moral temptation. If Satan was there, then so was Christ, who had found angels as well as wild beasts during His sojourn in the desert. In the wilderness the boundaries between human and nonhuman, between natural and supernatural, had always seemed less certain than elsewhere. This was why the early Christian saints and mystics had often emulated Christ's desert retreat as they sought to experience for themselves the visions and spiritual testing He had endured. One might meet devils and run the risk of losing one's soul in such a place, but one might also meet God. For some that possibility was worth almost any price.

By the eighteenth century this sense of the wilderness as a landscape where the supernatural lay just beneath the surface was expressed in the doctrine of the *sublime*, a word whose modern usage has been so watered down by commercial hype and tourist advertising that it retains only a dim echo of its former power. In the theories of Edmund Burke, Immanuel Kant, William Gilpin, and others, sublime landscapes were those rare places on earth where one had more chance than elsewhere to glimpse the face of God. Romantics had a clear notion of where one could be most sure of having this experience. Although God might, of course, choose to show Himself anywhere, He would most often be found in those vast, powerful landscapes where one could not help feeling insignificant and being reminded of one's own mortality. Where were these sublime places? The eighteenth-century catalog of their locations feels very familiar, for we still see and value landscapes as it taught us to do. God was on the mountaintop, in the chasm, in the waterfall, in the thundercloud, in the rainbow, in the sunset. One has only to think of the sites that Americans chose for their first national parks—Yellowstone, Yosemite, Grand Canyon, Rainier, Zion—to realize that virtually all of them fit one or more of these categories. Less sublime landscapes simply did not appear worthy of such protection; not until the 1940s, for instance, would the first swamp be honored, in Everglades National Park, and to this day there is no national park in the grasslands. . . .

But even as it came to embody the awesome power of the sublime, wilderness was also being tamed—not just by those who were building settlements in its midst but also by those who most celebrated its inhuman beauty. . . . As more and more tourists sought out the wilderness as a spectacle to be looked at and enjoyed for its great beauty, the sublime in effect became domesticated. The wilderness was still sacred, but the religious sentiments it evoked were more those of a pleasant parish church than those of a grand cathedral or a harsh desert retreat. The writer who best captures this late romantic sense of a domesticated sublime is undoubtedly John Muir, whose descriptions of Yosemite and the Sierra Nevada reflect none of the anxiety or terror one finds in earlier writers. Here he is, for instance, sketching on North Dome in Yosemite Valley:

> No pain here, no dull empty hours, no fear of the past, no fear of the future. These blessed mountains are so compactly filled with God's beauty, no petty personal hope or experience has room to be. Drinking this champagne water is pure pleasure, so is breathing the living air, and every movement of limbs is pleasure, while the body seems to feel beauty when exposed to it as it feels the campfire or sunshine, entering not by the eyes alone, but equally through all one's flesh like radiant heat, making a passionate ecstatic pleasure glow not explainable. . . .

. . . The sublime wilderness had ceased to be a place of satanic temptation and become instead a sacred temple, much as it continues to be for those who love it today.

But the romantic sublime was not the only cultural movement that helped transform wilderness into a sacred American icon during the nineteenth century. No less important was the powerful romantic attraction of primitivism, dating back at least to Rousseau—the belief that the best antidote to the ills of an overly refined and civilized modern world was a return to simpler, more primitive living. In the United States, this was embodied most strikingly in the national myth of the frontier. The historian Frederick Jackson Turner wrote in 1893 the classic academic statement of this myth, but it had been part of American cultural traditions for well over a century. As Turner described the process, easterners and European immigrants, in moving to the wild unsettled lands of the frontier, shed the trappings of civilization, redis-covered their primitive racial energies, reinvented direct democratic institutions, and thereby reinfused themselves with a vigor, an independence, and a creativity that were the source of American democracy and national character. Seen in this way, wild country became a place not just of religious redemption but of national renewal, the quintessential location for experiencing what it meant to be an American.

One of Turner's most provocative claims was that by the 1890s the frontier was passing away. Never again would "such gifts of free land offer themselves" to the American people. "The frontier has gone," he declared, "and with its going has closed the first period of American history." Built into the frontier myth from its very beginning was the notion that this crucible of American identity was temporary and would pass away. Those who have celebrated the frontier have almost always looked backward as they did so, mourning an older, simpler, truer world that is about to disappear forever. That world and all of its attractions, Turner said, depended on free land—on wilderness. Thus, in the myth of the vanishing frontier lay the seeds of wilderness preservation in the United States, for if wild land had been so crucial in the making of the nation, then surely one must save its last remnants as monuments to the American past—and as an insurance policy to protect its future. It is no accident that the movement to set aside national parks and wilderness areas began to gain real momentum at precisely the time that laments about the passing frontier reached their peak. To protect wilderness was in a very real sense to protect the nation's most sacred myth of origin.

Among the core elements of the frontier myth was the powerful sense among certain groups of Americans that wilderness was the last bastion of rugged individualism. Turner tended to stress communitarian themes when writing frontier history, asserting that Americans in primitive conditions had been forced to band together with their neighbors to form communities and democratic institutions. For other writers, however, frontier democracy for communities was less compelling than frontier freedom for individuals. By fleeing to the outer margins of settled land and society—so the story ran—an individual could escape the confining strictures of civilized life. . . .

The mythic frontier individualist was almost always masculine in gender: here, in the wilderness, a man could be a real man, the rugged individual he was meant to be before civilization sapped his energy and threatened his masculinity. . . . [T]he comforts and seductions of civilized life [seemed] especially insidious for men, who all too easily became emasculated by the femininizing tendencies of civilization. More often than not, men who felt this way came, like [writer Owen] Wister and [President Theodore] Roosevelt, from elite class backgrounds. The curious result was that frontier nostalgia became an important vehicle for expressing a peculiarly bourgeois form of antimodernism. The very men who most benefited from urban-industrial capitalism were among those who believed they must escape its debilitating effects. If the frontier was passing, then men who had the means to do so should preserve for themselves some remnant of its wild landscape so that they might enjoy the regeneration and renewal that came from sleeping under the stars, participating in blood sports, and living off the land. The frontier might be gone, but the frontier experience could still be had if only wilderness were preserved. . . .

There were other ironies as well. The movement to set aside national parks and wilderness areas followed hard on the heels of the final Indian wars, in which the prior human inhabitants of these areas were rounded up and moved onto reservations. The myth of the wilderness as "virgin," uninhabited land had always been especially cruel when seen from the perspective of the Indians who had once called that land home. Now they were forced to move elsewhere, with the result that tourists could safely enjoy the illusion that they were seeing their nation in its pristine, original state, in the new morning of God's own creation. Among the things that most marked the new national parks as reflecting a post-frontier consciousness was the relative absence of human violence within their boundaries. The actual frontier had often been a place of conflict, in which invaders and invaded fought for control of land and resources. Once set aside within the fixed and carefully policed boundaries of the modern bureaucratic state, the wilderness lost its savage image and became safe: a place more of reverie than of revulsion or fear. Meanwhile, its original inhabitants were kept out by dint of force, their earlier uses of the land redefined as inappropriate or even illegal. To this day, for instance, the Blackfeet continue to be accused of "poaching" on the lands of Glacier National Park that originally belonged to them and that were ceded by treaty only with the proviso that they be permitted to hunt there.

The removal of Indians to create an "uninhabited wilderness"— uninhabited as never before in the human history of the place—reminds us just how invented, just how constructed, the American wilderness really is. To return to my opening argument: there is nothing natural about the concept of wilderness. It is entirely a creation of the culture that holds it dear, a product of the very history it seeks to deny. Indeed, one of the most striking proofs of the cultural invention of wilderness is its thoroughgoing erasure of the history from which it sprang. In virtually all of its manifestations, wilderness represents a flight from history. Seen as the original garden, it is a place outside of time, from which human beings had to be ejected before the fallen world of history could properly begin. Seen as the frontier, it is a savage world at the dawn of civilization, whose transformation represents the very beginning of the national historical epic. Seen as the bold landscape of frontier heroism, it is the place of youth and childhood, into which men escape by abandoning their pasts and entering a world of freedom where the constraints of civilization fade into memory. Seen as the sacred sublime, it is the home of a God who transcends history by standing as the One who remains untouched and unchanged by time's arrow. No matter what the angle from which we regard it, wilderness offers us the illusion that we can escape the cares and troubles of the world in which our past has ensnared us. . . .

But the trouble with wilderness is that it quietly expresses and reproduces the very values its devotees seek to reject. The flight from history that is very nearly the core of wilderness represents the false hope of an escape from responsibility, the illusion that we can somehow wipe clean the slate of our past and return to the tabula rasa that supposedly existed before we began to leave our marks on the world. The dream of an unworked natural landscape is very much the fantasy of people who have never themselves had to work the land to make a living—urban folk for whom food comes from a supermarket or a restaurant instead of a field, and for whom the wooden houses in which they live and work apparently have no meaningful connection to the forests in which trees grow and die. Only people whose relation to the land was already alienated could hold up wilderness as a model for human life in nature, for the romantic ideology of wilderness leaves precisely nowhere for human beings actually to make their living from the land.

This, then, is the central paradox: wilderness embodies a dualistic vision in which the human is entirely outside the natural. If we allow ourselves to believe that nature, to be true, must also be wild, then our very presence in nature represents its fall. The place where we are is the place where nature is not. If this is so—if by definition wilderness leaves no place for human beings, save perhaps as contemplative sojourners enjoying their leisurely reverie in God's natural cathedral—then also by definition it can offer no solution to the environmental and other problems that confront us. To the extent that we celebrate wilderness as the measure with which we judge civilization, we reproduce the dualism that sets humanity and nature at opposite poles. We thereby leave ourselves little hope of discovering what an ethical, sustainable, *honorable* human place in nature might actually look like.

Worse: to the extent that we live in an urban-industrial civilization but at the same time pretend to ourselves that our *real* home is in the wilderness, to just that extent we give ourselves permission to evade responsibility for the lives we actually lead. We inhabit civilization while holding some part of ourselves—what we imagine to be the most precious part—aloof from its entanglements. We work our nine-to-five jobs in its institutions, we eat its food, we drive its cars (not least to reach the wilderness), we benefit from the intricate and all too invisible networks with which it shelters us, all the while pretending that these things are not an essential part of who we are. By imagining that our true home is in the wilderness, we forgive ourselves the homes we actually inhabit. In its flight from history, in its siren song of escape, in its reproduction of the dangerous dualism that sets human beings outside of nature—in all of these ways, wilderness poses a serious threat to responsible environmentalism at the end of the twentieth century.

By now I hope it is clear that my criticism in this essay is not directed at wild nature per se, or even at efforts to set aside large tracts of wild land, but rather at the specific habits of thinking that flow from this complex cultural construction called wilderness. It is not the things we label as wilderness that are the problem—for nonhuman nature and large tracts of the natural world *do* deserve protection—but rather what we ourselves mean when we use that label. . . .

Indeed, my principal objection to wilderness is that it may teach us to be dismissive or even contemptuous of . . . humble places and experiences. Without our quite realizing it, wilderness tends to privilege some parts of nature at the expense of others. Most of us, I suspect, still follow the conventions of the romantic sublime in finding the mountaintop more glorious than the plains, the ancient forest nobler than the grasslands, the mighty canyon more inspiring than the humble marsh. . . . By teaching us to fetishize sublime places and wide open country, these peculiarly American ways of thinking about wilderness encourage us to adopt too high a standard for what counts as "natural." If it isn't hundreds of square miles big, if it doesn't give us God's-eye views or grand vistas, if it doesn't permit us the illusion that we are alone on the planet, then it really isn't natural. It's too small, too plain, or too crowded to be *authentically* wild. . . .

If the core problem of wilderness is that it distances us too much from the very things it teaches us to value, then the question we must ask is what it can tell us about *home,* the place where we actually live. How can we take the positive values we associate with wilderness and bring them closer to home? I think the answer to this question will come by broadening our sense of the otherness that wilderness seeks to define and protect. In reminding us of the world we did not make, wilderness can teach profound feelings of humility and respect as we confront our fellow beings and the earth itself. Feelings like these argue for the importance of self-awareness and self-criticism as we exercise our own ability to transform the world around us, helping us set responsible limits to human mastery—which without such limits too easily becomes human hubris. Wilderness is the place where, symbolically at least, we try to withhold our power to dominate. . . .

Wilderness gets us into trouble only if we imagine that this experience of wonder and otherness is limited to the remote corners of the planet, or that it somehow depends on pristine landscapes we ourselves do not inhabit. Nothing could be more misleading. The tree in the garden is in reality no less other, no less worthy of our wonder and respect, than the tree in an ancient forest that has never known an ax or a saw—even though the tree in the forest reflects a more intricate web of ecological relationships. The tree in the garden could easily have sprung from the same seed as the tree in the forest, and we can claim only its location and perhaps its form as our own. Both trees stand apart from us; both share our common world. The special power of the tree in the wilderness is to remind us of this fact. It can teach us to recognize the wildness we did not see in the tree we planted in our own backyard. By seeing the otherness in that which is most unfamiliar, we can learn to see it too in that which at first seemed merely ordinary. If wilderness can do this—if it can help us perceive and respect a nature we had forgotten to recognize as natural—then it will become part of the solution to our environmental dilemmas rather than part of the problem.

This will only happen, however, if we abandon the dualism that sees the tree in the garden as artificial—completely fallen and unnatural—and the tree in the wilderness as natural—completely pristine and wild. Both trees in some ultimate sense are wild; both in a practical sense now depend on our management and care. We are responsible for both, even though we can claim credit for neither. Our challenge is to stop thinking of such things according to a set of bipolar moral scales in which the human and the nonhuman, the unnatural and the natural, the fallen and the unfallen, serve as our conceptual map for understanding and valuing the world. Instead, we need to embrace the full continuum of a natural landscape that is also cultural, in which the city, the suburb, the pastoral, and the wild each has its proper place, which we permit ourselves to celebrate without needlessly denigrating the others. We need to honor the Other within and the Other next door as much as we do the exotic Other that lives far away—a lesson that applies as much to people as it does to (other) natural things. In particular, we need to discover a common middle ground in which all of these things, from the city to the wilderness, can somehow be encompassed in the word "home." Home, after all, is the place where finally we make our living. It is the place for which we take responsibility, the place we try to sustain so we can pass on what is best in it (and in ourselves) to our children.

. . . Calling a place home inevitably means that we will *use* the nature we find in it, for there can be no escape from manipulating and working and even killing some parts of nature to make our home. But if we acknowledge the autonomy and otherness of the things and creatures around us—an autonomy our culture has taught us to label with the word "wild"— then we will at least think carefully about the uses to which we put them, and even ask if we should use them at all. Just so can we still join Thoreau in declaring that "in Wildness is the preservation of the World," for *wild*ness (as opposed to wilderness) can be found anywhere: in the seemingly tame fields and woodlots of Massachusetts, in the cracks of a Manhattan sidewalk, even in the cells of our own bodies. As [poet] Gary Snyder has wisely said, "A person with a clear heart and open mind can experience the wilderness anywhere on earth. It is a quality of one's own consciousness. The planet is a wild place and always will be." To think ourselves capable of causing "the end of nature" is an act of great hubris, for it means forgetting the wildness that dwells everywhere within and around us.

Learning to honor the wild—learning to remember and acknowledge the autonomy of the other—means striving for critical self-consciousness in all of our actions.

It means that deep reflection and respect must accompany each act of use, and means too that we must always consider the possibility of non-use. It means looking at the part of nature we intend to turn toward our own ends and asking whether we can use it again and again and again—sustainably—without its being diminished in the process. It means never imagining that we can flee into a mythical wilderness to escape history and the obligation to take responsibility for our own actions that history inescapably entails. Most of all, it means practicing remembrance and gratitude, for thanksgiving is the simplest and most basic of ways for us to recollect the nature, the culture, and the history that have come together to make the world as we know it. If wildness can stop being (just) out there and start being (also) in here, if it can start being as humane as it is natural, then perhaps we can get on with the unending task of struggling to live rightly in the world—not just in the garden, not just in the wilderness, but in the home that encompasses them both.

ψ *F U R T H E R   R E A D I N G*

Horace M. Albright, as told to Robert Cahn, *The Birth of the National Park Service* (1985)

Craig W. Allin, *The Politics of Wilderness Preservation* (1982)

Donald N. Baldwin, *The Quiet Revolution: Grass Roots of Today's Wilderness Preservation Movement* (1972)

Mark Daniel Barringer, *Selling Yellowstone: Capitalism and the Construction of Nature* (2002)

Frank Bergon, ed., *The Wilderness Reader* (1957)

Paul Brooks, *The Pursuit of Wilderness* (1971)

———, *Speaking for Nature: How Literary Naturalists from Henry Thoreau to Rachel Carson Have Shaped America* (1980)

Philip Burnham, *Indian Country, God's Country: Native Americans and the National Parks* (2000)

Lloyd Burton, *Worship and Wilderness: Culture, Religion, and Law in the Management of Public Lands and Resources* (2002)

J. Baird Callicott, ed., *The Great New Wilderness Debate* (1998)

Kendrick A. Clements, "Politics and the Park: San Francisco's Fight for Hetch Hetchy, 1908–1913," *Pacific Historical Review* 48 (1979), 185–215

Michael P. Cohen, *The Pathless Way: John Muir and the American Wilderness* (1984)

William Cronon, "The Trouble with Wilderness; or, Getting Back to the Wrong Nature" in William Cronon, ed., *Uncommon Ground: Rethinking the Human Place in Nature* (1995)

Thomas Dunlap, *Saving America's Wildlife* (1988)

Susan Flader, *Thinking Like a Mountain: Aldo Leopold and the Evolution of an Ecological Attitude Toward Deer, Wolves, and Forests* (1974)

Steven Fox, John Muir and His Legacy: *The American Conservation Movement* (1981)

Michael Frome, *Battle for the Wilderness* (1974)

Doug Goodman and Daniel McCool, eds., *Contested Landscape: The Politics of Wilderness in Utah and the West* (1999)

William L. Graf, *Wilderness Preservation and the Sagebrush Rebellions* (1990)

Kristina K. Groover, *The Wilderness Within: American Women Writers and Spiritual Quest* (1999)

Hans Huth, *Nature and the American: Three Centuries of Changing Attitudes* (1957)

John Ise, *Our National Park Policy: A Critical History* (1961)

Robert Keller and Michael Turek, *American Indians and National Parks* (1998)

David Kowalewski, *Deep Power: The Political Ecology of Wilderness and Civilization* (2000)

Robert Ben Martin, *The Hetch Hetchy Controversy: The Value of Nature in a Technological Society* (1982)

Rick McIntyre, *A Society of Wolves: National Parks and the Battle over the Wolf* (1996)

John McPhee, *Encounters with the Archdruid* (1971)

Howard Frank Mosher, ed., *Songs of the North: A Sigurd Olson Reader* (1987)

Roderick Nash, *Wilderness and the American Mind,* 4th ed. (2001)

Max Oeschlager, *The Idea of Wilderness from Prehistory to the Age of Ecology* (1991)

John F. Reiger, *American Sportsmen and the Origins of Conservation,* 3rd ed. (2001)

Jeff Rennicke, *Treasures of Alaska: Last Great American Wilderness* (2001)

James M. Ridenour, *The National Parks Compromised: Pork Barrel Politics & America's Treasures* (1994)

Janet Robertson, *The Magnificent Mountain Women: Adventures in the Colorado Rockies* (1990)

Alfred Runte, *National Parks: The American Experience* (1979)

———, *Yosemite: The Embattled Wilderness* (1990)

———, *Trains of Discovery: Western Railroads and the National Parks* (1990)

Susan Schrepfer, *The Fight to Save the Redwoods: A History of Environmental Reform, 1917–1978* (1983)

Mark Spence, *Dispossessing the Wilderness: Indian Removal and the Making of the National Parks* (1999)

Deborah Strom, ed., *Birdwatching with American Women: A Selection of Nature Writings* (1986)

Douglas H. Strong, *Trees—Or Timber? The Story of Sequoia and Kings Canyon National Parks* (undated)

———, *Dreamers and Defenders: American Conservationists* (1988)

Donald C. Swain, *Wilderness Defender: Horace M. Albright and Conservation* (1970)

Peter Wild, *Pioneer Conservationists of Western America* (1979)

———, ed., *The Desert Reader* (1991)

Dennis Williams, *God's Wilds: John Muir's Vision of Nature* (2002)

CHAPTER
12

Cities, Industries, and Pollution in the Twentieth Century

❦

Rapid industrialization in the late nineteenth and early twentieth centuries promoted both urbanization and pollution. Smoke spewed forth from chimneys, effluents poured into lakes and rivers, garbage piled up on sidewalks, and diseases spread, threatening human health. In 1860, 60 percent of Americans lived in cities; by 1970 the urban population had spurted to 72 percent. Along with the growth of cities came water pollution, smog, and disease. Writing in 1898, Robert Woods saw the city as a social wilderness; Booth Tarkington, in his novel The Turmoil *(1914), described it as grimy, dingy, and dirty. Urban pollution and disease affected affluent and working-class neighborhoods differently. Nature within the inner-city environment differed from nature in rural and suburban areas, but the two were connected by air and water flows. During the twentieth century, streetcar suburbs became automobile suburbs, and suburban sprawl used additional resources and added to pollution. The automobile also spurred tourism, linking suburbia with the national parks and wilderness areas that offered fresh air as an antidote to the stress of living in a fast-paced industrial society.*

An urban-reform campaign that focused on health, sanitation, parks, and beautification took shape in the twentieth century. Members of civic groups and women's clubs, scientists, politicians, lawyers, and engineers all participated in efforts to improve urban environments. The settlement house movement attempted to provide healthy domiciles for laborers and immigrants. Diseases of industrial workers received the attention of public health scientists. However, progress came slowly, owing to industry resistance, technological problems, ineffective legislation, and lack of enforcement. Also, since this was primarily a middle-class movement to improve middle-class life, these reform initiatives embraced quality-of-life rather than social-justice issues; for the working class, problems of racism, labor unrest, immorality, and poor living conditions persisted. Nevertheless, urban environmental reform in this era marked the first phase of a citizens' action movement dedicated to improving the environment and human health. (See Map 10 in the Appendix.)

The documents in this chapter illustrate the efforts of reformers to address urban pollution and environmental health. Document 1, an article written in 1901 by Mrs. C. G. Wagner, treasurer of the Women's Health Protective Association of Brooklyn, New York, details the problems arising from refuse accumulation and describes citizens' clean-up efforts. The unregulated growth of the meatpacking industry was such that by 1905 muckraker Upton Sinclair was documenting labor exploitation and cattle abuse in the packinghouses. The revelations in his exposé *The Jungle,* excerpted in Document 2, shocked the nation. In Document 3, reformer Jane Addams, the founder of Chicago's Hull House, a poor people's refuge, discusses women's efforts to organize garbage-collection reforms in tenement-house neighborhoods. Document 4, by Mrs. Ernest Kroeger, president of the Women's Organization for Smoke Abatement of St. Louis, details women's efforts to enforce state laws against the smoke nuisance.

Beginning in the early twentieth century, the invention of the automobile enabled middle-class Americans not only to escape urban pollution by moving to the suburbs, but also to escape the urban environment for recreation and to engage with nature in the national parks and forests. The automobile had contradictory effects: It both contributed to urban pollution and led those who used it to appreciate and thereby to save nature. Document 5, by Henry Ford, recounts Ford's early life on a farm and the ways in which nature, roads, and farm machinery inspired him to develop the automobile.

Racial and ethnic minorities, including blacks, bore the brunt of urban pollution and social stigma. In Document 6, writer Richard Wright, an African American migrant from the South who arrived in Chicago in 1927, compares the blackness of urban soot to his own blackness. To many northern urbanites, both blacks and pollution seemed an invisible and inevitable part of the city landscape. Document 7 is from the 1943 autobiography of public health scientist Alice Hamilton, who had worked alongside Jane Addams at Hull House. She describes her efforts to assist laborers and immigrants who had acquired industrial diseases through daily contact with chemicals while working in "the dangerous trades."

In Document 8, President Dwight D. Eisenhower, in an address to Congress in 1955, outlines the features of and rationale for an interstate highway system. Passed the following year, the Federal-Aid Highway Act of 1956 created the Dwight D. Eisenhower System of Interstate and Defense Highways, requiring that all interstate highways be divided highways with a minimum of two lanes in either direction, moderate grades with high-speed curves, no traffic lights, and conveniently located rest areas.

1. A Woman Reformer Advocates Civic Cleanliness, 1901

Because of the indifference on the part of many of our voters, combined with the exactions of business for others, and the neglect of our city officials in matters pertaining to the betterment of the city, it was forced upon the minds of a number of thinking women that something ought to be done to remedy the existing evils. For this reason, in April, 1890, the Women's Health Protective Association of Brooklyn, N.Y., was incorporated.

Its attention was first drawn to the unsanitary methods of collection and disposal of garbage and ashes. At that time the garbage was carried beyond the harbor

From Mrs. C. G. Wagner, "What the Women Are Doing for Civic Cleanliness," *Municipal Journal and Engineer* 11, no. 1 (July 1901), p. 35.

and dumped into the sea, only to be washed back again upon the south shore, leaving an unsightly and ill-smelling beach. It was frequently placed upon the walk in paper boxes, grape boxes, and even newspapers have been used for the unfortunate collector to handle, but by constant agitation, to some extent that has been corrected; for, at present, in most localities the receptacles are more in accordance with the city ordinance: "That it should be put in unleakable vessels." The larger portion of the garbage is now cremated, and the association looks forward to the day when it shall all be disposed of in that way.

Another line of work was that of getting the householder to keep the ash cans within the fence line, and when it is complied with, is certainly an improvement on the old way of having a long row of unsightly barrels and boxes lining the edge of the walks, filled to overflowing with worn-out pots and kettles, old brooms, rubbers, umbrellas, and various articles of household waste too numerous to mention.

And now the association has secured the separate removal of rubbish, although not done to its satisfaction, yet hoping some day to reach the point it aims for. . . .

The agitation against the slovenly manner in which the street cleaning was done brought about a better state of affairs, thanks to Col. [George E.] Waring [New York City street cleaning commissioner], for surely the present system far exceeds the old, when the dirt was swept into heaps and left sometimes for days before its gathering, for the winds and wagons to scatter it again. Though fallen below Col. Waring's standard, still it is in great advance of the past.

The unsanitary plumbing in some of the public schools was brought to the notice of the association as being detrimental both to the morals and the health of the pupils. On investigating, a sad state was found in some of them and continues the same to-day. Lack of funds was the excuse given for the condition of the buildings, though languages and the higher branches could be taught at a great expense to the taxpayers. Very little has been done, and the association intends to continue its efforts until these things are remedied.

Among the minor reforms of the association was getting the piggeries removed beyond the city line. The placing of cans on the street corners for waste paper is another reform, and the overflowing condition of some show how useful they are and how much would otherwise be distributed in the streets. An uncleanly obstruction on the edge of the walk was the grocers' coal boxes; they are now placed against the house. To a great extent the association has succeeded in having carts that were left standing in the streets stabled elsewhere. The distribution of circulars on the streets has claimed its attention for years, but success in that direction has not come yet.

"The secret of success is constancy of purpose."

2. Upton Sinclair Describes the Chicago Stockyards, 1905

It was in the stockyards that Jonas' friend had gotten rich, and so to Chicago the party was bound. They knew that one word, Chicago—and that was all they needed to know, at least, until they reached the city. . . .

From Upton Sinclair, *The Jungle*. New York: Harper & Brothers, 1905, pp. 24–26, 32–36.

A full hour before the party reached the city they had begun to note the per-plexing changes in the atmosphere. It grew darker all the time, and upon the earth the grass seemed to grow less green. Every minute, as the train sped on, the colors of things became dingier; the fields were grown parched and yellow, the landscape hideous and bare. And along with the thickening smoke they began to notice another circumstance, a strange, pungent odor. They were not sure that it was unpleasant, this odor; some might have called it sickening, but their taste in odors was not developed, and they were only sure that it was curious. Now, sitting in the trolley car, they real-ized that they were on their way to the home of it—that they had traveled all the way from Lithuania to it. It was now no longer something far off and faint, that you caught in whiffs; you could literally taste it, as well as smell it—you could take hold of it, almost, and examine it at your leisure. They were divided in their opinions about it. It was an elemental odor, raw and crude; it was rich, almost rancid, sensual, and strong. There were some who drank it in as if it were an intoxicant; there were others who put their handkerchiefs to their faces. The new emigrants were still tasting it, lost in wonder, when suddenly the car came to a halt, and the door was flung open, and a voice shouted—"Stockyards!" . . .

Then the party became aware of another strange thing. This, too, like the odor, was a thing elemental; it was a sound, a sound made up of ten thousand little sounds. You scarcely noticed it at first—it sunk into your consciousness, a vague disturbance, a trouble. It was like the murmuring of the bees in the spring, the whisperings of the forest; it suggested endless activity, the rumblings of a world in motion. It was only by an effort that one could realize that it was made by animals, that it was the distant lowing of ten thousand cattle, the distant grunting of ten thousand swine. . . .

There is over a square mile of space in the yards, and more than half of it is oc-cupied by cattle pens; north and south as far as the eye can reach there stretches a sea of pens. And they were all filled—so many cattle no one had ever dreamed existed in the world. Red cattle, black, white, and yellow cattle; old cattle and young cattle; great bellowing bulls and little calves not an hour born; meek-eyed milch cows and fierce, long-horned Texas steers. The sound of them here was as of all the barnyards of the universe; and as for counting them—it would have taken all day simply to count the pens. . . .

"And what will become of all these creatures?" cried Teta Elzbieta.

"By tonight," Jokubas answered, "they will all be killed and cut up; and over there on the other side of the packing houses are more railroad tracks, where the cars come to take them away."

There were two hundred and fifty miles of track within the yards, their guide went on to tell them. They brought about ten thousand head of cattle every day, and as many hogs, and half as many sheep—which meant some eight or ten million live creatures turned into food every year. One stood and watched, and little by little caught the drift of the tide, as it set in the direction of the packing houses. There were groups of cattle being driven to the chutes, which were roadways about fifteen feet wide, raised high above the pens. In these chutes the stream of animals was contin-uous; it was quite uncanny to watch them, pressing on to their fate, all unsuspicious— a very river of death. . . .

They climbed a long series of stairways outside of the building, to the top of its five or six stories. Here was the chute, with its river of hogs, all patiently toiling upward; there was a place for them to rest to cool off, and then through another passageway they went into a room from which there is no returning for hogs.

It was a long, narrow room, with a gallery along it for visitors. At the head there was a great iron wheel, about twenty feet in circumference, with rings here and there along its edge. Upon both sides of this wheel there was a narrow space, into which came the hogs at the end of their journey; in the midst of them stood a great burly Negro, bare-armed and bare-chested. He was resting for the moment, for the wheel had stopped while men were cleaning up. In a minute or two, however, it began slowly to revolve, and then the men upon each side of it sprang to work. They had chains which they fastened about the leg of the nearest hog, and the other end of the chain they hooked into one of the rings upon the wheel. So, as the wheel turned, a hog was suddenly jerked off his feet and borne aloft.

At the same instant the ear was assailed by a most terrifying shriek; the visitors started in alarm, the women turned pale and shrank back. The shriek was followed by another, louder and yet more agonizing—for once started upon that journey, the hog never came back; at the top of the wheel he was shunted off upon a trolley, and went sailing down the room. And meantime another was swung up, and then another, and another, until there was a double line of them, each dangling by a foot and kicking in frenzy—and squealing. The uproar was appalling, perilous to the eardrums; one feared there was too much sound for the room to hold—that the walls must give way or the ceiling crack. There were high squeals and low squeals, grunts, and wails of agony; there would come a momentary lull, and then a fresh outburst, louder than ever, surging up to a deafening climax. It was too much for some of the visitors—the men would look at each other, laughing nervously, and the women would stand with hands clenched, and the blood rushing to their faces, and the tears starting in their eyes.

3. Jane Addams Works to Control Garbage in Chicago, 1910

One of the striking features of our neighborhood twenty years ago, and one to which we never became reconciled, was the presence of huge wooden garbage boxes fastened to the street pavement in which the undisturbed refuse accumulated day by day. The system of garbage collecting was inadequate throughout the city but it became the greatest menace in a ward such as ours, where the normal amount of waste was much increased by the decayed fruit and vegetables discarded by the Italian and Greek fruit peddlers, and by the residuum left over from piles of filthy rags which were fished out of the city dumps and brought to the homes of the rag pickers for further sorting and washing.

The children of our neighborhood twenty years ago played their games in and around these huge garbage boxes. They were the first objects that the toddling child learned to climb; their bulk afforded a barricade and their contents provided missiles in all the battles of the older boys; and finally they became the seats upon which absorbed lovers held enchanted converse. We are obliged to remember that all children

From Jane Addams, *Twenty Years at Hull-House*. New York: Macmillan, 1930 [1910], pp. 281–287, 293–294.

eat everything which they find and that odors have a curious and intimate power of entwining themselves into our tenderest memories, before even the residents of Hull-House can understand their own early enthusiasm for the removal of these boxes and the establishment of a better system of refuse collection.

It is easy for even the most conscientious citizen of Chicago to forget the foul smells of the stockyards and the garbage dumps, when he is living so far from them that he is only occasionally made conscious of their existence but the residents of a Settlement are perforce constantly surrounded by them. During our first three years on Halsted Street, we had established a small incinerator at Hull-House and we had many times reported the untoward conditions of the ward to the city hall. We had also arranged many talks for the immigrants, pointing out that although a woman may sweep her own doorway in her native village and allow the refuse to innocently decay in the open air and sunshine, in a crowded city quarter, if the garbage is not properly collected and destroyed, a tenement-house mother may see her children sicken and die, and that the immigrants must therefore, not only keep their own houses clean, but must also help the authorities to keep the city clean.

Possibly our efforts slightly modified the worst conditions but they still remained intolerable, and the fourth summer the situation became for me absolutely desperate when I realized in a moment of panic that my delicate little nephew for whom I was guardian, could not be with me at Hull-House at all unless the sickening odors were reduced. I may well be ashamed that other delicate children who were torn from their families, not into boarding school but into eternity, had not long before driven me to effective action. Under the direction of the first man who came as a resident to Hull-House we began a systematic investigation of the city system of garbage collection, both as to its efficiency in other wards and its possible connection with the death rate in the various wards of the city.

The Hull-House Woman's Club had been organized the year before by the resident kindergartner who had first inaugurated a mothers' meeting. The members came together, however, in quite a new way that summer when we discussed with them the high death rate so persistent in our ward. After several club meetings devoted to the subject, despite the fact that the death rate rose highest in the congested foreign colonies and not in the streets in which most of the Irish American club women lived, twelve of their number undertook in connection with the residents, to carefully investigate the condition of the alleys. During August and September the substantiated reports of violations of the law sent in from Hull-House to the health department were one thousand and thirty-seven. For the club woman who had finished a long day's work of washing or ironing followed by the cooking of a hot supper, it would have been much easier to sit on her doorstep during a summer evening than to go up and down ill-kept alleys and get into trouble with her neighbors over the condition of their garbage boxes. It required both civic enterprise and moral conviction to be willing to do this three evenings a week during the hottest and most uncomfortable months of the year. Nevertheless, a certain number of women persisted. . . .

With the two or three residents who nobly stood by, we set up six of those doleful incinerators which are supposed to burn garbage with the fuel collected in the alley itself. The one factory in town which could utilize old tin cans was a window weight factory, and we deluged that with ten times as many tin cans as it could use—much less would pay for. We made desperate attempts to have the dead animals removed by the contractor who was paid most liberally by the city for that purpose but who, we slowly discovered, always made the police ambulances do the work, delivering the carcasses upon freight cars for shipment to a soap factory in Indiana where they were sold for a good price although the contractor himself was the largest stockholder in the concern. Perhaps our greatest achievement was the discovery of a pavement eighteen inches under the surface in a narrow street. . . . This pavement became the *casus belli* between myself and the street commissioner when I insisted that its restoration belonged to him, after I had removed the first eight inches of garbage. The matter was finally settled by the mayor himself, who permitted me to drive him to the entrance of the street in what the children called my "garbage phaëton" and who took my side of the controversy.

. . . Perhaps no casual visitor could be expected to see that these matters of detail seemed unimportant to a city in the first flush of youth, impatient of correction and convinced that all would be well with its future. The most obvious faults were those connected with the congested housing of the immigrant population, nine tenths of them from the country, who carried on all sorts of traditional activities in the crowded tenements. That a group of Greeks should be permitted to slaughter sheep in a basement, that Italian women should be allowed to sort over rags collected from the city dumps, not only within the city limits but in a court swarming with little children, that immigrant bakers should continue unmolested to bake bread for their neighbors in unspeakably filthy spaces under the pavement, appeared incredible to visitors accustomed to careful city regulations.

4. A Woman Reformer Promotes Smoke Abatement, 1912

The smoke nuisance in St. Louis had grown almost intolerable when the Wednesday Club, a strong, fine organization of five hundred women, took up the question and cast about to see what could be done. This was in December, 1910. Up to that time there had been sporadic attempts, with considerable results from these efforts, made by the Smoke Abatement Committee of the Civic League. The Missouri State Law, a strong law covering all aspects of the question excepting that of locomotives, was passed as a result of their work.

The State Law was excellent, but the work of the Civic League in enforcing the law was almost completely hampered by an ineffective City Smoke Abatement Department and indifference on the part of the public. The City Department had combined the Smoke Abatement Department with the Boiler and Elevator Department, and placed at the head of both a Chief Inspector of Boilers and Elevators, with several deputy boiler inspectors, and *no* deputy smoke inspector. The consequence was that there was no force to look after the smoke nuisance.

The Wednesday Club made tentative inquiry of the Civic League as to the necessity of energetic effort, and received in reply a cordial invitation to cooperate with its Smoke Abatement Committee to secure the enforcement of the (existing) smoke ordinance. After accepting the invitation of the Civic League, the Wednesday Club

From Mrs. Ernest Kroeger, "Smoke Abatement in St. Louis." *The American City* 6 (June 1912), pp. 907, 909.

realized that the movement should be larger and more general than a club movement, and, further, felt the necessity of arousing public opinion. With this end in view a mass meeting of the women of St. Louis was called in the Auditorium of the Wednesday Club and a program provided touching on the smoke nuisance from the standpoint of health, cleanliness, housekeeping, city planning, etc. The program included men and women speakers, some of whom were city officials.

At this meeting, which was crowded, the Women's Organization for Smoke Abatement in St. Louis was formed with 250 paid members. By the next afternoon there were 400 members, and at the present time the membership numbers 1,300. An executive board of twelve women was elected and has had charge of the planning and directing of all the organization's work. These women met weekly the first season and fortnightly the second, and have been enthusiastic and tireless in their crusade against the smoke nuisance.

The first work they took up was districting the city in districts of about five square blocks with volunteer members of the organization as reporters of the smoking chimneys in their districts. Colonel James Gay Butler, one of St. Louis' most public-spirited citizens, came to the assistance of the women with an open purse, stating that he would spend $50,000 if necessary to make St. Louis a clean city. He employed a lawyer and six smoke inspectors to supplement the work of the city, and offered to coöperate with the women in securing legal evidence from their district reports.

These district reports were mailed to the Executive Board of the Women's Organization, where copies were made and forwarded to the newspapers, Colonel Butler's lawyer and the City Department. These cases were then followed up, taken into court and required to comply with the law. For fifteen months Colonel Butler's lawyer and inspectors have secured convictions against offending chimneys, until now the manufacturing districts are pretty well cleaned up. The locomotives, residences and small apartment houses are at present our greatest offenders, and the combined efforts of the women, the Civic League, Colonel Butler and the newspapers are being directed against them. The newspapers have been most powerful allies in the smoke work and have given thousands of dollars of free advertising to the campaign.

The City Department has done all that it could do to coöperate with the Civic League and the Women's Organization. About a year ago the Mayor replaced the former Inspector of Boilers and Elevators with an able man who is doing all he possibly can under his present restrictions.

5. Henry Ford Recalls the Invention of the Automobile, 1922

We have only started on our development of our country—we have not as yet, with all our talk of wonderful progress, done more than scratch the surface. The progress has been wonderful enough—but when we compare what we have done with what there is to do, then our past accomplishments are as nothing. When we consider that more power is used merely in ploughing the soil than is used in all the industrial establishments of the country put together, an inkling comes of how much opportunity

From Henry Ford, *My Life and Work.* Garden City, N.Y.: Doubleday, 1922, pp. 1, 9, 21–32.

there is ahead. And now, with so many countries of the world in ferment and with so much unrest everywhere, is an excellent time to suggest something of the things that may be done—in the light of what has been done.

When one speaks of increasing power, machinery, and industry there comes up a picture of a cold, metallic sort of world in which great factories will drive away the trees, the flowers, the birds, and the green fields. And that then we shall have a world composed of metal machines and human machines. With all of that I do not agree. I think that unless we know more about machines and their use, unless we better understand the mechanical portion of life, we cannot have the time to enjoy the trees, and the birds, and the flowers, and the green fields. . . .

The economic fundamental is labour. Labour is the human element which makes the fruitful seasons of the earth useful to men. It is men's labour that makes the harvest what it is. That is the economic fundamental: every one of us is working with the material world which we did not and could not create, but which was presented to us by Nature. . . .

On May 31, 1921, the Ford Motor Company turned out Car No. 5,000,000. It is out in my museum along with the gasoline buggy that I began work on thirty years before and which first ran satisfactorily along in the spring of 1893. I was running it when the bobolinks came to Dearborn and they always come on April 2nd. There is all the difference in the world in the appearance of the two vehicles and almost as much difference in construction and materials, but in fundamentals the two are curiously alike—except that the old buggy has on it a few wrinkles that we have not yet quite adopted in our modern car. For that first car or buggy, even though it had but two cylinders, would make twenty miles an hour and run sixty miles on the three gallons of gas the little tank held and is as good to-day as the day it was built. The development in methods of manufacture and in materials has been greater than the development in basic design. The whole design has been refined; the present Ford car, which is the "Model T," has four cylinders and a self starter—it is in every way a more convenient and an easier riding car. . . .

It was life on the farm that drove me into devising ways and means to better transportation. I was born on July 30, 1863, on a farm at Dearborn, Michigan, and my earliest recollection is that, considering the results, there was too much work on the place. That is the way I still feel about farming. There is a legend that my parents were very poor and that the early days were hard ones. Certainly they were not rich, but neither were they poor. As Michigan farmers went, we were prosperous. The house in which I was born is still standing, and it and the farm are part of my present holding.

There was too much hard hand labour on our own and all other farms of the time. Even when very young I suspected that much might somehow be done in a better way. That is what took me into mechanics—although my mother always said that I was born a mechanic. I had a kind of workshop with odds and ends of metal for tools before I had anything else. In those days we did not have the toys of to-day; what we had were home made. My toys were all tools—they still are! And every fragment of machinery was a treasure.

The biggest event of those early years was meeting with a road engine about eight miles out of Detroit one day when we were driving to town. I was then twelve years old. The second biggest event was getting a watch—which happened in the same year. I remember that engine as though I had seen it only yesterday, for it was the first vehicle other than horse-drawn that I had ever seen. It was intended primarily for driving threshing machines and sawmills and was simply a portable engine and boiler mounted on wheels with a water tank and coal cart trailing behind. I had seen plenty of these engines hauled around by horses, but this one had a chain that made a connection between the engine and the rear wheels of the wagon-like frame on which the boiler was mounted. The engine was placed over the boiler and one man standing on the platform behind the boiler shovelled coal, managed the throttle, and did the steering. It had been made by Nichols, Shepard & Company of Battle Creek. I found that out at once. The engine had stopped to let us pass with our horses and I was off the wagon and talking to the engineer before my father, who was driving, knew what I was up to. The engineer was very glad to explain the whole affair. He was proud of it. He showed me how the chain was disconnected from the propelling wheel and a belt put on to drive other machinery. He told me that the engine made two hundred revolutions a minute and that the chain pinion could be shifted to let the wagon stop while the engine was still running. This last is a feature which, although in different fashion, is incorporated into modern automobiles. It was not important with steam engines, which are easily stopped and started, but it became very important with the gasoline engine. It was that engine which took me into automotive transportation. I tried to make models of it, and some years later I did make one that ran very well, but from the time I saw that road engine as a boy of twelve right forward to to-day, my great interest has been in making a machine that would travel the roads. . . . It is not possible to learn from books how everything is made—and a real mechanic ought to know how nearly everything is made. Machines are to a mechanic what books are to a writer. He gets ideas from them, and if he has any brains he will apply those ideas. . . .

In 1879—that is, about four years after I first saw that Nichols-Shepard machine—I managed to get a chance to run one and when my apprenticeship was over I worked with a local representative of the Westinghouse Company of Schenectady as an expert in the setting up and repair of their road engines. The engine they put out was much the same as the Nichols-Shepard engine excepting that the engine was up in front, the boiler in the rear, and the power was applied to the back wheels by a belt. They could make twelve miles an hour on the road even though the self-propelling feature was only an incident of the construction. . . .

Even before that time I had the idea of making some kind of a light steam car that would take the place of horses—more especially, however, as a tractor to attend to the excessively hard labour of ploughing. It occurred to me, as I remember somewhat vaguely, that precisely the same idea might be applied to a carriage or a wagon on the road. A horseless carriage was a common idea. People had been talking about carriages without horses for many years back—in fact, ever since the steam engine was invented—but the idea of the carriage at first did not seem so practical to me as the idea of an engine to do the harder farm work, and of all the work on the farm ploughing was the hardest. Our roads were poor and we had not the habit of getting around. One of the most remarkable features of the automobile on the farm is the way that it has broadened the farmer's life. We simply took for granted that unless the errand were urgent we would not go to town, and I think we rarely made more than one trip a week. In bad weather we did not go even that often. . . .

But I did not give up the idea of a horseless carriage. The work with the West-inghouse representative only served to confirm the opinion I had formed that steam was not suitable for light vehicles. That is why I stayed only a year with that company. There was nothing more that the big steam tractors and engines could teach me and I did not want to waste time on something that would lead nowhere. . . .

The gas engine interested me and I followed its progress, but only from curiosity, until about 1885 or 1886 when, the steam engine being discarded as the motive power for the carriage that I intended some day to build, I had to look around for another sort of motive power. In 1885 I repaired an Otto engine at the Eagle Iron Works in Detroit. No one in town knew anything about them. There was a rumour that I did and, although I had never before been in contact with one, I undertook and carried through the job. That gave me a chance to study the new engine at first hand and in 1887 I built one on the Otto four-cycle model just to see if I understood the principles. "Four cycle" means that the piston traverses the cylinder four times to get one power impulse. The first stroke draws in the gas, the second compresses it, the third is the explosion or power stroke, while the fourth stroke exhausts the waste gas. The little model worked well enough; it had a one-inch bore and a three-inch stroke, operated with gasoline, and while it did not develop much power, it was slightly lighter in proportion than the engines being offered commercially. I gave it away later to a young man who wanted it for something or other and whose name I have forgotten; it was eventually destroyed. That was the beginning of the work with the internal combustion engine. . . .

It was in 1890 that I began on a double-cylinder engine. It was quite impractical to consider the single cylinder for transportation purposes—the fly-wheel had to be entirely too heavy. Between making the first four-cycle engine of the Otto type and the start on a double cylinder I had made a great many experimental engines out of tubing. I fairly knew my way about. . . .

I had to work from the ground up—that is, although I knew that a number of people were working on horseless carriages, I could not know what they were doing. The hardest problems to overcome were in the making and breaking of the spark and in the avoidance of excess weight. For the transmission, the steering gear, and the general construction, I could draw on my experience with the steam tractors. In 1892 I completed my first motor car, but it was not until the spring of the following year that it ran to my satisfaction. This first car had something of the appearance of a buggy. There were two cylinders with a two-and-a-half-inch bore and a six-inch stroke set side by side and over the rear axle. I made them out of the exhaust pipe of a steam engine that I had bought. They developed about four horsepower. The power was transmitted from the motor to the countershaft by a belt and from the counter-shaft to the rear wheel by a chain. The car would hold two people, the seat being suspended on posts and the body on elliptical springs. There were two speeds—one of ten and the other of twenty miles per hour—obtained by shifting the belt, which was done by a clutch lever in front of the driving seat. Thrown forward, the lever put in the high speed; thrown back, the low speed; with the lever upright the engine could run free. To start the car it was necessary to turn the motor over by hand with the clutch free. To stop the car one simply released the clutch and applied the foot brake. There was no reverse, and speeds other than those of the belt were obtained by the throttle. I bought the iron work for the frame of the carriage and also the seat and the springs. The wheels were twenty-eight-inch wire bicycle wheels with rubber tires. The balance wheel I had cast from a pattern that I made and all of the more delicate mechanism I made myself. One of the features that I discovered necessary was a compensating gear that permitted the same power to be applied to each of the rear wheels when turning corners. The machine altogether weighed about five hundred pounds. A tank under the seat held three gallons of gasoline which was fed to the motor through a small pipe and a mixing valve. The ignition was by electric spark. The original machine was air-cooled—or to be more accurate, the motor simply was not cooled at all. I found that on a run of an hour or more the motor heated up, and so I very shortly put a water jacket around the cylinders and piped it to a tank in the rear of the car over the cylinders.

Nearly all of these various features had been planned in advance. That is the way I have always worked. I draw a plan and work out every detail on the plan before starting to build. For otherwise one will waste a great deal of time in makeshifts as the work goes on and the finished article will not have coherence. It will not be rightly proportioned. Many inventors fail because they do not distinguish between planning and experimenting. The largest building difficulties that I had were in obtaining the proper materials. The next were with tools. There had to be some adjustments and changes in details of the design, but what held me up most was that I had neither the time nor the money to search for the best material for each part. But in the spring of 1893 the machine was running to my partial satisfaction and giving an opportunity further to test out the design and material on the road.

6. A Black Migrant Experiences the Urban Environment, 1927

My first glimpse of the flat black stretches of Chicago depressed and dismayed me, mocked all my fantasies. Chicago seemed an unreal city whose mythical houses were built of slabs of black coal wreathed in palls of gray smoke, houses whose foundations were sinking slowly into the dank prairie. Flashes of steam showed intermittently on the wise horizon, gleaming translucently in the winter sun. The din of the city entered my consciousness, entered to remain for years to come. The year was 1927.

What would happen to me here? Would I survive? My expectations were modest. I wanted only a job. Hunger had long been my daily companion. Diversion and recreation, with the exception of reading, were unknown. In all my life—though surrounded by many people—I had not had a single satisfying, sustained relationship with another human being and, not having had any, I did not miss it. I made no demands whatever upon others.

The train rolled into the depot. Aunt Maggie and I got off and walked slowly through the crowds into the station. I looked about to see if there were signs saying: For White—For Colored. I saw none. Black people and white people moved about, each seemingly intent upon his private mission. There was no racial fear. Indeed, each person acted as though no one existed but himself. It was strange to pause before a crowded newsstand and buy a newspaper without having to wait until a white man was served. And yet, because everything was so new, I began to grow tense again, although it was a different sort of tension than I had known before. I knew that this machine-city was governed by strange laws and I wondered if I would ever learn them.

As we waited for a streetcar to take us to Aunt Cleo's home for temporary lodging, I looked northward at towering buildings of steel and stone. There were no curves here, no trees; only angles, lines, squares, bricks and copper wires. Occasionally the ground beneath my feet shook from some faraway pounding and I felt that this world, despite its massiveness, was somehow dangerously fragile. Streetcars screeched past over steel tracks. Cars honked their horns. Clipped speech sounded about me. As I stood in the icy wind, I wanted to talk to Aunt Maggie, to ask her questions, but her tight face made me hold my tongue. I was learning already from the frantic light in her eyes the strain that the city imposed upon its people. I was seized by doubt. Should I have come here? But going back was impossible. I had fled a known terror, and perhaps I could cope with this unknown terror that lay ahead.

The streetcar came. Aunt Maggie motioned for me to get on and pushed me toward a seat in which a white man sat looking blankly out the window. I sat down beside the man and looked straight ahead of me. After a moment I stole a glance at the white man out of the corners of my eyes; he was still staring out the window, his mind fastened upon some inward thought. I did not exist for him; I was as far from his mind as the stone buildings that swept past in the street. It would have been illegal for me to sit beside him in the part of the South that I had come from.

The car swept past soot-blackened buildings, stopping at each block, jerking again into motion. The conductor called street names in a tone that I could not understand. People got on and off the car, but they never glanced at one another. Each person seemed to regard the other as a part of the city landscape. The white man who sat beside me rose and I turned my knees aside to let him pass, and another white man sat beside me and buried his face in a newspaper. How could that possibly be? Was he conscious of my blackness?

7. Alice Hamilton Discusses Industrial Poisons, 1943

It was . . . my experience at Hull-House that aroused my interest in industrial diseases. Living in a working-class quarter, coming in contact with laborers and their wives, I could not fail to hear tales of the dangers that workingmen faced, of cases of carbon-monoxide gassing in the great steel mills, of painters disabled by lead palsy, of pneumonia and rheumatism among the men in the stockyards. Illinois then had no legislation providing compensation for accident or disease caused by occupation. (There is something strange in speaking of "accident and sickness compensation." What could "compensate" anyone for an amputated leg or a paralyzed arm, or even

From Alice Hamilton, *Exploring the Dangerous Trades: The Autobiography of Alice Hamilton.* Boston: Little, Brown and Company, 1943, pp. 114, 125–126.

an attack of lead colic, to say nothing of the loss of a husband or son?) There was a striking occurrence about this time in Chicago which brought vividly before me the unprotected, helpless state of workingmen who were held responsible for their own safety. . . .

In 1912, I wrote this in the *Journal of the American Medical Association:*

> The contrast was brought vividly home to me by a description which I found in T. Weyl's *Handbuch der Arbeiter-Krankheiten.* He is drawing what he considers a shocking picture of "lead tabes" or "lead cachexia" as it used to be found years ago, but which is now almost never seen, thanks to prophylactic measures. He describes the striking pallor, the hanging head, bowed shoulders, hands that hang limply and can hardly be raised; the shambling gait, trembling movements of all the muscles of the body, the emaciation which is extreme.

> From my own experiences I can unfortunately testify to the fact that, thanks to the lack of prophylactic measures, Weyl's lead tabes is far from being a rare condition in our country; that instances of it can be found in every town where there are lead industries of a dangerous character, and that it is not even a vanishing condition, for new instances of lead tabes are being added to the number every year. Surely there is every reason why we should devote to this disease the same intelligence and energy that we devote to other preventable diseases.

Life at Hull-House had accustomed me to going straight to the homes of people about whom I wished to learn something and talking to them in their own surroundings, where they have courage to speak out what is in their minds. They were almost always foreigners, Bulgarians, Serbs, Poles, Italians, Hungarians, who had come to this country in the search for a better life for themselves and their children. Sometimes they thought they had found it, then when sickness struck down the father things grew very black and there were no old friends and neighbors and cousins to fall back on as there had been in the old country. Often it was an agent of a steamship company who had coaxed them over with promises of a land flowing with jobs and high wages. Six hundred Bulgarians had been induced to leave their villages by these super salesmen, and to come to Chicago. Of course they took the first job they could find and if it proved to be one that weakened and crippled them— well, that was their bad luck!

It sometimes seemed to me that industry was exploiting the finest and best in these men—their love of their children, their sense of family responsibility. I think of an enameler of bathtubs whom I traced to his squalid little cottage. He was a young Slav who used to be so strong he could run up the hill on which his cottage stood and spend all the evening digging in his garden. Now, he told me, he climbed up like an old man and sank exhausted in a chair, he was so weary, and if he tried to hoe or rake he had to give it up. His digestion had failed, he had a foul mouth, he couldn't eat, he had lost much weight. He had had many attacks of colic and the doctor told him if he did not quit he would soon be a wreck. "Why did you keep on," I asked, "when you knew the lead was getting you?" "Well, there were the payments on the house," he said, "and the two kids." The house was a bare, ugly, frame shack, the children were little, underfed things, badly in need of a handkerchief, but for them a man had sacrificed his health and his joy in life. When employers tell me they prefer married men, and encourage their men to have homes of their own, because it makes them so much steadier, I wonder if they have any idea of all that that implies.

8. Dwight D. Eisenhower Promotes the Interstate Highway System, 1955

TO THE CONGRESS OF THE UNITED STATES:

Our unity as a nation is sustained by free communication of thought and by easy transportation of people and goods. The ceaseless flow of information throughout the Republic is matched by individual and commercial movement over a vast system of inter-connected highways criss-crossing the Country and joining at our national borders with friendly neighbors to the north and south.

Together, the uniting forces of our communication and transportation systems are dynamic elements in the very name we bear—United States. Without them, we would be a mere alliance of many separate parts.

The Nation's highway system is a gigantic enterprise, one of our largest items of capital investment. Generations have gone into its building. Three million, three hundred and sixty-six thousand miles of road, travelled by 58 million motor vehicles, comprise it. The replacement cost of its drainage and bridge and tunnel works is incalculable. One in every seven Americans gains his livelihood and supports his family out of it. But, in large part, the network is inadequate for the nation's growing needs.

In recognition of this, the Governors in July of last year at my request began a study of both the problem and methods by which the Federal Government might assist the States in its solution. I appointed in September the President's Advisory Committee on a National Highway Program, headed by Lucius D. Clay, to work with the Governors and to propose a plan of action for submission to the Congress. At the same time, a committee representing departments and agencies of the national Government was organized to conduct studies coordinated with the other two groups.

All three were confronted with inescapable evidence that action, comprehensive and quick and forward-looking, is needed.

First: Each year, more than 36 thousand people are killed and more than a million injured on the highways. To the home where the tragic aftermath of an accident on an unsafe road is a gap in the family circle, the monetary worth of preventing that death cannot be reckoned. But reliable estimates place the measurable economic cost of the highway accident toll to the Nation at more than $4.3 billion a year.

Second: The physical condition of the present road net increases the cost of vehicle operation, according to many estimates, by as much as one cent per mile of vehicle travel. At the present rate of travel, this totals more than $5 billion a year. The cost is not borne by the individual vehicle operator alone. It pyramids into higher expense of doing the nation's business. Increased highway transportation costs, passed on through each step in the distribution of goods, are paid ultimately by the individual consumer.

Third: In case of an atomic attack on our key cities, the road net must permit quick evacuation of target areas, mobilization of defense forces and maintenance of

From Dwight D. Eisenhower, "Special Message to the Congress Regarding a National Highway Program, February 22, 1955," in *Public Papers of the Presidents: Dwight D. Eisenhower, 1955*. Washington, D.C.: Government Printing Office, 1959, p. 39.

every essential economic function. But the present system in critical areas would be the breeder of a deadly congestion within hours of an attack.

Fourth: Our Gross National Product, about $357 billion in 1954, is estimated to reach over $500 billion in 1965 when our population will exceed 180 million and, according to other estimates, will travel in 81 million vehicles 814 billion vehicle miles that year. Unless the present rate of highway improvement and development is increased, existing traffic jams only faintly foreshadow those of ten years hence.

To correct these deficiencies is an obligation of Government at every level. The highway system is a public enterprise. As the owner and operator, the various levels of Government have a responsibility for management that promotes the economy of the nation and properly serves the individual user. In the case of the Federal Government, moreover, expenditures on a highway program are a return to the highway user of the taxes which he pays in connection with his use of the highways.

Congress has recognized the national interest in the principal roads by authorizing two Federal-aid systems, selected cooperatively by the States, local units and the Bureau of Public Roads.

The Federal-aid primary system as of July 1, 1954, consisted of 234,407 miles, connecting all the principal cities, county seats, ports, manufacturing areas and other traffic generating centers.

In 1944 the Congress approved the Federal-aid secondary system, which on July 1, 1954, totalled 482,972 miles, referred to as farm-to-market roads—important feeders linking farms, factories, distribution outlets and smaller communities with the primary system.

Because some sections of the primary system, from the viewpoint of national interest are more important than others, the Congress in 1944 authorized the selection of a special network, not to exceed 40,000 miles in length, which would connect by routes, as direct as practicable, the principal metropolitan areas, cities and industrial centers, serve the national defense, and connect with routes of continental importance in the Dominion of Canada and the Republic of Mexico.

This National System of Interstate Highways, although it embraces only 1.2 percent of total road mileage, joins 42 state capital cities and 90 percent of all cities over 50,000 population. It carries more than a seventh of all traffic, a fifth of the rural traffic, serves 65 percent of the urban and 45 percent of the rural population. Approximately 37,600 miles have been designated to date. This system and its mileage are presently included within the Federal-aid primary system.

In addition to these systems, the Federal Government has the principal, and in many cases the sole, responsibility for roads that cross or provide access to Federally owned land — more than one-fifth the nation's area.

Of all these, the Interstate System must be given top priority in construction planning. But at the current rate of development, the Interstate network would not reach even a reasonable level of extent and efficiency in half a century. State highway departments cannot effectively meet the need. Adequate right-of-way to assure control of access; grade separation structures; relocation and realignment of present highways; all these, done on the necessary scale within an integrated system, exceed their collective capacity.

If we have a congested and unsafe and inadequate system, how then can we improve it so that ten years from now it will be fitted to the nation's requirements?

A realistic answer must be based on a study of all phases of highway financing, including a study of the costs of completing the several systems of highways, made by the Bureau of Public Roads in cooperation with the State highway departments and local units of government. This study, made at the direction of the 83rd Congress in the 1954 Federal-aid Highway Act, is the most comprehensive of its kind ever undertaken. . . .

The Governors' Conference and the President's Advisory Committee are agreed that the Federal share of the needed construction program should be about 30 percent of the total, leaving to State and local units responsibility to finance the remainder.

The obvious responsibility to be accepted by the Federal Government, in addition to the existing Federal interest in our 3,366,000-mile network of highways, is the development of the Interstate System with its most essential urban arterial connections.

In its report, the Advisory Committee recommends:

1. That the Federal Government assume principal responsibility for the cost of a modern Interstate Network to be completed by 1964 to include the most essential urban arterial connections; at an annual average cost of $2.5 billion for the ten year period.
2. That Federal contributions to primary and secondary road systems, now at the rate authorized by the 1954 Act of approximately $525 million annually, be continued.
3. That Federal funds for that portion of the Federal-aid systems in urban areas not on the Interstate System, now approximately $75 million annually, be continued.
4. That Federal funds for Forest Highways be continued at the present $22.5 million per year rate. . . .

The extension of necessary highways in the Territories and highway maintenance and improvement in National Parks, on Indian lands and on other public lands of the United States will continue to be treated in the budget for these particular subjects.

A sound Federal highway program, I believe, can and should stand on its own feet, with highway users providing the total dollars necessary for improvement and new construction. Financing of interstate and Federal-aid systems should be based on the planned use of increasing revenues from present gas and diesel oil taxes, augmented in limited instances with tolls.

I am inclined to the view that it is sounder to finance this program by special bond issues, to be paid off by the above-mentioned revenues which will be collected during the useful life of the roads and pledged to this purpose, rather than by an increase in general revenue obligations.

At this time, I am forwarding for use by the Congress in its deliberations the Report to the President made by the President's Advisory Committee on a National Highway Program. This study of the entire highway traffic problem and presentation of a detailed solution for its remedy is an analytical review of the major elements in a most complex situation. In addition, the Congress will have available the study made by the Bureau of Public Roads at the direction of the 83rd Congress.

These two documents together constitute a most exhaustive examination of the National highway system, its problems and their remedies. Inescapably, the vastness of the highway enterprise fosters varieties of proposals which must be resolved into a national highway pattern. The two reports, however, should generate recognition of the urgency that presses upon us; approval of a general program that will give us a modern safe highway system; realization of the rewards for prompt and comprehensive action. They provide a solid foundation for a sound program.

DWIGHT D. EISENHOWER

THE WHITE HOUSE,
February 22, 1955.

ꙮ *E S S A Y S*

The essays in this chapter examine the history of urban pollution and environmental reform from several perspectives. In the first selection, urban environmental historian Robert Gottlieb of Occidental College in Los Angeles discusses the character of urban pollution and industrial poisons and shows how a growing moral consciousness led supporters of the working classes to try to reform the system. As the twentieth century progressed and people moved to the suburbs, the suburban home itself created new forms of pollution and energy demands. The second essay, by environmental historian Adam Rome of Pennsylvania State University, details some of the environmental consequences of suburban development. The first streetcar suburbs were confined to walking distances from train and streetcar stations. However, the automobile not only made the extended suburb possible, but also intensified class and race differences as suburbs attracted more affluent whites away from inner cities. The third essay, by professor emeritus James Flink of the University of California at Irvine, chronicles the development of roads under the incentives of automotive travel and the ways in which the automobile promoted access to nature in the national parks and monuments. Together the essays reveal the environmental and social problems arising from increasing dichotomies between industrialized cities and suburbanized home places linked by transportation systems.

Industrial Pollution and Reform

ROBERT GOTTLIEB

Exploring the Dangerous Trades

A tenacious reformer, a compassionate advocate, a cautious and careful researcher, Alice Hamilton was this country's first great urban/industrial environmentalist. Born in 1869 in New York City and raised in Fort Wayne, Indiana, Hamilton decided to study medicine, one of the few disciplines available to this first generation of women able to enter the universities and embark on a professional career. "I chose medicine," Hamilton would later say in her autobiography, *Exploring the Dangerous Trades,* ". . . because as a doctor I could go anywhere I pleased—to far-off lands or to city slums—and be quite sure that I could be of use anywhere." . . .

Excerpts from Robert Gottlieb, "Urban and Industrial Roots: Seeking to Reform the System" in *Forcing the Spring: The Transformation of the American Environmental Movement.* Washington, D.C.: Island Press, 1993, pp. 47–61, 64–65, 67. Reprinted by permission of Island Press.

During the first decade of the new century, there had been few investigations of occupational health and even fewer reforms of industrial practices in the United States, though occupational hazards were present in a wide range of industries. In 1908, Hamilton's interest in the subject was stimulated by an encounter at Hull House with John Andrews, the executive secretary of the American Association for Labor Legislation (AALL). Andrews had investigated more than 150 cases of phossy jaw, a debilitating and disfiguring disease prevalent in American match factories. Jane Addams of Hull House had been familiar with phossy jaw, having attended during the 1880s a mass meeting in London where several people had shown their scars and deformities. Until 1908, little had been done even to explore the problem in this country, since the American medical establishment argued that American factories were cleaner and less susceptible to occupational hazards. Andrews' report, however, not only documented the problem but pointed to a reasonably inexpensive substitute for white phosphorus and helped set in motion a high-profile campaign around the issue. It eventually led to the passage in 1912 of legislation that effectively eliminated all white phosphorus use through taxes and regulatory requirements. . . .

Though Hamilton was faced with a lack of documentation and information, few resources, company resistance, and workers' fears, her investigations, first with the Illinois survey [of industrial hazards] and subsequently with the Bureau of Labor within the U.S. Department of Commerce, demonstrated an extraordinary resourcefulness and persistence as she pursued her "shoe-leather epidemiology." Her search for data led her to undertake numerous interviews, home visits, and discussions with physicians and apothecaries, undertakers, charity workers, visiting nurses, and countless others. It required long hours and uncertain information, but it was a duty, she felt, "to the producer, not to the product." Hamilton recognized that her compassion as a woman for the victims of the dangerous trades gave her certain advantages in soliciting information through more informal settings. "It seemed natural and right that a woman should put the care of the producing workman ahead of the value of the thing he was producing," Hamilton remarked. "In a man it would have been [seen as] sentimentality or radicalism." . . .

By the 1920s, with the publication of her classic text *Industrial Poisons in the United States,* her increasing prominence in issues of occupational and environmental health, and her participation in organizations such as the Workers' Health Bureau, Alice Hamilton had become the country's most powerful and effective voice for exploring the environmental consequences of industrial activity. Her interest touched on issues of class, race, and gender in the workplace and the long-term hazards of the production system. She was concerned not only about the visible, acute problems of occupational hazards but also generational issues associated with "race poisons," reproductive toxins such as lead whose "effects are not confined to the men and women who are exposed to it in the course of their work, but are passed on to their offspring." She was able to communicate effectively with industry and government figures because of her sincerity in the goals and substance of her research, while developing a sympathetic relationship with workers due to her compassion and her commitment to change. A reformer in the mold of the settlement house worker (even while at Harvard, Hamilton maintained a "home" at Hull House), and a powerful environmental advocate in an era when the term had yet to be invented, Alice Hamilton situated the question of the environment directly in its urban and industrial context.

The Environment of Daily Life in the Industrial City

The rise of what Lewis Mumford has called the "industrial city" of the nineteenth and early twentieth centuries represents a chronicle of new and pervasive forms of environmental degradation. Though celebrated as a period of great economic expansion, industrial growth, and urban reconfiguration, the period from the 1860s through World War I can be seen as laying in place the contemporary environmental hazards of daily life in urbanized and industrialized America. The triumph of fossil fuels as dominant energy sources, the diminishing of wilderness areas and open urban spaces through the railroads and then with gasoline-powered vehicles, the growth of new industries such as steel, rubber, and chemicals, and the discharge and disposal of vast urban and industrial by-products contributed to the massive human and environmental toll accompanying the more celebrated changes in this period. H. L. Mencken, writing about the industrializing Monongahela Valley in the late nineteenth century, expressed this ironic juxtaposition directly: "Here was the very heart of industrial America, the center of its most lucrative and characteristic activity, the boast and pride of the richest and grandest nation ever seen on earth—and here was a scene so dreadfully hideous, so intolerably bleak and forlorn it reduced the whole aspiration of man to a macabre and depressing joke."

The hazards of the workplace paralleled the hazards of the city in communities adjacent to the factories subject to their stench, noise, and foul air, as well as in neighborhoods overcrowded with immigrants seeking to work and survive in the great urban centers of the East and Midwest. Jane Addams, in a famous passage describing Halsted Street on Chicago's west side, captured this quality of the urban environment near the turn of the century: "The streets are inexpressibly dirty," she wrote in *Twenty Years at Hull House,* "the number of schools inadequate, sanitary legislation unenforced, the street lighting bad, the paving miserable and altogether lacking in the alleys and smaller streets, and the stables foul beyond description. Hundreds of houses are unconnected with the street sewer."

The environmental problems endemic to the period—water quality, sewage and sanitation, solid and hazardous waste generation and disposal, ventilation and air emissions, occupational and public health issues—parallel the items of a contemporary environmental agenda. Water was a particularly critical issue. It was needed for urban expansion, used for municipal and industrial discharges, and was a deadly source of infection and disease once contaminated. With the expansion of the industrial city, urban areas became dependent on fresh supplies of water, once existing sources such as local wells or stream beds became contaminated. Water quality and water supply issues became intertwined. Better-quality sources allowed for more growth, while a sufficient supply helped improve the quality of urban life through such tasks as hosing down the streets and settling the dust, thereby reducing the threat of pestilence and disease in main thoroughfares and back alleys.

Most cities decided to confront the problems of degraded water supplies by opting to secure new, more pristine supplies, often imported from distant, nonurbanized areas. As a consequence, original water sources, such as local rivers, were allowed to become a kind of nineteenth-century Superfund site. Municipal leaders assumed that industries should be largely exempt from discharge controls and that property owners, as Pennsylvania governor Daniel Hastings complained in 1897, "had the right to develop anything they wished in water bodies fronted by their property." Lewis Mumford, in his epic study *The City in History,* wrote about how the early industrial city subordinated all details of daily life to the requirements of the factory, leading to urban and industrial discharges that fouled the waters of rivers and streams. "There are myriads of dirty things given it to wash, and whole wagonloads of poisons from dye houses and bleach yards thrown into it to carry away," Mumford quoted one nineteenth-century source about an urban river. "Steam boilers discharge into it their seething contents, and drains and sewers their fetid impurities; till at length it rolls on—here between tall dingy walls, there under precipices of red sandstone—considerably less a river than a flood of liquid manure."

As urban rivers, streams, and wells came to resemble open sewers, community leaders were forced to confront the enormity of the public health hazards and environmental degradation such practices represented. Infectious disease epidemics—yellow fever, then cholera and typhoid—plagued the industrial city up through the 1890s, striking seemingly at will. The problems were exacerbated by an unwillingness to control industrial and municipal discharges, because to do so might, as Philadelphia's chief engineer put it, "interfere with the large manufacturing interests which add so greatly to our permanent prosperity." Instead, municipalities searched for ways to accommodate industry and locate better-quality water sources. During the 1870s, the City of Newark, for example, sought to prevent discharges into the Passaic River, its primary source of drinking water. This included restrictions on upstream sources, such as a large paper mill, and such downstream practices as dumping dead animals and refuse directly into the river. But by the 1880s, the increase in industrial activities, particularly factories along the lower stretch of the river that poured out their own "peculiar filth," overwhelmed the local water departments. By the end of the decade, the Passaic River had become subject to uncontrolled discharges, its waters unfit to drink or even to be used by those industries, such as Newark's large breweries, that relied on fresh water sources. In 1889, city officials, under pressure from local industrial interests, contracted with a private company to deliver water from an upland tributary of the Passaic, bypassing and ultimately abandoning the main stem of the river to continuing contamination.

Water discharges represented only one type of environmental hazard: releases into the air and disposal onto the land were also poorly regulated and widely prevalent. In the industrial city, the minimal, often disorganized street collection of solid wastes and the lack of an effective and comprehensive sewer system for liquid wastes intensified the environmental problems of daily life already magnified by contaminated water. The city's streets were strewn with horse manure, mounds of uncollected garbage in alleyways, and slag and rubbish heaps from factories. Solid-waste disposal practices at the turn of the century involved locating the most convenient area for dumping wastes—often open pits directly within the urban area, or available bodies of water, such as the ocean for coastal communities. Garbage collection remained uncertain, with rotting mounds of garbage and ash a common sight in immigrant neighborhoods and industrial zones. The sewer system, where available, represented yet another uncontrolled source of wastes released by industries and cities.

The absence of any effective policy mechanism to distinguish between wastes also meant that a large volume of what we would today call hazardous wastes were entering the environment without restrictions. By World War I, heavy metals such as lead, organic chemicals such as benzene and naphtha, and a variety of other toxic substances used in steel mills, dye and munitions manufacture, paper and pulp mills, metallurgical processes, and mining were being discharged in significant amounts into the air, water, and land. These, in turn, were causing a wide variety of occupational and community-based environmental and public health problems largely ignored by industry and government officials alike. Environmental degradation was seen as a necessary by-product of urban and industrial growth, with industrial and civic leaders seeking to shift the burden of response to the worker and community resident rather than the industry or municipality. Sanitation, occupational hazards, and environmental and industrial poisoning all became defined as results of poor individual habits, creating a kind of environmental victimization. The experience of environmental degradation thus took on a class dimension. On the one hand, the industrial city became a source of great wealth and a symbol of progress for those directly benefiting from the industrial and urban expansion of the period. On the other hand, this very same expansion, with its belching factories, polluted waterways, and untreated and sometimes uncollected wastes, became, for many poor and industrial workers, an environmental nightmare that seemed impossible to escape.

Environmental Order: The Rise of the Professionals

Despite the great power of industrial interests in shaping the industrial city, the urban environment was still a protracted political battleground during the Progressive Era (1880s–1920s). Efforts to address environmental degradation were slow to develop at first, but grew in scale after the turn of the century, becoming especially significant by World War I. By then, two urban environmental approaches had emerged: professionalization and reform. Paralleling the conservationist and preservationist movements of the same era, professional and reform groups defined themselves in response to the environmental conditions brought by changes in the urban and industrial order.

First and foremost, urban and industrial conditions raised new public health problems. The environmental problems of the industrial city—limited and contaminated water supplies, inadequate waste and sewage collection and disposal, poor ventilation and polluted and smoke-filled air, overcrowded neighborhoods and tenements—provided the means to spread disease, the social and physical environment for it to flourish, and the arena in which problems were contested and solutions sought. These environmental and public health issues generated new social movements, most situated outside the medical profession and formed in response to specific disease epidemics. Seeking to link such issues as sanitation and public health, the new groups pushed for the establishment of municipal and statewide boards of health and other municipal and national public health and environment agencies. They hoped to initiate sanitary campaigns, check food and water supplies, and institute special measures, such as community quarantine programs. . . .

By 1912, at the height of the Progressive Era, a new public health agenda seemed more imminent. With the acceptance and initial implementation of certain disease treatment and prevention programs, the position of the growing professional class of physicians and other public health "experts" effectively shifted. More powerful coalitions incorporating the public health and sanitary movements as well as the insurance industry began to promote a broad package of public health reforms.

With the passage of legislation establishing the U.S. Public Health Service in 1912 and the development of its bacteria-based water quality standards two years later, the institutionalization of public health seemed secure. . . .

The rise of professional groups in the areas of sanitation and solid waste collection and disposal also reflected the development of a reform agenda focused on the inadequacies and corruption associated with sanitation efforts. The first major sanitation reformer, George Waring, the commissioner of sanitation for the City of New York during the 1890s, was an engineer who sought to rationalize and make more efficient (and equitable) the city's nearly nonexistent garbage collection system. At the same time, Waring explored new disposal technologies first developed in Europe and subsequently introduced in this country. Similar to Waring's interests, engineering and public health journals as well as popular publications such as *Cosmopolitan* printed articles during the 1890s and early 1900s about fusing engineering concerns with reform objectives in the municipal solid waste collection and disposal area. "Cleaning up the city" became at once an engineering strategy and a political metaphor.

Like the resource-oriented conservationists, solid waste reformers in the Progressive Era, partly through newly organized professional associations of sanitary engineers, emphasized concepts of efficiency and "multiple use," including the idea that garbage in its reusable forms was "gold." New technologies, such as reduction (the heating of garbage to extract raw materials or resources), reinforced the conservationist theme that production could be more "productive," as opposed to the wastes and excesses associated with early industrialization. Solid waste management, in this context, became not only a professional objective but constituted one element in the overall attempt to rationalize the production system.

The professionalization theme was perhaps most pronounced in the area of water quality, where the introduction of new forms of treatment and engineering became linked to both the science-based bacteriological and sanitary revolutions. By 1914, filtration and chlorine disinfection were seen as the best means of reducing exposure to bacterial agents of infectious disease. These new, successful methods of water treatment, advocated by and increasingly enforced by sanitary or civil engineers, not only reshaped municipal water department responsibilities for securing "clean" water supplies but effectively decoupled the issue of contaminated streams and other bodies of water from the quality or purity of drinking water after treatment. . . .

What industries produced and how they produced it—the direct concern of Alice Hamilton—had become, in the era of professionalization, a question of managing and controlling the by-products of industry rather than changing its processes and outcomes. In contrast, the social reform agenda in the urban and industrial environmental arena came to be associated more with passion than technique, the "producer" rather than the "product." . . .

Socializing Democracy: The Settlement Idea

When Jane Addams established Hull House on the west side of Chicago in 1888, new movements for social and environmental reform appeared ready to emerge as a major social force in the industrial city. Chicago, a major manufacturing, resource, transportation, and ethnic crossroads, seemed a particularly appropriate choice for a social and environmental reform movement. For many reformers, it had become symbolic of the new urban and industrial order, a city "first in violence, deepest in dirt, loud, lawless, unlovely, ill-smelling, new; an overgrown gawk of a village, the teeming tough among cities," as muckraker Lincoln Steffens characterized it.

Addams wanted Hull House to become a center for Chicago's reform movements, a neighborhood home at once part of and an alternative to the urban and industrial order. Her notion of the "social settlement," though partly derived from the upper-class orientation of the English settlement house movement of the 1880s, was quickly adapted to the conditions of the industrial city and the neighborhoods in which settlements located. Centers for ideas and reform, settlements would provide a "higher civic and social life," as the Hull House charter put it, an arena for advocates "to investigate and improve the conditions in the industrial districts of Chicago." Hull House itself quickly became a "colony of efficient and intelligent women living in a workingmen's quarter with the house used for all sorts of purposes by about a thousand persons a week," as one key Hull House figure wrote in a letter at the time. Though the settlement house was by no means the only force for social and environmental reform in the Progressive Era, it became both the meeting ground and a key symbol of the movements for change contesting the urban and industrial order of the period.

Focused on the conditions of daily life in their neighborhoods, the settlements immediately confronted questions of housing, sanitation, and public health. Concerns about overcrowded tenements, inadequate paving, and lack of crucial services such as garbage collection dominated the discussions and framed the actions of settlement workers. The immigrant wards and industrial neighborhoods adjacent to factories seemed most especially at risk, given the frequent breakdown of the urban infrastructure in those areas.

The initial response to this breakdown in services at the neighborhood level was to try to correct abuses by exposing the problems and bringing them to public attention. The dissemination of solid research and information along with greater accountability were central to the settlement concept of reform. Hull House resident Alice Hamilton's typhoid investigation, which pointed to the corruption and failure to act on the part of board of health personnel, was considered a model of success, as it led to the dismissal of eleven of the board's twenty-four inspectors and pressure for improved sanitary measures.

Similarly, Hull House figures focused on inadequate garbage collection as one key symptom of environmental breakdown. The garbage problem seemed so severe— "the greatest menace in a ward such as ours" according to Jane Addams—that the settlement workers sought a major investigation into the city's overall garbage system as a first step toward reform. As a result of that investigation, undertaken by the Hull House Woman's Club, Addams decided to submit her own bid to collect the garbage in the nineteenth ward. Though the bid was thrown out on a technicality, the ensuing publicity forced the mayor to appoint the Hull House founder to the position of garbage inspector for the nineteenth ward.

The appointment proved to be an extraordinary affair. The forceful, well-known Addams, along with her assistant, Amanda Johnson, a young University of Wisconsin graduate student, formed their own garbage patrol, driving around in what the children in the ward called "Miss Addams' garbage phaeton." Up at 6:00 A.M., the two would follow the huge trucks to the dump, keep charts and maps, make citizen arrests of landlords, complain to contractors, and raise enough of a stink that restructuring the garbage collection system quickly rose to the top of the agenda for both city hall and reform movement alike.

The garbage issue was also a central concern to the settlement workers in Chicago's "back of the yards" industrial and residential section, where the city's largest garbage dump was located. The settlement workers from the area were led by Mary McDowell, daughter of a prosperous Chicago steel man and a one-time kindergarten teacher at Hull House who had also helped organize and lead the Hull House Woman's Club. Known as the "garbage lady" because of her continuous advocacy of better disposal practices, McDowell sought to mobilize neighborhood and civic organizations, women's clubs (who formed their own "garbage committees"), and other public sanitarians to explore more effective scientific and technical solutions, such as reduction. McDowell also insisted that industry take responsibility for its trash and sewage disposal practices by funding some of the costs of developing new disposal and treatment techniques. . . .

The settlement movement also became adept at helping bring about broad reform agendas by linking workplace hazards with community and consumer concerns. This was best exemplified by the scandals surrounding the meat-packing industry. . . . Settlement reformers first became involved with the conditions in "Packingtown," as the stockyards community was known, through the establishment of a settlement house at the University of Chicago near the stockyards. This settlement house was headed by the ersatz "garbage lady," Mary McDowell. In her new location, McDowell was immediately appalled at the back-of-the-yards environment and sought to develop what one reform publication characterized as a "neighborhood consciousness" about the surrounding area.

In this small, dense, urban neighborhood was an extraordinary mix of environmental hazards. It was bounded on the north by the stagnant backwater of the South Fork of the Chicago River, where putrefying refuse filled in the river bed and formed "long, hideous shoals along the bank." The decaying organic matter released quantities of carbonic acid gas, which continually broke through the "thick scum of the water's surface," causing this section of the river to be named "Bubbly Creek." To the west lay the city's garbage dumps, four huge holes from which the clay had been dug for neighboring brickyards. These vast, open pits were fed daily by horse-drawn wagons carrying trash from throughout the city. This included waste from the packers that was then burned, creating a permanent stretch of fire surrounded by a moat to keep it from spreading. To the east was vacant land used as "hair fields," containing animal hair and other incidental slaughterhouse wastes that putrefied while drying. And, finally, to the south lay an open prairie. Without paved streets, without trees, grass, or shrubbery, with no sewer connections or regular trash pickup, and with its densely polluted air and powerful odors, Packingtown had become an urban environmental catastrophe by the turn of the century. "No other neighborhood in this, or perhaps in any other city, is dominated by a single industry of so offensive a character," wrote two settlement figures in 1911.

Once established in the stockyards neighborhood, McDowell and her settlement workers rapidly became active concerning local environmental and social conditions. Beginning with her efforts to improve garbage disposal practices, McDowell pushed much of the settlement agenda: sanitation reform, support for municipal bathhouses,

playgrounds, summer schools, kindergartens, adult education, and overall neighborhood improvement. But McDowell's most significant activities stemmed from her
recognition of the industrial character of her community and the link between the
conditions of work and the conditions of daily life in the community. In that context,
she became a pivotal supporter and figure of solidarity during the famous (and unsuccessful) stockyards strike of 1904 over union recognition.

In this same period, McDowell's Northwest Settlement also became a retreat
for muckraker journalist Upton Sinclair, who ate his meals at the settlement, discussing life in the back-of-the-yards neighborhood with McDowell and others while
preparing the material for his thinly fictionalized account of stockyard conditions,
The Jungle. Published in 1906, the book immediately caused a sensation, not so
much about the working and living conditions in the stockyards as about the quality of the meat provided the consuming public. For Sinclair, the inadvertent focus
on impure food undercut his intention to expose environmental conditions in the
workplace. But for the settlement reformers, including McDowell and Jane Addams,
the impure food controversy and other consumer issues provided an effective way to
bring about the reform of overall living environments, beginning with passage of the
Pure Food and Drug Act in 1906. As progressive (though not necessarily radical)
reformers, the settlement workers sought to define and legislate what they considered to be the "certain minimum requirements of well-being" in an industrial city.
This could be brought about by making available information to help empower the
poor and working classes, and by creating efficient, bureaucratic, managerial structures to help implement reform programs. . . .

Over time, the settlement reformers and their ideas would become subject to
much simplification and romanticization, transforming Jane Addams especially into
a kind of national myth. Still, women such as Addams, Alice Hamilton, Florence
Kelley, Grace Abbott, and Julia Lathrop had been able to force their issues onto the
national agenda, making them "objectively important in the life of the American
people," as one Hull House participant put it. Their issues cut to the heart of urban
and industrial change. And while the settlements themselves faded or were absorbed
into less threatening, apolitical forms, the issues of daily life and urban and industrial environments that had preoccupied the movement remained as crucial and unresolved as ever.

Suburbs and Pollution

ADAM ROME

[T]he design and construction of shelter, like the production of food and fuel, always has had important environmental consequences. In different ways at different
times, the process of home building has transformed plant and animal communities,
changed the quality of the air and the water, and shaped patterns of natural resource
consumption. . . .

From Adam Rome, "Building on the Land: Toward an Environmental History of Residential Development
in American Cities and Suburbs, 1870–1990." *Journal of Urban History* 20, no. 3 (May 1994) pp.
408–409, 412–426. Copyright © 1994 by *Journal of Urban History*. Reprinted by permission of Sage
Publications, Inc.

. . . At home, people consume energy, use water, and produce waste and pollution, but the parameters of those day-to-day decisions are set—literally built–in—by the design of houses and neighborhoods. . . .

. . . In 1870, almost all homes were heated with wood. But by 1900, wood accounted for only 37 percent of residential energy use; coal accounted for 62 percent. By 1920, the share for coal and natural gas combined was 79 percent; wood was just 21 percent. Thus the comfort of the nation's residences began to depend on nonrenewable fuels. . . .

In the decades after 1870, the number of homes served by municipal water systems increased rapidly, and the demand for water skyrocketed. Between 1856 and 1882, per capita daily water use (including nonresidential use) jumped from 33 to 144 gallons in Chicago and from 55 to 149 gallons in Detroit. At first, water was not even metered. Perhaps more important in the long run, the tap hooked up to a centralized source encouraged the use of clear, drinkable water even for activities that did not require so high a standard of quality. In effect, the planners of the new plumbing systems assumed that water was infinitely available. But, in fact, water was a precious resource, and cities in the twentieth century often have procured supplies only at considerable environmental and economic cost. San Francisco flooded the stunningly beautiful Hetch Hetchy valley to secure a naturally pure and abundant source of water, and Boston destroyed a valley of farm towns to build the Quabbin Reservoir.

In the last decades of the nineteenth century, the sewer hookup also became part of the infrastructure of most urban homes. By 1880, sewers served 67 percent of the nation's urban population; by 1900, the figure had reached 81 percent. For the residents of sewered neighborhoods, the change from the old world of cesspools and privy vaults was dramatic: Yards and streets no longer had to serve as depositories for excrement, kitchen slops, and wastewater.

Sewers solved one problem but created another: Disposal of raw sewage in rivers and lakes quickly became a major source of water pollution. By the turn of the century, the incidence of waterborne disease had risen sharply in several cities that drew their drinking water from sources downstream of sewer outlets. In Trenton, for example, the death rate from typhoid doubled between 1890 and 1900. Even after sanitary experts recognized the danger, only a handful of cities began to treat their sewage. Instead, cities overcame the problem of waterborne disease by securing new water supplies or by installing systems to disinfect water taken from tainted sources. Thus the pollution of urban rivers and lakes continued. Although there is as yet no systematic historical study of the harm done to aquatic life by sewage, there is enough evidence scattered in scientific and historical works to make clear that the damage was considerable.

The character of city streets also changed radically in the decades after the Civil War, and the transformation had important environmental consequences. In 1880, less than half of all urban streets were paved. By 1924, almost all were. In large part, of course, the new street surfaces were designed to ease the movement of traffic. But the paving of streets also facilitated the removal of water and waste. Instead of slowly soaking into the ground or collecting in annoying and often manure-fouled puddles and pools, rain simply ran down the streets. But where did the water end up? By 1920, most large cities had combined sanitary and storm sewer systems; a few cities had separate storm drains; and in a few large cities and in many smaller cities, there were no storm sewers at all, so runoff from streets simply drained into the nearest low-lying water bodies, including harbors. But in one important respect, the differences made no difference: The dirty runoff from city streets ended up polluting the waters in and around the nation's metropolitan areas.

In the period from 1870 to 1945, then, a number of the major patterns of residential development were especially costly to the environment. But there were some important mitigating or compensating factors. In the postwar period, in contrast, the story is almost all of a piece: The rush of new homes came at a greatly increased environmental cost. . . .

In the postwar years, the territory of cities and suburbs expanded by leaps and bounds. From 1950 to 1980, the officially defined "metropolitan" area jumped from 6 percent to 16 percent of the U.S. land mass. In the 1960s, urban development took roughly 900,000 acres a year—a territory larger than Rhode Island. Although that figure includes office buildings, shopping centers, factories, and schools, housing accounted for most of the new urban acreage. In many new suburbs, indeed, residential structures, lots, and streets claimed nearly two-thirds of the land. To some extent, of course, the increase in metropolitan land area after 1945 simply reflected the increase in urban population. But the rise of the low-density middle-class suburb accounted for much of the sprawl of urban territory. In the streetcar suburbs of the 1880s and 1890s, the average house lot was 3,000 square feet; in the automobile suburbs of the 1920s, the average was 5,000 square feet; but in the subdivisions of the 1940s and 1950s, the lots were between 4,000 and 8,000 square feet.

There is considerable evidence that an increased percentage of homes were built after World War II on land with a high environmental cost. The larger scale of many developments made the filling of marshes more economical, and even wetlands the size of the Florida Everglades became attractive to private developers. As a result, almost a million acres of marshes, swamps, bogs, and coastal estuaries were destroyed for urban development between the mid 1950s and the mid 1970s. With the help of bulldozers, builders in many areas of the country began to construct more homes on steep hillside sites. Indeed, the split-level house of the 1950s was designed, in part, to suit lots on steeply sloped ground. Thus the problems of landsliding and erosion grew worse. In one Philadelphia suburb, for example, the construction of homes on hilly pasture and forest land caused enough erosion to narrow the width of a nearby reservoir from 700 feet to 25 feet and shorten its length by nearly half a mile. In the postwar years, there also was an increase in floodplain construction, and floods soon began to do more serious damage to residential areas.

The loss of prime farmland to urban development also accelerated in the postwar years. In the megalopolis of the Northeast, the rate of conversion was twice as great in the five years from 1949 to 1954 as in the twenty years before. Santa Clara County, California, lost almost a fifth of its pear, peach, apricot, cherry, prune, and walnut lands in just five years. Although the loss nationwide was only a small fraction of the total agricultural acreage, a number of experts began to worry about the long-term impact of suburbanization on agricultural output. By 1970, indeed, 15 percent of the nation's best farmland was within the census-determined standard metropolitan statistical districts. Seventeen percent of the corn crop came from fields at the outskirts of the nation's largest cities; in several regions of the country, roughly two-thirds of the fruit and vegetable harvest also came from farms in metropolitan districts.

The use of factorylike methods of construction enabled some large builders to reduce waste of materials on-site. But otherwise, the new techniques and technologies increased the environmental impact of construction. To remove vegetation and flatten terrain, many builders bulldozed hundreds of acres at a time and so put the bare ground at the mercy of the wind and the rain. The result was more erosion and more silt damage to nearby streams, rivers, and lakes. Indeed, the rate of soil erosion from home building in the postwar years often was as severe as from clear-cut logging or strip-mining. By clearing away all vegetation and by filling or channeling all streams, builders also eliminated habitats for wildlife. Not surprisingly, a number of ecological studies later found significant reductions in the populations of birds, snakes, and frogs in postwar suburbs.

In many of the fastest growing areas at the urban fringe, there were no sanitary sewers. Accordingly, the number of homes relying on septic tanks and cesspools began to rise. In 1960, the figure was fourteen million; in 1970, it was seventeen million. When properly designed, sited, and maintained, on-site systems of liquid waste disposal were safe and efficient, but as many as a third of the systems installed in the 1950s and 1960s failed. They were put in unsuitable soil, above shallow aquifers, or near fresh water; they leaked; and they overflowed. As a result, they contaminated groundwater, polluted streams, or caused lakes to eutrophy in many metropolitan areas. By the mid 1980s, indeed, on-site waste disposal systems had polluted water in thirty-six states. The most dramatic threat was to drinking water, but septic tank and cesspool failures also harmed populations of fish, reptiles, and amphibians.

In many suburban subdivisions, there also was no public water supply, and the reliance on wells caused environmental problems. Often, the use of wells reduced flows in nearby streams and thus threatened fish and wildlife communities. In some coastal areas—the suburbs of Miami, Florida, most notably—the siting of wells near the ocean led to saltwater contamination of aquifers. . . .

The resource-consuming, pollution-producing lawn became ubiquitous. To be sure, the idea of the lawn had begun to take hold well before 1945. Frank Scott published the first important guide to suburban lawn care in 1870. By 1874, a New York company was manufacturing 15,000 lawnmowers a year. But until the mass suburbanization of the 1940s, the lawn was common only in well-to-do neighborhoods. For most urban residents, the lot was a functional yard. It was a place to dispose of waste, to sink a well, to wash and dry clothes, to grow crops, even to raise chickens or pigs, but it was not a tiny park. In many yards, indeed, there was no grass, only gravel. But invariably postwar yards were made into lawns. Although only 139,000 lawnmowers were sold in 1946, 3,800,000 were sold in 1960 and 6,130,000 were sold in 1972. By the 1980s, the acreage in residential lawns was four-fifths the size of Pennsylvania. Of course, the great increase in the number of lawns after 1945 led to a sharp increase in water consumption in many communities, especially in the arid Southwest. In some places, water used for lawns was 150 percent greater than that used for all other household uses, such as flushing, drinking, cooking, and cleaning. Like farmers, homeowners began in the postwar years to use prodigious quantities of chemical fertilizers and pesticides, and runoff from lawns soon became a leading cause of lake eutrophication and groundwater contamination. With the rise of the gasoline-powered lawnmower, the lawn also became a significant source of air pollution. In California alone, lawnmowers now produce as much pollution every year as 3,500,000 cars driving 16,000 miles apiece. The lawn contributed as well to the garbage crisis, as yard waste was the second largest item in urban landfills in the 1980s. . . .

For the first time, the design of most houses assumed a seemingly endless supply of energy. Architects and builders abandoned traditional ways of adapting design to regional climatic conditions. In most postwar homes, there were no porches, no basements, no high ceilings, no oversized Southern doors and windows to increase ventilation, no broad eaves to block the hot summer sun, no breezeways, no functional shutters, and no thick walls to protect against northern winters. Instead, the slab-style California ranchhouse became the norm in new neighborhoods across the nation: With the development of relatively cheap air conditioning units and central heating systems, every home could rely on utilities to provide Mediterranean comfort year-round. Because very little of the nation was naturally blessed with a California climate, the standardization of design contributed to a sharp rise in residential energy use in the 1950s and 1960s. . . .

[There was also a] trend toward electric heating, which generally had a higher environmental cost than the common alternatives. From 1950 to 1970, the average use of electricity per residential customer increased nearly 400 percent. Of course, the change was due partly to greater use of a host of household appliances, but increased use of electric heating accounted for the largest share of the overall increase in residential electricity use. To supply electric heat to homes, however, utilities generated radioactive waste, poured sulfur into the air, and sent fish-killing streams of hot water into rivers. For technical reasons, electricity also was less efficient as a heating source than the major alternatives in the 1950s and 1960s—natural gas and fuel oil. Although electric systems lost no heat up a furnace flue, there were huge inefficiencies in the generation and distribution of electricity. Even in the 1980s, only 29 percent of the energy used by utilities to generate electricity ultimately was usable in the home. With gas or oil heating, in contrast, the overall energy efficiency ranged from 50 to 65 percent.

In many ways, then, the environmental impact of the homes designed and built after 1945 was unprecedented both in scale and scope. But there was little concern about that impact until the late 1960s and early 1970s, when the modern environmental movement became a major political, social, and cultural force. In those years, environmentalists, architects, engineers, planners, and builders began to publish guides to more environmentally sensitive ways of designing and building homes. At all levels of government, especially after 1970, there were new laws and regulations intended to reduce the environmental impact of residential development. . . .

In principle, the most comprehensive federal reform was the National Environmental Policy Act of 1970, which required developers to file an environmental impact statement (EIS) in order to receive government loan guarantees. . . .

To some extent, federal antipollution legislation also had the potential to reform the process of home building. The Clean Air Act of 1970 required the Environmental Protection Agency (EPA) to review all proposals for new construction that might degrade the air of cities or regions with serious pollution problems—a requirement that could have led regulators to call for changes in housing and subdivision design to reduce residential emissions of pollutants. There is little evidence, however, that the EPA has used the law's powers for that purpose.

The Federal Water Pollution Control Act of 1972 required states to draw up plans to control water pollution from nonpoint sources, including septic tanks, storm runoff, and construction activities, but it is not clear whether the plans have led to effective action. Thus far, government agencies at all levels have spent far more money to improve treatment of municipal and manufacturing effluent than to improve control of nonpoint source pollution. . . .

Throughout the 1970s, environmentalists sought national legislation to regulate land use, but the effort failed. As a result, the federal role in overseeing the type of land open to development is limited to a few carrot-and-stick efforts to prod state governments into restricting the uses of coastal wetlands and estuaries, controlling building in floodplains, and protecting lands next to officially designated wild-and-scenic rivers. In most cases, the states have taken the carrot. In a few cases, states have even set minimum environmental standards for all development. In recent years, in consequence, there has been noteworthy progress in the protection of some sensitive lands. From the mid 1970s to the mid 1980s, for example, the rate of loss of wetlands to urban development was about one-fourth the rate of loss in the period from the mid 1950s to the mid 1970s. . . .

By 1990, to be sure, there were countless models around the nation of ways to design and construct subdivisions without steep environmental costs. In *The Granite Garden,* landscape architect Anne Whiston Spirn describes a model suburb—Woodlands, Texas—that was designed with a complex system of woods, streams, and creeks to sustain wildlife, to protect water quality, to prevent flooding, and to ensure that rain replenishes the underground aquifer. During construction, the use of earthmoving equipment was limited to avoid extensive disturbance of the soil. Trees along the tract's two natural creeks were left standing. The floodplain in the 20,000-acre development was left open, and homes and roads were sited to fit the topography. Because the homes were clustered, the surrounding open space was more extensive and richer in wildlife habitat. As a result, the development was able to support white-tailed deer, opossum, armadillos, and even bobcats. But Woodlands still was a rarity in the mid 1980s. In the judgment of two authorities on the planning of residential developments, "For every well-designed subdivision, there were scores that were poorly planned."

In at least two areas of residential design and construction, however, a combination of environmental concern and economic calculation led to significant breaks with postwar trends. Across the country, cities and suburbs in the 1960s and 1970s revised zoning and subdivision codes to allow "planned unit developments," which made more efficient use of land and resources by allowing higher-density neighborhoods. The housing in the new complexes was mostly multifamily, on small lots, with the units clustered around common recreation areas or open space. Because of changes in the economics and demographics of home buying, the planned unit development appealed to many developers. It reduced the per-unit cost of land at a time when land prices were rising rapidly. It also opened up a number of new markets, especially among the young and the old. As a result, planned unit developments quickly became common. . . .

Although there have been some recent changes in the design and construction of housing, a quick survey shows clearly that the past still has a formidable presence. Many of the most environmentally destructive forms of development today first took shape in the 1940s or in the decades around the turn of the century.

Automobiles and Roads

JAMES FLINK

Before the automobile revolution, extended vacations away from home were the privilege of the rich. The average middle-class family could not afford railroad fares to a remote national park and a long stay at a luxury hotel. With the advent of the Model T and improved roads, the automobile outing and the automobile vacation became middle-class American institutions. As Foster Rhea Dulles points out in his history of American recreation, the automobile "greatly stimulated the whole outdoor movement, making camping possible for many people for whom the woods, mountains, and streams were formerly inaccessible."

Until the late 1920s, however, automobile touring, especially to remote western parks, was severely limited by poor roads. Despite the efforts of bicycle organizations, automobile clubs, and farmers, the good-roads movement had accomplished little up to the outset of the Model T era. Roads meandered from town to town without forming a system of interconnected highways. They were poorly marked when marked at all. Roadside services for tourists were virtually nonexistent. Over 90 percent of the roads were unsurfaced, and impassable much of the year. Only 8.66 percent of the roads in the United States were surfaced at all in 1909, a gain of only 1.5 percent over 1904, when the first census of American roads was taken. These few improved roads most commonly had gravel surfaces, which automobile traffic quickly destroyed by sweeping the gravel into windrows, rather than packing it down as did much slower horse-drawn traffic. Macadam was no solution, for the weight and speed of motor vehicles quickly broke down macadamized surfaces too. Brick roads were satisfactory, but their cost was prohibitive. Until 1909 there was not a single section of paved road in a rural area.

At the Second Annual Good Roads Convention in 1909 at Cleveland, Ohio, "the two dominating influences . . . were the American Automobile Association, representing the autoists and the cities, and the National Grange, representing the farmers. Cooperating with these organizations were the American Road Makers' Association, the National Association of Automobile Manufacturers, and the American Motor Car Manufacturers' Association." Automobile interests predominated in the Lincoln Highway Association, organized on July 1, 1913, to promote the construction of a coast-to-coast highway taking "the shortest, best, and most direct route." The first demonstration "seedling" mile of the Lincoln Highway was opened at Malta, Illinois, in October 1914.

Through the combined lobbying efforts of automobile interests and farmers newly made mobile by the Model T, the primitive road network of 1910 was transformed into an interconnected system of concrete highways by 1930. By the end of 1912 a number of major road-building projects were under way; outstanding county/township road bonds totaled over $155.6 million and authorized state good-roads expenditures totaled nearly $136.9 million. By the end of 1914 the United States had 257,293 miles of surfaced roads, of which 75,400 miles were paved with macadam, 1,591 with brick, and 2,349 with concrete. . . .

From James J. Flink, "On the Road," in *The Automobile Age* (Cambridge, MA: MIT Press, 1988), pp. 169–175, 179–180, 182. Reprinted by permission of MIT Press.

The federal government gave its first support to building a national system of roads with passage of the 1916 Federal Aid Road Act, which appropriated $75 million to be spent over a five-year period by the secretary of agriculture for the improvement of post roads. Then, following World War I, the federal government made available as military surplus to state highway departments for road building some 25,000 heavy trucks and 1,500 caterpillar tractors. Demonstration of the value of long-distance trucking during the war and growing automobile registrations after the war led to passage of the Federal Highway Act of 1921, which provided federal aid to the states, through fifty-fifty matching grants, for building an interconnected interstate system of highways. Some $75 million was appropriated for 1922 alone, and that year 10,247 miles of federally financed highways were built, 3.5 times more than in the preceding five years under the 1916 legislation. States were required to select and designate not more than 7 percent of their highways as part of an interconnected system eligible for federal aid. In 1924 the amount of federal aid per mile was stabilized at $15,000. In 1925 a uniform plan was adopted for designating and numbering the U.S. highways that were part of the system. . . .

. . . Stephen T. Mather, the first director of the NPS [National Park Service], recognized that park development was linked intimately to the growth of tourism, so he energetically built a . . . "pragmatic alliance" . . . between the NPS and automobile interests throughout the country. The early impact of automobility on the national parks has been summarized succinctly by Robert Shankland in his biography of Mather: "The auto reached swarming ubiquity fast—faster than people now remember. As the auto prospered so did the national parks." Preservationist Edward Abbey claimed that the slogan "Parks are for people" decoded came to mean that "Parks are for people-in-automobiles."

Automobiles were first admitted into Mount Rainier in 1908, General Grant in 1910, Crater Lake in 1911, Glacier in 1912, Yosemite and Sequoia in 1913, Mesa Verde in 1914, and Yellowstone in 1915. As early as 1916 more visitors entered Yosemite by automobile than by railroad, and the largest source of revenue for the newly formed NPS already was automobile admission fees—levied for paying for park roads and improvements. Along with other prominent preservationists, Mather welcomed the automobile into the parks: he recognized the potential political power of the automobile industry, automobile clubs, and the growing number of automobile tourists. A broad base of popular support was deemed essential to the parks both to obtain adequate congressional funding for development and maintenance and to thwart mounting pressure for the exploitation of park resources from commercial interests and other governmental agencies. The main opposition to opening the parks to the automobile came, significantly, not from the preservationists but from park concessionaires who operated horse-drawn stage lines. Their fears were borne out when Mather ordered Yellowstone's stage lines motorized in 1917, a scant two years after the automobile was admitted into that park. Automobilists also were prominent in many preservationist organizations, a prime example being that the Save the Redwoods League originated at the Pacific Auto Show of 1920.

The Federal Highway Act of 1921 and the universal adoption of the gasoline tax to fund highway improvement by 1929 resulted in an interconnected system of paved highways that made even the more remote western parks accessible from the east coast. Moreover, as the outcome of agitation by the National Parks Highway

Association, formed in 1915, a route that interconnected all of the national parks had been laid out and signposted by the early 1920s. This interpark route was not totally paved. Nevertheless, it served as a psychological as well as a physical link among the national parks and encouraged people to travel to them.

Until at least the mid-1930s, however, good roads ended at the boundaries of the national parks. In 1915 Yellowstone was the only park with sufficient road mileage to make driving worthwhile, and all park roads not only were unpaved but were too narrow and had grades too steep for automobile traffic. By 1924 a total of only $3.5 million had been spent on park roads; there were only 12 miles of paved road in the entire National Park System, and Glacier and Mount McKinley still lacked through roads. Although by 1924 Yosemite had 138 miles of rutted wagon road, all except 20 miles were private. With 356 miles of unpaved road for a land area larger than several of our eastern states, Yellowstone still had the best road system of any national park.

The turning point came in 1923, when Congress appropriated $7.5 million for road building in the national parks between 1924 and 1927. Altitude, a short working season, rocky terrain, and preservationist considerations made the cost of building new paved park roads extremely high—$20,000 to $60,000 a mile. Consequently, although some 360 miles of new park roads were planned, paving the bulk of either these or existing park roads was out of the question. So the appropriation was used primarily to reduce grades, straighten sharp curves, and widen existing wagon roads to handle automobile traffic. . . .

. . . From 1933 to 1940 the National Park Service received $220 million from a variety of New Deal agencies. The major use of these funds was for a massive program of rebuilding and paving park roads, as well as for the addition of several impressive new scenic through roads, including the Zion–Mount Carmel Road and Tunnel, the Wawona Tunnel and Road in Yosemite, the Cape Royal Road in Grand Canyon, the Paradise Valley and Yakima Park Highway in Mount Rainier, the Sylvan Pass Road in Yellowstone, and the Going-to-the-Sun Highway in Glacier.

This represented only a small part of huge New Deal expenditures on road construction from 1933 to 1942. After Roosevelt came to power, federal aid was extended from designated sections of interstate highways to urban segments of primary roads in 1934 and to secondary "feeder" roads in 1936. John Rae points out that this represented "a major change in national highway policy." As a "time-honored method of relieving unemployment," the federal government attempted to offset declines in state and local expenditures for roads and streets. "By 1939 relief and recovery accounted for 80 percent of all federal expenditures for roads and 40 percent of the total outlay on highways from all sources," Rae reports. "Between 1933 and 1942 federal relief agencies spent $4 billion on roads and streets." . . .

Even though coach-class [rail] fares between Chicago and points west were halved between 1921 and 1926, automobile travel still was cheaper and more convenient for a family than travel by train. "The automobile represented a new democratization of vacation travel," Earl Pomeroy writes. "In the same years [the 1920s] when the average American had more time for trips away from home and more money to spend on them, he could buy gasoline to carry his whole family from his own front door for what he alone would have to pay to ride the train. The growing western highway systems, growing in response to his demands, represented his expanding opportunity and the opportunity of the sections that they fed." Pomeroy continues, "What the motor cars and the motorists did to the outdoors would be long debated, but there is little doubt that the age of the automobile was the age in which the average American vacationer first found the West within his reach." With this democratization of travel, "a mass market became more important to the tourist industry as a whole than the patronage of the elite. The great profits in the western tourist and vacation industry came not from serving squab to the few but from selling gasoline, hamburger sandwiches, and postcards to the many." . . .

Although rail travel to the national parks continued to increase into the 1930s, it had been surpassed in volume by cheaper automobile travel to the parks a decade earlier. The railroads managed to hang on, providing alternative transportation to the parks, until the 1960s, when one by one they discontinued service. The western national parks are still linked, about a day's travel apart, by a system of railroad tracks that fell into disuse with massive indirect government subsidization of competing highway transportation after 1956. Visitation to the western national parks is largely a summer business, whereas the profitable running of an unsubsidized inter-park railroad system would require year-round passenger traffic. With the cost of rail transportation estimated at $50 to $75 per person per day in the early 1980s, access to the national parks by motor vehicle remains much cheaper as well as much more convenient for families. Consequently, over 90 percent of the visitors to the national parks continue to arrive in motor vehicles. . . .

During the 1970s about one fourth of all travel over 100 miles from home by Americans was for purposes of outdoor recreation or sightseeing. Government statistics make evident the central role that the national parks and other public lands, such as state parks and the national forests, played in encouraging this recreational travel. Even if . . . some three fourths of the visitors to our national parks in 1977 were among the richest 15 percent of our population, on the other hand government statistics on participation in outdoor recreation for the bicentennial period July 1, 1976, through June 30, 1977, reveal that fully 62 percent of Americans twelve years old and over participated in sightseeing at historic or scenic national sites, 30 percent camped in developed and an additional 21 percent in undeveloped areas, and 28 percent hiked or backpacked.

Tourism, then—fostered by increased affluence and expanding automobile ownership in the post-World War II period . . . —is an essential part of American life and the American economy. And that democratic access to wilderness has remained compatible with wilderness preservation in the form of our national parks is both a signal achievement of American civilization and a major benefit of the automobile revolution.

❈ FURTHER READING

Stephen B. Adams and Orville R. Butler, *Manufacturing the Future: A History of Western Electric* (1999)

Ellis C. Armstrong, Michael Robinson, and Suellen Hoy, eds., *History of Public Works in the United States, 1776–1976* (1976)

Moses N. Baker, *The Quest for Pure Water: The History of Water Purification from the Earliest Records to the Twentieth Century* (1948)

Brian Black, "Oil Creek as Industrial Apparatus: Re-creating the Industrial Process Through the Landscape of Pennsylvania's Oil Boom," *Environmental History* 3, no. 2 (April 1998), 210–229

———, *Petrolia: The Landscape of America's First Oil Boom* (2000)

Russell Bourne, *Americans on the Move: The History of Waterways, Railways, and Highways* (2000)

John Bradley, ed., *Learning to Glow: A Nuclear Reader* (2000)

Marvin Brienes, "Smog Comes to Los Angeles," *Southern California Quarterly* 58 (1976)

Craig E. Colten, *The Road to Love Canal: Managing Industrial Waste Before EPA* (1996)

Gail Cooper, *Air-Conditioning America: Engineers and the Controlled Environment, 1900–1960* (1998)

Albert E. Cowdry, "Pioneering Environmental Law: The Army Corps of Engineers and the Refuse Act," *Pacific Historical Review* 44 (1975), 331–349

William Cronon, *Nature's Metropolis* (1991)

Mike Davis, *City of Quartz: Excavating the Future in Los Angeles* (1990)

———, *Dead Cities, and Other Tales* (2002)

———, *Ecology of Fear: Los Angeles and the Imagination of Disaster* (1998)

Alan Derickson, *Black Lung: Anatomy of a Public Health Disaster* (1998)

Scott Hamilton Dewey, *Don't Breathe the Air: Air Pollution and U.S. Environmental Politics, 1945–1970* (2000)

Mona Domosh, *Invented Cities: The Creation of Landscape in Nineteenth Century New York and Boston* (1997)

Robert J. Duffy, *Nuclear Politics in America* (1997)

James J. Flink, *The Car Culture* (1975)

Robert Gordon, "Poisons in the Fields: The United Farm Workers, Pesticides, and Environmental Politics," *Pacific Historical Review* 68 (November 1999), 51–78

Edward Greer, "Air Pollution and Corporate Power: &&Municipal Reform Limits in a Black City," *Politics and Society* 4 (1974), 483–510

Angela Gugliotta, "Class, Gender, and Coal Smoke: Gender Ideology and Environmental Injustice in Pittsburgh, 1868–1914." *Environmental History* 5, no. 2, (April 2000), 165–193

Spenser W. Havlick, *The Urban Organism: The City's Natural Resources from an Environmental Perspective* (1974)

Suellen M. Hoy, "'Municipal Housekeeping': The Role of Women in Improving Urban Sanitation Practices, 1880–1917," in Martin Melosi, ed., *Pollution and Reform in American Cities, 1870–1930* (1980)

Andrew Hurley, "The Social Bases of Environmental Change in Gary, Indiana, 1945–1980," *Environmental Review* 12 (1988), 1–19

Jane Jacobs, *Death and Life of Great American Cities* (1961)

Tom Lewis, *Divided Highways: Building the Interstate Highways, Transforming American Life* (1997)

Wesley Marx, *Man and His Environment: Waste* (1971)

Tom McCarthy, "The Coming Wonder?: Foresight and Early Concerns About the Automobile." *Environmental History* 6, no. 1, (January 2001), 46–74

Martin V. Melosi, *Garbage in the Cities: Refuse, Reform, and the Environment, 1880–1980* (1981)

———, ed., *Pollution and Reform in American Cities, 1870–1930* (1980)

———, *The Sanitary City: Urban Infrastructure in America from Colonial Times to the Present* (2000)

H. Wayne Morgan, *Industrial America: The Environment and Social Problems, 1776–1920* (1974)

David E. Nye, *Consuming Power: A Social History of American Energies* (1998)

———, ed., *Technologies of Landscape: From Reshaping to Recycling* (2000)

John Opie, *Nature's Nation: An Environmental History of the United States* (1998)

Jacob Riis, *How the Other Half Lives* (1890)

Adam Rome, *The Bulldozer in the Countryside: Suburban Sprawl and the Rise of American Environmentalism* (2001)

George Rosen, *A History of Public Health* (1958)

Charles S. Rosenberg, *The Cholera Years: The United States in 1832, 1849, and 1866* (1962)

Barbara G. Rosenkrantz, ed., *Sewering the Cities* (1977)

Edmund Russell, *War and Nature: Fighting Humans and Insects with Chemicals from World War I to Silent Spring* (2001)

Peter J. Schmitt, *Back to Nature: The Arcadian Myth in Urban America* (1969)

Christopher C. Sellers, *Hazards of the Job: From Industrial Disease to Environmental Health Science* (1997)

Upton Sinclair, *The Jungle* (1905)

Raymond W. Smilor, "Personal Boundaries in the Urban Environment: The Legal Attack on Noise, 1865–1930," *Environmental Review* 3 (1979)

Theodore Steinberg, *Nature Incorporated: Industrialization and the Waters of New England* (1991)

Bayrd Still, *Urban America: A History with Documents* (1974)

David Stradling, *Smokestacks and Progressives: Environmentalists, Engineers and Air Quality in America, 1881–1951* (1999)

Joel A. Tarr, "Historical Turning Points in Municipal Water Supply and Wastewater Disposal, 1850–1932," *Civil Engineering* 47 (1977), 82–91

———, "Out of Sight, Out of Mind: A Brief History of Sewage Disposal in the United States," *American History Illustrated* 10 (1976), 40–47

———, *The Search for the Ultimate Sink: Urban Pollution in Historical Perspective* (1996)

Sam Bass Warner, *Urban Wilderness* (1976)

CHAPTER
13

The Emergence of Ecology
in the Twentieth Century

Ψ

Although ecological modes of relating to nature have roots among both indigenous and preindustrial peoples, the emergence of ecology as a science belongs to the industrial era. The term oekologie, *from the Greek word* oikos *("home"), was coined by German biologist Ernst Haeckel in 1866. In America, chemist Ellen Swallow first publicized the word—changing it to oekology—in 1892, and in a book on sanitary chemistry published in 1907, she expanded the term to human ecology. Aldo Leopold's land ethic, defined in his 1949 book* A Sand County Almanac, *brought the idea of ecology to a wider public audience. But it was the publication of Rachel Carson's* Silent Spring *in 1962 that made ecology a household word and sparked the modern environmental movement.*

The development of ecology as a science, however, was not monolithic. Several schools of thought with different underlying assumptions about nature and its management have emerged in the twentieth century. For Swallow, nature was a home, and ecology described the larger home to which human homes were connected by the movements of air, water, and soil. To botanist Frederic Clements, writing in 1916, nature was organic: A plant formation was a complex organism, growing, maturing, and dying independently of humans and their activities. For British biologist Arthur Tansley, working in the 1930s, nature comprised a multitude of interconnected physical systems, from universe down to atom, of which one—the ecosystem— exhibited constant interchange among organic and inorganic components. In the view of ecologist Eugene Odum, writing in the 1950s, nature was a balanced homeostatic system, much like a thermostat, stabilized and maintained through biological diversity. And for late-twentieth-century population biologists, nature is a chaotic, random series of individual events whose behavior is predictable only in unusual, narrowly defined circumstances. Embedded in such fundamental metaphors as home, organism, machine, homeostatic system, and chaos are different ethical and political relationships between humans and nonhuman nature. This chapter's documents and essays reveal a number of possible connections between and among scientific assumptions, metaphors, policies, and ethics as the science of ecology evolved in the twentieth century. Such changing definitions of ecology pose dilemmas for environmental historians as well as for scientists, conservationists, and policymakers. (See Maps 2 and 3 in the Appendix.)

❦ D O C U M E N T S

In Document 1, an excerpt from her *Sanitation in Daily Life* (1907), chemist Ellen Swallow defines the meaning of human ecology. Document 2, from Frederic Clements's fundamental work *Plant Succession* (1916), describes ecology in terms of the similarity between the life processes of a plant community and those of a complex organism. However, in Document 3, botanist Henry Gleason sharply attacks Clements's organism metaphor and substitutes the individual plant association and the mosaic mixture. Document 4, by British botanist Arthur Tansley, likewise attacks Clements's use of the vegetative organism and substitutes the term *ecosystem,* which encompasses not only the biotic, but also the inorganic, physical factors that make up the whole environment.

In Document 5, published in 1949 just after his death, ecologist and game manager Aldo Leopold uses Clements's concept of the biotic community to develop a land ethic. Breaking with the utilitarian conservation ethic of Gifford Pinchot, which focused on commodity production to provide "the greatest good for the greatest number for the longest time," Leopold boldly asserts an ethic that enlarges "the boundaries of the community to include soils, waters, plants, and animals, or collectively: the land."

The contemporary environmental movement exploded in 1962 with the publication of Rachel Carson's *Silent Spring,* excerpted in Document 6. Carson graphically describes the transformation of life after the introduction of radioactive fallout from atomic-bomb testing and as a result of the widespread use of such pesticides as DDT, totally new to biologic experience. Document 7 is an excerpt from a 1969 paper by ecologist Eugene Odum on the role of humans in maintaining stable ecosystems. Drawing on Clements's concept of succession, Tansley's idea of the ecosystem, and the idea of the food chain, Odum argues that ecosystems develop toward diverse, stable systems whose balance humans may maintain or upset. Odum thus brings the concept of ecology back to Swallow's concept of the home, or *oikos*—a place in which humans must maintain clean air and water and live as a part of, not apart from, the environment.

During the 1970s and 1980s, ideas that were basic to Odum's approach to conservation, such as the diversity-stability hypothesis, equilibrium, and the "balance of nature," were challenged by concepts such as Gleason's patch dynamics, mosaics, disturbances, perturbations, and chaos. The final document, by ecologists S. T. A. Pickett and P. S. White, argues that equilibrium landscapes are the exception, not the rule, and that constant change poses a paradox for conservationists.

1. Ellen Swallow Richards Defines
Human Ecology, 1907

Sanitary science teaches that mode of life which promotes health and efficiency.

The individual is one of a community influencing and influenced by the common environment.

Human ecology is the study of the surroundings of human beings in the effects they produce on the lives of men. The features of the environment are natural, as climate, and artificial, produced by human activity, as noise, dust, poisonous vapors, vitiated air, dirty water, and unclean food.

From Ellen Swallow Richards, *Sanitation in Daily Life.* Boston: Whitcomb & Barrows, 1910 [1907], pp. v–viii.

The study of this environment is in two chief lines:

First, what is often called municipal housekeeping—the co-operation of the citizens in securing clean streets, the suppression of nuisances, abundant water supply, market inspection, etc.

Second, family housekeeping. The healthful home demands a management of the house which shall promote vigorous life and prevent the physical deterioration so evident under modern conditions.

The close interrelation of these two parts of sanitation should be borne in mind. Even if a man has been so blessed as to be born into favorable conditions, he must nevertheless face the problem of retaining health and strength under the strain of modern progress and civilization. Formerly a man's occupation in the fields and woods kept him in health, but now he must ordinarily give what strength he has to his occupation, and rely upon other sources from which to secure a healthy body. It is possible to understand the effect that is produced by unfavorable environment, if we compare the difference in physical stature between the Scotch agricultural worker and the inhabitant of certain manufacturing towns in England. There is an average of five inches in height and thirty-one pounds in weight in favor of the Scotchman. H. G. Wells, in speaking of the responsibility for man's physical efficiency, compares the city dweller in crowded streets and tenements with the man living in the freer, more open country, and makes the difference from three and one-half to five inches in stature and from twenty to thirty pounds in weight in favor of the country dweller. The former belongs to the physically unfit for the struggle of life.

A casual observer visiting the poorer parts of one of our large cities must necessarily be impressed with the stunted appearance of the children on the streets.

Since physical strength and power have always been desired by man; and since, in these modern days, women wish to be not far behind their brothers in endurance, the facts just given should furnish food for serious thought as to the means of acquiring a body physically fit, capable of securing the greatest capacity for work and for play—for life.

Is this physical fitness and consequent mental power so good a thing, so desirable, that the pupils in our schools and colleges are ready to give their attention to habits of right living when the methods of acquiring these habits are presented to them? Is it worth their while? Let the habits be once acquired, then the attention may be turned in other directions. It has been said, "Sow a habit and reap a character." This is true of the physical and mental as of the moral. Habits become fixed. It is necessary, then, that they be good habits. Right habits of living are the foundations of health of body and mind.

To secure and maintain a safe environment there must be inculcated habits of using the material things in daily life in such a way as to promote and not to diminish health. Avoid spitting in the streets, avoid throwing refuse on the sidewalk, avoid dust and bad air in the house and sleeping room, etc.

It is, however, of the greatest importance that every one should acquire such habits of *belief* in the importance of this material environment as shall lead him to insist upon sanitary regulations, and to see that they are carried out.

What touches my neighbor, touches me. For my sake, and for his, the city inspector and the city garbage cart visit us, and I keep my premises in such a condition as I expect him to strive for.

The first law of sanitation requires quick removal and destruction of all wastes—of things done with.

The second law enjoins such use of the air, water, and food necessary to life that the person may be in a state of health and efficiency.

This right use depends so largely upon habit that a great portion of sanitary teaching must be given to inculcating right and safe ways in daily life.

2. Frederic Clements Describes Plant Succession, 1916

Developmental aspect.—The essential nature of [plant] succession is indicated by its name. It is a series of invasions, a sequence of plant communities marked by the change from lower to higher life-forms. The essence of succession lies in the interaction of three factors, namely, habitat, life-forms, and species, in the progressive development of a formation. In this development, habitat and population act and react upon each other, alternating as cause and effect until a state of equilibrium is reached. The factors of the habitat are the causes of the responses or functions of the community, and these are the causes of growth and development, and hence of structure, essentially as in the individual. Succession must then be regarded as the development or life-history of the climax formation. It is the basic organic process of vegetation, which results in the adult or final form of this complex organism. All the stages which precede the climax are stages of growth. They have the same essential relation to the final stable structure of the organism that seedling and growing plant have to the adult individual. Moreover, just as the adult plant repeats its development, *i.e.,* reproduces itself, whenever conditions permit, so also does the climax formation. The parallel may be extended much further. The flowering plant may repeat itself completely, may undergo primary reproduction from an initial embryonic cell, or the reproduction may be secondary or partial from a shoot. In like fashion, a climax formation may repeat every one of its essential stages of growth in a primary area, or it may reproduce itself only in its later stages, as in secondary areas. In short, the process of organic development is essentially alike for the individual and the community. The correspondence is obvious when the necessary difference in the complexity of the two organisms is recognized.

Functional aspect.—The motive force in succession, *i.e.,* in the development of the formation as an organism, is to be found in the responses or functions of the group of individuals, just as the power of growth in the individual lies in the responses or functions of various organs. In both individual and community the clue to development is function, as the record of development is structure. Thus, succession is preeminently a process the progress of which is expressed in certain initial and intermediate structures or stages, but is finally recorded in the structure of the climax formation. The process is complex and often obscure, and its component functions yield only to persistent investigation and experiment. In consequence, the student of succession must recognize clearly that developmental stages, like the climax, are only a record of what has already happened. Each stage is, temporarily at least, a stable structure, and the actual processes can be revealed only by following

From Frederic Clements, *Plant Succession: An Analysis of the Development of Vegetation.* Washington, D. C.: Carnegie Institution of Washington, 1916, pp. 6–7.

the development of one stage into the succeeding one. In short, succession can be studied properly only by tracing the rise and fall for each stage, and not by a floristic picture of the population at the crest of each invasion.

3. Henry Gleason Explains Plant Associations, 1926

Plant associations exist; we can walk over them, we can measure their extent, we can describe their structure in terms of their component species, we can correlate them with their environment, we can frequently discover their past history and make inferences about their future.

We attempt to classify associations, as individual examples of vegetation, into broader groups, again basing our methods on various observable features and arriving accordingly at various results. We even enter the domain of philosophy, and speculate on the fundamental nature of the association, regard it as the basic unit of vegetation, call it an organism, and compare different areas of the same sort of vegetation to a species. . . .

Let us then throw aside for the moment all our pre-conceived ideas as to the definition, fundamental nature, structure, and classification of plant associations. . . . An area of vegetation which one ecologist regards as a single association may by another be considered as a mosaic or mixture of several, depending on their individual differences in definition. Some of these variations in structure (if one takes the broader view of the association) or smaller associations (if one prefers the narrower view) may be correlated with differences in the environment. . . .

We know that no two areas, supposed to represent the same association-type, are exactly the same, and we do not know which one to accept as typical and which to assume as showing the effects of geographical variation. We find fragmentary associations, and usually have no solid basis for deciding whether they are mere accidental intruders or embryonic stages in a developing association which may become typical after a lapse of years. We find variation of environment within the association, similar associations occupying different environments, and different associations in the same environment. It is small wonder that there is conflict and confusion in the definition and classification of plant communities. Surely our belief in the integrity of the association and the sanctity of the association-concept must be severely shaken. Are we not justified in coming to the general conclusion, far removed from the prevailing opinion, that an association is not an organism, scarcely even a vegetational unit, but merely a *coincidence?* . . .

. . . [T]he vegetation of an area is merely the resultant of two factors, the fluctuating and fortuitous immigration of plants and an equally fluctuating and variable environment. As a result, there is no inherent reason why any two areas of the earth's surface should bear precisely the same vegetation, nor any reason for adhering to our old ideas of the definiteness and distinctness of plant associations. As a matter of fact, no two areas of the earth's surface do bear precisely the same vegetation, except as a matter of chance, and that chance may be broken in another year by a continuance of the same variable migration and fluctuating environment which

From Henry Gleason, "The Individualistic Concept of the Plant Association," *Bulletin of the Torrey Botanical Club* 53 (1926), pp. 7–16, 23–26.

produced it. Again, experience has shown that it is impossible for ecologists to agree on the scope of the plant association or on the methods of classifying plant communities. Furthermore, it seems that the vegetation of a region is not capable of complete segregation into definite communities, but that there is a considerable development of vegetational mixtures. . . .

In conclusion, it may be said that every species of plant is a law unto itself, the distribution of which in space depends upon its individual peculiarities of migration and environmental requirements. Its disseminules migrate everywhere, and grow wherever they find favorable conditions. The species disappears from areas where the environment is no longer endurable. It grows in company with any other species of similar environmental requirements, irrespective of their normal associational affiliations. The behavior of the plant offers in itself no reason at all for the segregation of definite communities. Plant associations, the most conspicuous illustration of the space relation of plants, depend solely on the coincidence of environmental selection and migration over an area of recognizable extent and usually for a time of considerable duration. A rigid definition of the scope or extent of the association is impossible, and a logical classification of associations into larger groups, or into successional series, has not yet been achieved.

4. Arthur Tansley Introduces the Ecosystem, 1935

At the outset let me express my conviction that Dr. Clements has given us a theory of vegetation which has formed an indispensable foundation for the most fruitful modern work. With some parts of that theory and of its expression, however, I have never agreed. . . .

The weakness of this discussion of Clements, which is both able and ingenious, seems to me to reside . . . very largely on the assumption which governs the whole argument, and, as it seems to me, is quite illegitimate, that vegetation *is* an organism and therefore *must* obey the laws of development of what we commonly know as organisms. . . .

The usual view is that under the "typical" climatic conditions of the region and on the most favourable soils the climatic climax is reached by the succession; but that on less favourable soils of special character different kinds of stable vegetation are developed and remain in possession of the ground, to all appearance as permanently as the climatic climax. These are called *edaphic climaxes,* because the differentiating factor is a special soil type. Similarly special local climates determined by topography (*i.e.,* land relief) determine *physiographic climaxes.* But we may go farther than this and say that the incidence and maintenance of a decisive "biotic factor" such as the continuous grazing of animals may determine a *biotic climax.* And again we may speak of a *fire climax* when a region swept by constantly recurrent fires shows a vegetation consisting only of species able to survive under these trying conditions of life; or of a *mowing climax* established as a result of the regular periodic cutting of grasses or sedges. In each case the vegetation appears to be in

Excerpts from Arthur Tansley, "The Use and Abuse of Vegetational Concepts and Terms," *Ecology* 16, 1935, pp. 284–285, 289–290, 292, 295–296, 299, 306. Reprinted by permission of *Ecology.*

equilibrium with *all* the effective factors present, including of course the climatic factors, and the climax is named from the special factor differentiating the vegetation from the climatic climax. . . .

I plead for empirical method and terminology in all work on vegetation, and avoidance of generalised interpretation based on a theory of what *must* happen because "vegetation is an organism." . . .

On linguistic grounds I dislike the term biotic *community.* A "community," I think it will be generally agreed, implies *members,* and it seems to me that to lump animals and plants together as *members* of a community is to put on an equal footing things which in their whole nature and behaviour are too different. Animals and plants are not common *members* of anything except the organic world (in the biological, not the "organicist" sense). One would not speak of the potato plants and ornamental trees and flowers in the gardens of a human community as members of that community, although they certainly enter into its constitution—it would be different without them. There must be some sort of *similarity,* though not of course *identity,* of nature and status between the members of a community if the term is not to be divorced too completely from its common meaning. . . .

. . . I cannot accept the concept of the *biotic* community.

This refusal is however far from meaning that I do not realise that various "biomes," the whole webs of life adjusted to particular complexes of environmental factors, are real "wholes," often highly integrated wholes, which are the living nuclei of *systems* in the sense of the physicist. Only I do not think they are properly described as "organisms" (except in the "organicist" sense). I prefer to regard them, together with the whole of the effective physical factors involved, simply as "*systems.*"

I have already given my reasons for rejecting the terms "complex organism" and "biotic community." Clements' earlier term "biome" for the whole complex of organisms inhabiting a given region is unobjectionable, and for some purposes convenient. But the more fundamental conception is, as it seems to me, the whole *system* (in the sense of physics), including not only the organism-complex, but also the whole complex of physical factors forming what we call the environment of the biome—the habitat factors in the widest sense. Though the organisms may claim our primary interest, when we are trying to think fundamentally we cannot separate them from their special environment, with which they form one physical system.

It is the systems so formed which, from the point of view of the ecologist, are the basic units of nature on the face of the earth. Our natural human prejudices force us to consider the organisms (in the sense of the biologist) as the most important parts of these systems, but certainly the inorganic "factors" are also parts—there could be no systems without them, and there is constant interchange of the most various kinds within each system, not only between the organisms but between the organic and the inorganic. These *ecosystems,* as we may call them, are of the most various kinds and sizes. They form one category of the multitudinous physical systems of the universe, which range from the universe as a whole down to the atom. . . .

The concept of the "complex organism" as applied to the biome is objectionable both because the term is already in common use for an individual higher animal or plant, and because the biome is not an organism except in the sense in which inorganic systems are organisms.

The fundamental concept appropriate to the biome considered together with all the effective inorganic factors of its environment is the *ecosystem,* which is a particular category among the physical systems that make up the universe. In an ecosystem the organisms and the inorganic factors alike are *components* which are in relatively stable dynamic equilibrium. Succession and development are instances of the universal processes tending towards the creation of such equilibrated systems.

5. Aldo Leopold Proposes a Land Ethic, 1949

The Ethical Sequence

Ethics, so far studied only by philosophers, is actually a process in ecological evolution. Its sequences may be described in ecological as well as in philosophical terms. An ethic, ecologically, is a limitation on freedom of action in the struggle for existence. An ethic, philosophically, is a differentiation of social from anti-social conduct. These are two definitions of one thing. The thing has its origin in the tendency of interdependent individuals or groups to evolve modes of co-operation. The ecologist calls these symbioses. Politics and economics are advanced symbioses in which the original free-for-all competition has been replaced, in part, by co-operative mechanisms with an ethical content. . . .

The first ethics dealt with the relation between individuals; the Mosaic Decalogue is an example. Later accretions dealt with the relation between the individual and society. The Golden Rule tries to integrate the individual to society; democracy to integrate social organization to the individual.

There is as yet no ethic dealing with man's relation to land and to the animals and plants which grow upon it. Land, like Odysseus' slave-girls, is still property. The land-relation is still strictly economic, entailing privileges but not obligations.

The extension of ethics to this third element in human environment is, if I read the evidence correctly, an evolutionary possibility and an ecological necessity. It is the third step in a sequence. The first two have already been taken. Individual thinkers since the days of Ezekiel and Isaiah have asserted that the despoliation of land is not only inexpedient but wrong. Society, however, has not yet affirmed their belief. I regard the present conservation movement as the embryo of such an affirmation.

An ethic may be regarded as a mode of guidance for meeting ecological situations so new or intricate, or involving such deferred reactions, that the path of social expediency is not discernible to the average individual. Animal instincts are modes of guidance for the individual in meeting such situations. Ethics are possibly a kind of community instinct in-the-making.

The Community Concept

All ethics so far evolved rest upon a single premise: that the individual is a member of a community of interdependent parts. His instincts prompt him to compete for his place in that community, but his ethics prompt him also to co-operate (perhaps in order that there may be a place to compete for).

The land ethic simply enlarges the boundaries of the community to include soils, waters, plants, and animals, or collectively: the land. . . .

In short, a land ethic changes the role of *Homo sapiens* from conqueror of the land-community to plain member and citizen of it. It implies respect for his fellow-members, and also respect for the community as such. . . .

Land Health and the A-B Cleavage

A land ethic, then, reflects the existence of an ecological conscience, and this in turn reflects a conviction of individual responsibility for the health of the land. Health is the capacity of the land for self-renewal. Conservation is our effort to understand and preserve this capacity.

Conservationists are notorious for their dissensions. Superficially these seem to add up to mere confusion, but a more careful scrutiny reveals a single plane of cleavage common to many specialized fields. In each field one group (A) regards the land as soil, and its function as commodity-production; another group (B) regards the land as a biota, and its function as something broader. How much broader is admittedly in a state of doubt and confusion.

In my own field, forestry, group A is quite content to grow trees like cabbages, with cellulose as the basic forest commodity. It feels no inhibition against violence; its ideology is agronomic. Group B, on the other hand, sees forestry as fundamentally different from agronomy because it employs natural species, and manages a natural environment rather than creating an artificial one. Group B prefers natural reproduction on principle. It worries on biotic as well as economic grounds about the loss of species like chestnut, and the threatened loss of the white pines. It worries about a whole series of secondary forest functions: wildlife, recreation, watersheds, wilderness areas. To my mind, Group B feels the stirrings of an ecological conscience.

In the wildlife field, a parallel cleavage exists. For Group A the basic commodities are sport and meat; the yardsticks of production are ciphers of take in pheasants and trout. Artificial propagation is acceptable as a permanent as well as a temporary recourse—if its unit costs permit. Group B, on the other hand, worries about a whole series of biotic side-issues. What is the cost in predators of producing a game crop? Should we have further recourse to exotics? How can management restore the shrinking species, like prairie grouse, already hopeless as shootable game? How can management restore the threatened rarities, like trumpeter swan and whooping crane? Can management principles be extended to wildflowers? Here again it is clear to me that we have the same A-B cleavage as in forestry.

In the larger field of agriculture I am less competent to speak, but there seem to be somewhat parallel cleavages. Scientific agriculture was actively developing before ecology was born, hence a slower penetration of ecological concepts might be expected. Moreover the farmer, by the very nature of his techniques, must modify the biota more radically than the forester or the wildlife manager. Nevertheless, there are many discontents in agriculture which seem to add up to a new vision of 'biotic farming.' . . .

The discontent that labels itself 'organic farming,' while bearing some of the earmarks of a cult, is nevertheless biotic in its direction, particularly in its insistence on the importance of soil flora and fauna.

The ecological fundamentals of agriculture are just as poorly known to the public as in other fields of land-use. For example, few educated people realize that the marvelous advances in technique made during recent decades are improvements in the pump, rather than the well. Acre for acre, they have barely sufficed to offset the sinking level of fertility.

In all of these cleavages, we see repeated the same basic paradoxes: man the conqueror *versus* man the biotic citizen; science the sharpener of his sword *versus* science the searchlight on his universe; land the slave and servant *versus* land the collective organism. . . .

The Outlook

It is inconceivable to me that an ethical relation to land can exist without love, respect, and admiration for land, and a high regard for its value. By value, I of course mean something far broader than mere economic value; I mean value in the philosophical sense. . . .

One of the requisites for an ecological comprehension of land is an understanding of ecology, and this is by no means co-extensive with 'education'; in fact, much higher education seems deliberately to avoid ecological concepts. An understanding of ecology does not necessarily originate in courses bearing ecological labels; it is quite as likely to be labeled geography, botany, agronomy, history, or economics. This is as it should be, but whatever the label, ecological training is scarce.

The case for a land ethic would appear hopeless but for the minority which is in obvious revolt against these 'modern' trends.

The 'key-log' which must be moved to release the evolutionary process for an ethic is simply this: quit thinking about decent land-use as solely an economic problem. Examine each question in terms of what is ethically and esthetically right, as well as what is economically expedient. A thing is right when it tends to preserve the integrity, stability, and beauty of the biotic community. It is wrong when it tends otherwise. . . .

I have purposely presented the land ethic as a product of social evolution because nothing so important as an ethic is ever 'written.' Only the most superficial student of history supposes that Moses 'wrote' the Decalogue; it evolved in the minds of a thinking community, and Moses wrote a tentative summary of it for a 'seminar.' I say tentative because evolution never stops.

The evolution of a land ethic is an intellectual as well as emotional process. Conservation is paved with good intentions which prove to be futile, or even dangerous, because they are devoid of critical understanding either of the land, or of economic land-use. I think it is a truism that as the ethical frontier advances from the individual to the community, its intellectual content increases.

The mechanism of operation is the same for any ethic: social approbation for right actions; social disapproval for wrong actions.

By and large, our present problem is one of attitudes and implements. We are remodeling the Alhambra with a steam-shovel, and we are proud of our yardage. We shall hardly relinquish the shovel, which after all has many good points, but we are in need of gentler and more objective criteria for its successful use.

6. Rachel Carson Warns of a Silent Spring, 1962

There was once a town in the heart of America where all life seemed to live in harmony with its surroundings. The town lay in the midst of a checkerboard of prosperous farms, with fields of grain and hillsides of orchards where, in spring, white clouds of bloom drifted above the green fields. In autumn, oak and maple and birch set up a blaze of color that flamed and flickered across a backdrop of pines. Then foxes barked in the hills and deer silently crossed the fields, half hidden in the mists of the fall mornings.

Along the roads, laurel, viburnum and alder, great ferns and wildflowers delighted the traveler's eye through much of the year. Even in winter the roadsides were places of beauty, where countless birds came to feed on the berries and on the seed heads of the dried weeds rising above the snow. The countryside was, in fact, famous for the abundance and variety of its bird life, and when the flood of migrants was pouring through in spring and fall people traveled from great distances to observe them. Others came to fish the streams, which flowed clear and cold out of the hills and contained shady pools where trout lay. So it had been from the days many years ago when the first settlers raised their houses, sank their wells, and built their barns.

Then a strange blight crept over the area and everything began to change. Some evil spell had settled on the community: mysterious maladies swept the flocks of chickens; the cattle and sheep sickened and died. Everywhere was a shadow of death. The farmers spoke of much illness among their families. In the town the doctors had become more and more puzzled by new kinds of sickness appearing among their patients. There had been several sudden and unexplained deaths, not only among adults but even among children, who would be stricken suddenly while at play and die within a few hours.

There was a strange stillness. The birds, for example—where had they gone? Many people spoke of them, puzzled and disturbed. The feeding stations in the backyards were deserted. The few birds seen anywhere were moribund; they trembled violently and could not fly. It was a spring without voices. On the mornings that had once throbbed with the dawn chorus of robins, catbirds, doves, jays, wrens, and scores of other bird voices there was now no sound; only silence lay over the fields and woods and marsh.

On the farms the hens brooded, but no chicks hatched. The farmers complained that they were unable to raise any pigs—the litters were small and the young survived only a few days. The apple trees were coming into bloom but no bees droned among the blossoms, so there was no pollination and there would be no fruit.

The roadsides, once so attractive, were now lined with browned and withered vegetation as though swept by fire. These, too, were silent, deserted by all living things. Even the streams were now lifeless. Anglers no longer visited them for all the fish had died.

In the gutters under the eaves and between the shingles of the roofs, a white granular powder still showed a few patches; some weeks before it had fallen like snow upon the roofs and the lawns, the fields and streams.

No witchcraft, no enemy action had silenced the rebirth of new life in this stricken world. The people had done it themselves.

This town does not actually exist, but it might easily have a thousand counterparts in America or elsewhere in the world. I know of no community that has experienced all the misfortunes I describe. Yet every one of these disasters has actually happened somewhere, and many real communities have already suffered a substantial number of them. A grim specter has crept upon us almost unnoticed, and this imagined tragedy may easily become a stark reality we all shall know. . . .

The history of life on earth has been a history of interaction between living things and their surroundings. To a large extent, the physical form and the habits of the earth's vegetation and its animal life have been molded by the environment. Considering the whole span of earthly time, the opposite effect, in which life actually modifies its surroundings, has been relatively slight. Only within the moment of time represented by the present century has one species—man—acquired significant power to alter the nature of his world.

During the past quarter century this power has not only increased to one of disturbing magnitude but it has changed in character. The most alarming of all man's assaults upon the environment is the contamination of air, earth, rivers, and sea with dangerous and even lethal materials. This pollution is for the most part irrecoverable; the chain of evil it initiates not only in the world that must support life but in living tissues is for the most part irreversible. In this now universal contamination of the environment, chemicals are the sinister and little-recognized partners of radiation in changing the very nature of the world—the very nature of its life. Strontium 90, released through nuclear explosions into the air, comes to earth in rain or drifts down as fallout, lodges in soil, enters into the grass or corn or wheat grown there, and in time takes up its abode in the bones of a human being, there to remain until his death. Similarly, chemicals sprayed on croplands or forests or gardens lie long in soil, entering into living organisms, passing from one to another in a chain of poisoning and death. Or they pass mysteriously by underground streams until they emerge and, through the alchemy of air and sunlight, combine into new forms that kill vegetation, sicken cattle, and work unknown harm on those who drink from once pure wells. As Albert Schweitzer has said, "Man can hardly even recognize the devils of his own creation."

It took hundreds of millions of years to produce the life that now inhabits the earth—eons of time in which that developing and evolving and diversifying life reached a state of adjustment and balance with its surroundings. The environment, rigorously shaping and directing the life it supported, contained elements that were hostile as well as supporting. Certain rocks gave out dangerous radiation; even within the light of the sun, from which all life draws its energy, there were short-wave radiations with power to injure. Given time—time not in years but in millennia—life adjusts, and a balance has been reached. For time is the essential ingredient; but in the modern world there is no time.

The rapidity of change and the speed with which new situations are created follow the impetuous and heedless pace of man rather than the deliberate pace of nature. Radiation is no longer merely the background radiation of rocks, the bombardment of cosmic rays, the ultraviolet of the sun that have existed before there was any life on earth; radiation is now the unnatural creation of man's tampering with the atom. The chemicals to which life is asked to make its adjustment are no longer merely the calcium and silica and copper and all the rest of the minerals washed out of the rocks and carried in rivers to the sea; they are the synthetic creations of man's inventive mind, brewed in his laboratories, and having no counterparts in nature.

To adjust to these chemicals would require time on the scale that is nature's; it would require not merely the years of a man's life but the life of generations. And even this, were it by some miracle possible, would be futile, for the new chemicals come from our laboratories in an endless stream; almost five hundred annually find their way into actual use in the United States alone. The figure is staggering and its implications are not easily grasped—500 new chemicals to which the bodies of men and animals are required somehow to adapt each year, chemicals totally outside the limits of biologic experience.

Among them are many that are used in man's war against nature. Since the mid-1940's over 200 basic chemicals have been created for use in killing insects, weeds, rodents, and other organisms described in the modern vernacular as "pests"; and they are sold under several thousand different brand names.

These sprays, dusts, and aerosols are now applied almost universally to farms, gardens, forests, and homes—nonselective chemicals that have the power to kill every insect, the "good" and the "bad," to still the song of birds and the leaping of fish in the streams, to coat the leaves with a deadly film, and to linger on in soil—all this though the intended target may be only a few weeds or insects. Can anyone believe it is possible to lay down such a barrage of poisons on the surface of the earth without making it unfit for all life? They should not be called "insecticides," but "biocides."

The whole process of spraying seems caught up in an endless spiral. Since DDT was released for civilian use, a process of escalation has been going on in which ever more toxic materials must be found. This has happened because insects, in a triumphant vindication of Darwin's principle of the survival of the fittest, have evolved super races immune to the particular insecticide used, hence a deadlier one has always to be developed—and then a deadlier one than that. It has happened also because . . . destructive insects often undergo a "flareback," or resurgence, after spraying, in numbers greater than before. Thus the chemical war is never won, and all life is caught in its violent crossfire.

Along with the possibility of the extinction of mankind by nuclear war, the central problem of our age has therefore become the contamination of man's total environment with such substances of incredible potential for harm—substances that accumulate in the tissues of plants and animals and even penetrate the germ cells to shatter or alter the very material of heredity upon which the shape of the future depends.

Some would-be architects of our future look forward to a time when it will be possible to alter the human germ plasm by design. But we may easily be doing so now by inadvertence, for many chemicals, like radiation, bring about gene mutations.

It is ironic to think that man might determine his own future by something so seemingly trivial as the choice of an insect spray. . . .

All this is not to say there is no insect problem and no need of control. I am saying, rather, that control must be geared to realities, not to mythical situations, and that the methods employed must be such that they do not destroy us along with the insects.

7. Eugene P. Odum Discusses the Stability of the Ecosystem, 1969

The principles of ecological succession bear importantly on the relationships between man and nature. The framework of successional theory needs to be examined as a basis for resolving man's present environmental crisis. . . .

Ecological succession may be defined in terms of the following three parameters. (i) It is an orderly process of community development that is reasonably directional and, therefore, predictable. (ii) It results from modification of the physical environment by the community; that is, succession is community-controlled even though the physical environment determines the pattern, the rate of change, and often sets limits as to how far development can go. (iii) It culminates in a stabilized ecosystem in which maximum biomass (or high information content) and symbiotic function between organisms are maintained per unit of available energy flow. In a word, the "strategy" of succession as a short-term process is basically the same as the "strategy" of long-term evolutionary development of the biosphere—namely, increased control of, or homeostasis with, the physical environment in the sense of achieving maximum protection from its perturbations. . . .

As the ecosystem develops, subtle changes in the network pattern of food chains may be expected. The manner in which organisms are linked together through food tends to be relatively simple and linear in the very early stages of succession, as a consequence of low diversity. . . . In contrast, food chains become complex webs in mature stages, with the bulk of biological energy flow following detritus pathways. . . .

There can be little doubt that the net result of community actions is symbiosis, nutrient conservation, stability, a decrease in entropy, and an increase in information. The overall strategy is . . . directed toward achieving as large and diverse an organic structure as is possible within the limits set by the available energy input and the prevailing physical conditions of existence (soil, water, climate, and so on).

[There is] a basic conflict between the strategies of man and of nature. . . . Man has generally been preoccupied with obtaining as much "production" from the landscape as possible, by developing and maintaining early successional types of ecosystems, usually monocultures. But, of course, man does not live by food and fiber alone; he also needs a balanced CO_2–O_2 atmosphere, the climatic buffer provided by oceans and masses of vegetation, and clean (that is, unproductive) water for cultural and industrial uses. Many essential life-cycle resources, not to mention recreational

Excerpts from Eugene P. Odum, "The Strategy of Ecosystem Development," *Science* 164 (1969), pp. 262–270. Based on an address presented before the annual meeting of the Ecological Society of America at the University of Maryland, August 1966.

and esthetic needs, are best provided man by the less "productive" landscapes. In other words, the landscape is not just a supply depot but is also the *oikos*—the home—in which we must live. Until recently mankind has more or less taken for granted the gas-exchange, water-purification, nutrient-cycling, and other protective functions of self-maintaining ecosystems, chiefly because neither his numbers nor his environmental manipulations have been great enough to affect regional and global balances. Now, of course, it is painfully evident that such balances are being affected, often detrimentally. The "one problem, one solution approach" is no longer adequate and must be replaced by some form of ecosystem analysis that considers man as a part of, not apart from, the environment.

8. Pickett and White Explain Patch Dynamics, 1985

Ecologists have always been aware of the importance of natural dynamics in ecosystems, but historically, the focus has been on successional development of equilibrium communities. While this approach has generated appreciable understanding of the composition and functioning of ecosystems, recently many workers have turned their attention to processes of disturbance themselves and to the evolutionary significance of such events. This shifted emphasis has inspired studies in diverse systems. We use the phrase "patch dynamics" to describe their common focus.

Focus on patch dynamics leads workers to explicit studies of disturbance-related phenomena—the conditions created by disturbance; the frequency, severity, intensity, and predictability of such events; and the responses of organisms to disturbance regimes. The phrase "patch dynamics" embraces disturbances external to the community as well as internal processes of change. Patch dynamics includes not only such coarse-scale, infrequent events as hurricanes, but also such fine-scale events as the shifting mosaic of badger mounds in a prairie. . . . The most basic theme is an evolutionary one: How does the dynamic setting of populations influence their evolution? What are the implications for communities and ecosystems? [This approach] form[s] an alternative to equilibrium concepts of the evolution of populations, composition of communities, and functioning of ecosystems. . . .

The sources of variation in disturbances include differences in ecosystem scale, differences in kinds of disturbances, and differences in disturbance regimes. Even for a single ecosystem and disturbance event, effects vary at different trophic levels and occur over a wide range of biological levels from suborganismal (e.g., physiological effects) and organismal (e.g., behavioral changes) to ecosystem-wide (e.g., nutrient availability). Most disturbances produce heterogeneous and patchy effects; these effects may themselves depend on the state of the community prior to the disturbance.

We have adopted the term "patch dynamics" . . . for the following reasons:

1. "Patch" implies a relatively discrete spatial pattern, but does not establish any constraint on patch size, internal homogeneity, or discreteness.

From S. T. A. Pickett and P. S. White, *The Ecology of Natural Disturbance and Patch Dynamics*. Orlando, Fla.: Academic Press, 1985, pp. xiii, 5, 12.

2. "Patch" implies a relationship of one patch to another in space and to the surrounding, unaffected or less affected matrix.
3. "Patch dynamics" emphasizes patch change. . . .

Equilibrium landscapes would . . . seem to be the exception, rather than the rule (for example, most North American landscapes have probably been influenced by changing disturbance regimes in the last several thousand to tens of thousands of years).

Patch dynamics has implications for applied ecology. . . . Preservation of natural systems necessarily involves a paradox: we seek to preserve systems that change. Success in a conservation effort thus requires an understanding of landscape patch structure and dynamics.

❦ E S S A Y S

The first essay, by writer Robert Clarke, credits scientist Ellen Swallow with the founding of American ecology, defined as the maintenance of a healthy environment by and for humans. In the second essay, Donald Worster, an environmental historian at the University of Kansas, explores the role of metaphors—organism, economy, and chaos—in the ethics and policies of environmental management. Ecology as a science is not distinct from human society but is given meaning through human responses to disasters such as the Dust Bowl of the 1930s and the environmental crisis of the 1970s. In the chapter's concluding essay, Linda Lear shows how Rachel Carson's *Silent Spring,* published in 1962, aroused the nation to the problems of pesticides in the food chain and their very visible implications for bird life, and indeed all life on the planet.

Ellen Swallow Richards's Human Ecology

ROBERT CLARKE

When Ellen Swallow [Richards] entered MIT [the Massachusetts Institute of Technology], science was in its fourth century of the explosion that began with the Renaissance. Founded by Hippocrates 2,000 years before, science slept in the shadow of the Church for 1,500 years until wakened by the printing press. The Reformation unpried the private grip on knowledge even more.

By the seventeenth-century Age of Reason, rapid acceleration and chaotic accumulation of knowledge had changed man's mind and his environment. Where was it going? What was the purpose? [Seventeenth-century philosopher] Sir Francis Bacon tried to answer those questions by "reorganizing the whole of knowledge upon a proper platform." To make sure mankind would benefit, rather than fall prey to exploitation of knowledge, Bacon joined science to philosophy.

This fruitful union mothered the eighteenth-century Enlightenment, which in turn sired the social sciences of economic and political theory used for the new world's democracy. Technology, the application of science and mechanics, was still new. The word itself was not yet in existence. But it was about to be born. . . .

Excerpts from Robert Clarke, *Ellen Swallow: The Woman Who Founded Ecology.* New York: Follett, 1973, pp. 26, 31–32, 33–34, 36, 39–40, 52–54, 99–100, 113–118, 120.

Ellen [Swallow] was not the only pioneer at MIT. She was merely the only female. Everyone from faculty to the lowest student was opening a controversial path in education. . . . Everyone connected with the school felt the pressures of their unpopular position. In a pecking order with sexual as well as scientific gravity, she was at the bottom of an inverted pyramid of pressure.

The faculty was small in number. But it comprised large, impressive figures to Ellen [Swallow]; courageous for allying themselves to a cause while fully aware of the enmity of their peers. She looked with admiration on the men she saw in the halls: men like Edward C. Pickering, Charles W. Eliot, Frank H. Storer, Silas W. Holman, and William Atkinson. She absorbed the words and motions of those assigned to teach: Professor Crafts, Ordway, and Nichols; she learned new and basic branches of chemistry and physics. Mining was a major field by which MIT hoped to connect with industry so she studied mineralogy under Professor Robert Richards. . . .

She was shocked by things she saw on the way to school and around town. Filth. Disease. Suffering. She'd read about the excessively high rates of death and illness, the epidemics that ran through the city. Now she saw why. Horse wagons carrying uncovered food over dirty, unpaved streets through pools of stagnant swill made of everything from animal waste, human spit, and garbage. Alleys were worse: open sewers. Indoors, many homes weren't much better. . . .

Cities: the best and worst of civilization, she thought; people crowding together for greater human opportunity and suffering. And not just disease, either; she read about the terrible fire in Chicago that year; how the winds had fanned the flames to turn a whole city to ash. She saw young children and women employed in inhuman labor in equally inhumane conditions. . . .

In 1869, . . . Massachusetts established America's first state board of health. The statement by which it was created made a permanent impression on Ellen [Swallow].

> *"No Board of Health,"* its preamble said, *"if it rightly performs its duty, can separate the physical from the moral and intellectual natures of man. . . . These three qualities are . . . indissoluble, and mutually act and react upon one another. Any influence exerted to the injury of one, inevitably, though perhaps indirectly, injures the other and are acted upon [in turn] by the forces of nature that surround us."* (Author's italics.)

The intelligence of that statement more than 100 years ago carries a comprehension on which Ellen Swallow would build the foundations of environmental science. To her, *the physical, moral, and intellectual natures of man* were the three relative forces of environment by which man lived and developed his physical, social, and perceptual environments. . . .

. . . It would be fifteen years [after 1872] before the complete examination of [Massachusetts's] water and sewage would give the world its first Water Purity Tables and the United States would be given its first state water quality standards. When that time came, Ellen Swallow would play a much more central role. . . .

If the years immediately before incubated environmental science, 1873 marked its birth. Water was the appropriate medium for this event. But it was a medium for more than Swallow's work. While the chemist studied water in America, a biologist at the University of Jena, in Germany, was approaching environmental science from another direction.

Ernst Haeckel in his lifetime coined the names for nearly a dozen new sciences. As early as the late 1860s he is credited with suggesting a science be developed to study organisms in their environment. By 1873, Haeckel had come up with a name for that science. Then, leaving "Oekologie" for others to develop, he concentrated on other sciences he named, particularly "Phylogeny," and conceived the Phylogenetic Scale of Life, a tree from the smallest life form up to man.

Fluent in German, Swallow traced the German word Oekologie to its origin—the Greek word for house. "Oik" for house; "Oek" for "every-man's house"—environment. The "Oe," she knew made it universal—"oecumenical." If Haeckel, a male biologist, saw that a science of everyone's house environment needed to be developed, the female chemist slowly began to take up residency in the structure. . . . [C]hemistry could provide a distaff side for environmental science, not just life but the environment that influences that life. It would take the organization of an irrefutable body of knowledge.

Haeckel and Ellen Swallow started at the same time and at the same place: with water, the source of all life and its first environment. In Oekologie—the "universal house"—biology was the science of life; chemistry, as Ellen Swallow saw it, was the science of environment.

MIT was a near perfect incubator for environmental science. In addition to Nichols's and Swallow's study of water, Professor Frank Storer had begun, in 1870, the study of air. She would study this element, too, and physics along with chemistry, at the Institute. In a vague but constant effort to put it all together, she also went to that part of the laboratory where another MIT professor studied the earth itself. From mineralogist Robert Richards she would add earth to air and water science, to build Oekologie. . . .

"Now all I need is $2,000 to have a special room fitted up for 10 or 12 women. . . . I am making a strong effort to interest people in it," she wrote in February 1876. She had become the [women's laboratory] project's fund raiser as well.

"Success is assured," she wrote in May. Then later that month: "I must tell you the good news. Yesterday, the government of the Institute passed a vote that hereafter special students in chemistry shall be admitted without regard to sex. . . . I can assure you I am very happy."

Again, the faculty hedged. ". . . without regard to sex" applied only to Swallow's ". . . special students in chemistry . . ." An old garage tabbed for renovation as a men's gymnasium was set aside to segregate the special students. The "cautious and reluctant authorities placed her and her small band of disciples in a sort of contagious ward located in what we students used to call the 'dump' . . .", remembered a male student who became an officer of the MIT Corporation.

Nevertheless, in November 1876, twenty-three women, most of them teachers, began training for careers in science through chemistry at MIT. . . .

The world's first women's science laboratory was put in John Ordway's charge. But its day-to-day operation was the responsibility of one Ellen Henrietta Richards, nee Swallow, A.B., S.B., A.M. . . . On June 5, 1875, Ellen Swallow [had] married Robert Hallowell Richards, professor of mining engineering and head of the new metallurgical laboratory that was opened at the Institute. . . .

Through 1878, when MIT abandoned its "special student" label for women, until 1884, when the old garage was torn down and the sexes integrated in the school, and ever after, women came from all parts of the United States to study and to take back the knowledge of science to instill in new generations. As MIT's men went on to careers in industry and government, its first women found their way into high schools, seminaries, academies, preparatory schools, colleges, and universities. There they founded, enlarged, and improved science departments that brought ever more students through the doors of science unhinged by Ellen Swallow; students who otherwise might never have had the chance or inclination for science.

She started the development that would play a major if unstated role in the nation's course: arming public education with the subject and substance by which America would grow to international scientific and technological supremacy in the next century. But for as long as Ellen Swallow lived, she worked to nurture a balance between exploiting and improving the environment with science.

Until the Women's Laboratory was fully established, however, it was her main interest. Soon after it opened, she began adding new disciplines, new projects, and new significance to its student portfolio. For all this, she was unpaid. Instead she paid out $1,000 a year of her own money to reduce the lab's operating cost. . . .

In 1878, the Institute recognized Ellen Swallow as an "assistant instructor." If they added a token financial reward—Robert Richards said they didn't—she waived it, continuing her annual contributions to the school. She continued to solicit funds from others for scholarships to help bright but poorer students.

She recruited them, gave crash courses to prep them for exams, found lodging, part-time work, and full-time careers. With Robert Richards she taught, chaperoned, counseled, and fed them. When they graduated she stayed in touch, recruiting their students and finding jobs for hers. . . .

. . . [In 1876,] Swallow . . . made her pilgrimage to the laboratory shrine of Ernst Haeckel, the world's greatest living biologist, who had proposed evolutionary theories before Darwin.

Haeckel, founder of the "new zoology," in 1873 had coined one of many names for new sciences to be developed. So far, Oekologie had been ignored, even by him, as he continued classifying more life forms than any man alive and tracing them to a common source. . . .

If Haeckel and Swallow met, no record of the meeting has been found. But she did meet his most ardent supporter and supplier, [Carl] Zeiss. If Zeiss didn't walk her up the hill to the famous laboratory, he could describe it in detail to the woman fluent in German. Whether she met the man who named new sciences, the woman who founded environmental science was well aware of his work. . . .

November 30, 1892. In seven years and thirty-one days the twentieth century would begin. The complexities of a new era would replace the simple existence of the old.

Ellen Swallow had worked at an unbelievable pace to develop the interdisciplines of an environmental science she believed the next 100 years required. She knew work alone was no guarantee of permanence for the knowledge she had pulled together. If anything, the changing world—specialized, mechanized, cosmetic—seemed to take things apart. . . .

The First Lady of Science had gone in the opposite direction, putting sciences together to nurture the roots of environment. But to perpetuate her conglomerate body of knowledge and its applications, a permanent structure was required. Ernst Haeckel had been right when he suggested the name for a science of everybody's home. Ellen Swallow began to fill the void that accompanied Oekologie's 1873 proposal with her collection of old knowledge cross-fertilized with new to build "home science" for environment and life within it. . . .

At the end of the nineteenth century, the environment was still essentially held in human hands. But from her vantage point at MIT, Ellen Swallow could see that environment was being transferred to technology. It must not be turned over completely, she believed. *People* must retain some control over the shape and change of their environment. The only way they could, she saw, was to be equipped for that function—the man on the street or at work, the woman in the home or in the community, the child in school. All must have the knowledge required to retain their traditional relationship with environment. . . .

. . . [S]he believed if people would work with the environmental principle superimposed on their daily lives, they would grow more conscious of what the environment is and what to do—and not do—with it.

She intended exactly that on the November evening in 1892 when she christened the science she had nurtured through nineteen years.

It was Thursday, a crisp, chilly, early winter day in Boston. As the sun began its slow slide behind the trees and brownstones on the Boston side of the Charles River, a parade of carriages carrying well dressed ladies and gentlemen began arriving at the corner of Commonwealth Avenue and Exeter Street. In less than an hour, some 300 fashionable people climbed the ornate staircase to the elegant Vendome Hotel. This was the annual meeting of the prestigious Boot & Shoe Club, the *creme de la creme* of the footwear industry in Boston, industrial capital of the world.

. . . Club President F. H. Nazro "rapped the spoons into silence." . . .

As the nineteenth century draws to a close, he observed, humanity has not solved the problem of living. "Pray God, the twentieth century may." Then Nazro introduced the woman who would propose *how* the new century should solve *what* problems . . .: "Mrs. Robert Richards, Instructor in Sanitary Chemistry in the Massachusetts Institute of Technology." . . .

NEW SCIENCE, headlined *The Boston Globe* the next day. "Mrs. Richards Names It Oekology." Just below, "Tis the Art of First-Class Living." . . .

. . . Alice Freeman Palmer . . . had come all the way from the University of Chicago to attend the unveiling of Oekology. The former president of Wellesley was a dean at the University of Chicago.

"Speaking without notes and with convincing seriousness lightened by many touches of humor," Ellen Swallow threw open environmental science to the public.

> I would like to have the gift of mind reading for a while, for I think the very best speech would be to know what each one present expected to hear, here tonight. As your president has said, we have not come to talk over the science of domestics. A Domestic Science is something broader. It is a comfort to know [however] that you believe there [can be] a science for the home.
>
> But before there can be a science, there must be an art. The art of living has been given a good deal of consideration, and for some time there has been formulating a science of living.
>
> Perhaps no one is to blame for the fact that the science to teach people how to live [in their environment] has been so long in getting any attention. . . . Men built houses long before they knew how to live in them safely.

The implication was clear. Before people build a new environment, they had better learn to live in this one. Otherwise, the very base of what is built will be flawed.

She suggested, subtly, that perhaps the real reason why man built houses without knowing how to live in them was that woman, the traditional caretaker of that environment, had been denied the education that would have augmented man's knowledge. . . .

"To relieve women from drudgery, fathers formerly sent [daughters] to finishing schools and gave them lessons in the fine arts. But all of these semi-polite accomplishments turned to dust and ashes literally and figuratively in the crucible of life . . ." that is the home environment.

"They walled up the beneficient fireplaces and introduced airtight stoves and put washbowls in rooms to save steps, but they forgot to make the plumbing safe." . . .

Then she "scathingly" attacked, not only the educational system that would permit this ignorance among men and women, but also the ignorance by which the learning environment itself was allowed to exist—"erecting improperly ventilated and unsanitary buildings" in which children are supposed to learn. . . .

"If that is the environment in which they learn, then that is the environment they learn to live in. How can we expect them to know, let alone teach or live a better way?"

Then she made her appeal:

And now I ask you here tonight to stand sponsors of the christening of a new science and to give the same your fostering care and generous support. . . .

For this knowledge of right living, we have sought a new name. . . . As theology is the science of religious life, and biology the science of [physical] life . . . so let *Oekology* be henceforth the science of [our] normal lives . . . the worthiest of all the applied sciences which *teaches the principles on which to found . . . healthy . . . and happy life.*

And, she might have added, to assure future environmental quality.

It was done. Acknowledging the comments and good wishes of the audience, Ellen and Robert [Richards] thanked their friends and left the Vendome. Walking the quarter mile to Back Bay station for a train to Jamaica Plain, she felt satisfaction. She had invested the labors of nineteen years in her presentation of Oekology.

Organic, Economic, and Chaotic Ecology

DONALD WORSTER

*Organic Ecology**

On a typical afternoon the wind on the Great Plains blows at a steady fifteen miles per hour. It is a constant presence, pressing down with relentless will the grasses and row crops, whistling with an eerie whine around the farmer's barn and fences. In the spring of 1934, however, the wind suddenly turned demonic. On April 14, a vast black blizzard of earth came rolling out of the north toward Texas, whirling and spinning in a giant bowl, darkening the sun and blanketing the land with drifts up to twenty feet high. Then less than a month later, on May 10, another great storm moved east toward Chicago. Twelve million tons of plains dirt were dumped on

*Excerpts from Donald Worster, "Grass to Dust: The Great Plains in the 1930s," *Environmental Review* 3 (1977), pp. 3–9. Reprinted with permission from *Environmental History Review,* © 1977, the American Society for Environmental History.

that city. Two days later the storm reached the eastern seaboard. Dust sifted into the White House and fell on ships standing out to sea.

The wind often carried dust over the land: that was a familiar enough sight to settlers on the plains. They had even seen a few serious dust storms in 1932, in 1913, and further back in 1894 and 1886. But none of these had been of more than local significance, and nothing in the past prepared them for the frequency or terror of these new storms: 22 of regional extent in 1934, 40 in 1935, 68 in 1936, 72 in 1937, before at last they began to drop off. By then it was obvious to the entire nation that something was wrong on the western plains. Soil scientists for the Department of Agriculture estimated in 1938 that one-half of the region—some 500,000 square miles—had been seriously damaged by wind erosion. As a farmer wrote to the *Dallas Farm News* the following year: "The prairie, once the home of the deer, buffalo, and antelope, is now the home of the Dust Bowl and the WPA [Works Progress Administration]."

For a full half century the pioneers had advanced with the good years onto the plains in recurring tides of optimism, only to fall back when the dry spells appeared. But during World War I and through the 1920's man seemed at last to lay permanent hold on this defiant, intractable landscape. Much of the western grassland quickly became a vast machine-age frontier, mass-producing wheat and cotton. Thousands of new Ford tractors were put to work breaking the virgin sod, even when the nation could not absorb all the crop output. As farmers habitually do, the High Plains settlers fixed their eyes on only one factor in nature, rainfall. Rain, or the lack of it, could send the tractors out or hold them back, and during a good year of precipitation the farmer would plow and plant, regardless of the market. In this simple, single-factor way of thinking only of the weather lay the sodbuster's unpreparedness for the Dust Bowl disaster. When the thirties brought severe drought to his fields, the most serious problem for the settler proved to be not too little rain but too much dust—the loss of his topsoil, which once had been held in place by the native sod. All along the farmer had ignored the essential grass that shielded the soil from the constant wind. His mastery over the land, consequently, was turned once more into defeat. . . .

During this decade the plains experience helped provoke a reevaluation of the nation's entire approach to conservation. It was no longer adequate to talk separately about forests or wildlife, grasslands or soils in resource management; all elements were discovered to be bound together in a single equation. Undoubtedly this shift in outlook owed something to the collapse of the Wall Street markets. The ensuing depression, so starkly coincidental with the Dust Bowl, put Americans in a more communal, integrative mood. It also engendered a new willingness to subordinate economic criteria to broader standards of value, including ecological sanctity. Hence this decade, so tragic for the landscape as well as for personal security, saw such initiatives as the Tennessee Valley Authority headed by David Lilienthal, the wildlife management work of Aldo Leopold, and the environmental philosophy of Lewis Mumford—all ecology-oriented departures from previous conservation thinking.

Another evidence of this shift toward ecology, and at the highest levels of public resource policy, was the report submitted by the Great Plains Committee to President Franklin Roosevelt in December, 1936. The committee's chairman was Morris Cooke, head of the Rural Electrification Administration. The other members were

Hugh Bennett of the Soil Conservation Service, Harry Hopkins of the Works Progress Administration, and Secretary Henry Wallace of the Department of Agriculture. Without qualification, the committee agreed that the Dust Bowl was a wholly man-made disaster produced by a history of misguided efforts to "impose upon the region a system of agriculture to which the Plains are not adapted." The essence of the tragedy as they understood it was a failure to heed the common sense lessons of ecology. "Nature," they argued, "has established a balance in the Great Plains by what in human terms would be called the method of trial and error. The white man has disturbed this balance; he must restore it or devise a new one of his own." Unless this were done, the committee warned, the land would become a desert, and the government would have on its hands a perennial, costly problem of relief and salvage. . . .

More influential than any of these in the shaping of an ecological approach to conservation in this formative decade was Frederic Clements. A native of Nebraska, the son of pioneers, he had studied ecology during the 1890's at the state university in Lincoln, and by the thirties was a research fellow at the Carnegie Institute in Washington. No one had been more important than he in getting ecology on its feet as an academic discipline during the first decades of the twentieth century. He had helped to introduce the avant-garde German ecologists to American readers, and he had trained a number of young scholars in this emerging field. More important, he had developed, even before 1910, a persuasive model of how nature works, an ecological paradigm that dominated this science in America, as well as Great Britain, for over three decades. So widely adopted was it that Anglo-American ecology until the 1940's was commonly identified in international circles as a unique, distinguishable tradition: the so-called historical or dynamic school. The central theme of this school was Clements's theory of the climax state of vegetation. On this particular model scientists and conservationists in the thirties would attempt to build a new land-use program, one that would have special relevance to the Great Plains.

According to Clements's model of nature, every region of the earth must pass through a series of vegetational changes, or a process of "ecological succession." From a youthful, unstable, pioneering stage, the plant life of any area evolves eventually toward a more complex, mature equilibrium state, the "climax." Deflect or disturb this pattern of succession, and nature will struggle mightily to get back on the right track. Leave nature alone, and she will produce at last a plant community of near-perfect adaptation that will go on reproducing itself through thousands of years. In the Clementsian model this climax stage is the child of climate: the final outcome of succession is almost wholly determined by the prevailing patterns of rainfall, wind currents, and temperature over any large expanse of space.

In the case of the Great Plains the climax vegetation was the primeval grass, curling and billowing over hundreds of millions of acres of land. Only this grass had proved capable of surviving the periodic droughts of this region and the perennially sparse rainfall. As Clements maintained, this grassland climax had endured for millennia, perhaps as far back as the upthrust of the Rocky Mountains. "There is no basis," he cautioned, "for assuming either that the earth itself or the life upon it will ever reach final stability." But within the span of human time-consciousness at least, nature could be said to achieve long periods of stasis that could be taken as proof of her superior workmanship. And this end product, the grass, deserved as much attention from man as the climate that produced it. . . .

Such recommendations mark an important shift in American perception of the land. In the climax model of Clements environmentalists had at last an apparently objective, scientifically calibrated yardstick by which man's intrusions into nature could be measured. From the thirties on they began to rely on it more and more in discussing both the Dust Bowl crisis and subsequent environmental problems. Generally the view gaining support was that land-use policy should leave the climax vegetation as undisturbed as possible. Whenever interference by man was necessary—and hardly anyone maintained that it was not, unless the population dropped abruptly and humans reverted to a hunting economy—then the best that could be done was to stick as tightly as possible to nature's design. . . .

Frederic Clements died in 1945, and the science of ecology has since then moved in radically different directions. The discipline is no longer dominated by the succession-climax model, with its emphasis on an evolutionary or historical perspective. Even before Clements's death, during the thirties, a few dissidents challenged his thinking and the strong respect for the natural order it implied. This "anti-climax" group, which centered around [Henry] . . . Gleason of the University of Michigan and Arthur Tansley of Oxford, found more adherents in science and beyond as the difficulties of applying Clements's approach to land policies became more apparent. The Kansas historian James Malin, for example, levelled an especially fierce blast against the Clementsian tradition and its implied criticism of plains farmers for creating the Dust Bowl.

Economic Ecology*

The scientist who laid the foundations for the New [Economic] Ecology was the Cambridge University zoologist Charles Elton. In 1927 Elton published his first major work, *Animal Ecology,* which Julian Huxley introduced to the scientific world as a tool of great promise in the more effective management of the plant and animal "industry." . . . In every community, plants, through the photosynthetic conversion of sunlight to food, form the first link in a chain of nutrition. Food, one might say, is the essential capital in the natural economic order. The remaining links—usually no more than two or three, and almost never more than four—include the herbivorous animals and their predators. A typical food chain in a North American oak woods might link acorns, quail, and foxes, or acorns, mice, and weasels; with some 200 species of birds and mammals alone feeding on the oaks, the potential number of food chains is extraordinarily large. . . . And the bottom of the chain, rather than the top, is the most important link: The plants make the whole system possible. Elton referred to the sum total of chains in any community as the "food web"—an exceedingly complex design of crisscrossed lines of economic activity. Such webs are easiest to analyze in the relatively unpopulated arctic zones and almost impossible to untangle in the warm, humid tropics, where life forms abound.

In every food chain certain roles must be performed. The plants, for example, are all "producers." Animals can be described as either first- or second-order "consumers," depending on whether they eat plants or other animals. Those animals that

---

*Excerpts from Donald Worster, *Nature's Economy,* Cambridge University Press 1985, orig. pub. 1977, pp. 295–311, Cambridge University Press.

feed on the most numerous plants in a habitat, like the bison on prairie grasses, or copepods on diatoms in the sea, are the "key industries" in those economies. In 1926, August Thienemann had introduced the terms "producer," "consumer," and "reducer," or "decomposer," to describe ecological roles in a specific ecological setting; Elton now generalized them for every food chain in nature. These labels emphasized the nutritional interdependence that binds species together—the corporateness of survival—and they became the cues from which ecology would increasingly take an economic direction. . . .

A second long step toward the New Ecology was taken by A. G. Tansley, the Oxford botanist. In a 1935 essay, Tansley attempted to rid ecology of all the lingering traces of organismic philosophy, expressed most recently in Clements's description of vegetation as a single living organism. Although Tansley himself had once gone so far as to describe the human community as a "quasi-organism," he now decided that this organismic talk had exceeded the bounds of legitimate scientific inquiry. The often-repeated notion that the plant assemblage is more than the sum of its parts, that it forms a whole which resists reductive analysis, he took to be a fiction worked up by an overexcited imagination. These "wholes," he wrote, "are in *analysis* nothing but the synthesized actions of the components in associations." A mature science, in his view, must isolate "the basic units of nature" and must "split up the story" into its individual parts. It must approach nature as a composite of strictly physical entities organized into a mechanical system. The scientist who knows all the properties of all the parts studied separately can accurately predict their combined result. In addition, Tansley wanted to strike the word "community" from his science's vocabulary because of connotations that he considered misleading and anthropomorphic; some, he feared, might conclude from such language that human associations and those in nature were parallel. Plants and animals in a locale cannot constitute a genuine community, he argued, for no psychic bond can exist between them, and thus they can have no true social order. In short, Tansley hoped to purge from ecology all that was not subject to quantification and analysis, all those obscurities that had been a part of its baggage at least since the Romantic period. He would rescue it from the status of a vaguely mysterious, moralizing "point of view" and make of it instead of hard-edged, mechanistic, nothing-but discipline, marching in closed ranks with the other sciences.

To replace these fuzzy analogies with the organism or the human community, Tansley came up with a new model of organization: the "ecosystem." It was an idea strongly influenced by that masterful science of physics, which early in the twentieth century had begun to talk about energy "fields" and "systems" as a way of getting a more precise handle on natural phenomena than was possible in traditional Newtonian science. Organisms indeed live in closely integrated units, Tansley agreed, but these can best be studied as physical systems, not "organic wholes." Using the ecosystem, all relations among organisms can be described in terms of the purely material exchange of energy and of such chemical substances as water, phosphorus, nitrogen, and other nutrients that are the constituents of "food." These are the real bonds that hold the natural world together; they create a single unit made up of many smaller units—big and little ecosystems. The outmoded concept of an ecological community suggested a sharp disjunction between the living and nonliving substances on earth (part of the Romantic legacy). In contrast, Tansley's ecosystem brought all nature—rocks and gases as well as biota—into a common ordering of material resources. . . .

All ecological kinships thereafter had to be reworked in terms of energy relations. No energy is created or destroyed by the ecosystem, but only transformed and re-transformed before escaping. Most important, the ecologist had to be tutored in the Second Law of Thermodynamics, first formulated by Rudolph Clausius in 1850. According to this law, all energy tends to disperse or become disorganized and unavailable for use, until at last the energy system reaches maximum entropy: a state of total randomness, total equilibrium, death. The ecosystem of the earth, considered from the perspective of energetics, is a way-station on a river of no return. Energy flows through it and disappears eventually into the vast sea of space; there is no way to get back upstream. And unlike water in the hydrological cycle, energy once passed through nature is forever, irretrievably lost. By collecting solar energy for their own use, plants retard this entropic process; they can pass energy on to animals in repackaged or reconcentrated form—some of it at least—and the animals in turn hold it temporarily in organized availability. Put another way, the ecosystem is comparable both to a chain of reservoirs that store running water, and to the dams that make it work before it is released again to rush downstream. But all along the way, some of that flow seeps into the ground and some evaporates into the air, and all that remains must at some point be released. So long as the sun goes on supplying a current of energy, the ecosystem can endure. When that supply runs out, however, the system will collapse.

What remained was to merge these overlapping ideas . . . into a comprehensive account of the energy-based economics of nature. That final step was taken in 1942, when a postgraduate student at Yale, Raymond Lindeman, published a scientific paper entitled "The Trophic-Dynamic Aspect of Ecology." This event may serve to mark the full-blown arrival of the New Ecology. . . .

The specific environment Lindeman studied was Cedar Bog Lake in Minnesota. Such lacustrine systems again and again proved to be the best exemplars of the processes of energy capture and use, chiefly because of the simplified plant populations and the ease of biomass measurement there. But Lindeman's paper was much more than a report on this lake as an isolated example; he wanted to pull together all the major ecological theorizing of the past several decades, including Clements's notion of succession toward climax, into one grand model of "energy-availing" relationships in nature. And he succeeded brilliantly. "Trophic-Dynamic" in the paper's title meant the ecosystem's food or energy cycle, the metabolism of the whole. All resident organisms, he pointed out, may be grouped into a series of more or less discrete "trophic levels": the familiar producers, primary consumers, secondary consumers, decomposers. . . . In the Minnesota lake, the producers were the macrophytic pond weeds and, more important, the microphytic phytoplankton. On these fed the browsers—tadpoles, ducks, certain fishes and insects, tiny copepods and other zooplankton—filling a niche similar to that occupied by terrestrial herbivores. On the browsers in turn depended the second-order consumers, which included other fish, crustaceans, turtles, frogs, and birds. A snapping turtle or an osprey, both carnivorous predators, might represent the third-order consumer. Last came the countless millions of decomposers, bacteria and fungi, which lived in the slimy bottom mud and worked to break down organic substance into recyclable nutrients.

The single most important fact about these trophic levels, in Lindeman's view, was that the energy in use at one level can never be passed on in its entirety to the next higher level. A portion is always lost in the transfer as heat escaping into the atmosphere. The chief goal of Lindeman's ecology was to quantify these losses: to make precise measurements of the shrinkage in available energy as it passes through the ecosystem. He wanted to know, that is, the "productivity" of each level in the food chain and the "efficiency" of energy transfers. Productivity in this case referred not to the numbers of a given species but to the accumulated biomass at any trophic level and the caloric energy required to support that amount of organic matter. . . .

Once the ecologist had these productivity figures in hand for all the trophic levels, he could discover what happens to the captured solar energy as it moves through the ecosystem. He could calculate, that is, the "ecologic efficiencies" of organisms: how much energy they are able to utilize from lower levels and how much of that they in turn pass on, as well as how much they use up in metabolism. . . .

These then are the formative episodes in the development of the New Ecology, an energy-economic model of the environment that began to emerge in the 1920s and was virtually complete by the mid-forties. It is safe to say that this model is overwhelmingly the dominant one followed now in Anglo-American ecology. Since Lindeman, a new breed of like-minded mathematical ecologists has appeared on the academic scene, and they have pushed their subject to the front ranks of the "hard sciences." Among the postwar leaders in this surge toward respectability have been Lindeman's teacher at Yale, G. Evelyn Hutchinson, as well as Edward Deevy, David Gates, John Phillipson, George Woodwell, Robert MacArthur, and probably most important of all, Eugene Odum. . . .

Chaotic Ecology*

In 1953 Odum published the first edition of his famous textbook, *The Fundamentals of Ecology.* In 1966 he became president of the Ecological Society of America.

By now anyone in the United States who regularly reads a newspaper or magazine has come to know at least a few of Odum's ideas, for they furnish the main themes in our popular understanding of ecology, beginning with the sovereign idea of the ecosystem. Odum defined the ecosystem as "any unit that includes all of the organisms (i.e., the 'community') in a given area interacting with the physical environment so that a flow of energy leads to clearly defined trophic structure, biotic diversity, and material cycles (i.e., exchange of materials between living and nonliving parts) within the system." The whole earth, he argued, is organized into an interlocking series of such "ecosystems," ranging in size from a small pond to so vast an expanse as the Brazilian rainforest.

What all those ecosystems have in common is a "strategy of development," a kind of game plan that gives nature an overall direction. That strategy is, in Odum's words, "directed toward achieving as large and diverse an organic structure as is possible within the limits set by the available energy input and the prevailing physical

---

*Excerpts from Donald Worster, "Ecology of Order and Chaos," *Environmental History Review* 14, no. 1–2 (Spring/Summer 1990), pp. 4–16 excerpts. Reprinted with permission from *Environmental History Review,* © 1990, the American Society for Environmental History.

conditions of existence." Every single ecosystem, he believed, is either moving to-ward or has already achieved that goal. It is a clear, coherent, and easily observable strategy; and it ends in the happy state of order.

Nature's strategy, Odum added, leads finally to a world of mutualism and coop-eration among the organisms inhabiting an area. From an early stage of competing against one another, they evolve toward a more symbiotic relationship. They learn, as it were, to work together to control their surrounding environment, making it more and more suitable as a habitat, until at last they have the power to protect themselves from its stressful cycles of drought and flood, winter and summer, cold and heat. Odum called that point "homeostasis." To achieve it, the living components of an ecosystem must evolve a structure of interrelatedness and cooperation that can, to some extent, manage the physical world—manage it for maximum efficiency and mutual benefit.

I have described this set of ideas as a break from the past, but that is misleading. Odum may have used different terms than Clements, may even have had a radically different vision of nature at times; but he did not repudiate Clements's notion that nature moves toward order and harmony. In the place of the theory of the "climax" stage he put the theory of the "mature ecosystem." His nature may have appeared more as an automated factory than as a Clementsian super-organism, but like its predecessor it tends toward order.

The theory of the ecosystem presented a very clear set of standards as to what constituted order and disorder, which Odum set forth in the form of a "tabular model of ecological succession." When the ecosystem reaches its end point of homeostasis, his table shows, it expends less energy on increasing production and more on fur-nishing protection from external vicissitudes: that is, the biomass in an area reaches a steady level, neither increasing nor decreasing, and the emphasis in the system is on keeping it that way—on maintaining a kind of no-growth economy. . . . The sugges-tion was implicit but clear that if one interfered too much with nature's strategy of development, the effects might be costly: a serious loss of nutrients, a decline in spe-cies diversity, an end to biomass stability. In short, the ecosystem would be damaged.

The most likely source of that damage was no mystery to Odum: it was human beings trying to force up the production of useful commodities and stupidly risking the destruction of their life support system.

> Man has generally been preoccupied with obtaining as much "production" from the landscape as possible, by developing and maintaining early successional types of ecosystems, usually monocultures. But, of course, man does not live by food and fiber alone; he also needs a balanced CO_2–O_2 atmosphere, the climatic buffer provided by oceans and masses of vegetation, and clean (that is, unproductive) water for cultural and industrial uses. Many essential life-cycle resources, not to mention recreational and esthetic needs, are best provided man by the less "productive" landscapes. In other words, the landscape is not just a supply depot but is also the *oikos*—the home—in which we must live. . . .

Of course not every one who adopted the ecosystem approach to ecology ended up where Odum did. Quite the contrary, many found the ecosystem idea a wonderful instrument for promoting global technocracy. Experts familiar with the ecosystem and skilled in its manipulation, it was hoped in some quarters, could manage the entire planet for improved efficiency. "Governing" all of nature with the aid of rational science was the dream of these ecosystem technocrats. But technocratic management was not the chief lesson, I believe, the public learned in Professor Odum's classroom; most came away devoted, as he was, to preserving large parts of nature in an unmanaged state and sure that they had been given a strong scientific rationale, as well as knowledge base, to do it. We must defend the world's endangered ecosystems, they insisted. We must safeguard the integrity of the Greater Yellowstone ecosystem, the Chesapeake Bay ecosystem, the Serengeti ecosystem. We must protect species diversity, biomass stability, and calcium recycling. . . .

That was the rallying cry of environmentalists and ecologists alike in the 1960s and early 1970s, when it seemed that the great coming struggle would be between what was left of pristine nature, delicately balanced in Odum's beautifully rational ecosystems, and a human race bent on mindless, greedy destruction. A decade or two later the situation has changed considerably. There are still environmental threats around, to be sure, and they are more dangerous than ever. The newspapers inform us of continuing disasters like the massive 1989 oil spill in Alaska's Prince William Sound, and reporters persist in using words like "ecosystem" and "balance" and "fragility" to describe such disasters. . . . But all the same, and despite the persistence of environmental problems, Odum's ecosystem is no longer the main theme in research or teaching in the science. A survey of recent ecology textbooks shows that the concept is not even mentioned in one leading work and has a much diminished place in the others. . . .

Ecology is not the same as it was. A rather drastic change has been going on in this science of late—a radical shifting away from the thinking of Eugene Odum's generation, away from its assumptions of order and predictability, a shifting toward what we might call a new *ecology of chaos*.

In July 1973, the *Journal of the Arnold Arboretum* published an article by two scientists associated with the Massachusetts Audubon Society, William Drury and Ian Nisbet, and it challenged Odum's ecology fundamentally. The title of the article was simply "Succession," indicating that old subject of observed sequences in plant and animal associations. With both Frederic Clements and Eugene Odum, succession had been taken to be the straight and narrow road to equilibrium. Drury and Nisbet disagreed completely with that assumption. Their observations, drawn particularly from northeastern temperate forests, strongly suggested that the process of ecological succession does not lead anywhere. Change is without any determinable direction and goes on forever, never reaching a point of stability. They found no evidence of any progressive development in nature: no progressive increase over time in biomass stabilization, no progressive diversification of species, no progressive movement toward a greater cohesiveness in plant and animal communities, nor toward a greater success in regulating the environment. Indeed, they found none of the criteria Odum had posited for mature ecosystems. The forest, they insisted, no matter what its age, is nothing but an erratic, shifting mosaic of trees and other plants. In their words, "most of the phenomena of succession should be understood as resulting from the differential growth, differential survival, and perhaps differential dispersal of species adapted to grow at different points on stress gradients." In other words, they could see lots of individual species, each doing its thing, but they could locate no emergent collectivity, nor any strategy to achieve one.

Prominent among their authorities supporting this view was the nearly forgotten name of Henry A. Gleason, a taxonomist who, in 1926, had challenged Frederic Clements and his organismic theory of the climax in an article entitled, "The Individualistic Concept of the Plant Association." Gleason had argued that we live in a world of constant flux and impermanence, not one tending toward Clements's climaxes. There is no such thing, he argued, as balance or equilibrium or steady-state. Each and every plant association is nothing but a temporary gathering of strangers, a clustering of species unrelated to one another, here for a brief while today, on their way somewhere else tomorrow. "Each . . . species of plant is a law unto itself," he wrote. We look for cooperation in nature and we find only competition. We look for organized wholes, and we can discover only loose atoms and fragments. We hope for order and discern only a mishmash of conjoining species, all seeking their own advantage in utter disregard of others.

Thanks in part to Drury and Nisbet, this "individualistic" view was reborn in the mid-1970s and, during the past decade, it became the core idea of what some scientists hailed as a new, revolutionary paradigm in ecology. To promote it, they attacked the traditional notion of succession; for to reject that notion was to reject the larger idea that organic nature tends toward order. . . .

As this assault on the old thinking gathered momentum, the word "disturbance" began to appear more frequently in the scientific literature and be taken far more seriously. "Disturbance" was not a common subject in Odum's heyday, and it almost never appeared in combination with the adjective "natural." Now, however, it was as though scientists were out looking strenuously for signs of disturbance in nature—especially signs of disturbance that were not caused by humans—and they were finding it everywhere. During the past decade those new ecologists succeeded in leaving little tranquility in primitive nature. Fire is one of the most common disturbances they noted. So is wind, especially in the form of violent hurricanes and tornadoes. So are invading populations of microorganisms and pests and predators. And volcanic eruptions. And invading ice sheets of the Quaternary Period. And devastating droughts like that of the 1930s in the American West. Above all, it is these last sorts of disturbances, caused by the restlessness of climate, that the new generation of ecologists have emphasized. As one of the most influential of them, Professor Margaret Davis of the University of Minnesota, has written: "For the last 50 years or 500 or 1,000—as long as anyone would claim for 'ecological time'—there has never been an interval when temperature was in a steady state with symmetrical fluctuations about a mean. . . . Only on the longest time scale, 100,000 years, is there a tendency toward cyclical variation, and the cycles are asymmetrical, with a mean much different from today."

One of the most provocative and impressive expressions of the new post-Odum ecology is a book of essays edited by S. T. A. Pickett and P. S. White, *The Ecology of Natural Disturbance and Patch Dynamics* (published in 1985). I submit it as symptomatic of much of the thinking going on today in the field. Though the final section of the book does deal with ecosystems, the word has lost much of its former meaning and implications. Two of the authors in fact open their contribution with a complaint that many scientists assume that "homogeneous ecosystems are a reality," when in truth "virtually all naturally occurring and man-disturbed ecosystems are mosaics of environmental conditions." "Historically," they write, "ecologists have been slow to recognize the importance of disturbances and the heterogeneity they generate." The reason for this slowness? "The majority of both theoretical and empirical work has been dominated by an equilibrium perspective." Repudiating that perspective, these authors take us to the tropical forests of South and Central America and to the Everglades of Florida, showing us instability on every hand: a wet, green world of continual disturbance—or as they prefer to say, "of perturbations." Even the grasslands of North America, which inspired Frederic Clements's theory of the climax, appear in this collection as regularly disturbed environments. One paper describes them as a "dynamic, fine-textured mosaic" that is constantly kept in upheaval by the workings of badgers, pocket gophers, and mound-building ants, along with fire, drought, and eroding wind and water. The message in all these papers is consistent: The climax notion is dead, the ecosystem has receded in usefulness, and in their place we have the idea of the lowly "patch." Nature should be regarded as a landscape of patches, big and little, patches of all textures and colors, a patchwork quilt of living things, changing continually through time and space, responding to an unceasing barrage of perturbations. The stitches in that quilt never hold for long. . . .

Nature, many have begun to believe, is *fundamentally* erratic, discontinuous, and unpredictable. It is full of seemingly random events that elude our models of how things are supposed to work. As a result, the unexpected keeps hitting us in the face. Clouds collect and disperse, rain falls or doesn't fall, disregarding our careful weather predictions, and we cannot explain why. Cars suddenly bunch up on the freeway, and the traffic controllers fly into a frenzy. A man's heart beats regularly year after year, then abruptly begins to skip a beat now and then. A Ping Pong ball bounces off the table in an unexpected direction. Each little snowflake falling out of the sky turns out to be completely unlike any other. Those are ways in which nature seems, in contrast to all our previous theories and methods, to be chaotic. . . .

Making sense of this situation is the task of an altogether new kind of inquiry calling itself the science of chaos. Some say it portends a revolution in thinking equivalent to quantum mechanics or relativity. Like those other 20th-century revolutions, the science of chaos rejects tenets going back as far as the days of Sir Isaac Newton. In fact, what is occurring may be not two or three separate revolutions but a single revolution against all the principles, laws, models, and applications of classical science, the science ushered in by the great Scientific Revolution of the 17th century. For centuries we have assumed that nature, despite a few appearances to the contrary, is a perfectly predictable system of linear, rational order. Give us an adequate number of facts, scientists have said, and we can describe that order in complete detail—can plot the lines along which everything moves and the speed of that movement and the collisions that will occur. Even Darwin's theory of evolution, which in the last century challenged much of the Newtonian worldview, left intact many people's confidence that order would prevail at last in the evolution of life; that out of the tangled history of competitive struggle would come progress, harmony, and stability. Now that traditional assumption may have broken down irretrievably. For whatever reason, whether because empirical data suggest it or because extrascientific cultural trends do—the experience of so much rapid social change in our daily lives—scientists are beginning to focus on what they had long managed to avoid seeing. The world is more complex than we ever imagined, they say, and indeed, some would add, ever can imagine. . . .

The entire study of chaos began in 1961, with efforts to simulate weather and climate patterns on a computer at MIT. There, meteorologist Edward Lorenz came up with his now famous "Butterfly Effect," the notion that a butterfly stirring the air today in a Beijing park can transform storm systems next month in New York City. Scientists call this phenomenon "sensitive dependence on initial conditions." What it means is that tiny differences in input can quickly become substantial differences in output. A corollary is that we cannot know, even with all our artificial intelligence apparatus, every one of the tiny differences that have occurred or are occurring at any place or point in time; nor can we know which tiny differences will produce which substantial differences in output. Beyond a short range, say, of two or three days from now, our predictions are not worth the paper they are written on.

The implications of this "Butterfly Effect" for ecology are profound. If a single flap of an insect's wings in China can lead to a torrential downpour in New York, then what might it do to the Greater Yellowstone Ecosystem? What can ecologists possibly know about all the forces impinging on, or about to impinge on, any piece of land? What can they safely ignore and what must they pay attention to? What distant, invisible, minuscule events may even now be happening that will change the organization of plant and animal life in our back yards? This is the predicament, and the challenge, presented by the science of chaos, and it is altering the imagination of ecologists dramatically.

John Muir once declared, "When we try to pick out anything by itself, we find it hitched to everything else in the universe." For him, that was a manifestation of an infinitely wise plan in which everything functioned with perfect harmony. The new ecology of chaos, though impressed like Muir with interdependency, does not share his view of "an infinitely wise plan" that controls and shapes everything into order. There is no plan, today's scientists say, no harmony apparent in the events of nature. If there is order in the universe—and there will no longer be any science if all faith in order vanishes—it is going to be much more difficult to locate and describe than we thought.

For Muir, the clear lesson of cosmic complexity was that humans ought to love and preserve nature just as it is. The lessons of the new ecology, in contrast, are not at all clear. Does it promote, in Ilya Prigogine and Isabelle Stenger's words, "a renewal of nature," a less hierarchical view of life, and a set of "new relations between man and nature and between man and man"? Or does it increase our alienation from the world, our withdrawal into postmodernist doubt and self-consciousness? What is there to love or preserve in a universe of chaos? How are people supposed to behave in such a universe? If such is the kind of place we inhabit, why not go ahead with all our private ambitions, free of any fear that we may be doing special damage? What, after all, does the phrase "environmental damage" mean in a world of so much natural chaos? Does the tradition of environmentalism to which Muir belonged, along with so many other nature writers and ecologists of the past—people like Paul Sears, Eugene Odum, Aldo Leopold, and Rachel Carson—make sense any longer? I have no space here to attempt to answer those questions or to make predictions but only issue a warning that they are too important to be left for scientists alone to answer. Ecology today, no more than in the past, can be assumed to be all-knowing or all-wise or eternally true.

Rachel Carson's Ecological Vision

LINDA LEAR

Rachel Carson was an improbable revolutionary, even an unlikely reformer, yet she challenged industrial empires, exposed a scientific establishment that cherished its elitism, and accused the government of being irresponsible. She consciously questioned the dominant system of institutional arrangements and the culture's unequivocal devotion to technological progress. Her crusade renewed the political power of homeowners and housewives. Most important, her message fundamentally altered the way Americans, indeed citizens of the planet, look upon the living environment.

By the eloquence of her prose and rigor of her synthesis, Rachel Carson educated the public and made the life sciences a vehicle for understanding complex technology. *Silent Spring,* published [in 1962], alerted the world to the invisible dangers of environmental poisoning. She intended to alarm and hoped to encourage change, but she did not anticipate becoming a public figure or inspiring a cultural revolution. . . .

Silent Spring indicted the chemical industry, the government, and agribusiness for indiscriminately using pesticides. Her claims seemed fantastic, but if proven, unthinkably frightening. "For the first time in the history of the world," she wrote, "every human being is now subjected to contact with dangerous chemicals, from the moment of conception until death." The book was an overnight sensation. It alarmed the public and was accused of gross distortions. *Time Magazine* charged the book of "oversimplifications and downright errors," calling it an "emotional and inaccurate outburst."

There are very few books that can be said to have changed the course of history, but this was one of them. It polarized government, science, and industry, and made people stop in their tracks and see the world in a new way. With its publication, "ecology" became part of everyday vocabulary. Amid the clamor of what the *New York Times* called the "noisy summer" of 1962, supporters and opponents alike wondered where this powerful critique had come from, and what had possessed gentle poet-naturalist Rachel Carson to take on such a distasteful cause?

For Carson, like many scientists of her generation, the atomic bomb forever changed the way she perceived the living world. "Only within the moment of time represented by the present century has one species—man—acquired significant power to alter the nature of his world." The technology that produced the atomic bomb gave humans the illusion of power. Now they had the ability to unleash forces which eventually would outrun their control. . . .

The hindsight [since 1962] reveals that the power of *Silent Spring* came only partly from the timeliness of its cultural critique. By 1962 Rachel Carson enjoyed an international reputation. She was the most highly regarded marine biologist writing for the general public. She had the unique combination of scientific expertise and public trust to take on such a controversial subject. One of the finest writers in the English language of her day, she combined a poet's voice with a scientist's dispassion. . . .

From Linda Lear, "Rachel Carson's *Silent Spring*." *Environmental History Review* 17, no. 2 (Summer 1993), pp. 23, 27–28, 30–42. Reprinted by permission of the author.

Carson entered professional science during the Great Depression. Although government service offered her greater flexibility than the academy, she still encountered what Margaret Rossiter calls the "rigid lines" of propriety which dictated what sort of science women could do. Biology rather than chemistry or physics was the preferred choice. The acceptability of the life sciences for women was apparent at Woods Hole in the summer of 1929 when Carson won a seat as a "beginning investigator." There she was one of thirty-one women in the biological sciences, which claimed the most female students by far at the Marine Institute.

Away from Woods Hole Carson was, like most other women in the field, nearly "invisible." This was especially so within the government where few women were employed exclusively as scientists. She was one of the first two women ever hired at the professional level at the Fish and Wildlife Service in the 1930s. However Carson was never employed even primarily as an aquatic biologist. Her assignments were exclusively public information, writing and editing agency publications; this work required her to know the scientific background of every subject that came across her desk. Breadth rather than specialized knowledge enabled her to excel as a government scientist during the Cold War. . . .

The three "sea books," *Under the Sea-Wind, The Sea Around Us,* and *The Edge of the Sea* of 1941, 1951, and 1955 respectively, displayed Carson's field research in the tidal pools and shores of the Atlantic and her acute powers of observation. But these eloquent studies were equally dependent upon the immense secondary literature Carson discovered and devoured. Like most great teachers, Carson's genius lay in synthesizing an enormous amount of information generated by other scholars, adding her unique vision and experience, and distilling it in prose that educated as it captivated. Had her writing been less graceful, Carson still would have been a great teacher. But because she was a scientist in love with the English language, and an observer of the natural world with few peers, her ability to communicate what she saw increased exponentially.

Carson's liabilities as a female biologist in an age which valued narrow, technical expertise and relegated even male biologists to the "soft" periphery of science were real. Although many in the academy admired and respected her ecological sophistication, especially as demonstrated in *The Sea Around Us,* Carson was never a scientific insider. This isolation, combined with her early impecuniousness and heavy familial obligation, ironically forced her to concentrate on what she did best: research and writing to inform. . . .

Like the earlier "sea books," *Silent Spring* abounds with images taken from the experiences with nature that were familiar to the middle-class in both urban and suburban settings. Carson's voice comes to us from familiar places, even while she is describing the invisible workings of chemicals and molecular change. Nature is at once familiar and intimate, yet mysterious and ephemeral; ultimately unknowable because it is uncontrollable. Her language and syntax derive from an epistemology rich in spiritual dimension and almost mystical in content. Reverence, awe, and wonder are the hallmarks of this encounter with the common yet wholly other elements of nature. This unique vision allows Carson to describe the frightening damage out of control technology was doing to the natural world while her spiritual apprehension of nature's economy was the source of her outrage at humankind's careless interference. . . .

. . . [T]hree unrelated events involving the aerial application of chlorinated hydrocarbon pesticides coalesced to persuade Carson the natural world as she knew it was in danger. The first involved the controversial campaign undertaken by USDA [U.S. Department of Agriculture] in 1957 to eradicate the imported fire ant from the southern states by massive applications of dieldrin and heptachlor, two of the most persistent and most toxic new pesticides. Reports of wildlife damage brought a chorus of criticism from conservation groups. Carson read these reports, discussed them with her friends, attended USDA briefings as an Audubon member, and followed the acrimonious pesticide debate within the National Academy of Science/National Research Council on which her friend and former supervisor Clarence Cottam served.

About the same time she also received information on bird mortality caused by the aerial spraying of DDT mixed in fuel oil for mosquito control in the coastal counties of northern Massachusetts. Friend and fellow writer Olga Owens Huckins' home and bird sanctuary in Duxbury had been subjected to that spraying. Saddened and angry over the numbers of birds that had perished, Huckins wrote to the Boston *Herald* in protest. She sent Carson a copy of the published letter in January 1958 urging her to find someone in Washington to help stop the spraying. In the course of sleuthing on Huckins's behalf Carson uncovered the enormity of the pesticide problem. She understood immediately that there was material for an article at least and perhaps for a book.

Finally, Carson's initial inquiries about aerial spraying took place not only during the height of the fire ant controversy, but also at a time when newspapers were full of accounts of a trial in Long Island involving shocking misuse of pesticides. Robert Cushman Murphy, noted ornithologist, director of the American Museum of Natural History, and one of Carson's early benefactors, pursued the novel strategy of attempting to enjoin the federal government from further aerial pesticide spraying. Testimony presented during the trial documented enormous damage that pesticides had done to fish, birds, wildlife, dairy cattle, gardens, livestock, and perhaps to children. The suit, which was eventually dismissed on technicalities after appeal to the Supreme Court, gathered testimony from a variety of experts. It provided Rachel Carson with "mountains of material," important collaborators such as Mary Richards and Marjorie Spock, and a wealth of expert contacts in medical and agricultural fields previously unknown to her.

Soon Carson was corresponding with every independent scientist who knew something about pesticides and every government scientist who was brave enough to answer her letters. The Long Island trial lent a sense of urgency to her inquiries, and as her research on the subject grew, so did her determination to find out the truth. "Knowing the facts as I did," she later recalled, "I could not rest until I had brought them to public attention." . . .

The June 16, 1962 issue of *The New Yorker* carried the first of three articles condensed from *Silent Spring*. It was Carson's second appearance in the "profiles" column. That distinguished periodical had a history of bringing important social issues and authors to the reading public and this was no exception. The serialization of *Silent Spring* assured it the widest and most influential readership.

The impact of *Silent Spring* on the highest levels of the Kennedy administration and the "informed public" was immediate. As other journalists picked up *The New*

Yorker story, Carson's exposé of the side effects of technological progress reached a mass audience. National media attention began with the acclaimed serialization and continued in the pages of the *New York Times,* which on July 3 editorialized:

> Miss Carson will be accused of alarmism, or lack of objectivity, of showing only the bad side of pesticides while ignoring their benefits. But this, we suspect, is her purpose as well as her method. . . . If her series helps arouse enough public concern to immunize government agencies against the blandishments of hucksters and enforce adequate controls, the author will be as deserving of the Nobel Prize as was the inventor of DDT.

The following week the *Washington Post* commented that "Carson's negative case is virtually as powerful as the poisons she deplores." Officials within the Department of Agriculture who took the brunt of Carson's attack were caught off-guard and were privately outraged. Departmental representatives who sat on the toothless Federal Pest Review Control Board (FPCRB), a formal advisory committee that co-ordinated and monitored all federal pesticide activities, "alternated between angry attacks on *Silent Spring* and nasty remarks about Miss Carson."

Gender was used to denigrate her science. Ezra Taft Benson, former Agriculture Secretary, privately suggested to former President Dwight Eisenhower that Carson was "probably a communist." Why was a "spinster . . . so worried about genetics" he wondered? Other male critics castigated her as a "bird and bunny lover," and some suggested that she was just an "hysterical female." Privately some officials worried that Carson's message could create a constituency potentially disruptive of the pesticide status quo. But other observers found in Rachel Carson's gentle femininity and quiet self-containment a credibility and stature that mocked appeals to gender stereotypes. Still, gender and professional status remained the targets of Carson's detractors. . . .

. . . Most industry spokesmen criticized Carson's "unbalanced" presentation while they waited to examine her evidence. The president of Monsanto Corporation set the tone of the ensuing debate, calling Carson "a fanatic defender of the cult of the balance of nature."

The attacks increased in early August when the Velsicol Corporation, one of the chief manufacturers of chlordane, threatened Houghton Mifflin with a libel suit if they persisted in publishing the book. Its corporate counsel suggested that Carson was an unwitting pawn of "sinister" Cold War influences. The National Agricultural Chemical Association set aside $25,000 for a major public relations blitz to combat Carson's alarming conclusions.

By the time Houghton Mifflin published the book on September 27th, the critics had coalesced. . . . [Among them were] . . . the USDA and their most powerful constituents, the chemical industry and "Big Farmers." Initially they viewed the controversy as a short-term, but expensive, public relations and education issue. Industry experts of all sorts emerged; each one refuted Carson's evidence of contamination, most rebutting things Carson never said, and all proclaimed the necessity of the present level of pesticides to feed the U.S. and the world. Advertising campaigns for government and industry programs emphasized the horrors of a future without pesticides and a world without enough food. Yet many of these industry critics had read little more of *Silent Spring* than its opening fable. . . .

During a press conference on August 29, 1962 President John Kennedy pledged an investigation of the abuses Carson cited in the *New Yorker* series. An astute politician, Kennedy saw Carson's charges as political dynamite. The President's attention immediately expanded the book's influence. In late July Kennedy assigned Jerome Weisner, his Science Advisor, to set up a special panel of the [President's] Science Advisory Committee [PSAC] to investigate. Pesticides and pesticide use became a public policy issue, an event which USDA, the agrichemical industry, and many scientists regarded with alarm.

As *Silent Spring* leaped to the top of the best-seller lists in the fall of 1962, selling more than 600,000 copies, Carson herself became the center of a "human interest" story. The specter of the government, and the scientific and corporate establishments ganging up on the reticent Miss Carson attracted large segments of the American public who never read *The New Yorker* or the book. They sympathized with the demure author who was subjected to such heavy-handed attack.

The Columbia Broadcasting System (CBS) announced late in 1962 that it would produce a special on the book the following spring. The USDA, FDA, and PHS were flooded with letters from citizens protesting government spraying programs. Conservation organizations, particularly the Audubon Society, reported record membership growth. In Congress, John Dingell (D-Mich.), announced that his patience with the anemic FPCRB was at an end and that he would reintroduce mandatory federal coordination measures. Similar measures were introduced in the Senate. Activity within the states was even more furious as bills were introduced to limit the broadcast use of pesticides.

In spite of a mysterious letter writing campaign designed to pressure CBS to withdraw the show, and despite the last minute withdrawal of several corporate sponsors, the CBS prime-time special "The Silent Spring of Rachel Carson" aired on April 3, 1963, dramatically escalating the debate. The show amounted to nothing less than a second printing of *Silent Spring.* Although the network and producer Jay McMullen went to great lengths to offer a wide range of opinions on the pesticide issue, what the viewers saw was a graphic, one-hour portrayal of Carson's simple and compelling thesis that "we know not what harm we face."

The visual impact of the quiet, self-assured author who reiterated her deep concern that humanity had begun a process that threatened both its own future and that of the living environment was deeply convincing to many viewers. The contrast between the calm and articulate Carson, who spoke about the interrelatedness of all life, and her loud, "wild-eyed" opponent, Dr. Robert White-Stevens, could not have been more striking. White-Stevens, a heavily spectacled scientist with a white lab coat and a proper British accent, represented the chemical industry and American Cyanamid Company. He dramatically predicted a return to the "dark ages" of starvation, disease, and death if pesticide use was restricted. Television allowed Carson and not her critics to define the issue. By the end of the broadcast, the environment had been added to the public agenda.

The next day Connecticut Senator Abraham Ribicoff announced that he would conduct a congressional review of environmental pollution, including federal regulation of pesticides and federal pesticide control programs. Hearings of the Senate Subcommittee on Reorganization and International Organizations began on May

16th. With exquisite timing, the White House released the long awaited report of the PSAC with Kennedy's emphatic endorsement the day before the hearings began.

The PSAC report, "The Uses of Pesticides," was not as harsh in its recommendations as many in government and industry feared. Nevertheless, in language that clearly vindicated Rachel Carson, it concluded that "the accretion of residues in the environment can be controlled only by orderly reductions of persistent pesticides." It urged an end to the use of all chemicals like DDT and heptachlor, but failed to specify how this should be done. The PSAC criticized the operative scientific paradigm specifically challenging the concept of pest eradication. The report recommended increased public education on the benefits and hazards of pesticide use, noting that "until the publication of *Silent Spring* by Rachel Carson, people were generally unaware of the toxicity of pesticides."

The Christian Science Monitor declared the following day "Rachel Carson Stands Vindicated!" That evening, CBS news commentator Eric Sevareid recalled that "Miss Carson had two immediate aims. One was to alert the public; the second, to build a fire under the government." She had accomplished this and much more.

Silent Spring and the controversy it produced brought science into the wide arena of public understanding and debate for the first time since the end of World War II. Carson convinced those who read her book that there was a fragile partnership between humans and nature, which once broken, could lead to the destruction of both. By providing an alternative vision of scientific progress, one that required an informed and vigilant citizenry, she launched a popular movement she never dreamed possible.

Rachel Carson eloquently testified before the Ribicoff committee hearings on June 4th. She accepted awards from the world of letters, arts, and science as graciously and quietly as she had faced the criticism which had been heaped upon her earlier. But her time was running out. On April 14, 1964 at the age of fifty-six she died of cancer at her home in Silver Spring, Maryland.

Yet as the public mourned her untimely passing, the world was reading translations of *Silent Spring*. A younger generation of ecology conscious activists moved by her courage and vision were taking up their own crusades and broadening the cause. Ralph Nader remembers as a student at Princeton his conscience had first been disturbed by the death of songbirds in the university commons after aerial spraying of DDT. Barry Commoner worked on DDT as a Navy scientist during World War II. He shared Carson's alarm and was inspired by her actions. . . .

Rachel Carson was an important role model for this younger generation of scientists and environmental activists. Stuart Udall, who was Secretary of the Interior when *Silent Spring* was published, considers Carson the "fountainhead" of the new environmental movement. For Udall what distinguishes this new group of activists is that they share Carson's ecological values and care about the whole of the living world. This new ethic of interconnectedness is her most enduring legacy, and it is this quality which, at its best, distinguishes the modern movement. In a speech near the end of her life Carson defined the moral problem:

> What is important is the relation of man to all life. This has never been so tragically overlooked as in our present age, when through our technology we are waging war against the natural world. It is a valid question whether any civilization can do this and

retain the right to be called civilized. By acquiescing in needless destruction and suffering, our stature as human beings is diminished.

Through her ability to make the complexities of the living world understandable, Carson helped "democratize" science and make scientists more accountable. She showed that the public could understand complex scientific principles if they were explained in simple but accurate terms. Her teaching proved that once informed the public would demand the right to know what was being done to them in the name of "progress." Carson's insistence that the ultimate directions of science and technology were debatable initiated other institutional challenges that have altered public policy and the national agenda.

Never dreaming that one book could alter the course of history, Rachel Carson simply spoke for what she herself held most precious and hoped others might listen. Thanks to her courage and vision, millions did.

ᴪ *F U R T H E R   R E A D I N G*

Charles C. Adams, *Guide to the Study of Animal Ecology* (1913)

Stephen Bocking, *Ecologists and Environmental Politics: A History of Contemporary Ecology* (1997)

Daniel Botkin, *Discordant Harmonies* (1990)

Anna Bramwell, *Ecology in the Twentieth Century: A History* (1989)

Robert Clarke, *Ellen Swallow: The Woman Who Founded Ecology* (1974)

Frederic Clements, *Plant Succession: An Analysis of the Development of Vegetation* (1916)

William Coleman, *Biology in the Nineteenth Century: Problems of Form, Function, and Transformation* (1977)

Peter Crowcroft, *Elton's Ecologists: A History of the Bureau of Animal Population* (1991)

P. K. Dayton, "Ecology: A Science and a Religion," in R. J. Livingstone, ed., *Ecological Processes in Coastal and Marine Ecosystems* (1971)

Thomas R. Dunlap, *DDT: Scientists, Citizens, and Public Policy* (1981)

Frank Egerton, "Ecological Studies and Observations Before 1900," in Benjamin Taylor and Thurman White, eds., *Issues and Ideas in America* (1976), Part V, Chapter 16, pp. 311–351

Susan L. Flader, *Thinking Like a Mountain: Aldo Leopold and the Evolution of an Ecological Attitude Toward Deer, Wolves, and Forests* (1974)

Frank Benjamin Golley, *A History of the Ecosystem Concept in Ecology: More Than the Sum of the Parts* (1993)

Joel B. Hagen, *An Entangled Bank: The Origins of Ecosystem Ecology* (1992)

H. Patricia Hynes, "Ellen Swallow, Lois Gibbs, and Rachel Carson: Catalysts of the American Environmental Movement," *Women's Studies International Forum* 8, no. 4 (1985), 291–298

Richard L. Knight and Suzanne Riedel, eds., *Aldo Leopold and the Ecological Conscience* (2002)

Kathleen V. Kudlinski, *Rachel Carson: Pioneer of Ecology* (1988)

Jean Langenheim, "The Path and Progress of American Women Ecologists," *Journal of the Ecological Society of America* 69 (1988), 184–197

Linda Lear, *Rachel Carson: Witness for Nature* (1997)

———, ed., *Lost Woods: The Discovered Writings of Rachel Carson* (1998)

Aldo Leopold, *A Sand County Almanac* (1949)

———, *The River of the Mother of God and Other Essays,* ed. Susan L. Falder and J. Baird Callicott (1991)

George Perkins *Marsh, Man and Nature; or, Physical Geography as Modified by Human Action* (1864)

Leo Marx, "American Institutions and Ecological Ideals," *Science* 170 (1970), 945–952

Robert McIntosh, "Ecology Since 1900," in Benjamin Taylor and Thurman White, eds., *Issues and Ideas in America,* (1976), Part V, Chapter 17, pp. 353–372

———, *The Background of Ecology: Concept and Theory* (1985)

Curt Meine, *Aldo Leopold: The Man and His Work* (1989)

G. Tyler Miller, Jr., *Living in the Environment: Concepts, Problems, and Alternatives* (1974)

Bernard J. Nebel, *Environmental Science: The Way the World Works,* 2nd ed. (1987)

Eugene P. Odum, *Fundamentals of Ecology,* 1st ed. (1953)

John H. Perkins, *Insects, Experts, and the Insecticide Crisis* (1982)

Leslie A. Real and James H. Brown, *Foundations of Ecology: Classic Papers With Commentaries* (1991)

Robert E. Ricklefs, *The Economy of Nature* (1976)

Paul Sears, *Life and Environment* (1932)

———, "Ecology—A Subversive Subject," *BioScience* 14 (1964), 11–13

Michael B. Smith, "Silence, Miss Carson!: Science, Gender, and the Reception of *Silent Spring,*" *Feminist Studies* 27, no. 3 (Fall 2001), 733–752

Ronald C. Tobey, *Saving the Prairies* (1981)

Robert van den Bosch, *The Pesticide Conspiracy* (1980)

Donald Worster, *Nature's Economy: The Roots of Ecology* (1977)

CHAPTER
14

Water, Energy, and Population
in the Twentieth Century

☙

Between 1950 and 2000, the American population grew from approximately 158 million to 281 million people. Basic needs for water, energy, food, and clothing as well as a consumption-driven capitalist society put increasing pressure on natural resources. This chapter looks at the linkages between the demand for water and energy and the ways in which the federal government responded to population growth and the need for environmental regulation. The distinction made by John Wesley Powel in the 1860s between the rain-rich East and the arid West became of vital importance during the twentieth century as increasing numbers of people settled in the Southwest, the Rocky Mountains, the Great Basin, and southern California. The federal government sponsored large energy and water control projects, such as the Hoover and Glen Canyon Dams on the Colorado in the Great Basin, the Grand Coulee Dam on the Columbia in the Pacific Northwest, and the Tennessee Valley Project in the East. But hydropower was only one source of energy. Steam, coal, oil, and nuclear power supplied the needs of an industrialized society and an automobile-driven consumer culture.

During the 1970s new legislation regulated industrial effluents and pollution more tightly, increased the protection of wilderness and wildlife, and imposed greater controls on the uses and disposal of pesticides, toxic substances, and hazardous wastes. The outcome was an ever more complex and tightly linked set of flows between human society and nature that was experienced at all levels, from rural to urban and local to global. (See Map 10 in the Appendix.)

☙ DOCUMENTS

The documents in this chapter discuss sources of energy, such as water power, coal, and nuclear power, and their environmental and human health impacts; methods of environmental regulation; and the problems of burgeoning population growth. In Document 1, a speech made at the dedication of Boulder (now Hoover) Dam in Colorado, President Franklin Delano Roosevelt lauds the engineering advances that brought water and electric power to the arid West in the years of drought and dust bowls.

During the 1960s and 1970s, a host of environmental laws were passed that regulated pesticides; set standards for clean air and water; preserved wilderness, marine mammals, and endangered species; and established procedures for waste disposal. One of the most sweeping of these new laws, the National Environmental Policy Act (NEPA) of 1969, signed into law on New Year's Day 1970 by President Richard Nixon, is excerpted in Document 2. Although the preamble sets out goals designed to ensure a safe, healthful environment, NEPA's most significant requirement is the establishment of the environmental impact statement (EIS) for every proposed federal action that would affect the quality of the human environment. Duplicated by state legislatures throughout the country, these procedures and reports have altered or mitigated many proposed local and federal development projects.

Indian reservations that contain natural resources such as uranium, coal, copper, and water are leased for development both by the federal government and by private corporations. That Indians themselves hold strongly divided opinions on whether to lease their lands is revealed in Document 3, a 1970 letter by a group of Hopi to President Nixon. The Indians were protesting coal mining on their reservation by the Peabody Coal Company, a subsidiary of Kennecott Copper. Document 4, by environmentalist Barry Commoner, is an analysis of the environmental and human health impacts of nuclear power.

Document 5 is excerpted from a 1983 speech by William Ruckelshaus, former director of the Environmental Protection Agency, discussing problems of scientific risk assessment and of drafting legislation that would provide adequate protection from chemical hazards and pollutants. Document 6 presents the industrialist's point of view. G. M. Keller, chairman of the board and chief executive officer of Chevron Corporation, discusses efforts on the part of industry to mitigate environmental problems. In Document 7, population scientists Paul and Anne Ehrlich argue that the fundamental problem facing the human quality of life on the planet is burgeoning population growth, raising the question of whether population growth can be slowed and stabilized by humane means or whether populations will be dramatically thinned by starvation and lack of resources. Considered as a group, the documents reveal the linkages between water, energy, population growth, and environmental regulation.

1. President Franklin D. Roosevelt Dedicates Hoover Dam, 1935

Speech by Roosevelt at the Dedication of Boulder [Hoover] Dam, September 30, 1935

Senator [Key] Pittman, Secretary [of the Interior, Harold] Ickes, Governors of the Colorado's States, and you especially who have built Boulder [now Hoover] Dam: This morning I came, I saw and I was conquered, as everyone would be who sees for the first time this great feat of mankind.

Ten years ago the place where we gathered was an unpeopled, forbidding desert. In the bottom of the gloomy canyon whose precipitous walls rose to a height of more than a thousand feet, flowed a turbulent, dangerous river. The mountains on either

---

From Franklin D. Roosevelt, *Franklin D. Roosevelt and Conservation, 1911–1945*. Ed. Edgar B. Nixon. 2 vols. New York, 1957, vol. 1, pp. 430–433, 438–441.

side of the canyon were difficult of access with neither road nor trail, and their rocks were protected by neither trees nor grass from the blazing heat of the sun. The site of Boulder City was a cactus-covered waste. And the transformation wrought here in these years is a twentieth century marvel.

We are here to celebrate the completion of the greatest dam in the world, rising 726 feet above the bedrock of the river and altering the geography of a whole region; we are here to see the creation of the largest artificial lake in the world—115 miles long, holding enough water, for example, to cover the whole State of Connecticut to a depth of ten feet; and we are here to see nearing completion a power house which will contain the largest generators and turbines yet installed in this country, machinery that can continuously supply nearly two million horsepower of electric energy. All of these dimensions are superlative. They represent and embody the accumulated engineering knowledge and experience of centuries, and when we behold them it is fitting that we pay tribute to the genius of their designers. We recognize also the energy, the resourcefulness and the zeal of the builders, who, under the greatest physical obstacles, have pushed this work forward to completion two years in advance of contract requirements. But especially, my friends, we express our gratitude to the thousands of workers who gave brain and brawn in this great work of construction.

Beautiful and great as this structure is, it must also be considered in its relationship to the agricultural and industrial development and in its contribution to the health and comfort of the people of America who live in the Southwest.

To divert and distribute the waters of an arid region so that there shall be security of rights and efficiency in service, is one of the greatest problems of law and of administration to be found in any government. The farms, the cities, the people who live along the many thousands of miles of this river and its tributaries all of them depend for their permanence in value upon the conservation, regulation, and the equitable and fair division of its ever-changing water supply. What has been accomplished on the Colorado in working out such a scheme of distribution is inspiring to the whole country. Through the cooperation of the States whose people depend upon this river, and of the Federal Government which is concerned in the general welfare, there is being constructed a system of distributive works and of laws and practices which will insure to the millions of people who now dwell in this basin, and to the millions of others who will come to dwell here in future generations, a safe, just, and permanent system of water rights. In devising these policies and the means of putting them into practice the Bureau of Reclamation of the Federal Government has taken and is destined to take in the future, a leading and helpful part. The Bureau has been the instrument which gave effect to the legislation introduced into the Congress by Senator Hiram Johnson and Congressman Philip Swing.

When in flood the river was a threatening torrent. In the dry months of the year it shrank to a trickling stream. For a generation the people of Imperial Valley had lived in the shadow of disaster from this river which provided their livelihood, and which is the foundation of their hopes for themselves and their children. Every spring they awaited with dread the coming of a flood, and at the end of every summer they feared a shortage of water would destroy their crops.

The gates of these great diversion tunnels were closed here at Boulder Dam last February and in June a great flood came down the river. It came roaring down the canyons of the Colorado, through Grand Canyon, Iceberg and Boulder Canyons, but it was caught, it was caught and held safely behind Boulder Dam.

Last year a drought of unprecedented severity was visited upon the west. The watershed of this Colorado River did not escape. In July the canals of the Imperial Valley went dry. Crop losses in that Valley alone totaled $10,000,000 that summer. Had Boulder Dam been completed one year earlier, this loss would have been prevented, because the spring flood would have been stored to furnish a steady water supply for the long dry summer and fall.

Across the San Jacinto mountains southwest of Boulder Dam the cities of Southern California are constructing an aqueduct to cost $200,000,000, which they have raised, for the purpose of carrying the regulated waters of the River to the Pacific Coast 250 miles away.

And across the desert and mountains to the west and south run great electric transmission lines by which factory motors, street and household lights and irrigation pumps can be operated in Southern Arizona and California. Part of this power will be used in pumping the water through the aqueduct to supplement the domestic supplies of Los Angeles and surrounding cities.

Navigation of the river from Boulder Dam to the Grand Canyon has been made possible, a 115-mile stretch that had been traversed less than half a dozen times in all history. An immense new park has been created for the enjoyment of all of our people. And that is why, my friends, those of you who are not here today but can hear my voice, I tell you—come to Boulder Dam and see it with your own eyes.

2. The National Environmental Policy Act, 1969

Pub. Law No. 91-190, 83 Stat. 852 (1970) codified at 42 U.S.C.§4331 (1982). Selected provisions.

§4331. Congressional declaration of national environmental policy

(a) The Congress, recognizing the profound impact of man's activity on the inter-relations of all components of the natural environment, particularly the profound influences of population growth, high-density urbanization, industrial expansion, resource exploitation, and new and expanding technological advances and recognizing further the critical importance of restoring and maintaining environmental quality to the overall welfare and development of man, declares that it is the continuing policy of the Federal Government, in cooperation with State and local governments, and other concerned public and private organizations, to use all practicable means and measures, including financial and technical assistance, in a manner calculated to foster and promote the general welfare, to create and maintain conditions under which man and nature can exist in productive harmony, and fulfill the social, economic, and other requirements of present and future generations of Americans.

The National Environmental Policy Act of 1969. Public Law No. 91-190, 83 stat. 852 (1970) (codified at 42 U. S. C. sec. 4331 [1982]), selected provisions.

(b) In order to carry out the policy set forth in this chapter, it is the continuing responsibility of the Federal Government to use all practicable means, consistent with other essential considerations of national policy, to improve and coordinate Federal plans, functions, programs, and resources to the end that the Nation may—

(1) fulfill the responsibilities of each generation as trustee of the environment for succeeding generations;

(2) assure for all Americans safe, healthful, productive, and esthetically and culturally pleasing surroundings;

(3) attain the widest range of beneficial uses of the environment without degradation, risk to health or safety, or other undesirable and unintended consequences;

(4) preserve important historic, cultural, and natural aspects of our national heritage, and maintain, wherever possible, an environment which supports diversity and variety of individual choice;

(5) achieve a balance between population and resource use which will permit high standards of living and a wide sharing of life's amenities; and

(6) enhance the quality of renewable resources and approach the maximum attainable recycling of depletable resources.

(c) The Congress recognizes that each person should enjoy a healthful environment and that each person has a responsibility to contribute to the preservation and enhancement of the environment.

§ 4332. Cooperation of agencies; reports; availability of information; recommendations; international and national coordination of efforts

The Congress authorizes and directs that, to the fullest extent possible: (1) the policies, regulations, and public laws of the United States shall be interpreted and administered in accordance with the policies set forth in this chapter, and (2) all agencies of the Federal Government shall—

(A) utilize a systematic, interdisciplinary approach which will insure the integrated use of the natural and social sciences and the environmental design arts in planning and in decisionmaking which may have an impact on man's environment;

(B) identify and develop methods and procedures, in consultation with the Council on Environmental Quality . . . , which will insure that presently unquantified environmental amenities and values may be given appropriate consideration in decisionmaking along with economic and technical considerations;

(C) include in every recommendation or report on proposals for legislation and other major Federal actions significantly affecting the quality of the human environment, a detailed statement by the responsible official on—

(i) the environmental impact of the proposed action,

(ii) any adverse environmental effects which cannot be avoided should the proposal be implemented,

(iii) alternatives to the proposed action,

(iv) the relationship between local short-term uses of man's environment and the maintenance and enhancement of long-term productivity, and

(v) any irreversible and irretrievable commitments of resources which would be involved in the proposed action should it be implemented.

Prior to making any detailed statement, the responsible Federal official shall consult with and obtain the comments of any Federal agency which has jurisdiction by law or special expertise with respect to any environmental impact involved. Copies of such statement and the comments and views of the appropriate Federal, State, and local agencies, which are authorized to develop and enforce environmental standards, shall be made available to the President, the Council on Environmental Quality and to the public as provided by section 552 of title 5, and shall accompany the proposal through the existing agency review processes;

(D) any detailed statement required under subparagraph (C) after January 1, 1970, for any major Federal action funded under a program of grants to States shall not be deemed to be legally insufficient solely by reason of having been prepared by a State agency or official, if:

(i) the State agency or official has statewide jurisdiction and has the responsibility for such action,

(ii) the responsible Federal official furnishes guidance and participates in such preparation,

(iii) the responsible Federal official independently evaluates such statement prior to its approval and adoption, and

(iv) after January 1, 1976, the responsible Federal official provides early notification to, and solicits the views of, any other State or any Federal land management entity of any action or any alternative thereto which may have significant impacts upon such State or affected Federal land management entity and, if there is any disagreement on such impacts, prepares a written assessment of such impacts and views for incorporation into such detailed statement.

The procedures in this subparagraph shall not relieve the Federal official of his responsibilities for the scope, objectivity, and content of the entire statement or of any other responsibility under this chapter; and further, this subparagraph does not affect the legal sufficiency of statements prepared by State agencies with less than statewide jurisdiction.

(E) study, develop, and describe appropriate alternatives to recommended courses of action in any proposal which involves unresolved conflicts concerning alternative uses of available resources;

(F) recognize the worldwide and long-range character of environmental problems and, where consistent with the foreign policy of the United States, lend appropriate support to initiatives, resolutions, and programs designed to maximize international cooperation in anticipating and preventing a decline in the quality of mankind's world environment;

(G) make available to States, counties, municipalities, institutions, and individuals, advice and information useful in restoring, maintaining, and enhancing the quality of the environment;

(H) initiate and utilize ecological information in the planning and development of resource-oriented projects; and

(I) assist the Council on Environmental Quality established by subchapter II of this chapter.

3. Hopi Leaders Protest the Desecration of Their Sacred Lands, 1970

Last year [1969] the Peabody Coal Company, a subsidiary of Kennecott Copper Company, began stripping coal from 65,000 acres it [had] leased from the Navajo and Hopi tribes. Company officials declared that this mining would not damage Indian lands and in fact would improve the lives of many Navajos and Hopis. In disagreement with this action a group of Hopi wrote the following letter to President Nixon:

Dear Mr. President:

We, the true and traditional religious leaders, recognized as such by the Hopi People, maintain full authority over all land and life contained within the Western Hemisphere. We are granted our stewardship by virtue of our instruction as to the meaning of Nature, Peace, and Harmony as spoken to our People by Him, known to us as Massau'u, the Great Spirit, who long ago provided for us the sacred stone tablets which we preserve to this day. For many generations before the coming of the white man, for many generations before the coming of the Navajo, the Hopi People have lived in the sacred place known to you as the Southwest and known to us to be the spiritual center of our continent. Those of us of the Hopi Nation who have followed the path of the Great Spirit without compromise have a message which we are committed, through our prophecy, to convey to you.

The white man, through his insensitivity to the way of Nature, has desecrated the face of Mother Earth. The white man's advanced technological capacity has occurred as a result of his lack of regard for the spiritual path and for the way of all living things. The white man's desire for material possessions and power has blinded him to the pain he has caused Mother Earth by his quest for what he calls natural resources. And the path of the Great Spirit has become difficult to see by almost all men, even by many Indians who have chosen instead to follow the path of the white man. . . .

Today the sacred lands where the Hopi live are being desecrated by men who seek coal and water from our soil that they may create more power for the white man's cities. This must not be allowed to continue for if it does, Mother Nature will react in such a way that almost all men will suffer the end of life as they now know it. The Great Spirit said not to allow this to happen even as it was prophecied to our ancestors. The Great Spirit said not to take from the Earth—not to destroy living things. The Great Spirit, Massau'u, said that man was to live in Harmony and maintain a good clean land for all children to come. All Hopi People and other Indian Brothers are standing on this religious principle and the Traditional Spiritual Unity Movement today is endeavoring to reawaken the spiritual nature in Indian people throughout this land. Your government has almost destroyed our basic religion which actually is a way of life for all our people in this land of the Great Spirit. We feel that to survive the coming Purification Day, we must return to the basic religious principles and to meet together on this basis as leaders of our people.

From *Touch the Earth: A Self Portrait of Indian Existence,* introduced and edited by T. C. McLuhan (New York: Simon & Schuster, 1971), pp. 170–171. Reprinted with the permission of Simon & Schuster Adult Publishing Group. Copyright © 1971 by T. C. McLuhan.

Today almost all the prophecies have come to pass. Great roads like rivers pass across the landscape; man talks to man through the cobwebs of telephone lines; man travels along the roads in the sky in his airplanes; two great wars have been waged by those bearing the swastika or the rising sun; man is tampering with the Moon and the stars. Most men have strayed from the path shown us by the Great Spirit. For Massau'u alone is great enough to portray the way back to Him.

It is said by the Great Spirit that if a gourd of ashes is dropped upon the Earth, that many men will die and that the end of this way of life is near at hand. We interpret this as the dropping of atomic bombs on Hiroshima and Nagasaki. We do not want to see this happen to any place or any nation again, but instead we should turn all this energy for peaceful uses, not for war.

We, the religious leaders and rightful spokesmen for the Hopi Independent Nation, have been instructed by the Great Spirit to express the invitation to the President of the United States and all spiritual leaders everywhere to meet with us and discuss the welfare of mankind so that Peace, Unity, and Brotherhood will become part of all men everywhere.

Sincerely,

(signed) Thomas Banyacya, for
Hopi Traditional Village Leaders:
Mrs. Mina Lansa, Oraibi
Claude Kawangyawma, Shungopavy
Starlie Lomayaktewa, Mushongnovi
Dan Katchongva, Hotevilla

4. Barry Commoner Discusses the Problems of Nuclear Energy, 1971

I learned about the environment from the United States Atomic Energy Commission in 1953. Until then, like most people, I had taken the air, water, soil, and our natural surroundings more or less for granted. Although I was a scientist working on the fundamental properties of living things, I had received hardly any training in the special branch of biology that deals with environmental relations—ecology. However, like most of the scientists who had worked for the U.S. war program during World War II, I was overwhelmingly concerned with the new, enormously destructive force of nuclear energy born during the war.

In 1946 the Atomic Energy Commission (AEC) was created, to take charge of a massive U.S. program to develop the military, scientific, and industrial potential of atomic and nuclear energy. By 1951 the United States had exploded sixteen test bombs and the Soviet Union, thirteen, and the following year Great Britain joined in with its first test.

These explosions took place in remote, uninhabited areas of the world and their results were blanketed in military secrecy. The AEC normally issued only a terse

From Barry Commoner, "Nuclear Fire," in *The Closing Circle: Nature, Man, and Technology.* New York: Alfred A. Knopf, 1971, pp. 49–53, 56–58, 60–61, 65. Copyright © 1971 by Barry Commoner. Used by permission of Alfred A. Knopf, a division of Random House, Inc.

announcement that a test had taken place, that a bomb's radiation had been confined to a local area, and in any case was "harmless" to the public. Public discussion of the nuclear arms race was muzzled by Cold War hysteria and McCarthyism. But nature broke through these barriers.

On April 26, 1953, the city of Troy, New York, was drenched with a sudden cloudburst. As the rain fell, physicists in nearby university laboratories who were experimenting with radioactivity noticed a sudden surge in their "background" radiation counts. They soon discovered that the rain was highly radioactive and surmised that radioactive debris—fallout—from nuclear tests in Nevada had been carried by winds across the country and brought to earth by the heavy rain. Some of the physicists warned their wives to bring the children inside; but they made no public report, for that would violate the secrecy rules. However, scientists have a strong tendency to communicate among themselves, and soon physicists in laboratories throughout the United States were privately testing the radioactivity in rainfall and in dust wiped off their cars. It was everywhere: air, rain, soil, food, and water were contaminated by the radioactivity from nuclear explosions. Despite official secrecy, atomic energy had made its environmental debut.

All atomic radiation is destructive to living things, and many biologists regarded fallout as a potential hazard to everything alive. But, as the AEC was quick to point out, the fallout radiation reaching a person from the air, dust, or soil was low—not much higher than the intensity of radiation naturally emanated in the external environment from radium in rocks and by cosmic rays from outer space. And much of it was incapable of penetrating very deeply into the body. The hazard of such radiation, from outside the body, was slight—or so it seemed.

Then a new fallout term turned up in private conversations among scientists—strontium 90. My own experience is probably typical of most nonphysicists who had no professional interest in environmental radioactivity. I recall several cryptic remarks by physicist friends that radioactive strontium—strontium 90—had been detected in fallout. More meaningful was the worried look that accompanied the information; for some reason, which was never stated, strontium 90 appeared to be a particularly dangerous form of radioactivity.

As it happens, strontium, a natural, harmless element, and its radioactive isotope, strontium 90, both move through the environment in concert with calcium, a chemically similar element. And calcium is avidly withdrawn from the soil by plants, becoming incorporated into food and then taken up in the human body. Once fallout appeared on the earth, inevitably strontium 90 would accompany calcium as it moved through the food chain, ultimately becoming concentrated, along with calcium, in vegetables, in milk, in the bones of people.

Radiation from strontium 90 cannot penetrate through more than a small fraction of an inch of living tissue. However, once it is incorporated into the body, the isotope becomes closely packed around the living cells of the bone. These cells then lie within easy reach of strontium 90 radiation, and the risk to them—for example, from cancer—becomes enormously more severe than the risk from the same amount of strontium 90 outside the body. Suddenly, many of us in the scientific community began to worry about the fallout, and by the end of 1953 this concern broke through the screen of secrecy, and the fallout problem became public. Then a serious accident during an AEC test in the Pacific Ocean in March 1954 helped to dramatize the fallout problem—the unexpected exposure to fallout of the crew of the Japanese fishing boat *The Lucky Dragon*. A number of sailors suffered serious radiation sickness; several later died of it. . . .

For many of us the meaning of the environment and its importance to human life was suddenly brought to light. With elaborate skill and enormous resources, the AEC—and its Soviet and British counterparts—had accomplished what they thought to be a specific, technological feat for the single purpose of producing huge, destructive explosions. No one had *intended* to poison the earth with radioactivity or to threaten the health of human beings. But now, for the first time in the history of man, children grew up with strontium 90 built into their bones and iodine 131 embedded in their thyroid glands.

What linked the secret, supposedly isolated, nuclear explosions to the children was the environment. Winds carried fallout debris from the test site across the face of the globe; rain and snow brought it to earth; the growth of grass and food crops drew it from the soil; foods carried fallout radioactivity into children's bodies; natural biological processes in their bones and glands intensely concentrated the radioactive elements and amplified the risk to the children's health. Each nuclear explosion thrust radioactivity into the environment, the elaborate communication network in which every living thing is [enmeshed]. Unwittingly, the military technicians had tied their bombs into the network, with results that no one wanted—or could have predicted.

The nuclear tests revealed how little we knew about the environmental network. When the test program began, it was assumed that fallout driven into the stratosphere by the force of a nuclear explosion would remain there for years, allowing time for much of the initial radioactivity to decay harmlessly. Only later was it learned that there are currents in the stratosphere that carry fallout to the earth in a matter of months and which, rather than allowing it to spread evenly over the globe, dump most of it in the North Temperate Zone. . . .

In 1963, much to the surprise of political observers, the United States Senate overwhelmingly confirmed the United States-USSR Limited Nuclear Test Ban Treaty ending the testing of nuclear weapons in the atmosphere by the two great nuclear powers. This unexpected event was a tribute to the political effectiveness of the scientists' campaign to inform the public about fallout.

The Nuclear Test Ban Treaty should be regarded, I believe, as the first victorious battle in the campaign to save the environment—and its human inhabitants—from the blind assaults of modern technology. It was only a small victory, for U.S. and Soviet nuclear tests continue in underground vaults, and China and France, which are not bound by the Treaty, continue atmospheric testing. But although the Nuclear Test Ban Treaty has failed to stop the nuclear arms race, it has had two important results. The first is that it has saved lives.

The human cost of fallout is not exactly known. What is known, and widely acknowledged, is that a number of serious hazards to human health—cancer, genetic defects, general life-shortening—are instigated by radiation. . . . Had nuclear testing continued until 1970 at the 1962 rate, the fallout radiation burden borne by human beings would now be much greater than it is—in the case of strontium 90, about eight to ten times greater.

The second important result of the treaty is that it established that nuclear weaponry is a *scientific* failure. We now know that nuclear weapons are, in fact, incapable of defending the nation: regardless of the outcome of a nuclear war between the two major powers, neither society would survive the holocaust. In this sense, the nuclear bomb is a useless weapon—a fact of which the government was apparently unaware when the decision to "go nuclear" was made sometime after 1945. . . .

The first full-scale nuclear power plant in the United States went into operation in 1957. By 1965 there were eleven operating plants. In 1970 fourteen plants were in operation, and seventy-eight more were under construction or in preparation. . . .

Unlike fossil-fuel power plants, nuclear power plants do not produce chemical pollutants such as sulfur dioxide or dust. However they do produce radioactive pollutants. The AEC claims that this is no cause for public concern because nuclear plants release radioactive materials into the environment in amounts which are well below AEC safety standards. Nevertheless, in recent years public concern has been sufficiently intense to delay, and in some cases block, the construction of several projected power plants. In the words of the then chairman of the AEC, Dr. Glenn T. Seaborg, "The public is up-tight about the environment." . . .

. . . Our experience with nuclear power tells us that modern technology has achieved a scale and intensity that begin to match that of the global system in which we live. It reminds us that we cannot wield this power without deeply intruding on the delicate environmental fabric that supports us. It warns us that our capability to intrude on the environment far outstrips our knowledge of the consequences. It tells us that every environmental incursion, whatever its benefits, has a cost—which, from the still silent testimony of the world's nuclear weapons, may be survival.

5. A Federal Director Explains Environmental Risk, 1983

The Environmental Protection Agency [EPA] is an instrument of public policy, whose mission is to protect the public health and the environment in the manner laid down by its statutes. That manner is to set standards and enforce them, and our enforcement powers are strong and pervasive. But the standards we set, whether technology- or health-related, must have a sound scientific base.

Science and the law are thus partners at EPA, but uneasy partners. The main reason for the uneasiness lies, I think, in the conflict between the way science really works and the public's thirst for certitude that is written into EPA's laws. Science thrives on uncertainty. The best young scientists flock into fields where great questions have been asked but nothing is known. The greatest triumph of a scientist is the crucial experiment that shatters the certainties of the past and opens up rich new pastures of ignorance.

But EPA's laws often assume, indeed demand, a certainty of protection greater than science can provide with the current state of knowledge. The laws do no more than reflect what the public believes and what it often hears from people with scientific credentials on the 6 o'clock news. The public thinks we know what all the bad pollutants are, precisely what adverse health or environmental effects they cause,

Excerpts from William D. Ruckelshaus, "Science, Risk, and Public Policy," *Science* 221 (September 9, 1983), pp. 1026–1028. Based on a speech given at the National Academy of Sciences on June 22, 1983.

how to measure them exactly and control them absolutely. Of course, the public and sometimes the law are wrong, but not all wrong. We do know a great deal about some pollutants and we have controlled them effectively by using the tools of the Clean Air Act and the Clean Water Act. These are the pollutants for which the scientific community can set safe levels and margins of safety for sensitive populations. If this were the case for all pollutants, we could breathe more easily (in both senses of the phrase); but it is not so.

More than 10 years ago, EPA had the Clean Air Act, the Clean Water Act, a solid waste law, a pesticide law, and laws to control radiation and noise. Yet to come were the myriad of laws to control toxic substances from their manufacture to their disposal—but that they would be passed was obvious even then.

When I departed EPA a decade ago, the struggle over whether the federal government was to have a major role in protecting our health, safety, and environment was ended. The American people had spoken. The laws had been passed; the regulations were being written. The only remaining question was whether the statutory framework we had created made sense or whether, over time, we would adjust it.

Ten years ago I thought I knew the answer to that question as well. I believed it would become apparent to all that we could virtually eliminate the risks we call pollution if we wanted to spend enough money. When it also became apparent that enough money for all the pollutants was a lot of money, I came to believe that we would begin examining the risks very carefully and structure a system that would force us to balance our desire to eliminate pollution against the costs of its control. This would entail some adjustment of the laws, but not all that much, and it would happen by about 1976. I was wrong.

This time around as administrator of EPA, I am determined to improve our country's ability to cope with the risk of pollutants over where I left it 10 years ago. It will not be easy, because we must now deal with a class of pollutants for which it is difficult, if not impossible, to establish a safe level. These pollutants interfere with genetic processes and are associated with the diseases we fear most: cancer and reproductive disorders, including birth defects. The scientific consensus is that any exposure, however small, to a genetically active substance embodies some risk of an effect. Since these substances are widespread in the environment, and since we can detect them down to very low levels, we must assume that life now takes place in a minefield of risks from hundreds, perhaps thousands, of substances. We can no longer tell the public that they have an adequate margin of safety. . . .

We . . . need to strengthen our risk assessment capabilities. We need more research on the health effects of the substances we regulate. I intend to do everything in my power to make clear the importance of this scientific analysis at EPA. Given the necessity of acting in the face of enormous scientific uncertainties, it is more important than ever that our scientific analysis be rigorous and the quality of our data be high. We must take great pains not to mislead people about the risks to their health. We can help to avoid confusion by ensuring both the quality of our science and the clarity of our language in explaining hazards. . . .

In the future, this being an imperfect world, the rigor and thoroughness of our risk analyses will undoubtedly be affected by many factors, including the toxicity of the substances examined, the populations exposed, the pressure of the regulatory timetable, and the resources available. Despite these often conflicting pressures, risk assessment at EPA must be based only on scientific evidence and scientific consensus. Nothing will erode public confidence faster than the suspicion that policy considerations have been allowed to influence the assessment of risk.

Although there is an objective way to assess risk, there is, of course, no purely objective way to manage it, nor can we ignore the subjective perception of risk in the ultimate management of a particular substance. To do so would be to place too much credence in our objective data and ignore the possibility that occasionally one's intuition is right. No amount of data is a substitute for judgment. . . .

To effectively manage the risk, we must seek new ways to involve the public in the decision-making process. Whether we believe in participatory democracy or not, it is a part of our social regulatory fabric. Rather than praise or lament it, we should seek more imaginative ways to involve the various segments of the public affected by the substance at issue. They need to become involved early, and they need to be informed if their participation is to be meaningful. We will be searching for ways to make our participatory process work better.

For this to happen, scientists must be willing to take a larger role in explaining the risks to the public—including the uncertainties inherent in any risk assessment. Shouldering this burden is the responsibility of all scientists, not just those with a particular policy end in mind. In fact, all scientists should make clear when they are speaking as scientists, ex cathedra, and when they are recommending policy they believe should flow from scientific information. What we need to hear more of from scientists is science. I am going to try to provide avenues at EPA for scientists to become more involved in the public dialog in which scientific problems are described. . . .

In sum, my goal is a government-wide process for assessing and managing environmental risks. Achieving this will take cooperation and goodwill within EPA, among Executive Branch agencies, and between Congress and the Administration, a state of affairs that may partake of the miraculous. Still, it is worth trying, and the effort is worth the wholehearted support of the scientific community. I believe such an effort touches on the maintenance of our current society, in which a democratic polity is grounded in a high-technology industrial civilization. Without a much more successful way of handling the risks associated with the creations of science, I fear we will have set up for ourselves a grim and unnecessary choice between the fruits of advanced technology and the blessings of democracy.

6. A Business Leader Discusses Industry's Environmental Responsibilities, 1987

[Let us] take an objective look at the history of environmental issues . . . and take stock of our situation today.

Look back 20 years, and I think it can be stated as a fact that our society *needed* environmental regulation. I don't think the roof will fall in if we acknowledge that.

Increased pollution of all types was a direct by-product of the population boom and the great surge in U.S. industrial activity that followed World War II.

Excerpts from G. M. Keller, "Industry and the Environment," *Vital Speeches of the Day*, No. 9, December 15, 1987, pp. 78–80. Reprinted by permission of City News Inc.

Communities and ecosystems need protection from that pollution . . . and it's unlikely that industry would have cleaned up without some legal imperative to do so.

That's no slur on the ethics of industry. The company that makes such expenditures unilaterally is courting financial disaster. When controls are mandatory, all players have more or less the same handicap.

The point is that industry must accept responsibility for the problems that can be legitimately laid at our doorstep . . . past or present . . . and we must acknowledge that, in a general sense, regulation to protect the environment has been necessary.

By the same token, industry deserves . . . and seldom receives . . . a large share of the credit for developing the technology to reduce wastes and control pollution.

As a nation, we have made tremendous progress in cleaning up the environment . . . and that, too, should be acknowledged. Pollution of all types has been significantly reduced . . . even as industrial activity has greatly increased.

There's an excellent example. . . . We read a lot about the problems of the San Francisco Bay; but the fact is that despite tremendous growth in population . . . as well as . . . the potential sources of pollution . . . the Bay today is far cleaner than it was in the 1960s.

Industry's record is particularly impressive. The Bay Area Regional Water Quality Control Board, in testimony before Congress, compared industrial discharges of 1960 to those of 1985. They found that the total volume of industrial wastes had been cut by about 75 percent in that period . . . and major types of conventional pollution reduced by more than 90 percent.

We need to get this kind of information across to the public . . . not as a way of saying "We've done enough" . . . "Everything is solved." But just as a way of illustrating that the situation is *not* out of hand . . . we *are* making progress . . . and we will *continue* to find solutions.

We also need to make the point that our search for solutions represents a true commitment . . . not merely an obligation. Our personal values are not really different from those of the general public. As individuals, we too want a safe and wholesome environment. . . .

Administrators of the Environmental Protection Agency have been trying to sell the notion of scientific risk assessment for the last four or five years now. Unfortunately, it's been a very tough sell.

The basic problem seems to be that a significant part of the general public seems to feel that all chemicals are risky . . . and no risks are acceptable.

It's certainly true that our ability to detect infinitesimal quantities of many substances has run far ahead of our knowledge of what those measurements really *mean*.

The popular assumption . . . and too often one played up for political purposes . . . is that *any* detectable impurities have to be harmful . . . that if we can measure it, we ought to get rid of it.

Ironically, one of the truths about our environment . . . emerging from the work of scientists like Dr. Bruce Ames at [The University of California] . . . is that all sorts of fearsome substances occur in nature. We human beings have been living with them throughout our evolution. In large quantities, they can hurt us . . . but in smaller concentrations, they are a part of nature itself . . . and we tolerate many of them without apparent harm.

The point is not that we can afford to be complacent . . . or ignore toxics in our environment. It's simply that we should base our environmental policies on *facts*.

Is compound x at exposure level y for duration z harmful or not? That's a scientific question. Let science try to answer it . . . and let our elected officials *listen* to the answer.

In essence, that's all that risk assessment means. We in industry have to help our neighbors understand that this is the best way . . . maybe the only way . . . of finding out what problems we need to address.

As a step in that direction, I'd like to announce today that Chevron is pledging $1 million over the next several years to support environmental risk assessment research at top universities around the nation.

Our objective is to help stimulate programs that will draw talented people into this field, support them in developing and improving the methodologies for this emerging discipline and . . . ultimately . . . to build a base of scientific knowledge that will help *all* of us better understand the true risks involved in toxics.

We want our contribution to have a direct and *practical* benefit for the public. We hope that the information base will be used by industry, environmental groups and government officials alike in choosing the best route to environmental protection.

7. Paul and Anne Ehrlich Warn of a Population Explosion, 1990

In 1968, *The Population Bomb* warned of impending disaster if the population explosion was not brought under control. Then the fuse was burning; now the population bomb has detonated. Since 1968, at least 200 million people—mostly children—have perished needlessly of hunger and hunger-related diseases, despite "crash programs to 'stretch' the carrying capacity of Earth by increasing food production." The population problem is no longer primarily a threat for the future as it was when the *Bomb* was written and there were only 3.5 billion human beings.

The size of the human population is now 5.3 billion, and still climbing. In the six seconds it takes you to read this sentence, eighteen more people will be added. Each hour there are 11,000 more mouths to feed; each year, more than 95 million. Yet the world has hundreds of billions *fewer* tons of topsoil and hundreds of trillions *fewer* gallons of groundwater with which to grow food crops than it had in 1968.

In 1988, for the first time at least since World War II, the United States consumed more grain than it grew. About a third of the country's grain crop was lost to a severe drought—roughly the fraction that is normally exported. Over a hundred nations depend on food imported from North America, and only the presence of large carryover stocks prevented a serious food crisis.

It is not clear how easy it will be to restore those stocks. World grain production peaked in 1986 and then—for the first time in forty years—dropped for two consecutive years. In just those two years, the world population rose by the equivalent of the combined citizenry of the United Kingdom, France, and West Germany.

Global food production per person peaked earlier, in 1984, and has slid downward since then. In Africa south of the Sahara, production per capita has been declining for more than twenty years and in Latin America since 1981. And the prospects for unfavorable weather for agriculture may be rising as burgeoning populations add more and more "greenhouse" gases to the atmosphere. . . .

In the early 1930s, when we were born, the world population was just 2 billion; now it is more than two and a half times as large and still growing rapidly. The population of the United States is increasing much more slowly than the world average, but it has more than doubled in only six decades—from 120 million in 1928 to 250 million in 1990. Such a huge population expansion within two or three generations can by itself account for a great many changes in the social and economic institutions of a society. It also is very frightening to those of us who spend our lives trying to keep track of the implications of the population explosion. . . .

Consider the *very* slow-motion origins of our predicament. It seems reasonable to define humanity as having first appeared some four million years ago in the form of australopithecines, small-brained upright creatures like "Lucy." Of course, we don't know the size of this first human population, but it's likely that there were never more than 125,000 australopithecines at any given time.

Our own species, *Homo sapiens,* evolved a few hundred thousand years ago. Some ten thousand years ago, when agriculture was invented, probably no more than five million people inhabited Earth—fewer than now live in the San Francisco Bay Area. Even at the time of Christ, two thousand years ago, the entire human population was roughly the size of the population of the United States today; by 1650 there were only 500 million people, and in 1850 only a little over a billion. Since there are now well past 5 billion people, the vast majority of the population explosion has taken place in less than a tenth of one percent of the history of *Homo sapiens.* . . .

The time it takes a population to double in size is a dramatic way to picture rates of population growth, one that most of us can understand more readily than percentage growth rates. Human populations have often grown in a pattern described as "exponential." Exponential growth occurs in bank accounts when interest is left to accumulate and itself earns interest. Exponential growth occurs in populations because children, the analogue of interest, remain in the population and themselves have children.

A key feature of exponential growth is that it often seems to start slowly and finish fast. A classic example used to illustrate this is the pond weed that doubles each day the amount of pond surface covered and is projected to cover the entire pond in thirty days. The question is, how much of the pond will be covered in twenty-nine days? The answer, of course, is that just half of the pond will be covered in twenty-nine days. The weed will then double once more and cover the entire pond the next day. As this example indicates, exponential growth contains the potential for big surprises.

The limits to human population growth are more difficult to perceive than those restricting the pond weed's growth. Nonetheless, like the pond weed, human populations grow in a pattern that is essentially exponential, so we must be alert to the treacherous properties of that sort of growth. The key point to remember is that *a long history of exponential growth in no way implies a long future of exponential growth.* What begins in slow motion may eventually overwhelm us in a flash.

The last decade or two has seen a slight slackening in the human population growth rate—a slackening that has been prematurely heralded as an "end to the population explosion." The slowdown has been only from a peak annual growth rate of perhaps 2.1 percent in the early 1960s to about 1.8 percent in 1990. To put this change in perspective, the population's doubling time has been extended from thirty-three years to thirty-nine. Indeed, the world population *did* double in the thirty-seven years from 1950 to 1987. But even if birthrates continue to fall, the world population will continue to expand (assuming that death rates don't rise), although at a slowly slackening rate, for about another century. Demographers think that growth will not end before the population has reached 10 billion or more.

So, even though birthrates have declined somewhat, *Homo sapiens* is a long way from ending its population explosion or avoiding its consequences. In fact, the biggest jump, from 5 to 10 billion in well under a century, is still ahead. But this does not mean that growth couldn't be ended sooner, with a much smaller population size, if we—all of the world's nations—made up our minds to do it. The trouble is, many of the world's leaders and perhaps most of the world's people still don't believe that there are compelling reasons to do so. They are even less aware that if humanity fails to act, *nature may end the population explosion for us*—in very unpleasant ways—well before 10 billion is reached.

Those unpleasant ways are beginning to be perceptible. Humanity in the 1990s will be confronted by more and more intransigent environmental problems, global problems dwarfing those that worried us in the late 1960s. Perhaps the most serious is that of global warming, a problem caused in large part by population growth and overpopulation. It is not clear whether the severe drought in North America, the Soviet Union, and China in 1988 was the result of the slowly rising surface temperature of Earth, but it is precisely the kind of event that climatological models predict as more and more likely with continued global warming. In addition to more frequent and more severe crop failures, projected consequences of the warming include coastal flooding, desertification, the creation of as many as 300 million environmental refugees, alteration of patterns of disease, water shortages, general stress on natural ecosystems, and synergistic interactions among all these factors.

Continued population growth and the drive for development in already badly overpopulated poor nations will make it *exceedingly* difficult to slow the greenhouse warming—and impossible to stop or reverse it—in this generation at least. And, even if the warming should miraculously not occur, contrary to accepted projections, human numbers are on a collision course with massive famines anyway. . . .

Global warming, acid rain, depletion of the ozone layer, vulnerability to epidemics, and exhaustion of soils and groundwater are all, as we shall see, related to population size. They are also clear and present dangers to the persistence of civilization. Crop failures due to global warming alone might result in the premature deaths of a billion or more people in the next few decades, and the AIDS epidemic could slaughter hundreds of millions. Together these would constitute a harsh "population control" program provided by nature in the face of humanity's refusal to put into place a gentler program of its own.

We shouldn't delude ourselves: the population explosion will come to an end before very long. The only remaining question is whether it will be halted through the humane method of birth cont[r]ol, or by nature wiping out the surplus. We realize that religious and cultural opposition to birth control exists throughout the world; but we believe that people simply don't understand the choice that such opposition implies. Today, anyone opposing birth control is unknowingly voting to have the human population size controlled by a massive increase in early deaths.

Of course, the environmental crisis isn't caused just by expanding human numbers. Burgeoning consumption among the rich and increasing dependence on ecologically unsound technologies to supply that consumption also play major parts. This allows some environmentalists to dodge the population issue by emphasizing the problem of malign technologies. And social commentators can avoid commenting on the problem of too many people by focusing on the serious maldistribution of affluence. . . .

America and other rich nations have a clear choice today. They can continue to ignore the population problem and their own massive contributions to it. Then they will be trapped in a downward spiral that may well lead to the end of civilization in a few decades. More frequent droughts, more damaged crops and famines, more dying forests, more smog, more international conflicts, more epidemics, more gridlock, more drugs, more crime, more sewage swimming, and other extreme unpleasantness will mark our course. It is a route already traveled by too many of our less fortunate fellow human beings.

Or we can change our collective minds and take the measures necessary to lower global birthrates dramatically. People can learn to treat growth as the cancer-like disease it is and move toward a sustainable society. The rich can make helping the poor an urgent goal, instead of seeking more wealth and useless military advantage over one another. Then humanity might have a chance to manage all those other seemingly intractable problems. It is a challenging prospect, but at least it will give our species a shot at creating a decent future for itself. More immediately and concretely, taking action now will give our children and their children the possibility of decent lives.

ψ *E S S A Y S*

The essays in this chapter look at key events in U.S. environmental history from the perspectives of water, energy, and environmental regulation in the context of growing populations and consumer demand for resources. In the first essay, Charles Wilkinson of the University of Colorado at Boulder discusses the ways in which water has been harnessed in the American West, the environmental impacts of big dams, and the problems of water regulation for Indian reservations. The second essay, by David E. Nye of Odense University in Denmark, discusses the history of different energy systems, from human and animal muscle to water, steam, and fossil fuels, and suggests that in the future energy choices based on solar, wind, and conservation will become increasingly important. The third essay, by Edmund P. Russell III of the University of Virginia, looks at the history of the U.S. Environmental Protection Agency (EPA) and how it addresses risks to both human health and environmental quality. How Americans choose to develop their water and energy sources and the regulations they put in place to preserve environmental quality for growing numbers of people will have profound effects on biotic life and human health in the future.

Water and the Environment

CHARLES WILKINSON

Hoover Dam was impressive by more than western standards. It was world-class, one of the greatest construction ventures ever undertaken. At 726 feet—the height of a sixty-story office building—Hoover Dam was the world's highest dam. It used 66 million tons of concrete. The reservoir behind the dam stored 28 million acre-feet of water, twice the annual flow of the Colorado River.

Today, still larger dams—Grand Coulee on the Columbia, the Aswan in Egypt, and a few others—have been built, relying in good measure on the engineering know-how and confidence generated by Hoover. Still, given that, given even the knowl-edge that 110 workers died from falls, explosions, landslides, and heat prostration, the modern visitor will feel a sense of awe at Hoover's long, graceful arch, the white cement playing off against the sheer black-rock canyon walls and restraining the wild Colorado River. This is a place where the human race met nature square on and humans prevailed.

Hoover Dam was named after the engineer-president whose administration began the project. To whom should the 108-mile-long reservoir be dedicated? The answer was easy: Elwood Mead, commissioner of reclamation from 1924 through 1936. But Lake Mead symbolized a very different spirit from that of the idealistic young man who tried to see that Wyoming water law would be permeated with the public interest, who saw the future of the West as symbiotic with the tillers of the soil, who railed against "that pulpy individuality called a corporation" that would subvert the agrarian ideal.

No, the Elwood Mead who ran the Bureau of Reclamation during these critical years might mouth the old devotion to the family farm—running the intensity and fer-vor of the original reclamation ideal up the flagpole remained a key ingredient in the recipe for a still bigger bureau budget—but this Elwood Mead was subservient to the agency's new constituency, big agriculture, big cities (read: big real estate devel-opers), and big industry. Perhaps Elwood Mead's heart still lay with the family farm, but in these waning days of his career, Mead became first and foremost a builder. As Interior Secretary Harold Ickes wrote in one memorandum, "Commissioner Mead, of course, is always in favor of any new reclamation project." This attitude meshed well with the plans of the Franklin Roosevelt administration, determined to spend its way out of the depression. Mead died in office in 1934—FDR eulogized him as "a builder with vision"—but he was succeeded by other zealous and able builders who served as reclamation commissioners, most notably Michael Straus, commissioner from 1945 until 1953, and Floyd Dominy, who held the office from 1959 through 1969.

The dam-building movement from the 1920s through the 1970s remade the face of the West. It was led by the Bureau of Reclamation but was also fueled by the Army Corps of Engineers, the Bonneville Power Administration, cities and towns, the state engineer's offices, and various irrigation districts and other special water districts. Private irrigators, energy companies, and developers of all sorts either participated

From Charles F. Wilkinson, *Crossing the Next Meridian: Land, Water, and the Future of the West*. Wash-ington, D.C.: Island Press, 1992, pp. 255–268, 286. Reprinted by permission of Island Press.

in the publicly funded efforts or went their own ways. The era bred hundreds of major projects, tens of thousands of smaller ones. Dams, reservoirs, and diversions reworked virtually every river in the region.

. . . [T]he Columbia River, all the way from Bonneville Dam near Portland, Oregon, to the Canadian border, is almost all reservoir—just a few short stretches of free-flowing river remain. On the Colorado River, Hoover Dam set off a rush to develop that reached throughout the basin. The other gargantuan structure, every bit the equal of Hoover, is Glen Canyon Dam. Seven hundred and ten feet tall, the dam created the 27-million-acre-foot Lake Powell, at 186 miles the longest reservoir in the world. Lakes Mead and Powell together hold almost exactly four years' flow of the Colorado River. Dozens of other major dams, lesser than the two Goliaths but giants nonetheless, plug up the Colorado and its tributaries. Massive canal and pipeline systems transport water hundreds of miles away from the river—the Colorado River Aqueduct to the Los Angeles–San Diego area, the $4 billion Central Arizona Project to Phoenix and Tucson, the San Juan–Chama Project to Albuquerque, and no fewer than nine major tunnels bored under the Continental Divide to export water from Colorado's Western Slope to the East Slope cities and suburbs of Denver and Colorado Springs and irrigation projects on the South Platte and Arkansas rivers. Every other western river basin—the upper Missouri, draining large parts of Montana, Wyoming, Colorado, and the Dakotas; the Sacramento–San Joaquin system of California; the Klamath of California and Oregon; the Rio Grande of Colorado, New Mexico, and Texas; and many smaller ones—saw project after project, diversion after diversion.

From the 1920s through the 1960s, reservoir capacity in the West mushroomed, expanding at the rate of 80 percent per decade. The dams of the Colorado River watershed hold back 72 million acre-feet of water in storage—nearly six times the annual flow of the river. Missouri River impoundments dam up 85 million acre-feet. In the Pacific Northwest, reservoirs capture 55 million acre-feet; in California, the figure is 39 million acre-feet. On the much smaller Rio Grande, 7.8 million acre-feet of water are held each year, more than twice the annual runoff of the river. The Bureau of Reclamation alone has built 355 storage reservoirs and 16,000 miles of canals, 1500 miles of pipelines, and 278 miles of tunnels. Apparently no one has tried to count the total number of miles (though they surely exceed 100,000) of canals that divert the flows of western rivers and deliver water to irrigators and other water users. Westwide, more than a million artificial reservoirs, lakes, and ponds store 294 million acre-feet. This is the equivalent of twenty-two Colorado Rivers backed up behind dams and over former canyons. It is enough to put Montana, Wyoming, Colorado, and New Mexico—an entire tier of states, from Canada to Mexico—under a foot of water.

The Costs of the Harvest

A great deal of good has come from this Herculean engineering effort. The Missouri, for example, was a killer river in its natural state, carrying whole trees down from the Rockies and blasting out of its banks in Montana, the Dakotas, Nebraska, and Iowa. Dams on that river and others have saved human lives and uncountable hundreds of millions of dollars in property damage. Almost 50 million acres of farmland are in irrigation. Cities and towns have been allowed to rise up and grow through domestic water supplies and hydroelectric, fossil fuel, and nuclear power facilities, which all depend on substantial water supplies. Westerners achieved the multibillion-dollar, job-producing building boom they so avidly sought. Some of the reservoirs afford fishing, boating, and other flat-water recreation opportunities. Some dams, while inundating miles of trout streams, actually improve the fishing on rivers below the dams by cutting the high runoffs in the early spring and releasing flows of cool water during the dog days of July and August. . . .

One pervasive problem is the waste of water. The combination of overbuilt water supplies, heavy subsidies, and a hands-off attitude toward individual water use has created a situation in which the arid American West has some of the worst water conservation practices in the world. Per capita water consumption in the West is three times greater than in the eastern states. Much of this is accounted for by irrigation, but even in the cities, westerners use 45 percent more water than their eastern counterparts. . . .

. . . In western cities, the high water use is attributable mainly to lush lawns and golf courses (both of which give rise to large evaporative losses in the arid climate when water is overapplied) and to excessive use inside homes and businesses. The greatest losses of all, however, take place in irrigation, due to inefficiencies in transportation from stream or reservoir to the fields and on-field application in agriculture.

The Truckee-Carson Irrigation District (or Newlands Project), which receives water bound for Pyramid Lake, and the Middle Rio Grande Conservancy District, which uses water from the other side of the Continental Divide, are typical of many irrigation operations across the West. The TCID and the MRGCD are old-style operations that work mostly on unlined, earthen irrigation canals and ditches. These leaky earthen conveyance systems allow extensive carriage loss through seepage. . . .

By and large, the states allow the irrigators—who . . . use 80 percent to 90 percent of all water in every western state—to continue their traditional practices. In a few cases, perhaps most notably in the Central Valley of California and the fields in the Phoenix-Tucson area, irrigators have begun to adopt conservation measures such as leveling fields by laser systems and installing cement-lined canals; drip and trickle irrigation, based on the use of corrugated pipes run down furrows between rows of crops; and sprinkler systems, which, due to precise application, use much less water than does flood irrigation. . . .

There are disagreements over the exact definition of water waste. Farmers cannot be expected to find a way for crops to consume every drop of water—to inject water into the plants by hypodermic needle. Still, by any standard, western irrigation is extraordinarily inefficient. Westwide, only 41 percent of diverted water is consumed by crops, while 46 percent returns to the streams as return flows and 13 percent is lost to the system through evaporation . . . or seepage into impervious underground formations. . . .

When excess water is diverted from a stream, the return flow will usually cause stream temperatures to rise, producing negative effects on fish life. Further, return flows are laden both with natural salts and soils and, often, with agricultural chemicals. Doris Ostrander Dawdy has correctly written: "To read the history of irrigation is to read the story of salt." The most severe problems are in the Colorado River basin, where the combination of return flows and out-of-basin diversions, which concentrate salts in the remaining flows, has begun to force farmland out of production. The salty water simply kills off the crops. In order to meet the United States's obligation to deliver water to Mexico (presumably usable water, although federal officials debated the point for decades), the federal government has been required to build one of the world's largest desalinization facilities at Yuma, on the lower Colorado River. . . .

Soil loss is gradual, and for most citizens, the damage is hard to detect. Yet soil is eroding at the rate of 4 billion tons per year. In-stream costs are already extravagant, and drops in agricultural production due to elimination of the soil base are expected in the first or second decade of the twenty-first century. [Scientist and conservationist] Aldo Leopold, saying that "soil is the fundamental resource, and its loss the most serious of all losses," called soil erosion "a leprosy of the land."

Agricultural runoff has caused still other problems, and unlike the slow sapping of the vitality of the land, some are visible, and dramatically so.

During the 1980s, investigations began to turn up new and macabre problems. Selenium, a nonmetallic, sulfuric chemical found in soils, is beneficial to humans in very small quantities and is used in some medications, but heavy concentrations are highly toxic to animals and humans. In the early 1980s, the U.S. Fish and Wildlife Service observed rapidly increasing numbers of deaths and deformities of aquatic birds in Kesterson National Wildlife Refuge in California's Central Valley. The cause was pinned to wastewater with high concentrations of selenium leached from the soils in the Westlands Water District. Federal biologists later determined that selenium poisoning had also been detected in Utah, Wyoming, and Nevada. The Nevada killings . . . occurred at the Stillwater National Wildlife Refuge, which received runoff from the Newlands Project near Pyramid Lake. . . .

Water law in the western states traditionally dealt only with water quantity, not quality. Those who built the system had an intense interest in a supply of water but virtually none in pollution controls. The tacit understanding that controls of any kind were to be avoided kept pollution matters, especially as to mining and agriculture, out of the statute books. When the federal government began to get serious about water pollution with the passage of the Clean Water Act of 1973, irrigators managed to lobby through an exemption from the "nonpoint source" provisions of the act. Thus, the Clean Water Act dealt with point source pollution (from discrete sources, such as industrial pipes) and with most forms of nonpoint sources (diffuse surface runoff, including soil erosion, such as from logging, grazing, and road building or other construction activity). The agribusiness lobby, however, had worked hard, and a conspicuous exception from the 1973 act was runoff from agriculture, the largest source of soil loss.

The 1973 act has been a resounding success for point source pollution: industrial discharges and other such pollution have been sharply reduced. But virtually no progress was made on nonpoint source pollution. The problem of nonpoint source pollution is more difficult to attack because of its diffuse nature and, politically, because farmers, ranchers, and timber companies have been able to stave off any significant alterations in their manner of operation. In 1987, Congress came up with a new nonpoint source program, this time including irrigated agriculture, but the effort mainly involves a handoff to the states, which are required, in general terms, to come up with programs to combat nonpoint source pollution. To date, the state efforts, especially among the western states, have had few teeth. In the West, the controlling idea about water pollution, as about other areas of western water law, is still that irrigators ought to have sway over the rivers. . . .

We also are depleting water resources deep underground. The nation's groundwater aquifers—formations of saturated sand, soil, or porous rock—hold an estimated 180 billion acre-feet of water. This dwarfs the 1 billion acre-feet in all of the nation's rivers and 27 billion acre-feet in all of the freshwater lakes in North America. There is a lot of groundwater, but four qualifications must be considered. First, most of it is too deep to be pumped economically with existing technology. Second, most groundwater aquifers renew themselves to some extent, but they are not renewable resources in the sense that surface waters are; total annual recharge to the aquifers is just 1 billion acre-feet, about one-half of 1 percent. Third, groundwater is disproportionately located in the East; the arid West has less groundwater. Fourth, groundwater use may be limited by contamination. . . .

Unregulated water development also has threatened whole societies. The victims have been land-based societies like the Hispanic town of Rosa and the Jicarilla Apache Tribe, both victims of the San Juan–Chama Project, and the Pyramid Lake Band of Paiutes, whose water was taken by the Truckee-Carson Irrigation Project. Another affected group has been rural communities burdened by metropolitan water projects, a dynamic witnessed with the Owens Valley and Los Angeles and with the upper end of the San Juan watershed and the San Juan–Chama water diverted under the Continental Divide to Albuquerque.

The most extensive impacts have involved American Indians, whose established water rights have been expropriated in every corner of the American West. Tribal water priorities were set by the United States Supreme Court in *Winters v. United States* in 1908. The famous case arose on the Milk River in northern Montana near the Canadian border. Henry Winter (the "s" was added to the end of his name in the official court proceedings because the Bureau of Indian Affairs misspelled his name) and other settlers began diverting Milk River water in the early 1890s. In 1898, the Fort Belknap Tribe, which was downstream of the homesteaders, put in a small irrigation project. In the dry year of 1905, there was not enough water to go around, and a courageous United States Attorney, on behalf of the tribe, sued the homesteaders in federal court to require them to close their headgates and let water flow down to the reservation. Of course, under Montana law, the outcome was clear. Winter and the others had actually diverted water out of the stream before the tribe. First in time, first in right.

But the federal judge in Montana held for the tribe, and so did a unanimous Supreme Court. The reasoning was the same as in *United States v. Winans,* the Indian fishing rights case handed down three years earlier, in 1905. There . . . the Supreme Court reasoned that the tribes possessed sovereignty and real property rights in their aboriginal territory long before any treaties with the United States; at treaty time, they reserved—kept—the right to take salmon and steelhead at their traditional sites in the Pacific Northwest. The right to fish was "not much less necessary . . . than the [air] they breathed."

So, too, with water in *Winters.* The Assiniboine and Gros Ventre tribes of the Fort Belknap Indian Reservation had inhabited the Milk River country for centuries before any contact with white people. As the *Winters* Court put it, "The Indians had command of the lands and the waters—command of all their beneficial use, whether kept for hunting, 'and grazing roving herds of stock,' or turned to agriculture and the arts of civilization." The tribes had ceded land in 1874 and in 1888, when the Fort Belknap Indian Reservation was slashed in half to allow homesteading by non-Indians. But the Court asked rhetorically: "Did they give up all this? Did they reduce the area of their occupation and give up the waters that made it valuable or adequate?" The answer was no; otherwise, the tribes would be left, in the Court's words, with a "barren waste." The tribes at Fort Belknap possessed reserved water rights, under federal law, dating to the establishment of the reservation. These Indian rights were superior to any rights under Montana law or, for that matter, under the law of any state.

Coming from the nation's high court or not, the *Winters* doctrine has provided few benefits to the tribes. *Winters* was common knowledge, but it was ignored, subverted, and circumvented. Water developers detested any rules outside of their tightly controlled state systems. Taking the cue, state officials effectively read *Winters* out of existence through a business-as-usual approach of granting state water rights and allowing diversions that directly conflicted with Indian rights. Federal officials, supposedly bound to act as trustees for Indian rights, were, if anything, worse. They pushed for federal subsidies for non-Indian projects on Indian rivers and ignored potential Indian projects. There were almost no exceptions. . . .

. . . Almost all . . . reform is limited in scope and, even when it applies, usually affects only the granting of new rights. The huge mass of rights granted during the long tenure of pure, monolithic prior appropriation has been little disturbed. A minimum stream flow to protect wildlife with a priority date of 1980 gets the public nothing on those many western streams for which a priority date of 1920, or even 1880, is needed to get wet water. "First in time, first in right." On the other hand, even an ancient priority can be insufficient to guarantee social equity. An Indian water right, like that of the Jicarilla Apaches, with an 1887 priority date, gets a tribe little or nothing when there is a competing project on the same river, built and subsidized for non-Indians under the 1902 Reclamation Act. Even after a long decade of reexamination and some impressive paper laws, most wet water is still allocated to the beneficiaries of the classic prior appropriation doctrine. It is still mostly business as usual.

Energy and the Environment

DAVID E. NYE

The first and most fundamental energy is human muscle. This was the primary motive force of pre-Columbian Native Americans, and it remained extremely important until the middle of the nineteenth century in industry and until 1920 in agriculture. Relying on muscle power alone, Native Americans modified the land only lightly. Europeans transformed it almost beyond recognition, aided by new forms of energy: small mills, sailing ships, and domestic animals. Continual improvements in the productivity of this second energy system created exports and supported the emergence of a small urban society in the eighteenth century.

Industrialization began in earnest with a third energy system, as nineteenth-century entrepreneurs developed large-scale dams and water-driven factories in a

From David E. Nye, *Consuming Power: A Social History of American Energies.* Cambridge, Mass.: MIT Press, 1998, pp. 251–260, 263–264. Reprinted by permission of MIT Press.

form of industrialization unlike that of Great Britain. Thomas Jefferson and other agrarians wished the United States to remain a rural nation, but their contemporaries made political and economic decisions to build factories and canals, which underpinned early geographical expansion and industrial development. However, the Americans dispersed their mills into the countryside, whereas the British built steam-driven factories in their cities. In 1840 most American cities still were primarily centers of trade, with many small workshops that had little more than muscle power at their command. Water power was not very portable, and the factories that relied on it had to be near the source. Manufacturing was usually located in steep upland areas where water power was abundant, rather than along navigable streams. Yet, despite these drawbacks, water power was a clean and renewable source of energy. The water turbine, which doubled the power of the traditional water wheel, remained competitive with steam power for much of the nineteenth century. Indeed, more water power was developed after 1850 than before. However, the mill town faced a structural barrier in its development: the water power available at any one site was limited, and its availability was hardly constant.

The fourth energy system was based on the steam engine. Though Americans were quick to develop the steamboat (from 1810) and the steam railroad (from 1830), steam engines only began to be important in manufacturing during the 1840s. The new power source emerged in part because entrepreneurs developed mines and national transportation systems to deliver coal to market. Steam power facilitated both large-scale production and the expansion of the newly invented American corporation. In established manufacturing centers, such as Lowell, steam did not so much supplant water as supplement it. Full adoption of steam manufacturing came in previously unindustrialized cities away from rushing streams—notably in the midwest, where water-power sites were scarce. Steam was also fundamental to the networked city, whose infrastructure (as in the case of Chicago) required more energy than local water sources could provide. Yet if access to coal made it possible for towns that lacked water power to industrialize, no technological imperative ordained that they must. Indeed, this cultural decision was not paralleled to nearly the same extent in other resource-rich plains regions, such as the interiors of Brazil and Russia. As steam railroads ensured regular year-round transportation and steam manufacturing ensured supplies of goods, the theory of a free market became a practical reality. American corporations throve in the energy-rich environment.

Early in the twentieth century, Americans developed three more power sources—electricity, oil, and natural gas—and achieved higher levels of production and consumption than any society had been capable of before. . . . By the 1920s Americans owned 90 percent of the world's automobiles. The demand for cars, electrified homes, and a wide range of high-energy products and services defined this energy regime, whose importance became obvious during the shortages of the 1970s. The decades since are the mature phase of this system based on oil, natural gas, and electricity.

A sixth energy system is slowly emerging that re-emphasizes renewable power sources. An eclectic bricolage of many technologies and conservation measures, coordinated by computer technologies, its development will be constrained by the myriad choices Americans have already made—choices expressed in factories, roads, cities, and suburbs. In the next 50 years, even if fossil fuel supplies are six or seven times larger than currently proven reserves, the ecological costs of fossil fuels will make renewable sources more attractive and perhaps imperative. . . .

In the twentieth century, Americans' energy choices have affected every area of production and consumption. Most farmers abandoned horses and oxen for tractors, though the Mennonites and the Amish demonstrated that this change was not mandatory. Likewise, most farmers decided to use increasing amounts of fertilizer and pesticides, until recent consumer pressures made organic farming financially attractive. Motorists preferred large cars with poor fuel economy; home buyers preferred ever-larger houses; consumers wanted a plethora of electrical gadgets. The federal government also made important energy choices. Congress chose to build extensive hydroelectric power systems on the Tennessee, Colorado, and Columbia rivers. The government also restricted the importing of inexpensive Middle East oil for several decades. It spent billions of dollars on interstate highways instead of on mass transit. Its agricultural policy at times favored large-scale enterprise more than family farms. It spearheaded the development of atomic energy. And during the 1970s the federal government signally failed to develop a coherent energy policy. As the result of all these decisions, made by the people or their institutions, the United States became the largest consumer of energy in world history. . . .

Cities have continued to lose population to outlying areas, and this has created demand for more highways, tunnels, and bridges for commuters. The result of such choices is a "hypercity" designed less to be lived in than to be moved through. This is the city of images, which began to emerge with the electrified skyline around 1900. The city as spectacle becomes an exhibition space for corporate logos, skyscrapers, illuminated landmarks, signs, brightly lighted store windows, and other displays. Most of these are designed to be seen at a distance while traveling in an automobile. The dense infrastructures of older cities, such as Boston or Baltimore, retain the form of the walking city at the core, which is circled by streetcar suburbs laid down late in the nineteenth century. But the outermost ring of such a city, defined by limited-access roads lined with computer companies, service industries, and malls, has much the same layout as Los Angeles. These multiple centers, accessible only by car, have more office space than the old downtown and provide all the shopping and services the suburbanite might require. Regardless of region, "edge city" is the dynamic margin of development.

Americans' preferences for sprawling growth, automotive movement, and individualistic heating and housing impose conditions on their future energy choices. As the United States prepares to enter a new century, the federal government and the major automobile manufacturers are investing billions of dollars in electric cars, hybrid cars, solar cars, and smart cars that will drive themselves. Such planning makes sense so long as consumers choose to remain spread out. The sheer horizontal expanse of even smaller cities, such as Omaha, Sacramento, and Hartford (which contrasts strikingly with more densely populated European cities, such as Utrecht, Florence, and Mainz) suggests that there is little alternative. Americans have built energy dependence into their zoning and their architecture. As a result, they think it natural to demand the largest per capita share of the world energy supply.

. . . With natural gas in large supply, new plants coming on line have undercut the profitability of older [electric power] facilities. Nuclear plants in particular have become only marginally competitive, leaving some utilities stuck with reactors that have high fixed costs whether they are in use or not. [The] deregulated market will likely eliminate some small companies and sacrifice some forms of generation in favor of others. . . .

A partial displacement of fossil fuels by renewable energies is becoming technically possible, but it may occur first in other nations, notably in Europe. Such a reorientation requires a higher tax on oil than Americans are willing to impose. Nor does it seem likely that Washington is ready to put a small tariff on deregulated electricity prices to subsidize renewables and conservation. Even so, wind turbines now have commercial applications inside the United States. In California three large wind farms generate enough energy to supply a city the size of San Francisco. Utilities once bullish on nuclear power, such as Niagara Mohawk, have begun to install wind parks. The United States will have almost 1000 megawatts of wind power on line by the year 2000. The European Union expects to have 4000 megawatts on line by then, and twice as much by 2005. Putting wind turbines on 0.6 percent of the land of the lower 48 states (primarily in the Great Plains) could satisfy one-fifth of America's current energy needs; however, with the energy market they have constructed, Americans are not likely to do that. Another option is to place wind turbines on platforms offshore, where winds are strong. The prices of such turbines are declining as production achieves economies of scale, and their efficiency can still be improved somewhat through use of new materials. Wind turbines that entered the market in 1994 generated between 300 and 750 kilowatts each, whereas those of the late 1980s averaged 100 kilowatts. The new turbines have lighter blades made of synthetic materials and adjust more to variations in wind speed. . . .

The market in photovoltaic cells is also becoming more competitive. In 1995 the American Solar Energy Society concluded that solar electricity was "now near the threshold of significant contribution to the world energy market." Annual shipments of photovoltaic cells increased every year from 1988 to 1994, from 11.1 to 25.6 megawatts. Most of these cells are still used "off grid" in special applications or in remote locations. As the desire for clean, self-sufficient energy grows stronger, and as the costs of other energy forms increase, solar technologies should become more competitive. Residents of Sacramento have already voted to close a nuclear plant in favor of alternative energies, despite the higher price. . . .

Awareness of energy alternatives has increased since the 1970s. Critics of the high-energy regime have developed institutions, including the Rocky Mountain Institute, the Worldwatch Institute, the Earth Island Institute, and the Global Action and Information Network, which spread alternative ideas and encourage change. . . .

To quantify these problems in a way that makes sense to policy makers, a new form of economics seeks to "take nature into account." Curbing personal energy use is hardly a simple matter of reducing individual power consumption. Every consumer product embodies the energy expended to extract the raw materials, to manufacture the product, and to bring it to market. Every product has a "lifetime," and after its obsolescence come new energy inputs for replacement and recycling. . . .

In a world driven by economics, "the ecological services performed by a standing forest—cleansing the air, moderating weather and climate, preventing erosion and flooding, supporting animal and plant communities—have no meaning." These things . . . are "externalities." Trees have value only if they are cut down, and by this logic forests are razed in the Philippines and in Brazil. Indeed, according to traditional economics even ecological problems have positive value if they create business opportunities. By this logic the *Exxon Valdez* oil spill was a boon to Alaska, creating jobs and adding to the gross national product. Some economists have been attempting to discover the value of externalities by assessing their "contingent valuation."

Typically, this involves surveys in which people are asked how much they would be willing to pay, for example, to preserve forests or wetlands. In practice, some parts of the rain forest have been saved in exchange for the World Wildlife Fund's paying off Third World foreign debts. But what is the value of the preservation of a species, or that of the protection of the ozone layer? Americans long took for granted the continuing existence of breathable air, potable water, sufficient biodiversity, and protection from solar radiation. Abandoning such assumptions in practice will require more political will than the United States demonstrated in the 1970s energy crisis.

The energy choices of the past have brought the United States prosperity, but no more than was achieved by some other countries that use far less. The choices made at the end of the twentieth century will determine whether the US continues to consume more power per capita than any other country. Americans must choose whether to tax gasoline in order to stimulate conversion to alternative energies. They must choose whether deregulation will be used simply to save money in the short term or whether it can be part of a larger strategy of becoming more efficient. They must choose whether to make environmental economics the basis of policy. Individually, they must choose whether they want to drive or to take mass transit, whether they will buy ever-larger houses, how well they will insulate their homes, whether they will invest in low energy light bulbs and appliances, and whether they will adopt solar water heating, heat pumps, and other energy-saving technologies. In designing their cities, Americans can decide whether to encourage cycling, pedestrian traffic, and local shopping. In the workplace, they must decide to what extent computers will be used to reduce commuting. At the polls, they must decide whether to endorse recycling, research on alternative energies, and more fuel-efficient vehicles. In short, they must decide whether they think energy choices matter now, or whether they expect ingenious technologies to solve emerging problems later. They can even choose to believe in technological determinism, which will apparently absolve them from any responsibility to make choices. Whatever Americans decide, in the twenty-first century their economic well-being, the quality of their environment, how they travel, where and how they work, and how they live together will be powerfully shaped by their consuming power.

Environmental Regulation

EDMUND P. RUSSELL III

In 1992, the *New Yorker* published a Gahan Wilson cartoon in which four horseback riders greeted a fifth with the comment, "Congratulations, Ecological Disaster—it's not often we admit another horseman into the Apocalypse!" The cartoon illustrated the extent to which fears of ecological problems permeated American culture in the last decades of the twentieth century. These fears influenced not only the way people viewed the world around them, but also the way they spent a great deal of their money. By 1993, citizens of the United States allocated about $115 billion a

From Edmund P. Russell III, "Lost Among the Parts per Billion: Ecological Protection at the United States Environmental Protection Agency 1970–1993," *Environmental History* (1996–) 2, no. 1 (January 1997), pp. 29–41, 43. Copyright 1997 by Forest History Society. Reproduced with permission of Forest History Society in the format Textbook via Copyright Clearance Center.

year to environmental protection. The U.S. Environmental Protection Agency (EPA) spent about $6.9 billion of that amount, and groups regulated by EPA spent much of the rest to comply with directives issued by that agency.

Because *environment* means *surroundings,* it would be logical to predict that EPA and the groups it regulated spent much or most of those billions to protect the surroundings for human beings rather than human beings themselves. Such surroundings presumably would include land, water, air, and nonhuman species. Many members of the public believed this to be the case. In the 1980 presidential campaign, Ronald Reagan charged that "environmental extremists" at EPA and other federal agencies sacrificed economic growth for "rabbits' holes and birds' nests."

Some observers argued that EPA focused on human health issues and ignored, or at least paid too little attention to, nonhuman species. The agency's Science Advisory Board, a group of outside experts, said in 1990 that EPA had displayed a "relative lack of concern" about "natural ecosystems" because it "considered the protection of public health to be its primary mission." Others were harsher: a more accurate name for the agency, they suggested, would be the Environmental Cancer Agency.

Were these views accurate? Through interviews with past and current EPA employees and the examination of published and unpublished documents, it is possible to determine the extent to which EPA tried to protect nonhuman species between 1970 and 1993 and the factors that encouraged or discouraged such efforts. . . .

In the end, both views summarized above—EPA as ecological warrior and EPA as human health agency—are oversimplifications. The agency tried to protect nonhuman species at times, and did so to a greater extent than some observers have suggested, but it focused most of its attention on protecting human health. Why did EPA allocate its resources the way it did? . . .

A word relatively new to the public and to politicians, *ecology,* found its way into the discussions of a White House task force in February 1970. Charged with drafting a "President's Message on the Environment" for Richard Nixon, the task force proposed the creation of a new Department of Natural Resources that would oversee both use and protection of natural resources. Previous administrations had proposed similar departments, but the 1970 proposal marked the debut of an ecological idea—the need to preserve ecological balance—to justify the creation of a new policy and department.

The term *ecology,* which came from the Greek word for *home,* was coined by a nineteenth-century German scientist [Ernst Haeckel] to refer to the study of organisms and their surroundings. The term migrated from science to the popular and political lexicon in the 1960s, when a series of widely publicized events left Americans convinced that humans, and especially industry, threatened the well-being of the planet. Rachel Carson's *Silent Spring* (1962) convinced many people that pesticides, like atomic weapons, could "destroy life on earth." An oil spill in Santa Barbara killed sea animals, rivers foamed with detergents and occasionally caught fire, and photos of Earth taken from space made many people pause and think that this one planet was all they had. These concerns culminated on 22 April 1970, when millions of people celebrated the first Earth Day. An estimated ten million school children at ten thousand grammar and high schools, and students at some two thousand university campuses, participated. Ten thousand people flocked to the mall in Washington, D.C., and crowds of up to twenty-five thousand people attended rallies in New

York, Philadelphia, and Chicago. *Time* called it the nation's "biggest street festival since the Japanese surrender in 1945."

The term *ecology* seemed tailor-made to the new environmental conscious-ness. As one observer put it, *ecology* became "the political substitute for the word 'mother.'" In popular usage, ecology referred not just to a scientific discipline, but to the interconnectedness of life, the balance of nature, the beneficent aspects of the planet that humans threatened, and the environmental movement, which was some-times called "the ecology movement." Biologist Barry Commoner popularized four "laws of ecology" in a book titled *The Closing Circle.* His first law stated, "Every-thing is Connected to Everything Else."

The U.S. Congress responded to interest in ecological issues by passing a num-ber of laws that committed the nation to protect both human and nonhuman species. The National Environmental Policy Act of 1969 made it national policy to "promote efforts which will prevent or eliminate damage to the environment and biosphere and stimulate the health and welfare of man." Congress said it intended the Clean Water Act "to restore and maintain the chemical, physical, and biological integrity of the Nation's waters." Among other things, the act specified concern with "all identifiable effects on health and welfare including, but not limited to, plankton, fish, shellfish, wildlife, plant life, shorelines, beaches, esthetics, and recreation." The Federal Insec-ticide, Fungicide, and Rodenticide Act allowed approval of pesticides only if they "will not generally cause unreasonable adverse effects on the environment."

President Richard Nixon also felt it wise to portray himself as protector of the nation's ecology, so he created the Environmental Protection Agency in 1970. Echoing public concerns, Nixon called for EPA to identify the effects of pollutants on "the entire ecological chain," including both "man and his environment."

When EPA began operating in December 1970, it became clear that personnel brought contrasting commitments to protecting "the entire ecological chain." Most employees came to EPA from agencies in the Departments of the Interior, Agricul-ture, and Health, Education, and Welfare. Training and experience led these workers to focus on human health, not on "ecological chains." Many of these employees felt that the Department of the Interior was the agency that should focus on wildlife and related matters.

Members of the one new division of EPA, the Office of General Counsel and Enforcement, brought to the agency an outlook similar to that voiced by Nixon. In-fluenced by *Silent Spring* and the ecology movement, these lawyers wanted to pro-tect the ecology of America as well as the health of its citizens. As it happened, this office became the de facto policy office for the newborn agency, which pursued aggressive legal enforcement of environmental laws. Some issues, such as pollu-tion from automobiles, lent themselves to a focus on human health effects. Other issues, including the "political hot potato" of pesticide regulation, left room for focusing on effects on both humans and the environment. . . .

The contrast between these approaches came to the fore when EPA struggled to decide the fate of several pesticides. Ever since publication of *Silent Spring,* environ-mentalists had viewed pesticides as symbols of the threat that humans could pose to ecological systems. Rachel Carson had pointed out, for example, that populations of western grebes at Clear Lake, California, plummeted after homeowners sprayed DDD, a chemical compound similar to DDT, to control gnats. She argued that DDD accumulated in ever higher concentrations as it traveled up the food chain, creating a "chain of poisoning" that devastated the grebes. Ecological damage to birds and other species prompted the Environmental Defense Fund to petition the federal government to ban DDT and two of its derivatives, dieldrin and aldrin. The petitions also mentioned that pesticides could cause cancer, but they focused primarily on ecological effects.

Lawyers in EPA's Office of General Counsel and Enforcement sympathized with the Environmental Defense Fund's position, which led to a disagreement with the Office of Pesticide Programs that exemplified the contrasting values held by personnel in the two offices. Members of the Office of Pesticide Programs had come to EPA from the Department of Agriculture, and they considered damage to birds and fish not to have been proved, or at worst to have been of minor importance compared to the benefits that pesticides provided by protecting crops from insect pests and humans from disease. They felt that the lawyers pursued the aldrin/dieldrin case for political reasons and as an attempt to grab power. To the lawyers in the Office of General Counsel, the scientists in the pesticide program appeared misguided. Like Rachel Carson, EPA lawyers believed that pesticide manufacturers unduly influenced entomologists and their assessments of the costs and benefits of chemicals.

In the end, EPA Administrator William Ruckelshaus sided with his attorneys and their goal of protecting birds. Announcing his intention to cancel most uses of aldrin and dieldrin in 1972, Ruckelshaus devoted but one sentence to health, a reference to tumors that developed in mice given high doses of dieldrin. He emphasized instead dangers to wildlife and the atmosphere. When he banned DDT on crops, Ruckelshaus said that evidence "compellingly demonstrates the adverse impact . . . on fish and wildlife," especially since DDT tended to cause birds to lay eggs with thin, easily broken shells. Ruckelshaus also mentioned, but did not highlight, DDT's carcinogenic potential. Use of DDD was also canceled. Critics charged that Ruckelshaus's decisions callously disregarded human health, for the chemicals that would substitute for DDT and its relatives were even more poisonous to humans. . . .

Ironically, pesticide cases that entered the legal process as efforts to prevent damage to birds emerged as efforts to protect humans from cancer, reducing EPA's emphasis on ecological protection. Traditionally, courts had deferred to executive agencies in matters of scientific judgment and emphasized procedural, not substantive, matters in judicial reviews. A Court of Appeals decision in the aldrin/dieldrin case, however, pointed out the strength of carcinogenicity as a legal argument: "[C]andor compels us to say that when the matter involved is as sensitive and fright-laden as cancer, even a court scrupulous to the point of punctilio in deference to administrative latitude is beset with concern when the cross-reference [to cancer in EPA's brief] is so abbreviated."

EPA lawyers took the hint. They incorporated seven "general principles applicable to determination of carcinogenic hazards" into their final brief in the DDT cancellation hearings. They also argued that no potential carcinogen should be sold. Their final brief in the aldrin/dieldrin case listed nine "established principles of carcinogenicity." EPA lawyers repeated the principles in subsequent hearings on heptachlor, chlordane, and other pesticides, in which they stood as powerful precedents. Ecological arguments faded into the background. . . .

. . . Public fears of toxic substances became more prominent during the 1970s. The media splashed stories in newspapers and on television about a toxic waste dump under a neighborhood called Love Canal, polybromated biphenyls [PBBs] in food in Michigan, PCBs [polychlorinated biphenyls] emitted from a General Electric plant on the Hudson River, and other chemical hazards. Citing the National Cancer Institute, books and news programs announced that environmental factors caused 60 to 90 percent of cancers. Congress responded by passing the Toxic Substances Control Act of 1976, which charged EPA with preventing "unreasonable risk of injury to health or the environment" from toxic chemicals.

EPA and other agencies responded with a risk assessment methodology for cancer. [EPA head Douglas] Costle and heads of other regulatory agencies, including the Food and Drug Administration, the Occupational Health and Safety Administration, and the Consumer Product Safety Commission, formed a working group early in the Carter administration to develop a way to regulate toxic substances. The working group found it impossible to develop a risk assessment methodology for all problems, so it focused on one of wide interest, cancer, for which risk assessment methods had already been developed. . . .

The arrival of the Reagan administration in 1981 did little to revive interest in ecological protection at EPA. Few EPA employees believed that Reagan regarded ecological protection fondly; he was quoted as saying that trees and other plants caused most air pollution. Under new administrator Anne Gorsuch, EPA cut enforcement actions in half and morale plunged. After Gorsuch resigned, Reagan replaced her with former administrator William Ruckelshaus. Ruckelshaus also focused primarily on human health during his second term as administrator. At the end of this term, Ruckelshaus questioned the priorities of agency leaders, including, by implication, himself: "What is the impact of all this chemical loading over the years on the ecological systems in which human culture is embedded? After decades of so-called pesticide control, we have not even begun to ask this question. Indeed, it is odd how little time is spent at the upper levels of EPA thinking about such things and how much time is spent worrying about tiny increases in the risk of a single human disease [cancer]." . . .

Before leaving EPA, and perhaps without foreseeing it, Ruckelshaus had facilitated concern with ecological issues through his promotion of risk assessment as the agency's regulatory approach. Concerned about the cost of pollution control, Ruckelshaus argued that the agency needed to balance costs and benefits of individual regulations and to compare the value of various programs. He promoted risk-benefit analysis as the best way to accomplish these goals. Like cost-benefit analysis, risk-benefit analysis emphasized quantitative measures of tradeoffs. The methodology used to estimate the danger that something, usually a carcinogenic chemical, posed to a population became known as *risk assessment*. The National Academy of Sciences helped advance this approach when it published the Red Book, a 1983 study that codified procedures for risk assessment.

Although developed to help protect human health, risk assessment helped put ecological protection on the agency's agenda by enabling scientists to describe ecological threats in the same language that the agency used to describe threats to human health. Partly under contracts from EPA's Office of Research and Development, Glenn W. Suter and Lawrence W. Barnthouse at Oak Ridge National Laboratory developed *environmental risk analysis,* a method for identifying and quantifying the probability of adverse changes in the environment from human activities. In 1982 and 1986, for example, they estimated risks associated with indirect coal liquefaction, including risks to fish, algae, timber, agriculture, and wildlife. . . .

Scientists faced large obstacles when developing an ecological risk assessment. Health risk assessments dealt with only one well-studied species, humans, while ecological risk assessment could involve all species on earth. Limits on time and money forced scientists to test chemicals on a handful of species. They usually tested those already identified through legislation as valuable to society. Scientists wondered, but were largely unable to investigate, whether other species would react differently from test species, and whether single-species testing would reveal effects on other levels of organization, such as ecosystems.

The biggest challenge to advocates for ecological protection at EPA arose from a simple question: "So what?" Americans agreed on the value of protecting human lives. Health risk assessments dealt with dangers already familiar and of concern to the public, such as cancer or birth defects, but scientists wondered to what extent the public understood or cared about ecological risks. Was it significant if a fish population lost 15 percent of its members? Perhaps so, perhaps not, depending on the species of fish and whether or not it was endangered. . . .

William Reilly [EPA director during the first Bush administration], was a career conservationist. He advanced ecological protection at EPA in . . . [several] ways. First, he announced that it would be a "matter of policy" not to tolerate "an unnecessary risk of regularly repeated bird kills" from pesticides without a countervailing benefit. Second, Reilly vetoed a one billion dollar dam project in Colorado known as Two Forks. . . .

. . . Reilly said that he understood the value of water for Colorado, but that he had to "respect other values important to Coloradans and all Americans: a beautiful free flowing trout stream of the highest quality, wetlands; a downstream habitat of endangered whooping cranes, and other environmental resources."

Reilly's move made the Two Forks debate a national symbol of struggles between developers and environmentalists. Supporters reportedly spent $150,000 per month in efforts to convince EPA not to veto the project. Even the President felt compelled to address the issue. After proponents and opponents of the project flooded the White House with correspondence and entreaties, Bush announced that he had not told EPA to consider stopping the project and that he would not intervene to save it. . . .

In 1991, EPA issued its *Summary Report on Issues in Ecological Risk Assessment,* which suggested changes in terminology from the health framework while retaining the same approach and sequence of steps. For example, the report substituted the term "stress-response" for "dose-response." This report laid the groundwork for a 1992 publication, *Framework for Ecological Risk Assessment,* which formalized the agency's ecological risk assessment procedure. The report defined ecological risk assessment as "a process that evaluates the likelihood that adverse ecological effects may occur or are occurring as a result of exposure to one or more stressors." The report divided ecological risk assessment into three phases: problem formulation, analysis, and risk characterization. The report divided each of those phases into smaller steps, most of which were analogues of steps in health risk assessment.

This effort marked enough of a change in EPA direction that *Science* reported it in a 1992 article: "As if trying to determine human health risks from radiation, dioxin, and other hazards isn't enough trouble, the Environmental Protection Agency (EPA) may soon try its hand at the even more difficult chore of assessing ecological risk." This approach sounded so novel that *Science* put quotes around "ecological risk assessment" in the article title. Difficult or not, ecological assessments had become part of what EPA did. By 1993, various programs at EPA, including the Office of Prevention, Pesticides, and Toxic Substances, Office of Solid Waste and Emergency Response, Office of Water, and Office of Air and Radiation, had undertaken ecological assessments. . . .

At least two factors stood in the way of ecological protection. Agency culture still emphasized human health. Interest in ecological issues had grown at EPA, but many employees, especially managers, who had critical influence but who often had no formal training in ecological disciplines, still felt most at home with human health issues. The agency also lacked the internal expertise and knowledge that would give leaders confidence to take actions on a wide range of ecological issues.

EPA also had to face Congress and the cultural and political climate in which it operated. Administrators always found it easier to justify EPA actions to hostile Congressional committees when they based actions on human health. Americans agreed that human health deserved protection, but debated the extent to which nonhuman species deserved protection. Perhaps, as one EPA employee suggested, this difference arose from the Western tradition that humans had souls and animals did not. Whatever its origins, the perceived dichotomy between humans and nature undermined belief in what William Ruckelshaus called "the essential unity of nature" and contributed to a focus on human well-being.

When EPA employees did argue for ecological protection, they often did so on the anthropocentric grounds that ecosystems provide "goods and services" to humans. Occasionally, like the Science Advisory Board, employees suggested that nonhuman species had "intrinsic value" worth protecting, but the absence of agreement on this value made it shaky ground on which to regulate economic activity. Perhaps, as one employee suggested, the value on which Americans might agree would be the right of each species, but not necessarily all individuals in that species, to survive and reproduce.

Gahan Wilson's fifth horseman of the apocalypse represented "ecological disaster," which implied a concern for the well-being of nonhuman species. But one should not forget that the original four horsemen of the apocalypse—war, famine, plague, and wild beasts—represented threats to human survival. Fears of ecological problems arose in the United States partly because of altruistic impulses toward other species, but also, and probably more importantly, because of the conviction that human well-being was linked to the well-being of other species.

❦ *F U R T H E R   R E A D I N G*

Kenneth Andrasko, *Alaska Crude: Visions of the Last Frontier* (1977)
Tom Brown, *Oil on Ice: Alaskan Wilderness at the Crossroads* (1971)
Lloyd Burton, *American Indian Water Rights and the Limits of the Law* (1991)
Rachel Carson, *Silent Spring* (1962)
Jeanne Nienaber Clarke and Hanna J. Cortner, *The State and Nature: Voices Heard, Voices Unheard in America's Environmental Dialogue* (2002)
Marion Clawson, *The Bureau of Land Management* (1971)
Joel E. Cohen, *How Many People Can the Earth Support?* (1995)
Barry Commoner, *The Closing Circle* (1971)
———, *Making Peace with the Planet* (1990)

Paul J. Culhane, *Public Lands Politics: Interest Group Influence on the Forest Service and Bureau of Land Management* (1981)

Samuel Trask Dana and Sally K. Fairfax, *Forest and Range Policy: Its Development in the United States* (1980)

Art Davidson, *In the Wake of the Exxon Valdez* (1990)

Scott Hamilton Dewey, *Don't Breathe the Air: Air Pollution and U.S. Environmental Politics, 1945–1970* (2000)

Thomas R. Dunlap, *Saving America's Wildlife* (1988)

Paul Ehrlich, *The Population Bomb* (1968)

—— and Anne Ehrlich, *The Population Explosion* (1990)

William C. Everhart, *The National Park Service* (1972)

Stephen Haycox, *Frigid Embrace: Politics, Economics, and Environment in Alaska* (2002)

Samuel P. Hays, *Beauty, Health, and Permanence: Environmental Politics in the United States, 1955–1985* (1987)

——, *A History of Environmental Politics Since 1945* (2000)

Douglas Helms and Susan L. Flader, eds., *The History of Soil and Water Conservation* (1985)

Harold Ickes, *The Secret Diaries of Harold Ickes*, 3 vols. (1953, 1955)

Susan Killin, *Nature's State: Imagining Alaska as the Last Frontier* (2001)

Frank N. Laird, *Solar Energy, Technology Policy, and Institutional Values* (2001)

David E. Lilienthal, *TVA: Democracy on the March* (1944)

Matthew J. Lindstrom and Zachary A. Smith, *The National Environmental Policy Act: Judicial Misconstruction, Legislative Indifference & Executive Neglect* (2001)

John Livingston, *Arctic Oil: The Destruction of the North?* (1981)

Thomas A. Lund, *American Wildlife Law* (1980)

Robert Marshall, *The People's Forests* (1933)

Arthur F. McEvoy, *The Fisherman's Problem: Ecology and Law in the California Fisheries, 1850–1980* (1986)

Thomas A. Morehouse, *Fish and Wildlife Protection in the Planning and Construction of the Trans-Alaska Pipeline* (1978)

Robert J. Morgan, *Government Soil Conservation: Thirty Years of the New Decentralization* (1965)

Eric Morgren, *Warm Sands: Uranium Mill Tailings Policy in the Atomic West* (2002)

Roderick Nash, ed., *The American Environment* (1976)

——, *The Rights of Nature: A History of Environmental Ethics* (1989)

Edgar B. Nixon, ed., *Franklin D. Roosevelt and Conservation, 1911–1945*, 2 vols. (1957)

E. Louise Peffer, *The Closing of the Public Domain: Disposal and Reservation Policies, 1900–1950* (1951)

John F. Reiger, *American Sportsmen and the Origins of Conservation*, 3d ed. (2001)

Marc Reisner, *Cadillac Desert: The American West and Its Disappearing Water* (1986)

Elmo R. Richardson, *Dams, Parks, and Politics: Resource Development and Preservation in the Truman-Eisenhower Era* (1973)

Roy Robbins, *Our Landed Heritage* (1950)

William G. Robbins, *Lumberjacks and Legislators: Political Economy of the U.S. Lumber Industry, 1890–1941* (1982)

George W. Rogers, ed., *Change in Alaska; People, Petroleum, and Politics* (1970)

William D. Rowley, *U. S. Forest Service Grazing and Rangelands: A History* (1988)

Ned Rozell, *Walking My Dog, Jane: From Valdez to Prudhoe Bay along the Trans-Alaska Pipeline* (2000)

John H. Salmond, *The Civilian Conservation Corps, 1933–1942* (1967)

Stewart Udall, *The Quiet Crisis* (1963)

T. H. Watkins, *Righteous Pilgrim: The Life and Times of Harold Ickes, 1874–1952* (1990)

James Whorton, *Before Silent Spring: Pesticides and Public Health in Pre-DDT America*

Donald Worster, *Dust Bowl: The Southern Plains in the 1930s* (1979)

——, *Rivers of Empire: Water, Aridity, and the Growth of the American West* (1985)

CHAPTER
15

Globalization: The United States in the Wider World

❦

The connections between the United States and the global environment became increasingly apparent in the 1990s as ozone depletion spiraled, evidence of global warming caused by the buildup of atmospheric carbon dioxide accumulated, species around the world became endangered or extinct, temperate and tropical forests vanished, and world population soared. Economic networks became more global in scope as U.S. companies shifted production operations overseas to take advantage of cheap labor and to avoid environmental regulation. Mergers between companies based in different countries created complex international linkages. The increasing power of the World Trade Organization (WTO) and the passage of the North American Free Trade Agreement (NAFTA) weakened the power of the U.S. Congress to pass and enforce environmental regulations covering processes and products beyond U.S. borders. In the 1980s, the dumping of toxic materials and the siting of landfills in poor neighborhoods led to the antitoxic and environmental justice movements, drawing people of color into the environmental movement. Environmental conferences included the First National People of Color Environmental Leadership Summit in Washington, D.C., in 1991, the Rio de Janeiro Earth Summit in 1992, the Kyoto Conference on Global Climate Change in 1997, and the Johannesburg Conference on Sustainable Development in 2003.

Social movements accompanied the global conferences. Environmentalists and labor activists took to the streets in Seattle in November 1999 to protest the loss of environmental enforcement and labor regulations under the WTO. Groups such as Greenpeace, Earth First!, and the Rainforest Action Network engaged in direct action to protect whales and dolphins, tropical and temperate rainforests, and watersheds. Philosophical challenges to the Western worldview and its liberal politics were made by deep ecologists, ecofeminists, bioregionalists, social ecologists, and environmental ethicists. This chapter examines the global environmental crisis and responses by social justice activists, environmentalists, and philosophers. (See Maps 9 and 10 in the Appendix.)

502

The documents in this chapter focus on developments, from the local to the global, from the 1990s to the early twenty-first century. At the local level, toxic pollution affects individual lives, especially those in minority and poor communities. Document 1 is a "Report on Toxic Wastes and Race," released in 1987 by Ben Chavis, executive director of the Commission on Racial Justice of the United Church of Christ, arguing that toxic waste sites were disproportionately located in communities of color. Such global and local issues are motivations for organizing by environmental groups to save the environment.

The next three documents look at environmental activism among blacks, Indians, and women. In Document 2, Carl Anthony, an African American architect and urban planner in Oakland, California, explains what is at stake for inner-city blacks and urges them to become environmentalists. Winona LaDuke, an Algonquin from northern Minnesota and a founder of Women of All Red Nations, in Document 3 considers Indian relationships with nature and discusses some current red-white environmental controversies. In Document 4, Irene Diamond and Gloria Orenstein, coauthors of a 1990 collection of articles on ecofeminism, delineate issues that connect women to the environment.

The final four documents look at efforts to solve the environmental crisis at the global level. Document 5 reveals the agenda resulting from the 1992 United Nations Earth Summit in Rio de Janeiro. Document 6 details the results of the United Nations conference on Global Climate Change, held in Kyoto, Japan, in 1997, which opened a process by which nations around the world can commit to reducing carbon dioxide emissions from industrialization, which have been implicated in raising global temperatures. On October 12, 1999, the world population reached 6 billion people, with a projected increase to 7.3 to 10. billion over the ensuing half century. Document 7 is a press release on "The Day of 6 Billion" looking at the implications for the planet of such a large population. It argues that in addition to humane methods of encouraging population stabilization, a viable future will depend on the ways in which development takes place. Document 8 is the Declaration on Sustainable Development resulting from the 2002 United Nations conference in Johannesburg. Together the documents reveal different approaches, from the global to the local, of resolving the ecological crisis and creating a healthy planet.

1. Ben Chavis Reports on Toxic Wastes and Race, 1987

Preface

The Commission for Racial Justice of the 1.7 million-member United Church of Christ is pleased to release this report, *Toxic Wastes and Race in the United States: A National Report on the Racial and Socio-Economic Characteristics of Communities with Hazardous Waste Sites.* We believe that this report is of utmost importance, not only to racial and ethnic communities, but also to the nation as a whole. It is the first national report to comprehensively document the presence of hazardous wastes in racial and ethnic communities throughout the United States.

Excerpt from Ben Chavis, in Commission for Racial Justice, United Church of Christ, "Toxic Wastes and Race in the United States: A National Report on the Racial and Socio-Economic Characteristics of Communities with Hazardous Waste Sites" (Public Data Access, Inc., 1987), pp. ix–xvi. Reprinted by permission.

Since 1982, we have investigated and challenged the alarming presence of toxic substances in residential areas across the country. These investigations led us to examine the relationship between the treatment, storage and disposal of hazardous wastes and the issue of race.

In January 1986, two cross-sectional studies were initiated, utilizing appropriate statistical techniques, to determine the extent to which African Americans, Hispanic Americans, Asian Americans, Pacific Islanders, Native Americans and others are exposed to hazardous wastes in their communities. These were the first national studies to examine this subject. One study focused on commercial hazardous waste facilities; the other focused on uncontrolled toxic waste sites. The data presented in this report are the result of both studies.

Much of the data exhibited in this report has never before been compiled for public review. It is our hope that this information will be used by all persons committed to racial and environmental justice to challenge what we believe to be an insidious form of racism. We share a common definition of racism with the National Council of Churches Racial Justice Working Group:

> Racism is racial prejudice plus power. Racism is the intentional or unintentional use of power to isolate, separate and exploit others. This use of power is based on a belief in superior racial origin, identity or supposed racial characteristics. Racism confers certain privileges on and defends the dominant group, which in turn sustains and perpetuates racism. Both consciously and unconsciously, racism is enforced and maintained by the legal, cultural, religious, educational, economic, political, environmental and military institutions of societies. Racism is more than just a personal attitude; it is the institutionalized form of that attitude.

This report is intended to better enable the victims of this insidious form of racism not only to become more aware of the problem, but also to participate in the formulation of viable strategies. Too often African Americans and other racial and ethnic peoples are the victims of racism but are relegated to a defensive or reactive response, rather than a proactive position.

We are releasing this report in the interests of the millions of people who live in potentially health-threatening situations. In particular, we call attention to the fact that race is a major factor relating to the presence of hazardous wastes in residential communities throughout the United States.

The United Church of Christ, through the Commission for Racial Justice, has made a long-term commitment to seeing that justice is done across the lines of race. As a national church-based civil rights agency, we believe that the time has come for all church and civil rights organizations to take this issue seriously.

We realize that involvement in this type of research is a departure from our traditional protest methodology. However, if we are to advance our struggle in the future, it will largely depend on the availability of timely and reliable information. We believe this data should be utilized by federal, state and municipal governments to prevent hazardous wastes from becoming an even greater national problem. No residential community, regardless of race, should ever be left defenseless in the midst of this mounting crisis.

We are grateful to the Special Appeals Committee of the Executive Council of the United Church of Christ for providing funding from the Neighbors In Need

Offering for the studies and for this report. Special recognition should be given to Charles Lee, Director, Special Project on Toxic Injustice of the Commission for Racial Justice, who was responsible for coordinating the publication of *Toxic Wastes and Race in the United States.*

Benjamin F. Chavis Jr.
Executive Director

Executive Summary

Recently, there has been unprecedented national concern over the problem of hazardous wastes. This concern has been focused upon the adverse environmental and health effects of toxic chemicals and other hazardous substances emanating from operating hazardous waste treatment, storage and disposal facilities as well as thousands of abandoned waste sites. Efforts to address this issue, however, have largely ignored the specific concerns of African Americans, Hispanic Americans, Asian Americans, Pacific Islanders and Native Americans. Unfortunately, racial and ethnic Americans are far more likely to be unknowing victims of exposure to such substances.

Public policies ushered in by the Reagan Administration signaled a reduction of domestic programs to monitor the environment and protect public health. Reduction of such efforts to protect public health is especially disturbing in light of the many citizens who unknowingly may be exposed to substances emanating from hazardous waste sites. According to a December 1986 U.S. General Accounting Office (GAO) report, the U.S. Environmental Protection Agency (EPA) "does not know if it has identified 90 percent of the potentially hazardous wastes or only 10 percent."

Issues surrounding the siting of hazardous waste facilities in racial and ethnic communities gained national prominence in 1982. The Commission for Racial Justice joined ranks with residents of predominantly Black and poor Warren County, North Carolina in opposing the establishment of a polychlorinated biphenyl (PCB) disposal landfill. This opposition culminated in a nonviolent civil disobedience campaign and more than 500 arrests. As a result of the protests in Warren County, the GAO studied the racial and socio-economic status of communities surrounding four landfills in southeastern United States. It found that Blacks comprised the majority of the population in three of the four communities studied.

Previous to the Warren County demonstrations, racial and ethnic communities had been marginally involved with issues of hazardous wastes. One reason for this can be traced to the nature of the environmental movement which has historically been white middle and upper-class in its orientation. This does not mean, however, that racial and ethnic communities do not care about the quality of their environment and its effect on their lives. Throughout the course of the Commission for Racial Justice's involvement with issues of hazardous wastes and environmental pollution, we have found numerous grassroots racial and ethnic groups actively seeking to deal with this problem in their communities.

Racial and ethnic communities have been and continue to be beset by poverty, unemployment and problems related to poor housing, education and health. These communities cannot afford the luxury of being primarily concerned about the quality of their environment when confronted by a plethora of pressing problems related to their day-to-day survival. Within this context, racial and ethnic communities become particularly vulnerable to those who advocate the siting of a hazardous waste facility as an avenue for employment and economic development. Thus, proposals that economic incentives be offered to mitigate local opposition to the establishment of new hazardous waste facilities raise disturbing social policy questions. . . .

"Hazardous wastes" is the term used by the EPA to define by-products of industrial production which present particularly troublesome health and environmental problems. . . .

"Uncontrolled toxic waste sites" refer to closed and abandoned sites on the EPA's list of sites which pose a present and potential threat to human health and the environment. . . .

Major Findings

Demographic Characteristics of Communities with Commercial Hazardous Waste Facilities

- Race proved to be the most significant among variables tested in association with the location of commercial hazardous waste facilities. This represented a consistent national pattern.
- Communities with the greatest number of commercial hazardous waste facilities had the highest composition of racial and ethnic residents. In communities with two or more facilities or one of the nation's five largest landfills, the average minority percentage of the population* was more than three times that of communities without facilities (38 percent vs. 12 percent).
- In communities with one commercial hazardous waste facility, the average minority percentage of the population was twice the average minority percentage of the population in communities without such facilities (24 percent vs. 12 percent).
- Although socio-economic status appeared to play an important role in the location of commercial hazardous waste facilities, race still proved to be more significant. This remained true after the study controlled for urbanization and regional differences. Incomes and home values were substantially lower when communities with commercial facilities were compared to communities in the surrounding counties without facilities.
- Three out of the five largest commercial hazardous waste landfills in the United States were located in predominantly Black** or Hispanic communities. These three landfills accounted for 40 percent of the total estimated commercial landfill capacity in the nation. . . .

This report firmly concludes that hazardous wastes in Black, Hispanic and other racial and ethnic communities should be made a priority issue at all levels of government. This issue is not currently at the forefront of the nation's attention. Therefore, concerned citizens and policy-makers, who are cognizant of this growing national problem, must make this a priority concern.

---

* In this report, "minority percentage of the population" was used as a measure of "race."
** In this report, the terminology used to describe various racial and ethnic populations was based on categories defined by the U.S. Bureau of the Census: Blacks, Hispanics, Asian/Pacific Islanders and American Indians.

2. Carl Anthony Explains Why African Americans Should Be Environmentalists, 1990

When Martin Luther King Jr. decided to raise his voice in opposition to the war in Vietnam, many of his friends, as well as his critics, told him he ought to stick to domestic issues. He should concentrate on securing civil rights of African Americans in the South and leave foreign policy to the professionals who knew best. But King decided to oppose the war because he knew it was morally wrong and because he understood the link between the brutal exploitation and destruction of the Vietnamese people and the struggle of African Americans and others for justice and freedom in our own land.

Today, African American leadership and the African American community face a similar situation. Every day the newspapers carry stories about the changing atmosphere and climate, threats to the world's water supply, threats to the biodiversity of the rainforest, and the population crisis in poor nations that are growing too fast to be supported by the carrying capacity of their lands. Can we afford to view the social and economic problems of African American communities in isolation from these global trends?

African Americans could benefit from expanding their vision to include greater environmental awareness. For example, a recent study of the deteriorating conditions within the African American community termed young African American males in America "an endangered species." "This description applies, in a metaphorical sense, to the current status of young African American males in contemporary society," writes Jewelle Taylor Gibbs. Her study . . . present[s] a comprehensive interdisciplinary perspective of the social and economic problems of these young people, providing valuable statistics on high school dropout rates, work skills and attitudes, unemployment, robbery, rape, homicide and aggravated assault, drug addiction as well as teenage parenthood. But Gibbs makes no mention of the utter alienation of these young people from the natural environment, which is, after all, the source of Earth's abundance and well-being. The loss of this contact with living and growing things, even rudimentary knowledge of where food and water comes from, must present serious consequences that we, as yet, have no way of measuring.

The study said nothing of the difficult days ahead as American society seeks to make the transition from its current levels of consumption of resources to the more sustainable patterns of the future. Developing an environmental perspective within the African American community could help smooth this transition in several ways:

• by promoting greater understanding of the productive assets of society, including land, water and natural resources,

• by strengthening collaboration with groups seeking to redirect public investment and economic development away from wasteful exploitation of nature toward urban restoration and meeting basic human needs,

• by gaining access to information and resources which enhance the potential of community survival,

---

Excerpts from Carl Anthony, "Why African Americans Should Be Environmentalists," *Earth Island Journal* (Winter 1990), pp. 43–44. Reprinted with permission of the author.

- by developing new knowledge and skills to be shared by groups of people who live in the city,
- by strengthening social and political organization and creating new opportunities for leadership within the community.

Environmental organizations in the United States should also modify recruitment efforts in order to expand their constituency to include African Americans and members of other minority groups as participants in shaping and building public support for environmental policies. With the exception of limited collaboration between environmentalists and Native American groups, as well as anti-toxics campaigns, there has been little communication between environmentalists and non-European minority groups in the US. Critical issues—such as population control, limiting human intervention in the ecosystem, or rebuilding our cities in balance with nature—have been discussed almost entirely from a European and often elitist perspective. . . .

The principle of social justice, however, must be at the heart of any effort aimed at bringing African Americans into the mainstream of environmental organizations in the United States. Such a vision must offer a real alternative to a view of the tropical rainforest as an inviolate preserve or a private laboratory for multinational pharmaceutical companies, ignoring the needs of indigenous populations. While recognizing limits to growth, it must avoid misuse of environmental information as a way of rationalizing the economic status quo. It must not misuse concern for endangered species as a way of diluting our responsibility to meet basic needs for human health care, food and shelter. It cannot manipulate terms so that the legitimate need for population control becomes a code word for preserving racial dominance and purity.

Environmental protection must be understood as intimately connected to efforts to eradicate injustice. Solutions must offer a practical guide for goals which can be accomplished in the short run as we seek a path toward a more sustainable future. Environmental organizations can no longer afford to take the view that they are unconcerned about who benefits and who loses from restrictions on economic growth. Shifting resources away from projects which are damaging to the ecosystem toward programs and projects which meet basic human needs must become the highest priority for the environmental movement. In the United States, organizations such as the National Association for the Advancement of Colored People and the Urban League have a real stake in these outcomes. They should be part of the environmental dialogue. New organizations dealing explicitly with urban habitat are needed. . . .

The American inner-city was once a wilderness. Today, islands, estuaries, forests, and riparian habitats that once existed in these locations have been replaced by asphalt, concrete, barbed wire fences, boarded-up stores, crack houses, abandoned factories, landfills and pollution. After generations of isolation and manipulation, the people who live in these places rarely remember what it once was—or speculate on what it might become.

Isolation of African Americans from stewardship of the environment has deep historic roots. It is hard to keep the faith. The African American population migrated to the cities to escape the four centuries of exploitation on the plantations, crop farms and in the coal mines of the South. Displacement from rural countryside is parallel to similar experiences in the Third World. Understanding of these experiences, however painful, is an important resource as we seek a path towards sustainable development. . . .

In order to meet responsibilities for citizenship, African Americans must have opportunities and learn to play a greater role in formulating environmental policies which affect all members of the community. We must find new ways to bridge the gap between environmental advocates and African American communities.

Some of the means to achieve this goal might include:

• Presentations to groups with sustainable memberships by existing environmental organizations and individual resource persons.

• Outreach programs by environmental organizations to promote active learning and exposure to the wilderness experience by minority youth.

• Networks among minority-based organizations, environmental groups, public schools, community colleges and institutions of higher learning in order to expand educational opportunities for minorities in environmental science and related fields.

• Working specifically with inner-city organizations fighting drug abuse to develop environmentally-related projects and therapeutic settings such as tree planting, restoration, urban farming, horticulture therapy, international exchanges, etc.

• Strengthening neighborhood-initiated efforts at law enforcement, prevention and treatment of drug abuse.

• Legislative initiatives linking inner-city needs and environmental projects.

There are some hopeful signs. Environmental concerns of minority groups are already an integral part of the planning [processes in several cities].

3. Winona LaDuke Considers Indians' Place in the Ecosystem, 1990

I want to talk about something from our own culture which is the Anishinabe culture, the Algonquin culture. We have an economic system, a whole value system, and part of that value system—part of our whole way of living—is a concept called *reciprocity.*

When I go out and I harvest wild rice up on our lakes in Northern Minnesota, on our reservation, I bring tobacco, *saymah,* and I put the tobacco out. I make an offering when I go out to harvest, and then I collect different things from the land. We do the same thing when we go out hunting—when we go out hunting, whether it's for *wapsh* or *atuk,* rabbit or deer, all the different parts of the creation, we give something in order to get something back from the creation. We have a reciprocal agreement, and this confirms our relationship to the creation—we're a part, an integral part of the creation. We're an integral part of the ecosystem in our areas. Reciprocity is an essential part of our value system, which is very contrary to the industrial value system and the industrial society in the United States. . . .

The tendency in the environmental movement (and the tendency generally) is not to look in a holistic manner at the future, and we need to get away from that. We need to look at things like cultural diversity and not just biological diversity. We don't just need places in the Amazon where the toucan and the jaguar can live. We need places where the Yanomama can live. Where the Kayapo can live, where the Ache can live. All of those indigenous people are integral parts of their ecosystem.

We also need places where the Anishinabeg can live, where the Yurok can live, where the Dakota and the Dene can live. *We* are an integral part of the ecosystem just as anything else. Since 1900, a tenth of the forest in the Amazon has disappeared, but

Excerpts from Winona LaDuke, "The Struggle for Cultural Diversity," *Race, Poverty, and the Environment* 1, no. 2 (July 1990), pp. 1, 12–13. Reprinted from *Race, Poverty, and the Environment,* 1990.

one indigenous nation per year has disappeared in the Brazilian Amazon. One-third of all groups—90 out of 270—have entirely disappeared from the Brazilian Amazon. Corporations cannot get to the forest unless they get rid of the people.

We need to look at a broader context of issues and we need to relearn how to think. Industrial society teaches people to compartmentalize, and many of us are beginning to resist that and look at things in a holistic manner. All of the issues are of course totally related. . . .

We have to look at the bigger picture. It is cultural diversity as well as biological diversity. . . . We need to look at things like industrial law versus natural law. In our experience, natural law looks more to the long term. And when we look to the new society, and the new way of living here, we have to look toward natural law as something that makes sense for all of us. We all have to change how people think in this society. We all have access to power at different levels and in different places— the people who read this have access to power. We need to use it. We need to use it to struggle, and we need to use it to change how people think.

We need to use it to make structural change in society. We are rich in North America because other people are poor. That is how society functions, how society works, and that is what we must change. The concept of reciprocity is critical in our culture, and we are asking you as people of conscience to embrace it. I don't associate the industrial society with a color, I associate it with a value system.

People who have lighter skin pigmentation tend to have more power and access to ways to struggle in this society. And what may be surprising to you is that although Indian people in a lot of communities may be poor, almost every day Indian people pray for white people. In our language we have to pray for everything, and I guess that's how we give back what we can in our reciprocal agreement. Because we can't necessarily do the same things in Congress that you can do, but we can pray. *Megwitch.*

4. Two Feminists Discuss the Emergence of Ecofeminism, 1990

Today, more than twenty-five years after Rachel Carson's *Silent Spring* first raised a passionate voice of conscience in protest against the pollution and degradation of nature, an ecofeminist movement is emerging globally as a major catalyst of ethical, political, social, and creative change. Although Carson was not an avowed feminist, many would argue that it was not coincidental that a woman was the first to respond both emotionally and scientifically to the wanton human domination of the natural world. Carson's 1962 text prefigured a powerful environmental movement that culminated in the nationwide Earth Day of 1970, but the notion that the collective voices of women should be central to the greening of the Earth did not blossom until the mid to late 1970s.

Ecofeminism is a term that some use to describe both the diverse range of women's efforts to save the Earth and the transformations of feminism in the West that have resulted from the new view of women and nature. With the birth of the

Excerpts from Irene Diamond and Gloria Orenstein, eds., *Reweaving the World: The Emergence of Ecofeminism.* San Francisco: Sierra Club Books, 1990, pp. ix–xii. Reprinted with permission of Sierra Club Books.

Women's Movement in the late 1960s, feminists dismantled the iron grip of biological determinism that had been used historically to justify men's control over women. Feminists argued that social arrangements deemed to be timeless and natural had actually been constructed to validate male superiority and privilege. They asserted that women had the right to be full and equal participants in the making of culture. In this process writers and scholars documented the historical association between women and nature, insisting that women would not be free until the connections between women and the natural world were severed.

But as the decade advanced and as women began to revalue women's cultures and practices, especially in the face of the twin threats of nuclear annihilation and ecocide, many women began to understand how the larger culture's devaluation of natural processes was a product of masculine consciousness. Writers as diverse as Mary Daly, Elizabeth Dodson Gray, Susan Griffin, Carolyn Merchant, Maria Mies, Vandana Shiva, Luisah Teish, and Alice Walker demonstrated that this masculine consciousness denigrated and manipulated everything defined as "other" whether nature, women, or Third World cultures. In the industrialized world, women were impelled to act, to speak out against the mindless spraying of chemicals, the careless disposal of toxic wastes, the unacknowledged radiation seepage from nuclear power plants and weapons testing, and the ultimate catastrophe—the extinction of all life on Earth. In the Third World, women had still more immediate concerns. For women who had to walk miles to collect the water, fuel, and fodder they needed for their households, the devastation wrought by patriarchal fantasies of technological development (for example, the Green revolution, commercial forest management, and mammoth dam projects) was already a daily reality.

In many ways, women's struggle in the rural Third World is of necessity also an ecological struggle. Because so many women's lives are intimately involved in trying to sustain and conserve water, land, and forests, they understand in an immediate way the costs of technologies that pillage the Earth's natural riches. By contrast, in the industrialized world, the connections between women's concerns and ecological concerns were not immediately apparent to many feminists. Community activists such as Rachel E. Bagby, Lois Gibbs, and Carol Von Strom, who were struggling to protect the health of their families and neighborhoods, were among the first to make the connections. Women who are responsible for their children's well-being are often more mindful of the long-term costs of quick-fix solutions. Through the social experience of caretaking and nurturing, women become attentive to the signs of distress in their communities that might threaten their households. When environmental "accidents" occur, it is these women who are typically the first to detect a problem. Moreover, because of women's unique role in the biological regeneration of the species, our bodies are important markers, the sites upon which local, regional, or even planetary stress is often played out. Miscarriage is frequently an early sign of the presence of lethal toxins in the biosphere.

Feminists who had been exploring alternatives to the traditional "woman is to nature as man is to culture" formulation, who were seeking a more fundamental shift in consciousness than the acceptance of women's participation in the marketplace of the public world, began to question the nature versus culture dichotomy itself. These activists, theorists, and artists sought to consciously create new cultures that would embrace and honor the values of caretaking and nurturing—cultures that would not perpetuate the dichotomy by raising nature over culture or by raising women over men. Rather, they affirmed and celebrated the embeddedness of all the Earth's peoples in the multiple webs and cycles of life.

In their hope for the creation of new cultures that would live with the Earth, many women in the West were inspired by the myths and symbols of ancient Goddess cultures in which creation was imaged as female and the Earth was revered as sacred. Others were inspired by the symbols and practices of Native-American cultures that consider the effects on future generations before making any community decision. The sources of inspiration were many and varied and led to a diverse array of innovative practices—from tree-planting communities, alternative healing communities, organic food coops, performance art happenings, Witchcraft covens, and the retelling of ancient myths and tales to new forms of political resistance such as the *Chipko* (hugging) tree actions and women's peace camps. Through poetry, rituals, and social activism that connected the devastation of the Earth with the exploitation of women, these activists reinvigorated both feminism and social change movements more generally. The languages they created reached across and beyond the boundaries of previously defined categories. These languages recognized the *lived* connections between reason and emotion, thought and experience. They embraced not only women and men of different races, but all forms of life—other animals, plants, and the living Earth itself. The diverse strands of this retelling and reframing led to a new, more complicated experiential ethic of ecological interconnectedness.

5. The Rio de Janeiro Earth Summit, 1992

The Earth Summit in Rio de Janeiro was unprecedented for a UN conference, in terms of both its size and the scope of its concerns. Twenty years after the first global environment conference, the UN sought to help Governments rethink economic development and find ways to halt the destruction of irreplaceable natural resources and pollution of the planet. Hundreds of thousands of people from all walks of life were drawn into the Rio process. They persuaded their leaders to go to Rio and join other nations in making the difficult decisions needed to ensure a healthy planet for generations to come.

The Summit's message—that nothing less than a transformation of our attitudes and behaviour would bring about the necessary changes—was transmitted by almost 10,000 on-site journalists and heard by millions around the world. The message reflected the complexity of the problems facing us: that poverty as well as excessive consumption by affluent populations place damaging stress on the environment. Governments recognized the need to redirect international and national plans and policies to ensure that all economic decisions fully took into account any environmental impact. And the message has produced results, making eco-efficiency a guiding principle for business and governments alike.

• Patterns of production—particularly the production of toxic components, such as lead in gasoline, or poisonous waste—are being scrutinized in a systematic manner by the UN and Governments alike;

From United Nations, "UN Conference on Environment and Development (1992)." New York: United Nations Headquarters: Department of Public Information, revised 1997. The United Nations is the author of the original material.

• Alternative sources of energy are being sought to replace the use of fossil fuels which are linked to global climate change;

• New reliance on public transportation systems is being emphasized in order to reduce vehicle emissions, congestion in cities and the health problems caused by polluted air and smog;

• There is much greater awareness of and concern over the growing scarcity of water.

The two-week Earth Summit was the climax of a process, begun in December 1989, of planning, education and negotiations among all Member States of the United Nations, leading to the adoption of Agenda 21, a wide-ranging blueprint for action to achieve sustainable development worldwide. At its close, Maurice Strong, the Conference Secretary-General, called the Summit a "historic moment for humanity." Although Agenda 21 had been weakened by compromise and negotiation, he said, it was still the most comprehensive and, if implemented, effective programme of action ever sanctioned by the international community. Today, efforts to ensure its proper implementation continue, and they will be reviewed by the UN General Assembly at a special session to be held in June 1997.

The Earth Summit influenced all subsequent UN conferences, which have examined the relationship between human rights, population, social development, women and human settlements—and the need for environmentally sustainable development. The World Conference on Human Rights, held in Vienna in 1993, for example, underscored the right of people to a healthy environment and the right to development, controversial demands that had met with resistance from some Member States until Rio.

Background

The relationship between economic development and environmental degradation was first placed on the international agenda in 1972, at the UN Conference on the Human Environment, held in Stockholm. After the Conference, Governments set up the United Nations Environment Programme (UNEP), which today continues to act as a global catalyst for action to protect the environment. Little, however, was done in the succeeding years to integrate environmental concerns into national economic planning and decision-making. Overall, the environment continued to deteriorate, and such problems as ozone depletion, global warming and water pollution grew more serious, while the destruction of natural resources accelerated at an alarming rate.

By 1983, when the UN set up the World Commission on Environment and Development, environmental degradation, which had been seen as a side effect of industrial wealth with only a limited impact, was understood to be a matter of survival for developing nations. Led by Gro Harlem Brundtland of Norway, the Commission put forward the concept of sustainable development as an alternative approach to one simply based on economic growth—one "which meets the needs of the present without compromising the ability of future generations to meet their own needs."

After considering the 1987 Brundtland report, the UN General Assembly called for the UN Conference on Environment and Development (UNCED). The primary goals of the Summit were to come to an understanding of "development" that would support socio-economic development and prevent the continued deterioration of the environment, and to lay a foundation for a global partnership between the developing and the more industrialized countries, based on mutual needs and common interests, that would ensure a healthy future for the planet.

The Earth Summit Agreements

In Rio, Governments—108 represented by heads of State or Government—adopted three major agreements aimed at changing the traditional approach to development:
* Agenda 21—a comprehensive programme of action for global action in all areas of sustainable development;
* The Rio Declaration on Environment and Development—a series of principles defining the rights and responsibilities of States;
* The Statement of Forest Principles—a set of principles to underlie the sustainable management of forests worldwide.

In addition, two legally binding Conventions aimed at preventing global climate change and the eradication of the diversity of biological species were opened for signature at the Summit, giving high profile to these efforts:
* The United Nations Framework Convention on Climate Change and
* The Convention on Biological Diversity

Agenda 21 addresses today's pressing problems and aims to prepare the world for the challenges of the next century. It contains detailed proposals for action in social and economic areas (such as combating poverty, changing patterns of production and consumption and addressing demographic dynamics), and for conserving and managing the natural resources that are the basis for life—protecting the atmosphere, oceans and biodiversity; preventing deforestation; and promoting sustainable agriculture, for example.

Governments agreed that the integration of environment and development concerns will lead to the fulfilment of basic needs, improved standards for all, better protected and better managed ecosystems and a safer and a more prosperous future. "No nation can achieve this on its own. Together we can—in a global partnership for sustainable development," states the preamble.

The programme of action also recommends ways to strengthen the part played by major groups—women, trade unions, farmers, children and young people, indigenous peoples, the scientific community, local authorities, business, industry and non-governmental organizations (NGOs)—in achieving sustainable development.

The Rio Declaration on Environment and Development supports Agenda 21 by defining the rights and responsibilities of States regarding these issues. Among its principles:
* That human beings are at the centre of concerns for sustainable development. They are entitled to a healthy and productive life in harmony with nature;
* That scientific uncertainty should not delay measures to prevent environmental degradation where there are threats of serious or irreversible damage;
* That States have a sovereign right to exploit their own resources but not to cause damage to the environment of other States;
* That eradicating poverty and reducing disparities in worldwide standards of living are "indispensable" for sustainable development;
* That the full participation of women is essential for achieving sustainable development; and

• That the developed countries acknowledge the responsibility that they bear in the international pursuit of sustainable development in view of the pressures their societies place on the global environment and of the technologies and financial resources they command.

The Statement of Forest Principles, the non-legally binding statement of principles for the sustainable management of forests, was the first global consensus reached on forests. Among its provisions:

• That all countries, notably developed countries, should make an effort to "green the world" through reforestation and forest conservation;
• That States have a right to develop forests according to their socio-economic needs, in keeping with national sustainable development policies; and
• That specific financial resources should be provided to develop programmes that encourage economic and social substitution policies.

At the Summit, the UN was also called on to negotiate an international legal agreement on desertification, to hold talks on preventing the depletion of certain fish stocks, to devise a programme of action for the sustainable development of small island developing States and to establish mechanisms for ensuring the implementation of the Rio accords.

6. The Kyoto Protocol on Global Climate Change, 1997

Kyoto Protocol to the United Nations Framework Convention on Climate Change

The Parties to this Protocol, Being Parties to the United Nations Framework Convention on Climate Change, hereinafter referred to as "the Convention," In pursuit of the ultimate objective of the Convention as stated in its Article 2, Recalling the provisions of the Convention, Being guided by Article 3 of the Convention, Pursuant to the Berlin Mandate adopted by decision 1/CP.1 of the Conference of the Parties to the Convention at its first session, Have agreed as follows:

Article 1

For the purposes of this Protocol, the definitions contained in Article 1 of the Convention shall apply. In addition:

1. "Conference of the Parties" means the Conference of the Parties to the Convention.
2. "Convention" means the United Nations Framework Convention on Climate Change, adopted in New York on 9 May 1992.
3. "Intergovernmental Panel on Climate Change" means the Intergovernmental Panel on Climate Change established in 1988 jointly by the World Meteorological Organization and the United Nations Environment Programme.
4. "Montreal Protocol" means the Montreal Protocol on Substances that Deplete the Ozone Layer, adopted in Montreal on 16 September 1987 and as subsequently adjusted and amended.

United Nations, "Framework Convention on Climate Change." New York: United Nations, 1997. The United Nations is the author of the original material.

5. "Parties present and voting" means Parties present and casting an affirmative or negative vote.
6. "Party" means, unless the context otherwise indicates, a Party to this Protocol.
7. "Party included in Annex I" means a Party included in Annex I to the Convention, as may be amended, or a Party which has made a notification under Article 4, paragraph 2(g), of the Convention.

Article 2

1. Each Party included in Annex I in achieving its quantified emission limitation and reduction commitments under Article 3, in order to promote sustainable development, shall:
   a. Implement and/or further elaborate policies and measures in accordance with its national circumstances, such as:
      i.   Enhancement of energy efficiency in relevant sectors of the national economy;
      ii. Protection and enhancement of sinks and reservoirs of greenhouse gases not controlled by the Montreal Protocol, taking into account its commitments under relevant international environmental agreements; promotion of sustainable forest management practices, afforestation and reforestation;
      iii. Promotion of sustainable forms of agriculture in light of climate change considerations;
      iv. Promotion, research, development and increased use of new and renewable forms of energy, of carbon dioxide sequestration technologies and of advanced and innovative environmentally sound technologies;
      v.   Progressive reduction or phasing out of market imperfections, fiscal incentives, tax and duty exemptions and subsidies in all greenhouse gas emitting sectors that run counter to the objective of the Convention and apply market instruments;
      vi. Encouragement of appropriate reforms in relevant sectors aimed at promoting policies and measures which limit or reduce emissions of greenhouse gases not controlled by the Montreal Protocol;
      vii. Measures to limit and/or reduce emissions of greenhouse gases not controlled by the Montreal Protocol in the transport sector;
      viii. Limitation and/or reduction of methane through recovery and use in waste management, as well as in the production, transport and distribution of energy;
   b. Cooperate with other such Parties to enhance the individual and combined effectiveness of their policies and measures adopted under this Article, pursuant to Article 4, paragraph 2(e)(i), of the Convention. . . .

Article 3

1. The Parties included in Annex I shall, individually or jointly, ensure that their aggregate anthropogenic carbon dioxide equivalent emissions of the greenhouse gases listed in Annex A do not exceed their assigned amounts, calculated pursuant to their quantified emission limitation and reduction commitments

inscribed in Annex B and in accordance with the provisions of this Article, with a view to reducing their overall emissions of such gases by at least 5 per cent below 1990 levels in the commitment period 2008 to 2012.

2. Each Party included in Annex I shall, by 2005, have made demonstrable progress in achieving its commitments under this Protocol.

3. The net changes in greenhouse gas emissions from sources and removals by sinks resulting from direct human-induced land use change and forestry activities, limited to afforestation, reforestation, and deforestation since 1990, measured as verifiable changes in stocks in each commitment period shall be used to meet the commitments in this Article of each Party included in Annex I. The greenhouse gas emissions from sources and removals by sinks associated with those activities shall be reported in a transparent and verifiable manner and reviewed in accordance with Articles 7 and 8. . . .

Article 24

1. This Protocol shall enter into force on the ninetieth day after the date on which not less than 55 Parties to the Convention, incorporating Parties included in Annex I which accounted in total for at least 55 per cent of the total carbon dioxide emissions for 1990 of the Parties included in Annex I, have deposited their instruments of ratification, acceptance, approval or accession.

2. For the purposes of this Article, "the total carbon dioxide emissions for 1990 of the Parties included in Annex I" means the amount communicated on or before the date of adoption of this Protocol by the Parties included in Annex I in their first national communications submitted in accordance with Article 12 of the Convention.

3. For each State or regional economic integration organization that ratifies, accepts or approves this Protocol or accedes thereto after the conditions set out in paragraph 1 above for the entry into force have been fulfilled, this Protocol shall enter into force on the ninetieth day following the date of deposit of its instrument of ratification, acceptance, approval or accession.

7. Reporters Announce a World Population of Six Billion People, 1999

Oct. 12, 1999—The world's population topped the 6 billion mark Tuesday, with the birth of a baby in Sarajevo. To some, that's cause for celebration. We are healthier and living longer than ever before. But others worry the milestone is actually a harbinger of doom: they fear further environmental degradation and human suffering. And still others say we are misinterpreting the number entirely by overlooking the downward trend in global birthrates.

WHATEVER THE truth, the United Nations Population Fund designated Oct. 12 as "The Day of 6 Billion." U.N. Secretary-General Kofi Annan symbolically welcomed

---

From Julia Sommerfeld, "World Population Hits 6 Billion: A Baby Born in Sarajevo Revives the Population Debate," MSNBC, Oct. 12, 1999. © 2004 MSNBCi.

a baby boy born in Sarajevo as number 6 billion. . . . The date, to be sure, is more symbolic than scientific, meant to mark the moment when the world's population passes that threshold. The figure, with all those zeros, has a millennial feel. . . . But what does the number mean? . . .

For one thing, it means that the population of the world has doubled in less than four decades. Similarly, it means that a tenth of all the people who have ever lived are now alive. Yet it also shows how quickly the rate of population growth has slowed since the alarms about the consequences of overpopulation began sounding in the 1960s. Since 1992, the United Nations has had to push back its 6 billion estimate by almost two years.

Will technology save us from overpopulation? "This slowing of population growth is not inevitable. The work of many people over the last 30 years made it possible. Whether it continues, and whether it is accompanied by increasing well-being or increasing stress, will depend on choices and action in the next 10 years," a U.N. population report issued last month said. . . .

U.N. demographers project 2.9 billion people will be added to the planet in the next half-century, fewer than the 3.6 billion added during the past 50 years. But, in contrast to 50 years ago, when populations were growing everywhere, growth is now primarily occurring in developing countries.

. . . The United Nations Population Fund and environmental groups like the Worldwatch Institute, Zero Population Growth and Population Action International are concerned about what a growing population means for the environment and for the quality of life in developing countries. Brian Halweil, a researcher at the World-watch Institute, said "The Day of 6 Billion" should be seen as a rallying point for population issues, the most pressing of which, he said, are freshwater shortages and unemployment.

U.N. Projections

The U.N.'s medium projection that the world population will hit 8.9 billion in 2050, while regarded as the most likely scenario, is not inevitable. U.N. demographers have issued a range of projections for the 2050 world population, from 7.3 to 10.7 billion. And the general consensus, as expressed by 180 nations in the 1994 Cairo population conference and reiterated in another U.N. conference this July, is that the world's population growth rate should be slowed by providing women with more educational and family planning opportunities.

But [a] U.N. report finds that international assistance is lagging and some of the world's richest nations are not providing the funds needed for programs aimed at curbing population growth. "Unless funding increases substantially, the shortfall could spell continued high rates of unwanted pregnancy, abortion, maternal and child deaths, and an even faster spread of HIV/AIDS. The shortage of funding also means that progress towards human rights and equality in health care will be slower than ever," the U.N. report said. . . .

Although women today are having half as many children as their mothers did, more than 78 million people are being added to the planet each year, far more than in 1963, when the growth rate peaked. And high fertility 20 years ago has resulted in around 1 billion people between the ages of 15 and 24—a larger group of people coming into their reproductive [years] than this planet has ever seen. "The decisions taken in the next decade will determine how fast the world adds the next billion people and the billion after that, whether the new billions will be born to lives of poverty and deprivation, whether equality will be established between men and women, and what effects population growth will have on natural resources and the environment," the report said. To critics like Sheldon Richman, editor of the libertarian publication "The Freeman," the hype surrounding Oct. 12 is misplaced. The pattern of increasing life expectancy and decreasing death rate is simply the result of progress, he said. "People are living longer and healthier lives than ever before and this is not consistent with the idea we can overpopulate the earth," he said. Skeptics like Richman say that since Malthus predicted war and famine 200 years ago in his "Essay on the Principle of Population," concerns about the consequences of overpopulation have been baseless. . . .

. . . It took all of time until 1804 for the world's human population to reach 1 billion. But at the population's current growth rate, it only takes 12 years to add a billion people to the planet. Despite the slowing rate of growth since the 1960s, the net population growth since World War II means that even though people are multiplying at a slower rate, there are so many more people multiplying that the total number of people on the planet continues to grow. Demographers call this phenomenon population momentum and compare it to having a huge amount of money in the bank— even if interest rates are low, your money will still grow. The U.N. estimates that the momentum will not expire until around 2050, when the declining birth rate will stabilize the world's population. [Alex] Marshall at the United Nations Population Fund admits that there are many questions remaining about how many people our planet can support, but said that is exactly why we need to slow population growth, to buy time in order to answer questions about the sustainability of the planet and solve problems like malnutrition and unemployment. Stanford ecologist Paul Ehrlich, whose 1968 book "The Population Bomb" echoed Malthusian scenarios and made "overpopulation" a topical issue, said population growth isn't the only concern. Ehrlich still argues our current population level is three times what it should be. He said that the earth's optimal population size is around 2 billion.

Economy vs. Ecology

The debate over how many people are too many has pitted ecologists and economists against each other since the 1960s. Joel Cohen, a populations professor at Rockefeller University and Columbia University, said that the disagreement is inherent in the way each of these disciplines looks at the world. "Ecologists look at it in terms of natural restraints and economists emphasize human choices and usually both sides are more confident that their sides are right than the facts warrant," he said. Much of the disagreement hinges upon the idea that there is a maximum number that the earth can support, known among ecologists as a carrying capacity.

"The idea of carrying capacity doesn't apply to the human world because humans aren't passive with respect to their environment," said Richman of "The Freeman." "Human beings create resources. We find potential stuff and human intelligence turns it into resources. The computer revolution is based on sand; human intelligence turned that common stuff into the main component of an amazing technology."

But Halweil of Worldwatch disagrees, "It's conceivable for economists to look at trends as going upwards infinitely, but natural systems don't behave in the same way. There are thresholds in terms of natural systems. Perhaps we could cut down all the rainforests and harvest all the ocean fish out of existence and we could replace them with other resources, but that doesn't really account for destroying two ecosystems." . . .

Ehrlich said that on top of the problems caused by the sheer numbers of people inhabiting the planet are those caused by increasing consumption patterns. "Super-consumption is the other problem," he said. "And this behavior may be more difficult to change. We have had some success with birth rates but we have no clue how to get off superconsumption." Cohen said the notion of a carrying capacity, which is closely tied to our consumption patterns, is a source of much debate because it isn't as obvious for humans as for other animals because humans are more adaptable to environmental changes. "When you overexploit an area people respond; people aren't like deer who will just starve to death," he said. "The notion of carrying capacity depends on how we want to live." This idea that overpopulation depends on what kind of world we want to live in summarizes the conclusion of Cohen's book "How Many People Can the Earth Support?" and the environmentalists' viewpoint. "When I hear the question 'How many people can the earth support?,' what I hear is, 'What level of environmental degradation and human suffering are we willing to put up with?'" said Halweil.

8. The Johannesburg Declaration on Sustainable Development, 2002

From Our Origins to the Future

1. We, the representatives of the peoples of the world, assembled at the World Summit on Sustainable Development in Johannesburg, South Africa, from 2 to 4 September 2002, reaffirm our commitment to sustainable development.
2. We commit ourselves to building a humane, equitable and caring global society, cognizant of the need for human dignity for all.
3. At the beginning of this Summit, the children of the world spoke to us in a simple yet clear voice that the future belongs to them, and accordingly challenged all of us to ensure that through our actions they will inherit a world free of the indignity and indecency occasioned by poverty, environmental degradation and patterns of unsustainable development.
4. As part of our response to these children, who represent our collective future, all of us, coming from every corner of the world, informed by different life experiences, are united and moved by a deeply felt sense that we urgently need to create a new and brighter world of hope.

From United Nations, "Johannesburg Declaration on Sustainable Development." New York: United Nations, 2002. The United Nations is the author of the original material.

5. Accordingly, we assume a collective responsibility to advance and strengthen the interdependent and mutually reinforcing pillars of sustainable development— economic development, social development and environmental protection—at the local, national, regional and global levels.

6. From this continent, the cradle of humanity, we declare, through the Plan of Implementation of the World Summit on Sustainable Development and the present Declaration, our responsibility to one another, to the greater community of life and to our children.

7. Recognizing that humankind is at a crossroads, we have united in a common resolve to make a determined effort to respond positively to the need to produce a practical and visible plan to bring about poverty eradication and human development.

From Stockholm to Rio de Janeiro to Johannesburg

8. Thirty years ago, in Stockholm, we agreed on the urgent need to respond to the problem of environmental deterioration. Ten years ago, at the United Nations Conference on Environment and Development, held in Rio de Janeiro, we agreed that the protection of the environment and social and economic development are fundamental to sustainable development, based on the Rio Principles. To achieve such development, we adopted the global programme entitled Agenda 21 and the Rio Declaration on Environment and Development, to which we reaffirm our commitment. The Rio Conference was a significant milestone that set a new agenda for sustainable development.

9. Between Rio and Johannesburg, the world's nations have met in several major conferences under the auspices of the United Nations, including the International Conference on Financing for Development, as well as the Doha Ministerial Conference. These conferences defined for the world a comprehensive vision for the future of humanity.

10. At the Johannesburg Summit, we have achieved much in bringing together a rich tapestry of peoples and views in a constructive search for a common path towards a world that respects and implements the vision of sustainable development. The Johannesburg Summit has also confirmed that significant progress has been made towards achieving a global consensus and partnership among all the people of our planet.

The Challenges We Face

11. We recognize that poverty eradication, changing consumption and production patterns and protecting and managing the natural resource base for economic and social development are overarching objectives of and essential requirements for sustainable development.

12. The deep fault line that divides human society between the rich and the poor and the ever-increasing gap between the developed and developing worlds pose a major threat to global prosperity, security and stability.

13. The global environment continues to suffer. Loss of biodiversity continues, fish stocks continue to be depleted, desertification claims more and more fertile land,

the adverse effects of climate change are already evident, natural disasters are more frequent and more devastating, and developing countries more vulnerable, and air, water and marine pollution continue to rob millions of a decent life.

14. Globalization has added a new dimension to these challenges. The rapid integration of markets, mobility of capital and significant increases in investment flows around the world have opened new challenges and opportunities for the pursuit of sustainable development. But the benefits and costs of globalization are unevenly distributed, with developing countries facing special difficulties in meeting this challenge.

15. We risk the entrenchment of these global disparities and unless we act in a manner that fundamentally changes their lives the poor of the world may lose confidence in their representatives and the democratic systems to which we remain committed, seeing their representatives as nothing more than sounding brass or tinkling cymbals.

Our Commitment to Sustainable Development

16. We are determined to ensure that our rich diversity, which is our collective strength, will be used for constructive partnership for change and for the achievement of the common goal of sustainable development.

17. Recognizing the importance of building human solidarity, we urge the promotion of dialogue and cooperation among the world's civilizations and peoples, irrespective of race, disabilities, religion, language, culture or tradition.

18. We welcome the focus of the Johannesburg Summit on the indivisibility of human dignity and are resolved, through decisions on targets, timetables and partnerships, to speedily increase access to such basic requirements as clean water, sanitation, adequate shelter, energy, health care, food security and the protection of biodiversity. At the same time, we will work together to help one another gain access to financial resources, benefit from the opening of markets, ensure capacity-building, use modern technology to bring about development and make sure that there is technology transfer, human resource development, education and training to banish underdevelopment forever.

19. We reaffirm our pledge to place particular focus on, and give priority attention to, the fight against the worldwide conditions that pose severe threats to the sustainable development of our people, which include: chronic hunger; malnutrition; foreign occupation; armed conflict; illicit drug problems; organized crime; corruption; natural disasters; illicit arms trafficking; trafficking in persons; terrorism; intolerance and incitement to racial, ethnic, religious and other hatreds; xenophobia; and endemic, communicable and chronic diseases, in particular HIV/AIDS, malaria and tuberculosis.

20. We are committed to ensuring that women's empowerment, emancipation and gender equality are integrated in all the activities encompassed within Agenda 21, the Millennium development goals and the Plan of Implementation of the Summit.

21. We recognize the reality that global society has the means and is endowed with the resources to address the challenges of poverty eradication and sustainable development confronting all humanity. Together, we will take extra steps to ensure that these available resources are used to the benefit of humanity.

22. In this regard, to contribute to the achievement of our development goals and targets, we urge developed countries that have not done so to make concrete efforts [to] reach the internationally agreed levels of official development assistance.

23. We welcome and support the emergence of stronger regional groupings and alliances, such as the New Partnership for Africa's Development, to promote regional cooperation, improved international cooperation and sustainable development.

24. We shall continue to pay special attention to the developmental needs of small island developing States and the least developed countries.

25. We reaffirm the vital role of the indigenous peoples in sustainable development.

26. We recognize that sustainable development requires a long-term perspective and broad-based participation in policy formulation, decision-making and implementation at all levels. As social partners, we will continue to work for stable partnerships with all major groups, respecting the independent, important roles of each of them.

27. We agree that in pursuit of its legitimate activities the private sector, including both large and small companies, has a duty to contribute to the evolution of equitable and sustainable communities and societies.

28. We also agree to provide assistance to increase income-generating employment opportunities, taking into account the Declaration on Fundamental Principles and Rights at Work of the International Labour Organization.

29. We agree that there is a need for private sector corporations to enforce corporate accountability, which should take place within a transparent and stable regulatory environment.

30. We undertake to strengthen and improve governance at all levels for the effective implementation of Agenda 21, the Millennium development goals and the Plan of Implementation of the Summit.

Multilateralism Is the Future

31. To achieve our goals of sustainable development, we need more effective, democratic and accountable international and multilateral institutions.

32. We reaffirm our commitment to the principles and purposes of the Charter of the United Nations and international law, as well as to the strengthening of multilateralism. We support the leadership role of the United Nations as the most universal and representative organization in the world, which is best placed to promote sustainable development.

33. We further commit ourselves to monitor progress at regular intervals towards the achievement of our sustainable development goals and objectives.

Making It Happen!

34. We are in agreement that this must be an inclusive process, involving all the major groups and Governments that participated in the historic Johannesburg Summit.

35. We commit ourselves to act together, united by a common determination to save our planet, promote human development and achieve universal prosperity and peace.

36. We commit ourselves to the Plan of Implementation of the World Summit on Sustainable Development and to expediting the achievement of the time-bound, socio-economic and environmental targets contained therein.
37. From the African continent, the cradle of humankind, we solemnly pledge to the peoples of the world and the generations that will surely inherit this Earth that we are determined to ensure that our collective hope for sustainable development is realized.

Adopted at the 17th plenary meeting of the World Summit on Sustainable Development, on 4 September 2002.

⚘ E S S A Y S

The essays in this chapter view economic globalization from the vantage points of changing social movements, worldviews, and global systems. The first essay, by Eileen McGurty of Johns Hopkins University, explores the origins of the environmental justice movement as it emerged in Warren County, North Carolina, in 1982 out of strategic coalitions between whites and blacks protesting the siting of a landfill for PCBs in a largely African American community. In the second essay, Peter Borelli, editor of *Amicus,* the journal of the Natural Resources Defense Council, describes recent environmental critiques of mainstream society and alternative philosophical proposals. The third essay, by writer and systems theorist Fritjof Capra, shows how the networks of global capitalism and trade include the environment and living nature and asks what kind of changes are required in order to create a sustainable society for the twenty-first century. Together the authors show that changes must take place on every level, from ecology, to economy, to worldviews, if people and the planet are to survive.

Environmental Justice

EILEEN McGURTY

In the summer of 1978, Robert Burns and his two sons drove liquid tanker trucks along rural roads in thirteen North Carolina counties and through remote sections of the Fort Bragg Military Reservation. Driving at night to avoid detection, they opened the bottom valve of the tanker and discharged liquid contaminated with polychlorinated biphenyls (PCBs) removed from the Ward Transformer Company in Raleigh onto the soil along the road shoulders. This violation of the Toxic Substance Control Act (TSCA) continued for nearly two weeks until 240 miles of road shoulders were contaminated. Robert Ward had hired the Burnses to illegally dispose of the contaminated liquid in an attempt to avoid the escalating cost of disposal that was due, in part, to increasing regulation of hazardous waste. Since the contamination occurred on state-owned property, North Carolina was responsible for remediation. Within a few months after detecting the contamination, the state devised a

From Eileen McGurty, "From NIMBY to Civil Rights: The Origins of the Environmental Justice Movement." *Environmental History* (1996–) 2, no. 3 (July 1997), 301–302, 305–310, 312–318. Copyright 1997 by Forest History Society. Reproduced with permission of Forest History Society in the format Textbook via Copyright Clearance Center.

plan calling for the construction of a landfill in Warren County, a rural area in north-eastern North Carolina with a majority of poor, African-American residents. Warren County also suffered the most contamination of any of the thirteen counties [affected] by the illegal disposal. A farmer in the small community of Afton, facing a foreclosure and bankruptcy, sold his property to the state for use as a final resting place for the contaminated soil.

The announcement of this disposal site sparked intense resistance from county residents concerned with the possible contamination of their groundwater and the potential threat to local economic development from the stigma of a hazardous waste facility. After three years of legal battles unsuccessfully waged by Warren County against North Carolina and the U.S. Environmental Protection Agency (EPA), the state was permitted to begin construction of the landfill in the summer of 1982. When it became apparent that the standard processes of recourse would not stop the forty thousand cubic yards of soil from being buried at the site, citizens of Warren County changed their oppositional strategy to disruptive collective action. In the process of planning for the protest events, they also shifted their primary rationale for opposing the site. While threats to groundwater and the local economy were still worries for the citizens, the disruptive action focused on environmental racism. Protesters argued that Warren County was chosen, in part, because the residents were primarily poor and African-American. As one activist put it, "The community was politically and economically unempowered; that was the reason for the siting. They took advantage of poor people and people of color." The citizens garnered support from regional and national civil rights leaders and organized protest events daily during the six-week period while soil was delivered to the landfill. The unrelenting protests resulted in a delay and disruption of the landfilling project, with nearly five hundred arrests and significant state and national media coverage, but they failed to stop the landfill.

Despite the failure of the protests to reach the immediate objective, the controversy over the Warren County landfill had a major impact on contemporary environmental activism and the environmental policy agenda. The events in Warren County are proclaimed by activists and policymakers alike as the birth of the environmental justice movement. Environmental justice activists argue that the inequitable distribution of environmental degradation and systematic exclusion of the poor and people of color from environmental decision making is perpetuated by traditional environmental organizations, also known as mainstream environmentalism, and by environmental regulatory agencies. The topic seemed to explode overnight, creating the perception that environmental justice has shaped an original challenge to the contemporary environmental discussion. In reality, potential negative social impacts of both environmental degradation and regulatory policies have been at the core of environmental discussions since the onset of the modern environmental era. . . .

During the six weeks of protests in Warren County, North Carolina, in the autumn of 1982, white land owners joined together with black residents and civil rights activists to produce a significant disruptive collective action. The process of coming together transformed the two parties in the coalition and loosened the strict boundaries between environmental and civil rights causes. Civil rights activists embraced an environmental perspective as a result of a toxic threat to the daily lives of African-Americans and through their direct conflict with government agencies responsible for environmental decisions. Local whites, who began their opposition

with the narrow focus of keeping hazardous waste out of their community, expanded their resistance to include a concern for inadvertent racist ramifications of
some environmental policies. The political landscape for African-Americans at the
local and national level, the emerging toxic construct, and the economic instability
of the county all contributed to the transformative moment. This new movement
for environmental justice emerged from the lived experience of the residents of this
rural, poor county in North Carolina and their connections to powerful African-
Americans, not from mainstream environmental groups. This union of two causes
which emerged from the Warren County events was partly in conflict with the traditional environmental organizations involved in the case. The conflict is still reflected
in the ongoing tension between the two causes as they seek common ground. . . .

The initial protest in Warren County began typically, as a narrowly defined,
self-interested response to a local threat: "We don't want that facility in our backyards." Residents were primarily concerned with public health repercussions from
potential groundwater contamination and negative economic impacts of a waste
facility near their homes. The fear of contamination was fueled by the timing of the
North Carolina incident: the dumping of the PCB-contaminated liquid occurred
exactly at the same time when hazardous waste became a household word as a result
of the Love Canal catastrophe in August 1978. In Love Canal, New York, a community just southeast of Niagara Falls, a housing subdivision and public school were
built adjacent to an area used by the Hooker Chemical Company to dispose of over
forty-three million pounds of industrial wastes. By the 1970s, this toxic material had
seeped into the homes and the school, creating significant health problems for residents, including asthma, lethargy, cancer, miscarriages, and birth defects. In August
1978, New York officials decided to evacuate 240 families from the area. Television
news coverage of these events showed how toxic contamination had destroyed normal suburban life by financially destroying families and creating significant social
disorder. One week after Love Canal first appeared in the national media, North
Carolina learned of the illegal dumping along the road shoulders. During the following week, network television news covered both Love Canal and the North Carolina
roadways in the same segments.

The infusion of the hazardous waste issue into public discourse through the
Love Canal news coverage had two impacts. First, the toxic threat itself was always
lurking in the background; no one had immunity from the silent killer, not whites,
not blacks, not the wealthy, not the poor. Second, the government was implicated
in the victimization of citizens by toxic materials. Distrust of the agency with the
official environmental label became the rallying cry for the new activists. The direct
connection of the North Carolina contamination with the Love Canal catastrophe
reinforced both of these notions. The already strong connection between the two
cases of contamination increased when PCBs were identified as part of the toxins at
Love Canal. In December 1978, when county residents read in the newspaper that the
state had submitted a permit application for a landfill site in Warren County, they responded based on these newly formed constructs and vehemently resisted the plan.

Warren County Citizens Concerned about PCBs (Concerned Citizens) became
one of many local groups opposed to the hazardous waste facility, countering "facts"
from the state and the EPA with their own data showing the flaws in the state's plan.
In this way, they were like numerous other opponents of locally unwanted land uses,

worried that a hazardous waste facility would ruin the natural resources upon which they depended and destroy their already shaky economy. The post–Love Canal activism also created an aggregate of resistance groups that developed a new synergy. On regional and national levels, networks sprang up quickly to put local activists in touch with each other and to disseminate the most up-to-date information about the emerging field of hazardous waste management and remediation. These groups had access to information and also had experience in organizing against toxic contamination. Concerned Citizens were in need of both, and the emerging activist networks provided the necessary information for them to organize significant resistance. . . .

. . . The technical arguments were clearly an "anywhere but here" discussion. Once the county entered the judiciary system with its civil suit against the state and the EPA, it was forced to continue in this vein, arguing over technical problems with the site and flaws in the design of the landfill. If the county did not agree that a safe disposal method was possible, as was presumed under the federal regulations, then what would the state do to remediate the problem? There had to be a solution; it was unthinkable that this situation could not be fixed with the application of sound science. As a result, once the court ruled that . . . design improvements transformed the Warren County property into an acceptable site, the county was forced to accept the landfill. In the spring of 1982, the county withdrew its suit after securing the design changes and gaining the deed to the 120 acres of the Pope farm which was not to be used for the landfill. The court lifted the injunction, and the state began construction of the landfill in June, with the contaminated soil scheduled to begin arriving at the site in September.

The Coalition Is Formed

Late in the summer of 1982, with the soil delivery looming, the citizens made a drastic shift in their strategy by moving toward disruptive collective action. Protests were not generally a part of the cultural experience of the white members of the group, and when faced with the reality of organizing a direct action, Concerned Citizens realized that it lacked expertise. In fact, demonstrations in the South were typically associated with black civil rights activism often leveled against local whites. During the tumultuous 1960s in Warren County, many confrontations between black and white residents occurred in the middle of Warrenton on Main Street. . . .

Given the long history of racial discrimination and tension, it was most astonishing that a largely white opposition group in a rural southern county would reach out to black protest leaders for help and advice to revive their movement. It was even more astonishing that many whites, although not all, stayed and participated in the meetings, marches, and acts of civil disobedience. The nature of toxic contamination, the political climate in the county, and the tenacity and coalition-building skills of opposition leaders made these unlikely partners collaborate. . . .

In addition to the factors motivating white members of Concerned Citizens and African-Americans in the county to join forces, participants and bystanders attributed the success of the coalition to Ken and Deborah Ferruccio, two well-educated and tenacious individuals who had moved to North Carolina from Ohio in 1975 in hopes of raising their children in a peaceful, rural setting. When it was time to contact civil rights leaders for assistance, neither Ferruccio had any direct ties to black leaders. They drew on their association, through Concerned Citizens, with the pastor of the nearby black Baptist church to make the initial contact with the powerful and influential United Church of Christ Commission on Racial Justice (UCC). Reverend Luther Brown of Coley Springs Baptist Church was not a politically active pastor; he did not believe that the spiritual well-being of his congregation depended on fundamental political and social change. In early 1979, concerned for the health of his parishioners, Reverend Brown met with the Ferruccios and several other Concerned Citizens. Although this type of action was unfamiliar to Reverend Brown, he continued to follow the activities of the group. Reverend Brown and Ken Ferruccio eventually contacted Reverend Leon White, the director of the North Carolina office of the UCC; while Brown did not know Reverend White well, his position as a black pastor proved essential in linking the two organizations.

Leon White, who had orchestrated much of the voter registration drive in Warren County, had many years of experience in organizing civil rights demonstrations and had the institutional support of the UCC behind him. One of the most significant impacts from the involvement of White was his connection with the Reverend Benjamin Chavis, the renowned leader of the "Wilmington Ten." As a member of White's UCC congregation located in Warren County, Chavis became an important symbolic leader for local blacks involved in the protests. He delivered a motivational speech to the group, and on the third day of the protests he was arrested while leading a group of activists in blocking Department of Transportation trucks.

Chavis evoked respect from African-Americans, caution from law enforcement, and intense interest from the media. Locals felt that participation from Chavis meant he was still connected to his roots in northeastern North Carolina. Because he had a national reputation, it also meant that their local struggle was meaningful in a larger arena. Although law enforcement officials were not surprised by his participation nor taken off guard by it, Chavis gave the action a serious connotation, with a potential for extreme disruption, and perhaps even violence. His position also gave the newly embraced environmental issue legitimacy among African-Americans. After his brief experience with the Warren County residents, Chavis became the chief crusader among civil rights leaders combating what he called "environmental racism." Several years later, he convinced the UCC to fund an extensive study of the relationship between the location of toxic waste and the racial composition of the surrounding community. The result, *Toxic Waste and Race,* became a cornerstone of the environmental justice movement. The participation of Chavis, his influential position with African-Americans, his influence in national policy arenas, and his dynamic personality catapulted the new linkage between environmentalism and civil rights into the minds and hearts of a multitude of Americans—blacks, whites, civil rights activists, and environmentalists.

In addition to expertise from the UCC, local opponents received support from the Southern Christian Leadership Conference (SCLC), the organization associated with Martin Luther King and the nonviolent civil rights actions of the 1950s and 1960s. The initial involvement of the SCLC led to the arrest of Walter E. Fauntroy, a nonvoting member of congress from the District of Columbia, and increased media attention associated with this unusual occurrence. When Fauntroy returned to Washington, he initiated the first government-sponsored inquiry into the correlation of race and income with landfill sites. The subsequent General Accounting Office

(GAO) study influenced Chavis to support the more extensive *Toxic Waste and Race* and started the drive toward documenting discrimination in siting and in environmental hazards. Although questions remain about the validity of the results and the use of the conclusions for forming public policy, the GAO study has had a large impact on the development of the environmental justice movement and on the resulting changes in policy. Because an influential black political leader like Fauntroy was in a position to marshal government resources on behalf of Warren County activists, the environmental justice movement took its first step toward documenting its central claim.

With the assistance of experienced civil rights organizers, a direct action campaign against the landfill was waged from September 15 through October 12, 1982. The number of participants ranged from a handful to several hundred, and the protest successfully disrupted the orderly and efficient completion of the landfill. Tensions were high in the county, particularly in late August after an unknown vandal slashed the landfill's plastic liner with a knife. This vandalism, coupled with the organizing support from well-known, even feared and notorious, civil rights leaders, convinced the state that the potential for violence was high; more than two hundred state patrol officers were posted at the scene and a battalion of the national guard was placed on alert.

The power of the protests came from the repertoire of actions honed by civil rights activists two decades earlier. Observers saw the similarities immediately:

> The whole thing was a revival of the whole civil rights stuff – the tone, the look, the cants, the point. It was more like a civil rights protest than any NIMBY ["not in my back yard"] opposition. I had been to other NIMBY type meetings in wealthy communities with all kinds of technical stuff about why not near them. There was some of that [in Warren County] but the tone of the marches was more "you are doing this to us because we're poor and black."

Participants were familiar with the pattern for activism and could easily fall into its rhythm. Although not all whites in the county were willing to join, the actions of the civil rights movement were familiar to both blacks and whites. Meetings at the local black Baptist church (located less than two miles from the landfill site), the high visibility of well-known African-American activists, the incorporation of prayer into all the protests, and the long distance march—from Warrenton to Raleigh—were all part of an established program of civil rights activism familiar to both county residents and activists from other places who joined the locals.

The landfill situation also presented an opportunity for dramatic action. When the Department of Transportation trucks brought the contaminated soil from the road shoulders to the landfill, the protesters lay down on the road in front of the oncoming vehicles. None of the Warren County residents participating in the protests had ever "put their bodies on the line" in such a literal sense. This tactic of symbolically blocking the source of the contamination delayed the project and raised the visibility of the events, inviting more extensive media coverage and encouraging others to join the protests. . . .

Changing discriminatory land use decisions had been part of an earlier civil rights agenda, but the civil rights framing of the Warren County case added environmental, social, economic, and political dimensions to the problem. The contamination was thrust upon the community by the state and federal governments. Since government had failed many times in the recent past to protect blacks, it was not difficult to believe that another failure was imminent. Civil rights activists adopted an environmental perspective to protect African-Americans, their health, and the resources upon which they depended. This environmental viewpoint was in opposition to the government agencies that were charged with taking protective action, but did not protect all citizens equally. . . .

The civil rights agenda extended itself to include an environmental agenda based on how activists redefined what constituted an environmental problem and who their opponents were. Alliances with traditional environmental organizations were not part of the extension into the environmental arena. When African-Americans spoke about the involvement of environmental organizations in the controversy, they only referred to the government agencies that made environmentally related decisions, especially the EPA. The "Group of Ten," the largest mainstream environmental policy groups in the nation, did not fit the definition of an "environmental organization" for blacks and did not touch the lives of the Warren County protesters with the same force as the EPA. Civil rights leaders depended on the information provided by the antitoxic organizers, but in 1982 these activists hardly had the same power and authority that the mainstream environmental organizations had in the environmental policy arena. . . .

The rising problem of hazardous waste management, the emergence of antitoxic activism, and the shifting politics of civil rights merged together in a place where the deteriorating economic condition of African-Americans was severe. Warren County, like many rural southern counties, was hit particularly hard by the recession of the early 1980s. Warren was attempting to make the transition from an agriculturally based economy to a mixed economy and was on the verge of some success at the time the landfill was proposed. The landfill threatened any hope for economic development in this largely black southern county. Growing difficulties with hazardous waste management and its emerging regulatory structure emphasized the impacts of environmental hazards on the daily lives of citizens. The inadequate implementation of hazardous waste reform provided opportunities for intensified political action, and this burgeoning activism helped to shape the fledgling Warren County opposition movement.

The political landscape for African-Americans was also changing. The election of Ronald Reagan created a significant increase in political action among African-Americans, especially in regard to the 1981 reauthorization of the Voting Rights Act of 1965. When the act was reauthorized and strengthened, African-American residents in Warren County seized this opportunity to change the county political structure to more closely resemble its racial demographics. The increased electoral activities among African-Americans in Warren County helped define the issue of the landfill as one of racial discrimination.

The heritage of civil rights activism in the county impacted the organizing of the landfill opposition. Warren County activists were able to link with powerful African-American elites by renewing associations with earlier civil rights activism. Through reforms resulting from this activism, these individuals had gained access to official political institutions. These positions of power enabled the fledgling movement to raise a new issue—distributive justice of environmental hazards—in public policy debates. . . .

Actions on behalf of environmental quality were not necessarily "distractions from the problems of black and brown Americans," but were instead an integral part of making daily life healthy, safe, and economically secure. Such a notion helped to blur the distinction between environmentalism and social justice causes. While this transformation did not eliminate elitism in the mainstream organizations or the potential regressive impacts from several environmental reforms advocated by these groups, challenges are now made by activists who have incorporated an environmental awareness into their cause and who can envision alternatives. Warren County and the unlikely coalition that formed there began the process of overcoming these limitations of the environmental movement.

Environmental Philosophy

PETER BORELLI

In 1948, the noted astronomer Fred Hoyle anticipated the current situation when he wrote, "Once a photograph of the Earth, taken from the outside is available . . . a new idea as powerful as any other in history will be let loose." That photograph is now available, and with it the understanding that the world we live in is both finite and interconnected.

More recently, Alvin Toffler described the eighties as the dawn of a new era of crisis and opportunity regarding the ultimate survival of the planet. "Humanity," he wrote in his best-seller *The Third Wave* (1980), "faces a quantum leap forward. It faces the deepest social upheaval and creative restructuring of all time. Without clearly recognizing it, we are engaged in building a remarkable new civilization from the ground up." . . .

Deep ecology is the most influential new way of interpreting the environmental crisis. Its principles, enunciated in 1972 by Norwegian philosopher Arne Naess, are defined principally in opposition to the established movement, which it terms "shallow" ecology: anthropocentric and utilitarian. In this view, shallows encourage the destructiveness and wastefulness of industrial society even as they seek to reform it. For example, deep ecologists argue that environmental regulations based on emissions standards and tolerances represent licenses to pollute. Thus, NRDC [Natural Resources Defense Council], National Audubon, the National Wildlife Federation, and other such groups are considered shallow by most deeps.

Naess's ideas have been developed in the United States by sociologist Bill Devall and philosopher George Sessions. (Both are Californians and active in the Sierra Club, despite its "shallowness.")

Deep ecology extends the ecological principle of interrelatedness to virtually every aspect of our daily lives. Human and nonhuman species are viewed as having inherent and equal value, from which it follows that humans have no right to reduce the natural diversity of the earth, either directly or indirectly. Direct actions include such things as agriculture, mining, forestry, and technology. Indirect actions include economic and social policies that impinge on other human or nonhuman

From Peter Borelli, "The Ecophilosophers," *The Amicus Journal* 10, no. 2 (Spring 1988), pp. 30–39. Reprinted with permission of *The Amicus Journal*.

life forms, as well as population growth, which is viewed as an impediment to "the flourishing of human life and cultures."

Deep ecologists do not specify what the optimal human population of the world should be, but Naess has suggested an unimaginable figure of 1 billion, roughly equal to the total world population in 1800. In 1986, Naess wrote with all serious-ness in the journal *Philosophical Inquiry:* "It is recognized that there must be a long range, humane reduction through mild but tenacious political and economic meas-ures. This will make possible, as a result of increased habitat, population growth for thousands of species which are now constrained by human pressures."

John Muir, who may have been this country's first deep ecologist, summed up the biocentric (some might say misanthropic) perspective in these words:

> Pollution, defilement, squalor are words that never would have been created had man lived conformably to Nature. Birds, insects, bears die as cleanly and are disposed of as beautifully. . . . The woods are full of dead and dying trees, yet needed for their beauty to complete the beauty of the living. . . . How beautiful is all Death!

According to Sessions and Devall, the goal of deep ecology is to achieve univer-sal ecological consciousness "in sharp contrast with the dominant world view of technocratic-industrial societies which regards humans as isolated and fundamen-tally separate from the rest of nature, as superior to, and in charge of, the rest of creation." [Former Sierra Club Executive Director Michael] McCloskey's response: "While many of the aims of deep ecologists are appealing as ideals, it is not clear how far or fast they want to go in pursuit of their ideals, nor whether they really want to engage in the process of real-world change."

Indeed, deep ecology is less a movement than a bundle of ideas held to a greater or less degree by a heterogeneous grouping of organizations and individuals. The most visible and best organized are the monkeywrenchers, Earth First!, who take direct action in a variety of wilderness and forestry controversies in the West by arguably nonviolent means. (Naess, incident[al]ly, is the author of two studies on Gandhi and reportedly engaged in nonviolent resistance against the Nazis.) Deeps also are found on campuses and in local grass-roots organizations, where their effec-tiveness is hard to measure.

McCloskey acknowledges that an attitudinal survey of five major environmen-tal groups (Environmental Action, Environmental Defense Fund, National Wildlife Federation, Sierra Club, and the Wilderness Society), conducted by Resources for the Future in 1978, suggests that about 19 percent of their members hold views "that might be associated with the deep ecology movement."

Bioregionalism resembles deep ecology in adopting a radically different world view but is more catholic and tied to a different social base. It is an outgrowth and resurgence of the sixties back-to-the-land movement, and in the spirit of E. F. Schumacher's *Small is Beautiful,* looks for inspiration to cultures and life styles of indigenous peoples and dwellers in the land such as the Amish. Currently, there are more than 100 bioregional groups from Oregon to Maine, which informally exchange information and ideas. Since 1984, there have been two North American Bioregional Congresses attended by representatives from thirty or more states, sev-eral Canadian provinces, and Native American tribes.

The term bioregionalism was coined in 1976 by Peter Berg, who, with his wife Judy Goldhaft, runs a bioregional clearinghouse in San Francisco's Mission District called the Planet Drum Foundation. (The drum figures in shamanic ritual.) During the sixties, Berg and Goldhaft were among the founders of the Diggers, an organization that offered refuge to thousands of young people descending on Haight-Ashbury. It was also during this period that they made a cross-country tour of back-to-the-land communes.

The underlying premise of bioregionalism is that the environmental crisis begins at home and revolves around individuals' perceptions of their place in the world. Being a bio requires bearing witness. "All the planetwide pollution problems originate in some bioregion," says Berg. "It's the responsibility of the people who live there to eliminate the source of them. If you strike a five-finger chord—by promoting more community gardens, more renewable energy, accessible public transportation, sustainable agriculture—and you are serious about it, rain forests will stop getting chopped down in direct proportion."

Poet Gary Snyder, whose Pulitzer Prize–winning *Turtle Island* captures the spirit of bioregionalism, told the *Amicus Journal* recently that he saw himself "living on Planet Earth, on Turtle Island, in Shasta Nation. I think in terms of where the plant communities shift, and know where the rivers reach better than I know the highways now. It's a wonderful way to see the world, and it'll outlast anyone's local political boundary."

Snyder has a bioregional quiz for guests. "Where does the water you drink come from? What is the soil series where you live? Name five edible plants in your region and their seasons. Where does your garbage go?"

Unlike the back-to-the-landers who tended to isolate themselves in self-supporting communes, bioregionalists for the most part live within existing communities where they carve out simplified life styles and become involved in regional land-use issues. While some try to live off the land as farmers, most are wage earners in a variety of trades and professions. In many respects, they are the opposites of yuppies. Young, well-educated, and potentially upwardly mobile, they have chosen to make their living where they want to live rather than the other way around.

In the Sierra Nevada foothills where Snyder lives, he and others have joined long-time residents in electing new planning commissioners concerned about controlling growth. They also are involved in the U.S. Forest Service's management plan for the Tahoe National Forest.

In Northern California's Mattole River area, friends of the Bergs are involved with a watershed bioregional council that has been working with local residents to restore the native king salmon population, destroyed by logging operations that had silted the river.

When drinking-water contamination got out of hand along the Missouri-Arkansas border, a group of people got together to form the Ozark Area Community Congress (OACC), which promotes the use of compost toilets. In 1980, OACC called the first large gathering of the "ecological nation," modeled after tribal consensus as practiced by the Iroquois Federation.

OACC's activities soon attracted attention in Kansas, where it inspired formation of the KAW Council based in Lawrence. Among its founders is thirty-year-old Kelly Kindscher. In 1983, he took a 690-mile "walk" from Kansas City to the foothills of the Colorado Rockies "in the tradition of the Indian vision quest" to get to know his prairie bioregion. KAW now has about 350 members, publishes a newsletter, and is involved in agricultural issues. . . .

Despite their willingness to work incrementally toward change, most bio-regionalists believe the trend toward ecological destruction will not be reversed until there is a spiritual awakening. Father Thomas Berry, director of the River-dale Center for Religious Research in New York and active with the Hudson Bio-regional Council, states, "If we do not alter our attitude and our activities, our children and grandchildren will live not only amid the ruins of the industrial world, but also amid the ruins of the natural world." What is needed, he says, is a "treaty" or spiritual bond between ourselves and the natural world similar to God's covenant with creation after the Flood (*I set my rainbow in the cloud, and it shall be a sign of the covenant between me and the earth.*—Genesis 9:13). Such a treaty would be based on the principle of mutual enhancement. "The [Hudson] river and its valley," he writes, "are neither our enemy to be conquered, nor our servant to be controlled, nor our mistress to be seduced. The river is a pervasive presence beyond all these. It is the ultimate psychic as well as the physical context out of which we emerge into being and by which we are nourished, guided, healed, and fulfilled."

Berry's writings have attracted considerable attention among clerics, scientists, and environmentalists who feel that the Church has turned its back on the biologi-cal sciences and belittles "nature worship." Brian Swimme, a California physicist who works with the Institute for Cultural and Creation Spirituality, credits Berry with having developed a "functional cosmology" that goes beyond both science and theology. By combining a contemporary biological view of life with a sense of mystery about the universe, Berry has given new meaning to spiritual devotion and religious responsibility.

Though not actually a movement, the Gaia hypothesis complements the thinking of many of today's environmentalists. First proposed in 1972 by British chemist James Lovelock, who had worked with the NASA [National Aeronautics and Space Administration] team investigating the possibility of life on Mars, it holds that "the evolution of the species of living organisms is so closely coupled with the evolution of their physical and chemical environment that together they constitute a single and indivisible evolutionary process." The idea was drawn from Love-lock's observation that despite being composed of an unstable mixture of reactive gases (such as oxygen and methane), the atmosphere for the entire 3,500 million years since life began has remained remarkably stable. From this he hypothesized that "living matter, the air, the oceans, the land surface, were parts of a giant sys-tem which seemed to exhibit the behavior of a living creature." Hence, Gaia, Greek goddess of the earth.

The idea is not new. It surfaced during the nineteenth century when the German geographer Carl Ritter postulated a galvanic force in nature by means of which its separate parts communicated. More recently, the hypothesis has been extended by the controversial work of Boston University biologist Lynn Margulis, who argues that symbiosis and cooperation among all organisms always have been integral to successful existence.

Whether metaphor or reality, Gaia is in serious trouble. The dynamic balance of the biosphere is being radically disrupted by human activities such as the destruction of tropical forests, fossil-fuel consumption, and the release of chlorofluorocarbons.

While there is a widespread belief these days that caring for the earth requires fundamental and even radical change, it is not at all clear that this must extend to electoral politics. In the United States, the environment has been a bipartisan issue with vast public support. As former Senator Gaylord Nelson observed in part one of this series, when he went to Washington in 1963, "There were not more than five broad-gauged environmentalists in the Senate." When he introduced a ban on DDT during his freshman year, he could find only a single sponsor for a companion bill in the House. Were such a bill introduced today, however, the list of sponsors would fill the title page. The environment is now called America's issue, which at the very least means that there is some kind of consensus about the importance of environmental issues, if not their solution.

In the democratic coalition governments of Europe, where representation in parliament is based on the percentage of the national vote won by each party, it has been another story. There, young activists and elements of the middle class have coalesced around the ideas of deep ecology and the goal of achieving *Ökopax* (eco-peace), campaigning for a nuclear-free Europe and against environmental abuses. In 1979, the West Germans formed a coalition: *die Grünen,* or the Greens. By 1983, the Green Party had won 5 percent of the national vote (the minimum share of the vote required to win seats in the Bundestag), and twenty-seven seats in the Bundestag.

The Greens' astonishing entrance onto the political stage was immediately followed by infighting among ecologists, counterculturalists, moralists, feminists, antinuclear activists, and Marxists—each insisting that his or her prescription for the world's ills was most effective. While demonstrating the party's broad base of support, the infighting, nevertheless, has diverted its energy. Less than a year after their entry into parliamentary politics, one of the most articulate of the Greens, a former general in the West German army named Gert Bastion, quit his seat in the Bundestag in disgust. A few months later, Petra Kelly, a founding member, was thrown out of the Bundestag by her own party for ignoring her Bavarian constituents.

Still, by not trivializing their agenda and constantly seeking political compromise, the Greens have survived. Buoyed by protests against a proposed nuclear reprocessing station in Wackersdorf, public reaction to Chernobyl, and progress toward nuclear arms reductions, the Greens won 8.3 percent of the popular vote and forty-two seats in last year's [1987] national election. . . .

Soon after the West German Greens' first electoral victory, Charlene Spretnak, a Berkeley activist and lecturer on spirituality and feminism, and Fritjof Capra, author of *The Tao of Physics* and founder of an ecological think tank called the Elmwood Institute, teamed up to write *Green Politics.* It called for a U.S. Green movement based not on the German model but on the spiritual insights of deep ecology. The idea was that ecological problems of America were not the direct fault of capitalism but of consumerism caused by an emptiness of spirit.

Though deep ecology disavows central control, Spretnak initiated a loose-knit grass-roots network called the Committees of Correspondence (as during the American Revolution), organized at a meeting of activists in St. Paul, Minnesota, in August

1984. They adopted a platform consisting of "ten key values": ecological wisdom, grass-roots democracy, personal and social responsibility, nonviolence, decentralization, community-based economics, postpatriarchal values (feminism), respect for diversity, global responsibility, and concern for the future. Since then, about seventy-five Green groups have been formed.

. . . [In 1987], about 1,500 Greens gathered in Amherst, Massachusetts, for their first national conference. The stage was set for the Greening of America, but by lunch-time of the first day, the meeting had dissolved into an unhappening, as shouting matches broke out among deep ecologists, feminists, animal liberationists, anarchists, antimilitarists, monkeywrenchers, and graying SDSers. There was little talk of national organization or coalition building.

The Greens face numerous problems in the United States, not the least of which is the entrenchment of a two-party political system. While there is room for new, even radical environmental thinking that challenges the underlying assumptions of modern technology and industrial societies, the Greens must cope with the reality of environmentalism already having been absorbed by American politics. The likelihood of the Greens becoming a third national party is extremely remote, but the possibility of their stimulating effective local coalitions of minorities, women, workers, neighborhood groups, and environmentalists involved in every-day challenges such as toxic exposure and community planning and development, is very real. . . .

An important faction among the Greens is social ecology, which holds that environmental problems are rooted in social conditions. The leading spokesman, Murray Bookchin, is a veteran of the old and new lefts and director emeritus of the Institute for Social Ecology in Plainfield, Vermont. Bookchin takes sharp issue with those who "deify" nature. . . .

"We must achieve not just the reenchantment of nature but the reenchantment of humanity," Bookchin told the Amherst conference. He argued that the deep ecologists view humanity as "an ugly 'anthropocentric' thing—presumably, a malignant product of natural evolution—that is 'overpopulating' the planet, 'devouring' its resources, destroying its wildlife and the biosphere.

"Our wholesale condemnation of technology," he continued, "is a condemnation of some of the best achievements of mankind. The problem begins with our hierarchical society, a monstrous society in which growth and wealth measure progress and culture does not." . . .

Dan Chodorkoff, also of the Institute for Social Ecology, echoed Bookchin's remarks. "We need not a mindless unity with the rest of nature, but an increased mindfulness . . . a humanistic tradition which looks at the vast fecundity and tremendous diversity of relationships in nature, which need to be developed and applied by human beings.". . .

Ecology is not only a science, but an ethical confirmation of the wisdom of the great religions. Wes Jackson, a brilliant thinker in the field of sustainable agriculture, reminds us in *Altars of Unhewn Stone* of God's words to Moses after he had delivered the Ten Commandments: *If you make me an altar of stone, you shall not build it of hewn stone; for if you use your tool on it, you have profaned it.*—Exodus 20:25. "The scripture must mean," writes Jackson, "that we are to be more mindful of the creation, more mindful of the original materials of the universe than of the artist." . . .

. . . [I]t is appropriate to consider if we have made the best use of our atomic- and space-age knowledge. Environmentalists, in particular, should be asking if they have sufficiently advanced their cause. There are many who believe we have not, either because our vision is too dim or our actions too timid. . . .

The answer to such questions lies in recognizing that pollution, plunder, consumption, and waste for the most part are the consequences of political and economic conditions that also account for much of the human misery and strife in the world. This will require a broader, more comprehensive vision on the part of national environmental groups and a pragmatic, more constructive strategy on the part of groups seeking radical change. More important, it will require greater commitment and courage on the part of all environmentalists to challenge the present direction of economic policy and politics.

Globalization and Environmental Sustainability

FRITJOF CAPRA

During the last decade of the twentieth century, a recognition grew among entrepreneurs, politicians, social scientists, community leaders, grassroots activists, artists, cultural historians, and ordinary women and men from all walks of life that a new world was emerging—a world shaped by new technologies, new social structures, a new economy and a new culture. "Globalization" became the term used to summarize the extraordinary changes and the seemingly irresistible momentum felt by millions of people.

With the creation of the World Trade Organization (WTO) in the mid-1990s, economic globalization, characterized by "free trade," was hailed by corporate leaders and politicians as a new order that would benefit all nations, producing worldwide economic expansion whose wealth would trickle down to all. However, it soon became apparent to increasing numbers of environmentalists and grassroots activists that the new economic rules established by the WTO were manifestly unsustainable and were producing a multitude of interconnected fatal consequences—social disintegration, a breakdown of democracy, more rapid and extensive deterioration of the environment, the spread of new diseases, and increasing poverty and alienation. . . .

In 1996, two books were published that provided the first systemic analyses of the new economic globalization. They are written in very different styles and their authors follow very different approaches, but their starting point is the same—the attempt to understand the profound changes brought about by the combination of extraordinary technological innovation and global corporate reach.

The Case Against the Global Economy is a collection of essays by more than forty grassroots activists and community leaders, edited by Jerry Mander and Edward Goldsmith, and published by the Sierra Club, one of the oldest and most respected environmental organizations in the United States. The authors of this book represent cultural traditions from many countries around the world. Most of them are well known among social-change activists. Their arguments are passionate, distilled from the experiences of their communities, and aimed at reshaping globalization according to different values and different visions.

The Rise of the Network Society by Manuel Castells, Professor of Sociology at the University of California at Berkeley, is a brilliant analysis of the fundamental processes underlying economic globalization, published by Blackwell, one of the largest academic publishers. Castells believes that, before attempting to reshape globalization, we need to understand the deep systemic roots of the world that is now emerging. "I propose the hypothesis," he writes in the prologue to his book, "that all major trends of change constituting our new, confusing world are related, and that we can make sense of their interrelationship. And, yes, I believe, in spite of a long tradition of sometimes tragic intellectual errors, that observing, analysing, and theorizing is a way of helping to build a different, better world."

During the years following the publication of these two books, some of the authors of *The Case Against the Global Economy* formed the International Forum on Globalization, a nonprofit organization that holds teach-ins on economic globalization in several countries. In 1999, these teach-ins provided the philosophical background for the worldwide coalition of grassroots organizations that successfully blocked the meeting of the World Trade Organization in Seattle and made its opposition to the WTO's policies and autocratic regime known to the world. . . .

Another important and rather mysterious aspect of globalization was the sudden collapse of Soviet communism in the 1980s, which occurred without the intervention of social movements and without a major war, and which came as a complete surprise to most Western observers. According to Castells, this profound geopolitical transformation, too, was a consequence of the Information Technology Revolution. In a detailed analysis of the economic demise of the Soviet Union, Castells postulates that the roots of the crisis that triggered Gorbachev's *perestroika* and eventually led to the breakup of the USSR are found in the inability of the Soviet economic and political system to navigate the transition to the new informational paradigm that was spreading through the rest of the world.

Since the demise of Soviet communism, capitalism has been thriving throughout the world and, as Castells observes, "it deepens its penetration of countries, cultures, and domains of life. In spite of a highly diversified social and cultural landscape, for the first time in history, the whole world is organized around a largely common set of economic rules." . . .

The process of economic globalization was purposefully designed by the leading capitalist countries (the so-called "G-7 nations"), the major transnational corporations, and by global financial institutions—most importantly, the World Bank, the International Monetary Fund (IMF) and the World Trade Organization (WTO)—that were created for that purpose.

However, the process has been far from smooth. Once the global financial networks reached a certain level of complexity, their nonlinear interconnections generated rapid feedback loops that gave rise to many unsuspected emergent phenomena. The resulting new economy is so complex and turbulent that it defies analysis in conventional economic terms. Thus Anthony Giddens, . . . director of the prestigious London School of Economics, admits: "The new capitalism that is one of the driving forces of globalization to some extent is a mystery. We don't fully know as yet just how it works." . . .

It is interesting to apply the systemic understanding of life to the analysis of this phenomenon. The new economy consists of a global metanetwork of complex technological and human interactions, involving multiple feedback loops operating far from equilibrium, which produce a never-ending variety of emergent phenomena. Its creativity, adaptability, and cognitive capabilities are certainly reminiscent of living networks, but it does not display the stability that is also a key property of life. The information circuits of the global economy operate at such speed and use such a multitude of sources that they constantly react to a flurry of information, and thus the system as a whole is spinning out of control.

Living organisms and ecosystems, too, may become continually unstable, but if they do, they will eventually disappear because of natural selection, and only those systems that have stabilizing processes built into them will survive. In the human realm, these processes will have to be introduced into the global economy through human consciousness, culture, and politics. In other words, we need to design and implement regulatory mechanisms to stabilize the new economy. As Robert Kuttner, editor of the progressive magazine *The American Prospect,* sums up the situation, "The stakes are simply too high to let speculative capital and currency swings determine the fate of the real economy." . . .

Global capitalism has increased poverty and social inequality not only by transforming the relationships between capital and labor, but also through the process of "social exclusion," which is a direct consequence of the new economy's network structure. As the flows of capital and information interlink worldwide networks, they exclude from these networks all populations and territories that are of no value or interest to their search for financial gain. As a result, certain segments of societies, areas of cities, regions, and even entire countries become economically irrelevant. In the words of Castells:

> Areas that are non-valuable from the perspective of informational capitalism, and that do not have significant political interest for the powers that be, are bypassed by flows of wealth and information, and ultimately deprived of the basic technological infrastructure that allows us to communicate, innovate, produce, consume, and even live, in today's world.

The process of social exclusion is epitomized by the desolation of American innercity ghettos, but its effects reach far beyond individuals, neighborhoods, and social groups. Around the world, a new impoverished segment of humanity has emerged that is sometimes referred to as the Fourth World. It comprises large areas of the globe, including much of Sub-Saharan Africa and impoverished rural areas of Asia and Latin America. The new geography of social exclusion includes portions of every country and every city in the world.

The Fourth World is populated by millions of homeless, impoverished, and often illiterate people who move in and out of paid work, many of them drifting into the criminal economy. They experience multiple crises in their lives, including hunger, disease, drug addiction, and imprisonment—the ultimate form of social exclusion. Once their poverty turns into misery, they may easily find themselves caught in a downward spiral of marginality from which it is almost impossible to escape. . . .

According to the doctrine of economic globalization—known as "neoliberalism," or "the Washington consensus"—the free-trade agreements imposed by the WTO on its member countries will increase global trade; this will create a global economic expansion; and global economic growth will decrease poverty, because its benefits will eventually "trickle down" to all. As political and corporate leaders like to say, the rising tide of the new economy will lift all boats. . . .

The central enterprise of current economic theory and practice—the striving for continuing, undifferentiated economic growth—is clearly unsustainable, since unlimited expansion on a finite planet can only lead to catastrophe. Indeed, at the turn of this century it has become abundantly clear that our economic activities are harming the biosphere and human life in ways that may soon become irreversible. In this precarious situation, it is paramount for humanity to systematically reduce its impact on the natural environment. As then-senator Al Gore declared courageously in 1992, "We must make the rescue of the environment the central organizing principle for civilization."

Unfortunately, instead of following this admonition, the new economy has significantly increased our harmful impact on the biosphere. In *The Case Against the Global Economy,* Edward Goldsmith, founding editor of the leading European environmental journal *The Ecologist,* gives a succinct summary of the environmental impact of economic globalization. He points out that the increase of environmental destruction with increasing economic growth is well illustrated by the examples of South Korea and Taiwan. During the 1990s, both countries achieved stunning rates of growth and were held up as economic models for the Third World by the World Bank. At the same time, the resulting environmental damage has been devastating.

In Taiwan, agricultural and industrial poisons have severely polluted nearly every major river. In some places, the water is not only devoid of fish and unfit to drink, but is actually combustible. The level of air pollution is twice that considered harmful in the United States; cancer rates have doubled since 1965, and the country has the world's highest incidence of hepatitis. In principle, Taiwan could use its new wealth to clean up its environment, but competitiveness in the global economy is so extreme that environmental regulations are eliminated rather than strengthened in order to lower the costs of industrial production.

One of the tenets of neoliberalism is that poor countries should concentrate on producing a few special goods for export in order to obtain foreign exchange, and should import most other commodities. This emphasis has led to the rapid depletion of the natural resources required to produce export crops in country after country—diversion of fresh water from vital rice paddies to prawn farms; a focus on water-intensive crops, such as sugar cane, that result in dried-up riverbeds; conversion of good agricultural land into cash-crop plantations; and forced migration of large numbers of farmers from their lands. All over the world there are countless examples of how economic globalization is worsening environmental destruction.

The dismantling of local production in favor of exports and imports, which is the main thrust of the WTO's free-trade rules, dramatically increases the distance "from the farm to the table." In the United States, the average ounce of food now travels over a thousand miles before being eaten, which puts enormous stress on the environment. New highways and airports cut through primary forests; new harbors destroy wetlands and coastal habitats; and the increased volume of transport further pollutes the air and causes frequent oil and chemical spills. Studies in Germany have shown that the contribution of nonlocal food production to global warming is between six and twelve times higher than that of local production, due to increased CO_2 emissions.

As ecologist and agricultural activist Vandana Shiva points out, the impact of climate instability and ozone depletion is born disproportionately by the South, where most regions depend on agriculture and where slight changes in climate can totally destroy rural livelihoods. In addition, many transnational corporations use the free-trade rules to relocate their resource-intensive and polluting industries in the South, thus further worsening environmental destruction. The net effect, in Shiva's words, is that "resources move from the poor to the rich, and pollution moves from the rich to the poor."

The destruction of the natural environment in Third World countries goes hand in hand with the dismantling of rural people's traditional, largely self-sufficient ways of life, as American television programs and transnational advertising agencies promote glittering images of modernity to billions of people all over the globe without mentioning that the lifestyle of endless material consumption is utterly unsustainable. Edward Goldsmith estimates that, if all Third World countries were to reach the consumption level of the United States by the year 2060, the annual environmental damage from the resulting economic activities would be 220 times what it is today, which is not even remotely conceivable.

Since money-making is the dominant value of global capitalism, its representatives seek to eliminate environmental regulations under the guise of free trade wherever they can, lest these regulations interfere with profits. Thus the new economy causes environmental destruction not only by increasing the impact of its operations on the world's ecosystems, but also by eliminating national environmental laws in country after country. In other words, environmental destruction is not only a side effect, but is also an integral part, of the design of global capitalism. "Clearly," Goldsmith concludes, "there is no way of protecting our environment within the context of a global 'free trade' economy committed to continued economic growth and hence to increasing the harmful impact of our activities on an already fragile environment."

♥ *F U R T H E R   R E A D I N G*

Murray Bookchin, *The Ecology of Freedom* (1982)

Michael Brown, *Laying Waste: The Poisoning of America by Toxic Chemicals* (1979)

Robert D. Bullard, ed., *Confronting Environmental Racism: Voices from the Grassroots* (1993)

———, *Dumping in Dixie: Race, Class, and Environmental Quality* (2000)

Manuel Castells, *The Rise of the Network Society* (1996)

Luke W. Cole, *From the Ground Up: Environmental Racism and the Rise of the Environmental Justice Movement* (2001)

Council on Environmental Quality, *The Global 2000 Report to the President: Entering the Twenty-First Century* (1981)

Angela Davis, "Inside/Outside: Women at the Borders of Globalization," in *AULA: Architecture and Urbanism in Las Américas* (Spring 1999)

Theodore Goldfarb, ed., *Taking Sides: Clashing Views on Controversial Environmental Issues,* 3rd ed. (1989)

Samuel P. Hays, *Beauty, Health, and Permanence: Environmental Politics in the United States, 1955–1985* (1987)

——, *A History of Environmental Politics Since 1945* (2000)

H. Patricia Hynes, *The Recurring Silent Spring* (1989)

Fredric Jameson, "Notes on Globalization as a Philosophical Issue," in Frederic Jameson and Masao Miyoshi, ed., *The Cultures of Globalization* (1998)

Benjamin Kline, *First Along the River: A Brief History of the U.S. Environmental Movement* (2000)

Frances Moore Lappé and Joseph Collins, *Food First* (1977)

James N. Levitt, ed., *Conservation in the Internet Age: Threats and Opportunities* (2002)

Jerry Mander and Edward Goldsmith, eds., *The Case Against the Global Economy* (1996)

Christopher Manes, *Green Rage* (1990)

John McCormick, *Reclaiming Paradise: The Global Environmental Movement* (1989)

John R. McNeill, *Something New Under the Sun: An Environmental History of the Twentieth Century World* (2000)

Donella H. Meadows et al., *The Limits to Growth* (1972)

G. Tyler Miller, Jr., *Living in the Environment: Concepts, Problems, and Alternatives* (1975)

Kathryn M. Mutz, Gary C. Bryner, and Douglas S. Kenney, eds., *Justice and Natural Resources: Concepts, Strategies, and Applications* (2002)

Robert Paehlke, *Environmentalism and the Future of Progressive Politics* (1989)

David Pepper, *The Roots of Modern Environmentalism* (1985)

Laura Pulido, "Rethinking Environmental Racism: White Privilege and Urban Development in Southern California," *Annals of the Association of American Geographers* 90, no. 1, (2000)

Philip Reno, *Mother Earth, Father Sky, and Economic Development: Navajo Resources and Their Use* (1981)

Dick Russell, "Environmental Racism: Minority Communities and Their Battle Against Toxics," *The Amicus Journal* 11 (Spring 1989), 22–32

C. Brandt Short, *Ronald Reagan and the Public Lands: America's Conservation Debate, 1979–1984* (1989)

Hawley Truax et al., "Beyond White Environmentalism: Minorities and the Environment," *Environmental Action* (January/February 1990), 19–30

World Commission on Environment and Development, *Our Common Future* (1987)

Worldwatch Institute, *State of the World 2003* (2003)

Eddie Yuen, Daniel Burton Rose, and George Katsiaficas, eds., *The Battle of Seattle: The New Challenge to Capitalist Globalization* (2001)

Glossary

☙

animism   A belief that everything in nature, including rocks, wind, plants, and other animals, is alive and has a soul, inner spirit, or organizing power.

anthropocentric   The idea that humanity is the most important entity in the universe and that all other parts of the natural world exist for the sake of humanity.

balance of nature   The position that abiotic and biotic processes in ecological systems return to a state of equilibrium if they are disturbed and tend toward self-regulation.

biocentric   The idea that all plants and animals, as centers of life, are worthy of moral consideration and have intrinsic value.

biogeochemical cycles   The flow of elements, such as oxygen, carbon, nitrogen, and phosphorus, through earth, air, and water.

biological determinism   The idea that biological or environmental factors carry greater weight than cultural factors in the causal sequence of events.

biomass   The total weight of all living material in a defined area.

biome   The complex of animal and plant communities that exists under the particular climatic conditions in a given area.

bioregionalism   The philosophy that holds that people and other living and non-living things are interdependent and that they should live as much as possible within the resources and ecological constraints of a particular geographical area, such as a watershed.

biota   The plant and animal life of a place or region.

biotic community   The complex of interdependent living organisms in a given place.

chaos theory   The mathematical theory that holds that a small effect can lead to a large effect that cannot be predicted by linear (first-power) differential equations (those dealing with infinitesimal differences between variable quantities), and that such complex events may be better described by nonlinear equations.

consciousness   An awareness of one's own thoughts, perceptions, and volition, or the collective awareness of a group of people.

conservation   The protection and use of natural resources for the benefit of present and future generations.

declensionist   Relating to a narrative structure, or plot, that portrays history as a movement from a better, more positive, or happier state to a worsened, negative, or sadder condition.

deep ecology   The idea, first proposed by Norwegian philosopher Arne Naess, that environmental problems require a shift in basic philosophical assumptions about human relationships with the nonhuman world and cannot be solved by legislation and regulation alone.

diversity-stability hypothesis   The theory that complex biological and physical systems result in the long-term maintenance of an ecosystem.

ecocentric   The idea that the natural world is an integrated ecological whole and as such is worthy of moral consideration.

ecofeminism   The idea that a historical and cultural association exists between women and nature, that both have been dominated in Western culture, and that women can liberate both themselves and nature through environmental activism.

ecological imperialism   The idea, proposed by environmental historian Alfred Crosby, that the European colonists, together with their animals, germs, varmints, and weeds, were both deliberately and inadvertently part of colonization, giving Europeans an advantage in settling the temperate regions.

ecological revolution   A concept developed by environmental historian Carolyn Merchant to characterize major transformations in the relationships between humans and nonhuman nature.

ecological succession   The replacement of one community of organisms in a particular environment by another community over a period of time.

ecology   A branch of science dealing with the interactions between and among organisms and their abiotic surroundings; it was named by Ernst Haeckel in 1866 and defined as "the whole science of the relations of the organism to the environment."

ecosystem   A community of animals, plants, and bacteria and their relationships with one another and with their physical and chemical environment.

environment   The surroundings, or external conditions, that affect a group of organisms and its development.

environmental ethics   A branch of moral philosophy that addresses questions of what ought to be done to save the environment.

environmentalism   Policies and actions taken to address environmental problems, such as pollution and resource depletion, for the benefit of present and future generations.

food web   Interlocking systems of organisms and nutrients in which energy in the form of food is transferred from one trophic (nutritional) level to another.

homeostasis   The tendency for an organism to maintain internal stability by compensating for external changes; for example, the maintenance of temperature by the human body.

homocentric   The idea that humans are the center of the natural world and should be given moral consideration over other parts of nature.

Hudson River school   A group of nineteenth-century American landscape painters who first concentrated on the Hudson River region but also depicted parts of New England, upper New York State, New Jersey, and Pennsylvania; they eventually extended their focus to Europe, the American West, and South America.

human ecology   The study of human communities and their interactions with other communities, species, and the natural environment over given time periods.

land ethic   A concept developed by ecologist Aldo Leopold that extended the ethics of the human community to include "soils, waters, plants, and animals, or collectively: the land."

mechanism   A system whose parts work together as do the parts of a machine. A philosophy of the seventeenth-century scientific revolution that characterized the world as a machine made up of inert parts that obey the laws of physics and chemistry.

monoculture   The cultivation of a single crop on a given piece of land.

nature   The physical universe, including all its physical features, processes, and organisms and their interactions. Although nature technically includes human beings, the word is often used to refer to the nonhuman world, exclusive of human beings and their social and cultural institutions.

organicism   A philosophy that holds that the world is like a living organism, such as the human body. Each part of nature, including animals, plants, and minerals, is part of a larger whole and participates in it.

plant associations   Groups of plants that are usually found together in areas with similar ecological conditions.

polyculture   The cultivation of a number of crops in a single field or piece of land.

portmanteau biota   The term used by environmental historian Alfred Crosby to characterize the animals, plants, weeds, pests, and pathogens that accompanied people on ships to the New World.

positivism   The philosophical theory that only mathematical statements and empirically verifiable statements are true and lead to positive knowledge of the external world.

preservation   The belief that natural areas should be left undisturbed by human beings.

resources   Money, property, or natural entities that can be used to the advantage of an individual or a country.

social ecology   The study of human social and economic institutions and communities and their interactions with other humans, other species, and the natural environment.

steady state   A dynamic balance between the inputs and outputs of a system, such as an organism or an ecosystem.

subsistence   The means of sustenance, support, or livelihood that enables an individual to continue to exist.

transcendentalism   The idealist, Platonist philosophy held by a group of individuals, of whom Ralph Waldo Emerson is the best-known representative, in the nineteenth-century United States. For the transcendentalists, it was the ideal that was actually real; the material world was only a constantly changing appearance. Symbols and emblems in the material world provided clues to ideal truths through visionary insight and spiritual intuition, enabling the human soul to transcend physical limitations and to gain insight into the Oversoul, or divine One.

trophic   Relating to food and nutritional processes that entail the transfer of energy from one organism to another.

wild   Existing in an undomesticated natural state; savage, uncultivated, uncivilized.

wilderness   An uncultivated, uninhabited, or densely forested region; a barren, empty, or open area.

Timeline

<table>
<tr><td>13,000 BP–1500</td><td>Settlement of North America</td></tr>
<tr><td>1492–1650</td><td>European exploration of North America</td></tr>
<tr><td>1580</td><td>Spanish settlement of Southwest</td></tr>
<tr><td>1585–1590</td><td>John White's depictions of Roanoke/Indians</td></tr>
<tr><td>1607</td><td>English settlement of Chesapeake Bay area</td></tr>
<tr><td>1620</td><td>English settlement of Massachusetts Bay area</td></tr>
<tr><td>1691</td><td>Broad Arrow Policy</td></tr>
<tr><td>1705</td><td>Robert Beverley's History and Present State of Virginia</td></tr>
<tr><td>1760–1820</td><td>Soil conservation experiments in Virginia</td></tr>
<tr><td>1773</td><td>Phillis Wheatley's poems about nature</td></tr>
<tr><td>1775–1783</td><td>The American Revolution</td></tr>
<tr><td>1776</td><td>Declaration of Independence</td></tr>
<tr><td>1785</td><td>General Land Ordinance of 1785</td></tr>
<tr><td>1787</td><td>Thomas Jefferson's Notes of the State of Virginia</td></tr>
<tr><td>1803</td><td>Louisiana Purchase</td></tr>
<tr><td>1804–1806</td><td>Lewis and Clark expedition</td></tr>
<tr><td>1808–1834</td><td>John James Audubon's depictions of birds and life in United States</td></tr>
<tr><td>1812–1815</td><td>The War of 1812</td></tr>
<tr><td>1836–1850</td><td>Hudson River School of painters</td></tr>
<tr><td>1844</td><td>George Catlin's paintings of American Indians and nature in the Great Plains</td></tr>
<tr><td>1844</td><td>Thomas Hart Benton's "Manifest Destiny"</td></tr>
<tr><td>1849</td><td>California Gold Rush</td></tr>
<tr><td>1854</td><td>Thoreau's Walden</td></tr>
<tr><td>1861–1865</td><td>The Civil War</td></tr>
</table>

1862	Homestead Act
1862	Morrill Land Grant Act
1863	Frances Anne Kemble's *Journal of a Residence on a Georgian Plantation in 1838–1839*
1878	John Wesley Powell's *Report on the Arid Lands of the United States*
1892	Founding of the Sierra Club
1892	Ellen Swallow introduces the term "Oekology" to America
1893	Frederick Jackson Turner's *Significance of the Frontier in American History*
1897	Louis Hughes' *Thirty Years a Slave*
1900–1913	Progressive Conservation Movement
1902	Reclamation Act
1905	Upton Sinclair's *The Jungle*
1908	Theodore Roosevelt's Conference of Governors
1910	Jane Addams' *Twenty Years at Hull-House*
1914–1918	World War I
1916	The National Parks Act
1916	Frederic Clements' *Plant Succession*
1925	Alice Hamilton's *Industrial Poisons in the United States*
1929–1938	The Great Depression and the New Deal
1933	Robert Marshall's *The People's Forests*
1933	Founding of the Civilian Conservation Corps
1935	Founding of the Wilderness Society
1936–1945	New Deal Conservation
1941–1945	World War II
1946	Creation of the Bureau of Land Mangement
1949	Aldo Leopold's *A Sand County Almanac*
1962	Rachel Carson's *Silent Spring*
1964	The Wilderness Act
1968	Paul Ehrlich's *The Population Bomb*
1968	Wild and Scenic Rivers Act
1969	The National Environmental Policy Act
1970	Earth Day/Environmental Movement
1970	Clean Air Act
1972	Federal Water Pollution Control Act
1973	Endangered Species Act
1980	Alaska National Interests Lands Act

1982	Environmental Justice Movement begins
1987	Montreal Protocol on Ozone Depletion
1989	Exxon Valdez oil spill, Prince William Sound
1991	First National People of Color and Environmental Leadership Summit
1992	Rio de Janeiro Earth Summit
1992	California Desert Protection Act
1996	Grand Staircase-Escalante National Monument
1997	Kyoto Protocol on Global Climate Change
2000	World population passes six billion people
2002	Johannesburg World Summit on Sustainable Development

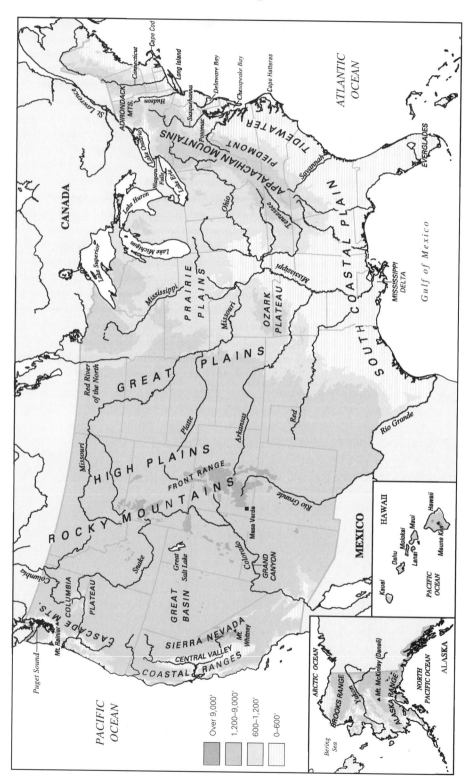

Map 2   Natural Vegetation of the United States   A-9

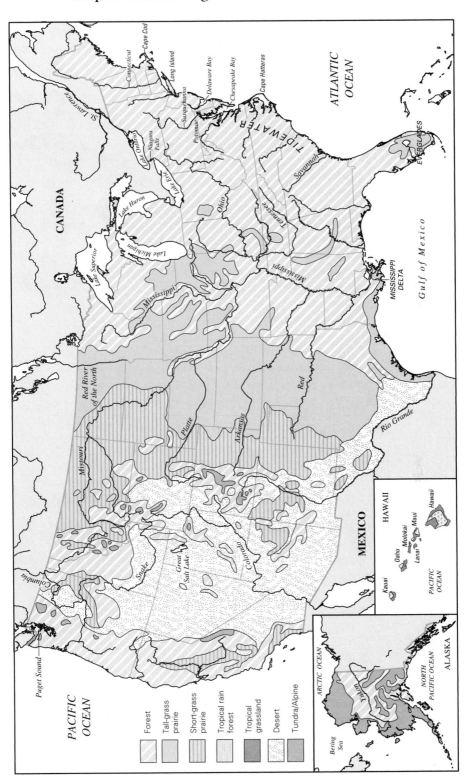

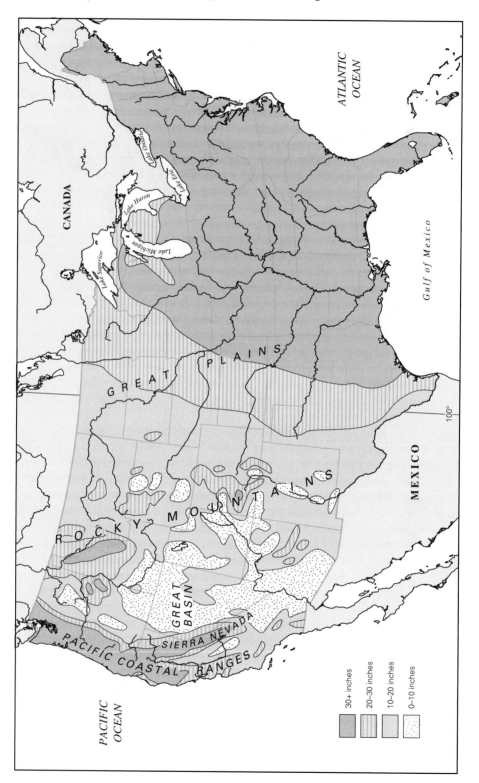

PACIFIC
OCEAN

CANADA

ATLANTIC
OCEAN

Lake Ontario

Lake Erie

Lake Huron

Lake Superior

Lake Michigan

Gulf of Mexico

G R E A T   P L A I N S

R O C K Y   M O U N T A I N S

GREAT
BASIN

SIERRA NEVADA

PACIFIC COASTAL   RANGES

MEXICO

100°

30+ inches

20–30 inches

10–20 inches

0–10 inches

Map 4   Cultural Areas of Native Americans   A-11

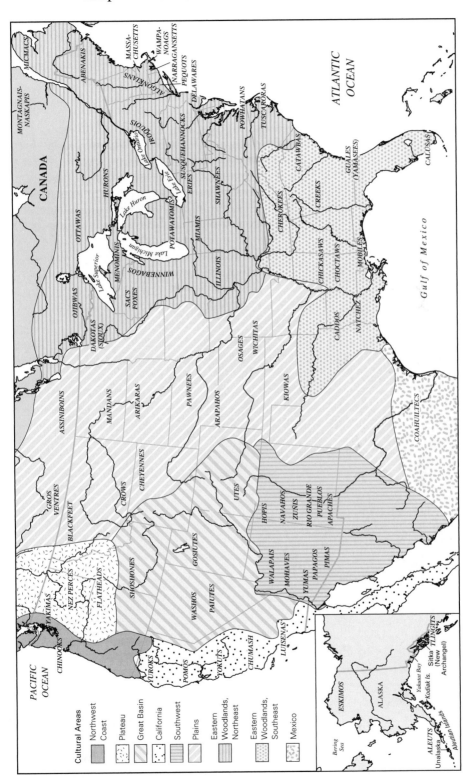

Cultural Areas

Northwest Coast

Plateau

Great Basin

California

Southwest

Plains

Eastern Woodlands, Northeast

Eastern Woodlands, Southeast

Mexico

MICMACS
MONTAGNAIS-NASKAPIS
ABENAKIS
MASSA-CHUSETTS
WAMPA-NOAGS
NARRAGANSETTS
PEQUOTS
ALGONKINS
DELAWARES
POWHATANS
TUSCARORAS
CATAWBAS
CHEROKEES
CREEKS
GUALES (YAMASEES)
CALUSAS
CANADA
OTTAWAS
HURONS
IROQUOIS
Lake Ontario
Lake Erie
ERIES
SUSQUEHANNOCKS
SHAWNEES
Lake Huron
POTAWATOMIS
MIAMIS
MENOMINIS
WINNEBAGOS
Lake Michigan
Lake Superior
OJIBWAS
SACS
FOXES
ILLINOIS
DAKOTAS (SIOUX)
CHICKASAWS
CHOCTAWS
MOBILES
NATCHEZ
CADDOS
OSAGES
WICHITAS
ASSINIBOINS
MANDANS
ARIKARAS
PAWNEES
KIOWAS
COAHUILTECS
GROS VENTRES
BLACKFEET
CROWS
CHEYENNES
UTES
HOPIS
NAVAHOS
ZUNIS
RIO GRANDE PUEBLOS
APACHES
SHOSHONES
GOSIUTES
WALAPAIS
MOHAVES
YUMAS
PAPAGOS
PIMAS
NEZ PERCES
FLATHEADS
YAKIMAS
CHINOOKS
YUROKS
POMOS
WASHOS
PAIUTES
YOKUTS
CHUMASH
LUISENAS
LUISENAS

ATLANTIC OCEAN

Gulf of Mexico

PACIFIC OCEAN

ESKIMOS
ALASKA
TLINGITS
Sitka (New Archangel)
Yakutat Bay
Kodiak Is.
ALEUTS
Unalaska
Aleutian Islands
Bering Sea

Map 5 The Colonial Economy

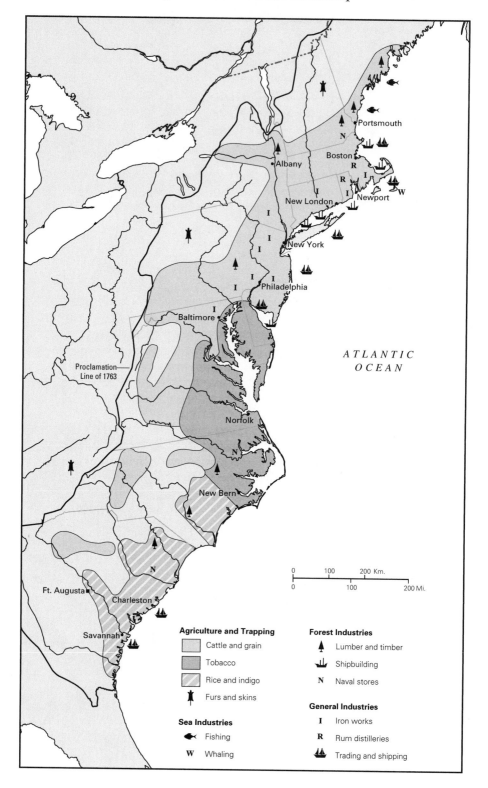

ATLANTIC OCEAN

Portsmouth

Albany

Boston

New London

Newport

New York

Philadelphia

Baltimore

Proclamation Line of 1763

Norfolk

New Bern

Ft. Augusta

Charleston

Savannah

0   100   200 Km.

0   100   200 Mi.

Agriculture and Trapping

Cattle and grain

Tobacco

Rice and indigo

Furs and skins

Sea Industries

Fishing

W   Whaling

Forest Industries

Lumber and timber

Shipbuilding

N   Naval stores

General Industries

I   Iron works

R   Rum distilleries

Trading and shipping

Map 6   Southern Cotton Production, 1820 and 1860   A-13

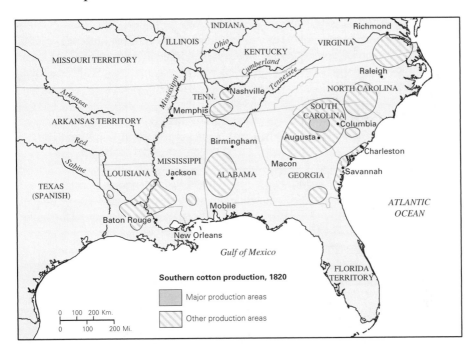

Southern cotton production, 1820

▨ Major production areas

▨ Other production areas

0   100 200 Km.

0   100   200 Mi.

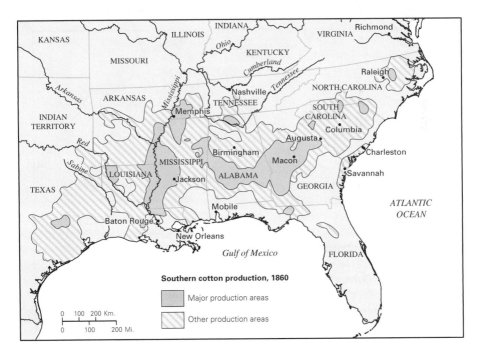

Southern cotton production, 1860

▨ Major production areas

▨ Other production areas

0   100 200 Km.

0   100   200 Mi.

Map 7   The Northwest, 1785–1787

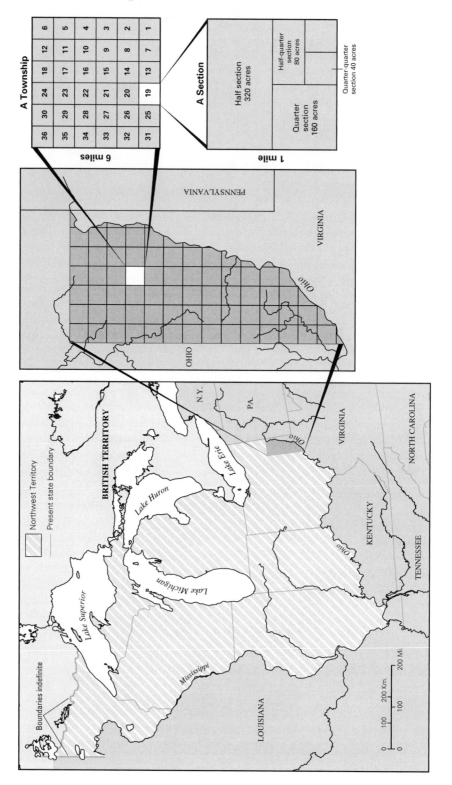

Map 8   Trails to the West, 1840   A-15

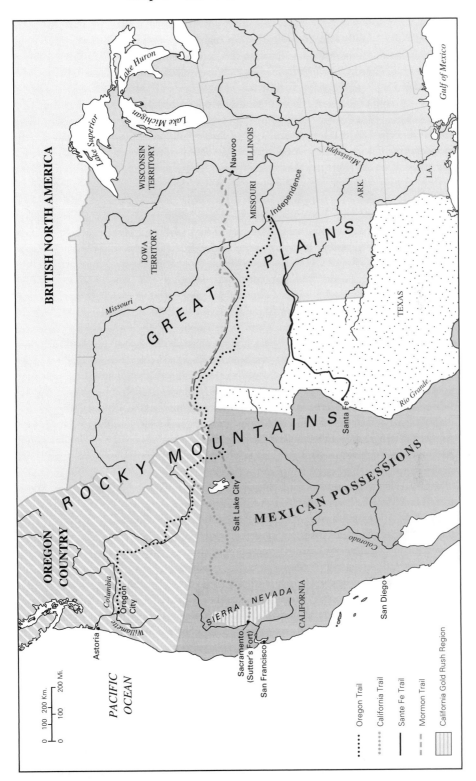

PACIFIC OCEAN

OREGON COUNTRY

BRITISH NORTH AMERICA

Lake Superior
Lake Huron
Lake Michigan

WISCONSIN TERRITORY

IOWA TERRITORY

Missouri

GREAT PLAINS

ROCKY MOUNTAINS

Columbia
Willamette
Astoria
Oregon City

SIERRA NEVADA

Sacramento (Sutter's Fort)
San Francisco

Salt Lake City

MEXICAN POSSESSIONS

CALIFORNIA

Colorado

San Diego

Santa Fe

Rio Grande

TEXAS

ARK.

LA.

Mississippi

MISSOURI

ILLINOIS

Nauvoo

Independence

Gulf of Mexico

0   100   200 Km.
0   100   200 Mi.

········· Oregon Trail
······· California Trail
——— Sante Fe Trail
– – – Mormon Trail
▨ California Gold Rush Region

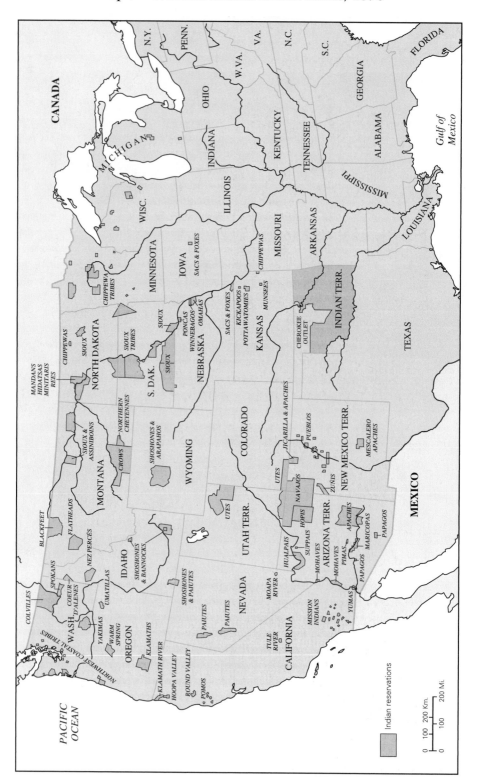

PACIFIC OCEAN

CANADA

N.Y. PENN.

MICHIGAN

OHIO

INDIANA

ILLINOIS

WISC.

MINNESOTA

IOWA

MISSOURI

ARKANSAS

W.VA. VA.

KENTUCKY

TENNESSEE

N.C.

S.C.

GEORGIA

ALABAMA

MISSISSIPPI

LOUISIANA

FLORIDA

Gulf of Mexico

CHIPPEWA TRIBES

SIOUX

NORTH DAKOTA

MANDANS HIDATSAS MINITARIS REES

CHIPPEWAS

SIOUX

SIOUX TRIBES

S. DAK.

SIOUX

SACS & FOXES

CHIPPEWAS

SACS & FOXES

PONCAS WINNEBAGOS OMAHAS

NEBRASKA

KICKAPOOS POTTAWATOMIES MUNSEES

KANSAS

INDIAN TERR.

CHEROKEE OUTLET

TEXAS

BLACKFEET

FLATHEADS

NEZ PERCES

SIOUX & ASSINIBOINS

NORTHERN CHEYENNES

CROWS

SHOSHONES & ARAPAHOS

MONTANA

WYOMING

COLORADO

JICARILLA & APACHES

PUEBLOS

UTES

NAVAJOS

ZUÑIS

NEW MEXICO TERR.

MESCALERO APACHES

MEXICO

COLVILLES

SPOKANS

COEUR— D'ALENES

WASH.

YAKIMAS

WARM SPRING

UMATILLAS

IDAHO

SHOSHONES & BANNOCKS

UTAH TERR.

UTES

HOPIS

SUPPAIS

HUALPAIS

ARIZONA TERR.

APACHES

MARICOPAS

PAPAGOS

PAPAGOS

NORTHWEST COASTAL TRIBES

KLAMATH RIVER

HOOPA VALLEY

ROUND VALLEY

POMOS

OREGON

KLAMATHS

SHOSHONES & PAIUTES

PAIUTES

PAIUTES

NEVADA

MOAPA RIVER

TULE RIVER

CALIFORNIA

MISSION INDIANS

MOHAVES

MOHAVES

PIMAS

PAPAGOS

YUMAS

Indian reservations

0   100   200 Km.

0   100   200 Mi.

Map 10   American Industry in 1900   A-17

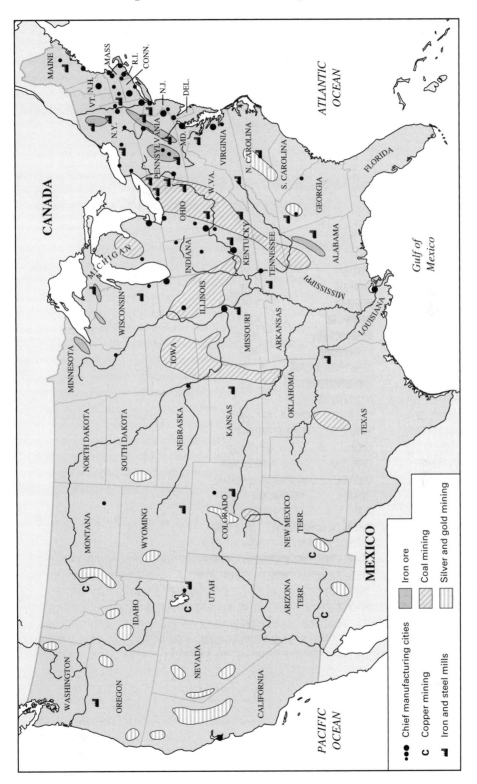

CANADA

MAINE
N.H.
VT.
MASS
R.I.
CONN.
N.Y.
N.J.
PENNSYLVANIA
DEL.
MD.
W. VA.
VIRGINIA
N. CAROLINA
S. CAROLINA
GEORGIA
FLORIDA
OHIO
KENTUCKY
TENNESSEE
ALABAMA
MISSISSIPPI
MICHIGAN
INDIANA
ILLINOIS
WISCONSIN
MINNESOTA
IOWA
MISSOURI
ARKANSAS
LOUISIANA
OKLAHOMA
TEXAS
NORTH DAKOTA
SOUTH DAKOTA
NEBRASKA
KANSAS
MONTANA
WYOMING
COLORADO
NEW MEXICO TERR.
IDAHO
UTAH
ARIZONA TERR.
WASHINGTON
OREGON
NEVADA
CALIFORNIA

ATLANTIC OCEAN

Gulf of Mexico

MEXICO

PACIFIC OCEAN

Chief manufacturing cities

C   Copper mining

Iron and steel mills

Iron ore

Coal mining

Silver and gold mining